The
John Updike
Encyclopedia

THE
JOHN UPDIKE
ENCYCLOPEDIA

Jack De Bellis

GREENWOOD PRESS
Westport, Connecticut • London

Library of Congress Cataloging-in-Publication Data

De Bellis, Jack.
  The John Updike encyclopedia / Jack De Bellis.
    p.   cm.
  Includes bibliographical references and index.
  ISBN 0–313–29904–8 (alk. paper)
  1. Updike, John—Encyclopedias.   2. Updike, John—Chronology.   I. Title.
  PS3571.P4Z459   2000
  813'.54—dc21   99–089163
   [B]

British Library Cataloguing in Publication Data is available.

Library of Congress Catalog Card Number: 99–089163
ISBN: 0–313–29904–8

First published in 2000

Greenwood Press, 88 Post Road West, Westport, CT 06881
An imprint of Greenwood Publishing Group, Inc.
www.greenwood.com

Printed in the United States of America

∞™

The paper used in this book complies with the
Permanent Paper Standard issued by the National
Information Standards Organization (Z39.48–1984).

10 9 8 7 6 5 4 3 2 1

Back cover photo courtesy of *Reading Eagle/ Times*.

Dedicated
to my mother, true Viking,
"Most near, most dear, most loved and most far"
(George Barker, "Sonnet to My Mother")

Contents

Preface

Nearly two decades ago critic George Hunt wondered at the temerity of a critic who would offer in regard to John Updike "an exacting critical study of such a prolific author who is still relatively young." The same consternation strikes this writer. The surprising turns Updike's career has taken would doom any critic who thinks that he or she can offer a "summing up" of Updike, for Updike is, like Rabbit, rich, but unlike Rabbit, he is hardly at rest, but rather still running. Although he has published about fifty books and, as he has said, has been tidying up his desk, his career is far from over, so this encyclopedia may certainly seem premature. In fact, this volume has been revised repeatedly during its five-year progress because Updike's extraordinary oeuvre has continued to expand in all directions, and because the more familiar a reader becomes with his work, the more his books speak to one another and to other books. This requires constant revision of ideas.

The aims of this encyclopedia are similar to those of W. H. Auden* in *The Dyer's Hand*, quoted by Hunt: to offer a comprehensive survey that reveals a vast oeuvre; to provide readings that indicate that complexity; to demonstrate Updike's artistic "making"; and to suggest connections of Updike's writing to many subjects, such as art, science, religion and history. Though this encyclopedia necessarily anatomizes Updike's oeuvre, I hope that the reader acquires a coherent sense of his remarkable accomplishments through the many cross-references offered, as well as the effort to suggest, in many entries, shared themes, ideas and matters of craft among Updike's books. His apostate minister Clarence Wilmot (*In the Beauty of the Lilies*) knew that the encyclopedist plays God by attempting to provide a "replica of Creation," but I hope that the reader will pardon this blasphemy. I am no apostate; I am a true believer in Updike.

John Updike's critics from the beginning have sought to rise to the level of Updike's quality. In dozens of books and hundreds of articles and reviews these commentators have provided detailed and ingenious interpretations and refined, patient judgments. Available to the inquiring reader are lengthy studies of Updike's interest in Karl Barth, Søren Kierkegaard and Carl Gustav Jung; of his similarities to Philip Roth; of his use of image clusters and computer language; of his employment of parables and fairy tales; of his religious symbolism and the epistolary form; of his use of the critical approach called deconstruction and his interest in the theories of Sigmund Freud; of his interest in the remote world of myth and the ubiquitous realm of popular culture in America; and of his characters' constant immersion in history. Yet many opportunities remain for the interested commentator.

The John Updike Encyclopedia seeks to facilitate further critical inquiry, as well as to offer a handy resource for the general reader about plots, characters, major themes, references, key ideas, biography and sources. Each entry for Updike's books provides a summary of that book and a modest exposition of its major ideas. Some entries are miniature essays, concerning, for example, the classical world, African Americans, magic realism, Nathaniel Hawthorne, film, John Cheever and hostile critics, as well as plots and characters, significant places and dates. To facilitate a full use of the encyclopedia entries, I have provided three kinds of cross-references: (1) an asterisk (*) next to a word refers the reader to another entry, and such items are starred only the first time they appear in each entry; (2) following many entries I have indicated other entries of interest under "*See*," but no asterisked item appears under "*See*"; and (3) the index. Updike works mentioned in the entries are never starred but should automatically lead the reader to entries for those books. To direct the reader unobtrusively to Updike's books in the entries, I have employed title abbreviations, the key for which is included following this preface. Also, the key for abbreviations for critical frequently mentioned books can be found there.

An exhaustive listing of every character and plot of every story, an analysis of every essay and poem or an explanation of every referent would make the encyclopedia unwieldy and perhaps self-defeating. Consequently, some readers may find that an allusion has not been explicated, that a quotation went untreated, or that a minor character has not been identified. My concern is not to list everything but to include only references, allusions and quotations that advance the reader's essential understanding of Updike's remarkable creative imagination. Inevitably, similar information needs to be repeated in several entries, since it is likely that most readers will read selectively. I have provided more extended entries on Updike's recent works, since they have not yet received ample critical attention. Since the "Rabbit" tetralogy contains his best-known and perhaps most enduring novels, many of my entries refer to those novels. Since *RA* is Updike's definitive edition of the four novels that comprise the Rabbit saga, I refer to this text even when I indicate the individual novels within it: *RR, RRed, RIR* and *RaR*.

Updike, one of the most intertextual of modern writers, has employed about 25,000 referents in his oeuvre (his favorite word for the shelf of his jacketless books that adorns his study), but entries for every allusion, reference and quotation in the oeuvre would be less useful than a grouping of such items, though for the most important, for example, Plato, I have provided a separate entry. So instead of listing hundreds of movies individually, the "Film" entry explains Updike's major uses of film and identifies the most important ones. Some referents like AIDS, unfortunately, need no definition. The entries on referents always explain them in terms of the context of Updike's use and are not intended to be as comprehensive as entries in other encyclopedias. Thus "Vietnam" is "defined" in terms of its importance to Updike's work, not as it might be described in the *Encyclopedia Americana*. It would be redundant to define that which Updike's context already defines, like the mythic figures in *C* who are contextually identified, or the Sanskrit in *S.*, which is defined in Updike's glossary. Also, I have relied upon, but not necessarily noted, Updike's omnibus interviews in *PP* ("One Big Interview") and *HS* ("On One's Own Oeuvre") and compilations of his personal commentary on his books in *OJ* ("Literarily Personal") and *MM* ("Personal Matters"). I have also made extensive use of James Plath's *Conversations with Updike* for other quotations.

Many entries contain a bibliography of works by and about Updike relevant to the specific entry. The Updike citations in the entry bibliographies are succinct: I use his last name followed by his relevant work (poem, story, article, review) and the volume in which it can be found if it is collected. This is a selected list, as are the secondary citations. Effort has been made to emphasize the most recent secondary material. The student wishing to be exhaustive will want to consult C. Clarke Taylor's *John Updike: A Bibliography* (Kent, OH: Kent State University Press, 1968) and my *John Updike: A Bibliography, 1967–1993* (Westport, CT: Greenwood Press, 1994). A general bibliography listing the most important sources of works about Updike will be found at the end of this volume. Appendix I, "A Chronological List of the Works of John Updike," enables the interested reader to pursue study of Updike. Appendix II, "Films and Film Personalities in the Works of John Updike," lists all films and film personalities mentioned in his work.

Acknowledgments

This book would have been very different and much less readable without the meticulous care of Professor Beverly Luzietti Tisdale and Jim Morrison. Bev's brilliance with language and clarity of mind can be read in any sentences or paragraphs that seem lucid and appealing. Her perseverance in giving patient attention repeatedly to many versions of this long work fills me with awe. Jim's depth of knowledge of John Updike has dazzled me, and his insights helped me more than once to open my eyes wider. Bev and Jim have made this book more than I perhaps deserve, and I hope that it is deserving of their time. My deepest appreciation also goes to my copyeditor, Mr. Charles Ekerline, for his unswerving effort to perfect the accuracy and stylistic consistency of this book. Various other persons have kindly answered queries, my colleagues Scott Gordon and Barbara Pavlock and fellow Updike critics James Schiff and James Yerkes among them. Former classmates of Updike's, especially Barry Nelson and his *Chatterbox* advisor, Mrs. Thelma Lewis, cheerfully guided me through Updike's early life. The index of this book was prepared, in part, with funds from Lehigh University's Office of Research and the staff of Lehigh's Linderman Library and the Allentown Public Library were kind enough to answer numerous queries. Excerpts from John Updike, *Collected Poems, More Matter, Odd Jobs, Picked-up Pieces, Rabbit, Run, Self-Consciousness*, and *Telephone Poles* are reprinted by permission of Alfred A. Knopf, a Division of Random House, Inc. As always, I acknowledge my resilient and forebearing wife, Patty, for her patience and fortitude. John Updike has been generous in providing a plentitude of information about his family and in reviewing the chronology. We are almost precise contemporaries, and it has been a joy to circle the sun with him these many years.

Introduction

If there is any writer who needs no introduction, it is John Updike. He has been foremost among American writers since his *PF* won the Rosenthal Prize Award for a first novel awarded by the National Institute of Arts and Letters.* Since then his career has taken unexpected turns from the sensational *Couples* to his *Bildungsroman IB* nearly thirty years later. He has been recognized as a triple-threat writer whose short fiction,* poetry* and reviews regularly appear in leading magazines such as the *New Yorker,* the *New York Times Book Review* and the *New York Review of Books*. Generations of high-school students have enjoyed his short fiction and light verse,* and dozens of graduate students have written theses about his work. He has won the acclaim of his fellow writers with awards* from the most prestigious societies and universities. Updike has been honored by an American president, a French premier and a Pennsylvania governor. Colleges and universities have given him honorary degrees and have called him to their campuses to speak, read, instruct students and be interviewed. His fiction and criticism are regularly taught in colleges, and critics have provided commentary on all phases of his work.

Updike has two characteristics that distinguish him from other contemporary American writers. He has been capable of writing remarkably detailed and affectionate fiction set in the world in which he grew up, and he has constantly developed new directions that keep the reader wondering what is coming next. Who could predict *C, Coup*, three novels derived from *The Scarlet Letter*, a book partly set during the Buchanan* administration, a series of stories about Jewish writer Henry Bech,* and books treating computer hackers and a businessman who transforms into St. Mark? Read chronologically, his books dazzle with the unexpected. Consider his first decade, 1958–68. Updike's first book, some forget, was a collection of light verse, *CH*. Who would predict his next book, *PF*, would be a novel about the elderly in a poorhouse, told with science-fiction overtones? Next came a realistic novel of censorable sex and youthful waste (*RR*). It hardly prepared for the tragicomic and experimental *C*. A novel of double adultery,* *Marry* was drafted at this time, though not published till much later, and then Updike produced *OF*, a compact tale of domestic betrayal and reunion. At the end of the decade, in 1968, came *Couples*, which earned Updike notoriety for the sexual escapades of ten couples, placed him on the cover of *Time* and made him a fortune. Meanwhile, Updike had produced another collection of increasingly serious poetry (*TP*, 1963), a volume of essays and parodies (*AP*) and three gatherings of short fiction (*SD*, 1959; *PigF*, 1962; and *MuS*, 1966), volumes of stories that traced his development from master of the *New Yorker* style to his "abstract-personal" "fugal weave" fiction. From 1958 to 1968 Updike moved swiftly and almost effortlessly from a young writer of promise to a writer in the forefront of his generation. His accomplishment in those ten years would seem brilliant were it not that the next three decades demonstrate even greater achievements.

Since 1968 Updike has hardly ever experienced a disabling writer's block. He has provided a continuous stream of dependably high-quality fiction, increasingly respected poetry, a play and surprising memoirs. He has also earned a reputation as one of the most deeply read reviewers of our time who immerses himself in world fiction, thereby assuring himself a vast readership. He has also plunged into major writers, several times reviewing work by and about James Joyce,* Marcel Proust,* Vladimir Nabokov,* Henry Green* and Jorge Luis Borges.* In addition, Updike has published introductions, prefaces, forewords and afterwords for, among others, individual novels by Edmund Wilson,* collections of short fiction by Herman Melville,* drawings by David Levine, a bibliography of his work and Karl Barth* on Mozart. Besides this, Updike has quietly assembled commentary on many major American writers with essays on Benjamin Franklin, Nathaniel Hawthorne,* Herman Melville, Walt Whitman,* Ralph Waldo Emerson,* William Dean Howells and Edith Wharton. Updike has also undertaken surveys of epic and tragedy. His range of interest is impressive, and his ability to write with a trustworthy voice on many subjects beyond the arts is arresting. His constant winning of awards for the best short fiction and nonfiction shows the high acclaim with which his work has been received by his peers.

Updike has been unfailingly helpful to former students such as Nicholas Delbanco, fellow writers such as John Cheever* and a great number of interviewers. He has assisted in the efforts of librarians, scholars and bibliographers. Critics who have approached Updike for help have been unanimous in their recognition of his generosity and concern. Graduate students send questionnaires, professors ask detailed questions, and all are answered with Updike's customary alacrity, accuracy and good humor. He is in turn a generous evaluator of criticism about him, having endorsed George Hunt's book. He once opened his home to one bibliographer and has written a foreword for another, and unlike Henry Bech, he sometimes responds to criticism sent to him. Apart from widespread critical and popular interest in his work, he is the most "collectible" of all modern American authors, with some of his work selling for prices in four figures. Small wonder Amazon. com has called him "incomparable."

Criticism from the start has been drawn to the philosophical themes in Updike's work. Thus existential theories are used by David Galloway in *The Absurd Hero in American Fiction* (1966; 2nd rev. ed., 1981), and by John Neary in *Something and Nothingness* (1992). From the beginning Updike critics have responded to his religious themes, and Alice and Kenneth Hamilton's *The Elements of John Updike* (1970) demonstrated that Updike's work is filled with religious imagery* and allusions. Then George Hunt's *John Updike and the Three Great Secret Things: Sex, Religion, and Art* (1980) related Updike's fiction to psychoanalytic theories, especially that of Carl Jung. The critical interest in Updike's philosophical and religious ideas evolved into a study of myth* and ritual in Edward Vargo's *Rainstorms and Fire* (1973) and Robert Detweiler's *John Updike* (1972; rev. ed., 1984). Detweiler also redirected attention to Updike's artistry and style,* which had been emphasized in Joyce Markle's study of imagery in the early novels, *Fighters and Lovers: Theme in the Novels of John Updike* (1973), and also in Larry Taylor's *Pastoral and Antipastoral Patterns in John Updike's Fiction* (1971), which had explored Updike's literary sources in the pastoral* tradition. Detweiler's varied approaches acted as a corrective to the long immersion in Updike's ideas.

Hamilton and Detweiler repeatedly wrote on Updike, and the pattern of a deep involvement among Updike critics through the course of several articles and books was continued by Donald Greiner in the 1980s and James Schiff and Dilvo Ristoff in the 1990s. Apart from offering an authoritative analysis of the novels in *John Updike's Novels* (1984), Greiner also wrote about Updike's theme of adultery and Updike's involvement with Nathaniel Hawthorne, and he provided the first serious attention to Updike's poetry and essays in *The Other John Updike* (1981). Greiner has also contributed several essential chapters to *The Dictionary of Literary Biography* and the *Contemporary Authors Bibliographical Series*. A dozen years later James Schiff explored Updike's criticism in an influential article, and then in *Updike's Version: Rewriting "The Scarlet Letter"* (1992) he examined Updike's use of Hawthorne in three novels. He then updated Detweiler in *John Updike Revisited* (1998).

Critics were clearly being tested by Updike's vigorous, varied writing, and collections of critical articles represented the many viewpoints of reviewers and critics toward Updike's work, such as that edited by William T. Stafford for *Modern Fiction Studies* (1974), David Thorburn and Howard Eiland's *John Updike: A Collection of Critical Essays* (1979) and William R. Macnaughton's *Critical Essays on John Updike* (1982). Stafford's compilation includes essays on the short fiction as well as the early novels, reviews of books of criticism on Updike and a bibliography. Thorburn and Eiland provide essentially thematic treatments of nearly all of Updike's books published to that time. The anthology of Macnaughton contains key reviews and essays on the first several novels, along with the first evaluative survey of criticism on Updike. Such attention to so many of Updike's works shows the gathering feeling that Updike was producing a total body of absorbing work.

Attention to love in Updike's work had been signaled in Joyce Markle's *Fighters and Lovers* (1973) and would be explored further by Mary O'Connell's feminist approach in *Updike and the Patriarchal Dilemma* (1996). This work, focusing entirely on the Rabbit tetralogy, would signal an increasing focus upon these four books as a fertile area of scholarship. Consequently, Stanley Trachtenberg's *New Essays on Rabbit, Run* (1993) and Lawrence R. Broer's *Rabbit Tales: Poetry and Politics in John Updike's Rabbit Novels* (1998) contain essays entirely dedicated to the saga. Dilvo Ristoff has applied the New Historicism to Updike's saga in two books, *Updike's America: The Presence of Contemporary American History in John Updike's Rabbit Trilogy* (1988) and *John Updike's "Rabbit at Rest": Appropriating History* (1998). The numerous critics involved in Updike study have thus applied varied approaches with remarkable results. Updike's impact on other areas is signaled by the collection of essays edited by James Yerkes, *John Updike and Religion. The Sense of the Sacred and the Motions of Graces* (1999).

All the while scholars have been supplying indispensable bibliographies of Updike's work, criticism about him, compilations of foreign publications and the texts of his interviews. The Updike "Centaurian" Website, overseen by Yerkes, garners over one hundred "hits" a day on the average. Updike is widely taught, and many of these students will someday add to the richness and complexity of Updike commentary, furthering the understanding and enjoyment of future generations of readers.

But despite numerous books and articles by energetic Updike scholars and commentators, much remains to be done. Full studies of the poetry, essays and criticism are required for a fuller understanding of Updike's position as a man of letters. Updated examinations of the short fiction and novels, offering a thorough evaluation of the trajectory of Updike's career, are overdue, and works that offer a comprehensive understanding of the interlocking relationship of his fiction, poetry, reviews, essays, drama and children's literature have yet to be attempted. Influence studies comparing Updike's work with that of James Joyce, Marcel Proust, Vladimir Nabokov, John Cheever, Joyce Carol Oates, Henry Green and others should reveal much about his creative process.* While critics are increasingly turning attention to Updike's interest in religion* and history,* more needs to be done with his use of popular culture* and fine art. Detailed analyses of his style would enable many readers to understand how Updike's wonderful effects are created. His international impact should be evaluated, along with the value of academic approaches to his work from feminists, deconstructionists and neohistoricists. On the other hand, Updike has long considered himself a "professional writer," one capable of writing about baseball, Hindu religion, computers or car dealers—whatever was assigned. So a study of Updike as journeyman writer is in order, with accompanying attention to his apprentice work in high school and at the *Harvard Lampoon*,* as well as his association of more than forty years with the *New Yorker*. No critic has yet made a systematic study of the evolution of a given work from drafts through various publications; Updike's papers are available for such an analysis. In some distant time a biography should appear to supplement understanding of Updike's oeuvre, and editions of his correspondence and notebooks, as well as drafts of his work, will eventually supply a firmer comprehension of the development of his art. Updike has already anticipated such needs by writing memoirs and cooperating readily with serious students and scholars. A new bibliography of primary and secondary work will of course be essential, as will a catalogue of the Updike holdings in Harvard's Houghton Library. Future Updike scholarship should be very busy and quite exciting.

As I write this in the spring of 2000 reflecting on John Updike's present position in American literature, I think about his frequent remark lately about how he is "tidying up" as his career draws closer to its close, and I wonder how this compares to his activities of the past two years. Since November 1998, he has published a massive collection of reviews and essays, *MM*, and a collection of short fiction, *BaB* (both Book-of-the-Month Club selections) and thus underwent numerous interviews. He also recorded two cassettes of readings of stories from his three collections about Henry Bech, *Bech at Bay and Before*, and when everyone thought that the saga of Henry Bech was finished, he published another Bech story only a few weeks later. Meanwhile, he published poems about slumlords and sexual politics, gave *Border's* Inside an interview that reflected on the recurrence in his work of characters such as Bech, Harry "Rabbit" Angstrom* and Joan* and Richard Maple,* printed a travel piece on his trip to China, and reviewed *A Man in Full*, by Tom Wolfe, an old nemesis, igniting a controversy about "entertainment" versus "art" on the eve of the National Book Award presentations, in which Wolfe was heavily favored to win the fiction award. Updike also provided coverage of major art shows of Jackson Pollack and Pieter de Hooch, introduced a special edition of his story *The Women Who Got Away*, reviewed several Robert Frost biographies and wrote an introduction and selected *The Best American Short Stories of the Century* for Houghton Mifflin. At the same time Updike was busy writing *Gertrude and Claudius*, a novel, while revising the children's poems of *A Child's Calendar*. Updike also received two major awards in November 1998, the National Book Foundation's award for distinguished contribution to American letters and the Thomas Cooper Library Medal from the University of South Carolina, and that same month was the keynote speaker at the Jewish Book Festival of the Atlanta Jewish Community Center. In addition, he gave readings at several universities from Pennsylvania to California and from New Jersey to Texas, and at Harvard he read the poetry of L. E. Sissman to honor his late friend. At some of these appearances Updike attended workshops and college classes. On most of these occasions he probably signed dozens of books and consented to interviews.*

This brief survey of Updike's recent activities shows unceasing industry and enjoyment. Updike's work continues to be of such quality that the appearance of one of his books is an event anticipated by a vast and devoted critical and popular following. He is a writer to be read for his beautiful, humorous and exacting style, whether the content includes esoteric discussions of quantum physics,* theological disputes or the work of pop artists.* In short, Updike shows little sign of slowing down or easing up, even though he has over fifty books behind him and one of the most distinguished careers in American literature. Though he has accepted an award for lifetime achievement, more of his writing life is still ahead of him, and though he tidies his desk, his next book, as he has often said, will be his most significant. Who would doubt this?

Abbreviations

UPDIKE'S WORKS

A	*The Afterlife*
AP	*Assorted Prose*
B	*Brazil*
BaB	*Bech at Bay*
BB	*Bech: A Book*
BD	*Buchanan Dying*
BIB	*Bech Is Back*
C	*The Centaur*
CC	*Concerts at Castle Hill*
CH	*The Carpentered Hen and Other Tame Creatures*
ChC	*A Child's Calendar*
Coup	*The Coup*
Couples	*Couples*
CP	*Collected Poems, 1953–1993*
FN	*Facing Nature*
GC	*Gertrude and Claudius*
GD	*Golf Dreams*
HA	*A Helpful Alphabet of Friendly Objects*
HH	*Hoping for a Hoopoe*
HS	*Hugging the Shore*
IB	*In the Beauty of the Lilies*

JL	*Just Looking*
LL	*Licks of Love*
M	*Midpoint and Other Poems*
Marry	*Marry Me: A Romance*
MF	*Memories of the Ford Administration*
MM	*More Matter*
MS	*A Month of Sundays*
MuS	*The Music School*
MW	*Museums and Women and Other Stories*
OF	*Of the Farm*
OJ	*Odd Jobs*
OL	*On Literary Biography*
OS	*Olinger Stories*
P	*Problems and Other Stories*
PF	*The Poorhouse Fair*
PigF	*Pigeon Feathers*
PP	*Picked-up Pieces*
RA	*Rabbit Angstrom*
RaR	*Rabbit at Rest*
RIR	*Rabbit Is Rich*
RR	*Rabbit, Run*
RRed	*Rabbit Redux*
RV	*Roger's Version*
S.	*S.*
SC	*Self-Consciousness*
SD	*The Same Door*
TE	*Toward the End of Time*
TF	*Too Far to Go*
TM	*Trust Me*
TP	*Telephone Poles*
TT	*Tossing and Turning*
V	*Verse*
W	*The Witches of Eastwick*

SECONDARY WORKS FOR THE ENTRY
BIBLIOGRAPHIES

Ancona, *WA*	Ancona, Francesco Aristide. *Writing the Absence of the Father: Undoing Oedipal Structures in the Contemporary American Novel.* Lanham, MD: University Press of America, 1986. 81–91.
Bloom, *JU*	Bloom, Harold, ed. *John Updike: Modern Critical Views.* New York: Chelsea House, 1987.
Broer, *RT*	Broer, Lawrence R., ed. *Rabbit Tales: Poetry and Politics in John Updike's Rabbit Novels.* Tuscaloosa: University of Alabama Press, 1998.
Burchard, *YS*	Burchard, Rachel C. *Yea Sayings.* Carbondale, IL: Southern Illinois University Press, 1971.
Campbell, *UN*	Campbell, Jeff. *Updike's Novels: Thorns Spell a Word.* Wichita Falls, KS: Midwestern State University Press, 1987.
Detweiler, *JU*	Detweiler, Robert. *John Updike.* Rev. ed. Boston: Hall, 1984.
Greiner, *Adultery*	Greiner, Donald J. *Adultery in the American Novel: Updike, James, and Hawthorne.* Columbia: University of South Carolina Press, 1985.
Greiner, *JU*	Greiner, Donald J. *John Updike's Novels.* Athens: Ohio University Press, 1984.
Greiner, *OJ*	Greiner, Donald J. *The Other John Updike: Poems/Short Stories/Prose/Play.* Athens: Ohio University Press, 1981.
Hamilton and Hamilton, *EJ*	Hamilton, Alice, and Kenneth Hamilton. *The Elements of John Updike.* Grand Rapids, MI: Eerdmans, 1970.
Hunt, *JU*	Hunt, George. *John Updike and the Three Great Secret Things: Sex, Religion and Art.* Grand Rapids, MI: Eerdmans, 1980.
Luscher, *JU*	Luscher, Robert M. *John Updike: A Study of the Short Fiction.* Boston: Hall, 1992.
Macnaughton, *CE*	Macnaughton, William R., ed. *Critical Essays on John Updike.* Boston: Hall, 1982.
Markle, *FL*	Markle, Joyce B. *Fighters and Lovers: Theme in the Novels of John Updike.* New York: New York University Press, 1973.

Neary, *SN*

Neary, John M. *Something and Nothingness: The Fiction of John Updike and John Fowles*. New York: Carbondale, IL: Southern Illinois University Press, 1991.

Newman, *JU*

Newman, Judie. *John Updike*. New York: St. Martin's, 1988.

O'Connell, *UP*

O'Connell, Mary. *Updike and the Patriarchal Dilemma*. Carbondale: Southern Illinois University Press, 1996.

Plath, *CU*

Path, James. *Conversations with Updike*. Jackson: University of Mississippi Press, 1994.

Ristoff, *JU*

Ristoff, Dilvo I. *John Updike's "Rabbit at Rest": Appropriating History*. New York: Lang, 1998.

Ristoff, *UA*

Ristoff, Dilvo I. *Updike's America: The Presence of Contemporary American History in John Updike's Rabbit Trilogy*. New York: Lang, 1988.

Schiff, *JU*

Schiff, James A. *John Updike Revisited*. Boston: Twayne, 1998.

Schiff, *UV*

Schiff, James A. *Updike's Version: Rewriting "The Scarlet Letter."* Columbia: University of Missouri Press, 1992.

Searles, *FP*

Searles, George J. *The Fiction of Philip Roth and John Updike*. Carbondale: Southern Illinois University Press, 1985.

Tallent, *MM*

Tallent, Elizabeth. *Married Men and Magic Tricks: John Updike's Erotic Heroes*. Berkeley, CA: Creative Arts, 1982.

Taylor, *PA*

Taylor, Larry E. *Pastoral and Anti-pastoral Patterns in John Updike's Fiction*. Carbondale: Southern Illinois University Press, 1971.

Thorburn, *JU*

Thorburn, David and Howard Eiland, eds. In *John Updike: A Collection of Critical Essays*, Englewood Cliffs, NJ: Prentice-Hall, 1979.

Uphaus, *JU*

Uphaus, Suzanne Henning. *John Updike*. New York: Ungar, 1980.

Vargo, *RF*

Vargo, Edward P. *Rainstorms and Fire*. Port Washington, NY: Kennikat Press, 1973.

Vaughn, *JU*

Vaughn, Philip H. *John Updike's Images of America*. Reseda, CA: Mojave, 1981.

Yerkes, *JU*

Yerkes, James, ed. *John Updike and Religion: The Sense of the Sacred and the Motions of Grace*. Grand Rapids, MI: Eerdmans, 1999.

John Updike: A Chronology

1932   An eleventh-generation American (an eighteenth-century ancestor was also named John Updike, and two Updikes fought in the Civil War [*AP*]), John Hoyer Updike was born March 18 in the Reading Hospital, West Reading, Pennsylvania, during "severe Depression-shock" (*SC*) to poor, well-read parents, Wesley Russell Updike,* who later taught mathematics at Shillington* High School (1934–74), and Linda Grace Hoyer Updike,* who worked at Pomeroy's Department Store and later published stories in the *New Yorker*.* In 1932 they lived with her parents, John* and Katherine Hoyer, at 117 Philadelphia Avenue, Shillington, a Reading* suburb, which was the subject of the memoir "A Soft Spring Night in Shillington" (*SC*) and was fictionalized as Olinger (pronounced "O, Linger!" [*OS*]), as Reading was named Brewer.* Updike described Reading, in southeastern Pennsylvania, as sitting "dreaming and declining in the center of a lozenge-shaped county of bosomy farmland, Berks. Its urban silhouette, in the shadow of Mount Penn,* is dominated by the eighteen-story courthouse that rose from the tight red-brick blocks in 1932. . . . The people are both conservative and fanciful; hex signs adorn the Berks barns, and a pagoda surprisingly perches atop Mount Penn" (*PP*). Reading was once, he notes, "a grand place—thriving downtown, factories pouring out smoke and textiles and steel and pretzels and beer . . . a town that made things" (Plath, *CU*). The Shillington house, bought by the Hoyers in 1922, was said to have been among many things that attracted Wesley Updike to Linda Hoyer and, as Updike said, "caused my card, a decade later in the game, to come up" (*SC*). Updike has noted: "When I was born, my parents and my mother's parents planted a dogwood tree in the side yard of the large white house in which we lived throughout my boyhood" (*AP*).

1936   Attends Shillington Elementary School, kindergarten through sixth grade. Publishes a collage in *Children's Activities*.

1938   First attack of psoriasis. Begins cartooning.*

1942   Takes drawing* and painting lessons from Clint Shilling at about this time.

1943   Enters seventh grade.

1944   Updike's paternal aunt Mary* gives the Updikes a subscription to the *New Yorker*, and James Thurber* sends him one of his dog drawings, which Updike still keeps in his study as "a great talisman."

1945   Updike's first publication, "A Handshake with the Congressman," appears February 16 in the Shillington High School (now Thomas E. Mifflin Regional High) *Chatterbox*.* On Halloween his family moves to the sandstone farmhouse originally owned by the Hoyers, eleven miles south of Shillington in Plowville.* Updike remarked, "Whatever creative or literary aspects I had were developed out of sheer boredom those two years before I got my driver's license" (Plath, *CU*).

1946   Writes a murder mystery, belatedly published in 1993, fables imitating Thurber's and light verse.* At about this time goes to New York* with his aunt Mary to visit the Museum of Modern Art.

1947   Contributes to the Shillington High School newspaper and serves as class president. The yearbook identifies him as "the sage of Plowville," who "hopes to write for a living."

1949   Publishes "I Want a Lamp," a poem in the *American Courier* 10 (July 1): 11. Has a leading role, the main romantic interest, in the junior play, as he will the following year in the senior play, which he writes. He plays the father in both plays.

1950   Graduates president and covaledictorian of the senior class at Shillington High School. Updike had contributed 285 drawings, articles and poems to the *Chatterbox*. This summer and the following two summers Updike works as a copy boy for the Reading *Eagle*,* where he writes a few feature stories and contributes poems to Jerry Lobrin's column. In part because his mother read an anthology that revealed that many great writers attended Harvard,* Updike enters Harvard on a tuition scholarship, eventually majoring in English. He later says that he chose Harvard over Cornell because he wanted to do cartoons for the *Harvard Lampoon*.* Charles Hemmig, the principal under whom his mother taught, writes a generous letter supporting his Harvard aspirations (*CP*). His first year at Harvard he writes more than forty poems and draws for the *Harvard Lampoon*.

1951   First prose, "The Different One," is published in the *Harvard Lampoon*. Updike discards a novel about two-thirds written called *Willow*, about a town like Shillington; it foreshadows his stories about Olinger.

1953   Named editor of the *Harvard Lampoon*. A story about an ex–basketball player receives an A from Albert Guerard. On June 26 marries Mary Pennington,* a Radcliffe (1952) fine arts student studying at the Fogg Museum, daughter of Rev. Leslie T. Pennington and Elizabeth Daniels Pennington. Her father is minister of the First Unitarian Church in the Hyde Park section of Chicago. They honeymoon in Ipswich,* Massachusetts, then work at a camp at Lake Winnipesaukee. Updike publishes many parodies, sketches and cartoons in the *Harvard Lampoon*. His maternal grandfather, John F. Hoyer, dies in September.

1954   Graduates from Harvard summa cum laude. His senior thesis is "Non-Horatian Elements in Robert Herrick's Imitations and Echoes of Horace." Wins a Knox Fellowship, enabling him to attend Ruskin School of Drawing and Fine Art,* Oxford,* England, September 1954–June 1955. While at Oxford he meets Joyce Cary, James Thurber and E. B. White and his wife Katharine White, fiction editor of the *New Yorker*, who offers him a job at the magazine. The *New Yorker* buys ten poems and four stories; his first story, "Friends from Philadelphia," appears there October 30.

1955   His daughter Elizabeth* is born, April 1. Updike is declared 4-F because of psoriasis. In August Updike moves in a pale blue Ford to New York City, living at West Eighty-fifth and Riverside Drive, the fifth floor, and becomes a "Talk of the Town" reporter for the *New Yorker* (until April 1957). In a few days he becomes a "Talk Writer," the title designating a writer whose copy does not go to a rewrite man.

1957   His son David* is born January 19. In April Updike leaves the *New Yorker* and New York for Ipswich, Massachusetts (site of fictional Tarbox of *Couples*), where he and his family live in a house called "Little Violet" on Essex Road. Receives Harper and Brothers' rejection of his 600-page novel *Home* begun after high school. *Go Away*, another novel, is written later.

1958   First book published, *The Carpentered Hen and Other Tame Creatures* (fifty-five poems) with Harper and Brothers, but he decides not to publish with that firm in the spring when Harper balks at the ending of *The Poorhouse Fair*. In the spring the Updikes purchase a seventeenth-century house at 26 East Street, Ipswich.

1959   First novel, *The Poorhouse Fair*, and first collection of stories, *The Same Door*, published with Alfred A. Knopf. Joins First Congregational Church in Ipswich. Updike reads Søren Kierkegaard* and Karl

Barth.* Wins a Guggenheim Fellowship to support the writing of *Rabbit, Run* (novel). After finishing a draft at the end of the year, he goes to Anguilla* for five weeks; while he is there, the book is provisionally accepted. His son Michael* is born May 14. "A Gift from the City" is selected for *The Best American Short Stories 1959*.

1960   *Rabbit, Run* published by Knopf after Updike reluctantly makes changes to avoid possible lawsuits for obscenity. *The Poorhouse Fair* wins the Rosenthal Award of the National Institute of Arts and Letters. Updike publishes in the *New Yorker* a famous tribute to Ted Williams, "Hub Fans Bid Kid Adieu."* Daughter Miranda* is born December 15.

1961   Updike now works in an office above a restaurant in the Caldwell Building on South Main Street. "Wife-wooing" included in *O. Henry Prize Stories 1961*.

1962   *Pigeon Feathers* (stories) and an adaptation for young people of Mozart's opera *The Magic Flute*, with illustrations, are published. "The Doctor's Wife" is included in *O. Henry Prize Stories 1962* and "Pigeon Feathers" in *The Best American Short Stories 1962*. Updike publishes an important memoir, "The Dogwood Tree," in *Five Boyhoods*. He teaches creative writing at Harvard during July and August. *Rabbit, Run* is published in London by Deutsch. Updike makes "emendations and restorations" for Penguin Books edition while living in Antibes, France, November–December. This text is later used for the Modern Library version and for the Knopf fifth printing; he makes further revisions in the 1995 *Rabbit Angstrom*, which brings together all four "Rabbit" novels. As Updike has said, "*Rabbit, Run*, in keeping with its jittery, indecisive protagonist, exists in more forms than any other novel of mine" (*RA*, "Introduction").

1963   *The Centaur* (novel) published and wins the National Book Award. The next year, *Telephone Poles and Other Poems* (sixty poems) also published. Updike marches in a civil rights demonstration.

1964   *Olinger Stories*, stories taken from the two previous collections, published by Vintage Books. *The Ring*, an adaptation of Wagner's *Ring of the Nibelung* cycle of operas, is published. Updike is elected to the National Institute of Arts and Letters, one of the youngest persons so honored. Receives an honorary doctor of letters degree from Ursinus College, June 8. Travels to Russia and Eastern Europe for the State Department in the U.S.-USSR Cultural Exchange Program.

1965   *Of the Farm* (novel), *Assorted Prose* (parodies, articles and reviews), *Verse* (a composite of his two previous verse collections, *Carpentered Hen* and *Telephone Poles*) and *A Child's Calendar* (twelve poems) are published. Updike wins Le prix du meilleur livre étranger for *The Centaur*. Attends a dinner at the White House in June. On a Sunday that same month the Ipswich Congregational Church is burned by lightning, as the First Congregational Church is burned in Tarbox

(*Couples*). Begins depositing his papers in Harvard's Houghton Library.

1966   *The Music School* (stories) published. "The Bulgarian Poetess," from *The Music School*, wins the First O. Henry Prize and is included in *O. Henry Prize Stories 1966*.

1967   Signs a letter urging Soviet writers to help restore Jewish cultural institutions. "Marching through Boston" is selected for *O. Henry Prize Stories 1967*. Receives an honorary Litt. D. from Moravian College, Bethlehem, Pennsylvania.

1968   *Couples* (novel) published, remains on the best-seller lists for a year and earns $360,000 in movie rights. Updike writes the Ipswich "Pageant" (*Three Texts from Early Ipswich*). Appears on the cover of *Time*, April 26, subject of the cover story "The Adulterous Society." "Your Lover Just Called" is included in *O. Henry Prize Stories 1968*. Takes his family to London to avoid Vietnam* War protests (among other reasons), and while there begins researching President James Buchanan.*

1969   *Midpoint and Other Poems* published. *Bottom's Dream*, an adaptation for children of Shakespeare's *A Midsummer Night's Dream*, with music by Felix Mendelssohn, published.

1970   *Bech: A Book* (a story cycle) published. Revised edition of *Rabbit, Run* published. Film *Rabbit, Run* appears, with James Caan, Carrie Snodgress, Anjanette Comer and Jack Albertson, directed by Jack Smight. Updike travels with daughter Elizabeth to Japan and Korea, where he gives a paper at the PEN conference in Seoul. Moves to 50 Labor-in-Vain Road, Ipswich. In May *The Fisherman's Wife* is produced, an opera with libretto by Updike and music by Gunther Schuller. "Bech Takes Potluck" is included in *O. Henry Prize Stories 1970*.

1971   *Rabbit Redux* (novel) published. Receives the Signet Society Medal for Achievement in the Arts.

1972   *Seventy Poems* published. *Museums and Women and Other Stories* published. Updike is appointed Honorary Consultant in American Letters to the Library of Congress (1972–75). March 8–14 lectures in Venezuela as a guest of Centro Venezolano Americano. Father dies April 16.

1973   Writes "Introduction" to *Soundings in Satanism*. Travels to Ghana, Nigeria, Tanzania, Kenya and Ethiopia on a Lincoln Lectureship from the Fulbright Board of Foreign Scholarships.

1974   *Buchanan Dying* (play) published. Updike and his wife Mary separate in September; he moves into an apartment at 151 Beacon Street, Boston, and teaches at Boston University in the fall. Contributes to an open letter to USSR Ambassador Anatoli Dobrynin to stop harassing Alexander Solzhenitsyn.

1975   *A Month of Sundays* (novel) published. *Picked-up Pieces* (articles and reviews) published. "Nakedness" is included in *O. Henry Prize Stories 1975*. Updike wins the Lotus Club Award of Merit. Undergoes PUVA (Psoráten Ultra-Violet "A") cure for psoriasis at Massachusetts General Hospital.

1976   *Marry Me: A Romance* (novel) published. *Buchanan Dying* premieres April 29 at Franklin and Marshall College, Lancaster, Pennsylvania. Updike is elected to the fifty-member American Academy of Arts and Letters* within the larger National Institute and is given the Special Award for Continuing Achievement in *O. Henry Prize Stories 1976*, which includes his "Separating." "The Man Who Loved Extinct Mammals" selected for *The Best American Short Stories 1976*. In March he and Mary Pennington Updike receive perhaps the first "no-fault" divorce awarded in Massachusetts.

1977   *Tossing and Turning* (poems) published. Revised edition with an introduction by Updike of *The Poorhouse Fair* published. On September 30 Updike marries Martha Ruggles Bernhard* at Clifton Lutheran Church, Marblehead, Massachusetts, and lives at 58 West Main Street, Georgetown, with her three sons. Takes Miranda and his mother to Spain and there writes "Spanish Sonnets."

1978   *The Coup* (novel) published. Updike testifies in Boston against government support of the arts before the House Subcommittee on Select Education and Labor.

1979   *Problems and Other Stories* published. *Too Far to Go: The Maples Stories* published and produced as an NBC two-hour movie directed by Fielder Cook, with Blythe Danner, Kathryn Walker and Michael Moriarty, and screenplay by William Hanley. *Talk from the Fifties* published.

1980   "Gesturing" included in *The Best American Short Stories 1980*. Film *The Music School* televised over the Public Broadcasting System as part of "The American Short Story" series the week of April 28. Updike has to be hospitalized for an emergency appendectomy that interrupts his trip to Kent State University for background information for *Rabbit Is Rich*.

1981   *Rabbit Is Rich* (novel) published (which in 1982, wins the National Book Critics Circle Award, the Pulitzer Prize for fiction and the American Book Award for fiction, the three major American literary fiction prizes). Updike is awarded the Edward MacDowell Medal for literature. "Still of Some Use" included in The *Best American Short Stories 1981*. Updike is the subject of a BBC documentary, "What Makes Rabbit Run?" which takes him to Berks County, Pennsylvania. Attends University of Rhode Island Summer Writers Conference, Kingston, Rhode Island, in July. Yields his chairmanship of the literary awards committee of the National Institute of Arts and Letters, and John Cheever* writes, "How splendid is his voice! How inestimable is the contribution he makes to western civilization! This is not to say that you have been forgiven for yielding your chairmanship" (Benjamin Cheever, ed., *The Letters of John Cheever*, New York: Simon and Schuster, 1988, 362).

1982   *Bech Is Back* (story cycle) published. On Updike's fiftieth birthday Knopf reissues, with revisions, *The Carpentered Hen*, the only trade book not published by Knopf. In May Updike moves to Beverly Farms, Massachusetts, about thirty miles from Harvard. Joins St. John's Episcopal Church. Receives an Albright College (Reading, Pennsylvania) honorary degree. For the second time he appears on the cover of *Time*, October 18, as subject of "Going Great at 50."

1983   *Hugging the Shore* (articles and reviews) published; the following year it wins the National Book Critics Circle Award for Criticism. In May Updike receives the Pennsylvania Distinguished Pennsylvania Artist Award from Governor Richard Thornburgh. "Deaths of Distant Friends" included in the *Best American Short Stories 1983*, and "The City" included in *O. Henry Prize Stories 1983*. Wins the Lincoln Literary Award bestowed by the Union League Club.

1984   *The Witches of Eastwick* (novel) published. Updike edits and introduces *The Best American Short Stories 1984*. Awarded the National Arts Club Medal of Honor. PBS film *The Roommate*, based on "The Christian Roommates" from *The Music School*, is shown January 27; it is produced by American Playhouse, directed by Neil Cox, with screenplay by Morton Miller, starring Barry Miller and Lance Guest. *Jester's Dozen* (twelve pieces from the *Harvard Lampoon*) published.

1985   *Facing Nature* (poems) published. "The Other" (*Trust Me*) included in *O. Henry Prize Stories 1985*. Updike receives Kutztown University Foundation's Director's Award "in recognition of leadership, dedication and service to others in the community, especially in the area of education." At the same ceremony his mother receives the university's Distinguished Alumni Service plaque.

1986   *Roger's Version* (novel) published. Updike attends the "Vienna Show" in Paris, featuring paintings by Gustav Klimt, Egon Schiele and Adolph Hitler.

1987   *Trust Me* (stories) published. Updike receives the Elmer Holmes Bobst Award for Fiction as well as the Peggy Varnadow Helmerich Award for life achievement. "The Afterlife" included in *The Best American Short Stories 1987*. Film *The Witches of Eastwick* premieres, directed by George Miller, starring Cher, Veronica Cartwright, Jack Nicholson, Michelle Pfeiffer and Susan Sarandon.

1988   *S.* (novel) published. "Leaf Season" selected for *O. Henry Prize Stories 1988*. PBS film *Pigeon Feathers*, an adaptation of "Pigeon Feathers" for American Playhouse, is directed by Sharon Miller, February 17.

Updike gives the PEN/Malamud Memorial Reading at the Folger Shakespeare Library, Washington, D.C., October. Brandeis University honors him with the Life Achievement Award.

1989 *Self-Consciousness* (memoirs) and *Just Looking* (essays on art) published. His mother dies, October 10. President Bush presents him the National Medal of Arts, November 17, at the White House. Updike gives the Reading Public Library a collection of sixty first editions and other books he had inscribed to his parents.

1990 *Rabbit at Rest* (novel) published; next year it wins the Pulitzer Prize for fiction and the Critics Circle Award. Only Booth Tarkington, William Faulkner and Updike among novelists have won the Pulitzer twice. Updike discusses his childhood and Rabbit books for *The South Bank Show* (London Weekend Television); the program dramatizes scenes from the four Rabbit novels.

1991 *Odd Jobs* (essays) published. Updike is awarded Italy's Scanno Prize for *Trust Me*. "A Sandstone Farmhouse" wins "First Prize" in *O. Henry Prize Stories 1991* and is included in *The Best American Short Stories 1991*.

1992 *Memories of the Ford Administration* published. Updike delivers keynote address at the Illinois Humanities Council's annual festival in Chicago, November 30. Receives an honorary Doctor of Letters degree from Harvard University.

1993 *Collected Poems, 1953–1993* published. In July in Key West, Florida, Updike is awarded the Conch Republic Prize for Literature because his life's work reflects "the daring and creative spirit of the Keys." *Love Factories* published. Receives the Common Wealth Award.

1994 *Brazil* (novel) and *The Afterlife and Other Stories* published.

1995 *Rabbit Angstrom: A Tetralogy* (gathering of the four "Rabbit" novels) published in Everyman's Library. *A Helpful Alphabet of Friendly Objects* (twenty-six poems with photographs taken by his son, David) published. Updike is awarded the Howells Medal from the American Academy of Arts and Letters, an award given to the best fiction work of the previous five years. Receives the French rank Commandeur de l'Ordre des Arts et des Lettres.

1996 *In the Beauty of the Lilies* (novel) published and receives the Ambassador Book Award. *Golf Dreams* (essays and stories) published.

1997 *Toward the End of Time* (novel) published. Updike begins and ends "Murder Makes the Magazine," a story whose body is composed of daily additions by winning entrants on the website Amazon.com. Receives the Campion Award September 11, given by the Jesuit magazine *America* to "a distinguished Christian person of letters." Wins the Ambassador Book Award.

1998   *Bech at Bay* (story cycle) published. Updike edits *A Century of Arts and Letters* and contributes the "Foreword" and a chapter, "1938–47: Decade of the Row." On May 2 receives the Harvard Arts First Medal. Receives the Thomas Cooper Library Medal from the University of South Carolina, November 13–14. Receives the National Book Foundation medal for distinguished lifetime achievement November 18 and publishes his speech as *Of Prizes and Print* (stories and the novella, "Rabbit Remembered"), a twenty-one-page booklet.

1999   *More Matter* (essays and reviews) published.

2000   *Gertrude and Claudius* published. *Licks of Love* published. *On Literary Biography* published, though dated 1999.

An encyclopedia . . . is a blasphemy—a commercially inspired attempt to play God, by creating in print a replica of Creation. . . . [I]t breaks your heart at the end, because it leaves you as alone and bewildered as you were not knowing anything.

—John Updike, from *IB*

"I am going from door to door trying to sell subscriptions to twenty-four volumes of more fact than fancy called *The Popular Encyclopedia*. I dare say you would have no use for it."

"Well, now, we can't be altogether sure without hearing about it."

—John Updike, from *IB*

Well, what about the *Encylcopedia Britannica*, its row of soldiers in leather uniform, that alphabetical universe of negotiable truths, of facts I can *use?* Bent low in the library wing chair, my aged eyesight strained, I consult, I memorize, I rush upstairs and pop the stolen tidbit still warm into the humming word processor, fortifying the stew of my own that therein simmers. Bliss!

—John Updike, from "Five Remembered Moments of
Utter Reading Bliss" (*MM*)

A

Abortion. Updike uses the subject of abortion often because it forces his characters* to face moral choices, and thus abortion helps to define character. When Ruth Leonard Byer* tells Harry "Rabbit" Angstrom* to leave his wife Janice* or she will abort his child, Rabbit returns to his family, but for the rest of his life he hopes that Ruth did not abort their child (*RR*). Abortion threatens Rabbit's hope of achieving perfection, glimpsed in his baby girl Rebecca, and he becomes convinced that Ruth lied about aborting his child. He decides that she bore him a daughter, and he seeks this daughter throughout his life, though he shies away from certain knowledge at the end in order to keep intact his dream of perfection. Rabbit is yoked to Ruth through the problem of abortion, yet in *RIR* Rabbit offers to arrange an abortion for Teresa "Pru" Lubell,* the fiancée of his son, Nelson Angstrom,* so Nelson will not be trapped into marriage as he had been. The personal problem is shown to be part of a national issue when Rabbit and his friends are outraged at the pope's conservative stand on abortion (*RIR*).

In *Marry*, begun shortly after *RR*, after Jerry Conant* decides that he must leave his wife, Ruth Conant,* for Sally Mathias, Ruth takes revenge by planning to terminate her imagined pregnancy; though she finds that she is not pregnant, her decision helps to clarify her feelings. In *RV* Roger Lambert* fails to argue Verna Ekelof* into an abortion by comparing her "baby" to a sardine, because, as Verna explains, she loves giving birth, feeling "split into two persons." Her decision underlines Lambert's failure to understand people he deems his inferiors. Also, Lambert is unmasked as a bigot since he hopes that the abortion will prevent the birth of a "tarbaby," since Verna has had black lovers. Piet Hanema* arranges an abortion for Foxy Whitman* (*Couples*), but only after their affair has ended and at the risk of ruining his marriage. Ironically, the abortion reunites Piet and Foxy and leads to marriage. *See* **Adultery; Feminism; Sex.**

Abraham (c. 1500 B.C.). The Book of Genesis states that God promised Abraham, the father of the Hebrews, that they would become a "great nation." When God told Abraham to sacrifice his son Isaac, Abraham's immediate compliance caused God to spare Isaac and formally renew his covenant with Abraham. Abraham has thus come to represent a man whose faith cannot be moved, and he may be an analogue for both Roger Lambert* and Dale Kohler,* each unwavering in his own notions of faith. Rebecca Abrams (her surname is another name for Abraham) reminds the committee deciding the merit of Dale's project that the God of Moses and Abraham was true objectively, not merely subjectively (*RV*). Dale's effort to objectively prove God's existence and his sly destruction by Lambert may provide an ironic parallel to the Abraham and Isaac story. *See* **Religion**.

Academia. Updike displays a sensitivity to the position of the teacher, attacks academic abstraction and the bureaucracy of knowledge and reveals an interest in the relationship of teaching to life. He saw the teacher's situation firsthand when he taught creative writing at Harvard* in the summer of 1962 and at Boston University in the fall of 1974. Nicholas Delbanco was a student of Updike's at Harvard and said that Updike served the "honorable role" of identifying talent when he saw it. He also claimed that he drove Updike from teaching. But Updike's research and readings have kept him close to colleges all over the world. Updike's portraits of teachers are not encouraging. He seems to favor teachers taking a personal interest in their students, but even then the immaturity of students does not assure that they will understand or value such interest. Teachers most often fail because they fail to relate their information or understanding in ways students can understand. In some cases, as with Updike at Harvard, the students are insufficiently valued—Updike failed three times to be accepted into Archibald MacLeish's writing course. In other cases, the student's values are slighted, as happened to Updike at Harvard when his religious convictions conflicted with his professor's view of the history of Western thought ("Humanities Course" [*CH; CP*, note]). A survey of Updike's treatment of teachers will make these various objections clearer.

As his father's student in science* class, he saw his father's hard work and the students' lack of respect for him, and he knew of his mother's fear when confronting a class. Also, he lived with his maternal grandfather, John Hoyer,* a former history* teacher, fictionalized as John Hook* in *PF*. His third novel, *C*, was written partly, as Updike said, to vindicate his father in the fictional guise of George Caldwell.* Hook and Caldwell are ineffective teachers; the former is too dogmatic, the latter too inventive. Ninety-four-year-old Hook debunks Abraham Lincoln* and defends traditional religious values rather patronizingly to prefect Stephen Conner,* who is deaf to such attitudes. Hook does not try to see Conner's views sufficiently to fully answer them. Caldwell's imaginative approach to the history of evolution is too sophisticated and rushed to capture his students' short attention span. Yet despite such ineffectuality, Caldwell is loved by his students for his personal concern about their lives. Updike reveals how susceptible teachers are to thoughtless adolescents in "Tomorrow and Tomorrow and So Forth" (*SD*) when Prosser, like Caldwell, fails to edify his high-school class and believes that a student loves him, despite contrary evidence. Another psychological probing showing the teacher's vulnerability concerns a Proustian* moment in which a failed love affair of years before is recalled when a student brings a chambered nautilus to "show and tell" ("More Stately Mansions" [*TM*]). Also, history professor Morrison learns to live with his fear that his career-long search for a "sweeping and unifying insight" will forever elude him ("Slippage" [*TM*]). Updike used college settings in *RV* and *MF* to attack the stale territorializing and ludicrous jargon rife in the disciplines of religion* and history. These novels may reflect Updike's reading of a mentor, Vladimir Nabokov,* whose *Pale Fire* (1962) parodied academic scholarship. Roger Lambert* merely blows the dust off his notes on the church fathers before lecturing (*RV*), and Lambert must later shield himself from the sexual seductiveness of Verna Ekelof* while he tries to teach her about death in poetry. Alf Clayton* is also distracted by his female student's efforts to arouse him while conferring about her paper on sexuality in Theodore Roosevelt (*MF*).

Teachers often act as foils for central characters. Thus in *Coup* Frederick Craven, Government Professor at McCarthy College, teaches "Plato to Pound: Totalitarianism as the Refuge for Superior Minds," which sounds fascistic to the Marxist Col. Felix Ellelloû.* An adulterer, Marty Tothero,* Harry "Rabbit" Angstrom's* coach, teaches him bromides about the "sacredness of achievement." Former teacher Freddy Thorne* becomes the leader of games* that are intended to disillusion friends like Foxy Whitman,* and he conducts therapeutic sessions that reveal Piet Hanema's* fear of death. Piet leaves his wife Angela Hanema,* an astronomy professor's niece who had only mild success trying to teach Piet about astronomy. After the divorce she teaches children.*

Teaching at the college level seems to be an exercise in self-concern. In *MF* and *RV* Updike shows theology and history professors obsessed with narrow specialties. Alf Clayton defends himself with wit and cunning against colleagues infatuated by current critical methods like deconstructionism (*MF*), but Roger Lambert cleverly ruins a rival, Dale Kohler* (*RV*). Though Clayton and Lambert are absorbed in their studies of President James Buchanan* and the church fathers, respectively, neither can wall out the world. Clayton blends his own failed love affair into Buchanan's broken engagement, and Lambert's translation of Tertullian* fosters fantasies of his wife in bed with Dale. Playing academic politics, Lambert argues his position, derived from Karl Barth,* against Dale, knowing that it will alienate committee members who fear being aligned with Barth; Lambert's "counterspin" succeeds. Other aspects of academe pass under Updike's eagle eye in *RV* and *MF*, like the academy's habit of professionalizing all knowledge, so that the study of the Holocaust becomes "Holocaustics." In *MF* debates rage that seek to expunge the author as Clayton's peers argue about "deconstructionism," which attempts to reveal the utter instability of any text, rendering the quest for the truth of any work impossible. As Updike remarked in a review, deconstructionists provide "plenty of reference to implied social constructs but little to enduring truthfulness."

On the moral scale of academic misuse of power, Lambert and Clayton sexually harass their students—Lambert through a tutorial with his stepniece on William Cullen Bryant's "Thanatopsis" and Clayton during a conference on phallic imagery in Teddy Roosevelt's speeches. Angela Hanema may well summarize the attitudes of Clayton and Lambert: "I like teaching. It's easier than learning" (*Couples*). That seems to be the implication of Updike's satirical poems about academe in *CH*, in which he transforms the daily science news into light-verse* burlesque ("V. B. Nimble, V. B. Quick"), and in "Humanities Course" he attacks Harvard professor Varder, who used a humanistic approach to undermine Christianity, and who, according to Updike, was the "personification" of Harvard. Additionally, "The Astronomer" (*PF*) describes a scientist-humanist clash when Bela, an astronomy professor, ridicules Plato* and Søren Kierkegaard* to mock a friend's spiritual crisis. Ministers* who are too humanistic are also treated critically as teachers. In "Pigeon Feathers" (*PigF*) a boy despairs when he is dissatisfied by his minister's version of the afterlife. Similarly, when Clarence Wilmot* loses his faith after reading modern German theology professors, American theology professors fail to help him restore it (*IB*). To Nelson Angstrom* Kent State University is merely a youth camp where students are taught how to intimidate the undereducated. Rabbit, though, is outraged when he learns that Kent would allow Nelson to major in geography. Rabbit's best tutor is his mistress, fourth-grade teacher Thelma Harrison,* who, through unconventional sex, provides him the knowledge of nothingness that eases his anxiety about death.*

Although Updike is noted for somewhat donnishly demonstrating erudition, from the Greek myths in *C* (which he called his "schoolish" novel) to the wisdom of the church fathers and computers in *RV*, his summer of teaching creative writing at Harvard left him frightened at not being able to distinguish his own writing from his students', and like Ernest Hemingway,* he feared that teaching might adversely affect his writing, since it was "truly depleting and corrupting." He has never supported his writing by teaching or any other nonwriting activity and has pointed to the great difficulties of teaching contemporary writing. Modern writers, he notes, show occasional "thinness" at the world's operations, except for the academic world. Updike admires John Barth, Joyce Carol Oates and Saul Bellow* for being able to teach as well as write, but he finds Bellow in his fiction sometimes a "little professor" who thus "muddles" his endings. Updike fears that no Hemingway will appear again because "print culture" has become academic. Even the writer lured to give a college reading, like Henry Bech,* risks humiliation when he finds that an adoring collector merely uses his signed books as a commodity ("Three Illuminations in the Life of an Author" [*BB*]), and he suffers an identity crisis similar to David Kern's* ("Pigeon Feathers" [*PigF*]) in "Bech Panics" (*BB*). But Updike has revised his earlier opinion of academia somewhat and in "Bech Presides" (*BaB*) has shown Bech supervising "The Forty," a group like the American Academy of Arts and Letters* within the National Institute of Arts and Letters, and trying (and failing) to resist efforts to dissolve that body. As Updike remarked in writing about the American Academy of Arts and Letters, because writers work in isolation and silence, they need collegiality more than other artists. Teaching has obviously afforded such collegiality to writers as different as Philip Roth* and Joyce Carol Oates, and Updike's close relation to dozens of colleges suggests that somehow academia is valuable to him as well.

Bibliography: Updike, *OJ*; "Man Is an Island," *New Yorker* 4 Dec. 1995: 103–4, 106–7.

Acheson, Dean (1893–1971). The Harvard* educated secretary of state (1949–53) under President Harry Truman and defender of Alger Hiss, an alleged Soviet spy, Dean Acheson faced Senator Joseph McCarthy's charges that he coddled State Department Communists. Acheson's recommendation to President Lyndon Johnson* in 1968 that he end the Vietnam* War helped halt the bombing of North Vietnam. In a dream Peter Caldwell,* when quizzed about cabinet secretaries, can only recall Acheson of all the members of the president's cabinet, though his mnemonic "St. Wapnical" should have brought them all to mind. Acheson's courage in combatting McCarthyism and recommending the end of the Vietnam War link him to George Caldwell,* who serves his principal loyally despite mistreatment. Like Acheson, Caldwell is remembered in his obituary as a man of good will and a patriot (*C*).

Adams, Nick. The hero of Ernest Hemingway's* *Nick Adams Stories*, Nick has been psychologically damaged in World War I and seeks to recover from his experiences by living honestly in his senses. Accordingly, his language and thinking are spare. In the poem "Meditation on a News Item," about how Fidel Castro places first in the Hemingway fishing tournament, Updike notes that Hemingway said to the Cuban leader, "You are a lucky novice." To the speaker this sounded like Nick Adams talking: "Succinct / Wry, ominous, innocent" (*TP*).

Adams, Samuel (1722–1803). An American patriot most famous for devising the Boston Tea Party, Samuel Adams was educated at Harvard* and supported the Sons of Liberty, whose demonstration against the Townshend Acts prompted the Boston Massacre. He was a force in generating the Revolutionary War and afterward became the governor of Massachusetts. Updike points to Adams in listing various rebels from whom he, as an American Protestant, had benefitted (*SC*). Adams's fidelity, in spite of opposition, to his published political views might have suggested to Updike a similarity to his unpopular stand on Vietnam,* as well as his concern for adhering to the truths he discovered about sex* and religion.*

Addams, Charles (1912–1988). A cartoonist and illustrator for the *New Yorker** (1930–90), Charles Addams was noted for his amusingly grotesque and macabre characters, later called the Addams Family, about whom a television series and two films were created. Though nightmarish, his ghouls are not threatening. Addams is mentioned by Sarah Worth* when she notes that her and her husband Charles's arrival and separation at parties resemble the Addams cartoon of a skier whose tracks go straight to a tree and appear again on the other side, to an onlooker's befuddlement. The cartoon implies that Sarah's transcendental strivings have left her husband confused as she magically divests herself of his material world. The cartoon may also symbolize her life with Charles, apparently stymied by his philandering (tree = phallus?) and only overcome when she has seduced the Arhat* (*S*.). See **Cartooning; Drawing and Painting**.

Adultery. Adultery is absent in Updike's one play and appears seldom in his poetry* but often in his stories and everywhere in his novels. In adultery all three parties are in the middle—sexually, socially and morally—and middleness* is Updike's key subject. Though some assume that Updike glorifies adultery, he really uses it as a negative example, since he vividly establishes its harm. Even when divorce* does not result, adultery can be harrowing, as *RR* and alternate endings in *Marry* show. For a family, the results can be emotionally devastating ("Separating" [*TF*]) and even lead to death*: Harry "Rabbit" Angstrom's* adultery results in his baby's drowning and perhaps an abortion* (*RR*), while in *RRed* adultery contributes to Jill Pendleton's* death. In *Couples* Piet Hanema's* affair brings about an abortion and the breakup of two homes; two families dissolve in one ending of *Marry*. Adultery and divorce bring to Joey Robinson* a new wife but to his mother a heart attack (*OF*). Discarded women of adulterers are wretched—Janice Angstrom* and Ruth Leonard Byer* (*RR*), Jill (*RRed*), Teresa Angstrom* (*RaR*), Angela Hanema,* Verna Ekelof* (*RV*), Norma Latchett* (*BIB*), Joan Maple* (*TF*)—and sometimes vindictive—Georgene Thorne (*Couples*), Jane Smart,* Sukie Rougemont* and Alexandra Spofford* (*W*) and Gloria Turnbull* (*TE*). Men are sometimes bitter when they are cast aside: Rabbit (in both *RR* and *RRed*), Freddy Thorne* and Ken Whitman* (*Couples*), Henry Bech* ("Bech Takes Pot Luck" [*BB*]), the Arhat* (*S.*) and Ronnie Harrison* (*RaR*).

Though Updike shows the harmful effects of adultery, he also explores how it can stem from a need for self-actualization. In *Couples* Piet Hanema says that he feels that his high valuation is verified when his lover speaks his name. For this an adulterer will risk wife and children (*RR, RRed, RaR, Couples, MF, TF*). Janice Angstrom clearly gains a greater confidence in evoking love (*RRed, RIR, RaR*), and if Ruth did not abort her baby, her daughter commemorates her romance. To Freddy Thorne, adulterers are heroic since they challenge the Puritan rejection of the body, and adultery humanizes people and creates a new religion* (*Couples*). In "The Music School" (*MuS*) the narrator says that we are "all pilgrims faltering toward divorce." Adultery is both a symptom of a post-Christian society and a way back to traditional values. Tom Marshfield* (*MS*) appears to work his way back to God through adultery with Ms. Prynne.*

Often riddled with guilt (Piet is the exception), the Updike adulterer can be reduced to abject distress (*TF*) or become obsessed about the end of the affair (*MF*). Updike's adulteresses are less troubled by adultery. Janice's affairs with Charlie Stavros* (*RRed*) and Webb Murkett* (*RIR*) clearly strengthen her. The affair with Charlie provides her a chance to bring her lover back from a life-threatening heart attack and then ends only because of Miriam Angstrom's* intervention. Janice cries after her night with Webb only from regret that her greatest night of sex will not be repeated. Sarah Worth* (*S.*) is comically impersonal as she seduces a professed holy man and tape-records the seduction. Isabel Leme* simply accepts her adulterous prostitution as an economic necessity, though it torments Tristâo Raposo,* whose affairs are intended to degrade her (*B*). Essie Wilmot/Alma DeMott* pragmatically accepts sex as the currency of Hollywood and thinks little of sleeping with her leading men while she is married: adultery is merely part of the economic situation, and meanwhile it also verifies the high valuation she places upon herself (*IB*). Gertrude awakens through adultery like a princess in a fairy tale (*GC*). Interestingly, in some cases women scorn men who resist straying (George Caldwell* [*C*]; Piet Hanema [*Couples*]; Darryl Van Horne* [*W*]). *See* **Abortion; Feminism; Sex.**

Bibliography: Markle, *FL*; Tallent, *MM*; Greiner, *Adultery*; Schiff, *UV*; O'Connell, *UP*.

Aesop (620?–560? B.C.). The Greek Aesop compiled beast fables from the oral tradition that were later written in Greek by Babrius in the form in which they are primarily known. Aesop's "The Ant and the Grasshopper" is the source of Updike's "Brother Grasshopper" (*A*), and Updike compares translations of the tale to decide that the grasshopper was not a cicada. *See* **Classical Literature; *The Tale of Peter Rabbit*; Thurber, James**.

Bibliography: Updike, "Introduction to *Brother Grasshopper*" (*MM*).

African Americans. African Americans act as a goad, forcing placid indifference to give way to communication and empathy. *RA* depicts the American evolution during 1959–90 from racial distrust and violence toward accommodation. Though African Americans are an absent presence in *RR*, in the grim, comic and brilliantly articulate Skeeter* of *RRed*, Updike provides one of the finest black characters in American fiction. (It has been suggested that Skeeter may have been based on the black Marxist Stokely Carmichael, later named Kwame Toure.) Harry "Rabbit" Angstrom* meets Skeeter in an African-American bar, Jimbo's Friendly Lounge, having been invited by a black coworker, Buchanan. There Rabbit becomes immersed in a new world in which the pianist Babe evokes profound emotions from him by her playing, in which marijuana is freely used, and in which he is introduced to Skeeter, who speaks in a language marked by biblical images and black argot. In a strange updating of the relationship of Huckleberry Finn and Jim, Updike uses Skeeter to instruct Rabbit about the black perspective on war, the Industrial Revolution and America. Updike has said that the encounter of Harry "Rabbit" Angstrom and Skeeter has a "religious meaning" and that if Skeeter proclaims himself Jesus, he ought to be taken seriously. But Rabbit's resistance to Skeeter's teaching goes very deep, and, like many whites, Rabbit thinks that even President Richard Nixon is trying "to make 'em [blacks] all rich without putting 'em to the trouble of doing any work." Even though Skeeter provides daily consciousness-raising sessions in the style of the 1960s and they share a woman, Jill Pendleton,* and experience homosexual feelings for each other, Skeeter ultimately makes little dent in Rabbit's racist armor. (Henry Bech,* a Jewish writer, feels more agreeable to African Americans. He notes at a party in which everyone dresses in white that the whitest person is a black woman painted, which he interprets as indicating that "America at heart is black. . . . The Negro lives deprived and naked among us as the embodiment of truth, and that when the castle of credit cards collapses a black god will redeem us" ["White on White" (*BIB*)]. Because most middle-class American whites Updike depicts are racist, even those who fought alongside African Americans in Vietnam,* Rabbit's house is burned in an effort to drive Skeeter out and teach Rabbit a lesson about middle-class values. (Updike relates in *SC* that in Shillington* a black family's home was burned under suspicious circumstances and with less provocation.) Even at a baseball game (the national pastime) fans yell, "Kill that black bastard" (*RRed*). Yet throughout *RA* Rabbit fantasizes about sexual integration with black women.

Certainly the birth of two sons to Updike's daughter and her Ghanaian husband, to whom he dedicated *SC*, encouraged his favorable depiction of African Americans and precipitated his use of magic realism* in *B* to enable whites and blacks to literally understand what it is like to live in the other's skin. *B* demonstrates Updike's vision of the future expressed in *SC*, though the novel has a tragic ending. Through magic realism this novel provides a more personal, but less ambitious achievement than Updike's meticulous re-creation of an imaginary black nation similar to Ethiopia in *Coup* and the education its leader receives at a midwestern American college. *See* **Black Muslims; Ellelloû, Col. Hakim Felix; Evers, Medgar; *The Same Door*.**

Bibliography: Detweiler, *JU*; Greiner, *JU*; Edward M., Jackson "Rabbit Is Racist," *College Language Association Journal* 28 (June 1985): 444–51; Ristoff, *UA*.

The Afterlife (New York: Knopf, 1994). The collection of stories in *A* (1987–94) treats primarily middle-aged men, roughly Updike's age. It is chiefly important for the stories modeled on Updike's mother, Linda Hoyer Updike,* who died in 1989, "A Sandstone Farmhouse," "The Other Side of the Street," "The Brown Chest," "His Mother Inside Him" and "The Black Room." All reveal helplessness in the face of a loved one's decline, as well as the subjective character of grieving. Powerful images from photographs or memory summarize a life and the mysterious bonds that tie one to it. Death is described with magic realism* in the unusual setting of England ("The Afterlife"), and the isolation of the dying is deepened through myth* ("The Journey of the Dead"). Updike's signature story of suburban sophis-tication, extramarital complications and musical expertise is displayed wittily in "The Man Who Became a Soprano." Homosexuality* is a new subject in "Cruise" and "The Rumor," and in "Grandparenting" Updike revisits Rich-ard* and Joan Maple* to witness their grandchild's birth, their old feelings and their new alignments. "Tristan and Iseult" uses the central myth of *Couples*, Tristan and Isolde,* but less seriously, and points toward *B*'s sym-bolic treatment of the myth. Like "The Afterlife," "Farrell's Caddie" applies magic realism comically to reveal the extrasensory prescience of a Scots golf caddie.

Bibliography: Michiko Kakutani, "Of Time, Loss and Death: The Vista Is Length-ening," *New York Times* 8 Nov. 1994: C-17; Jay Parini, "All His Wives Are Mother," *New York Times Book Review* 8 Nov. 1994: 7; Paul Gray, "Doglegs of Decrepitude," *Time* 14 Nov. 1994: 96.

Aga Khan (1800–1881). Thought to be a descendant of Muhammad, Aga Khan governed Kerman Province in Iran until 1840, when he fled to British-controlled India after an unsuccessful Iranian coup. For helping Britain con-trol frontier tribes, Aga Khan became the leader of the Ismailis in India, Pakistan, Africa and Syria. Roger Lambert* says that Aga Khan exemplifies how people may still believe that a person is divine despite sybaritic excesses

(*RV*), and Lambert's observation is borne out in the charismatic Jesse Smith* of *IB*. Religious persons like Tom Marshfield* (*MS*), Ed Parsley* (*W*) and the Arhat* (*S.*) who represent the divine though they are sexually quite active recur in Updike's novels. *See* **Ministers; Religion**.

Agnew, Spiro (1918–1996). Thirty-ninth vice president of the United States (1969–73) under Richard Nixon, Spiro Agnew became the first U.S. vice president to resign because of criminal charges that he accepted bribes while governor of Maryland. The political opposite of Marxist Col. Félix Ellelloû,* Agnew is discussed by Kutunda,* Ellelloû's mistress, in order to upset Ellelloû because she feels estranged from him (*Coup*). A demagogic speaker who claimed to speak for the "silent majority," Agnew delighted in coining such alliterative phrases as "nabobs of negativism," which Updike notes in *SC*. Agnew also insisted that despite the protests against the Vietnam* War, Nixon had the support of most Americans, the same assumption upon which Ellelloû bases his rule, and which leads to his ouster. *See* **American History**.

AIDS. Acquired immune deficiency syndrome (AIDS), mentioned as putting an end to the idyllic sex of the 1960s since it is spread mainly by sexual contact (*SC*), is a pandemic that is nearly always fatal. When a person is infected by the human immune deficiency virus (HIV), which does not always lead to AIDS, that person gradually loses protection from pneumonia and other diseases. An estimated twenty million persons were infected by HIV worldwide in 1995. Though Harry "Rabbit" Angstrom,* like most heterosexuals, assumes that HIV and AIDS are entirely homosexual diseases and resents the sympathy consequently accorded homosexuals, he is empathetic toward his son Nelson's* homosexual friend Lyle, an AIDS victim (*RaR*). Nelson had helped Lyle pay for AIDS drugs with money embezzled from Springer Motors.* Since Lyle is dying and Rabbit has life-threatening heart trouble, Rabbit's homophobia diminishes, and Lyle becomes for Rabbit a guide in facing death.* *See* **Homosexuality**.

Airplanes. Airplanes function symbolically throughout Updike's work and particularly in *RA* as angelic assistants for lovers or harbingers of death.* Harry "Rabbit" Angstrom* feels that the "five windows" of his senses are not enough to experience his new freedom when he leaves the "dead and living alike" five miles below as his plane carries him to a Caribbean vacation (*RIR*). Yet in *RaR* "Rabbit" fears that his son, daughter-in-law, grandson and granddaughter will die as their plane lands in Florida.* The feared plane crash mirrors Rabbit's vision of "his own death, shaped vaguely like an airplane," (*RaR*). The vision resembles that of Piet Hanema,* who dreams of dying in a plane crash, payment, Piet thinks, for his adultery (*Couples*). Rabbit's fear of death is underlined by his frequent graphic recall of the December 1988 crash of Pan Am Flight 103 over Lockerbie, Scotland, killing 270.

But when Jerry Conant* and Sally Mathias plan a sexual liaison in Washington, their British Overseas Airlines Corporation (BOAC) plane seemingly lifts them toward heaven (*Marry*), and when United Airlines punningly carries them back from their affair, their souls seem as united as their bodies had been. Later, when they end their affair, a plane soars overhead, a shadow of their "flight," placing them distinctly on the ground. (Similarly, a plane flies overhead as Rabbit lies stricken on the Florida basketball court [*RaR*]). In "A Constellation of Events" (*TM*) Betty flies with her husband on business to Philadelphia and distracts herself from fear of flying by reading a book lent to her by a man about to become her lover. Since Updike had written an important favorable review of Erica Jong's novel *Fear of Flying*, he may have made a wry allusion to it in this incident. *See* **Science**.

Bibliography: Ristoff, *JU*.

Algeria. The Algerian War is mentioned by Col. Félix Ellelloû* in *Coup* because he played a decisive role in winning Algerian independence. A league of French generals, the OAS, determined to keep Algeria French through terrorism, but newly elected president of France Charles de Gaulle executed several generals in order to assure the former colony its freedom.

Allentown, Pennsylvania. A Pennsylvania city thirty miles east of Reading* noted for its cultural and intellectual life, Allentown housed the Liberty Bell during the Revolutionary War. Janice Angstrom* lies when she tells her parents that Harry "Rabbit" Angstrom,* her husband, has gone to Allentown to sell a car in order to pretend that Rabbit has not deserted her again (*RR*). Allentown is not given a fictitious name, contrary to Updike's usual practice in *RA*, in which Reading is Brewer* and Mt. Penn* is Mt. Judge.* In his stories and *C* fictional Olinger is based on Shillington.*

"Alphonse and Gaston." "Alphonse and Gaston" was a popular comic strip by Frederick Burr Opper (1857–1937), the American cartoonist for the *New York Journal* who also created Happy Hooligan and illustrated books by Mark Twain. His witty situations often featured excessively polite characters, as in the courtesies of the civilized centaurs George Caldwell* and Phillips unable to decide who should go through a door first (*C*). *See* **Art; Cartooning; Comedy; Drawing and Painting**.

Alter ego. Alter ego is a psychological term that refers to an artist's creation of a character* similar to himself. Thus Updike's Peter Caldwell* (*C*), Joey Robinson* (*OF*), Richard Maple* (*TF*), Piet Hanema* (*Couples*) and Alf Clayton* (*MF*) resemble Updike in a few biographical details, enabling him to use personal material while distancing himself from his imaginary character. Peter Caldwell most closely resembles Updike, since Peter's town of Olinger is based on Shillington,* the school he attends resembles Updike's Shillington High School and Peter's father teaches science* at Olinger High as Updike's father had at Shillington High. George Caldwell,* Peter's father, is so close to Updike's own father that Wesley Updike* admitted that Updike got him "right" as Caldwell. In addition, Peter's home in Firetown* is very similar to Updike's in Plowville.* In *OF* Joey's connection to Updike is less direct than Peter's since he is in advertising and married for the second time, but he becomes an alter ego when he visits a farm in a location resembling Plowville, and Mrs. Robinson* resembles Updike's mother. His alter ego is even clearer when he appears in "The Other Side of the Street" in *A*. Richard Maple, the hero of stories collected as *TF*, like Updike, is recently married, lives in both New York* and a small Massachusetts town, has four children and is separated and then divorced in order to remarry. A third alter ego, Piet Hanema, a contractor, has two girls, as Updike does, and lives in an upper-middle-class town with many friends conflicted in their marriages. Piet, significantly, like Updike, respects craftsmanship. Alf Clayton (*MF*) is a comic alter ego, since, like Updike, he is involved with President James Buchanan* and distrusts the literary approach called deconstructionism. Other characters bear transposed traces of an alter ego, such as Essie Wilmot*/Alma DeMott* (*IB*) in her meteoric career in film,* which Updike loves. Henry Bech* (*BB, BIB, BaB*) can be considered both alter ego and anti–alter ego, since he is a fictionalist like Updike but is Jewish, far more publicly visible, husband to a woman nearly half his age, and a murderer and winner of the Nobel Prize.* Bech's trips to Eastern Europe, Africa and Asia resemble those of Updike, though his writer's block and his novels' subjects do not. In *Travel Light* Bech created a book similar to Jack Kerouac's* *On the Road*, a book Updike has publicly denounced.

Perhaps because of Updike's personal style* and vivid characterizations, he has had to remind his readers that Harry "Rabbit" Angstrom* (*RA*) is not an alter ego, but an anti–alter ego, an experiment in writing about a person who might have been he had he not gone to Harvard* and become a writer. Although Updike has insisted that "he was never a basketball star like Harry Angstrom;" still, both men are golfers, live in a suburb of Reading* and experience spiritual crises. Though Updike explains, "For a novel there has to be something out of the autobiographical to excite the author," nevertheless, alter egos supply a special power to his characterizations. Updike has also remarked that he created for his reviews and essays "an alter ego, a kind of sage younger brother, urbane and proper, with none of the warts, tics, obsessions, and compulsions that necessarily disfigure an imaginative writer, who must project a world out of a specific focus and selected view—whose peculiarities, indeed, *are* his style, his personality, his testimony, his peculiar value . . . a kind of lawyer in the family" (*OJ*).

Alton. A fictitious town based on Reading,* Pennsylvania, used in the early short stories of *SD* and *PigF* and the novel *C*, Alton is the city in which George Caldwell* and his son Peter Caldwell* are forced to spend the night (*C*). Alton is called Brewer* in *RA*. Alton is described as having a great department store, Foy's, the fictitious name for Pomeroy's, where Updike's mother, Linda Hoyer Updike,* had worked. John Nordholm, the hero of "The Happiest I've Been" (*SD*), calls Alton "The suburb of a city like "Pandemonium."* *See* **Firetown; Shillington.**

Bibliography: Hamilton and Hamilton, *EJ*; Greiner, *OJ*.

Amazon.com. Amazon.com is an Internet Website on which segments of Updike fiction appeared during a contest inviting writers to contribute to a "chain story," "Murder Makes the Magazine."*

Amazons. In myth* Amazons ("breastless" in Greek) removed their right breasts to facilitate drawing their bows. Roger Lambert* recalls that the Amazons' self-mutilation contradicts the soft views of women that have dominated male thinking (*RV*). The queen of the Amazons, Penthesilea, was killed during the Trojan War by Achilles. *See* **Classical Literature.**

American Academy of Arts and Letters. Resembling the Académie Française, the American Academy of Arts and Letters was created in 1898 in order to gather together the greatest writers, artists and composers in America. It was founded by Archer M. Huntington, who gave the group an endowment and a mansion where it still meets. Two tiers of membership were created in the original National Institute of Arts and Letters and the Academy of Arts and Letters, a general body of recently voted members (the institute) and a small legislative group elected from the institute (the academy); by the 1980s a single body, the American Academy of Arts and Letters, emerged. The National Institute was conservative and opposed avant-garde and liberal artists; some of its members were racist, sexist and anti-Semitic. Consequently, H. L. Mencken* vigorously opposed it, and Sinclair Lewis* and Ezra Pound,* though members, were opposition leaders from within. Since the academy seemed to resist originality, it served little purpose to some members except to give grants to emerging writers, artists and musicians. But until recently it failed to provide grants to avant-grade writers. In 1964 Updike became one of the youngest members elected to the National Institute. He joined the academy in 1976 and served as secretary from 1978 to 1981, and chancellor (president) from 1987 to 1990. John Cheever* wrote in a letter that he would not forgive Updike for relinquishing the presidency: "How inestimable is the contribution he makes to western civilization!" (Cheever, *Letters*, 362).

Updike's "*Scarlet Letter* trilogy" gained impetus when he presented the essay "Hawthorne's Religious Language" to the academy; it was published in the *Proceedings of the American Academy and Institute of Arts and Letters* 30 (1979):21–27, the outgrowth of interests in Hawthorne* begun in 1975 with *MS*. In 1995 Updike was awarded the W. D. Howells Medal from the academy for having written the best fictional work of the previous five years, a period that included the novels *RaR*, *MF* and *B* and the stories in *A*.

Updike's first contact with the academy might have been when *PF* won the Rosenthal Award given by the National Institute of Arts and Letters for the best first novel. Thirty years later he edited the history of the academy, *A Century of Arts and Letters*, providing a "Foreword" and the chapter "1938–1947: Decade of the Row." (Updike's talent as historian had been shown previously in his research into President James Buchanan* for *BD* and into his family in *SC*.) The "Decade" essay provides a careful analysis of the period in which the academy liberalized, stymied a split between the institute and the academy and overcame the racism, sexism, anti-Semitism and fascism of some members. Its election of Ezra Pound showed that its veneration for art* went beyond politics and personality. In his "Foreword" Updike states that arts organizations are antithetical to "the American grain," yet Updike's presence in the academy represents not only the acknowledgment of his extraordinary powers by his peers, but also his own active participation in benefitting younger writers. In the New York*–based academy Updike had found the literati he had avoided when he lived in New York. This club included such Nobel* laureates as T. S. Eliot,* William Faulkner,* Eugene O'Neill and Toni Morrison and enabled Updike to forge even stronger bonds with writers he already admired, some of whom were friends, like John Barth (whom he had nominated for membership in 1973), John Cheever, James Dickey, John Hollander, Joyce Carol Oates, Philip Roth* and Kurt Vonnegut. Updike also notes writers who refused membership to whom he feels indebted: Vladimir Nabokov,* James Thurber,* J. D. Salinger* and Edmund Wilson.* Updike had written of his own ancestors what could be his view of the hundreds of academy members who preceded him: "We reverence them because they participate in the mystery of our own being" (*SC*).

In "Bech Enters Heaven," Henry Bech's* dream of reaching heaven on earth is attained ironically when he becomes part of the famous academy. Yet he feels "tricked by a false ideal" and believes that he "entered heaven through sacrificing his selfhood and his ability to love" (*BIB*). In "Bech Presides" (*BaB*) Bech is tricked into taking the presidency of "The Forty," which resembles the American Academy. He doesn't realize that he has been used to help destroy the academy because the valuable real estate can be used by the brother-in-law of a greedy member.

Bibliography: Updike, *A Century of Arts and Letters* (New York: Columbia University Press, 1998).

American History. Throughout his career Updike has so integrated history with his narratives that a virtual chronicle of America could be constructed from his work. He also reopens debate on historical events and uses the past to reveal the present. In *W*, for example, Updike examines the Puritanism of America, wittily projecting Satan's appearance in 1970s Rhode Island. Updike has noted that each of his novels* identifies a "reigning" president,* and his first novel, *PF*, attempts to restore President James Buchanan's* reputation through debates between John Hook* and Stephen Conner,* who discuss Buchanan's role in ending slavery, Hook insisting that Abraham Lincoln* had ignored Buchanan's negotiated peace with the South. Updike revisits Buchanan in *BD*, the play, and *MF*, the novel, each focusing on how domestic tragedy brought Buchanan into politics—the play dramatizing zones of Buchanan's consciousness to explore his guilt for the death of his fiancée Ann Coleman,* and the novel suggesting parallels between dissent during Buchanan's period and President Gerald Ford's problems with civil distress and Vietnam* War protests. Besides personalizing history and rescuing Buchanan's reputation, the two works offer parallels to contemporary politics.

Updike uses American history most extensively in *RRed* and *IB*. In the former novel he examines the civil rights and "Black Power" movements of the 1960s, the moon landing, and the "sexual revolution"—issues that refute the claim that Updike is not a socially conscious novelist. In *RRed* Updike returns to the Civil War–Vietnam parallel with a fresh insight as he provides the perspective of an African American,* Skeeter,* who considers American history a cynical manipulation of blacks. Skeeter quotes Frederick Douglass and others to show how blacks, ostensibly free, were kept chained, but as a Vietnam veteran, he reveals that the war is a harbinger of the next development in American history, apocalyptic race war. Skeeter fails to persuade Harry "Rabbit" Angstrom,* who sometimes echoes ideas expressed by Updike (see "On Not Being a Dove" [*SC*]). *IB* particularizes American history, 1910–90, by evoking the daily life of a small town, probably modeled on Shillington,* and the rise to movie stardom of Essie Wilmot* while encapsulating events in the manner of John Dos Passos's newsreels or headlines in his novels in the *USA* trilogy. *IB*'s first segment traces the rise of the trade unions and the professionalizing of theology. The last segment delineates a religious cult, the CIA's involvement with other nations and the Watergate scandal. Throughout *IB* Updike provides a running history of the American film* industry, occasionally using real persons to heighten the sense of actuality.

Elsewhere, the contradictions of American foreign policy during the Cold War form the background of *Coup*, in which an East African country resists manipulation by Eastern and Western powers. Israeli-Arab conflicts are alluded to in "The Holy Land" (*BIB*) and the Korean War* in *RR*, as are the Cuban missile crisis* and the Bay of Pigs invasion in *Couples*. In this novel the tension of nuclear blackmail forms the context of Piet Hanema's* fear of death.* On the other hand, Updike imagines that some aspects of history, like the Gerald Ford administration, cannot be recalled even by professional historians (*MF*). History for Updike's world of "middleness"* is cultural, sometimes focusing on popular culture,* as in popular science* and the computer (*C, RV, TE*), music (*RA*), magazines (*RA*) and film* (*RA, IB*).

Bibliography: Vaughn, *JU*; Newman, *JU*; Ristoff, *UA*; Ristoff, *JU*.

American Literature. Of modern American writers, Updike has been among the most omnivorous readers in American literature. As a book reviewer and as part of his own exploration of his culture, he has steeped himself in past and contemporary American writers. Admitting in an interview* that as a young writer he had neglected American writers except for the humorists James Thurber* and Robert Benchley, Updike has since published commentary on Benjamin Franklin, Ralph Waldo Emerson,* Nathaniel Hawthorne,* Herman Melville,* Walt Whitman,* William Dean Howells and Edith Wharton. He presented these essays as readings, published some as separate books and revised others into introductions, afterwords or prefaces. Hawthorne particularly affected Updike's imaginative writing when he undertook a trilogy of novels based on *The Scarlet Letter* (*MS, RV* and *S*.). This investigation of America's Puritan heritage enabled Updike to explore the strengths and weaknesses of modern religious impulses and various attitudes toward women and sex. Such explorations helped Updike to immerse himself in what he called "American reality" and to replicate it, but he also delighted in revisiting Puritan authors such as Anne Bradstreet in writing the program notes for an Ipswich* pageant. He has often turned his attention to Melville, evaluating in one essay his entire work and in another concentrating on Melville's short fiction. Updike has stated that Whitman inspired *IB*, and he has often drawn American writing directly into his narrative, as in *MF*, which mentions a play based on Emily Dickinson, *TE*, which uses one of her poems, *RV*, in which Roger Lambert* tutors Verna Ekelof* in William Cullen Bryant's "Thanatopsis," and in the consciousness-raising session in which Skeeter* dramatizes and quotes extensively from Frederick Douglass (*RRed*).

In his chapter "1938–1947: Decade of the Row" in *A Century of Arts and Letters*, Updike provides a summary of American writing during these years and offers the epithet "workmanlike" to characterize this work, contrasting it to the better writing produced before and after this period. He had done a similar survey in "Bech Enters Heaven" (*BB*), and in each case he notes the mutability of fame. Relying heavily upon quotations from American writers since the 1920s, Updike's "The Glittering City" (MM) offers a panorama of the problems and excitements of New York.* His "An Ohio Runaway" (MM) provides a deft survey of writers of the 1920s, focusing on a sweeping study of the neglected Dawn Powell; Edmund Wilson* had failed to revive her career in 1962. Updike also provides a retrospective of the career of W. M. Spackman, a writer likened to Henry Green* and Vladimir Nabokov,* and he quotes with approval novelist Carolyn See's *phrase juste* about Spackman, "a literary stylist of dizzying refinement." In his talk "Glittering City" Updike stitches together extracts from Edmund Wilson, F. Scott Fitzgerald, Edith Wharton, Hart Crane and Ernest Hemingway.* The result is an interesting mosaic of the city. In an "Introduction" to Wharton's *Age of Innocence*, he detects her responses to Marcel Proust* in her "crystalline perspective" and mixture of "enchanted caricature" with "presiding philosophical temper."

Updike frequently refers to various American masters, championing the cause of Ernest Hemingway's masterful style, explaining why Henry James* may have been right about the difficulties of writing historical fiction (*BD*), quoting Wallace Stevens* and revering his impact on modern poetry, and humorously exploring the panoply of enshrined authors through Henry Bech* ("Bech Enters Heaven" [*BB*]). Bech himself is a composite of Norman Mailer,* Philip Roth* and Saul Bellow,* while Bech's adventures are sprinkled with references to Edgar Allan Poe,* Melville, Sidney Lanier, Mark Twain, John Barth, Jack London, Ezra Pound* and William Faulkner* (*BB, BIB, BaB*). In *S.* the Arhat* tells Sarah Worth* that J. D. Salinger* and Allen Ginsberg got him interested in Eastern religion, and the witty Jane Smart* jokes with allusions to T. S. Eliot* and Gertrude Stein (*W*). Perhaps the most unacknowledged major influence on Updike, according to critic Larry Taylor, is Henry David Thoreau,* for Thoreau is America's leading writer of the pastoral* and applies antipastoral slants to pastoral values, as Updike does in *RIR* and *TE*. Taylor also suggests that John Barth may have contributed to Updike's antipastoralism.

Despite his stated reluctance to comment on American contemporary writers (his reviews of non-American writers form a plentitude), Updike has reviewed (among many others) beat-generation authors (Jack Kerouac,* William Burroughs, Seymour Krim, Herb Gold), hippies* (Ken Kesey), Jewish writers (Saul Bellow, Norman Mailer, Bernard Malamud, J. D. Salinger), Southerners (James Agee, Peter Taylor, Barry Hannah), poets (L. E. Sissman, Robert Lowell), modernists (Vladimir Nabokov), postmodernists (Donald Barthleme), women (Alice Adams, Marge Piercy, Anne Tyler, Ann Beattie, Ursula Le Guin, Joyce Carol Oates, Erica Jong) and friends (E. B. White, John Cheever,* Philip Roth, Kurt Vonnegut).

Updike's acquaintance with American writers has been quite extensive. He has also written on Henry Wadsworth Longfellow, James Branch Cable, Sherwood Anderson, F. Scott Fitzgerald, John O'Hara, Theodore Dreiser,* T. S. Eliot, Eugene O'Neill, Robert Frost, John Marquand, Dorothy Parker, Thornton Wilder, James Gould Cozzens and Edmund Wilson, among others. He examines Fitzgerald in particular detail in reviewing not only biographies but his most important works quoting a passage in which Jay Gatsby balances gracefully on his car's dash board (*MM*). Updike used works by Sinclair Lewis* and Wallace Stevens for epigraphs for *RIR*. He expresses sympathy for the depiction of marriage in Cheever, Oates and Roth, as one might expect. Updike has noted that the writers still exciting him are those he read when young—Malamud, Bellow, Roth and Cheever—and that they are the models against which he rates himself. George Searles has drawn close comparisons between Updike and Cheever and Updike and Roth, and Updike has been linked with modern social realists like F. Scott Fitzgerald by Taylor, as well as with writers describing spiritual crises and those confronting absurdity, like J. D. Salinger. In "The Importance of Fiction" (*OJ*) Updike provides a breezy evaluation of the "shapely lies" of modern fiction, making epigrammatic comments on a great many American writers. He also provides interesting views of many writers (some non-American) in his "Introduction" to the seventh volume of *Paris Review* interviews. He notes that Philip Roth is "especially zealous in directing attention away" from himself to his work, and he remarks that Roth's defense of the "free-world writer against the charge of triviality is worth the price of this book." *See* **African Americans; Brer Rabbit; Influences**.

Bibliography: Updike, "The Importance of Fiction" (*OJ*); "The Glittering City," "Introduction to *The Age of Innocence* by Edith Wharton," "Introduction to *The Paris Review Interviews*," "An Ohio Runaway," "This Side of Coherence," "Introduction to *The Writer's Desk*," "Remarks in Acceptance of the National Book Critics Circle Award for Fiction," "Remarks Delivered in Acceptance of the Howells Medal" (*MM*); Searles, *FP*.

Amleth (also *Hamblet*). *See* **Hamlet, Prince of Denmark**.

Andrews Sisters. Three sisters—Patty (1920–   ), Maxene (1916–1995) and Laverne (1913–1967) Andrews—formed a singing trio in the 1940s, appearing in many Hollywood musicals and selling many records. They are mentioned in *RV* by Roger Lambert* as containing "an element of brass," a tradition passed on to singers like Cher and Bette Midler.

Andromeda Galaxy. Nearly two million light-years away, the spiral Andromeda galaxy in the constellation Andromeda is a companion to our Milky Way galaxy. It is the only other galaxy visible to the naked eye. Piet Hanema* sees the galaxy setting when he thinks that he has fallen out of love with Foxy Whitman* (*Couples*). Piet is aware that the constellation represents the "Chained Lady" of astrology who is freed by the hero Perseus, something he feels that he has been asked to achieve in freeing Foxy of her unsatisfying marriage. Elsewhere, Updike has remarked that if a "self" existed even on this galaxy, the idea of God would accompany it (*SC*).

Angel Falls. Angel Falls is a waterfall in eastern Venezuela, mentioned in *SC*, on which Updike and his party crash-landed their helicopter as they descended, seeking a picnic site on Ayuân Tepuî, a great mesa from which the waterfall descends. Updike related that in acting "cool," he was responding to his confirmed sense that he was protected from disaster by luck. But this sense of having luck, some of his critics thought, might have weakened his writing by hardening him to other people's suffering in his fiction.

Angst. The family name of Updike's most famous character, Harry "Rabbit" Angstrom,* is a compound of *angst*, a German word that suggests anguish, remorse, self-hatred and dread, and *Strom*, German for stream. Thus the family name is a "stream of dread or anguish." Awaiting his daughter's funeral, Rabbit feels that "his insides are a clenched mass of dread." The German *angst* is rooted in Latin *angere*, "to cause pain," popularized by Søren Kierkegaard* in *Fear and Trembling, the Sickness unto Death*. Anxiety is certainly a trait of rabbits. The entire Angstrom family expresses anxiety: Rabbit's father, Earl Angstrom,* agitated at Rabbit's actions; his mother, Mary Angstrom,* easily upset by his wife Janice Angstrom*; his son, Nelson Angstrom,* so unstable he needs cocaine to relax; his sister Miriam Angstrom,* so anxious over sexual relationships she creates artificial rules to keep uninvolved; and even those marrying into the Angstrom family, like Teresa "Pru" Lubell Angstrom,* who out of anxiety and despair sleeps with her father-in-law. Anxiety, though, is typical of those in the middle class because of the stress of "middleness."* Updike's remark that our age may be "anxiety-prone" echoes W. H. Auden's* poem *The Age of Anxiety* (*SC*). As a dual pun, the word "angstrom" is also a term from physics indicating a unit of length equal to one ten-billionth of a meter, used primarily for light, waves. As applied to the Angstroms, it suggests that the anguish felt in being so small must be immense, though dimly illuminating. *See* **Barth, Karl; Names**.

Bibliography: Taylor, *PA*; Jack De Bellis, "The 'Extra Dimension': Character Names in Updike's 'Rabbit' Trilogy," *Names* 36 (Mar.–June 1988): 29–42.

Angstrom, Earl (1905–1975). Earl Angstrom is the father of Harry "Rabbit" Angstrom* and works as a printer at Verity Press. He vigorously sides against his son for deserting his family (*RR*). Earl gets Rabbit a job at Verity Press in *RRed* and informs him about the progress of the Parkinson's disease Rabbit's mother, Mary Angstrom,* has developed. He also passes along Mary's correct suspicion that Janice Angstrom* has been seeing another man. Since Rabbit views his mother as having the most "force" in the family, his father seems weak to him. In resisting his father and gravitating toward his mother, Rabbit extended his Oedipal phase. Not only would this inhibit Rabbit from developing male friendships (consider his difficulties with Ronnie Harrison,*

Rev. Jack Eccles,* Skeeter* and Charlie Stavros*), but it also would contribute to his son Nelson's* reliance upon Janice precisely as Rabbit had relied on his own mother. Earl's name suggests a relation to heroic "eorls" or chiefs, but he is not even the head of his family. Ironically, a descendant of Earl ("eorl") is a Roy* ("roi" or king), the name of his grandson, who, when he was as young as two, illustrated the family's decline and fall even further. Yet Updike uses Earl Angstrom as a contrast to his son's irresponsibility, because like George Caldwell* (C), he shoulders his burdens with minimal complaint. Thus he neither understands nor accepts his son's unwillingness to take up his traditional responsibilities. Having married a woman less in love with him than he was with her, as he admits in the presence of Eccles, they often quarrel. Since Rabbit avoided their arguments by playing basketball,* which led to his sense of importance and his dissatisfaction with his wife, part of the blame for Rabbit's delinquency is traceable to the imbalance of love in Rabbit's parents. *See* **Freud, Sigmund**.

Bibliography: Detweiler, *JU*; Greiner, *JU*; Jack De Bellis, "Oedipal Angstrom," *Wascana Review* 24 (1989): 45–59; O'Connell, *UP*.

Angstrom, Harry "Rabbit" (1933–1989). Updike's most famous character,* Harry "Rabbit" Angstrom is the hero of the "Rabbit" tetralogy (*RR, RRed, RIR* and *RaR*, collected as *RA*). In *RR* he has been trapped into marriage by Janice Springer Angstrom's* premarital pregnancy, but deserts her and his two-year-old son Nelson.* After an abortive trip south he returns to Brewer* to live with a prostitute, Ruth Leonard Byer.* He returns to Janice when she delivers their second child, Rebecca,* three months later. When Rabbit leaves Janice again, she accidentally drowns Becky. He returns for the funeral, only to run back to Ruth when he feels falsely accused of the baby's death.* Pregnant by Rabbit, Ruth gives him an ultimatum: divorce Janice and marry her, or she will abort their baby. Instead, Rabbit runs. In *RRed* we learn that Rabbit had returned to Janice and worked for a while at Springer Motors* before joining his father as a linotyper at Verity Press. Janice leaves Harry for Charlie Stavros,* a car salesman, and Rabbit accepts into his home Jill Pendleton,* a runaway, and Skeeter,* a Black Power advocate, who lures Jill into heroin addiction. Rabbit drifts into experimentation with marijuana, loses his job, contributes to Jill's accidental death and helps Skeeter escape. Alienated from Nelson, who loved Jill, Rabbit takes Janice back when her affair with Stavros founders, and they restart their life.

In *RIR*, after another decade has passed, Rabbit has become part-owner of his deceased father-in-law's Toyota dealership, Springer Motors. Fearing that Nelson has been trapped into marriage by impregnating a Kent State University secretary, Teresa "Pru" Lubell Angstrom,* Rabbit warns him not to follow in his footsteps, but Nelson does not listen. Still sure that Ruth bore him a child, a daughter, Rabbit spies on her farm for evidence, but she insists that she aborted their child. Rabbit schemes to sleep with Cindy Murkett,* his friend Webb Murkett's* wife, and though he gets a chance during a wife-swapping spree in the Caribbean, Rabbit draws his rival Ron Harrison's* wife, Thelma Harrison,* instead. Before the rotation of wives can bring Cindy to him, Rabbit is forced to return to Brewer when Nelson returns to Kent State University, deserting Pru. While Nelson is gone, Pru delivers a daughter and presents Rabbit with his grandchild. Another decade passes, and in *RaR* Rabbit has retired to Florida,* leaving Nelson in charge of the car agency. But his effort to entertain his granddaughter Judy* during a Christmas visit from his son and his family leads to a catastrophe. Rabbit's Sunfish capsizes, and in the effort to save his granddaughter from drowning, he suffers a heart attack. Rabbit returns to Pennsylvania in order to have an angioplasty operation in Brewer. There he learns that Nelson's cocaine habit has nearly bankrupted Springer Motors. After Nelson is rehabilitated, Janice becomes a real-estate saleswoman, and Rabbit, recovering from his operation, makes love to a distraught Pru. Rabbit flees to Florida after she confesses their episode to Janice and Nelson, and he dies there while playing a basketball* game.

Updike's complex hero had his roots in Updike's earlier fictional and poetic treatments of athletes who illustrate the fallacy of the belief that athletic prowess assures success in life. Yet Rabbit's brush with greatness on the basketball court had given him a vision of first-ratedness he yearns to relive. Convinced of his "specialness" because "something" wants him to find it, he thinks that maturity is death and detests the "national rhythm" of work and family. Because he cannot be false to himself, he becomes enmeshed in tragedies. Yet Updike shows that the advice he is given is rooted in his inability to find meaningful work that provided a sense of usefulness. It is also rooted in failing institutions, like the church, that had traditionally encouraged transformation from self-centeredness to selflessness. Even though Rabbit essentially upholds religious and social values, he finds himself forced to rely upon his emotions to provide honest patterns of action. Rabbit also relies upon traditional concepts of his position as a white male and thus adopts his culture's sexism, racism, and patriotism, leading him to support the war in Vietnam* and bigotry in Brewer. Yet his zest for life gives people like Rev. Jack Eccles,* Mrs. Smith, Ruth and Thelma hope in something beyond day-to-day existence.

Gradually Rabbit's will to resist his culture, or rather to return it to its previous stability, gives way to comfort within it and skepticism about his efforts to find the "thing." In the end he accommodates himself to death, persisting in eating* habits that are killing him while rejecting any reconciliation with his family after sleeping with Pru. His heart grows harder as he admits that he never loved Thelma, his decade-long mistress, and he feels discomfort at the new lives his wife and son have carved for themselves with no help from him. He is at home in neither the past nor the future because he is not content with either marriage or illicit love. Yet Rabbit may be a symbol of America itself, for like America, as James Schiff notes, he is large, rich, optimistic, self-indulgent, "culturally unsophisticated" and yearning. He marches in the July Fourth parade as Uncle Sam,* and though Uncle Angstrom totters on stilts and feels his beard detach and his hat topple, he still stands though his feet reel, accepting the crowd's cheers. Updike has taken an ordinary character from middle-class America and by presenting him in the present tense has provided a sense of "presentness" and urgency to his hero. Also, by modulating his point of view from distance to intimacy, he presents Rabbit with all his imperfections, but also with a poetic core. Though Rabbit may do things sufficient to earn the title "monster" from some characters, he is also capable of seeing a golf* shot or Bradford pear trees with a sense of wonder. Updike's hero is thus ambiguous, and consequently, he has stirred much controversy and produced in a generation of readers intense, ambivalent reactions.

Since Updike sees Rabbit as a representative man, he was pleased that Knopf published the four novels under the Everyman imprint. For the Everyman edition Updike made hundreds of changes, particularly to clarify Rabbit's character, and added a valuable introduction, making this the definitive "Rabbit saga." *See* **Angst; Names**.

Bibliography: Elmer F. Suderman, "The Right Way and the Good Way in *Rabbit, Run*," *University Review* 26 (Oct. 1969): 13–21; Joseph Waldmeir, "It's the Going That's Important, Not the Getting There: Rabbit's Questing Non-Quest," *Modern Fiction Studies* 20 (Spring 1974): 13–27; Detweiler, *JU*; Greiner, *JU*; Jack De Bellis, "Oedipal Angstrom," *Wascana Review* 24 (1989): 45–59; O'Connell, *UP*; Schiff, *JU*.

Angstrom, Janice Springer. The wife of Harry "Rabbit" Angstrom* in *RA*, Janice Angstrom evolves from what Rabbit calls a "dumb mutt" who tricked him into marriage by becoming pregnant to a working woman who grows in independence. In *RR* Janice, who had met Rabbit while working at Kroll's Department Store* in Brewer,* became pregnant by him and married him; two years later she becomes pregnant again. An indifferent housewife, Janice watches television* and drinks in the afternoon. Rabbit, feeling that his marriage has grown second-rate, leaves her to follow his dream of again becoming first-rate. Janice waits patiently, going to movies with a girlfriend and hoping that her minister,* Rev. Jack Eccles,* can talk Rabbit into returning home. When she delivers her baby, Rabbit comes home, but problems with feeding the baby and tending to Rabbit's sexual needs revive tensions. He leaves her again, and Janice, partly drunk, accidentally drowns their baby. Quite shaken, she attends the funeral with Rabbit and is stunned by his assertion that she, not he, killed the baby. Rabbit flees again, but we later learn that he returns and they resume their marriage. Partly because of Rabbit's virtual abstention from sex for fear of producing another child who might die, Janice, in *RRed*, has an affair with one of her father's salesmen, Charlie Stavros,* and leaves home to live with him after a beating by Rabbit. She becomes alarmed that Rabbit is providing a dangerous home life for their son Nelson Angstrom* when she discovers that two outcasts Rabbit has befriended, Jill Pendleton* and Skeeter,* are using drugs.* Janice returns home only after Rabbit's sister Miriam* seduces Stavros, Jill dies, and Skeeter disappears. In *RIR* she inherits, with her mother, control of Springer Motors,* maneuvers the marriage of her son over Rabbit's objections and helps arrange spouse swapping in order to sleep with contractor Webb Murkett.* Janice also installs her son in the firm over Rabbit's opposition. In *RaR* Janice extricates Nelson from cocaine addiction, saves the car agency from bankruptcy, assists Rabbit following his heart attack, becomes a real-estate salesperson and tries to restore Rabbit to the family after he and Nelson's wife make love. As Janice rises from insignificance to authority, Rabbit descends from greatness to pathos, ineffectuality and isolation.

Janice serves two functions. She guides evaluations of Rabbit, and she reveals the changes in American women through four decades. As a mediocre housewife, she prompts Rabbit's decision to desert his family, but in her interior monologue in *RR* Janice reveals insecurities related to her parents that are similar to Rabbit's. If he feels that their marriage is second-rate, part of the reason can be traced to his insensitivity to her fears and needs. Rabbit, like other men, keeps alive his sense of first-ratedness by rejecting Janice. Her effort to revive their love by taking a lover in *RRed* and her warnings about the effect on Nelson of Rabbit's unsavory guests show her willingness to apply extreme measures to save her marriage and family. Even her scheme to swap spouses allows her to deliver Rabbit to a woman who adored him, Thelma Harrison.* Her sporadic but well-intentioned concern for Rabbit's diet after his heart attack only highlights Rabbit's self-destructiveness in resisting her good advice.

Janice's second function charts her personal development as a woman and a representative of ordinary middle-class women from 1960 to 1990. As a dependent 1950s housewife attached to her parents, she readily accepted her role as subordinate to her husband. But Janice learns independence in the 1960s, discovering natural talents in bookkeeping and real estate and acquiring confidence in her creative ideas. Like other women in the 1970s, Janice learns how to win in a man's world, plotting with equal facility Nelson's wedding and Murkett's seduction. She keeps the mutual hostility of Rabbit and Nelson from splitting the family. As other women did in the 1980s, Janice develops pragmatic ways of meeting life: she treats Nelson with tough love and Rabbit with sensitivity when she is not involved in her own pursuits. She also becomes alert to ways of dealing with her own problems by attending to sound bites of psychological self-help from television and magazines. Thus she overcomes her fear of her mother and gains heightened self-esteem. Despite her shock at Rabbit's affair with their daughter-in-law, she does not abandon him when he is dying. Janice shows that ordinary women in a patriarchal society can learn to develop untapped resources and take pleasure in small but real accomplishments. Updike's focus on her fumbling but successful effort to forestall Charlie's angina attack in *RRed* reveals her as a life force superior to Rabbit's mother, and this stands as a symbol of the distance women have traveled in *RA*. Her willingness to assert herself in a male world without losing her femininity shows also that she has avoided her mother's hardness. Her development in *RA* thus reveals Updike's maturity in the treatment of women over the course of thirty-two years. *See* **Angstrom, Mary; Angstrom, Rebecca; Springer, Bessie; Springer, Fred**.

Bibliography: O'Connell, *UP*.

Angstrom, Judy (1982–   ). The daughter of Nelson* and Teresa "Pru" Angstrom,* Judy Angstrom is called "another nail in the coffin" by Harry "Rabbit" Angstrom* when Pru presents her to him at the end of *RIR*, and in *RaR* Judy nearly precipitates his death. Judy apparently pretends that she is in danger of drowning, and Rabbit's strain in saving her unleashes a heart attack. She also unwittingly provides Rabbit with information about Nelson's drug addiction while they channel-surf television programs. When Rabbit works to earn her affection and interest, she becomes a point of contention between father and son, as Jill Pendleton* had been in *RRed*. Judy is typical of women upon whom Rabbit places a high valuation, that is, those who reflect his own sense of his specialness. Female babies* provide a physical reality to his own life force. He perceived this first in his baby Rebecca who died (*RR*), then in the wonder of being able to create a female from his male body in the daughter he thinks was not aborted by Ruth Leonard Byer* (*RIR*) and now in discovering his own physical "specialness" embodied in his granddaughter Judy.

Angstrom, Mary. The mother of Harry "Rabbit" Angstrom* and Miriam Angstrom* and the wife of Earl Angstrom* in *RR*, Mary Angstrom counters her husband's argument that Rabbit has become a "Brewer* bum" in deserting his family. She insists that Rabbit had been trapped by Janice Angstrom's* pregnancy, and she tells Rev. Jack Eccles* what he finds indefensible, that Janice was calculating and half-crazy. Rabbit has thought of his mother as the person with the most force in his life, so it is logical that her accusing face at the grave of his daughter causes Rabbit to feel shunned for the baby's death. Rabbit's mother-in-law Bessie Springer* contends that Mary has filled Rabbit's head with pride, thus creating his marital unhappiness and desertion. In *RRed* Mary, dying of Parkinson's disease (from which Updike's paternal grandmother suffered), hints that Janice is having an affair, but she cannot convince Harry to abandon his family and look out for himself. After Mary's death Janice tells Rabbit that she had always hated

Mary for her interference. Mary thus provided Rabbit with his best and worst characteristics; a sense of importance and a selfish egotism. These traits are transmitted to his son Nelson Angstrom,* but after Nelson has indulged his selfish habits, he becomes a person with a mission to help other addicts. Rabbit's attachment to Mary is a source of his rejection of his father and son.

Bibliography: Jack De Bellis, "Oedipal Angstrom," *Wascana Review* 24 (1989) 45–59; O'Connell, *UP*.

Angstrom, Miriam "Mim." The sister of Harry "Rabbit" Angstrom* and daughter of Mary* and Earl Angstrom,* Mim Angstrom quarrels often with Rabbit, who dislikes signs that she enjoys dating and drinking. Rabbit prefers to think of her as ecstatic when he drove her on the handlebars of his bike or while they were treading on the edge of the local quarry (*RR*). In *RRed*, after seeking a Hollywood career and working as a Disneyland guide, Mim becomes a Las Vegas call girl for gangsters. (Essie Wilmot* in *IB* will become the successful film* star Mim failed to be.) Mim learns to depersonalize love and sex* by playing roles and establishing rules about involvement with her clients. At Disneyland she worked among automatons of Presidents* Abraham Lincoln* and George Washington and amuses her family by imitating them (Mim the mime). Still loyal to her family, Mim helps return Janice* to Rabbit by sleeping with Janice's lover, and she comforts their ailing mother. Mim offers Rabbit the insight that "God died on the trail west," and so young westerners have grown shells hard as cockroaches. But Rabbit resists such a cynical attitude, though he is willing to profit from it when she cold-bloodedly seduces Janice's lover and hastens the end of Janice's affair. When Mim returns for her nephew Nelson Angstrom's* wedding in *RIR*, she suggests that Rabbit find a mistress his own age, which in fact he does after swapping wives later in the narrative. Mim does not return in *RaR*, though she becomes blended in Rabbit's mind with his supposed daughter, Annabelle Byer,* as Rabbit struggles to tell his son Nelson with his dying words that he has a sister. Mim represents another version of the "working woman" in *RA*, and though she is disreputable, she demonstrates a self-reliance that enables her to make her way in a man's world. She also contrasts with Rabbit by pragmatically selecting what is possible over what is dreamed.

Bibliography: O'Connell, *UP*.

Angstrom, Nelson (1956–). The son of Janice* and Harry "Rabbit" Angstrom,* Nelson Angstrom is deserted by his father in *RR* when he is two years old, and then by his mother when he is twelve (*RRed*). Thus Nelson is the living evidence of his parents' delinquency, since he was conceived before their marriage and suffered from their infidelities. Nelson witnesses his sister's accidental drowning, his parents' alienation, his father's infidelity with a woman he is drawn to, Jill Pendleton,* the frightening monologues of Skeeter* and Rabbit's use of drugs.* In addition, Rabbit's mother rejects him. The result is a hostility toward his father and a dependency upon his mother, along with greater identification with the Springers (his mother's family) than with the Angstroms. In *RRed* he blends his need for a mother with his growing sexual desire and directs these to Jill, his father's young mistress. Since Nelson shares Jill's disaffiliation from parents, he forms a strong bond to her. The resulting conflict with Rabbit repeats their conflict over Janice and foreshadows Rabbit's infidelity with Nelson's wife, Teresa "Pru" Angstrom.* Nelson correctly perceives that Rabbit does not love Jill or Janice, and that he has placed Jill in jeopardy by admitting Skeeter into their home, so when Jill dies, Nelson accuses Rabbit of responsibility for her death.*

In *RIR* Nelson decides that his father was guilty of his sister Rebecca's* death too and grows openly rebellious and dreams of his father's death. But at Kent State University Nelson replicates Rabbit's mistake by his premarital impregnation of Pru, and although he is planning to marry Pru, he sleeps with her friend Melanie and resists Rabbit's effort to warn him away from marriage. Like his father, Nelson has difficulty following advice. Unable to adjust to college and resenting married life, Nelson insists on working under Rabbit at Springer Motors,* with the support of his grandmother, Bessie Springer.* Nelson nearly ruins the agency by alienating customers and negotiating unwise trades, and, enraged by his father's criticism, he smashes cars. Later, while his parents are vacationing, he deserts his wife and forces Rabbit and Janice to curtail their spousal sharing and return to Brewer.* A decade later, in *RaR*, tension between Nelson and Rabbit has deepened, despite Pru's effort to make Nelson understand his father. As addicted to cocaine as Rabbit is to fattening food,* Nelson nearly destroys Springer Motors through embezzlement, and while he seeks treatment, Pru, by now alienated, makes love with Rabbit. Despite Nelson's rehabilitation and scheme to make restitution, Rabbit retains a cynical view of his reformed son. Yet Nelson is at his side when he dies, and Rabbit's last words apparently tell him that Nelson has a sister and that death is not so bad. Though Nelson's Oedipal entanglement had once turned murderous, he is shaken by Rabbit's death. Nelson's marital life had been even more reckless than Rabbit's and his neglect of his son Roy Angstrom* more severe than Earl Angstrom's* neglect of Rabbit or Rabbit's neglect of him. It would seem that the Oedipal complex has become the modern equivalent of the "sin" of the father visited upon his children. Nelson is the living embodiment of Rabbit's wayward emotion and a constant goad to his sense of specialness. By repeating Rabbit's errors, Nelson also reminds Rabbit of the gap between his desire for first-ratedness and the reality of his life. Yet Nelson's journey from a whining, egotistical brat to a person concerned with helping others with similar problems of addiction emphasizes the lack of such positive direction in Rabbit's life. *See* **Freud, Sigmund**.

Bibliography: Detweiler, *JU*; Jack De Bellis, "Oedipal Angstrom," *Wascana Review* 24 (1989): 45–59; O'Connell, *UP*.

Angstrom, Rebecca June "Becky" (1959–1959). The daughter of Janice Angstrom* and her husband Harry "Rabbit" Angstrom,* Becky Angstrom was born shortly after Rabbit's return from his spring affair with Ruth Leonard Byer.* Rev. Jack Eccles's* notification of her impending birth causes Rabbit to run from Ruth, and when he sees Becky, he intuits that the baby embodies the kind of perfection he had long been seeking. "She knows she's good," Rabbit thinks. When Rabbit runs after a sexual problem with Janice, she inadvertently drowns Becky while bathing her. Though at the baby's grave Rabbit accuses Janice of the inadvertent death, the family assumes that he was at fault, since his running drove Janice to drink and thus caused Becky's death. Ruth, who knows no details, dubs Rabbit "Mr. Death." Though Rabbit returns to his wife, for ten years in *RRed* he avoids sex with her from fear that he will create another baby destined to die. Janice, though, may have been absolved by the appearance of the "star child" in the film she and her family see, *2001: A Space Odyssey*.* Later in this novel the death of Jill Pendleton* through Rabbit's carelessness symbolically balances the death of Becky. In *RIR* the image of the drowning child in the bathtub metaphorically now includes the Gulf of Mexico when Rabbit capsizes a Sunfish and needs to rely upon Cindy Murkett* to save him. When another Sunfish tips over and Rabbit, suffering a heart attack, is saved by his granddaughter Judy, it is as though Becky through Judy has saved Rabbit (*RaR*). Becky represents an objectification of Rabbit's sense of his own "specialness," glimpsed and then lost. Rabbit's ability to free himself from guilt marks a major turn toward maturity.

Bibliography: O'Connell, *UP*.

Angstrom, Roy Frederick (1986–   ). Roy Frederick Angstrom, the four-year-old son of Teresa "Pru"* and Nelson Angstrom* (*RaR*) is nearly the same age as his Father when his grandfather, Harry "Rabbit" Angstrom,* deserted Nelson and his mother in *RR*. Roy conveys hostility toward Rabbit, as if acting out what Nelson might have felt, by wrenching the oxygen mask from his face and digging into the leg upon which Rabbit was operated in the angioplasty procedure. Rabbit cannot conceal his sadistic impulses toward Roy, partly because he favors his granddaughter Judy,* mostly because he always sees men of any age as competitors. Yet after he runs from his family, Rabbit tries to give Roy advice for living over the phone, though, naturally, little communication is possible.

Angstrom, Teresa "Pru" Lubell (1955–   ). Teresa "Pru" Lubelle works as a secretary at Kent State University, where she meets and is impregnated by Nelson Angstrom.* She marries him in September 1979 (*RIR*), but Nelson abuses her while she is pregnant and causes her to fall and break her arm. After he deserts her, Pru has her first child, Judy.* A decade later, in *RaR*, Pru is disillusioned by the twin pressures of raising two demanding children and witnessing Nelson's alienation, adultery,* drug* habit and thievery. She confides her problems to her father-in-law, Harry "Rabbit" Angstrom,* the night he returns from angioplasty, and they make love, though afterwards she confesses the infidelity to Nelson and works with Janice Angstrom* and Nelson to restore her marriage. Though Pru and Rabbit are not blood relatives, Pru has undertaken the "incest"* with cool deliberation at a moment when Rabbit, feeling deserted by Janice and fearing death, is most vulnerable. With the red hair of the "mermaid" Rabbit thought beckoned to him in West Virginia (*RR*) and the green eyes of Lucy Eccles* (*RR*), Pru represents Rabbit's ideal woman. (Updike notes in *SC* that the redheadedness of his father's brother Archibald suggested "a ball of fire, a powerhouse.") Her subsequent betrayal of Rabbit to Nelson undermines his faith in the momentarily restored "first-ratedness" he has always felt with women, especially daughters. For him, the incest symbolizes his sense of union with the daughters he felt sprang magically from his male body, and when he first sees Pru naked, he thinks of Brewer's* Bradford pear trees, which for him represented paradise. It is possible that Pru purposefully seduced Rabbit in order to prevent Janice from going through with her plan to unite all the Angstroms under one roof. *See* **Femmes fatales**.

Bibliography: O'Connell, *UP*; Judie Newman, "*Rabbit at Rest*: The Return of the Work Ethic," in Broer, *RT*.

Anguilla. One of the British Virgin Islands east of Puerto Rico, Anguilla was the place where Updike spent a winter ("To Evaporation" [*FN*]). He visited the island in September 1959, after finishing *RR*, in order to treat his psoriasis by sunbathing. While he was there, he discovered "the black races," a "magnificent enlargement of all my world" (*SC*). *See* **African Americans**.

Bibliography: Updike, "Letter from Anguilla," "P.S." (*PP*); "A Letter to My Grandsons" (*SC*).

Anselm, St. (c. 1033–1109). Mentioned as an advocate of the "locked-in God" in *SC*, Anselm, influenced by St. Augustine,* philosophized about the nature of God. He is credited with having created the ontological argument, which argues that to doubt God's existence, one would have to agree first that God would have to exist outside human intelligence and therefore could not be grasped or doubted by human intelligence. To doubt God would thus be self-contradictory because it would doubt what cannot be doubted, since it is not possible to think of something greater than a being than which nothing greater can be thought. So God would have to exist. Thomas Aquinas* most notably challenged his argument. *See* **Religion**.

Anthony, Susan B(rownell) (1820–1906). A foremost abolitionist, temperance advocate and founder of the National Woman Suffrage Association, Susan B. Anthony was internationally active in promoting women's rights. On July 2, 1979, the U.S. Mint issued the Susan B. Anthony dollar coin to honor her. Updike's poem "On the Recently Minted Hundred-Cent Piece" finds that the unpopular coin was the victim of luck, time and Uncle Sam,* who "done done our doll dollar in" (*FN*). *See* **American History; Poetry**.

Antinomianism. Antinomianism, meaning "against law," opposed the need to subscribe to the laws of the Old Testament in the belief that Christ's sacrifice freed man from those laws. St. Paul's emphasis on faith rather than law for salvation shows traces of antinomianism, but the Apostles early realized the social danger in such a belief. In *RV* Roger Lambert* notes Pelagius's worry about Augustine's* antinomianism. Martin Luther's opposition to antinomianism led to its adherents abandoning it, though Anabaptists later espoused it. Updike in *W* alludes to Anne Hutchinson, who preached antinomianism in America, and such practitioners laid the foundation for transcendentalism,* since some of its concepts, like Ralph Waldo Emerson's* "over-soul," are similar to antinomianism's intuitive revelation of indwelling grace. Updike describes his position as "rather Antinomian Christianity" (*SC*), and Rev. Jack Eccles* accuses Updike's alter ego* Harry "Rabbit" Angstrom* of a similar belief (*RR*). *See* **Religion**.

Apartheid. Meaning "separateness," apartheid was a segregationist system, informally part of the political reality of South Africa for decades, that became law in 1948, giving the minority whites political and social control over all others. Apartheid declared which work one could do, where one could live and what education one would get and attempted to create a separate development for nonwhites, though far from equal. As a result of strikes and violence the government began to relax its measures, and when countries like the United States invoked sanctions against South Africa, apartheid was ended. Updike's experiences with blacks in Anguilla* caused his first important revision of his illusion of a "happy apartheid" he had maintained in Shillington.* Though he professed liberal ideas of full equality, they had never been tested by personal relations with nonwhites, as he says in *SC*. *See* **African Americans;** *The Coup; Rabbit Redux;* **Skeeter**.

"Aperto, Chiuso." Italian for "open, closed," "Aperto, Chiuso" is the title of the first part of a two-part story, "George and Vivian" (*A*). The phrase refers to the business hours of gas stations sought by George and Vivian Allenson, as well as their lurching marriage.

Apollo 11. After President John Kennedy* announced in 1961 America's plan to land a man on the moon and return him safely, a series of manned rockets led to the moon landing by *Apollo 11* on July 20, 1969. The July 16 launch is watched by Harry "Rabbit" Angstrom* with his father in the Phoenix bar at the opening of *RRed*, and the lunar landing with Neil Armstrong's famous words, "That's one small step for a man, one great leap for mankind," is watched with his mother and son, though the message is garbled. In fact, the entire moon shot is fairly meaningless to Rabbit, who finds it a mere technological and political stunt that lifts the astronauts but cannot raise the spirits of those on earth, and that is directed at a "nothing" in the sky. Though the astronauts landed in the Sea of Tranquility, to Rabbit they merely fled the social disorders on earth. (Mission Control inappropriately named the mission since Apollo was the sun god, not the moon god.) As Robert Detweiler pointed out, Updike uses imagery* from the moon flight throughout *RRed*. In *C* Updike uses the god Apollo as an analogue for Doc Appleton,* the physician who treats George Caldwell's* stomach disorder and finds no cancer.* *See* **Science**.

Bibliography: Detweiler, *JU*.

Appleton, Doc. In *C* Doc Appleton treats George Caldwell* for a stomach ailment at first thought to be cancer.* Updike indicates that Apollo, the healer, was the mythical analogue for Appleton. Updike's father's personal doctor, Dr. Ernie Rothermel, was the model for Doc Appleton, as Updike noted in *SC*.

Apprenticeship. As he shows in *SC*, as a child, Updike was fascinated by his mother's typing short fiction, making an immediate connection between the raised letters on his blocks and the type that struck the page. Since he had shown talent for drawing,* his mother had him take lessons from a Shillington* artist named Clint Shilling, and later, when they began receiving the *New Yorker* in 1944, Updike found James Thurber* and Robert Benchley cartoonists and writers he could learn from. He submitted drawings and writing to the Shillington High School *Chatterbox* from 1945 to 1949, his first publication being "A Handshake with the Congressman," February 16, 1945. Updike eventually contributed 285 poems, articles, reviews and drawings to the *Chatterbox*. During this time he published a poem, "I Want a Lamp," in the *American Courier* (July 1, 1949) and in 1946 wrote a murder mystery unpublished until 1993. Before graduating from high school Updike helped create the yearbook and started *Home*, which occupied him into the 1970s. Though his work for the Reading *Eagle** in the summers of 1950–52 did not include writing, it kept him around writers. At Harvard,* chosen partly because of the chance to work on the *Harvard Lampoon,** Updike published dozens of poems, stories, articles and drawings (1951–54). In June 1954 the *New Yorker* accepted a poem and a story, and his first *New Yorker* story, "Friends from Philadelphia," was published October 30, 1954. After graduating from Harvard, Updike joined the *New Yorker* staff, working in the "notes and comments" department. At about this time Updike began in New York a 600-page novel, *Home*, and *Willow*. Both were unfinished and unpublished.

Updike's apprentice work shows invention, humor and craftsmanship. His poetry* is closely tied to his aptitude for cartoon drawing, with its amusing selection of subjects from the everyday, witty turn of phrase, visual suggestiveness and comic rhyming. Also, his articles reveal an interest in religion* and film,* later staples of his work. Updike's abandoned novels indicate that the starting place for most of his fiction would be autobiographical. His early work also shows the lifelong pattern: the marriage of high productivity to polished craft.

Bibliography: Updike, "Note on 'Separating' " (*MM*); *First Words: Earliest Writing from Favorite Contemporary Authors*, ed. Paul Mandelbaum (Chapel Hill: Algonquin Books, 199), 420–71; Hamilton and Hamilton, *EJ*; Greiner, *OJ*; Stuart Wright, "John Updike's Contributions to *Chatterbox*," *Bulletin of Bibliography* 42 (Dec. 1985): 171–78.

Archimedes (287–212 B.C.). A Greek mathematician who anticipated integral calculus, Archimedes elucidated the principles of the lever and pulley and discovered Archimedes' principle (an immersed body displaces an amount of fluid equal to its body weight), a staple of modern science.* Archimedes is reputed to have boasted that he could move the earth if he were given a proper position for a lever. Updike suggests that he seeks an "Archimedean point outside the world from which to move the world," an Archimedean formulation of faith (*SC*). See **Classical Literature**.

Argus. A hundred-eyed giant of Greek myth* who is killed by Hermes when he is guarding Io from Zeus, Argus is associated with the peacock and the building of Jason's ship, the *Argo*. The Cube, the theological seminary's central computer building in *RV*, is compared to Argus by Roger Lambert* because it seems like a beast with many eyes. Its "peacock" associations connect Argus to Christ in the religious aviary, but the mythical ship recalls Argus to a doomed pursuit of material wealth. The mythic and Christian implications apply to the building where Dale Kohler* tries to prove the existence of God and fails. See *The Centaur;* **Classical Literature**.

Arhat (Arthur Steinmetz). In *S.* Arthur Steinmetz impersonates the holy
man or Arhat at the ashram Sarah Worth* attends. At first Sarah reveres the
Arhat for his wide knowledge of Hindu religion and Sanskrit and is flattered
that he explains the myth of Kundalini (a snake, the source of female sexual
power, which lives in her spine), but later she discovers that he is a Jewish
Armenian from Watertown, Massachusetts, who lived in India for fifteen
years, established an ashram at Ellora,* was deported and decided to create
his own ashram. When she discovers that he has betrayed her, Sarah embezzles from the cult and flees to an island.

The surname "Steinmetz" refers to Charles Proteus Steinmetz, an electrical engineer and inventor who emigrated to America because of political
oppression. Arthur's father called him a genius and his mother a dwarf,
perhaps because of Charles Steinmetz's hunchback. The two designations
suggest the dual nature of man, always a concern to Updike. In addition,
the similarity of "Arhat" and Arthur doubles the force of the allusion of his
name to Hawthorne's* Arthur Dimmesdale and Updike's "*Scarlet Letter* trilogy" (*MS, RV* and *S.*). The locals call the Arhat a devil and pun by calling
him "a rat," but his first name "Art" may indicate his craftiness in disguise,
like "the Artful Dodger." He is thus a comic version of Updike's other devil
figures, Freddy Thorne* (*Couples*), Darryl Van Horne* (*W*) and Claudius*
(*GC*). *See* **Buddha, Gautama**.

Art. Painting and sculpture, whether as fine art or popular art, appear regularly in all of Updike's work because as a child Updike created many drawings,* particularly after becoming acquainted with the *New Yorker** when he
was young and modeling his works on those of its cartoonists. At that time
he discovered the Reading* Museum and became immersed in the fine arts
seen in *C* and "Still Life" (*PigF*). There he encountered a fountain sculpture
of a woman trying to drink from a shell, the water forever out of reach,
described in *C*. Peter Caldwell* is struck by "the patience of its weight, the
mildness of its denial," a symbol of Prometheus and art. A frequenter of the
Museum of Modern Art when he lived in New York,* shown graphically in
"My MOMA Done Tole Me" (*JL*), Updike has reviewed art shows from
John Singleton Copley to Egon Schiele and art books from James Whistler
to Claes Oldenburg. His formal appraisals of artists from medievalism to
pop art* have been collected in *JL*. Besides reviews of fine art, he has written
prefaces for cartoonist Al Capp,* illustrator Ralph Barton and caricaturist
David Levine. In his essay "1938–1947: Decade of the Row" in *A Century
of Arts and Letters*, Updike gives an overview of the art of the decade, which
included the "superb pro-American propaganda" of Norman Rockwell. In
"Acts of Seeing" he praises Rockwell for his extraordinary photorealism that
constantly causes Updike to see new things in "Shuffleton's Barber Shop."
Updike has noted that "I am a sort of frustrated painter" who, with a feeling
for composition, sees the book "as a canvas with things disposed on it."

Updike's interest in art has provided a virtual history of modern painting, but he has also written on Pieter de Hooch and Michelangelo, whose paintings in the Sistine Chapel are "the greatest feat of painting in the history of the world."

Updike has enriched the texture of his work with references to painters and sculptors, especially in *Couples, Marry* and *W*. His characters* often have artistic backgrounds, especially first wives like Angela Hanema,* who learned male anatomy from Michelangelo (*Couples*), and Ruth Conant,* who thinks of her husband Jerry Conant* as David by Michelangelo (*Marry*). Well educated and sophisticated, Harold little-Smith owns reproductions of engravings by Albrecht Dürer, Rembrandt, Giambattista Piranesi and Pablo Picasso and explains pop art and hard edge (*Couples*). Ruth crashes her car because she is so involved in comparing the natural landscape to those of Claude Monet and Paul Cézanne, and she sees Georges de La Tour lighting effects and Marc Chagall sky. The National Museum in Washington is a trysting places for lovers Jerry Conant and Sally Mathias (*Marry*). Jerry sees them reflected in Jan Vermeer's* exact positioning of colors. Vermeer's respect for natural beauty is shared by Cézanne's quest for the exact shades of fruit. Images from the medieval Unicorn Tapestry, which depicts a virgin's capture of Christ the Unicorn, import a chivalric tone to the adulterer's courtship (*Marry*). When Ruth prepares to tell Jerry of her planned abortion* of his baby, her evidence of menstruation in the "manner" of a modern abstractionist is not a metaphor of her, but her. Ruth attacks her husband's mistress by calling "pretentious trash" Sally's picture of Hans Arp, Andrew Wyeth and Käthe Kollwitz. Darryl Van Horne,* however, is enthralled by pop art because to him, in accordance with his fixation upon entropy, it reveals modern man, as he says, "going down with a smile." He thinks that the sculpture of Edward Keinholz has replaced the Mona Lisa, but admits that his affection for Jasper Johns stems from a love of "junk." The narrative voice* calls his collection "permanized garbage." Van Horne fails to turn Alexandra Spofford's* simple ceramics into monumental sculptures resembling Niki de Saint-Phalle's. Elsewhere, in "Leaf Season" (*TM*) a Vermont barn is compared to op art sculpture, and Rob takes his wife to the Philadelphia Museum of Art to see Augustus Saint-Gaudens's *Diana* and Marcel Duchamp's *Nude Descending a Staircase*, each a sophisticated double entendre.

Updike's many special editions contain works by illustrators he has admired, including *A Child's Calendar* (Ekholm Burkert); *Bottom's Dream* (Warren Chappell); *In Memoriam Felis Felis* (R. B. Kitaj); *The Twelve Terrors of Christmas* (Edward Gorey); *Down Time* (Barry Moser); *January* (Thomas Bewick); and *The Women Who Got Away* (Barry Moser). Updike has been involved in the production of his books, often suggesting art for his dust jackets (Constantin Brancusi for *TT*, William Blake for *Couples* and others in *BD*, *B*, *IB* and *TE*), and he designed the jackets of *C, P, FP, W, TM, A, S., RIR* and *BD* and made suggestions for that of *RaR*. The most interesting of these selections was that of Blake's *Adam and Eve Sleeping*. Critic Larry Taylor notes its "luxuriant portrayal of our first parents languorously asleep in the . . . dreamless sleep of uncorrupted innocence . . . but the disturbing elements of the drawing are a waning moon in the background, and a fat, bug-eyed toad in the foreground, inches away from Eve's face. . . . And we know that this first 'couple' will awaken to enact the terrible motions which will plunge them and the race into sin, death, and corruption" (Taylor, *PA*). *See* **Cartooning; Thurber, James**.

Bibliography: Updike, "Acts of Seeing," "Cubism's Marketeer," "The Sistine Chapel," "The Frick" (*MM*); Michael Paul Nesset, "John Updike and Andrew Wyeth: The Nostalgic Mode in Contemporary American Art," University of Minnesota, 1978.

Assorted Prose (New York: Knopf, 1965): Updike's first collection of non-fiction, mostly from the *New Yorker*,* contains subjects, themes and styles that recur throughout his work. Updike's wit, exemplified in poems in *CH* and *TP*, is shown in several light pieces like the parodies reflecting the style of James Thurber.* Updike's review of a book of parodies virtually defines the genre. The clarity and observation often noticed as integral to Updike's style* are displayed in the much-anthologized "Central Park" and "Beer Can." They reveal Updike's typical love of ordinary things, coupled to a nostalgia for the vanished 1950s, according to Donald Greiner. The philosophical background of *Couples* and *Marry* is evident in Updike's review of Denis de Rougemont's books on love in history, and his immersion in history is signaled by pieces on the assassination of President John F. Kennedy.* A benchmark for America's loss of heroes, JFK's death is a crucial event in *Couples*. Updike's reviews are critically discerning. He finds Vladimir Nabokov* a modernist worth emulating; *RR*, *Couples* and *Coup* reflect Nabokov's influence, and Updike's later reviews continue his enthusiasm. Updike always speaks his mind in order to direct the writer toward his strengths and the reader toward what is most valuable. Conversely, he suggests that J. D. Salinger* and Samuel Beckett* were incorrectly enshrined because of their silence. For Updike, Salinger, an influence on Updike's early fiction, had become a sentimentalist in *Franny and Zooey*, while Beckett became self-indulgent in *How It Is*. Irked by Jack Kerouac's* naïve recklessness, Updike parodies him in "On the Sidewalk," yet he found Kerouac's writing in the present tense worth emulating in *RR*. But these writers "risk excess," and for this Updike admires them as true "artists."

Important positions in his spiritual development that radiate throughout his fiction are revealed in explorations of Karl Barth* and Paul Tillich.* "More Love in the Modern World" reviews two studies by Denis de Rousemont in the philosophy of love, particularly the myth of Tristan and Isolde.* Updike refutes de Rousemont's claims that love is narcissistic by asserting that in love one's own high valuation of the self is asserted and accepted, making one "lovable" and providing a proof that one exists. Such a view would fuel early works like *RR*, *C*, *Couples* and "The Music School," (*MuS*). Updike inspects his own formative life in "The Dogwood Tree: A Boyhood,"* a prologue to the later memoirs of *SC*. Critic Robert Regan finds Updike placing his young self in this essay at the center of the universe as James Joyce's* Stephen Dedalus had, as if he were a Jungian* collective unconscious. "Hub Fans Bid Kid Adieu,"* a frequently anthologized monument of sports reportage, was the prelude to his dozens of articles, poems and stories about sports.* His passion for art,* begun as a child and shown in "Modern Art," has established Updike as a notable art-show reviewer (*JL*), while forming an ingredient of characterization in *C*, *Couples*, *Marry* and *W*. Critics of *AP* noted that Updike's brilliant style brought a new power to nonfiction that would interest writers like Norman Mailer,* Joyce Carol Oates and Philip Roth.* *See* **Criticism by Updike;** *Hugging the Shore;* **Light Verse;** *More Matter;* *Odd Jobs;* *Picked-up Pieces;* **Poetry; Presidents**.

Bibliography: Walter Sullivan, "Updike, Spark and Others," *Sewanee Review* 74 (Summer 1966): 711–13; Robert A. Regan, "Updike's Symbol of the Center," *Modern Fiction Studies* 20 (Spring 1974): 77–96; Greiner, *OJ*; Schiff, *JU*.

Athanasian Creed. Mentioned in *RV*, the Athanasian Creed's articles of faith, like the method of performing sacraments like baptism, were embraced by members of the early Catholic church. The Athanasian Creed, attributed to the Alexandrian theologian St. Athanasius (450–525 A.D.), stated the articles of faith required for salvation concerning the Trinity and the Incarnation, elaborating on doctrines in the Apostles' and Nicene creeds about the life of Jesus Christ. Though the Apostles' Creed has been the basic creed since the second century, the Athanasian and Nicene creeds are still used by Catholics, Anglicans and the Russian Orthodox liturgy. When Dale Kohler* insists on belief in "the Creed," Roger Lambert* heatedly replies that Dale neglects the way the creeds disagree with each other, which brings Dale to accuse him of blasphemy (*RV*). *See* **Anselm, St.; Antinomianism; Augustine, St.; Religion; Thomas Aquinas, St**.

Atlantis. The large island of Atlantis is described in Plato's* *Timaeus* and *Critias* as having had a utopian civilization, destroyed about 10,000 B.C. Although most scholars think that the tale is fictitious, some archaeologists today have offered as candidates for Atlantis America and the island of Thera, destroyed by a volcanic eruption around 1500 B.C. George Caldwell* refers to his mouth after a tooth extraction as "like the lost Atlantis" (*C*). The story "Atlantises" (*P*) describes how the Farnhams, refugees from Atlantis, look back upon their hedonistic past. Updike uses extracts from Plato's

Critias to provide a mythic quality to the Farnhams' past at the same time that they relinquish it for the realistic present.

Bibliography: Luscher, *JU.*

Auden, W(ystan) H(ugh) (1907–1973). The most influential poet in England after 1945, W. H. Auden supported socialist causes, reflected in *Poems* (1930), which attacked the social and psychological hardships endured under England's conservative system. *The Age of Anxiety* (1947) earned him the Pulitzer Prize and titled the age that would later include America's premier character of angst,* Harry "Rabbit" Angstrom.* Like Updike, Auden was influenced by Søren Kierkegaard* and was a master of style who explored religious subjects with psychological insight. Auden, like Updike, hoped for a negotiated peace to the Vietnam* War (*SC*). *See* **English Literature.**

Augustine, St. (Aurelius Augustinus) (354–430). Though early in his life he was a Manichaean* who believed that equally balanced forces of good and evil were in conflict, St. Augustine, bishop of Hippo, later showed the place of free will in cooperation with grace. Augustine also fought the Pelagians who denied original sin, a point Updike makes in "Augustine's Concubine" (*P*). Augustine revealed that original sin and divine grace, divine sovereignty and predestination were not incompatible, and he insisted on divine grace. Thus he influenced John Calvin* and Martin Luther, leaders of the Reformation. In "Augustine's Concubine" Updike interlaces quotations from Augustine's *Confessions* with a modern-dress re-creation of the affair of Augustine and his Carthaginian lover (369–84) who gave him a son, Adeodatus, whom Augustine took to Milan. After studying with St. Ambrose there, Augustine converted to Catholicism (387). Updike suggests that Augustine's lover was also a saint, since she made it possible, through Augustine's rejection, for modern man to sublimate sexual desire into attacks upon heresies that solidified the church. In *RV* Roger Lambert* invokes both Calvin and Augustine to suggest that babies* can be evil. *See* **Religion; Thomas Aquinas, St.**

Bibliography: Updike, "Lust" (*MM*).

Auntie Mame. The autobiographical novel *Auntie Mame* by Patrick Dennis describes how his flamboyant aunt teaches him a great deal about life quite unconventionally. Richard Maple* notices the novel in Rebecca Cune's apartment, and the book thus forms an ironic reference to the sexual tension between the aggressive Rebecca (Mame) and the cautious Richard (Patrick) ("Snowing in Greenwich Village" [*SD*]).

Austen, Jane (1775–1817). Jane Austen was an English novelist of manners, regarded by critic Lionel Trilling* as one of the greatest of all novelists, noted for witty, precise observation best seen in *Sense and Sensibility* (1811), the story of two sisters and their love affairs; *Pride and Prejudice* (1813), in which five Bennet sisters seek husbands; and *Emma* (1816), mentioned in *S.* and "A Constellation of Events" (*TM*). Emma Woodhouse, like Austen's other heroines, uses her intelligence and strong will to negotiate the pitfalls of upper-middle-class courtship while seeking a suitor for the illegitimate Harriet Smith. Emma's situation suggestively parallels Betty of Updike's story, who intends to consummate an adultery.* The go-between in her situation is a copy of Austen's *Emma*, lent by her would-be lover. Unlike Emma Woodhouse, Betty begins her affair with very few illusions, easily skirts her difficulties and continues the affair with a richer sense of love's complexity. In *S.* Sarah Worth* likes to imagine her daughter Pearl as reading Austen at college, without recognizing that her interference in Pearl's marital plans reenacts a similar interference Emma and Harriet face in *Emma*. Critic David Galloway likens the early Updike fiction to that of Austen, and Updike finds that Austen "haunts" Ann Beattie's *Love Always* (*OJ*). See **English Literature.**

Bibliography: David Galloway "The Absurd Hero as Saint," in *The Absurd Hero in American Fiction: Updike, Styron, Bellow, Salinger*, 2nd rev. ed. (Austin: University of Texas Press, 1981).

Autobiography. Updike has not yet authorized a biography, and to discourage an unauthorized biography he has supplied various observations about himself at widely spaced intervals. The earliest of these memoirs is "The Dogwood Tree: A Boyhood,"* which recounted his life with his parents and maternal grandparents and his awareness of three great "secret" things: sex, religion* and art.* A decade later he added two pieces: "A Soft Spring Night in Shillington," a nostalgic reflection on his hometown, to which he remains attached (Shillington* was fictionalized in "One More Interview" [*P*]); and "At War with My Skin," concerning his long battle against psoriasis. In *SC* (1989) he collected "A Soft Spring Night in Shillington" and "At War with My Skin" and added four others that examined matters as mundane as teeth problems and as complex as the continuation of the self after death.* Such essays greatly enhance an understanding of Updike's interface with his artistic self, and he includes footnotes and other references to provide useful connections between his art and life. "Literarily Personal" (*OJ*), a compilation of various interviews and reflections, supplies autobiographical material, as do a great many personal essays in *MM* and the appendices to *CP*. But Updike has not gone beyond these essays, and he has said that exploration of the writer's life in his work attests to critical morbidity. Epigrammatically he remarked, "My life is, in a sense, trash; my life is only that of which the residue is my writing" (*PP*). He has taken a playful approach to the issue as well, writing in "Updike and I," an essay in the manner of Jorge Luis Borges's* "Borges and I," that "Updike" works "only in the medium of the written word," where "other principles apply," and "I" fears the day Updike fails to show up and "I" must do his work, though "no one would be fooled" (*MM*).

Updike has remarked that a writer is given his first subject, his life through his adolescence, and that a submerged thread of autobiography connects some of his fiction. He notes in *SC* that to use the "living model" of someone close to him is to invite giving offense: "parents, wives, children—the nearer and dearer they are, the more mercilessly they are served up. So my art . . . has a shabby side." Such a harsh judgment does not invalidate the truth he searched for among those players in his autobiography. He has used the Reading* area in many works and used his maternal grandfather in his portrait of John Hook* (*PF*), his paternal grandfather in creating Clarence Wilmot* (*IB*), his father as the model for George Caldwell* (*C*) and his mother and her Plowville* farm in making Mrs. Caldwell and Mrs. Robinson* (*C, OF, A*). Both *C* and *OF* take place on a farm purchased by the mother because it was her parents' home. Updike's mother also purchased her parents' former home and moved the family from Shillington to Plowville. Updike has indicated that *C* was written partly to avenge his father's various humiliations as a teacher; he suggested that the same impulse partly governed the portrait of his mother in *OF*, continued in later stories like "A Sandstone Farmhouse" (*A*) and "The Cats" (*The New Yorker*, 9 Dec. 1996: 92–102). In various guises his first wife and children appear in stories from the first collection (*SD*) to that of "Grandparenting" (*TM*), and his second wife is fictionalized in "Separating" (*P*). In addition, since Updike has suggested that another woman tested his marriage about 1962, the novels *OF* and *Marry* (begun after *C*) may also contain biographical roots. Shillington High School classmates like Barry Nelson and Donald A. Van Lieu can spot other classmates in novels and stories like "Lunch Hour" (*The New Yorker* 18 Dec. 1995: 96–99). Of course, sometimes Updike's style* blurs the line between fiction and essay. "Lucid Eye in Silver Town" can be read as a story, as Updike says, but it also resembles an essay. The event it depicts seems factual, and the quest for Jan Vermeer's* paintings and an allusion to this situation as fact occur in *C*. Again, "My Father on the Verge of Disgrace" (*The New Yorker* 10 Mar. 1997: 80–85) seems composed of real anecdotes, similar to those concerning Updike's father in *SC*. (An anecdote from *SC* is repeated almost exactly in the novel *TE*.)

Though Updike has insisted that his characters* should not be thought mere codes for living people, a thread of a "fictional autobiography" could be construed that reveals the underpinnings of the real life transmuted into art. For example, the early stories "Son" (*P*) and "Flight" (*PigF*) contain elements of setting that resemble Updike's Shillington, characters who resemble him and family members, and the escape from the small town through the agency of a forceful mother that agrees with the facts of Updike's movement from Plowville to Harvard.* Also, in "Pigeon Feathers" (*PigF*) a bookish young boy has a religious crisis; his books and the crisis accord with facts in Updike's life. Readers have been teased to discover real persons and events behind the fictional surfaces of *Couples*, since the characters of the stories of divorce* and remarriage forming *TF* seem very close to Updike's own experiences. The Updike oeuvre reveals a repeated adulterous situation involving the shifting from one family to another through divorce and remarriage, a parallel to Updike's divorce and remarriage. Obviously, Updike's travels to Eastern Europe, Africa and Brazil have been turned into fiction; they are, in a sense, research. Henry Bech's* Bulgarian poetess, for example, may be Elizavieta Bagriana. Bech himself is a composite of many writers Updike has known, yet the critics he slays in "Bech Noir" (*BaB*) may be traceable to specific critics of Updike, Harold Bloom, for example. Surely Updike was using his own experience with the American Academy of Arts and Letters* in "Bech Presides" (*BaB*), though of course the situation could not be the same. Apart from his memoirs, the most deliberate Updike has been in using himself in his work is in the poem "Midpoint" in (*M*), in which he supplies photographs of himself and his family as well as his philosophy of life. Updike traces his first thirty-five years with candor in this poem.

But at the same time that he was fictionalizing elements of his life, Updike also created persons totally different from himself with backgrounds unlike his own. He has called such characters "alter egos"* (though they seem more like anti–alter egos), the most famous of which are Harry "Rabbit" Angstrom,* Col. Félix Ellelloû,* a black dictator, Darryl Van Horne,* a warlock, Rev. Tom Marshfield,* a minister,* Dale Kohler,* a computer expert, Alf Clayton,* a history professor, and Jesse Smith,* a religious fanatic. The alter egos no doubt enabled him to adjust the limits of his use of his personal life in his work. Yet in *MF* and *RR* even the alter egos engage in the same basic plot that drives so many of the works based on his biography, adultery* and remarriage. The two story cycles Updike's mother Linda Hoyer Updike* published also use alter egos to control biographical material. Finally, the reader in search of autobiographical material within Updike's work must always be aware of how reductive this is; his works and their characters remain intersections between reality and imagination. The biographical reader should also take care not to read the fiction as biography when nonfictional supporting evidence is unavailable. As Updike remarked, "In the end I'm as mysterious as the next person." *See Assorted Prose*; **Hoyer, John; Hugging the Shore; Odd Jobs; Picked-up Pieces; Self-Consciousness; Updike, David; Updike, Elizabeth; Updike, Mary; Updike, Michael; Updike, Miranda; Updike, Wesley.**

Bibliography: Hunt, *JU*; Peter Bailey, "Notes on the Novel-as-Autobiography," *Genre* 14 (1981): 79–83; Jack De Bellis, "Oedipal Angstrom," *Wascana Review* 24

(1989): 45–59; Peter J. Bailey, "Why Not Tell the Truth?" *Critique 32* (Summer 1991): 211.

Automobiles. Automobiles, like airplanes,* television* and other inventions of modern technology, are universal in Updike's work and are invested with images of status, mobility and personal identity. Automobiles often function as symbols of what Updike described in an essay on John O'Hara as "status symbol, as love nest, as contemplation cell, as communal sign" (*OJ*). Cars are especially prominent in his early work. In *PF* a truck driver impatiently backs into a wall, precipitating a confrontation between the poorhouse inmates and prefect Stephen Conner.* In "Ace in the Hole" (*SD*) Fred "Ace" Anderson parks cars and loses his job when he scrapes one. In *C* George Caldwell* drives a "hearse-like" black 1936 Buick, but his indifferent maintenance and erratic handling of it get him and his son Peter Caldwell* stuck in snow and bring on Peter's fever. In *RR* Harry "Rabbit" Angstrom* finds the kids he shoots hoops with suspicious since he does not have a car. He argues with his wife about having left the car at her mother's, and when he flees in it, Rabbit drives in a circle from Mt. Judge* to West Virginia and back, a repetition underlining others, as the circle reiterates other circular images like basketball* hoops, golf* holes, car tires and female sex organs. Dilro Ristoff thinks that the widespread use of the car in America shows the intimate effects of the economy on Rabbit. Rabbit first makes love in a car, but his trip in it shows that though the car permits the force of individual power to be directed willfully, it also isolates him from others. He leaves his wife Janice Angstrom* the car while he lives with Ruth Leonard Byer.* *RRed* finds Rabbit stripped of his car because when Janice deserts him, she takes his Falcon. The car's name suggests Rabbit's hawkish stand on Vietnam.* Jill Pendleton's* Porsche exemplifies her ironic means of escaping her privileged life; when it "seizes up" and is casually discarded, the car's fate foreshadows her own fate as a drugged, abandoned woman. The symbolically named Fury of Rabbit's adulterous partner Margaret Fosnacht becomes the escape car ("underground railroad"?) for Skeeter* the black drug pusher and possible murderer of Jill. In *RIR* Rabbit, who has married the car dealer's daughter, gets rich by selling gas-stingy Toyotas. But his son Nelson Angstrom,* angry at his father's criticism of him as a car salesman, smashes a few cars (*RIR*), then nearly destroys the dealership by manipulating car sales to finance his cocaine addiction (*RaR*). In *RIR* Rabbit cruises the area in a luxury Toyota to spy on Ruth Byer's farm, then in *RaR* realizes his dream of *RR* by driving to Florida.* Rabbit's shift from serviceable Fords to Japanese cars, from thrifty to luxury autos, traces his developing affluence; his political shift from anti-Vietnam to pro-Japan shows that his politics follow his bank balance. The one constant is the car radio flooding him with popular music* and easing him back to his days of glory on the basketball court.

Another symbolically defining vehicle is Joey Robinson's* tractor (*OF*), which parallels the pulling and hauling he must do to achieve his mother's approval; his method of cutting the grass with it contrasts to his mother's method and helps to define their characters. Darryl Van Horne's* coffin car (*W*) foreshadows the death of Jenny Gabriel, and Sarah Worth's* forklift truck (*S*.) establishes her as someone capable of lifting weight, physical, emotional and spiritual. Henry Bech's* Rumanian driver nearly kills him, suggesting power without control in the Rumanian regime ("Bech in Rumania"/*[BB]*). Piet Hanema's* conspicuous truck advertises him as a man of construction, but leads to the destruction of two marriages (*Couples*). In *Coup* Col. Félix Ellelloû* reveals his conflicted attitude toward capitalism when he makes his desert trek in a Mercedes; like Rabbit's his motoring takes him away from the source of real danger. After her crash in *Marry* Ruth Conant* gets a pumpkin-colored Volvo and like Cinderella* reclaims her husband (in one of the book's endings). Her straying husband Jerry Conant* drives a Mercury, named for the trickster god who is incapable of strong feeling; his mistress Sally Mathias's punning Saab underscores the tearful failure of her affair (in one of the book's endings). The white Porsche convertible of Sally's husband, Richard Mathias, perhaps recalls a radio soap opera Updike would have known, *Portia Faces Life*, undercutting the tragedy of his affair. Wittily, Updike proposes that after atomic war the only viable infrastructure will be that of FedEx (*TE*).

Bibliography: Updike, "My Life in Cars" *Architectural Digest*: Ad Motoring *Supplement* (Oct. 1999): 28, 30, 32. Priscilla Lee Denby, "The Self Discovered: The Car in American Folklore and Literature, *Dissertation Abstracts International*" 42/08A (1981): 3703, Indiana University; Newman, *JU*; Ristoff, *UA*.

Awards and Honors. Updike has continually received recognition for his broad popular appeal and the exactitude of his artistry. His promise was first acknowledged when Harvard* awarded him a tuition scholarship ($400) in 1950. Its faith in Updike was repaid when he graduated summa cum laude in 1954, and his distinguished undergraduate career led to the winning of a Knox Fellowship, enabling him to pursue his interest in art* at the Ruskin School of Drawing and Fine Art,* Oxford,* England (1954–55). His first novel, *PF*, won the Rosenthal Award given to the best first novel, awarded by the National Institute of Arts and Letters. In 1959 he was awarded a Guggenheim Fellowship to support the writing of what would become his most famous novel, *RR*. "A Gift from the City" was selected for "*The Best American Short Stories 1959*." Updike's short story, "Wife-wooing," was chosen for *O. Henry Prize Stories 1961*, "The Doctor's Wife" was selected for *O. Henry Prize Stories 1962*, and "Pigeon Feathers" for *The Best American Short Stories 1962*. In 1964 Updike received four honors. First, *C* garnered the prestigious National Book Award given by the Association of American

Publishers, and since Updike was one of very few writers earning his living completely by his pen, the $10,000 prize validated his decision to support his wife and his four children by writing. Second, Updike was elected to the National Institute of Arts and Letters, a society of 250 artists, writers and composers founded by the American Social Science Association in 1898 to advance literature and the fine arts in the United States. He was the youngest member ever elected, and the honor thus acknowledged the extraordinary capabilities demonstrated in the first decade of his professional writing career. (Updike later became a member of the Academy of Arts and Letters within the National Institute and presided over it from 1978 to 1981.) For the third honor of 1964, Updike was invited by the State Department to visit Russia, Rumania, Bulgaria and Czechoslovakia as part of the U.S.-USSR Cultural Exchange Program. The trip not only intensified Updike's interest in non-American writers, but also was a resource for the story cycles *BB*, *BIB* and *BaB*. Fourth, Updike received his first honorary degree, from Ursinus College.

Such travelling and his election to the international American Academy of Arts and Sciences in 1965 may well have increased awareness of Updike in Europe (he had been translated since 1960) and promoted his winning Le prix du meilleur livre étranger for *C* in that same year. From 1966 to 1970 he won the First O. Henry Prize several times: "The Bulgarian Poetess" (*O. Henry Prize Stories 1966*); "Marching through Boston" (*O. Henry Prize Stories 1967*); "Your Lover Just Called" (*O. Henry Prize Stories 1968*); and "Bech Takes Potluck" (*O. Henry Prize Stories 1970*). Updike received an honorary Litt. D from Moravian College, Bethlehem, Pennsylvania, in 1967. He was featured in the April 26, 1968, *Time* magazine cover story, "The Adulterous Society."

In 1971 Updike received the Signet Society Medal for Achievement in the Arts, and the following year he was appointed Honorary Consultant in American Letters to the Library of Congress (1972–75). Ensuing research there on President James Buchanan* enabled Updike to write *BD* and *MF*. In 1972 he was one of one hundred American poets recorded by *The Spoken Arts Treasury of 100 American Poets*, and he was the guest of the Centro Venezolano Americano for lectures March 8–14 in Venezuela. In 1973 his Lincoln Lectureship from the Fulbright Board of Foreign Scholarships took him to Ghana, Nigeria, Tanzania, Kenya and Ethiopia, where he researched material for *Coup*, and 1974 found "Son" included in *The Best American Short Stories 1974*. In 1974 Lafayette College awarded him an honorary Doctor of Literature degree. "Nakedness" was selected for *O. Henry Prize Stories 1975*. In the same year, he won the Lotus Club Award of Merit. In 1976 Updike was given the Special Award for Continuing Achievement for "Separating" (*O. Henry Prize Stories 1976*), and "The Man Who Loved Extinct Mammals" appeared in *The Best American Short Stories 1976*. He was also elected to the fifty-member American Academy of Arts and Letters within the larger National Institute. "Gesturing" appeared in *The Best American Short Stories 1980* and "Still of Some Use" in *The Best American Short Stories 1981*.

These many awards for short fiction* fueled the argument that Updike might be most successful in that genre, but he revealed that he was still a preeminent novelist when *RIR* won all three of the major American literary prizes for fiction—the Pulitzer Prize (awarded for outstanding achievement in "letters" by Columbia University), the National Book Critics Circle Award and the American Book Award (formerly the National Book Award). In 1981 he was awarded the Edward MacDowell Medal for achievement for literature and was the subject of a BBC documentary, "What Makes Rabbit Run?" That year he appeared on the cover of *Time* for the second time, October 18, for the feature story "Going Great at 50." In 1982 Albright College awarded Updike an honorary degree. After such plaudits from so many discriminating sources, few would disagree that Updike was in fact going great.

In 1983 his home state honored him with the fourth Distinguished Pennsylvania Artist Award, and he won the Lincoln Literary Award given by the Union League Club. "Deaths of Distant Friends" was selected for *The Best American Short Stories 1983*, and "The City" was included in *O. Henry Prize Stories 1983*. The following year he was chosen to write the "Introduction" for *The Best American Short Stories 1984* and edit that volume. Also in 1984 his collection of essays and reviews, *HS*, won the National Book Critics Circle Award for Criticism, and his peers acknowledged his eminence by awarding him the National Arts Club Medal of Honor. In 1985 "The Other" was included in *O. Henry Prize Stories 1985*, and he received the Kutztown University Foundation's Director's Award "in recognition of leadership, dedication and service to others in the community, especially in the area of education." He was honored with an exhibit of his work at the M. D. Anderson Library of the University of Houston. In 1987 Updike won the Peggy Varnadow Helmerich Award for his life's work and the Elmer Holmes Bobst Award for Fiction, and "The Afterlife" was selected for *The Best American Short Stories 1987*. The next year he received the Life Achievement Award from Brandeis University, and "Leaf Season" was included in *O. Henry Prize Stories 1988*. Also in 1988 Updike gave the first annual PEN/Malamud Memorial Reading at the Folger Shakespeare Library in Washington, D.C.

National acknowledgment again arrived with the 1989 National Medal of Arts, given by President George Bush. In 1991 "A Sandstone Farmhouse" was awarded the First O. Henry Prize and was included in *O. Henry Prize Stories 1991* and in *The Best American Short Stories 1991*, while the story collection *TM* received Italy's Scanno Prize. Like *RIR* in 1981, *RaR* won the National Book Critics Award, the Critics Circle Award, and the Pulitzer Prize, making Updike only the third novelist to win the Pulitzer twice, with Booth Tarkington and William Faulkner. (Harvard University honored Updike with a Doctor of Letters degree in 1992.) In 1993 he won the Conch

Republic Prize for Literature as well as the Common Wealth award. Two years later he was awarded the Howells Medal from the American Academy of Arts and Letters,* and received the French rank Commandeur de l'Ordre des Arts et des Lettres. In 1996 he became a member of the Society for the Arts, Religion and Contemporary Culture, one of 300 elected fellows, and received the Ambassador Book Award for *IB*. In 1997 Updike received from the Jesuit magazine *America* the Campion Award, which had also been won by T. S. Eliot.* In 1998 he received the Harvard Arts First Medal, the Thomas Cooper Library Medal from the University of South Carolina and the National Book Foundation Medal for "distinguished contribution to American letters." Some believe that he will one day be awarded the Nobel Prize,* though Updike doubts this.

Bibliography: Updike, *A Century of Arts and Letters* (New York: Columbia University Press, 1998); "Accepting the Bobst Award," "Remarks in Acceptance of the National Book Critics Circle Award for Fiction," "Remarks Delivered in Acceptance of the Howells Medal," "Accepting the Campion Medal," "Accepting the Life Achievement Award from the National Book Foundation" (*MM*); "American Arts Academy in Annual Honors to 63," *New York Times* 24 May 1979: C20; Rhoda Koenig, "Feminism and Foolishness at PEN," *New York* 19 (3 Feb. 1986): 40.

B

Babbage, Charles (1792–1871). Charles Babbage was a British mathematician and inventor whose development of a machine that could do mathematical calculations led to the computer. It was built in 1991 using his specifications, calculating up to thirty-one digits. Babbage's analytical engine specifications aptly adorn the wall of the museum in the Cube (*RV*). In a "Special Message" about *RV*, Updike noted that Babbage's "visionary principles quite outraced the era's resources of machined metal and pasteboard." The computer, Updike suggests, may encourage writers to "tinker . . . excessively" (*OJ*). *See* **"Murder Makes the Magazine."**

Babies. Updike has written about the joy and pain of having a child and the first impression it makes upon the parents. In *RR* Janice Angstrom* fixates upon the delicious experience of childbirth and explains to her husband Harry "Rabbit" Angstrom,* "It was like having *you*." Rabbit is convinced that when his baby's eyes open, she will "see everything and know everything." In *RV* Verna Ekelof* explains that she loves the feeling of being split in two so that suddenly there are two of "you," and Sarah Worth* echoes this sentiment in *S*. when she insists on the wonderful feeling of reproducing yourself, a creature with a womb reproducing a creature with a womb. In "Grandparenting" (*A*) Updike describes the birth of the first grandchild to Richard* and Joan Maple,* perhaps based on Trevor Leonard Updike, to whom this book is partly dedicated. (Updike dedicated three books, in whole or in part, to babies [*SC, CP, A*]). Richard Maple interprets this baby's first thoughts in language resembling Rabbit's last thoughts. Looking at Richard the baby, Richard thinks, "We'll both get through it"; looking at his son, Rabbit says, "It isn't so bad" (*RaR*). After the birth of Updike's grandchildren, babies appear more often in Updike's work, most emphatically in "Bech and the Bounty of Sweden," in which Henry Bech's* daughter Golda messes her diapers while she delivers a concise speech on "The Nature of Human Existence" (*BaB*). *See* **Children**.

Babylon. Babylon (literally, "gate of God") was the powerful capital of Babylonia in the second and first millennia B.C. It is famous for the Hanging Gardens and the law code of its leader Hammurabi. Perhaps because legend also ascribes to it the Tower of Babel, Babylon was referred to in the Bible* as a synonym of wickedness, and because the Bible describes how the Jews were exiled there (597–528 B.C.), it also represents alienation and captivity in James's encounter with a homeless person that causes him to fear New York,* with its "steep Babylonian surfaces" and "godless millions" ("A Gift from the City" [*SD*]). (James may reflect Updike's own attitude, which contributed to his decision to leave New York.) Roger Lambert,* an expert in the church fathers, says that his Barthian* God laughs at the Tower of Babel humanity built to Him (*RV*).

Bacchantes. Roger Lambert,* worried about the harm Verna Ekelof* inflicted on her daughter (*RV*), thinks of other "murderous mothers, frenzied Bacchantes," referring to the first Bacchantes who dismembered Pentheus, cousin of Dionysus, for spying on them as they performed the rituals Pentheus had rejected. Their ecstasies made them appear to know magic, and miracles were alleged at Dionysian festivals (the Bacchanalia), which the Roman Senate prohibited in 186 B.C. for their licentiousness. *See* **Classical Literature**.

Bach, Johann Sebastian (1685–1750). A German composer of instrumental and liturgical vocal music, Johann Sebastian Bach is considered by some as the greatest musical genius, particularly for his mastery of counterpoint and his ability to compose in every musical form. From Dietrich Buxtehude Bach discovered new possibilities in baroque organ music. In Leipzig after 1723 he wrote 295 cantatas, the Christmas Oratorio, the B Minor Mass and Passions according to St. John and St. Matthew. The revival of interest in Bach's music, begun by Felix Mendelssohn in 1829, was abetted by scholars and performer-critics like Albert Schweitzer. Since Bach's music is almost architectural in its intricate structure, it enables some performers to transcend personal problems. Such is the case with Sitinna (*Coup*) and Ruth Conant* (*Marry*), who plays *The Well-tempered Clavier* (a tour de force written 1717–23), and Jane Smart,* who plays a cello suite (*W*). Piet Hanema* listens to the organist rummage through a Bach fugue (*Couples*), and Lee's wife puts on a Bach piece while reading ("Incest" [*SD*]). In playing Bach's second suite for unaccompanied cello, written after the death of Bach's wife, Jane Smart discovers death* to be a male secret (*W*); stringed instruments are traditionally associated with demonism. Roger Lambert* dryly notes the confluence of "civilization and health" when he witnesses the Kriegman family doing aerobics to a Bach fugue (*RV*). *See* **Classical Music**.

Bibliography: Updike, *Concerts at Castle Hill* (Northridge, CA: Lord John Press, 1993).

Bacon, Francis (1909–1992). The Irish painter Francis Bacon is mentioned as an artist who saw that "people are meat," and Updike connects him to Francisco Goya and Georges Rouault, who also employed anger and shocking images. For all of them, "pain is paint" ("Spanish Sonnets II" [*FN*]). *See* **Art**.

Baez, Joan (1941–   ). The American "Barefoot Queen of Folk Singers," Joan Baez took an outspoken stand against the Vietnam* War and founded Humanitas to study nonviolence as a method of social protest. Baez is scornfully named as typical of the "American-style culture" Isabel Leme* received in college (*B*). Updike himself resisted Baez and others who opposed the reelection of President Lyndon Johnson* (*SC*). *See* **Popular Music; Presidents**.

Baldwin, James (1924–1987). An African-American* novelist and essayist, James Baldwin established himself as a major spokesman for black social protest and homosexuality* in his novel *Giovanni's Room* (1956) and essays in *The Fire Next Time* (1963). His smoldering rage fueled the "Black Power" movement. For their tutorial session, Roger Lambert* invites Verna Ekelof* to read Baldwin, probably ironically, because Verna had a child by a black lover (*RV*). *See* **American Literature**.

Barbarella. An erotic comic strip set in the forty-first century, *Barbarella* was serialized in *Playboy* (in which Updike has published) and then made into a film in 1968 featuring Jane Fonda, recently married to the director Roger Vadim. After this, Fonda turned to more serious roles and also became an antiwar activist, visiting North Vietnam* in 1972 against State Department advice and thereby earning the nickname "Hanoi Jane," alluded to in *Coup*. She married political activist Tom Hayden in 1973 and withdrew from acting permanently after 1991. Fonda won an Academy Award for best actress in the antiwar film *Coming Home* (1978). *Barbarella* is mentioned as part of the sexual revolution of the 1960s in *SC*. *See* **Cartooning; Film**.

Barth, Karl (1886–1968). A Swiss Protestant theologian who taught "dialectical theology" at the University of Basel, Karl Barth became a major influence on Updike when Updike experienced anxiety on entering marriage while studying at Harvard* and embarking on his career. Feeling "existential terrors" in England (1954–55), Updike read Hilaire Belloc,* G. K. Chesterton, C. S. Lewis, Søren Kierkegaard* and Barth, and he continued to read Barth into the 1970s. Like Roger Lambert* (*RV*), Updike first read *The Word of God and the Word of Man* and the philosopher Bertrand Russell (whom Burton places along with Barth in his library ("Dentistry and Doubt" [*SD*]). Barth popularized the idea of the *Deus absconditus* ("absent God") who communicates with man only through prayer, and this can be seen in stories like "Pigeon Feathers" and "The Astronomer" (*PigF*), in which Updike's heroes are gripped by the physical horror of death* and the dread of cosmic loneliness and find no real cure for these feelings. Barth, Updike said in an interview,* "thought concrete action was more or less hopeless in producing any absolute result."

The most important novels Updike wrote under Barth's influence were *C, RR, OF* and *RV*. For *C* Updike provides an epigraph* from Barth stating that anxiety is produced when man on his boundary tries to reach God on His. But in the last chapter of *C* sky and earth are united in the imagery,* just as the images of pastoral* nature alternate with the realistic winter story. Updike's mythical analogies in *C* underline the union of boundaries by showing men as part animal, part god. Even in George Caldwell's* description of evolution, Barthian ideas emerge, according to critic George Hunt. Harry "Rabbit" Angstrom* is likewise a creature struggling to move from the human to the spiritual boundaries, toward the "thing that wants me to find it" (*RR*), and his minister,* Fritz Kruppenbach,* a character modeled on Barth, apparently helped to give him that realization that God is "wholly other," and that His chief proof of His existence is through the desire to know Him. Pascal, who provided the epigraph to *RR*, paid homage, like Barth, to the absent God. It has been argued that *RR* proceeds from Barthian ideas. A paraphrase of Barth's "Man and Woman" from his *Church Dogmatics: A Selection* was written as a separate piece and then turned into a sermon* about Adam and Eve. After Joey Robinson* and his mother Mrs. Robinson* hear it delivered by a young minister, their discussion of the sermon aids their reconciliation (*OF*). Roger Lambert accepts Barth's God as wholly other, and he finds his own safety in being placed "totally on the other side of humanity" (*RV*). Updike's most Barthian character, Lambert quotes Barth from memory, identifies his titles in German, and, prompted by thoughts about structure from an offhand remark from Verna Ekelof,* glosses it with Barth's observation that those who have willed chaos have no right to order. Lambert is relieved, after failing to recall a Barth title, to recover the book and spot the important passage from "The Task of the Ministry" in *The Word of God and the Word of Man*, in which he discovers the insight, "The God who stood at the end of a human way would not be God." As a scholar of the church fathers, Lambert finds comfort in the fact that like Tertullian,* Barth saw that "the flesh is man." This idea carries with it the biblical understanding that "the flesh" includes the intellect's rebellion against God, not merely lust (*RV*). Clarence Wilmot* (*IB*) reiterates this view of the absent God, but both he and Dale Kohler* fail to accept Him totally: Wilmot loses his faith and accepts the pseudogod of movies as a "present god"; and Kohler seeks to force God out of hiding by his computer experiments.

Updike has repeatedly remarked that a God who is not part of daily human affairs is not very real for him. Barth provided him with a God who infuses himself in all aspects of his Creation, thus enabling Updike to "open to the world again." So Barth, with T. S. Eliot,* G. K. Chesterton and Miguel Unamuno, helped him "believe" (SC). Though Updike would say that he affects a style of "Barthian dandyism" (SC), Barth clearly offered him a way to master anxiety, as shown in his "Ode to Entropy" (FN), in which Barth insists that the prayer for stronger faith is the one prayer never denied. Updike's characters like Jerry Conant* seemingly read Barth (along with Gabriel Marcel and Nikolai Berdyaev) to recover such faith (Marry).

Updike's early essay on Barth, reprinted in AP, shows that Updike preferred Barth's ideas over those of the more socially oriented theologian Paul Tillich* or even the crisis theologian Kierkegaard, because from Barth Updike had learned to say that "the worst about our earthly condition" can only be changed by "scandalous supernatural redemption" (SC). Also, Barth suggested the possible divorcing of theology from morality, something that Lambert discovers connects him to Tertullian's "the flesh is man" (RV). This idea motivates men like Piet Hanema* (Couples). In addition, Barth's sensitivity to ambiguity, paradox and "nothingness" was dramatized by Updike in W and explored in his introduction to Soundings in Satanism (PP). Updike often links Barth and Kierkegaard in praising the theologians who most influenced him. They are named saints in "Die Neuen Heiligen" (TP) and heroes in "Midpoint" (M). Updike's introduction to Barth's Wolfgang Amadeus Mozart notes Mozart's ability to say "Yea" was "the exact texture of God's world" (OJ). See **Classical Literature; Religion**.

Bibliography: Updike, "Deliverance to the Captives," New Yorker 41 (9 Sept. 1961): 155; Updike, New Yorker 42 (26 Nov. 1966): 247; "To the Tram Halt Together" (HS); "Introduction" to Wolfgang Amadeus Mozart, by Karl Barth (OJ); Gary Waller, "Updike's Couples: A Barthian Parable," Research Studies 40 (1972): 10–21; William Ray Neal, "The Theology of Karl Barth as an Interpretive Key to the Fiction of John Updike," Dissertation Abstracts International 38/03A (1977): 1382, University of Mississippi Hunt, JU; Ralph C. Wood, "Karl Barth, John Updike and the Cheerful God," Books and Religion 16 (Winter 1989): 5, 26–31.

Basketball. Harry "Rabbit" Angstrom* is the most famous basketball player in literature, and the sport is described in thrilling personal details that establish its rich meaning to his inner life. But Updike also uses basketball to reveal that despite its promotional efforts, it cannot build character or friendship or provide values useful to the American success myth. Instead, it creates a premature relation between a physical achievement and an overvaluation of self. Updike's treatment of the sport is thus both emotionally enthusiastic and socially critical, and Rabbit balances on this fulcrum.

Updike's conception of Rabbit began at the start of his career with a story, "Ace in the Hole" (written at Harvard* for professor Albert Guèrard published in 1955 and collected in *SD*), and a poem, "Ex–Basketball Player" (published in 1957, reprinted in *CH*). In "Ace in the Hole," Fred "Ace" Anderson has problems reconciling his past basketball glory with the demands of his wife, baby and job parking cars. Like Rabbit, Ace has problems with authority and prefers to follow his memories, while dreaming that his daughter will follow his fame. Though he tries to charm his wife, Eve, with such notions, she is clearly losing patience, and their marriage looks doomed. "Ex–Basketball Player" describes the emptiness of "Flick" Webb's life as he works at a gas station. His hands had been "birds" on the court, the narrator painfully recalls, but they now are used to change tires. The story and poem, like *RR*, ask why society encourages people to perfect talents of no value in the everyday world, and why it encourages young people to build their sense of identity around values that stunt their maturity.

Like Ace and Flick, Rabbit tries to settle into the world of buying and selling, first with the MagiPeel Kitchen Peeler, a gadget he can hold in his hand like a basketball, then with automobiles,* which emulate in horsepower what he had supplied in leg power, the capacity to cover ground fast. The salesman, like the sports hero, makes people happy and is rewarded by them. But Rabbit learns that the contrasts are more important: the salesman must lie, if only by hiding the truth, and he contaminates his sense of first-ratedness by transferring the "sense that he can do anything" to the realization that he is ineffectual. When Rabbit injects himself into a kids' pickup game on his way home from work, the visceral feeling of the game revives his athletic sense of first-ratedness, energizing a reconnection with his lapsed "first-ratedness." It is no accident that he seeks his former coach, Marty Tothero,* for help, and he fortifies his rising sense of the past by telling Tothero of his pride of accomplishment, of being "in the zone." His actions afterwards show a futile attempt to revive the dormant dream that various institutions have contaminated. Marriage has pulled him down to life with a drunken wife and a toddler with broken plastic toys. Religion* conspires to deprive him of what Rabbit called his "inner light trip."

Businessmen like his father-in-law threaten to trap him with laws and police. Nature* itself seems to conspire against him, driving his sexual desire, eroticizing basketball and discarding him when he has reproduced. Rabbit knew that any game brings order to chaotic experience, and without the game the contrast between this past certainty and the ambiguity of domestic problems traps him like a rabbit. The decades that follow pull Rabbit further from the game and the "inner light trip" associated with it: he sees his records broken by black players and grows irked by the new style of play (*RRed*). Even his sister beats him in a casual game in *RIR*. In *RaR* Rabbit revives his old passion for basketball by playing pickup games with black kids. But he can win a game of one-on-one only by pushing his enlarged "athlete's heart," rising to the occasion with one last ascent to the sky toward the "thing" that wanted him to find it, his past sense of specialness. Oddly enough, the game ends with Rabbit ahead 20–19, but since the game was to be played to 21, it never, appropriately, ended.

Thematically, basketball reveals problems with the American success dream, because although Tothero preaches that the sport builds character for the "greater game of life," it also gave Rabbit the chance to "run" from the society that requires nesting of its athletes. Rabbit has been taught contradictories. Another aspect of the American success myth is the mystique of male bonding, but *RA* shows that Rabbit detests his teammate Ronnie Harrison* (the only Mt. Judge* player ever named), who fouled so Rabbit could shoot unmolested. He is Rabbit's other-self and his lifelong antagonist. Rabbit pays back Ronnie's intimacies with Ruth Leonard Byer,* Rabbit's girlfriend and a former prostitute, by sleeping with Ronnie's wife Thelma* for ten years without loving her, as though she were a concubine. In *RR* Rabbit had found Tothero a pathetic philanderer; later he learns that Tothero thought Ronnie a better team player. Rabbit's treatment of Thelma emulates Tothero's misuse of women. Yet the flight of the basketball from Rabbit's fingers symbolized not just the way to score, but the way to lift his spirit. The ball's flight concertized his spiritual hopes of resurrection and eternal life, and those witnessing might feel in their hero a vicarious thrill of ascent. Thus basketball contains metaphors of sexual, spiritual and mythical achievement balanced against the false aspects of the American dream. *See* **Games; Sports**.

Bibliography: Jack B. Moore, "Sports, Basketball and Fortunate Failure in the Rabbit Tetralogy," in Broer, *RT*.

Baskin, Leonard (1922–). An American sculptor and graphic artist, Leonard Baskin uses ugly bodies and faces to portray modern depravity. His wood engravings employ powerful, often-tortured images of death* and compassion, resembling William Blake's. Updike mentions Baskin's illustrations of Blake's *Auguries of Innocence* ("Transaction" [*P*]). Baskin, like Updike a member of the American Academy of Arts and Letters,* is also interested in integrating type, paper, illustrations and binding to make aesthetically pleasing total book designs. *See* **Art**.

Batman. A comic-book character by Bob Kane and Bill Finger who first appeared in *Detective Comics* in 1939, Batman is the disguise adopted by socialite Bruce Wayne as the "caped crusader." He wears a bat costume to combat criminals in the city of Gotham with his young companion Robin (Dick Grayson). They fight colorful villains like the Joker and Penguin and speed about town in a Batmobile housed in a Batcave. The television* series spoofed *Batman* (1966–68), and three serious Batman films appeared in 1989 and the 1990s. In "Bech Noir" (*BaB*) New York* writer Henry Bech,* responding to the films, kills four hostile critics,* the last with his mistress Robin while he is dressed as Batman. As "Bechman" he aims to rid "Gotham" of its villainous critics. *See* **Popular Culture**.

Bauhaus. The German Bauhaus school of design has been highly influential on modern architecture, from industry to theater design. Founded in 1919 by Walter Gropius, Bauhaus blurred the distinction between fine and applied arts. It attracted such teachers as Paul Klee and Lyonel Feininger, who were guided by architect and director Ludwig Mies van der Rohe's slogan "More Is Less." After the Nazis closed the school in 1933, its artists came to the United States and, led by László Moholy-Nagy, dominated art* and architecture teaching. When Fergusson takes his son to visit colleges, he is not surprised that many campuses are neo-Bauhaus ("The Egg Race" [*P*]).

Beauvoir, Simone de (1908–1986). A French novelist, feminist and lifelong companion to Jean-Paul Sartre, beginning in 1929, Simone de Beauvoir wrote fiction with existential themes, particularly *The Mandarins* (1954), which won the Prix Goncourt. She explored her own life in *Memoirs of a Dutiful Daughter* (1958) and addressed her womanhood from a feminist perspective in *The Second Sex* (1949), aging in *The Coming of Age* (1970) and her relationship with Sartre in *Adieux: A Farewell to Sartre* (1981). Sarah Worth* admits that while majoring in French philosophy she fantasized being Simone de Beauvoir, and her own "autobiography" (*S.*), with its various existential concerns, reveals some of what she might have imagined. *See* **French Literature**.

Bech, Henry. The title character of the story collections *BB*, *BIB* and *BaB* and the interviewer of Updike on the publication of *RRed*, *RIR*, *MF* and *BaB*, novelist Henry Bech is a critical and popular success who suffers writer's block. While awaiting inspiration in *BB*, Bech tours several countries, reads at a college, then in *BIB* changes mistresses, is inducted into a prestigious literary society and writes a smash novel. In *BaB* he presides at the dissolution of the literary society, faces a libel charge, kills a few critics and receives the Nobel Prize.*

Updike has said of his acknowledged alter ego* that Bech "was the anti-Updike as far as I could conceive of one." So Bech is also the reverse of Updike, a Jewish liberal who served in World War II, and who has had enormous notoriety but now waits out his writer's block by accepting offers to speak or read anywhere. He never realizes, as Updike did when he left New York* in 1957, that being lionized interferes with a serious writer's commitment. His ascent to the society of writers at the end, however, suggests that Updike does envision Bech's recovery in "Bech Enters Heaven," though the writers he is associated with there are not Updike's personal choices for literary greatness: none of his acknowledged favorites are there, neither Vladimir Nabokov* nor Ernest Hemingway* nor Saul Bellow.* But in *BaB* Bech is worshipped by dissidents, helps destroy a venerable literary society, beats a libel rap, gets away with murder, marries a sexy twenty-six-year-old and has a baby, and wins the Nobel Prize. In short, Bech must have entered heaven because he can do no wrong.

Updike, working improvisationally, has recycled, as he would say, Henry Bech throughout his career. Updike remarked that he used Nabokov's *Pnin* for the idea of turning stories about a single character into a "half novel." After his initial treatment of Bech in "The Bulgarian Poetess," written from his experiences on visiting the Soviet bloc in 1964–65, Updike fleshed out notes for other stories to make *BB*. Trips to other foreign countries in 1973 and 1978 netted material for Bech's adventures in Asia and Africa; with a mock bibliography and notes (which Updike called "padding") he composed the book of stories *BIB*. Updike's visit to Kafka's* grave in Prague formed the basis for "Bech in Czech" (1985), which was inserted into *BaB*. While Updike's personal situations were mined for "Bech Presides" and "Bech Pleads Guilty," "Bech Noir" was fashioned from long-brewing attempts to reinstruct wayward critics, and "Bech and the Bounty of Sweden" from predictions that he would win the Nobel Prize by a German critic Updike admired. *See* **Autobiography; Comedy; Short Fiction.**

Bibliography: Updike, "Bech Meets Me," "One Big Interview" (*PP*); "On One's Own Oeuvre" (*HS*); "Henry Bech Interviews John Updike" (*MM*); "Questions of Character: There's No Ego as Wounded as a Wounded Alter Ego," *New York Times* 1 Mar. 1999: E1, E7; Hunt, *JU*; Greiner, *OJ*; Sanford Pinsker, "John Updike and the Distractions of Henry Bech, Professional Writer and Amateur American Jew," *Modern Fiction Studies* 37 (Spring 1991): 97–111; Luscher, *JU*; David Lodge, "Bye-Bye Bech," *New York Review of Books* 19 Nov. 1998: 8–10.

Bech, Mrs. Hannah. Henry Bech's* mother, Mrs. Hannah Bech, impresses upon her son the importance of literature by taking him out of school and, apparently, to the American Academy of Arts and Letters* ("Bech Enters Heaven" [*BB*]). The impact of his trip with her is so profound that later in this story he thinks that he sees her ghost in the audience when he joins that "pantheon." Meddlesome in the stories, the backstage mother supplies her child with a great sense of importance. Mrs. Bech, a stereotypical Jewish mother, like other backstage mothers (*SD*, *PigF*, *OF*, *RA* and *IB*), firmly guides Henry Bech to a fierce dedication to art.

Bech: A Book (New York: Knopf, 1970): Called both a novel and a story collection by Updike, the seven loosely related tales of *BB* introduce the middle-aged Jewish novelist Henry Bech,* an alter ego* as different from

Updike as a writer as Harry "Rabbit" Angstrom* is as an athlete. Henry Bech thus represents to Updike what Keats called, speaking of Shakespeare, "negative capability," the power to create characters* utterly unlike himself. Bech also serves as an example of a major force in American fiction, the Jewish novelist. In an interview* Updike called Jewish writing the chief glory of postwar American literature, and he thought that it might be "a lot of fun" to be an urban Jewish writer. With Bech, Updike vicariously becomes a Jewish writer who is loosely modeled on Norman Mailer,* Saul Bellow* and Philip Roth.* (Bech, who claimed that he disliked puns, called *BB* a "little *jeu* of a book" [italics his]). Criticism by Cynthia Ozick that Bech is not Jewish enough, however, led Updike to argue this point with Henry Bech when interviewed by his creation, that he meant to create a Jewish *writer*, not a *Jewish* writer (Updike, "Questions of Character," *New York Times*, 3 Mar. 1999, E1, 7). The book is also a fine vehicle for Updike's verbal humor, comic caricature and farce, which Jewish writers from Shalom Aleichem to Woody Allen have perfected.

Bech establishes his comically acerbic character in a "Foreword" written as a letter to his creator, Updike, a punning "Dear John" letter in which Bech tells his creator that it is better to have a book "about me than about you." Since he has read the stories "John" wrote about him, Bech offers him a series of editorial suggestions, including "falsifications." An italicized editorial note in brackets assures the reader of this book that all of Bech's demands were met.

Henry Bech has a mighty reputation but a major writer's block. Awaiting inspiration, he reads, travels, lectures and moves from woman to woman. Satirical, ironic and brusque, Bech makes his way through Bulgaria, Russia, Rumania and England on a government junket, never quite aware how he has been exploited by others or how he has avoided breaking out of his stagnation.

To treat the stories specifically, in "Rich in Russia," Updike gives a mock lecture about Bech's Russian jaunt five years before. Like Vladimir Nabokov,* Updike addresses the readers as "students." Bech's defensiveness and naïveté are unveiled in "Rich in Russia," providing comedy at Bech's expense. His condescending attitude toward the Russians and the "loot" he gets from them illustrates his indifference to how he presents himself and his inability to understand what he observes. Bech's ugly-American flaunting of his money only highlights his appearance as another example of American decadence. He blithely insults Russian writers when he tells them that his favorite American novelist is Nabokov, whose family had emigrated to France and then to America to avoid being persecuted by the Communists. Bech's mock enthusiasm for a painting of a turbine is seen through by his translator, Kate (as Bech Americanizes her name). In another illumination of Bech's faulty vision, Kate tells Bech that his women are unreal, like "extraterrestrial life." Bech is so involved with his caricature of Russia that he fails to realize that he was expected to sleep with Kate. Yet this revelation may be only one more case of sexism, one more way that Bech reduces real persons to stereotypes; he fails to see her true attraction to him and the role she might have played in helping him through his writer's block. To be "rich" in Russia, for Bech, is to be nearsighted.

"Bech in Rumania" again shows Bech stereotyping for his own self-protection. He sees Rumania as Dracula's lair, not a place where writers might forfeit their freedom by insisting on truth. In contrast to Updike, who has made it a matter of professional duty to know the difficulties under which other writers labor, Bech knows Rumania only through the "official briefing"; the only Rumanian he has read is Eugène Ionesco. His lack of interest makes him quizzical to Rumanian writers and American guides alike. His high anxiety when he is being driven through the streets by a seemingly insane driver symbolizes both his and Rumania's plight, energy going no-where. Bech permits himself sophomoric ironies, for example, in mimicking the broken English of his guide, Petrescu. When drunken Bech describes how Herman Melville* "defended our native terror," Bech's intoxication with his eloquence keeps him from seeing that the present situation of the Rumanian writer is "native terror." He makes nothing of his meeting with "the hottest red writer this side of Solzhenitsyn," as an American official puts it. Bech has floated on the surface of another country, and Updike's self-reflexive irony reveals Bech's unwillingness to put aside his private fears and see things as they are.

The award-winning "Bulgarian Poetess" (*MuS*), the first story Updike ever wrote about Bech, focuses upon another missed opportunity in which Bech meets the poetess, Vera, and is attracted to her as the "central woman" he had long sought to lead him from his writer's block. He gives a long summary of how he writes, and turns her attention from "love" as a literary subject to his quip that the orgasm is "perfect memory," but of what is unclear. When he leaves her at the airport, he gives to her one of his books inscribed with his regret that they must live "on opposite sides of the world." But he writes this as a reflex after she gives him one of her books inscribed, apparently, with love. He fails to see that she had been offering to shorten the distance he thinks hopeless.

The four remaining stories place Bech in American settings. A philan-derer, Bech is sexually territorial, and in "Bech Takes Pot Luck" he imagines that an idolizing former student, Wendell, might be after his mistress, Norma Latchett.* Wendell is writing a novel influenced by the film (which Updike dislikes), of James Joyce's* *Ulysses* and he talks a good deal about giving Bech and Norma LSD* once they have smoked marijuana. Bech imagines that Norma has gone off to sleep with Wendell, not realizing until later that Wendell has destroyed the LSD. He had told her of Bech, "He's my God," but Bech's misjudgment of him and his mistress again reveals Bech's inability to see beyond himself. Bech had gotten the idea that Norma would be unfaithful from her sister, Bea Latchett,* who becomes his new mistress that night.

Bech is duped again by desire in "Bech Panics," a story told as a "slide show," a device Nabokov had used in a chapter of his autobiography, *Speak Memory*. Bech agrees to read at a Southern women's school, and as Bea correctly sees, he wants to "sack out with Scarlett O'Hara," although he protests that he sees himself as an "apostle to the Gentiles." At the college he finds the "massed fertility" overwhelming, but he looks at the women as a "Martian" might, becoming himself an "extraterrestrial," perhaps having learned something from Kate's stinging remark in "Rich in Russia." Instead of taking up with Scarlett O'Hara, Bech promises an administrator that he will judge a poetry contest. Meanwhile, Bech's old fear of death* returns; he throws himself on the ground begging for mercy from an indifferent universe. His dread humanizes Bech and explains in part why he has developed his shell of buffoonery.

Bech doesn't realize that his shell cannot protect him from his own vanity. In "Bech Swings" a London gossip columnist thinks that he is a swinger, and an interviewer plies him with praise, only to double-cross him in print. The writer has become the butt of a joke. His plan to release himself from bondage to writer's block by falling in love had never included his becoming ridiculous in the process. Bech never realized that "he had become a character by Henry Bech."

Bech continues his transformation in "Bech in Heaven." When he was thirteen, his mother took him from class to visit an academy resembling the American Academy of Arts and Letters,* where he saw the names of "immortals" like Shakespeare and Plato.* Years later he is inducted into this academy and is greeted by other writers he thought long dead, many of whom are analogues to real American writers. He has "made it" to "Heaven," finishing Bech's journey, begun in the first story, from clown to angel. Updike has played a last joke—on himself—since he had been installed in the National Institute of Arts and Letters in 1964.

In a mock Henry Bech bibliography, Updike thickens the book into marketable size, gives Bech further historical presence and settles old scores with a few of his hostile critics, notably John Aldridge and Norman Podhoretz, the editor of *Commentary* and long-time foe of Updike's work. Updike creates an inside joke by revealing that Bech had written many pieces for *Commentary* and that Podhoretz had praised Bech's work. Having given Bech a quasi-reality through the "Preface" and bibliography, Updike allowed Bech to interview him four times at the publication of *Red, RIR, MF* and *BaB*. See **Comedy; Updike John, in His Work**.

Bibliography: Updike, "Bech Meets Me," "One Big Interview" (*PP*); Thomas R. Edwards, "Bech: A Book," *New York Times Book Review* 21 June 1970: 1, 38; Jack Richardson, "Keeping Up with Updike." *New York Review of Books* 15 (22 Oct. 1970):

46–48; Hunt, *JU*; Greiner, *OJ*; Detweiler, *JU*; Sanford Pinsker, "John Updike and the Distractions of Henry Bech, Professional Writer and Amateur American Jew," *Modern Fiction Studies* 37 (Spring 1991): 97–111; Luscher, *JU*.

Bech at Bay (New York: Knopf, 1998). *BaB*, the third collection of short fiction about Henry Bech,* which Updike calls a "quasi-novel," charts the Jewish writer from 1986 to 1999 and finds him playing multiple roles, as a celebrity tourist meeting dissidents and apparatchiks ("Bech in Czech"), as the president presiding over an arts and letters group ("Bech Presides"), as the defendant in a libel trial ("Bech Pleads Guilty"), as an avenger upon villainous critics ("Bech Noir") and as a Nobel Prize* recipient ("Bech and the Bounty of Sweden"). Some of the stories echo those in *BB* and *BIB*: "Bech in Czech" continues the foray into Eastern Europe of "Bech in Rumania" (*BB*), and the attack of dread Bech experienced in "The Bulgarian Poetess" (*BB*) reappears in "Bech Panics" (*BB*). "Bech and the Bounty of Sweden" ends the writer's journey from the major national award in "Bech Enters Heaven" (*BB*) to the greatest world honor. "Bech Noir" recalls "Macbech" (*BIB*) in its emphasis on atrocity. As in *BB* and *BIB* Bech finds attractive young women eager to share his bed and adventures. Bech shares with other Updike male characters* a willingness to be manipulated by women and a reliance on his own intuition.

The stories of *BaB* have a comic-mordant tone, beginning in a cemetery ("Bech in Czech") and ending with a wave goodbye ("Bech and the Bounty of Sweden"), while in between treating the relation of writing to government and of money to art, the instability of writers' language, ruthless murders and writer's block. The book is leavened by Updike's customary stylistic brilliance, making indelible a Czech palace or a baby's bottom, the creation of a literal poison-pen letter and the mimicking of children's writing styles. Updike considers the state of writing in a satellite country, where books are sacred: dissidents lovingly bind carbon copies of works that could put them in prison. But how do Bech's books fare in translation? A Swede reads him in French to better savor his style. Updike plays with aesthetic distance when his creation, Bech, worries that his creator might make him disappear if he bores his author, a reasonable worry, since Updike has Bech dress as comicbook hero Batman* in "Bech Noir." *BaB* is filled with name dropping, from Nobel writers to obscure Japanese novelists thought to resemble Bech, and "Bech Noir" is a "key" story, in which fictional critics are really Updike's own hostile critics.* In his own list of important American writers, Bech casually inserts the name "John Updike," and why not, since Bech interviewed Updike four times and wrote a "Preface" to *BB* in which he wondered if the book was really "more about me than about you"? Part of the fun of *BaB* lies in watching Updike drift in and out of his alter ego.*

In the first story, "Bech in Czech," Bech visits Franz Kafka's* grave in Prague but is more moved by the newer cemetery where Jews rest who died before and after the Holocaust. The cemetery is closed to them until the attendants recognize Bech and shout the titles of his novels. (This incident actually happened to Updike: the gatekeepers shouted, *"Rabbit, Run."*) They tell him that they prefer Bech (*Herz*) to Kafka (*Schmerz*). He discovers that in Prague writing "poetry of small feelings" could result in imprisonment, and he sees dissidents' books made by hand with such daring and love that he nearly cries at the medieval character of such craft, literature lovingly passed from hand to hand. Yet Bech is so careless he uses the names of dissidents, despite warnings that his limousine might be bugged. He is similarly insensitive to the plight of his adoring translator, telling him that he does not really care how the Czech translation reads. Bech imagines, perhaps fatuously, that because his work is being read, this "fractured society" is "healing beneath his influence." Yet alone he feels terror that such people as the dissidents have mythologized him and fears that his creator's boredom will not even allow him to cleanse his "primordial terror" by giving him an erection. The creation of Updike or God, Bech is affecting in his limitations and torment and intuits the distance between American writers and dissidents: "Without guilt there is no literature."

"Bech Presides," a nearly suffocating depiction of literary infighting and backbiting, finds Bech asked to contribute to a festschrift for Isaiah Thornbush, a writer he despises, when he is beguiled by Aesop Press's editor, Martina O'Reilly, whom Bech meets at the festschrift party, at which the reader tries to match living writers to the characters. Lucy Ebright may be Joyce Carol Oates; she earlier appeared in "White on White" (*BIB*). When Martina and Bech become lovers, she urges him, as Thornbush had, to accept the presidency of their arts club, "The Forty," which resembles the thirty-to-fifty-member "academy" within the National Institute and Academy of Arts and Letters. After a lifetime as a renegade, Bech now defends establishment values when a vocal minority wants to dissolve "The Forty" (which happened to the institute and academy in 1992; after this, the group was renamed the American Academy of Arts and Letters). Eventually "The Forty" is disbanded, and the building is sold—to Thornbush's brother-in-law. Bech was duped into presiding over the destruction of a gathering that honored the arts. Bech had been deceived by his belief that money could make truth and beauty possible, but his shift from the subversive writer he had been surprises him. A few years later Bech is rewarded with a festschrift to which Thornbush contributes the same double-tongued praise Bech had written for him. Bech's loss of values may be disillusioning, but Bech might reply with one of his epigrams, "Sour grapes, the champagne of the intelligentsia."

The third story, "Bech Pleads Guilty," finds Bech in court in 1972 facing a charge of libel for having written that Hollywood agent Morris Ohrbach was an "arch-gouger" because he had bled singer Lanna Jerome of millions. (Updike himself was sued, unsuccessfully, in Los Angeles in 1982.) Bech apparently had quixotically defended Lanna because he had fallen in love with a girlfriend, Claire, while Lanna's songs played in the background. The trial pits New York* against Los Angeles, books against movies, and cunning against feeling, and though Ohrbach wins the jury at first, he loses in the end when his kindness toward Bech causes him to fail to follow his lawyer's leading questions. Since Bech feels that the white-haired old man had been offering him forgiveness as Jew to Jew, and repeatedly links Ohrbach to his father, "filial affection" is awakened, and Bech pleads guilty—to himself. Bech recedes into the distance in this tale so that the machinery of law can be exposed as a manipulation of words, just as fiction writing is. Yet the value of Bech's words stems from sources as vague as his feeling for Lanna and attachment to Ohrbach. Updike draws a sharp contrast to the value of words when a philology expert explains the derivations of "arch" and "gouger." By focusing upon the complex impulses that brought Bech to write the offending phrase, Updike restores the importance of the author and questions the way his words are construed beyond his intentions. The court case is a metaphor for the writer's abuse by critics, the subject of "Bech Noir."

In the fourth story, "Bech Noir," Bech, now seventy-four, revenges himself on his hostile critics* after reading of the natural death of critic Lucas Mishner. After helping Raymond Featherwaite fall under a subway train, Bech kills Debora Frueh, a writer of children's books, by sending a request for an autograph and poisoning the return envelope's flaps. Thrilled, his mistress, Robin, helps him murder Aldous Canon (whose name puns on "oldest canon," an out-of-touch keeper of the literary canon and an antique weapon) by having Robin put in Canon's computer a "Trojan Horse" virus of subliminal Buddhist* messages and the word "jump." Canon leaps to his death, and Bech and Robin become Bechman and Robin as he dons a cape as the scourge of "Gotham" and she a cat-woman outfit. In his black costume and dark designs he is truly "Bech Noir." They visit Orlando Cohen, who at eighty is smothering from emphysema, though still feisty enough to repeat his previous attacks on Bech, which focus on his "squeamishness" for refusing to make his writing Jewish, thus causing him to "miss the boat to America." Bech tears away Cohen's oxygen tubes, justifying the killing by arguing that Cohen's vicious reviews had drained away his creative air. Ironically, Bech has poured his creativity not into his novels, but into destructive action. Though Bech as killer may alarm some readers, he had previously provided a list of his hostile critics in the bibliography of *BB*, so his revenge is not that surprising, and figuratively Bech acts out the fantasies of many other writers. But in the end Bech is persuaded to stop scourging his critics, partly through Robin's ultimatum (recalling Ruth Leonard Byer's* in *RR*) that she will tell the cops if Bech does not give her a baby and settle down. Unlike fellow New Yorker Darryl Van Horne* (*W*), Bech gives up marauding. (The story's title contains two puns. "Bech Noir" resembles the French *bête noire*, something hated—a phrase Updike uses in his essay in *A Century* *of Arts and Letters.* Since, "noir" means "black"; thus "Bech Is Black" rhymes with *Bech is Back*.)

The final story, "Bech and the Bounty of Sweden," describes how Bech's winning the Nobel Prize prompts the reemergence of his writer's block; he cannot produce the obligatory "lecture" for the Nobel Academy, so he uses his block as the substance of his lecture. But he also includes, like Darryl Van Horne,* an ultimate sermon,* "The Nature of Human Existence." In its brevity, it recalls the minimalist Samuel Beckett,* whose name and themes resemble Bech's, and it is given by his infant daughter Golda. She squeals "Hi!" into the microphone and signals "bye-bye" with closing hand, all the while messing her diapers. Bech effectively tells the dignitaries what life is: hello, goodbye and a mess in between. The audacity has its truth, since life is appallingly brief and all life is messy. It is Bech's farewell and his metaphorical suicide, the ultimate writer's block.

The critics alluded to in "Bech Noir" who had attacked Updike create a special interest for the Updike reader. As Jim Morrison speculates in "The Centaurian" Updike Website, Lucas Mishner might be Harold Bloom. In 1987 Bloom wrote an unflattering introduction to his edition of essays on Updike that included this remark about Updike: "The American sublime will never touch his pages." Mishner's comment echoed Bloom: "Bech will never, never be touched by the American sublime." The remark is doubly galling because "American sublime" is taken from Wallace Stevens,* whom Updike much admires. Raymond Featherwaite could be Fred Inglis, professor at the University of Warwick, England, who accused Updike in a review of *SC* of having "piled malodorous offerings beside the mirror of his narcissism." Debora Frueh may have elements of Diana Trilling, who caviled at Updike's use of sex,* especially "suckling." But most likely Updike had Dorothy Rabinowitz in mind, since Updike mentioned her as a critic who went out of her way to attack him. Aldous Canon might be John Aldridge, who attacked Updike for having nothing to say, and Orlando Cohen appears to be Alfred Kazin, with a touch of Cynthia Ozick, who scored Updike for not making Bech Jewish enough. *BaB* is a daring and innovative continuation of Henry Bech's adventures, but not his farewell, since Updike published "His Oeuvre" in the *New Yorker** in 1999, tracing Bech's memories of his mistresses while he gives a reading (*LL*). *See* **The Novel; Short Fiction**.

Bibliography: Updike, "Bech Meets Me," "One Big Interview" (*PP*); "On One's Own Oeuvre" (*HS*); "Henry Bech Interviews John Updike" (*MM*); "Questions of Character: There's No Ego as Wounded as a Wounded Alter Ego," *New York Times* 1 Mar. 1999: E1,E7; Bloom, *JU*; James Schiff, "When the Writer Strays from His Desk," Cincinnati *Enquirer* 20 Oct. 1998: C4; James Yerkes, "Wound Down and Winding Up," *Christian Century* 21 Oct. 1998: 97; Jack De Bellis, "Bech Battles Back," Centaurian Website, 9 Nov. 1998; David Lodge, "Bye-Bye Bech," *New York Review of Books* 19 Nov. 1998: 8–10.

Bech Is Back (New York: Knopf: 1982). *BIB*, a collection of seven short stories, or what Updike called a "quasi-novel," continues the career of the Jewish writer Henry Bech* begun in *BB*. *BIB* provides a series of comic reversals for the peripatetic novelist: on visiting an autograph hound, Bech discovers that his works have been collected merely for investment value. When he is lecturing in the "third world," his moderate attitudes and formalist aesthetic approaches alienate his politically engaged audiences. Making whirligig visits to Australia and Canada, Bech finds that he cannot clearly distinguish either his lovers or the cities in which he is interviewed and feted. He finds himself ironically disillusioned by the Holy Land yet drawn to Scottish Presbyterianism. But marriage helps Bech break his writer's block with a quasi-obscene blockbuster in which Bech the man and Bech the writer "wed" in "Bech Wed." In a side glance at Truman Capote's famous black-and-white party, Updike fashions a "White on White" party to portray Bech's fall into notoriety. Like *BB*, *BIB* shows how vulnerable a serious modern writer can be. However, the comedy* of the first collection has diminished, and Updike employs little postmodern fun like the "Foreword" and "Bibliography" of *BB*.

The first story, "Three Illuminations in the Life of an American Author," makes a three-pronged attack on Bech's self-importance. The first episode treats his visit to one Federbusch, to whom he had been signing books for years. Bech imagines himself appearing before him "—whimsical as Zeus, radiant as Apollo." Instead, Bech finds that the collector does not even read the books, just hoards them, along with signed Philip Roths,* Norman Mailers* and John Barths. Bech's flaw was that, "not content with adoration in two dimensions [he] had offered himself in a fatal third." The second episode finds Bech yearning for a female character who might "redeem" his effort to finish a novel; he settles on a woman who recalls to him Poe's "lost" Lenore. Their affair (she loved only the literary Bech) destroys "Lenore," and his novel grinds to a "grateful halt." There were good reasons why Bech received the "Melville Prize," given to the writer with "the most meaningful silence." Bech's third illumination occurs in an episode in which he signs 28,500 copies of *Brother Pig* on a tropic isle with a girlfriend. Bech eventually freezes so that he cannot write his own name. The writer had been progressively deluded by the collector's adulation, by his own fiction made flesh in Lenore and by making money on the strength of writing merely his name.

"Bech Third-Worlds It" follows, its snappy title suggesting that Bech's breezy New York* style underestimates his new challenges. In Ghana he asks, "Did we do something wrong?" as the villagers disappear on the arrival of his embassy car. Of course, anyone more politically sensitive than Bech would not have to ask. In Venezuela he is told that he is being watched by Indians who can see him "all too well." On the Cape Coast he cannot tell if the laughter is hostile or friendly when he defines an American writer as one simultaneously writing and holding American citizenship. At a conference on humor in Korea he sees a young satiric poet mugged by police. He is told in Kenya that his books are weeping, "but there are no tears," and Bech thinks that he has finally found a critic who understands him. Bech weaves in and out of countries, in and out of bewilderment and in and out of the question, what is he doing here facing societies he does not care to understand and answering questions he never considered? Bech's "dread" does not vanish until he is flying home.

"Australia and Canada" again employs what Updike called a fugal weave of incidents and scenes at so whirling a pace that the two countries blend, sometimes in a single paragraph. In Toronto the "exquisitely unprolific" Bech discovers, when interviewed by Vanessa, that "his words were a shell, an unreal umbrella." His escort, Glenda, introduces him to Peter, a Mc-Luhanite* whom Glenda rejects, telling Bech, "I want to have your baby," which only convinces Bech that he needs to marry his mistress, Bea Latchett,* when he gets back to New York. Updike makes the reader feel Bech's displacement by rapidly shifting from Toronto to Sidney, Australia, sometimes in the same paragraph without transition. Bech finds himself "down under" in the thrall of two guides, Hannah and Moira, and with their friend Peter, who had been the lover of both of them. The two Peters become a composite "fulcrum character," swinging Bech from Toronto to Sydney as Bech loses his identity as a writer in the oscillations. The only sign of his vocation is a copy of his novel *Brother Pig*, whose title page he uses to stuff his ears.

"The Holy Land" finds Bech honeymooning with Bea, an Episcopalian, in what she calls, and he derides, "the Holy Land." Bech's lack of response to the area and her overresponse to it form the central irony, and Updike yokes their differing reactions to their differing senses of their marriage. Bech feels that the marriage is like the Zionist state, "a mistake long deferred." He walks the Via Dolorosa responding to irony rather than to spirituality. While Bea stares at the Mount of Olives, Bech reads a sign warning against leaving valuables unattended. Bea has to beg him to touch the Wailing Wall, and he thinks that the more Jewish he became, the more she liked him. He quips about the Church of the Holy Sepulcher's ugliness, "You should have let the Arabs design it for you." He feels claustrophobic among the "Christly vapors" that were "inhaled" by every despot persecuting Jews. He tells Bea that the church was "God-forsaken." He finds Israel depressing, "a ghetto with farms." Ironically, Bech, the wandering Jew, is happier in New York than in Israel, while Bea considers emigrating there.

"Macbech" continues Bech's wandering, and in another reversal he finds himself more at home in "raw, grimy, lush, mysterious" Scotland, where he had taken Bea for her birthday, than he had been in Israel. Bea resents his feeling that Scotland is heaven, and she grows defensive when he tries to implicate her in the seventeenth-century "Clearances," the removal of the poor so their land could be used for grazing, what Bech calls the worst genocide before Hitler. He insists that they go to a castle he thinks is related to her ancestors, the Sinclairs. Again Bech's happiness seems to demand offending his wife. A visit to the Sinclair farms takes them to cliffs that Bech calls "my kind of place," and with bravado he goes to the edge, but feels dread and terror. When he insists that it is where "they" belong, she counters, "Where I belong," outraged that as a writer he has appropriated her ancient homeland. Bea correctly recognizes that she has become a "character" by Bech, while Bech had become a character by Bech in "Bech Swings" (*BB*)—a sign, perhaps, that he is regaining his power as writer; it is also an example of his fear of commitment and an indication of his cruelty.

"Bech Wed," a story of novella length, shows Bech, now secure in Westchester, aboard the "ark of suburban living." He becomes "wed" figuratively to his writing, to publishing and to notoriety. While Bech labors on the ground-breaking novel *Think Big*, Updike explores the process of writing—its false starts, alterations, tortures and joys. The intense isolation required to write the book contrasts to the way the world reads his book. Thus Bea seeks biographical meaning behind what Bech calls a "fantasy" of egotism. Bea also finds his work a symbolic attack on her, and Bech's confrontation of his Jewishness; he cannot reassure her that the book is neither of these. When Bech approaches a publisher, he is wed to a new world of editors and advertising: *BIB* derives its title from the ad campaign, "Bech Is Back." Updike provides parody reviews to show how a book becomes what a reader wishes: Gore Vidal sniffs, "not quite as *vieux chapeau* as I feared," and George Steiner uses the book to make vast cultural generalizations. As Updike had been, Bech is interviewed by Michiko Kakutani, caricatured by David Levine and photographed by Jill Krementz. As the book becomes a hit, the world robs him of privacy (which Bech will again endure when he wins the Nobel Prize* ["Bech and the Bounty of Sweden" (*BaB*)]. Bech encounters his former mistress Norma Latchett,* who assures him that her sister Bea had gotten him to write a sellout best-seller. Since this accords with Bech's own view, he sleeps with Norma, delighted that marriage has allowed him to know the happiness of adultery.*

The last story, "White on White," reveals the price of Bech's fame. He attends a party in which everything is white, given by a photographer resembling photographer Richard Avedon, who had photographed Updike. Bech discovers in the new mud-wrestling craze that his satire on the television* industry was really true, he is told that the point to fiction is to "hasten the Revolution," and he meets literary celebrity Lucy Ebright, who seems to be based on Joyce Carol Oates and will return in "Bech Presides" in *BaB*. (This blend of real and fictitious persons had been used in "Bech in Heaven" [*BB*], and Updike will use it again throughout *BaB*.) A black woman painted white seems to Bech "truth," for "America at heart is black." It is Holy Week, but Bech feels "unclean" by the end of the party, anticipating sex* with a female mud wrestler, Lorna, whose name combines the names of Bech's mistress Norma and two of his fictional women, Lenore and Thelma. Updike thus comically exposes the confusion between a writer and his world, but he shows that in society's exploitation of art,* the artist can and will cooperate.

Bibliography: Updike, "On One's Own Oeuvre" (*HS*); "Questions of Character: There's No Ego as Wounded as a Wounded Alter Ego," *New York Times* 1 Mar. 1999, E1, E7; Greiner, *OJ*; Detweiler, *JU*; Martin Amis, "John Updike: Rabbitland and Bechville," in *The Moronic Inferno and Other Visits to America* (New York: Viking, 1987), 155–59; Luscher, *JU*.

Beckett, Samuel (1906–1989). Irish-born, French avant-garde playwright and novelist Samuel Beckett later translated his work into English. He was James Joyce's* secretary, and when he won the Nobel Prize* (1969), his life work was called a "miserere" for mankind. Updike's reviews of Beckett's *Mercier and Camier*, *How It Is* and *Stirrings Still* attest to Beckett's fascination with those he called "sons of Joyce," such as Vladimir Nabokov* and Jorge Luis Borges.* As Joyce's secretary, Beckett undoubtedly learned a good deal about stream-of-consciousness style, which he used in novels like *Malone Dies*, and which Updike employed in *PF*, *RR* and *C*. In *C* and *Coup* Updike relied upon Beckett's comic grotesque and linguistic ingenuity. He may have taken Beckett's *Krapp's Last Tape* as a model for *BD*, since President James Buchanan,* like Krapp, is immobile in his pain and in reviewing his life makes the past real on stage. Updike said that he sought a "Beckettian tone" in *MF*, the novel based on Buchanan. In *MS* Updike created in Tom Marshfield* a Beckettian character obstinately staying alive while reduced to nothing but memory, desire and talk. Ben Turnbull* of *TE* also resembles Krapp in his physical deterioration and fluid movement through time. Since Updike was aware of the grotesque comedy in Beckett as well, he might have punned on his name in creating his novelist Henry Bech.* Beckett is mentioned in "The Bulgarian Poetess" (*BB*). *See* **English Literature**.

Beerbohm, Max (1872–1956). The English essayist and parodist Max Beerbohm is also known for caricature that impressed the young Updike. Perhaps his greatest parody was that of Henry James.* His witty drawings portrayed English political and literary celebrities. *Zuleika Dobson* (1911), his sole novel, satirized Oxford* University and romantic love. Beerbohm is among "irrelevant associations" made by Burton while his teeth are drilled ("Dentistry and Doubt" [*SD*]). In "Incest" (*SD*) Lee staves off insomnia by creating a word game in which he recalls names of persons alphabetically, recollecting Zuleika Dobson (*SD*). Updike's "Rhyming Max" (*AP*) reviews a biography of Beerbohm, and Updike establishes the quality of Beerbohm's poetry by examining his rhymes. *See* **Art; Drawing and Painting; Poetry**.

Bibliography: "Updike, Beerbohm and Others" (*AP*).

Beiderbecke, Bix (1903–1931). An American trumpeter and one of the first significant white jazz musicians, Bix Beiderbecke played with Louis Armstrong and was famous for his tone, phrasing and harmonies. Peter Caldwell* sees his film biography, *Young Man with a Horn*, while awaiting the results of his father's X rays. (In fact, the film was released in 1949, two years after Peter saw it in January 1947.) In the movie Beiderbecke resists the blandishments of a wealthy lady for a faithful woman who enables him to develop his art. The story parallels the resistance of George Caldwell* to Vera Hummel and his preference for fidelity to his wife and family. The plot also parallels the story of Peter Caldwell, who has become an artist partly because of the love of beautiful women, particularly the statue of a "naked green lady" in the Alton museum and the women of Jan Vermeer.* *See* **Film; Popular Music**.

Being There. A film (1979) with Peter Sellers, *Being There*, made from a novel by Jerzy Kosinski, is considered in "A Soft Spring Night in Shillington," (*SC*). Updike was touched by Sellers's portrayal of an idiot savant whose simple remarks remembered from television* pass for political wisdom among gullible Washingtonians. Updike recounts how he was struck by how Sellers captured Chancy Gardner's innocence while subtly satirizing Washington politics and American culture. Updike especially noted that the end credits of the film revealed the plasticity of being, since Sellers repeatedly breaks the barrier between the film's artifice and his reality. The performance and the "out-takes" focused attention for Updike upon his own *Dasein*, his being-in-the-world. *See* **Film; Shillington, Pennsylvania; Television**.

Belloc, Hilaire (1870–1953). The English politican and writer Hilaire Belloc is best known for his sardonic and humorous verse like *The Bad Child's Book of Beasts* (1896) and *Cautionary Tales for Children* (1907), alluded to in *RR*. Jack Eccles* and his wife Lucy Eccles* quarrel over his choice of bedtime reading for their three-year-old daughter Joyce (probably Belloc's "Jim—Who Ran Away from His Nurse and Was Eaten by a Lion"), since she has dreamed that a child ate a boy. This quarrel may indicate one reason why they later divorced, alluded to in the scene added to *RRed* for *RA*. Another story in Belloc's collection describes the miserable perishing of a child named Rebecca. Since this is the name the Angstroms give their daughter, her death* may be foretold in Belloc's volume. Belloc is also referred to forlornly by Burton when, at the dentist, he thinks about his religious skepticism, marked by his books by Karl Barth* and Bertrand Russell, who had superseded Belloc ("Dentistry and Doubt" [*SD*]). In his "Afterword" to *B* Updike acknowledges his use of Joseph Bédier's *The Romance of Tristan and Iseult*, translated by Paul Rosenfeld and Belloc. *See* **Ministers**.

Bibliography: Newman, *JU*.

Bellow, Saul (1915–   ). An American novelist and winner of the Nobel Prize* (1976), Saul Bellow is called by Updike "the American writer supreme," and he quotes Bellow in the epigraph to *SC* from his "What Kind of Day Did You Have?" as Updike's way of notifying the reader that his memoirs will deal with ordinary events. Bellow propelled the rise of the Jewish writer after 1945, which Updike charted in Henry Bech.* Bellow revived the picaresque novel with *The Adventures of Augie March* (1953) (which Updike says established him as "our most exuberant and melodious postwar novelist") and rectified the lack of intellectual engagement in American fiction with idea-packed novels like *Herzog* (1964), *Mr. Sammler's Planet* (1970) and *Humboldt's Gift* (1975). Bellow's use of intellectual probing to address America's loss of spiritual values may have influenced Updike's interest in this theme in *PF, MS, RV, TE* and the stories "The Music School" (*MuS*) and "Augustine's Concubine" (*P*). *See* **Novel**.

Bibliography: Updike, "An Interesting Emendation" (*PP*).

Berra, Harold "Yogi" (1922–   ). Hall of Fame catcher for the New York Yankees, 1946–65, then manager of the Yankees (1964) and the New York Mets (1972–75), Yogi Berra is mentioned in the poem "Tao in the Yankee Stadium Bleachers" (*CH*), which names him in the last line because of the witty connection between Eastern philosophy and a ballplayer named "Yogi." Like a yogi, "Berra flies," but to left field. Richard Maple* in "Snowing in Greenwich Village" (*SD*) refers to Berra merely as a rich celebrity met as an advertising contact. *See* **Religion; Sports**.

Bethlehem Steel. At one time an important steelmaker in Bethlehem, Pennsylvania, Bethlehem Steel sold wooded areas near Updike's Plowville* to developers for processing Philadelphia's trash (*SC*). This is one of many negative changes Updike detects in his hometown world, a major theme in his fiction. *See* **Reading; Shillington, Pennsylvania**.

Bhagavad-Gita. A long Sanskrit poetic dialogue, the *Bhagavad-Gita* reveals the essence of Hindu belief. In it the god Krishna* explains to Prince Arjuna before a battle why he should wage war against friends and family. Krishna tells Arjuna that his duty as a soldier is related to his path toward God through reincarnation and the need to renounce the "fruits of action." Krishna further reveals that spirit and matter are united and shows the link between sacrifice and renunciation. He enables Arjuna to see his form briefly, thus showing the union of creation and destruction. Updike uses the *Bhagavad-Gita* to defend his "hawkish" position on Vietnam* in *SC* and when he speaks through Harry "Rabbit" Angstrom* that to be alive is to kill, that in some sense existence itself is "wrong."

Bible. Updike uses both testaments of the Bible habitually, filling his work with quotations, sermons* and allusions. He uses sermons like the temptation in the wilderness in *RR*, Adam and Eve in *OF*, the woman taken in adultery and the raising of Lazarus in *MS* and the parable of the tares in *IB*. The most extensive use of the Bible is made in *IB*, in which the charismatic cult leader Jesse Smith* leads his followers into Armageddon. Smith seems to be a modern version of St. Augustine,* whose conversion occurred when a voice drove him to read Romans 13:14: "Put on the Lord Jesus Christ, and make no provision for the flesh, to gratify its desires" ("Augustine's Concubine" [*P*]). In ordinary life, however, biblical characters are merely answers to word games like "Who am I?" (Magdalene and Delilah in *Couples*).

Other characters* like George Caldwell,* Piet Hanema* and Dale Kohler* are used as models for Christ. Updike has explained that he used the analogue of the centaur Chiron in *C* partly because Chiron's sacrifice resembled Christ's. The novel blends both Christ's story and many allusions to the Bible with classical myths. Piet Hanema as a carpenter provides a Christic analogue, and his allusions to "the Loaves and Fishes" and quoting "Time to love, time to die" strengthen this image, as does his carrying of the church cross after the Tarbox church burns (*Couples*). Similar images create a Christic image for Dale Kohler (*RV*), while associations with deception, smoking and resistance to Dale's project to reveal God place Rogar Lambert* in the devil's camp. The many arguments between Lambert and Kohler are marked by dissensions about biblical stories like that of Job (*RV*).

Sally Mathias uses the Adam and Eve story to characterize her and her lover, and Jerry Conant* attacks his wife by demanding to know why she doesn't believe in Jesus or the resurrection of Lazarus. To establish a tone and point of view, Updike frequently uses epigraphs* taken from the Bible, like Psalm 45 in *MS*: Tom Marshfield's* story illustrates the meaning of how he learned to praise God with his tongue. Some of Updike's uses of the Bible may come through literary sources, for example, T. S. Eliot.* Updike's maternal grandfather, with whom he lived for many years, had read the Bible "to tatters" and often quoted from it (*SC*). Yet Updike feels that the Bible has fallen into a certain disrespect, "like a once-fearsome lion that, now toothless and declawed, can be petted and teased" (*MM*). See **Ministers; Religion**.

Bibliography: Updike, "Lust," "Stones into Bread" (*MM*); Hamilton and Hamilton, *EJ*; Hunt, *JU*; Campbell, *UN*.

Bibliography. Several bibliographies have provided the student and scholar with listings of Updike's voluminous work and writing about him. His publications at Shillington* High School can be found, as can his writings for the *Harvard Lampoon*.* The latter are listed by C. Clarke Taylor, who supplies a list of primary sources and brief annotated entries on secondary works, each to about 1968. Jack De Bellis takes up primary and secondary material to 1993, and his bibliography also includes interviews,* letters, manuscripts, graphics, readings and translations.* His listing of secondary works includes theses and dissertations, and a compilation of Updike's translated works is provided, as well as caricatures, parodies and audio and video recordings. Updike's "Foreword" to De Bellis's book includes items unlisted elsewhere. Ray Roberts provides in-depth descriptions of Updike works that are of particular use to collectors. *See* **Collecting Updike.**

Bibliography: Updike, "Autobibliographical Note" (*HS*); "A Foreword to *John Updike: A Bibliography, 1968–1993*" (*MM*); C. Clarke Taylor, *John Updike: A Bibliography* (Kent, OH: Kent State UP, 1968); Michael A. Olivas, *An Annotated Bibliography of John Updike Criticism, 1967–1973, and a Checklist of His Works* (New York: Garland, 1975); Ray A. Roberts, "John Updike: A Bibliographical Checklist Section A—Primary Publications," *American Book Collector* 1, new series (Jan.–Feb. 1980): 5–12, 40–44, and Mar.–Apr. 1980: 39–47; Stuart Wright, "John Updike's Contributions to *Chatterbox*," *Bulletin of Bibliography* 42 (Dec. 1985): 171–78; Jack De Bellis, *John Updike: A Bibliography, 1967–1993* (Westport, CT: Greenwood Press, 1994).

Biographical Anecdotes Related to Updike. Most people who have met John Updike report that he leaves an indelible mark for his charm, wit and gracious interest in other people. Those who have encountered him professionally praise his value as a colleague. In the following anecdotes, his friends, peers and ordinary readers offer testimony to Updike as a person and artist.

Updike's close relation to friends from Shillington* is well documented in *SC*, and Barry Nelson and Don Van Liew in particular recall how Updike would hang from the stairwell railings in Shillington High School to gain the attention of girls changing classes. They also recall how he would drive the family car down Coughdrop Hill steering from the running board or intentionally spinning the car in gravel. Nelson had an Updike conference in Shillington several years ago, and three women who attended were former classmates of Updike's, who still correspond with him. He often returns to Shillington for class reunions, and when asked how he is received on such occasions, Van Liew remarked, twinkling, "We put him in his place." Shillington, Updike has often remarked, makes him feel most himself. To keep him in touch, a former teacher, Mrs. Thelma Lewis, regularly sends him a batch of clippings.

Those who write to Updike know that he is a remarkably prompt correspondent. In one such letter he clarified for a bookseller the meaning of the death* of the centaur in *C*. For a graduate student he answered a questionnaire concerning his point of view in *RR*. When Professor Jay Parini was in high school, he wrote praising *PF* and received, to his shock, a very amiable response. When I curated a "Visual Art" show, Updike was the first of a hundred authors to reply, and he placed no restrictions on how his work should appear. Patricia Bozeman, now head librarian at the University of Houston, recounts how her first task there was to arrange an exhibit of Updike's work for his appearance. She finished only a few hours before he arrived, but, as she recalls, "John Updike very graciously invited me to accompany him as he travelled through that case-by-case chronology of his work." At another such exhibit Updike assented to a request that he correct an error that had been made in the printing of the broadside, "Styles of Bloom." The poem was taken from its frame, disassembled, corrected and replaced on the wall while Updike joked and the crowd watched.

People who have eagerly awaited his signature after a reading have been surprised at the delightful way he approaches what other writers consider a chore. He converses with each person, even though he might be tired from a day of interviews, class appearances, panels and readings. An instructor has reported that when Updike was handed nine books by a collector who felt sufficiently embarrassed to hand off six of the books to his wife and her friend, Updike looked at him sternly and asked, "How did you get two such attractive women to carry your books? I've never had such luck," and then he exploded in laughter. A Princeton student told me that at a reading she managed to have a private and prolonged conversation about how *W* had personally given her a feeling of "empowerment." For those concerned with how he manages to publish one or two books a year in addition to writing a steady stream of reviews and making personal appearances, James Schiff has shed some light. Schiff glimpsed Updike's use of odd bits of time when, after a typical packed day at the University of Pittsburgh, he observed Updike in a corner of the hotel lobby quietly writing.

Many have commented on Updike's unfailing fairness as a reviewer and mentor. Stephen Jay Gould said, "[I] was never more flattered in my professional life than by the very kind reviews that John Updike wrote about my work for the *New Yorker*." Erica Jong noted that Updike's review of *Fear of Flying* turned her career around. Garrison Keillor said succinctly that Updike "stands head and shoulders above the others." Novelist Nicholas Delbanco reported that Updike has served "wonderfully" the role of an exemplary writer for him, and that since he took a course at Harvard* from Updike in 1962, Updike has continued to read and comment on Delbanco's work. Updike admires writers of conviction, as the following anecdote shows. In the later 1970s or the 1980s, according to Larisa Anubis, an acquaintance of Armenian film director Sergei Paradjanov, in the documentary film *Paradjanov: A Requiem* (1994) Paradjanov speaks of Updike as helping to get him released from the Soviet authorities. Updike described Paradjanov in a letter to me as a "live wire among those very insulated ones in the good old USSR."

When he received the Conch Republic Prize for Literature at Key West in 1993, James Plath reports, Updike sat for his portrait, painted by Ernest Hemingway's* grandson. When Edward Hemingway could not finish after three years, Updike said, "Let the young genius simmer." To the emerging novelist Leonard Chiang, Updike suggested that he "keep an agent out" of his work and showed clearly why an agent would not advance Chiang financially. Alec Guinness wrote in *My Name Escapes Me* (New York: Viking, 1997) that Updike's "minute observations" "take one's breath away. It seems to me he always sees the truth of things and expresses that truth brilliantly." Jack Smight, the director of the film *Rabbit, Run*, concurs, saying, "Updike is truly an encyclopedia of life." The publisher of Lord John Press, Herb Yellin, has said that Updike is "unique [crossed out], great [crossed out], a genius. Stet."

Black Humor. A literary method as old as Chaucer, black humor has been used extensively since the 1960s to make serious or repugnant subjects comic. It has been practiced by John Barth, Thomas Pynchon, Kurt Vonnegut, Joseph Heller and many others. Updike calls such a "mingling of pathos and laughter" a "symptom of recovery from nuclear phobia" ("Beerbohm and Others" [*AP*]). In *C* black humor is used to reveal the naïveté of Peter Caldwell* when he expects his girlfriend to think his psoriasis a delightful surprise. Sometimes Updike combines shocking humor with tragedy, for example, when an American diplomat is immolated on a towering pile of cases of cereal (*Coup*). The most continuous use of black humor, however, is in *W*, in which the witches cause floor sweepings magically to emerge from the mouth of the local newspaper editor's wife while she decries the decline of morality, and devil figure Darryl Van Horne* gives the antisermon "This Is a Terrible Creation" in the Unitarian church. Probably Updike's most comic use of black humor is in "Bech Noir" (*BaB*), in which Henry Bech* systematically, ingeniously and wittily murders his harshest critics. *See* **Magic Realism; The Novel.**

Bibliography: Updike, "Beerbohm and Others" (*AP*), Thomas Le Clair, "Death and Black Humor," *Critique* 17.1 (1975): 5–40.

Black Muslims. One of various "Negro improvement movements" begun shortly after World War II, the American Islamic religious organization of the Black Muslims was led by Elijah Muhammad (1897–1975). Its most famous representative was the magnetic Malcolm X, who was assassinated in 1965 for contesting the leadership of Elijah Muhammad. Later Louis Farrakhan reasserted the principles of black separatism and the "doing-for-self" philosophy of drug* rehabilitation. In *Coup* Oscar X, a Black Muslin, disapproves of Col. Félix Ellelloû's* relationship with white Candace Cunningham* as much as white racists do. Ellelloû, who repudiated the Muslims and their separatist policy, fought for the French in Indochina. *See* **African Americans**.

Boethius (c. 480–524). The Roman philosopher Boethius, befriended by King Theodoric, was erroneously thought to be a traitor and while awaiting execution wrote *The Consolation of Philosophy*. Though Boethius was not Christian, he explained Christian morality so effectively that his influence continued for centuries and established the supremacy of Christianity as a philosophy in Western Europe. Since Boethius, Updike observed, Western civilization has transpired under Christian enchantment (*SC*). *See* **Plato; Religion**; *Roger's Version*.

Bonhoeffer, Dietrich (1906–1945). A German Lutheran theologian who practiced in Berlin and publicly criticized Hitler's effort to impose anti-Semitism on the Lutheran church and German society, Dietrich Bonhoeffer conducted anti-Nazi reforms as director of the Confessing church, which the Nazis closed. He was accused of plotting Hitler's assassination and was hanged in 1945. Since Bonhoeffer, like Karl Barth,* supported "the positivism of revelation," according to Roger Lambert,* Lambert could admire him for not being mired in pointless philosophizing about God's nature and existence (*RV*). *See* **Religion**.

The Book of Common Prayer. The official prayer book of the Church of England and the Episcopal church in the United States, *The Book of Common Prayer* was written in 1549 as an English version of the Roman Catholic liturgical books. Updike notes that the text supports life as constant change, going from "strength to strength," thus seeming to refute the idea of eternal stasis after life. Updike quotes "There is no health in us" as he recalls dental work (*SC*). *See* **Religion**.

The Book of Kells. An Irish illuminated manuscript (mid-eighth century) noted for its elaborate ornamentation and striking colors, The Book of Kells was found disappointing by Roger Lambert* during his "squint" at the book in Trinity College, Dublin, probably because the arabesques of design and the daring muted pastels offended Lambert's ascetic sense (*RV*). *See* **Art; Religion**.

Books of Updike. Updike's books share similarities that collectively stamp "Updike books" on them, particularly in their uniform appearance. When Henry Bech* interviewed his creator, he noticed that Updike had two sets of books, those in jackets and those without. The regularity of the spines of the jacketless books made Bech conclude that Updike intended to create an "oeuvre." Updike uses the word *oeuvre* to characterize the work of William Faulkner* and Honoré de Balzac, who deliberately set out to create a fictional world or to place all the world they knew between covers of books. (Humorously, Updike has also used the word to indicate the "masterworks" of Henry Bech—his mistresses.)

After leaving Harper and Brothers for Knopf in 1960, Updike requested that his books be bound with the title horizontally on the spine, his name above the title and Alfred Knopf's below, each separated by horizontal lines and his name and the publisher's in a different color than the title. Updike's name alone appears on the cover with a long line under it. Some effort has been made to match the color of the cover and spine to the subject: green, the color of grass, for *RR*; gold, the color of gold, for *RIR*; "saucy pink" for *S.*; and what he called "diabolic purple" for *W*. (This is also true of Knopf signed, limited editions of these trade books.) The top stain generally follows the cover color, but this changes to express different printings. Knopf's brief biography of Updike has always contained the same basic information since *RR*, listing Updike's date and place of birth, the schools he attended, his Knox Fellowship, his tenure at the *New Yorker** and a brief family note on his residence and number of children. Sometimes this is reprinted on the inside rear jacket. The books always explain the selection of the typeface, which has always been Janson. The back of the jacket often carries quotations from favorable critics. The jackets are often designed by Updike. The inside jacket flap contains a brief description of the book's contents, sometimes written by Updike; note, for example, the witty way he has his character Henry Bech endorse a reissue of *PF* as "surely his masterpiece."

Inside, the books' title pages are uniform, and Updike sometimes dedicates the book, usually to a family member or, as in *CP*, to everyone from his grandfather to his grandchildren, but he has dedicated his book to editors four times. The books invariably include epigraphs.* Chapter divisions are usually signaled with upper- or lowercase roman numerals or arabic numerals. Only *RR* contains unnumbered sections, and only *RV* contains subdivisions of roman capitals. *W* is unique with three divisions in lowercase roman, each with section titles and epigraphs. Collections usually have forewords or prefaces.

The dust jackets show variations, but those for the Rabbit saga contain the same horizontal stripes, with the moon in *RRed* and a tombstone in *RaR*. Some covers tease the reader, showing Updike in a rowboat to accompany the title *HS*, the face of baby Updike on *SC* and the double face of President James Buchanan* on *MF*. The "S." on the cover of *S.* is Sarah Worth's signature initial, but it also alludes to Hester Prynne's "scarlet letter" (as well as Hawthorne's* novel *The Scarlet Letter*) and symbolizes Kundalini, the serpent as the seat of female sexual power. The jacket of *RV* contains the symbol of a cross composed of the computer's "1" and "0," as though the sources of the power of Christianity and the computer were integrally related. Often the jackets are decorated with thematic art: Dürer witches grace *W*, Blake's antipastoral paradise *Couples*. The dust jackets might otherwise be embellished with museum pieces (*FN, A, TE*), paintings (*IB, TM, B*), household items (*CH*) or caricatures (*BB, BIB, BaB, GD*). The cover of *JL* shows two sides of Updike as he tries to make head and tail of works of art, and his design for *P* shows a geometry problem.

Updike has actively participated in the production of his books, in one case even going to the Scranton, Pennsylvania, bindery to see the books pass through that process. He provides a vivid and affectionate description of the process of book assembly, entranced by the "angelic beauty of human engineering." He has selected numerous layouts and pictures for dust jackets and written their blurbs. He has chosen the cover and top stain colors, and he has specified the type, Janson, one of those "influential and sturdy Dutch types," according to the note. When asked to name favorites, he thinks "most fondly" of *HS* and *BD* because they were good examples of book production, "good margins, nice cover, pleasant heft." Updike has said that "fussing with the type, the sample pages, the running heads, the dust jacket, the flap copy, the cover cloth—has perhaps been dearer to me than the writing process" ("Me and My Books" [*MM*]). *See* **Collecting Updike; Titles of Updike's Works**.

Bibliography: Updike, "His Oeuvre," *New Yorker* 25 Jan. 1999: 74, 76–81; "Me and My Books," "Foreword to *Love Factories*" (*MM*).

Boreas. In Greek myth Boreas was the god of the north wind, whose brothers were Zephyrus, god of the west wind, and Notus, god of the south wind. Updike's narrator imagines that women think that Boreas impregnated Night ("Wind" [*TT*]). *See* **Classical Literature**.

Borges, Jorge Luis (1899–1986). A blind avant-garde Argentinean poet and antirealist story writer and director of the Buenos Aires library until he was fired and exiled by a fascist government, Jorge Luis Borges specialized in writing brief philosophical works, detective stories and essays, often blending the genres. He abhorred novels and found Marcel Proust* tedious. Updike's reviews of Borges's works reveal Updike's critical acumen in finding genius in writers distinctively different from himself; his review "The Author as Librarian" was influential in establishing Borges's reputation in the United States. Updike may have found suggestions for what he called his "personal-abstract" stories "The Music School," "Harv Is Plowing Now" and "Leaves" (*MuS*) in Borges's works. Borges's glosses on historical figures and his reuse of myths* might also underlie Updike's "Augustine's Concubine" (*P*) and his several treatments of Tristan and Isolde.* Tristão Raposo's death in *B* resembles that of Borges's gaucho in "The South." *See* **European Literature; Kafka, Franz; Literary Influences; Magic Realism; Nabokov, Vladimir**.

Bosch, Hieronymus (1450?–1516). Hieronymus Bosch was an artist of the Netherlands school whose fantastic figures and strange melding together of organic and inorganic images, along with arcane religious symbolism, have made him attractive and baffling. His work contains a maze of conventional images of the Nativity and the Crucifixion, along with depictions of witchcraft and alchemy. Bosch achieves power through his graphic delineation of punishment for sin as well as serene, luminescent visions of heaven. Roger Lambert* may allude to Bosch's *Garden of Earthly Delights* in his vision of his wife's adultery* in the messy room of Dale Kohler.* Lambert is unaware, though, of the fact that Esther Lambert* may have been impregnated in this "garden" (*RV*). *See* **Art**.

Boston, Massachusetts. The capital of Massachusetts, Boston is the largest city in New England and the source of American Puritanism as well as the crucible of American democracy. Boston contains the first public school and university, Harvard,* in America. It was the home of the "Boston Brahmins," the aristocratic educated elite, the "Fireside Poets," like William Cullen Bryant, and transcendentalists Ralph Waldo Emerson* and Henry David Thoreau.* Boston is the site of a liaison between Janet Appleby and Horace little-Smith (*Couples*) and is where Ben Turnbull has his office in *TE*. Although the latter novel takes place in the year 2020, the vast construction to convert elevated roads to underground throughways begun in the 1990s remains unfinished; Updike's joke or reasonable guess?

Bibliography: Updike, "Sunday in Boston" (*TI*).

Botticelli Game. In Botticelli a person chosen by the group must discover his assigned "identity" by asking questions, such as "Is this person in politics?" The group's answer may contain clues leading to disclosure. In *Couples* Foxy Whitman* is asked to discover her identity as Christine Keeler, a "tart" who involved John Profumo,* a member of Parliament, in scandal. Foxy is shamed by the association and by the awareness that people have guessed that Piet Hanema* is her lover. The end of the game is confusing in the British edition, since all references to the scandal were suppressed for legal reasons. *See* **Games**.

Bottom's Dream (New York: Knopf, 1969). *Bottom's Dream*, an adaptation for children of Shakespeare's *Midsummer Night's Dream* (1969), uses only the plots of the fairies and Bottom and his friends. One of several works Updike composed for children, it may shed light on the children* in *RR*, *RaR* and *RV*. *See* **Babies**.

Bibliography: Nora L. Magid, "Clear the Stage for a Repeat Performance," *New York Times Book Review* 9 Nov. 1969: 2, 65; William Heyen, "Sensibilities," *Poetry* 115 (Mar. 1970): 428–29.

Braque, Georges (1882–1963). A French painter who was at first influenced by the brilliant colors of the fauvists* like Henri Matisse, Georges Braque, by 1908, under the impact of Paul Cézanne's blend of formal structure and strange perspective, became a cubist, reducing buildings to cubes and prisms that looked flat yet three-dimensional. In 1909 he met Pablo Picasso, who was also interested in reducing objects to facets. Both invented "collage," using ordinary material like newspapers glued into the painting. In "Toward Evening" (*SD*), to reduce boredom, Rafe creates a game* in which he associates house numbers with historical moments, connecting "1902" with Braque's journey to Le Havre to study painting. Like a collage, the story blends the ordinary homeward bus trip to Rafe's family after work with unusual connections. Thus at one point Rafe becomes entranced by a woman whom he examines as if she were a work of art.*

Brazil (New York: Knopf, 1994). *B* treats the story of Tristan and Isolde* (acknowledged in Updike's "Afterword"), which had preoccupied him for some time, shifting the location from medieval Ireland to Brazil (it is Updike's only novel named entirely after a locale) and the time period from the Middle Ages to the present. The setting keeps the tale exotic and suggests its universality; the time shift reveals the modernity of the subject. While marriage supplies the hurdle the lovers must leap in the ancient story, differences in color (the hero is black and the heroine white) create an impediment to adultery* in *B*. The novel is more than an updating of the legendary lovers, though, for the violence and manners of Rio and the mysterious folkways of Brazil's interior are crucial determinants in the tragedy.

Isabel Leme,* the daughter of a rich businessman, selects a handsome lower-class black, Tristão Raposo,* to initiate her into sex.* Partly because her family objects to him, she moves in with his suspicious family and later elopes with Tristão. Isabel's uncle sends a henchman to bring her back and kill Tristão if necessary, so the lovers flee into the jungle. Tristão eventually kills their pursuer, mines gold and becomes increasingly disillusioned when Isabel becomes a prostitute to support them and several children of mixed parentage. In order to elude her uncle with a perfect disguise, Isabel changes her skin to black and Tristão's to white in a remarkable instance of magic realism.* They return to Rio, and the magic works. Ironically, however, Tristão then desires Isabel less, and she discovers that she enjoyed sex more as a black woman. Tristão turns arrogant and is killed by a poor black boy to whom he still feels psychological kinship, but for whom, as a white man, he feels tragic disdain.

The novel shows once again how willing Updike is to take risks. As he had created an entire black nation to investigate the political intricacy of Africa in *Coup*, Updike now exploits the black erotic folk experience. In both books he drew upon inventions akin to those of Vladimir Nabokov,* using Asian travels described in Nabokov's *The Gift* in *B*. Deeply researched, the texture of *B* provides a powerful sensory experience of Brazil, enclosing the tragic love affair within the fecund beauty and indifferent violence of nature,* from which love had arisen. Also, Updike writes the story in an approximation of the courtly language of the medieval tale of the lovers. Consequently, it gives the impression of having been translated from another language. Some incidents, particularly the encounters with the Guaicuru and the Pualista *bandeiras* in the interior of Brazil, also seem to come from another time.

B shows interesting connections to the Rabbit saga, which Updike had just finished. As in *RR* and *RRed*, a visceral need for freedom leads to a need for flight from authority. Like Janice Angstrom* (*RRed*), the runaway Isabel follows a dream of love too long suppressed. As Harry "Rabbit" Angstrom* discovered the importance of speculating in gold and silver in *RIR*, Tristâo unearths a huge nugget in the mine. Like Rabbit in *RaR*, Tristâo isolates himself from his wife, places himself in jeopardy with blacks and dies. *B* is thus an example of Updike's transformation of his career-long interest in the ex–basketball* player from Brewer,* while ironically portraying the transforming power of men through women's protective love. In contrast to *RA*, however, Updike's impressions of Brazil were valid for 1992, but not for the 1960s, when the action takes place. In *RA* Updike is scrupulously accurate about day-to-day historical events and impressions. *See* **African Americans**.

Bibliography: Michiko Kakutani, "Tristan and Iseult as Latin Lovers," *New York Times* 25 Jan. 1994: C19; Barbara Kingsolver, "Desire under the Palms," *New York Times Book Review* 6 Feb. 1994: 1, 26; Tom Shone, *Times Literary Supplement* No. 4748 (1 Apr. 1994): 21; Schiff, *JU*; Dilvo Ristoff, "When Earth Speaks of Heaven," The Future of Race and Faith in Updike's *Brazil*, in Yerkes, *JU*.

Brer Rabbit. "Brer Rabbit" is an African American folk tale included by American writer Joel Chandler Harris (1848–1908) in his *Uncle Remus, His Songs and His Sayings* (1880) and *Uncle Remus and Br'er Rabbit* (1906). Harris discovered the story during the Civil War while working on a Southern plantation as a reporter, and he was the first to attempt to wed the reproduction of black dialect to indigenous tales. Harris's Uncle Remus, a former slave, tells stories of humanlike animals, including Br'er Fox and Br'er Bear. Roger Lambert* explains to his wife Esther* that for his half-niece Verna Ekelof,* who has had black lovers, the ghetto where she lived was to her as the "briar patch was to Br'er Rabbit" (*RV*). But Lambert does not see that Verna may only seem weak like Br'er [*sic*] Rabbit; her ingenuity enables her to overcome strong foes like Lambert: she seduces the ex-cleric into quasi-incest. Brer Rabbit is also mentioned in "Minority Report" (*M*), in which the narrator discovers that Brer Rabbit was right: "Freedom is made of brambles." *See* **African Americans; Incest**.

Brewer, Pennsylvania. The fifth-largest city in Pennsylvania, called the "flowerpot city" (*RR*) because of its extensive use of red brick, Brewer was modeled on Reading,* thirty-five miles northwest of Philadelphia, Pennsylvania. Updike meticulously describes Brewer's homes and apartments, schools, factories, pretzel and beer industries, bars and churches, ballparks and restaurants, newspapers and vacant lots, maple trees and strip malls. In *RA* Brewer is the site of the love affair between Ruth Leonard Byer* and Harry "Rabbit" Angstrom* that drives Rabbit away from his wife Janice Angstrom.* With their son Nelson Angstrom,* Janice watches at Ruth's window, hoping for a glimpse of Rabbit (*RR*). A decade later Nelson will bicycle to Charlie Stavros's* apartment at 1204 Eisenhower Street, hoping to glimpse his mother when she has gone to live with him (*RRed*). Brewer is also a center of racial unrest and urban blight, and it grows more seedy throughout *RA* as palatial movie theaters become skin-flick houses. But it also welcomes high-tech industries and corresponding upscale housing developments. The suburb Mt. Judge,* modeled on Mt. Penn,* is Rabbit's hometown in *RR*, looming over Brewer, with its Pinnacle Hotel resembling a pagoda. Ruth and Rabbit walk there on Palm Sunday after their first night together, and Rabbit feels that "the true space in which we live is upward space." The Angstroms eventually move to the more fashionable suburb of Penn Villas (*RIR*), thus placing distance between themselves and the source of their success, since Springer Motors* is on Route 111 (probably Pennsylvania Route 222) in Brewer.

Brewer represents a typical middle-class American town reflecting all the changes in America from 1959 to 1989: altering family patterns (an increase in divorce,* working mothers, family counseling), changing institutions (the church and its ministers* becoming more socialized), declining and emerging businesses (linotyping gives way to printing technology; American cars lose markets to Japanese imports; electronics firms emerge), changing styles in sports (baseball games become more exciting on television,* blacks dominate basketball*; golf* becomes accessible to the middle class), entertainment (great movies of the past have made room for porno flicks; television has brought social comedy and war into the living room), rising new classes and groups (African Americans,* Latinos, women, gays and lesbians, white-collar workers), changing styles of leisure (country club, Caribbean vacations, Florida retirement, recreational drugs*) and increasingly visible vice (sex,* drugs, riots, white-collar crime). Rabbit is conflicted about most of these changes, but Janice accommodates them by taking part in a real-estate boom, adopting the therapeutic language of television talk shows—achieving "closure" with her lover—and participating in the shifting markets in automobiles,* finances and real estate. Nelson exploits Brewer's shifting fortunes by stealing from Springer Motors, then accepting drug counseling so he can work with addicted youth. Updike's Brewer is said to be as real as William Faulkner's* Jefferson. *See* **Plowville, Reading, Shillington, Pennsylvania.**

Brezhnev, Leonid (1906–1982). The general secretary of the Communist party of the USSR from 1964 to 1982, Leonid Brezhnev supervised experimental cultivation of arid lands under Premier Nikita Khrushchev,* whom he later helped depose. Brezhnev's reduction of tensions with the United States ("détente") and agreement to limit strategic arms (SALT) marked greater Soviet conciliation toward the West. By 1970 Brezhnev became the supreme Soviet leader. Col. Fêlix Ellelloû* in *Coup* thought Brezhnev instrumental in helping to establish Islamic Marxism in Kush.

Brook Farm. The cooperative community in Brook Farm, Massachusetts, founded by George Ripley in 1841, advocated share and share alike, division of labor, sexual equality without sexual exclusivity and the spiritual attitudes of transcendentalism.* Nathaniel Hawthorne* was attracted to Brook Farm for a while, but repudiated the community in *The Blithedale Romance*. This novel influenced the writing of *S.*, and Updike becomes a modern Hawthorne when he explores the moral and psychological confusion of the community and its fraudulence and hypocrisy. Updike repeatedly unmasked deception and self-deception in unconventional living groups, no matter how well intended. His first novel exposed the misguided humanism that creates regimentation restricting freedom (*PF*). In *Couples* suburban living virtually parodied the good intentions of communal bonding, and in *MS* Updike showed that an enforced society of reprobates does not necessarily encourage reclamation. Country-clubbers are satirized when Harry "Rabbit" Angstrom* joins the Flying Eagle Tee and Racquet Club in *RIR*. The college world in *Coup*, *RV* and *MF* seems to encourage narcissism in the faculty and students alike. *IB* exposes a tragic view of a Branch Davidian–style compound that in the name of religion forces armed confrontation. That novel contrasts the compound's Brook Farm style to conventional communities resembling Shillington,* like Basingstoke. The film* colony is also described in *IB*. Mini-commune types enable Updike to reveal his dissatisfactions with all but the most traditional styles of living. Some include the squatters on Ben Turnbull's* land (*TE*), the literary academy (*BB*, *BaB*), the drug* subculture (*RaR*, "Bech Takes Pot Luck" [*BB*]) and the trio of Harry "Rabbit" Angstrom, Skeeter* and Jill Pendleton* (*RRed*). Conversely, he favors the marginalized communities of blacks in *RRed* and *Coup* and of Brazilian Indians in *B*.

Bibliography: Schiff, *JU*.

Buchanan, James (1791–1868). The fifteenth president of the United States (1857–61), James Buchanan is variously credited with preventing or postponing the Civil War and with appeasement of the South that led to the war. He is the protagonist of *BD*, a major figure in *MF* and the subject of a debate in *PF*, in which John Hook* calls him the last president to represent "the entire country." *See* **Coleman, Ann; Presidents**.

Buchanan Dying (New York: Knopf, 1974). Updike originally projected the play *BD* as a novel fitting into two vast schemes. First, it would complete a "tetralogy" in which four books took up four different aspects of time (*PF*, the future; *RR*, the present; *C*, the remembered past; and *BD*, the historical past). Second, each book would record four views of Pennsylvania and say farewell to his native state. The projected novel would also fit into a plan to write twenty-six novels, each dominated by a word whose initial letter formed a letter of the alphabet: "boys" is the first word of *RR* and "Caldwell" of *C*. But Updike suffered his only serious writer's block when the novel would not "get legs," as he put it, after his immense research in the late 1960s, a "penance," as he called it, for writing the commercially successful *Couples*.

Updike feared that the warnings Henry James* had given Sarah Orne Jewett about historical fiction containing a "fatal *cheapness*" (*MM*) and a "vigorous fakery" (*RA*, "Introduction") might apply to *BD*, so he considered writing a play instead of a novel. This was not an unlikely idea since Updike had originally considered *RR* as a movie and had offered to write the screenplay after selling the novel to Hollywood. Although Updike had always felt "unease" attending a play because of the artificiality of listening to words memorized by actors, he hated wasting six years' effort and undertook his sole drama. Updike decided to "let the designers of sets and costumes solve the surfaces. Let theatrical unreality equal historical unreality. Let the actors themselves be the 'veins.' Let speech, which is all impalpable that remains to us of the dead, be all" (*BD*). Because of *BD*'s rather static quality ("three talkative acts," he called them), Updike refers to it as a closet drama; it has rarely been produced. The struggle to turn unmanageable material into fiction resembles Henry Bech's* writer's block.

The play concerns the waning days of Buchanan's life in 1868. He is tormented by two events in his life that overwhelmed him: the mysterious estrangement and death of his fiancée, Ann Coleman,* and the Civil War, which he had tried to forestall. The two are yoked together, since her death in part led to his political career. By concentrating on Buchanan's reflections on these things and introducing fragments from the past on stage as part of his revealed memory, Updike establishes what he called a "Beckettian* tone."

Buchanan recalls how after a business trip he stopped at the home of a mutual female friend instead of visiting Ann, whose jealous fury caused her to flee Lancaster for Philadelphia, resulting in illness. Her treatment with laudanum precipitated her death, and her family tacitly considered Buchanan to be responsible for the tragedy (as Harry "Rabbit" Angstrom's* family had considered him guilty of the death of his baby in *RR*). Buchanan is thus Updike's typical hero, a man caught in the middle—in this case, between guilt and innocence, between the political forces of North and South, between his interest in farming and the law and between his honest affection for a woman from a higher class and his inability to assure her family of his intentions to marry.

Buchanan in fact had one nearsighted and one farsighted eye and was thus constantly aware of the immediate and distant contexts of his observation. This double vision created a relativistic viewpoint and results in inaction, since the near-at-hand seems to have the same value as the far-reaching, the pragmatic as the idealistic. (Updike notes in an epigraph* the philosophic importance of this visual problem to Søren Kierkegaard.*) Buchanan also resembles Updike's customary protagonist, immersed in domestic tragedy while absorbed by larger problems (Rabbit in *RRed*, Col. Félix Ellelloû* in *Coup*, Clarence Wilmot* in *IB*, Ben Turnbull* in *TE*). Buchanan, however, is tortured by these problems to the end.

Stylistically, Updike departed from his customary epigrammatic or lyric styles* for a Victorian "upholstered" style, as one critic called it. Also, Updike mixes historical figures with imagined characters for the first time in a novel and speculates about motives with considerable latitude, particularly Ann Coleman's. In the end, Updike felt that he failed to grasp the "poignancy" of Buchanan because he had forgotten that the nostalgia of time passing could be grasped neither by history, what he called "the determined study of past events," or memory, "the form of nostalgia." Apparently, Updike found that his material was unsuitable for analysis in the style of Marcel Proust.*

Updike may have been drawn to the 1850s because he found the period similar to the 1960s in forcing debates on national issues that created strain in personal relationships. Seeing another way to reveal the modernity of Buchanan's tragedy, Updike blended it with events in the 1970s and 1990s in *MF*. In writing *MF* he drew upon his "copious afterword" (*MM*), nearly as long as the play, which he could not get into the drama. At least he was relieved of his "unease" with the "*theatricality*" of the stage's artifice. Though the dust jacket asserts that the "Afterword" "rounds out the portrait" of Buchanan, it is also a mine of informative quotes from his research, speculations about his characters' motives and explanations of Updike's aims, treatments and understandings both of history* and his own creative process,* as well as notes about his family. The "Afterword" is thus a valuable document for understanding Updike, as useful as his comments in *SC* and many special introductions to his work. It has never been reprinted.

Bibliography: Updike, "Afterword" (*BD*); Arthur Schlesinger, Jr., "The Historical Mind and the Literary Imagination," *Atlantic* 233 (June 1974): 54–59; Stanley Weintraub, "Closet Drama," *New Republic* 170 (22 June 1974): 26; Irvin Ehrenpreis, "Buchanan Redux," *New York Review of Books* 21 (8 Aug. 1974): 6, 8; "John Updike's *Buchanan Dying*: A Chamber Theatre Production," *Readers Theatre* 7 (Fall/Winter, 1979): 7, 8, 37; Greiner, *OJ*.

Buddha, Gautama (563?–483? B.C.). Called "the Enlightened One," Gautama Buddha founded Buddhism after leaving his privileged family in search of understanding. This "Great Renunciation" was the defining moment in history, according to Buddhists. He rejected the asceticism of the Hindu caste system, but experienced "the Great Enlightenment" and delivered a sermon rejecting metaphysical and logical thinking. In *RV* Roger Lambert* cynically explains modern youth's detached religious commitment by finding Buddhism's "non-attachment" to be the cause of the generation of the 1980s excusing theft. *See* **Berra, Yogi;** *Bhagavad-Gita;* **Religion.**

Burckhardt, Jakob (1818–1897). Jakob Burckhardt was a historian of art and culture. His work *The Civilization of the Renaissance in Italy* (1860) attributed the shift from medievalism to Renaissance modernism to the development of idealized individualism. Professor Morrison knows that he will never achieve such an insight ("Slippage" [*TM*]).

Byer, Annabelle. The daughter of Ruth Leonard Byer,* Annabelle Byer appears at Springer Motors* to buy a car with a friend in *RIR*, leading Harry "Rabbit" Angstrom* to speculate that she might be his and Ruth's daughter, though Ruth insists that she is not. Later in this novel Annabelle meets Rabbit's son Nelson Angstrom* at a party, and Nelson complains about Rabbit to her. She tries unsuccessfully to direct his attention toward his father's motives, and for a while Nelson shows an interest in her, perhaps because his wife, Teresa "Pru" Angstrom,* is dancing, though she is pregnant. In *RaR* Annabelle nurses Rabbit after his angioplasty procedure, yet he decides not to pursue her offer to have him meet her mother; he wants no definitive resolution. While he is dying, he may intend to reveal to his son Nelson that she is his sister, but this is ambiguous.

Bibliography: O'Connell, *JU*.

Byer, Ruth Leonard. Harry "Rabbit" Angstrom's* mistress in *RR*, Ruth provides him with confirmation of his own high valuation of himself, matches his own flair for neatness, gives up part-time prostitution for him, becomes pregnant by him and is abused by Rabbit when he learns that she had been the lover of his foe Ronnie Harrison.* She loved Rabbit because, as she told him, "In your stupid way you're still fighting" (*RA*), and because of his spontaneity and "mildness." Yet Rabbit leaves her when his wife Janice Angstrom* has their baby, Rebecca June.* When he returns after the baby dies, Ruth calls him "Mr. Death" and offers an ultimatum: if he leaves Janice and his son Nelson Angstrom,* she will marry him and have his child, but if he returns to his family, she will have an abortion.* Ruth reappears in *RIR*, now married to Frank Byer, a farmer who operates a school bus. (Has Ruth sold herself to a "Frank" buyer?). She refuses to confirm Rabbit's suspicion that she had not had the abortion and that Annabelle Byer,* whom he had met at Springer Motors,* is their daughter. Though he keeps alive his feeling that love with Ruth was paradise, he refuses to see her when Annabelle offers to arrange it and dies keeping alive a dream that cannot be destroyed (*RaR*).

Bibliography: O'Connell, *JU*.

C

Cain. In Genesis Cain, son of Adam and Eve, kills his brother Abel when God prefers Abel's offering. God then marks Cain as an outcast to keep anyone from killing him. Cain's mark is mentioned in *Coup* by the Islamic Col. Félix Ellelloû, who, exiled, has figuratively become Cain. Updike repeatedly uses the outcast in his work; for example, Harry "Rabbit" Angstrom,* George Caldwell,* Peter Caldwell,* Skeeter,* Jill Pendleton,* Tom Marshfield,* Dale Kohler,* the Arhat,* Clarence Wilmot,* Clark DeMott* and Jesse Smith.* Henry Bech* might also qualify as an outcast. *See* **Bible; Characters**.

Calder, Alexander (1898–1976). Alexander Calder was a Philadelphia, Pennsylvania, sculptor whose wire circus characters established his reputation for wit. Under the influence of Joan Miró, he helped to bring abstraction to sculpture in his mobiles, which balanced arrangements of abstract metals, and his stabiles, which fixed abstract forms. In "Toward Evening" Rafe brings home a simple bird mobile for his infant Liz, to the displeasure of his wife, who seemed to expect a Calder (*SD*). Updike used this mobile in the poem "Mobile of Birds," revealing his baby daughter Elizabeth's* indifference to it. In another poem, "Calder's Hands," which Updike probably wrote to commemorate the exhibit Calder created at the Whitney Museum and his death immediately thereafter, Updike describes the restlessness and accuracy of Calder's hands, shown in a short film. In *W* Alexandra Spofford* reveals her sense of inadequacy in making figurines when Darryl Van Horne* insists that she do more monumental things in the spirit of Calder and Henry Moore. *See* **Art**.

Caldwell, George. George W. Caldwell teaches general science* at Olinger High School, which his son Peter Caldwell* attends (*C*). In the first chapter

Caldwell lectures on cosmic and biological evolution leading to the arrival of man. He asserts that man is tragic because he can foresee death,* and death haunts Caldwell through the narrative; he fears that he has cancer,* says that nature* itself reminds him of death, and is haunted by the proverb "Time and tide wait for no man." His foe, the principal Louis Zimmerman,* writes his (premature) obituary. Though Caldwell is something of a joke to his students and an embarrassment to his son for his classroom comic inventions, he is personally concerned with them all. He nearly gives away the answers to a geology test to a slow student and, as the swimming coach, inspires another student to become a teacher. Peter suffers at his hands when his father goes out of his way to help a hitchhiker who steals Caldwell's gloves. Peter is tortured further when his father mishandles the car twice; first they must stay in a seedy hotel where they are mistaken for homosexuals, and the second time Peter contracts a fever from walking in the January snow. Meanwhile, the gym teacher propositions Caldwell, but he is faithful to his dominating wife, and despite thinking that he has lost basketball* tickets in his care and witnessing the principal's apparent infidelity, Caldwell manages to hold his job. He is a survivor.

Updike presents Caldwell in four ways: as a character modeled on Updike's own father, as a teacher, as a father and as a "centaur." Updike has said in interviews* that he created Caldwell because he had decided that his first novels would describe family members, starting with his maternal grandfather in *PF*. He also intended to "avenge" Shillington's* injustices to his father (*SC*), and indeed his father Wesley Updike* acknowledged that Updike's portrayal of him is accurate. Second, Caldwell's eccentric teaching devices have become part of the school's oral tradition, and the students recognize his teaching as a blend of knowledge, caring, play and common sense. As a result, when one of his swimmers earns a perfect score in a contest, perfection descends from the clouds to Olinger. Third, from the perspective of his teenage son, Caldwell is so much larger than life that he is an impediment to his own growth. Seen from the child's perspective, Updike has noted, people surrounding a child seem "god-sized." Yet Peter is made uncomfortable and self-conscious by the disrespect directed at his father and by his father's willingness to submit to unjust authority and to befriend unworthy strangers who take advantage of him. Also, Peter sees Caldwell as blocking his happiness with his mother and his girlfriend. Peter fantasizes that the family would be happier if Caldwell would die, and he is humiliated when his father speaks before Peter's girlfriend of his psoriasis. Fourth and last, Caldwell is an analogue for Chiron,* the centaur who instructs the young and gives up immortality in order to end Prometheus's pain. Updike's technique of alternating chapters that take place in Olinger with chapters set in Olympus displays the gap between gods and men, but it also suggests that Caldwell's suffering and struggle are not so different from the mythic centaur's pain. In the last chapter Chiron kills himself to protect Prometheus, and this led early reviewers to conclude that Caldwell had killed himself as well. But Updike has insisted in interviews that Caldwell metaphorically dies daily by working for his family; thus Caldwell, like Chiron, sacrifices himself for others. The narrative, composed by his son, Peter, lovingly re-creates three days in the winter when Peter felt utterly confused and painfully afraid of his father's suffering. Perhaps the psoriasis-suffering Peter had recognized that he needed, like the mythical figure in the print *The Flaying of Marsyas*, to suffer to become an artist, and his recollection of his father is dual suffering: his father's and his own memory of it. Yet it is also a dual purgation, for Peter discovers the godlike in all men through his father, and he shapes his pain into art that transcends it. In *SC* Updike describes his father in detail and remarks on how his white-collar suit seemed "a Nessus's shirt to him." The reference is ironic since Nessus was a centaur and Wesley Updike* was used as a model for Caldwell who was himself modeled on a centaur. Nessus's shirt, stained with blood, was responsible for Hercules's death.

Bibliography: Ronald Wesley Hoag, "*The Centaur*: What Cures George Caldwell?" *Studies in American Fiction* 8.1 (1980): 88–98; Detweiler, *JU*; Greiner, *JU*.

Caldwell, Peter. Peter Caldwell is a dual figure, an Olinger High School student in a small Pennsylvania town, Olinger, and an artist living with a mistress in New York* whose recollections of his fifteen-year-old self form the narrative (*C*). In January 1947 Peter studies at the school where his father teaches and witnesses his father's humiliation by a disorderly class, manipulation by a dull student and denigration by the principal. He worries that his father might have cancer*; throughout the novel he is haunted by his father's imminent death.* At school Peter is mortified when his father casually refers to Peter's psoriasis, a secret he intends to reveal only to a girl as a token of his love. Peter is embarrassed by the stories told by fellow students—Caldwell once affixed a snowball to a chalkboard to show a period at the end of an equation—and Peter is aware that his father's colleagues demean him. At one point, Peter confronts the principal, Louis Zimmerman,* about the same question he says his father inadequately addressed in his class: what are the humanistic values implicit in the sciences? Yet Peter wishes that his father would not insert himself between him and his mother, but his Oedipal problem is countered by fear of his father's death, and he pleads, "Please don't die!" Peter is thus a typically conflicted adolescent beset by identity crises and fears of abandonment while searching for love. Peter becomes infuriated when his father's indifference to his car causes them to become stuck in a snowdrift, and the walk in the snow for a safe haven makes Peter ill. In a sense, George Caldwell is the eagle to Peter's Prometheus.

A dozen years later, Peter, now a twenty-seven-year-old New York second-rate abstract expressionist with a black mistress, examines those three days in January in order to understand his father's ongoing sacrifice for him and his family. The last chapter makes clear that Peter has been recalling his life in order to recover the reality of his father, both as he appeared through the adolescent distorting glass and as Peter has come to appreciate him. The mature Peter Caldwell can thus unveil the mythical teacher Chiron who had always resided within his father. He now understands his father, symbolically, as a centaur, a man with his feet in the swamp and his head afloat in the stars. As an artist, Peter envelops his narrative with dozens of mythological references in order to rediscover the child's perspective from the vantage point of his artistic sophistication.

Bibliography: James M. Mellard, "The Novel as Lyric Elegy: The Mode of Updike's *The Centaur*," in Bloom, *JU*.

Calendar. As a social realist, Updike roots his fiction in a specific time by providing a clear chronology for his novels. He often supplies symbolic overtones to his timetable; for example, *PF* takes place one August day: the brevity of the day, of the summer and of the life of the elderly are encapsulated in one symbolic day.

Updike carefully reviewed the calendar of the four Rabbit novels in creating *RA*, as an extensive description of it will make clear. Harry "Rabbit" Angstrom's* desertion of his family starts on Friday, March 20, 1959, the beginning of spring and two days before Palm Sunday. His spring idyll with Ruth Leonard Byer* ends about June 21, the start of summer. His daughter is born and dies in June. The season of spring is thus ironic; rather than being fecund and regenerative, spring is a season of death.*

RRed begins with the day of the *Apollo 11** moon launch, July 16, 1969, another false start, since the space age is merely a technological stunt in which scientists have discovered a way to land a spaceship on what Rabbit considers "nothing," the dead moon, which operates on an alien calendar. During the summer and fall Rabbit's life disintegrates: his wife Janice* leaves him, Jill Pendleton,* a rich runaway, challenges his values, and Skeeter,* a black militant, squats in his home, making him an outlaw and placing his home at the mercy of neighborhood violence. But July 20, the day of the lunar landing, the birthday of the space age, is also the birthday of Rabbit's mother, who is dying of Parkinson's disease, and the day Janice and Rabbit begin life apart. Their son Nelson Angstrom* also starts a new life not only with the figurative death of his mother but the discovery of his infatuation with Jill and his conflict with his father. A new age has begun for them all that summer. Rabbit's house is burned and runaway Jill is killed on Columbus Day Eve, another ironic American calendar date. Around Halloween Rabbit dreams of Jill's ghost, buries the ghost of his baby who died a decade before and reconciles with Janice, who had nearly caused her lover's death.

RIR also begins in the summer (1979) and ends by ushering in a new decade with Super Bowl Sunday as Rabbit is presented his granddaughter. Summer is again a time of problems, as Nelson's working at Springer Motors* renews the hostility between father and son. Nelson's already-pregnant fiancée, Teresa "Pru" Lubelle,* arrives on a date she embodies, Labor Day Eve, and they marry on September 22, the first day of fall. She "falls" (with Nelson's help) and breaks her arm the day before the anniversary of the cessation of hostilities ending World War I, November 10. On Webb Murkett's* advice Rabbit gambles on the rise of the price of gold and silver, and the calendar thus becomes a way of charting the growth of wealth, though at Christmas Rabbit becomes overburdened by gold that he strains to carry to the bank. The new year brings mostly happy developments. On New Year's Day the Angstroms decide to leave the house of Janice's mother, Bessie Springer,* and buy a new home, thus putting space between a difficult parent and a nervous son, since Nelson and Pru are also living at Mrs. Springer's. Vacationing in the Caribbean with money earned from the precious metals during the fortunate fall, the Angstroms swap spouses with Ronnie* and Thelma Harrison* and Webb and Cindy Murkett," and a ten-year affair begins between Thelma and Rabbit. During this time Nelson deserts Pru and his baby, but intends to return to Kent State University. On Super Bowl Sunday, January 20, Rabbit sees his granddaughter Judy for the first time, and though this is Rabbit's symbolic victory over death, Judy is also Rabbit's "nail in his coffin."

RaR starts with another Christmas vacation, this time for Nelson's family, and Rabbit and Janice await them in Florida* like children with expectations of Santa. But their gift for Rabbit is a heart attack and for Janice heartsickness as she learns of Nelson's drug* addiction and embezzlement from her father's firm. The new year begins with Rabbit's near death, and spring finds Rabbit in Pennsylvania, where he was born. The return from the South recalls *RR*, in which Rabbit drove back from West Virginia on March 21, 1959. Spring truly symbolizes recovery, as Rabbit has angioplasty in May, Janice earns her real-estate license, and Nelson completes drug rehabilitation. But summer finds Rabbit fleeing from the disclosure of his intimacy with Pru. he dies at summer's height in Florida, nine months after the action had begun, as if he had experienced a gestation of death, as James Schiff surmises.

Although Palm Sunday is mentioned in *RR* and Christmas is alluded to in *RaR*, Updike's wittiest use of the religious calendar is in *RV*, in which Dale Kohler* apparently resurrects God with the computer on April 5, the first Friday in April, but he gives up in despair about the time of the June equinox, roughly the time of Pentecost. But most narratives celebrate secular rather than religious holidays. In "The Kid's Whistling" (*SD*) Christmas is anticipated. In "The Happiest I've Been" (*SD*) New Year's Eve is celebrated, suggesting the unsteady way in which hometown kids return to college. On Memorial Day, a day to honor the heroic dead, we learn that Ruth is pregnant by Rabbit (*RR*). Sarah Worth* is remembered by her daughter on Mother's Day, and she starts her new life by reviving an old affair on December 21, the winter solstice (*S.*) Roger Lambert's* Thanksgiving guest is Dale Kohler. He and Esther Lambert* give thanks by falling in love (*RV*).

Updike obviously worked with almanacs and yearbooks to provide historical references for *IB*. He said that news and sports scores in *RR* were copied directly from the radio as he wrote. Updike clearly intends to give as much actuality to the passing of time as he does to spatial reality and ordinary things. Other works such as *Marry* and *Couples* deliberately situate the narrative in a time of national significance. *Marry* takes place between March and November 1962, during the "Camelot"* period of what Updike called "John Kennedy's* reign." Before Kennedy's death, Updike asserted, America was innocent. *Couples* takes place in 1963–64 and describes the death of innocence in the assassination of JFK. Meanwhile, a self-imposed discipline caused Updike to write *MS* with a chapter for each day of the month. An opposite impulse caused him to embrace eighty years of American history in *IB*, and in this novel Updike fortifies the narrative with specific public events to emphasize the time-bound character of the action.

Updike has created an interesting symbolic calendar in *W*. The action takes place early in the 1970s when the Vietnam* War raged and possibly gave rise to Eastwick's* witchery. The narrative begins in the fall: on Halloween a Walpurgisnacht takes place as Darryl Van Horne* entertains the three witches in his hot tub (*W*). Denying the fertility of the season, they destroy Jenny Gabriel in the spring. The witches convene on Thursdays, the day devoted to Thor, the Norse god of thunder, son of Odin and the earth goddess Jord. Thunder, such as that Alexandra Spofford* creates to dispel annoying Frisbee players, was the sound of Thor's chariot.

In *TE* the year carries daily symbolic significance. Ben Turnbull* shows scrupulous interest in nature's* daily changes since he fears that he may be dying of cancer* and this may be his last chance to observe the birth and death of the year 2020, a time for perfect, if punning, hindsight. Updike's artistic interest in the calendar may have led him to review Stephen Jay Gould's study of the millennium.

Bibliography: Updike, "Millennium Fever," *New Yorker* 20–27 Oct. 1997: 160, 163–166; Ristoff, *UA*; Schiff, *JU*.

Calpurnia. After Julius Caesar's wife Pompeia apparently violated the mysteries of the Bona Dea, the scandal forced him to divorce her, saying, "Caesar's wife must be above suspicion." For political reasons he then married Calpurnia. Gloria Turnbull's* Boston club is named "in honor" of Calpurnia, clearly a feminine effort to undo Caesar's injustice. In a dream Ben Turnbull* sees himself and his wife leave "The Calpurnia" and walk across the terrifying rubble of a freeway long under construction. Since Caesar had not married for love, and since Calpurnia follows a woman devoted to "the mysteries," she and her fellow clubwomen are characterized as loveless opportunists. The dream of rubble on a "freeway" and the club name underline the reasons why Turnbull seeks other women (*TE*). *See* **Classical Literature**.

Calvin, John (1509–1564). A theologian and French leader of the Reformation, John Calvin was driven from Paris in 1535 for supporting Martin Luther and then experienced a spiritual crisis in Switzerland. In 1560 he helped write Geneva's constitution and later wrote an extensive biblical commentary, the Bible* being for him the source of all knowledge in religion.* His *Institutes of the Christian Religion* (1536–59) showed how biblical theology was not in conflict with the Apostles' Creed. He insisted that man could know God through Jesus Christ, and that this is the way to overcome man's innate depravity. Calvin founded his teaching on predestination since it was supported by biblical authority. In *C* Reverend March insists that Calvinism is just as "Christocentric" as Lutheranism and argues that the doctrine of predestination is balanced by God's infinite mercy. George Caldwell* unhappily observes that such infinite mercy must also be infinitely far away. In *RV* Roger Lambert* fails to convince Verna Ekelof* that St. Augustine* and Calvin believed that even babies* were evil, because without such a concept the world is not fallen and there is no need for redemption. Lambert also meditates on how persons like Verna Ekelof do not find property sacred as Calvin did, since it is an "outward sign and a sacred symbol." Rev. Clarence Wilmot* owns forty-four volumes of Calvin's *Commentaries*, but he still loses his faith (IB). Calvin's doctrines influenced Puritanism and thus Nathaniel Hawthorne's* *Scarlet Letter*, which Updike used as the model for his trilogy, *MS*, *RV* and *S*. This trilogy thus comments upon Calvinism from a modern perspective.

Camelot. In the legends of King Arthur, Camelot is the seat of Arthur's court, where he took Queen Guenivere. Arthur's reign of peace was enforced by knights like Galahad, Percival and Gawain, and the love triangle of Arthur, Guenivere and Lancelot formed the basis of the musical *Camelot* (1960) by Alan Jay Lerner and Frederick Lowe. The musical was a favorite of President John Kennedy,* who often saw his administration as similar to Camelot, as Updike says in *SC*. Updike's use of Kennedy in *Couples* thus may be connected to the story of Tristan and Isolde,* which Updike said he used as the inspiration for the love of Piet Hanema* and Foxy Whitman* in *Couples*.

Cancer. Cancer occurs in Updike's work in order to identify hidden corruption. The disease is mainly symbolic of an insidious malfunction of the otherwise reliable body that grows within but may have no external symptoms until it is too late. In *PF* Stephen Conner* fantasizes about finding a cure for cancer and thus receiving the Nobel Prize. George Caldwell* fears (needlessly) that he has cancer (*C*), and the witch Alexandra "Lexa" Spofford* is also convinced that she has the disease despite her sister witches' remonstrances. Caldwell and Lexa share a loss of faith in nature,* and the witches magically try to induce cancer in Jenny Gabriel (*W*), though Jenny's work as a radiologist, or even atomic energy in the atmosphere, may have caused her cancer; thus witchcraft may have emerged because of the "cancer" of technology's interference with nature. Ironically, Eastwickians see witchcraft metaphorically as a modern cancer. Ben Turnbull* suffers from prostate cancer, which both increases his desire for a young girl and impedes his pleasure with her (*TE*).

Bibliography: Newman, *JU*.

Capp, "Al" Alfred (1909–1979). Al Capp created the comic strip "Li'l Abner" (1934–77), a satire* featuring odd types from hillbilly Dogpatch. Updike says that he never missed reading it, loving its "headlong outrageousness" of invention and its bravura drawing* blended to "literary wit" and the energy of Dickens. The earth seemed less populous, he noted in the poem "The Shuttle," with Al Capp dead. Capp was born in Connecticut, the site of *Marry*, in which Richard Mathias says that Jerry Conant* never had any real talent as a cartoonist. *See* **Art; Cartooning;** *Harvard Lampoon*.

Capri, Italy. An island in the Bay of Naples, Italy, Capri has limestone cliffs and many caverns, including the Blue Grotto, a magical place of blue water whose color is caused by the sun's refraction in the water outside the cave. In speaking of his love of Shillington,* Updike clarifies that he does not love it as one would Capri or New York,* because they are special, but rather because Shillington is synonymous with being (*SC*). Capri and New York are famous for their elite rulers (the emperor Tiberius,* 42 B.C.–A.D. 37, built twelve villas during his ten years there), and Updike prefers the ordinary person. *See* **Classical Literature.**

Carlyle, Thomas (1795–1881). A Scottish essayist and social critic, Thomas Carlyle wrote articles for the *Edinburgh Encyclopedia*, translated Goethe, and published a philosophical satire, *Sartor Resartus* (1833–34) that described his personal passage from "Everlasting Nay" to "Center of Indifference" to the "Everlasting Yea." As a literary force, Carlyle influenced writers like John Stuart Mill and Ralph Waldo Emerson,* who responded particularly to Carlyle's *Heroes, Hero-Worship, and the Heroic in History* (1841). It argued that heroes have made civilizations what they are. Updike observed that Carlyle told Emerson that Henry James's* stammer was customary of great men— something perhaps consoling to Updike, who also stammered (*SC*). *See* **English Literature.**

The Carpentered Hen (New York: Harper, 1958). *CH*, Updike's first book, contains fifty-five poems, thirty-eight of which were first printed in the *New Yorker*.* It is Updike's sole trade book published by a press other than Knopf; its reissue by Knopf (1982) contains many changes, in accord with Updike's customary practice when reprinting anything. Many of the poems in this collection illustrate Updike's creative process* at work, since he altered them with each reprinting in *HH* and *V* and provided notes for many in *CP*. The poem "Vacuum Cleaner" saw three separate versions. The title, *CH*, is explained in the poem "A Wooden Darning Egg," which shows Updike's love of craftsmanship in both poetry* and everyday objects; note the love shared for wood craftsmen of the past by John Hook* and Piet Hanema.* The volume exhibits the light verse* that created Updike's reputation before he ever published a book. Some humorous poems concern science.* "V. B. Nimble, V. B. Quick" springs from a news story about V. B. Wigglesworth, a scientist appointed Quick Professor of Biology. Seizing the pun, Updike describes his day as a whirligig of symposia and lab experiments. "White Dwarf" describes cosmic fright, using as a model "Twinkle, Twinkle, Little Star." Such a deft touch on deep subjects recalls the poets Updike first read, Phyllis McGinley, Arthur Guiterman, Robert Service, Ogden Nash and Morris Bishop.

Verse reflecting his wider reading in poetry at Harvard* is nostalgic and thoughtful. The most anthologized poem of this collection, "Ex–Basketball Player," is a sympathetic portrait of Flick Webb. Like Updike's most famous fictional character, Harry, "Rabbit" Angstrom,* Flick's court triumphs have poorly prepared him for life after basketball.* Now a garage attendant, he kills time in a luncheonette, where the rows of candies seem to him tiers of adoring fans. The narrator recalls that Flick's hands were "like wild birds," but now they dribble inner tubes "as a gag." Similarly reflective, "Tao in the Yankee Stadium Bleachers" explores an insight during a baseball game in which a "yogi" "flies," but it is Yogi Berra,* not a Brahman. The poems closing the book, "A Cheerful Alphabet of Pleasant Objects," were written for Updike's one-year-old son David,* the subject of "The One-Year-Old." The "Alphabet" poems display Updike's love of puns when "Vacuum Cleaner" makes something of "Nothing," and the poems also reveal his feeling that light verse is "cartooning* in print," so the physical appearance of the poem on the page can create an added dimension to its force, changes in the visual field, as in "Letter Box" and "Nutcracker." Updike's penchant for the unexpected rhyming word, sometimes combined with an allusion ("man/Cézanne" and "use/Camus"), recalls that, for *Harvard Lampoon** poets like Updike, *Punch* was an important model.

Bibliography: Louise Bogan, "Books: Verse," *New Yorker* 35 (18 Apr. 1959): 170; Virginia Busha, "Poetry in the Classroom: 'Ex–Basketball Player,' " *English Journal* 59 (5 May 1970): 643–45; Patrick Bowles, "Updike's 'Vacuum Cleaner,' " *Explicator*

37 (1978): i, 42–43; Greiner, *OJ*; Margaret Manning, "John Updike Redux," *Boston Sunday Globe* 21 Mar. 1982: A-19; Edward A. Kopper, Jr., "A Note on Updike's 'Ex-Basketball Player,' " *Notes on Contemporary Literature* 21–5 (Nov. 1991): 6.

Carson, Johnny (1925–). A comedian and host of *The Tonight Show* (1962–92), Johnny Carson was noted for his relaxed humor and "cool" attitude. Outstanding show-business personalities as well as literary and scientific celebrities like Truman Capote and Carl Sagan appeared as Carson's guests. Harry "Rabbit" Angstrom,* inveterate watcher of television,* thought that Carson, like other television hosts, had "nothing to sell but their brass. Making millions on sheer gall" (*RRed*). Carson continues the tradition of Jimmie the Big Mousketeer,* from whom Rabbit tried to learn things that might make him a better salesman, while realizing, "Fraud makes the world go round" (*RR*). Ironically, Rabbit through his "gall" becomes a success, and his son Nelson Angstrom* through fraud nearly brings down Springer Motors.*

Carthage. According to legend, Carthage, near Tunis, Tunisia, was founded by Queen Dido, and Virgil explains in the *Aeneid* that Aeneas stayed with Dido a short while but was forced by the gods to continue to Italy to found Rome, whereupon Dido immolated herself. After more than one hundred years of war Rome destroyed Carthage. Later, Roman Carthage accepted Christianity, and by 400 A.D. St. Augustine* became bishop of Hippo near Carthage. Augustine, like Aeneas, left Carthage and in Milan codified church law, helping to end the Roman Empire. In "Augustine's Concubine" (*P*) Updike quotes various passages from *The Confessions of St. Augustine* describing Augustine's immersion in vice in Carthage, in which the Carthaginians "boil" in sensual delights. There he meets the austere Scythian beauty who becomes his mistress, but he leaves her because he feels called by God to Italy. Like T. S. Eliot* in *The Waste Land*, Updike selected from *The Confessions* the quote "To Carthage I came." Eliot's poem, like Updike's story, also tries to show the difficulties of spiritual life within modern materialism. *See* **Antinomianism; Classical Literature**.

Cartooning. Cartooning came naturally to Updike at an early age, but after his aunt Mary gave his family a subscription to the *New Yorker** when he was twelve, he tried to model his cartoons on artists like James Thurber* and Charles Addams* and took lessons from a Shillington* artist. At his request James Thurber and Saul Steinberg sent him signed drawings. While drawing for the Shillington High School *Chatterbox** and the *Harvard Lampoon** (1945–54), Updike hoped to work for Walt Disney,* and so before the *New Yorker* accepted his first stories and poems, Updike considered himself primarily a cartoonist. In "The Old Movie Houses" (*MM*) he said, "To create motion, frame by frame, appeared Godlike." Updike quipped that though writing free-verse poems was "cartooning in print," cartoonists needed to have many more ideas than novelists. In his "Foreword" to *Jester's Dozen*, Updike said that looking back on his *Lampoon* drawings gave him pleasure (*OJ*). As his writing on Mickey Mouse and Al Capp* show, he has displayed continuous interest in cartoon characters, and he has occasionally published drawings. Though he has written a poem about "Superman," his favorite cartoon figure is Spiderman because of its realism. Updike has said that he feels "shyly happy among texts" because of his "yen to draw talk balloons in ruled-off panels" (*OJ*).

Merging with Updike's interest in cartoons is his delight in movies, and among the long list of film* personalities mentioned throughout Updike's work, Warner Brothers' wisecracking artful dodger Bugs Bunny seems the most important, a parody of the anxiety-driven Harry "Rabbit" Angstrom.* The hero of the story "Intercession" (*SD*) is a cartoonist. Updike supplied an introduction and selected the drawings of David Levine for a volume of the artist's caricatures, *Pens and Needles*, and Levine has rendered several caricatures of Updike, who appeared in 1962 with cartoonist Walt Kelly on television.* See **Art; Comedy; Drawing and Painting**.

Bibliography: Updike, "Five Days in Finland at the Age of Fifty-Five" (*OJ*); "Introduction to *The World of William Steig*," ed. Lee Lorenz (New York: Artisan, 1998); "Introduction, *"The Art of Mickey Mouse,"* "Note for an Exhibit of *New Yorker* Cartoons at the Art Institute of Boston, January 28th–March 8th, 1993," "The Old Movie Houses," "My Cartooning," "Cartoon Magic," "Lost Art," "Introduction to *My Well-Balanced Life on a Wooden Leg*" (*MM*); David Astor, "Updike Is Honored by Cartoonists," *Editor and Publisher* 15 Dec. 1990: 36; Jack De Bellis, " 'It Captivates . . . It Hypnotizes': Updike Goes to the Movies," *Literature/Film Quarterly* 23.3 (1995): 169–87.

Casablanca. Updike often mentions the romantic film* *Casablanca* (1942), released one week before the Casablanca Conference at which President Franklin Roosevelt* and Prime Minister Winston Churchill* agreed to demand unconditional surrender from Germany. The film's narrative features an ex–concentration-camp victim, Victor Laszlo, who marshals support in neutral Morocco. Seeking an exit visa from an influential American, Rick Blaine, he discovers that they each love the same woman, Lisa Lund. Rick chivalrously steps aside and provides the visas, knowing that he will never see Lisa again. In *S.* Sarah Worth* recalls perfectly a key scene between the stars Humphrey Bogart and Ingrid Bergman, showing a more romantic attachment to the exotic Moroccan setting than her practical demeanor might suggest. In *IB* Clark DeMott* is fixated by Bogart's line "Go ahead and shoot, you'll be doing me a favor," finding in it a focus for his sense of futility and a tough-guy pose. The line has ironic resonance when Clark is killed while shooting religious zealot Jesse Smith.* In the process he supplies freedom for the children of Smith's cult fanatics. See **Film**.

Bibliography: Jack De Bellis, " 'It Captivates . . . It Hypnotizes': Updike Goes to the Movies," *Literature/Film Quarterly* 23.3 (1995): 169–87.

Cathars. The most important of various sects called Cathars, from the Greek word for "pure," were the thirteenth-century Albigensians, who were ruthlessly persecuted for appearing to advocate that good and evil were equal in power. They generally believed that the body itself was evil, since it was material, not spiritual. The same was true of the church itself, which had great material wealth; therefore, the clergy could corrupt those wishing to be pure. Roger Lambert,* who has left the ministry for unspecified reasons, realizes that the Cathars would have found him guilty of heresy for widening his range of sins in order to evoke even more forgiveness from God (*RV*). *See* **Augustine, St.; Manichaeanism; Tertullian; Thomas Aquinas, St**.

Catullus (84?–54? B.C.). A Roman poet, Catullus wrote passionately of a mysterious Lesbia in self-critical verse, as well as in poems about marriage. Updike mentions Catullus in "George and Vivian I: *Aperto, Chiuso*" (*A*) as an ironic comment about a failing marriage. *See* **Classical Literature**.

The Centaur (New York: Knopf, 1963). Updike's novel *C*, set in Olinger High School during January 1947, was originally intended to be one of four related novels modeled on his grandparents and parents. *PF* and *OF* used his maternal grandfather and his mother as models. In *C* Updike modeled George Caldwell* on his father, Wesley Updike.* It is Updike's most personal and most experimental novel, and nowhere else are comedy* and tragedy blended so successfully. In an obituary to Caldwell, many elements of the Updike family saga appear. The novel was also intended to be a companion to *RR*, exemplifying responsible commitment that contrasts to Harry "Rabbit" Angstrom's* irresponsible social behavior. When Updike came to the end of Rabbit's journey in *RaR*, however, he noted in his "Introduction" to *RA* that "the dodgy rabbit had become the suffering horse," suggesting that a blending had occurred between Rabbit and Caldwell. While Rabbit is in flux because of his inability to settle for ordinary life, and his social world is stable, George Caldwell in *C* is stable, but his world is in upheaval.

During three January days in 1947, George Caldwell is struck by an arrow, teaches a wildly unruly science* class, is propositioned by the gym teacher, gives a student test answers, coaches the swimming team, oversees the sale of basketball* tickets (which he thinks he has lost), fears that he has cancer* and discovers that he does not, gets caught in a blizzard, is mistaken for a homosexual seducer, has his gloves stolen by a hitchhiker, has a tooth removed, detects that his principal is having an affair, worries about his inability to care for his wife and her father and befriends strangers. Meanwhile, his fifteen-year-old son Peter* grows increasingly anxious over his father's health, tries to deepen his girlfriend's commitment to him by showing her his skin disease, waxes jealous of his father's attentiveness to his students, struggles with Latin translation and contracts a high fever. Such incidents in this father/son story suggest the tumultuousness of adolescence and the multifariousness of Caldwell. To add to the intensity, Updike provides highly realistic, sometimes satiric portraits of persons from Shillington,* the model for the fictional Olinger.

Updike carries the narrative to another level of richness by entwining the narratives of George Caldwell and his son with the myth of Chiron* the centaur (George Caldwell), who sacrificed himself for Prometheus (Peter) and the good of man. Updike counterpoints the first and third chapters with contrasts in teaching: the realistic class is chaotic as Caldwell authoritatively struggles to explain the "Creation Clock"; but Chiron's class is a summer arcadia taught by a nurturing teacher to attentive students like Achilles. The first and last chapters are mosaics with mythical and realistic material combined: in the first chapter Caldwell transforms from man to centaur and back, while in the last chapter Caldwell is specifically linked to Chiron and his protection of Prometheus through suicide. Peter and George Caldwell share aspects of both Christ and Prometheus as well, particularly in chapter 6.

The novel blends comedy and tragedy. It is comic in disclosing the absurdities of an educational system trying to harness adolescent energy and in its satiric depiction of academic infighting. It is tragic in revealing how ordinary good people are misunderstood, how young men are trapped in Oedipal entanglements, and how men fare against nature.* Thus when Caldwell fears that the principal may fire him and worries about his inability to please his wife, he is an ordinary man facing injustice. But Caldwell is also an example of the tragedy embodied in man because of his power to foresee his death.* Yet fifteen-year-old Peter sees Caldwell as weak and foolish and is outraged that his father would give rides to a vagrant thief when they are late for school, infuriated that he would allow the car to break down in a blizzard and perplexed that he would misplace the basketball-game tickets entrusted to him to sell. The novel thus reveals Peter's understandable fear and frustration toward his father for failing as a protective parent while charting Peter's gradual awareness of his father's humanity and his necessary death. Conflicted, Peter hopes that his father will die and allow him uncontested love for his mother, but he also fears his death because he loves him.

Peter's appreciation of his father takes place in hindsight, for he tells the story a dozen years after leaving his family and becoming an artist. His recreation of those three critical days in January 1947 helps him to understand how he can repay his father's sacrifice and forces him to understand his own transformation. His personal struggle and the sacrifice he finally perceives in his father create a dreamlike blend of the realistic and the surrealistic, the actual and its magnification, the mythic.

The story of Chiron the centaur, erroneously thought to be Updike's parading of irrelevant erudition, which his epigraph,* taken from a school-book on myth* is intended to dislodge, is a necessary parallel to Caldwell's story. Chiron had instructed Prometheus, who stole fire from the gods and brought it to man in the form of knowledge, and then sacrificed himself for Prometheus. Like Caldwell, Chiron risks repression for his decision to transmit his knowledge of nature. Updike has said that for him, this was the heart of the book, a rare instance of self-sacrifice in the classical world paralleling Christ's sacrifice; even the names echo: Chiron/Christ. (In his Harvard* thesis Updike found that Robert Herrick transformed the images he borrowed from Horace through his "Christ-like tenderness.") Some might feel uneasiness with this experiment in parallelism, which seems the reverse of James Joyce's* *Ulysses*, because rather than encoding the classical analogues to his characters, Updike supplies the parallels in an appendix of analogues. Updike has insisted, however, on the psychological aptness of perceiving everyday persons in mythic roles because children see the world as larger than life, partly because the world of adult actions and motives always seems enigmatic to them. This is reinforced when Peter as an adult nostalgically relives his adolescence and replays his father's symbolical laying down of his life for him.

The use of mythical figures and allusions also underlines Updike's conviction that the events of everyday life contain larger implications, and *C*'s epigraph from Karl Barth* suggests this in drawing attention to the human and heavenly boundaries. Thus all men are centaurs, bound to the earth and conscious of death while yearning for the sky and immortality. (Chiron himself is half-divine.) Also, myth provides relief from the drabness of actuality. Meanwhile, the incongruous distance between the ordinary and the mythic provides the basic comic disjunction while keeping alive the serious sense that everyone carries a possibility for greatness, no matter how ridiculous or childish he or she seems. The appearance of mythical figures, rooted in Peter's need to understand his father, is personally based, unlike the fantasy of witches in modern Rhode Island, which stems from social sources (*W*). Critic Larry Taylor translates the Greek sentence at the end, between "Now" and "Chiron accepted death," as "And having received an incurable wound, he went off to the cave. And he willingly went there to die; and although he was immortal and thus not able to die, when Prometheus exchanged fates with him, in order that Chiron might die in his stead, then the Centaur died." *See* **Academia; Autobiography; Classical Literature**.

Bibliography: Taylor, *PA*; Edward P. Vargo, "The Necessity of Myth in Updike's *The Centaur*," *PMLA* 88 (May 1973): 452–60; John B. Vickery, "*The Centaur*: Myth, History and Narrative," *Modern Fiction Studies* 20 (Spring 1974): 29–43; Hunt, *JU*; Detweiler, *JU*; Greiner, *JU*; Newman, *JU*; Schiff, *JU*.

Challenger. The U.S. space shuttle *Challenger* exploded on lift-off January 28, 1986, killing the crew of seven and suspending the program for two years. In the story "The Man Who Became a Soprano" (*A*), the recorder group is so dedicated that it meets even on the day of the Challenger disaster. Various alliances and disaffiliations of members of the group cause similar challenges to their success, forcing one instrumentalist to change from tenor to soprano recorder. *See* **Airplanes**.

Characters. Updike's characters have followed the development of their author as a person and as a writer. Four phases of characterization can be construed: 1954–67, 1968–80, 1981–87, and 1988–present. Updike has remarked that the author's first subject, his early life, is his given subject; the rest needs to be imagined and researched. In his first phase, the "Pennsylvania material" (1954–67), Updike clearly models many characters in his stories and novels upon family members—John Hook* on his maternal grandfather, John Hoyer* (*PF*); Clarence Wilmot* on his paternal grandfather, Hartley Updike* (*IB*); George Caldwell* on his father, Wesley Updike* (*C*); Mrs. Caldwell and Mrs. Robinson* (*OF*) on his mother Linda Hoyer Updike* (*C, OF*). His early work also focuses on heroes who are searchers trying to establish their personal values against social conventions ("A & P," "Flight" and "Pigeon Feathers" [*PigF*], and Harry "Rabbit" Angstrom* [*RR*], Peter Caldwell* [*C*] and Joey Robinson* [*OF*]), and who are surprised by the unclear answers they receive to moral and spiritual questions. The young hero (at times loosely based on Updike, at times his alter ego*) is often in conflict with his parents—the forceful mother who interferes with his quest, and the preoccupied father, frequently an Oedipal rival (*C*). Many of the early narratives chart the problems of young marrieds ("Ace in the Hole," "Toward Evening," "Sunday Teasing," "Snowing in Greenwich Village" [*SD*]; "Should Wizard Hit Mommy?" [*PigF*], "The Music School" [*MuS*], and *OF*). Teachers appear in "Tomorrow and Tomorrow and So Forth" (*SD*), *C* and "The Astronomer" (*PigF*), along with Henry Bech,* a Jewish novelist ("The Bulgarian Poetess" [*MuS*]) who reappears in later novels. Ministers* are prominent ("Dentistry and Doubt" [*SD*]; *RR; C; OF*; "Pigeon Feathers" [*PigF*]) and will continue as important characters. Updike's early fiction shows serious concern for women in the interior monologues of Ruth Leonard Byer,* Lucy Eccles* and Janice Angstrom* (*RR*) and only marginal interest in children,* African Americans,* homosexuals and Native Americans.

In the second phase (1968–80) Updike continues his core interest in young married men in their twenties experiencing emotional distress (*Marry*) and obsessions with death* and failure (*Couples*). They, like their wives and lovers, often seek psychoanalysis (*Couples*; "The Fairy Godfathers," "Problems" [*P*]). Updike's interest in marginalized characters expands his interest in Henry Bech; a rich runaway, Jill Pendleton* (*RRed*); and a traduced president, James Buchanan* (*BD*). Ministers become major figures (*MS*). Wives and lovers become complications in the pursuit of personal identity (*Couples, RRed,*

MuS, Coup). In *Couples* Updike amplifies his use of the female viewpoint established in *RR*, and he also introduces the "devil-figure" Freddy Thorne* (developed from Stephen Conner* of *PF* and precursor of Darryl Van Horne* of *W*, Roger Lambert* of *RV*, and Claudius* of *GC*). The use of a literary alter ego emerges decisively in Bech (*BB*). Outcasts continue to govern Updike's regard: in *RRed* Updike uses an African American character, Skeeter,* as a major figure for the first time, a Vietnam* War veteran and racist; and *Coup* uses the first-person viewpoint of a black African. Political personalities arrive in Pennsylvania's lone president James Buchanan (*BD*) and Col. Félix Ellelloû* (*Coup*). Children play a more important role also, dominating some of the stories of *TF*, providing innocent ironic commentary on the adult world (*Couples*) and becoming adversarial (*RRed*). What Updike calls the "insider" character emerges in Thorne and Charlie Stavros,* who lead to Webb Murkett* (*RIR*), Van Horne (*W*) and Jesse Smith* (*IB*).

The third phase (1981–87) emphasizes social characters, like those in *Couples*; sometimes they are academics (*BIB, RV, MF*), artistic charlatans (*BIB, W*) or middle-class businessmen (*RIR*). Women become central and increasingly independent (*RIR, W*). Updike's ministers turn increasingly ineffectual, like Rev. "Soupy" Campbell in *RIR*. Unitarian* activist Ed Parsley* is destructive and reckless (*W*), and Van Horne mocks ministers by sermonizing unchallenged against God in the Unitarian church (*W*). The scientist/technologist of earlier stories ("The Music School" [*MuS*]), poetry ("V. B. Nimble, V. B. Quick" [*CH*]) and novels (Ken Whitman* [*Couples*]) becomes a major character in Dale Kohler* (*RV*). Like science* teacher George Caldwell (*C*), Kohler is inept when addressing spiritual matters (*RV*). The stories of *TM* repeatedly describe men in decline who look back with nostalgia at past lovers and crucial misunderstandings with parents and wives.

The fourth phase (1988–present) presents the decline and fall of Updike's strongest characters. Though strong women are depicted with zest, an elegiac tone cloaks many of his heroes. In *S*. Sarah Worth* tells her own story of a rejection of materialism for enlightenment, and she has both the courage to explore her inner self and the practicality to capitalize on the weakness of men. Isabel Leme* (*B*) illustrates raw sexual power; she chooses her sexual initiator, and does not flinch from selling her body and indulging in magic to protect him. In *IB* actress Essie Wilmot/Alma DeMott* finds that she can reach a higher plane through her film* career and becomes a model for all women. Updike also explores the decline and death of a powerful woman, Rabbit's mother Mary Angstrom,* who resembles Updike's own mother. A still photograph of her running to a trolley captures the urgent vitality of a woman who lived much on her own terms ("A Sandstone Farmhouse" [*A*]). Queen Gertrude* contains elements of all these women (*GC*). The decline and death of Updike's mother accompanies the decline and death of Updike's most famous hero, Rabbit Angstrom (*RaR*). Rabbit's death was anticipated by President Buchanan's, who dies again when he is scrutinized by the second-rate academic Alf Clayton* (*MF*). In addition, Rev. Clarence Wilmot* fails as a minister most dramatically by losing his faith and his voice (his hardier wife finishes his sermon), then faces a lingering death from tuberculosis, leaving his family impoverished (*IB*). Other religious men in this recent phase of characters are either liars or murderers: the phoney Arhat* who is unmasked by Sarah Worth (*S.*) and the fanatic Jesse Smith who is killed by Clark DeMott* (*IB*). If Bech was a sardonic if dedicated artist, Alma DeMott of *IB* is the most serious artist Updike has created, perhaps his greatest alter ego. She alters a pattern that had concerned Updike since *C*; Peter Caldwell* had called this the "classic degeneration" of priests, teachers and artists (*C*). Though the priests and teachers have been increasingly worsened, Updike's portrait of the artist has provided hope. Early in his career Updike had said in his essay "The Dogwood Tree: A Boyhood"* (*AP*) that art* was a method of riding a thin pencil line into "unborn hearts," a task, he announced in his poem "Midpoint" (*M*), that has kept him "knocking on the doors of days."

As has been suggested, these types of characters developed through Updike's career are not entirely isolated from each another—scientists, blacks, ministers and women had always interested Updike. In *SC* footnotes reveal the sources of characters in his family and in himself. He notes how "The Journal of a Leper" recorded his own treatments for psoriasis. Of course, Updike alludes to his wives and children (*SD*, *PigF*, *P*, *TM*, *MuS*, *TF*, *TE*) and sometimes uses their physical traits and interests. Yet his creative imagination uses everyone to construct his characters. As Updike notes in *CP*, the principal of Shillington* High School was the model for a character in a discarded novel, then for James Buchanan. Also, Updike sometimes alludes to hostile critics* (*W*) or friendly professors (*RaR*).

A classification of Updike's characters might include these categories: searchers, finders, reality instructors and the trapped. Searchers often pursue a specific or nonspecific quest, lured by some sense of perfection or order in nature.* On a personal scale, George and Peter Caldwell seek to understand nature and art, and Peter Caldwell seeks the meaning of his father. Colonel Ellelloû safaris into Kush to learn his place in the heart of his people. But searchers are teased by larger goals: John Hook perceives patterns in quilts that indicate vast meaning (*PF*); and Rabbit Angstrom feels that a "thing" wants him to find it (*RR*). Tom Marshfield* through enforced diary writing seeks God, and Skeeter uses Jill Pendleton's experience with hallucinogens to gain God's support for a race war (*RRed*). Dale Kohler, like Hook, thinks that by devoted attention to nature's patterns he will see God (*RV*). Sarah Worth, Clark DeMott and Alma DeMott (*IB*), Ben Turnbull,* (*TE*) and Claudius all seek something transcendent as well, though only Alma finds it. Sarah, Alma, Ben, and Claudius are also finders, since they are sure that they have discovered an absolute truth. Sarah discovered it in unveiling the fake Arhat, Alma in her portrayal of screen roles and Ben in his willing movement through time. In addition, Piet Hanema* found through love a "radical" confirmation of the significance of his existence, and Peter Caldwell has recognized that if his submission as an artist is perfect, he will discover "a beautiful and useful truth." Skeeter discovered God's revelations in the "black hole" of Vietnam, as Jesse Smith had in the Bible* and Claudius in Byzantium.

Reality instructors attempt to teach the searchers, but they are often confusing, self-absorbed parents like Rabbit, Caldwell, Jack Eccles* (*RR*), Mrs. Robinson (*OF*), Verna Ekelof* (*RV*), Alexandra Spofford* (*W*), Sarah Worth and Alma DeMott. Reality instructors fail in other ways. They are inconsistent, like Marty Tothero* in *RR*, who promises help but doesn't give it, calls Rabbit a monster and later instructs him about morality; doctrinaire (Reverend, March in *C*); authoritarian (Joey Robinson's mother and Isabel Leme's uncle); dangerous (Freddy Thorne, Darryl Van Horne, Jesse Smith, Claudius); devious (Roger Lambert); fakes (the Arhat); dehumanizing or confused heads of state (Connor [*PF*]; President Buchanan [*BD*]; Enzana [*Coup*]); or smug businessmen (Webb Murkett [*RIR*]). Sometimes reality instructors are valuable: the gas-station attendant in *RR* who tells Rabbit he needs directions, the former poorhouse supervisor Mendelssohn who gives the poor reason to live and die (*PF*) and Nelson Angstrom,* who struggles to alert Rabbit to the dangers of Skeeter (*RRed*). Several women act as positive reality instructors for Rabbit: Ruth Leonard, who tells Rabbit that in his way he is still "trying," but also warns him that he is Mr. Death (*RR*); Jill Pendleton, who tries to clarify for him ways in which he can pursue his own inner light (*RRed*); and Thelma Harrison,* who tries to acquaint Rabbit with unselfish love (*RaR*).

Finally, many of Updike's characters could be called "the trapped." Some are trapped by circumstances: the elders in the poorhouse are snared by the well-meaning welfare state, as the people of Kush are caught between communism and capitalism. Bech is enmeshed in the commercial and social images of the writer, which contribute to his being stymied by a writer's block. Piet Hanema, Tristão Raposo,* Jerry Conant,* Tom Marshfield, Darryl Van Horne, Richard Maple,* Alf Clayton, and Claudius are slaves of passion. Ben Turnbull is deluded by "business as usual" after atomic war. Dale Kohler is netted by the computer. Rabbit is the typical trapped man, first with what his mother calls the only "trick" Janice knew, getting Rabbit to make her pregnant, then in dead-end jobs and, most cruelly, by his own dream of the return to the paradise of his "specialness." Piet Hanema and Foxy Whitman,* like Ruth Leonard Byer and Rabbit, were also trapped by premarital pregnancy, and Rabbit tries to arrange an abortion* to keep his son Nelson from being similarly trapped. Rabbit's jobs trap him, whether print setting, because he hates manual labor and disrespects his father, who got him the job, or selling cars, because he associates it with dishonesty. The Hanemas (*Couples*), Maples (*TF*), Conants (*Marry*), Claytons (*MF*), Lamberts (*RV*),

Worths (*S.*) and Turnbulls (*TE*) are entangled in unhappy marriages, as are the early Janice and Rabbit Angstrom and his parents. Clarence Wilmot (*IB*) and Roger Lambert are captive to the ministry whose purpose has eluded them. Nearly everyone is trapped in the middle class, and women (but not men) who are in the upper class are anxious to flee it (Jill Pendleton, Isabel Leme and Sarah Worth). Naturally, many of the trapped also become outcasts, a group that includes Rabbit of *RR*, Tom Marshfield (*MS*), Darryl Van Horne at the end of *W*, Claudius, Clarence Wilmott (*IB*) and Tristâo Raposo and Isabel Leme (*B*). Such a grouping of Updike's characters provides, of course, only a skeletal view of some of the most complex and interesting figures created in this century by any novelist. Updike's great range of individuals reveals his omnivorous interest in the *comédie humaine* while proving his contention that just as anyone can become a hero in a democracy (Plath, *CU*), anyone can be a character in his novels. *See* **Cain**.

Bibliography: Burchard, *YS*.

Chatterbox. The Shillington* High School newspaper *Chatterbox* published 285 items by Updike, including poetry,* stories, film reviews, essays and drawings.* Updike's experience there aided him when he helped produce *Hi-Life*, the yearbook in 1950 and when he wrote for and edited the *Harvard Lampoon.* His teacher in grades 8–12 and first editor, Mrs. Thelma Lewis, recalls how Updike devised a prank, "Ode to Seniors" that amused the students and befuddled the principal. Updike was feature editor and art editor in his junior and senior years. *See* **Apprenticeship**.

Bibliography: Stuart Wright, "John Updike's Contributions to *Chatterbox*," *Bulletin of Bibliography* 42 (Dec. 1985): 171–78.

Cheever, John (1912–1982). An American fictionalist best known for his short fiction, John Cheever was an early influence on Updike. They mutually respected and admired each other's work. Perhaps because they both published in the *New Yorker** and published books together at Knopf, Cheever called Updike a "colleague," though Cheever was twenty years older. To Updike, Cheever was the quintessential *New Yorker* short story writer of the 1950s. Cheever and Updike chronicled "the urban and suburban disappointments," as Updike remarked in a Cheever review, so comparably that Cheever was complimented for writing *RRed* and, misidentified as the writer of the "Maple stories" (*TF*), was invited to speak at Notre Dame in 1979. Updike was sometimes called an "under-or-over-a-Cheever." Having read Cheever since 1949, Updike wrote him a fan letter, and their eventual correspondence (1970?–82) reveals a literary and personal meeting of minds. Cheever recognized when he read *PF* that Updike was "a winner" and recommended him to the National Institute of Arts and Letters. In 1963, as a National Book Award judge, Cheever helped to award *C* the prize, but at the ceremony in 1964, Cheever was miffed that the *New Yorker* had printed his "Swimmer" a few pages after Updike's story "The Morning," though he knew that shorter stories always preceded longer ones in that magazine.

Updike found that Cheever "thought fast, saw everything in bright true colors, and was the arena of a constant tussle between the bubbling *joie de vivre* of the healthy sensitive man and the deep melancholy peculiar to American Protestant males" (*OJ*). Yet that exuberance could hide envy, as Cheever played rude pranks at Updike's expense during formal dinners in Russia and Washington. Though their ten days together in Russia in October 1964 began their friendship, Cheever wrote in a letter about a year later that he found Updike "arrogant," that they spent "most of our time back-biting," that Updike tried to upstage him by reading his "nonsense verse," that Updike's poems on Russian cities were "asinine," and that Updike would kill his wife if he knew she was secretly reading Cheever's *The Brigadier and the Golf Widow* (*OJ*). Cheever's exaggerations may have stemmed from his "deep melancholy," perhaps prompted by Updike's ascendancy. Such worry may have been reflected in a 1964 journal entry in which Cheever records a dream about Updike trying to murder him. If Updike was aware of Cheever's fears, he did not make them public, insisting instead in an interview in 1966, "I've never met anyone quicker on his feet, both fictional and real, than Cheever." Speaking about *Couples* in 1968, Cheever was quick enough to recommend the "great advances" Updike had contributed in writing about "venereal sport" with "freedom, discovery and newness."

In 1970 Cheever and Updike served as delegates to the Thirty-seventh International PEN Congress in South Korea, Cheever asserting that "John's paper was brilliant and so was John," and in that year Updike wrote the short story "The Orphaned Swimming Pool," which he said "owes the most" to Cheever of all his stories. (Arguably, Updike's "Snowing in Greenwich Village" may owe something to Cheever's "Torch Song.") In 1971 each contributed to *Atlantic Brief Lives* (Ed. Louis Kronenberger. Boston: Atlantic-Little, 1991). Cheever pronounced *Red* "great" in 1971, and in 1974 he wrote Updike that writing students at the University of Iowa were enthusiastic about his work. Aware of his lessening impact as newer writers took the limelight, Cheever was as reassured by Updike's constantly warm, if nevertheless impartial, reviews of his books as he was by Updike's friendship in the mid-1970s when Cheever needed support through his marital and drinking crises. Despite an aversion for teaching, Updike substituted for Cheever at Boston University in the fall of 1974, when Cheever was unfit. Updike charts the sad deterioration at this time in his review of Cheever's journals, but adds, "Even at his lowest ebb Cheever can write like an angel and startle us with offhand flashes of unblinkered acumen." In fact, Updike declares that the "indispensable" Cheever was written "when all his conflicts were unresolved." Updike admits to difficulty in trying to reconcile the "sprightly, debonair, gracious man" he knew with "the crushing sense of shame and despond" revealed in the journals ("Cheever on the Rocks" [*MM*]).

Although Cheever complained of their "conspicuous ego clash" in May 1975, he helped Updike enter the National Institute and Academy of Arts and Letters, an indication of how he could be, Updike wrote, "instinctively magnanimous." Though he might make Updike the butt of jokes, when he was told by another novelist on June 1, 1976, that Updike had been killed in a car crash, Cheever, taken in by the hoax, sobbed that Updike "was a man I so esteemed as a colleague and so loved as a friend that his loss is indescribable," and he praised Updike's gift for communicating "his most elated and desperate emotions" and his "immense and uncommon intelligence." Updike felt by this time that Cheever had become "less a mortal man than an enviable prose style," and his praise of Cheever's *Falconer* prompted from Cheever, "There is almost no one I would sooner please and you have been very generous since you wrote, years ago, about the hang of Honoria's dress," referring to Updike's 1949 letter.

Yet in 1978 he could hope that the publication of books by his daughter Susan and her friend Calvin Tompkins would put "some consternation in the Updike camp" as when Updike was about to be honored by Knopf at the St. Regis hotel. But Cheever and Updike demonstrated their mutual respect on *The Dick Cavett Show*, November 17, 1981, before a national audience, Cheever declaring that *RIR* was one of the best American novels in years. He privately observed that Updike looked "comely" on television. In thanking Updike for his positive review in 1982 of *Oh What a Paradise It Seems*, Cheever said, "Your magnanimity is overwhelming," and he told Philip Roth* in his last letter that *BIB* was "first-rate." Updike read a tribute at Cheever's funeral, June 22, 1982. Two years after winning the William Dean Howells Medal in 1995 (which Cheever had won in 1965), Updike indicated that Cheever was among the writers who "still excite me the most."

Updike attests to direct influence when he says that his first published story, "Friends from Philadelphia," was written in response to what he then thought was misanthropic satire in Cheever's "O Youth and Beauty!" Cheever's images and situations in "Torch Song" seemed to reappear in Updike's "Snowing in Greenwich Village" [*SD*]). More debatable are the impact of Cheever's story "Swimmer" on Updike's "Lifeguard," the similarities of suburban scandal in Cheever's Shady Hill and Bullet Park and Updike's Brewer* (*RA*) and Tarbox (*Couples*), and the relation of Updike's Janice Angstrom* to Cheever's "Janice," a hamlet near New York City* in *Oh What a Paradise It Seems*. If Updike found in Cheever's *Wapshot Chronicle* "pervading nostalgia" and "a magnificent old man's journal," was this somehow behind *TE*?

Reviewing *Bullet Park*, Updike remarked that Cheever had no peer among contemporary American fiction writers "in the coining of images and incidents." Updike said, "All is fabulous from the start" in his review of *Oh What a Paradise It Seems*, and he found a "broad streak of the fantastic" in

Bullet Park. Such reviews place Cheever with such "fabulists" as John Barth, Thomas Pynchon, John Hawks and James Purdy, writers Updike feared were elbowing Cheever off the literary scene. So close were the two writers that Updike's summing up of Cheever could stand as self-reflexive: "His very acuity and ardor . . . were excited by any scent and found the heart's prey trembling in every patch of experience. He was of an ever-rarer breed, a celebrant." The comment in fact seems to characterize Ben Turnbull* (*TE*), causing one to wonder if Turnbull might contain aspects of Cheever. Updike's Jewish novelist Henry Bech* lived in Ossining, New York, where Cheever lived from 1961 to 1982. *See* **American Literature, Literary Influences**.

Bibliography: Updike, *OJ*, 108–17; "Cheever on the Rocks" (*MM*). George W. Hunt, "Religious Themes in the Fiction of John Updike and John Cheever," *New Catholic World* 1979: 248–51; Nicki Sahlin, "Manners in the Contemporary American Novel: Studies in John Cheever, John Updike and Joan Didion," *Dissertation Abstracts International* 41/12A (1980): 5102, Brown University; Kathryn Riley, "The Use of Suburbia as a Setting in the Fiction of John O'Hara, John Cheever, and John Updike," *Dissertation Abstracts International* 42/09A (1981): 4002, University of Maryland, College Park.

Chess. An Eastern game appropriated during the Crusades and brought back to the courts of Europe, chess was often used in medieval tales as a metaphor for knightly combat and lady worship in chivalry. The lovers Tristâo Raposo* and Isabel Leme,* who approximate Tristan and Isolde,* are frequently described with chivalric imagery and at one point themselves are referred to as "two squares of the chessboard, come to give us a game!" by a bandit leader. Updike also describes a table inlaid with a chessboard in the house of Isabel's uncle (*B*). This tradition is used ironically when Jerry Conant* and Richard Mathias play chess, and Jerry uses the game as a metaphor for Richard's tactics as they discuss Jerry's love affair with Richard's wife Sally Mathias* (*Marry*). But when Richard puts Jerry in a "knight fork" in which Jerry must lose a "piece," the sexual puns provide an ironic distance from ancient chivalry. Jerry must lose either Sally or his wife Ruth Conant,* in vulgar parlance, a "piece." "Fork" connotes a man forked by a woman in a sexual embrace. In the end Jerry is "forked" by his own weak will when he refuses to stand by Sally. Updike learned chess when he was eleven and for a while loved the game; this might form another link between him and Vladimir Nabokov,* who published books of chess problems.

Child Psychologists. Richard Mathias* seduces Ruth Conant* (*Marry*) partly through his knowledge of such child psychologists as Jean Piaget, Benjamin Spock and Anna Freud, the daughter of Sigmund Freud,* whose theories emphasized the need to overcome repression. Freud's own interest in children* is referred to by Lucy Eccles* (*RR*) and Piet Hanema* (*Couples*).

Children. When John Updike and his wife Mary Updike* had children, he felt that "I should in some way be writing for them," so he created children's stories from Shakespeare's *Midsummer Night's Dream*, fashioned an opera libretto from Hans Christian Andersen's "Fisherman and His Wife" and wrote an introduction to *The Young King and Other Fairy Tales* by Oscar Wilde, as well as children's versions of Mozart's *Magic Flute* and Wagner's *Ring*. Updike also wrote twenty-six poems, "A Cheerful Alphabet of Pleasant Objects" (*CH*), for his one-year-old son David Updike.* Nearly forty years later he wrote *A Helpful Alphabet of Friendly Objects*, illustrated by David's photographs. It was dedicated to his grandchildren. In addition, Updike reviewed the children's literature of Randall Jarrell (*HS*).

In his fiction Updike uses children to reflect adult tensions. In *RR* Janice* and Harry "Rabbit" Angstrom* are enchanted by television's* *Mickey Mouse Club*, about which Rabbit, though miffed that his wife wastes her time watching the show, admits that the Mouseketeer children are "cute," though he has seen the program so often that it has begun to cloy. Also in *RR*, Joyce, the daughter of Jack* and Lucy Eccles,* has nightmares after a bedtime reading of Hilaire Belloc's* "Jim—Who Ran Away from His Nurse and Was Eaten by a Lion," from *The Bad Child's Book of Beasts* and *Cautionary Tales for Children*. This becomes a source of disagreement between Jack and Lucy in *RR* and may indicate one reason why they later divorced (*RRed*). Also in *RR*, Joyce and her mother discuss "bosoms," and the word stays in Rabbit's mind as he wonders about Lucy's interest in him.

In "Should Wizard Hit Mommy?" (*SD*) a bedtime story forms a parable in which an insightful child becomes acquainted with the capricious world of adults and uses the story as a way of revealing the conflicts their tensions produce in her. The child's understanding of how punishment meted out in the bedtime story can be used to administer punishment to her own mother shows a precocious effort to insist on fair play. In "Bech Noir" (*BaB*) Updike turns this around when Henry Bech* uses a child to administer justice; Bech enters the child's mind in order to dupe a hostile critic.* To murder Debora Frueh, a writer of children's stories, Bech adopts the persona of several children. First a young child asks for an autograph. (Bech holds a ballpoint pen in his fist to imitate the child's handwriting and moistens the return envelope's flap with poison.) When that fails, Bech tries the same ruse in the style of an older girl, adopting her sentiments and adding a happy face. When this also fails, Bech imitates a teenage boy, and when Frueh responds to this ruse, she licks the return envelope and dies. Diabolical Bech has hoisted her on her own sentimental treatment of children. A writer of children's stories also appears in *RV* when Sue Kriegman taps out her books on the typewriter while Esther Lambert* commits adultery* next door. When the adultery of Georgene Thorne and Piet Hanema* is referred to as "Hansel and Gretel abandoned," the allusion to the children's tale may also convey, as Larry Taylor claims, ironic lyricism, since it shows that they are "involved in a fairy tale of their own making."

Such tales can be used to screen out adult behavior, but they may also explain it. Eleven-year-old Richard retells science-fiction stories that involve the wonders of evolution and the loss of magical powers (*OF*). The stories enable him to withdraw from the fierce adult quarrels of Joey Robinson,* Peggy Robinson and Mrs. Mary Robinson. In contrast, Joey Robinson tells his stepson a fable of a frog who seeks a treasure within his stomach. He descends into himself to find it, disappears, then returns. Richard identifies the story as sounding like a Dr. Seuss tale, but he is too young to note its resemblance to the archetype of the "hero's quest," in this case the quest for inner treasures.

Clearly, such unsentimentalized children help to focus attention upon misplaced adult feeling and to show how adults usually fail to discover clues to their regeneration through children. Children are neglected in *RA*, *Couples*, and *W*, but in *IB*, *OF*, *TF* and *RV* they impel adults to be honest, and they focus the ability of adults to teach in *SD*, *C*, *Couples* and *RV*. Children are sources of guilt for Rabbit and others, and sometimes foci of Oedipal competition (*RA*, *W*). Perhaps the most provoking of the children is Verna Ekelof's* daughter Paula,* who speaks one word: "Da?" she asks every man, seeking her father, her mother's black lover who abandoned her (*RV*). Paula represents dual abuse, that of children and blacks. Also, her name recalls St. Paul and Nathaniel Hawthorne's* hope, at the end of *The Scarlet Letter*, the novel on which *RV* is based, of a woman prophet who could lead men and women out of the frailty and sorrow that seem to be the relation of the sexes. George Hunt asserts that children in *Couples* and *Marry* are used for ironic counterpoint to the lives of their parents, like a Greek chorus. But even the inarticulate infant Golda can be a resounding presence as she provides Bech with his Nobel Prize* speech, "The Nature of Human Existence," saying "Hi!" and waving "bye-bye" ("Bech and the Bounty of Sweden" [*BaB*]).

The child is sometimes an "absent presence." The accidentally drowned Rebecca Angstrom* had driven sex from the lives of Janice and Rabbit; their search for sex* with others produces chaos and more death (*RRed*). Becky seems to have revenge on Rabbit through his granddaughter Judy, whose pretense of drowning brings on Rabbit's great exertion and heart attack (*RaR*). The absent presence of the child appears again in *S*, in which Sarah Worth* writes letters to her college daughter and attempts to interfere in her marriage.

Bibliography: Updike, "Owlish and Fishy" (*HS*); Taylor, *PA*; Newman, *JU*.

A Child's Calendar (New York: Knopf, 1965). The poems for each month in *A Child's Calendar* demonstrate Updike's ability to adopt the simplicity and playfulness of a child while using images of precision and sophistication (*CH*). Updike remarked that he himself had found children's books depressing; perhaps *A Child's Calendar* attempts to offer children something more lively. A new edition .(New York: Knopf, 1999) changed certain words for updating and additional amusement (*HA*). *See* **Children**.

Bibliography: Updike, "A Cheerful Alphabet of Friendly Objects" (*CH*); "Should Wizard Hit Mommy?" (*PigF*); "The Updike Year," *Christian Science Monitor* 57 (4 Nov. 1965): B2.

Chiron. The centaur in *C*, used as an analogue to George Caldwell,* Chiron is a lover of nature,* knows the pharmacopoeia and instructs Greek heroes like Achilles and Asclepios. Updike's epigraph* to the novel explains that Chiron, unlike other bawdy and violent centaurs, taught peace. His resistance to Zeus's domination brought him to champion the new creation man and thus to be forced into suicide. Updike notes that Zeus relented afterward and placed Chiron in the sky as the zodiacal constellation Sagittarius, a parallel to George Caldwell's daily sacrifice for his family. As if he were Zeus, Caldwell's son Peter* makes his father immortal by placing him in a novel. Updike, who discovered the myth in a book belonging to his first wife, Mary Updike,* notes a similarity between Chiron's self-sacrifice for man and Christ's. *See* **Classical Literature**.

Chomsky, Noam (1928–   ). An American linguist, Noam Chomsky founded transformational grammar in order to express in formulas how languages are generated and spoken. He also contributed to the opposition to the Vietnam* War through many publications and articulate leadership. Roger Lambert* describes Isaac Spiegel's struggles with machine translation, using "Chomskyite charts" to aid him, a parallel to Dale Kohler's* hopeless attempt to reach God through computer programs (*RV*). Spiegel had begun his study at MIT, where Chomsky has taught since 1955.

Christie, Agatha (1891–1976). The English detective novelist Agatha Christie was a staple of Updike's early reading and influenced plays* written at Shillington* High School. Her detectives, Hercule Poirot and Miss Marple, are as eccentric as her strange, twisting plots. Christie's play *The Mousetrap* has run in London since 1952. Fulham in "The Wallet" (*TM*) rereads one of her Poirot novels, and Ruth Leonard Byer* probably reads Christie after she gives up prostitution (*RR*). Updike commended Christie for spying out murder in the vicarage and acquitting the innocent in his poem "Agatha Christie and Beatrix Potter" (*TP*). *See* **"Murder Makes the Magazine."**

Churchill, Sir Winston (1874–1965). Great Britain's prime minister during World War II whose bulldog tenacity kept England fighting and won America's support, Sir Winston Churchill had been active in British politics since World War I, when he was disgraced for supporting the Gallipoli campaign. He cleverly understood Hitler's plans for war and became prime minister (1940–45). During the war he kept morale high despite German rocket bombs attacking many cities during the "Blitz," vowing that if his country were invaded, it would never surrender. He also helped fuse relations of the United States and the USSR to British interests, but after the war he was alarmed by Stalin's seizure of Eastern Europe, which created what he called an "Iron Curtain." In *C* George Caldwell* disputes Minor's popular anti-Communist claim that Churchill had intended to have troops march on Moscow after World War II. Caldwell rejects this because he believes that his beloved president Franklin Roosevelt* had no such intentions. Such conversations occur repeatedly in the novels, showing how ordinary people strive to understand the intentions of great world leaders (*PF, RRed, RIR, BD, MF, Coup, W*).

Cinderella. The fairy tale of Cinderella, codified from oral traditions by French writer Charles Perrault (1628–1703), is mentioned when Sally Mathias feels as if she has been awakened by her lover Jerry Conant* (*Marry*).

Classical Literature. As befits a writer who enjoys displaying his learning, Updike's work is filled with references to Greek and Roman writers, particularly in the early works. Because of James Joyce's* impact upon him, perhaps, he frequently focuses on the inability of the modern world to continue classical insights. But Updike recognizes too that the classics can be treated with levity without compromising the discoveries made about man's condition, as when he refers to Archimedes,* Seneca, Ovid, Catullus,* and Publius Vergilius Maro (Virgil) examines Roman portrait busts and the Venus de Milo, and salts his poems with mythical allusions, like Acheron, Cerberus, Eurydice, the Titans and the Gorgons, as well as Roman figures like the Caesars (Tiberius,* Julius Caesar,* Caligula) and wives of Caesars (Calpurnia,* Livia and Octavia), and cities like Pompeii. The story "Pygmalion" (*TM*) treats myth* ironically when a woman chosen to supplant a first wife is found to contain the same qualities as her predecessor.

In his most extended use of classical myth, *C*, Updike alternates between humor and seriousness in paralleling ordinary people of Olinger with the Greek gods. What Joyce conceals, Updike reveals: in some chapters Updike simply inserts myth with no reference to the realistic plot of three ordinary days in the life of a high-school boy and his father. The first sentence shows that teacher George Caldwell,* who lectures on evolution, is a modern Chiron* who will later sacrifice himself. As Chiron, Caldwell must resist the temptations of the gym teacher (Aphrodite) and outwit the antagonistic principal (Zeus). As Updike moves between Caldwell and Chiron, he produces an ironic tone that is often humorous and sometimes tragic. Updike repeatedly counterpoints the extraordinary against the ordinary. When Chiron resists Aphrodite, for example, he refreshes her mind on the names of the gods, a comic epic catalogue. To refresh his readers' memory, Updike appends a list of analogues in the appendix; this tactic also spoofs academic pedantry and supplies the reader with richer understanding and enjoyment. Though some readers, like Updike's first wife Mary Updike,* found the mythic analogues cumbersome and unnecessary, the serious theme of man existing on a boundary separate from God is turned to comical advantage by the gap between the immortal and the quotidian. Larry Taylor has shown in detail how Updike relies upon the *Idylls* of Theocritus in providing the form and style of the pastoral* elegy to *C*, and how the Chiron/Prometheus story underlines the story of Christ's sacrifice; as Updike indicated, even the names chime: Chiron/Christ. Since one critic has suggested that Virgil's *Georgics*, a poem praising the pastoral life, might contribute a subtext to *OF*, Virgil's poem might also account for the given name of George Caldwell and his marriage to a Ceres analogue. Virgil's *Aeneid* is studied in Peter Caldwell's Latin class, and Peter stumbles through the segment in which Aeneas meets his mother, Venus. The confrontation prepares for the pathos of Peter exposing his psoriasis to his girlfriend as a sign of his trust and affection. Updike uses the *Aeneid* (as well as Homer's *Odyssey*) to supply a contrast between ancient and modern ways of facing death* in "The Journey to the Dead" (*A*).

Other allusions to myth and Homer supply ironic undercurrents. In *Couples* Piet Hanema's* wife Angela Hanema* not only shows him the constellation named for the mythical character Andromeda, but also assumes the "classic position" Andromache used to console Hector in Homer's *Iliad*. But Piet is no Hector, since he is about to ruin his family by leaving her for Foxy Whitman.* As Andromache was given to Achilles' son after the fall of Troy, Angela is offered to Freddy Thorne* in payment for procuring an abortion* for the child of Piet and Foxy. But Thorne, who earlier, when he appeared in a scuba suit, was described as a Cyclops, is no Polyphemus; he is impotent with Angela.

Potent, however, is Harry "Rabbit" Angstrom,* who, when he sprinkles gold Krugerrands on his wife Janice Angstrom* before making love to her, mimics Zeus's encounter with Danaë as Ovid describes it in *The Metamorphoses*. Updike calls Janice and Rabbit "gods bedded among stars." Elsewhere, when Richard Mathias* offers retsina wine to his wife Sally and her lover Jerry Conant* during their divorce negotiations, he remarks, "The Greeks knew how to meet their fate," possibly referring to Odysseus's burial of Elpenor (*Marry*). Another way to meet fate was by following the injunction of a "wise old Greek," "Know thyself," uttered by Jimmie, the "Big Mouseketeer,"* to attentive Janice and Rabbit (*RR*). But Jimmie not only converts the injunction to simply mean "Be yourself" but winks, suggesting to Rabbit that the oracle's advice should not be taken too seriously. Rabbit seems to take the modern debasement of the message to heart when he explains to Ruth Leonard Byer* that he has "the guts" to be himself. These classical allusions show that modern couples are not so sure how to meet their fates, and Updike smiles and grimaces at this fact.

Updike's characters often employ Plato* in an effort to reduce anxiety, and they rely on Lucretius, Virgil and other Roman authors to fortify themselves against the unknown. David Kern's* wish to survive death physically, not just as an idea, is not alleviated when his mother tells him to read Plato's allegory of the cave ("Pigeon Feathers" [*PigF*]), and Stephen Conner* (referred to with the Latin title "prefect") mockingly alludes to the allegory of the cave as "cartoons painted on a waterfall" and uses the materialistic arguments of Lucretius to counter the spiritualized universe John Hook* proposes (*PF*). But Col. Félix Ellelloû* does seek the "hard stone within Plato's cave" to indicate substances that seem unreal (*Coup*). Quotations from Lucretius embellish the tryst of Venus and Mars (the gym teacher and minister) in *C*, and Clyde Gabriel reads *De rerum natura* to learn how human beings, like atoms, are random creations (*W*). "The Journey to the Dead" (*A*) includes part of Virgil's *Aeneid* in Latin. But most spectacularly, Roger Lambert* quotes two pages in Latin from Tertullian* that, like the Greek on the last page of *C*, are untranslated, perhaps to force the reader to feel the exotic language in which Lambert was immersed, or to apprehend the strange boundary Caldwell had crossed in becoming immortal. It may be these things that Alfred Schweigen misses when the Mass is no longer said in Latin ("The Music School" [*MuS*]).

Appropriately, the witches of Eastwick* use Latin to cast spells, most cleverly when Sukie Rougemont* changes milk to cream by saying, "Sator arepo tenet opera rotas."* The sentence merely means, "Sower Arepo holds the wheels at his work." It is not only a palindrome, but the most splendid ever conceived, a magic cube, which reads the same up, down and backward when the words are placed one beneath the other. It was featured in George Ripley's *Believe It or Not*, a book Updike alludes to in *Marry*. Since it was thought to contain a phrase etched into church floors, "Pater Nostra A O," a reference to the Alpha and Omega of Christ, it is a measure of Sukie's blasphemy that she uses this palindrome for such a trivial purpose. Another blasphemous magic cube is "the Cube" in *RV*, a building housing computers that Dale Kohler* uses to reach God. But Sukie's Latin palindrome is not only an index of Updike's cleverness, but a measure of his willingness to use such knowledge to amuse and instruct. The Latin word "redux" used in the title *RRed* reappeared ten years later in *RIR*, the word having become popular with journalists in that decade. Updike has Rabbit recoil at a word whose meaning he does not understand but detests because of its overuse. Updike has often given characters names rooted in Greek: Jack Eccles* (*RR*) or

Latin: Amy Mortis (*PF*), Angela Hanema (*Couples*), Essie Wilmott/ Alma DeMott* (*IB*) and Gloria Turnbull* (*TE*). For fun, Foxy Whitman declines the name of Vietnam* leader Ngo Dinh Diem* as if it were a Latin noun: "Diem. *Dies. Diei. Diei. Diem*" (*Couples*). Also, Updike fashioned a translation from the Latin poem "Basium XVI" by Ioannes Secundus, a sixteenth-century poet influenced by Catullus. Professor Barbara Pavlock describes Updike's translation of "Kiss XVI" as a free, lyrical translation with a more expansive tone than the original. At Harvard* Updike's thesis was written on Horace and English poet Robert Herrick, and Horace is alluded to in *PF*. Updike has provided an extensive analysis of Homer and the Greek tragedians in tracing the interrelationship of literature and religion* in "Religion and Literature" (*MM*).

Bibliography: John J. White, *Mythology in the Modern American Novel: A Study of Prefigurative Techniques* (Princeton: Princeton University Press, 1971); W. W. de Grummond, "Classical Influence in *The Poorhouse Fair*," *American Notes and Queries* 13 (1974): 21–23; James Ellis, "Plato's Allegory of the Cave in *Rabbit, Run*," *Notes on Modern American Literature* 2 (1978): item 15; James Ellis, "Karl Barth and Socrates as Mousketeers in *Rabbit, Run*," *Notes on Contemporary Literature* 3 (1977): 10–13.

Classical Music. Updike often uses classical music to establish the purported upper-class sophistication of his characters. Thus Harold little-Smith mimics conducting works by Richard Wagner and Wolfgang Amadeus Mozart, Frank Appleby likes only baroque composers, Terry Gallagher plays "Greensleeves" on both recorder and lute, and Carol Constantine plays the lute and loves compositions for cello by Johann Sebastian Bach* (*Couples*). Two other cellists recognize the link between the cello and death.* The daughter of Alfred Schweigen ("The Music School" [*MuS*]) plays while he contemplates death and insanity, and Jane Smart* understands that "the male voice of death" is the subject of Bach's Second Suite for unaccompanied cello (*W*). Darryl Van Horne* asserts that Ludwig van Beethoven, Franz Liszt and Niccolò Paganini sold their souls to compose their music, and he should know (*W*). "The Man Who Became a Soprano" (*A*) describes the political intrigue and covert eroticism* within a recorder group. (Updike himself played the recorder for a time.) Updike reviewed classical music concerts at Castle Hill, Massachusetts, from 1961 to 1965. Ben Turnbull* listens to Jacques Offenbach and Dietrich Buxtehude on the radio as he drives to Boston (*TE*). In his essay "1938–1947: Decade of the Row" in *A Century of Arts and Letters*, Updike describes the classical music of the decade, noting how American composers moved from the eastern conservatories to colleges throughout the country. See ***2001: A Space Odyssey***.

Bibliography: Updike, *Concerts at Castle Hill* (Northridge, CA: Lord John Press, 1993); "Introduction to *Concerts at Castle Hill*" (*MM*).

Claudius. Claudius is the King of Denmark in *GC*. (He is called Fengon in Part I of the novel, Feng in Part II and Claudius in Part III; for convenience he is called Claudius in this entry.) After realizing he loves Gertrude,* the wife of his brother King Horwendil of Denmark, Claudius exiles himself to Byzantium. There everything seems contradictory and ambiguous: lunatics and saints are indistinguishable, excess and asceticism reign side by side. Returning to Denmark, he enraptures Gertrude with stories of his adventures, and he excites her with his knowledge of falconry. But again he stifles his feelings and leaves for Italy. On his return, Claudius, now fifty-nine years old, gives Gertrude a peacock brooch, a chalice and a silk gown. The gifts secure her seduction, and they each recognize the dangerous and incestuous nature of their union. Claudius believes his passion for Gertrude has enabled him to experience a Byzantine transcendent love, a "gift from Eden's shadows." She is his "holy wisdom." Discovered by King Horwendil, Claudius cleverly poisons the king but never tells Gertrude he has murdered him. Claudius then successfully lobbies for the kingship and marries Gertrude. Denmark flourishes under his rule, and Claudius schemes to end his stepson Hamlet's* estrangement from him, from Gertrude and from court affairs. Claudius's last thought is quite ironic: "All would be well."

Claudius resembles other Updikean villains, such as Stephen Conner,* Roger Lambert* and Darryl Van Horne,* in his refined intellect and ambition. But like them he will be overcome by forces beyond his control. Claudius also recalls tragic Tristan* who falls in love with Isolde* (Gertrude) and brings about both of their deaths. Although the pattern appears in other Updike novels, such as *B*, in no other work of his does Tristan commit murder to secure his love. Like Harry "Rabbit" Angstrom* with his daughter-in-law Teresa "Pru" Angstrom,* Claudius also uses Edenic imagery* to define his incestuous sexual experience. *See* **Adultery; English Literature; Tristan and Isolde.**

Clayton, Alfred ("Alf") Landon (1936–   ). The chief character of *MF*, Alf Clayton teaches history at Wayward Junior College in New Hampshire and has been writing a book on President James Buchanan* since 1964. In 1974 he became estranged from his wife when he took a history colleague's wife as his mistress. From the vantage point of 1991, Clayton tries and fails to reconstruct both the Buchanan administration and his domestic crisis of 1974. Asked to reply to a questionnaire concerning his memories of President Gerald Ford's* administration, Clayton records his personal problems during that time, mixed with a digression on the progress of his Buchanan study, including re-creations of key scenes focusing on Buchanan's failed courtship, which Clayton thinks led to Buchanan's presidency and thus impeded the progress toward civil war. Intertwined with his thoughts on Buchanan, Clayton recalls his domestic "civil war" in which union with his wife was ultimately preserved. *See* **Presidents.**

Cockaigne. In medieval legend the Land of Cockaigne supported the idle rich, graphically described in a thirteenth-century poem, "The Land of Cockaygne," which satirized monastic life. Ben Turnbull* imagines that a wandering deer on his land has been browsing there in a "dream of Cockaigne" (*TE*). Pieter Brueghel the Elder painted *The Land of Cockaigne* (1567), in which a scholar snores, a peasant slumbers, and a soldier sleeps. The three sleeping figures in the painting resemble figures from Turnbull's time travel, St. Mark, a Nazi and a Neanderthal. Empty eggshells near the soldiers symbolize spiritual emptiness, while pigs and geese trot along, already partly roasted. Everywhere pudding and cakes are ready to eat. Ironically, Turnbull's own home becomes the Land of Cockaigne after his wife Gloria Turnbull* leaves him or dies—or did he dream this? In reality, Turnbull himself, rich and retired, is living in the Land of Cockaigne, despite atomic war. In a review of M. Ageyev's *Novel with Cocaine* (*OJ*) Updike mentions the rumor that the book may have been written by Vladimir Nabokov,* but decides that it is unlikely. *See* **Drugs**.

Coleman, Ann. Ann Coleman is the fiancée of James Buchanan* in *BD* and *MF* who, Updike surmises, died mysteriously when she imagined that Buchanan had fallen out of love with her. Speculation in these books suggests that her overdose of laudanum led to Buchanan's immersion in law, his presidency and perhaps a postponing of the Civil War. *See* **Presidents**.

Bibliography: Greiner, *OJ*.

Coleridge, Samuel Taylor (1772–1834). An English romantic poet, Samuel Taylor Coleridge published with William Wordsworth *Lyrical Ballads* (1798), containing "The Rime of the Ancient Mariner." Sarah Worth* describes her mother's aged suitor, a retired admiral, as an "ancient mariner," but the image is ironically self-reflexive, since Coleridge's mariner told a tale of spiritual loss and renewal, roughly the same tale Sarah describes in her letters in *S*. Also, though Sarah protects her mother against a supposed imposter, Sarah herself has succumbed to the Arhat,* a religious fraud. She warns her mother that the "mariner" will exploit her savings, but she herself has given amply to the Arhat, though once she recognizes her mistake, she recovers, by theft, a considerable amount of her financial loss. Like the Arhat, Coleridge at one point hoped to create a utopian community. Coleridge hoped to situate his community in Pennsylvania, perhaps because he was a Unitarian.* *See* **English Literature**.

Collected Poems, 1953–1993 (New York: Knopf, 1993). The compilation *CP* contains most of the poems from Updike's five previous volumes of poetry* and useful notes on many of them. Apart from bringing together Updike's own selection of forty years of his poetry, it also includes his final revisions, for example, in "Moons of Jupiter" and "Midpoint." Such revising is typical of Updike's lifelong effort to make each opportunity to reprint his works a chance to perfect them. The volume is also another indication of Updike's bringing his lifework to closure, as in the completion of the Rabbit novels and his third volume concerning Henry Bech. He has even rounded off the 1957 poem cycle "A Cheerful Alphabet of Pleasant Objects," dedicated to his one-year-old son David,* with *HA*, poems for his grandson illustrated by David in 1995. Even the recycling of President James Buchanan* in *MF*, the memoirs in *SC* and his multigenerational novel *IB*, as well as the collections of essays on art,* music and golf* suggest that Updike is gathering his work to a close. When a bibliography of a quarter-century of work by and about him appeared in 1994, he wrote a "Foreword" to it, attesting to another sense of closure. *See* **Light Verse**.

Bibliography: Updike, *A Helpful Alphabet of Friendly Objects* (New York: Knopf, 1995), George J. Searles, *Christian Century* 110 (1 Dec. 1993): 1215; Boyd Tonkin, *New Statesman and Society* 7 (7 Jan. 1994): 42; *Economist* 330 (29 Jan. 1994): 92; Thomas Disch, *Poetry* 163 (Feb. 1994): 285; Mark Ford, "Backside of the Tapestry," *Times Literary Supplement* 25 Feb. 1994: 21.

Collecting Updike. Updike is one of the most collectible of all modern American writers, and some of his texts are sold for thousands of dollars. Collecting Updike is made difficult because of the number of special editions of his work, from signed Knopf special editions accompanying the regular trade publications to the Quality Paperback Club and privately printed editions. Many of his poems and stories have been printed themselves as special editions, like "Brother Grasshopper" (*A*) and "Dog's Death" (*M*). In addition, the collector needs to acquire variant editions, like the second state of the first edition of *MS*, which corrects an error in a poetic quatrain, or the corrected edition of the poem "Query." The serious collector will want to acquire manuscripts and uncorrected proofs. The uncorrected proof of "His Mother Inside Him" (*A*) contains a sentence not in the Knopf trade edition. Since Updike routinely made alterations and additions in already-published pieces he wished to incorporate in a new volume, his original manuscripts or typescripts thus supply another version of his work that the collector would want, though most are now in the archives at Harvard.* Of course, the very involved purchaser would want to add foreign editions, since Updike has been published in two dozen languages, sometimes in editions not available in America, like the gathering of the first two books about Henry Bech* published in England, *The Complete Henry Bech*. The collector would also want to acquire magazines in which Updike has published, which number close to two thousand. Records, cassettes, audio tapes, video tapes and paperbacks may also attract the collector, perhaps along with interviews from a Website and CD-ROMs to come. Paperbacks sometimes correct errors in the trade editions, and Updike has published original paperbacks, *OS*, *V* and *TF*. "Association books" would also be of interest—works of writers Updike has read, or works of his from the library of a friend like Joyce Carol Oates, or books which carry Updike blurbs. Naturally, the collector, if he is a "completist," will want the several hundred books that have reprinted Updike essays, poems and stories.

Updike's work should be acquired in the best condition; the price frequently changes dramatically because of a good or bad dust jacket. The price-clipped jacket usually demotes the price of the book. The same is true of a remaindered book that contains a defacing mark. Naturally, the book or magazine rises in value when it is signed, and even more so when Updike supplies an inscription. The "completist" collector would want to own every printing of every edition, and every state from manuscript to final publication. The collector might also want photographs, letters from Updike, books owned by him and books about him. After this, one leaves book collecting and enters the acquisition of memorabilia, things owned by Updike or related to him. One might buy shingles from the Shillington* house he lived in, for example.

Updike provides some wry observations about his time as a bookseller for a charity, running across his own books: "battered copies of *Couples*, rubbed and rain-damaged *Rabbits*, and foxed, dogeared *Witches of Eastwicks*, the diabolic purple I chose for the cover cloth faded by the passing years to an innocent mauve" ("Me and My Books" [*MM*]). About signing these books he writes, "The fetish of the signature is surely one of the more pathetic features of contemporary religion" (*MM*).

Bibliography: Updike: "Me and My Books" (*MM*); Ray A. Roberts, "John Updike: A Bibliographical Checklist: Section A—Primary Publications," *American Book Collector*, n.s. 1 series (Jan.–Feb. 1980): 5–12, 40–44; Ray A. Roberts, "John Updike: A Bibliographical Checklist: Section B—Secondary Publications," *American Book Collector*, n.s. 1, (Mar.–Apr. 1980): 39–47; *The Works of John Updike: Catalogue Number One* (Winston-Salem: Lovett & Lovett [1986]) (Bookseller's catalogue with 310 items and illustrations); Charles Michaud, "Gleanings from an Updike Collection," *Firsts: Collecting Modern First Editions* 3 (Jan. 1993); 12–15; Herb Yellin, "On Collecting John Updike," *Firsts: Collecting Modern First Editions* 3 (Jan. 1993): 20 (includes "An Informal Checklist with Approximate Prices for First Editions," 20–25).

Comedy. Updike's drawings and cartoons (which slowed to a trickle after he left the *Harvard Lampoon**) no doubt honed the wit he employs in his writing. In one self-portrait, for example, Updike draws a mouth full of teeth (*SC* tells us that his teeth have given Updike a lifetime of trouble) composed of his upside-down name in Courier type. His light verse,* which he still occasionally publishes ("Venetian Candy" uncollected), provided a long foregrounding of wit. He continues to write humorous essays ("Car Talk,"

[*MM*]) and stories ("Grandparenting" [*A*]), and he prankishly started and finished the chain story "Murder Makes the Magazine"* (1997).

Updike employs comedy for its own pleasure, but he often uses it, like other devices, both to relieve tension and to emphasize the multiple possibilities of viewpoint in any human situation. Viewed from a large perspective, even death* can be turned to comic account. Thus Updike sometimes resembles the laughing clown who hides a breaking heart. Laughter provides a palliative and also underscores his serious themes, most notably in *C*, *Couples*, *BB*, *BIB*, *RIR*, *W* and *S.*, as well as in the stories "Who Made Yellow Roses Yellow?" (*SD*), "Problems" (*P*) and "The Man Who Became a Soprano" (*A*). He even ends *BaB* with a joke that proves Sigmund Freud's* dictum that every good joke has a tragic side.

Updike's first appearance as a professional writer was as a writer of light verse penned in frank homage to favorite writers from the *New Yorker** like Richard Armour, Robert Benchley and Ogden Nash, who showed how light verse could be subversive, turning newspaper items, for example, into satiric jabs at the silliness of daily life, from science* to breakfast cereals and from sex to pedantry. The fiction of James Thurber,* P. G. Wodehouse and Max Beerbohm* aided the skewering of middle-class pretensions in *Couples*. Perhaps Franz Kafka* and James Joyce* were sources for the grotesque incongruity of high-school personages serving as classical parallels that makes *C* Updike's funniest novel. The zany and macabre humor of Charles Addams,* Thurber and S. J. Perelman may have sparked Updike's keen sense of gallows humor, which contributes to the ludicrous pranks of the witches in *W*. Updike's reading in Joyce and Vladimir Nabokov* might have contributed to his creation of Sarah Worth,* a first-person narrator who unwittingly discloses her meretricious values in *S*. No doubt Updike saw in Nabokov's comic academics of *Pale Fire* a professor like Alf Clayton* (*MF*) and perhaps a murderer like Henry Bech* (*BaB*), just as Saul Bellow's* delineation of Jewish intellectuals also lay behind Bech. The social comedy of ministers* and salesmen, of hippies* and recalcitrant sons in *RIR* and *RaR* might be traceable to satirists like Henry Fielding, Jane Austen,* Charles Dickens, Anthony Trollope, Joyce, Kafka, Kingsley Amis, Barbara Pym and P. G. Wodehouse.

Formal jokes, like that of the lost motorcycle (*RR*) or the golfed goose, often lay "eggs" (*RIR*), but unintentional silliness like eating parrot food (*RaR*) and deliberate mayhem like Rabbit's son Nelson Angstrom's* car derby, (*RIR*) become part of the comic mythology of the Angstrom family. Updike's Rabelaisian humor is reserved for sex, especially in *RIR* in scenes in which Rabbit makes love while *Consumer Reports* commentary swirls in his head, and in which he places Krugerrands all over his wife Janice Angstrom's* body before sex, only to be alarmed later that one of them might have been mislaid. Black humor,* possibly influenced by Kurt Vonnegut and Donald Barthelme, sometimes enables Updike to heighten a sense of evil at the same time it is exposed. Thus with gallows humor Updike describes in *W* how Clyde Gabriel hangs himself, a proofreading correction signaling his death when the blackness in his skull gave way "with the change of a single letter, to blankness." Comic irony controls the structure of *S.*, since it is framed by the joke of mistaken identity: the Arhat* is a fake. The sudden revelations at the end of *MS* and *RV* provide a similar ironic shock: the apparently repentant Rev. Thomas Marshfield* has used the journal intended to lead him back to God as a means of seducing Ms. Prynne*; and Esther Lambert's* pregnancy may bring Roger Lambert* to raise as his own child the baby fathered by Dale Kohler,* the student he helped to ruin. The reader who knows William Shakespeare's *Hamlet* will find the end of *GC* ironic indeed. *See* **Cartooning; Drawing and Painting; Poetry**.

Bibliography: Updike, "Lost Art," *New Yorker* 15 Dec. 1997: 75–76, 78–80.

Con. In Italian *con* means "with," but as George Allenson observes in the story "Aperto, Chiuso"* (*A*), *con* in French is slang for "vagina," about which Updike had written two poems, "Cunts" (1973) and "Klimt and Schiele Confront the Cunt" (1988), and which Harry "Rabbit" Angstrom* often contemplates (*RA*).

Conant, Jerry. The hero of *Marry*, Jerry Conant, a cartoonist, has an affair with Sally Mathias. Her husband in turn has an affair with Jerry's wife. Jerry is a courtly lover who thinks of Sally in angelic terms. Though his wife Ruth allows him a summer to consider a divorce* and remarriage, with the stipulation that he not see Sally, Jerry betrays his pledge and sees Sally anyway, yet in the end his bond to his children* keeps him from leaving his family. But in an alternate ending to the novel, Jerry leaves Ruth and marries Sally. The reader is asked to choose. *See* **Adultery**.

Conant, Ruth. The wife of Jerry Conant* in *Marry*, Ruth Conant, threatens him with abortion* of their child in retaliation for his affair, but discovers that she is not pregnant. Meanwhile, she is so upset by Jerry's affair and her own with his mistress's husband, Richard Mathias, that she drives off the road and is nearly injured. *See* **Adultery**.

Concerts at Castle Hill (Northridge, CA: Lord John Press, 1993). *Concerts at Castle Hill* consists of twenty-two reviews from the *Ipswich** *Chronicle* (1961–65) that were signed "H. H." The signature doubles Updike's middle initial for "Hoyer," which he used in signing his drawings for the *Harvard Lampoon** "JHU." The reviews represent his interest in everything from folk music to classical music,* from Pete Seeger to Peter Serkin, a catholicity of taste reflected throughout his fiction and poetry.* Music comforts the aged in *PF* when they sing with the prefect Mendelssohn, the songs growing progressively more religious. Popular music* supplies a sense of actuality in all his novels. It is part of the air Harry "Rabbit" Angstrom* breathes in *RA*. In *RR* radio songs ironically counterpoint his flight from his family ("The Man Who Got Away"), while bongo music from the film *Bell, Book and Candle* accompanies his affair with Ruth Leonard Byer.* In *RRed* soul music of the black singer Babe frees Rabbit for a fuller sensory experience, while Jill Pendleton's* "talking blues" explains her life without the impediment of discussion (*RRed*). Disco songs from Donna Summer ("Gimme Hot Stuff!") in *RIR* comment upon Rabbit's effort to discover if he has a daughter. Rabbit's granddaughter Judy* sings commercial jingles to shift her attention away from his heart attack and help save his life (*RaR*). "The Music School" (*MuS*) and *W* describe cello playing; the novel is so rich in insider detail that it seems that Updike himself might have played the cello. He did play the recorder, and "The Man Who Became a Soprano" (*A*) shows this clearly in citations not only of composers and works but editions. Dance music is often used as a prelude to seduction in *Couples*, but in *RIR* Nelson Angstrom* seethes as his pregnant wife dances, and he cannot "let the devil of the music" enter him. Darryl Van Horne* plays the piano demonically, provides expert analysis of Jane Smart's* cello playing and accompanies her in the Dvorak Cello Concerto. Some Updike poems have been set to music for soprano and instruments such as the tuba. *See* **Bach, Johann Sebastian; Classical Music; Popular Music**.

Conner, Stephen. The prefect of the poorhouse in *PF*, Stephen Conner, unlike his predecessor Mendelssohn, is determined to run the poorhouse as a modern institution, with efficiency taking priority over the individuality of the poor. He dreams of a Nobel Prize for his humane work, and he reveals his plans in discussions with ninety-four-year-old John Hook.* Since Hook represents past humanistic values, Conner's values are revealed as uncaring. Conner is indifferent to concrete things like the weather, and this indifference causes him to assume that a storm will not interfere with the fair. It does, and Hook could interpret the signs that Conner is blind to. Conner is rational when he is instructing an aide to shoot a suffering cat, but he secretly harbors a hope that the poor themselves may be similarly exterminated. He thoughtlessly ignores the poor's need for personhood and bluntly rejects religion* as unrealistic, despite the solace it provides the aged. However, Hook scoffs at Connor's scientific program to eliminate pain, reminding Conner that pain is caused by transgressing God's commandments. Hook condemns Conner's fear of waste as "busy-ness," the work of the Devil.

With the Conner-Hook disputes Updike begins his career as a novelist by inviting the reader into a debate concerning the nature of goodness and good men. Conner is so clearly a loser in the debate to some critics that they consider the novel unbalanced and ineffective as a novel of ideas. But

Conner, whom Updike called a preliminary study for George Caldwell,* represents the first of many characters dedicated, with good intentions, to the mind to the exclusion of the heart, like doctors (Freddy Thorne* [*Couples*]), ministers* (Roger Lambert,* [*RV*]) and artists/scientists (Darryl Van Horne,* [*W*]). *See* **Nobel Prize in Literature**.

Bibliography: Updike: "Introduction to the 1977 Edition," in *The Poorhouse Fair* (New York: Knopf, 1977), vii–xvii; Hunt, *JU*; George J. Searles, *"The Poorhouse Fair:* Updike's Thesis Statement," in Macnaughton, *CE*, 231–36; Detweiler, *JU*; Greiner, *JU*.

The Contras. In 1986 the Central Intelligence Agency (CIA) was implicated in "the Iran-contra affair," in which arms were sold to Iran and the Iranian money went to right-wing rebels known as the contras fighting the Marxist Sandinista government in Nicaragua. In "The Man Who Became a Soprano" (*A*) the scandal is a preoccupation of Maury Sutherland, who drowns out soprano recorder player Jessie Bridgeton. Jessie's husband, Terry Bridgeton, solves the problem by switching his tenor recorder for Jessie's soprano recorder, thus "becoming" a soprano.

The Coup (New York: Knopf, 1978). Updike's novel *The Coup* visits new terrain by creating an African country, Kush, modeled on Ethiopia. ("Kush" was old Egyptian for "Ethiopia.") Updike had visited Ethiopia in 1973, and the drought ravaging Kush resembles the one in progress in Ethiopia while he was there. *Coup* was the first novel Updike undertook after he remarried.

Updike explores the efforts of Col. Félix Ellelloû,* president of Kush, to resist the blandishments of the United States, mainly concerned with Kush's oil deposits, and to keep his Islamic people aware of Marxist ideals. To discover subversives, Ellelloû travels throughout his famine-stricken wasteland in several disguises (beggar, insurance adjuster, vendor); the masks replicate his name, which means "freedom" in Berber. He enters a magical world in which the decapitated head of King Edumu becomes not only a totem, but also the central image of an American-style theme park created by subversives who have accepted the gifts of the West while staging a coup in his absence and naming a city for him. Meanwhile, a flashback discloses that Ellelloû learned Marxism in America while he was an exchange student. His hatred of America is thus ironically abetted by capitalism. As James Schiff suggests, Ellelloû's journey of a black man entering an evil white world has been the reverse of that of Joseph Conrad's hero Kurtz in *Heart of Darkness*, a white man probing a dark world.

Updike thus explores the New Left with the same fervor with which he had examined the Black Power of Skeeter* in *RRed* and would examine the New Left students in *B*, but he is more careful to indicate the comic incongruities of a leader who prefers that his people starve rather than accept

American aid, and who is undone by his mistress Kutunda* and his assistant Ezana.* Updike also traces the quest of Ellelloû for a satisfactory woman, while his four wives, according to critic George Hunt, act as mother (Kadongolimi), temptress (Candace "Candy* Cunningham*), virgin (Sittina), and spirit (Sheba). Yet Ellelloû ignores the good advice of Kadongolimi, his mistress Kutunda betrays him, and his American wife Candy only reminds him of the seductiveness of the America he so hates. Through Candy he is married to the nation he hates ideologically. Updike uses Ellelloû's experience in America to focus on the racism and materialism that Skeeter also condemned, customary targets throughout Updike's work. The book is really less about Africa than America, and Ellelloû's inability to save his country from capitalism is a dire forecast of America's inability to resolve its own self-destructiveness. Ellelloû is a familiar Updike hero, a man determined to follow his instincts even if the social fabric unravels, but unlike Harry "Rabbit" Angstrom* or Essie Wilmot/Alma DeMott,* Ellelloû does so with some of the most brilliant language of any Updike first-person narrator; Updike's narrative voice is thus very close to Ellelloû's. When Ellelloû draws attention to the uselessness of such a verbal gift to effect social change, Updike may be admitting the difficulties faced by any socially conscious novelist, like those he had met on trips to the Soviet bloc or in Africa.

Since Updike's attempts to research a novel about President James Buchanan* failed (*BD*), *Coup* was his first successful effort to use the library and the physical site to create a book based neither in Pennsylvania nor New England and not concerned with domestic tragedy. Updike was continuing his interest in historical, social and political ideas evident in *BD*, *BB* and *RRed*. His research also included children's books, travellers' accounts and African novels. Such omnivorous reading would characterize his research for *RIR*, *RV*, *S.*, *B* and *IB*. Since some critics have questioned the accuracy of Updike's description of his African country and it is unlikely that he was simply careless, some "inaccuracies" may be intended ironically, something the reader of other researched novels will want to remember. Certainly realism is not Updike's only concern, for Updike has called *Coup* an allegory of Watergate, with the coup paralleling President Richard Nixon's resignation; for example, a statesman's name is "Klipspringer," reminiscent of Henry Kissinger, Nixon's secretary of state. Also, Updike supplies mythic overtones in Ellelloû's name, which may derive from the great-grandfather of the prophet Samuel, Elihu, meaning "he is God" (Samuel 1.1). The mythic implications are contained in larger patterns as well as in the stories of the Fisher King and Oedipus Rex.

Bibliography: Joyce Carol Oates, "*The Coup*," *New Republic* 180 (6 Jan. 1979): 32–35; Hunt, *JU*; Joyce Markle, "*The Coup*: Illusions and Insubstantial Impressions," in Macnaughton, *CE*; Detweiler, *JU*; Greiner, *JU*; Schiff, *JU*.

Couples (New York: Knopf, 1968). *Couples* is Updike's greatest commercial success and most notorious book in its examination of the erotic lives of ten upper-middle-class couples in Tarbox, Massachusetts, a "post-pill" (and pre-AIDS*) suburban "paradise." Thanks to a frank approach to sex* that is comic, lyric, celebratory, satiric and philosophical, *Couples* became an instant best-seller and *cause célèbre*. For Larry Taylor, "to miss the satiric point is to miss much of the novel and mistake it as pornographic." The novel blends what Updike identified in "The Dogwood Tree"* as his "three great secret things"—sex, religion* and art*—in audacious ways that prompted much favorable criticism. The couples include Marcia and Harold little-Smith; Janet and Frank Appleby; Irene and Ben Saltz; Carol and Eddie Constantine; Georgene and Freddy Thorne*; Angela* and Piet Hanema*; Foxy* and Ken Whitman*; Bernadette and John Ong; Terry and Matt Gallagher; and Bea and Roger Guerin. Their interconnections are amusing, surprising and instructive, making *Couples* a deft social analysis by America's literary authority on domestic affairs.

Updike has said that due to the failing of religion, society had made a "monstrous" inflation of the private versus the social life, a contrast he had already described in the irresponsibility of Harry "Rabbit" Angstrom* (*RR*) and the heroic social commitment of George Caldwell* (*C*). He was thus intrigued by a new "camaraderie" that often led to adultery* and divorce* but that promised a refreshing new start in the wake of the collapse of traditional religion. In *C* adultery was resisted; in *RR* adultery brought tragedy, but marriage remained intact. *Couples*, Updike observed, is about a divorce, as *OF* was about the consequences of a divorce. While writing these four novels, Updike was also creating short stories concerning Joan* and Richard Maple* that depicted the decline and fall of a marriage into divorce and remarriage (*TF*). The narrative of *Couples* concerns the love affair of Piet Hanema and Foxy Whitman, which brings about the dissolution of both marriages and the remarriage of Piet to Foxy. Afterward they leave Tarbox and become "just another couple." Their love began partly as an antidote to Piet's fear of death,* and apparently it healed him as religion could not.

Piet Hanema, a carpenter and contractor commissioned to renovate the Whitman home, has become sensitized to death after his parents' fatal car accident, which confirms his feeling that religion has failed. As a consequence of this despair, his wife Angela's sexual apathy and the constant company of the other couples at parties and games, Piet beds several of his friends' wives, using sex as a confirmation of his identity and his very existence. He begins an affair with Foxy Whitman, even though she is pregnant at the time. After she delivers, they continue their affair, end it and, in a moment of weakness, again make love. This time Foxy becomes pregnant by Piet, who seeks an abortion* through his dentist Freddy Thorne. For his help, Thorne demands a night with Angela Hanema. She complies, but divorces Piet for having asked this of her. Meanwhile, Ken Whitman divorces

Foxy when he learns of her affair from Piet's former mistress, Georgene Thorne. Contrasting subplots satirize the emptiness of adultery as the Applebys and Smiths (assisted by psychotherapy) swap spouses, as do the Saltzes and Constantines (regarded by the others as the "Saltines"). The affairs show that the most private acts inevitably become communal, and this seems to support Thorne's notion that, religion having failed, sex has become the new religion, a way in which people humanize one another. Updike often explained that his graphic sex scenes were intended to take coitus out of the bedroom and place it in the parlor, to demythologize it and to see it as both whole and holy, part of the deepest recesses of humans, as D. H. Lawrence and James Joyce* understood. *Couples* thus predicates, like the story "The Music School" (*MuS*), that only intimate human contact can replace the loss of God, so the couples, according to Thorne, "make a church of each other" and proclaim sex the modern religion. Through sex the couples can humanize one another in a way religion no longer can. In an apocalyptic conclusion the Tarbox church burns down, but the weathercock is salvaged. *PF* had described a future in which communities were run without regard to religion, and Updike describes communities in *S.* and *TE* in which sex is central to phony religious cults. Updike is not optimistic about communities grounded in modern humanism.

Craft may also act as a substitute for religion. As a carpenter, Piet Hanema loves the eighteenth-century artisans of the Tarbox Congregational Church, and while carrying on their tradition and renovating Foxy's house, he begins his life-regenerating affair. But in addition, Piet learns that he cannot build structures that keep death away, since to protect his daughter Ruth's hamster he had built a beautiful cage, yet through Ruth's sister Nancy's spitefulness the hamster escaped and was killed. No artistry can preserve the church from lightning nor the cage from Nancy's spite. The renovation of Foxy's home destroys the "house of Whitman" and the "house of Hanema," though it creates a new "house" by the marriage of Foxy and Piet. In *Couples* the fear of death and salvation through sex are merged, as Piet is forced to confront death and sex in his unresolved Oedipal entanglement that persists though his parents are dead.

Updike weaves together these many strands and knits the love of Piet and Foxy to other deaths, like that of their aborted baby, with its public parallel, the miscarriage of President John F. Kennedy's* baby and the assassination of the young president. The nation's security, partly invested in its celebration of the First Family, is unstable, and symbolically the Kennedys oversee all other couples. The Kennedy gusto for life also provides a sense of a First Party safely guarding the Tarbox parties. The night of JFK's death, which Updike said was the inspiration for *Couples*, signifies the fragility of public protection, leaving the couples to build their lives existentially; but only Piet and Foxy can meet this challenge. Updike also moves the affair of Foxy and Piet beyond the national to the universal by using the myth* of Tristan and

Isolde.* Though such mythical love leads to death, it is counterpointed in the novel by the myth of the waste land and the regeneration of the Fisher King. This fertility-rejuvenation story encloses the narrative of Piet's redemption through love of an earthy "foxy" woman after having failed to reach the "angelic" Angela. Piet is a kind of Fisher King of the middle class, and Updike defines "Hanema" as a name containing "letters" of his fate: "Me, a man amen, ah." The words are odd fragments bound within Piet; it is up to him to put himself together. Against the myth of regeneration by love is the theme that neither God's nor man's artistry can forestall death and the failure of traditions. Thorne remarks sardonically that man is "born to get laid and die." For Piet that is not enough. Interestingly, this thought is also articulated by Isabel Leme* in *B*, another novel built on the structure of the Tristan and Isolde myth. But Isabel, unlike Thorne, accepts the spiritualized view of her lover, Tristâo Raposo,* and struggles to unite with him in death.

Piet's love of Foxy, rather than Angela, underlines Updike's conviction that God must be perceived in finite particulars, that the spiritual must come through the terrestrial, yet the distance between the two reminds us of the ludicrousness of man's transcendent efforts. Thus Piet leaps from the bathroom where pregnant Foxy had been suckling him on hearing Angela at the door. This parody of Eden is also dangerous. If achieved, Eden may destroy personhood. As Updike has remarked, "Unfallen Adam is an ape" (Plath, *CU*). Perhaps Piet in his new life is also "in a sense dead," as Updike noted, since "to be a person is to be in a situation of tension" (Plath, *CU*). Man with his new religion is hard to define and this accounts for why critics see Piet Hanema as both Adam in Eden and Adam after the fall. In treating Piet as a "fallen ape," Updike continues a long tradition in American literature* of the American Adam. Like Natty Bumpo or Ishmael, Piet is embarking on a new terrain requiring new resources.

For a similar, if slighter, treatment of couples, see "Leaf Season" (*TM*), in which several families congregate in Vermont for an October weekend of games and intrigue, and "The Man Who Became a Soprano" (*A*), about the political and sexual intrigues in a recorder group. In its broad interest in community structures, *Couples* resembles *PF*, *MS* and *S*.

Bibliography: "View from the Catacombs," *Time* 91 (26 Mar. 1968): 66–68, 73–75; Robert Detweiler, "Updike's Couples: Eros Demythologized," *Twentieth Century Literature* 17 (Oct. 1971): 235–46; Markle, *FL*, Hunt, *JU*; Detweiler, *JU*; Greiner, *JU*; Burchard, *YS*; Newman, *JU*.

Creative Process. Updike has commented on the stages of his creative process in various interviews* and essays as composed of germinating ideas, work habits, revising routine and participating in the publishing process, from revisions in uncorrected proof and advance reading copies to the dust-jacket design. The bedrock of his work is daily consistency. He has remarked that he aims for about three pages of fresh material a day: like snowflakes falling, he has said, a certain accumulation will result.

The inception of his fiction and poetry* always contains a desire to describe perfectly an aspect of experience that will be acknowledged by others as the way we live. Sometimes it comes right the first time, "like ice riding on its own melting" (Plath, *CU*), as Updike says, quoting Robert Frost. When Updike is writing fiction, he tries to get something suspenseful going and waits for the subconscious to work on it, and certain sites have stimulated this incubation: *Couples* was outlined on the backs of envelopes in church; the poem "Seagulls" was written with charcoal on driftwood at the beach. Reprinting his own personal favorite story "Leaves" also occasioned comments on his inspiration, particularly his concerted effort to create a different kind of short story. He has said that his deepest satisfactions in novel writing are in keeping a mass of images moving forward and the creation of a substantial universal image like Tarzan; Harry "Rabbit" Angstrom,* a modern Everyman, may be such an image.

Updike has offered bibliographical comments that often indicate how a work first occurred to him in *CP*, *RA* and several special editions. Remarks on *MF* for the Franklin edition and *RA* are particularly elucidating, revealing that he wrote the names of the songs as he heard them while composing the segment in *RR* in which Rabbit drives south, or noting that a black family was "burned out" by racists in his own town. He has footnoted his memoirs with connections between events in his life and fictional uses of those events (*SC*), noting for example, how his home in Shillington* was quite close to the poorhouse, and that his father said that when they were completely broke, at least they could walk there. Updike explains that when he is writing long works, he does not begin until he knows the ending, and he is usually prompted by a sense of graphic design: *Couples* is a "sandwich," *RR* a zigzag shape. The joy of creation, he noted, comes when the work takes on its own life, though his characters* can come too close, as when Updike experienced cardiac symptoms similar to those Rabbit Angstrom suffered (*RaR*).

Updike believes that discipline assists creation. He writes fiction and poetry in longhand, prose at a typwriter and final revisions at the computer. Once the hard copy appears, the computer files are erased. Though he once wrote in a rented office above a restaurant in Ipswich,* he now uses four different rooms in his home for different projects. Poetry is often written on airplanes or in terminals: the poem "Exposure" was written on the back of a tune-up receipt. Though Updike's immense productivity often seems to have endured little reworking, revisions on proof sheets and galleys show relentless revising. Reproductions of his manuscript pages, as in Elizabeth Falsey's *The Art of Adding and the Art of Taking Away* (1987), dispel the rather romantic illusion that Updike never blots a line or alters a page. When Updike is reprinting work published in magazines or books, he will always find something to perfect. (A wrenched sentence in *A* appears to have resulted when marginal corrections were misunderstood by the typesetter.) When he is republishing a book, he will sometimes reinstall material altered originally (as in *RR*, in which material altered to meet Knopf's objections festooned the book with attached notes for its English publication; and the ending of "Trust Me" was changed to suit *New Yorker** editor William Shawn but restored for the book *TM*). Sometimes previously published books are revised for accuracy or stylistic refinement: to insure a more precise chronology of events in *RA*; to permit last-minute ideas, as when the poems of *CH* were published by Harper, then in England as *HH* and later by Knopf; or to clarify "science-fiction" elements of *PF* when it was reissued. Often essays in *PP*, *HS*, *OJ* and *MM* contain footnotes that update or clarify comments made in magazine publication. (A political essay written in 1993 contains a footnote in 1998 referring to the Clinton/Lewinsky affair.) Updike keeps the jacketless copies of all books published by Knopf before him as he works, occasionally making corrections of typos or matters of fact to perfect later editions or paperback printings.

Often he resurrects discarded material. The short story "Couples" became the novel *Couples*, the play *BD* was reshaped to fit into the novel *MF*, and essays on William Dean Howells and Edmund Wilson* were "thriftily," recycled, as Updike put it, through many versions. Probably one reason he has had so few writer's blocks lies in his working out problems away from the writing desk, then either abandoning intractable material that does not "have legs" or working on a solution: the 600-page novel *Home* that occupied him for several years, had no "legs," and so went unpublished to Harvard's* Houghton Library Updike archives.

Updike has also provided clues about his creative process in forewords, introductions, prefaces and afterwords written for special editions. *OF*, he notes, was composed with the image of an "X" in mind, and also as "chamber music for four voices" that, like "musical instruments," echo, have narrative solos and "recombine in argument or harmony." He notes a similar "musical pattern" in the "advance and retreat" of his characters in *TF*. Of "Hub Fans Bid Kid Adieu"* he notes that since Ted Williams's last day in baseball was "soaked in love," his own paragraphs must contain a similar love. In another special edition he explains that he conceived of *RR* as experimental both because it was written with the daring innovation of present tense, and because he had conceived it as a film and intended to call it *A Movie*. Admitting that he did well at the *New Yorker* because of his and his editors' "respect for facticity," he directs attention to his passionate concern for correct details in his fiction, and he sometimes uses a fact-checking service. Nevertheless, fiction is not fact, and he has left untouched "errors" like describing an Eisenhower summit meeting as taking place at Gettysburg rather than at Camp David.

Updike explains why he decided against consistency from story to story when he collected several for *OS*, and he shares his source for *PF*, Henry Green's* *Concluding*, indicating his indebtedness to Green's style. He distinguishes books that were useful to him from those that were not in writing *Coup*. He traces the long gestation of *Marry*: a chapter published in 1968 was in fact begun in 1964, before *OF*. Since he says in the 1983 edition of *CH* that he no longer writes light verse,* he offers a historical overview of the form, connecting light verse to the psychological theory of Henri Bergson. After reviewing a work about Tristan and Isolde,* Updike immediately tried to apply what he had learned to a novel undertaken after *C*. The work was not published until 1976, *Marry*. Updike considers the text an "object" with its own shape and texture, and he sees the work in print similarly—the print of the *New Yorker* delighted him as much as the writers and cartoonists published there. He takes an active role in creating dust jackets and selecting cover colors, type fonts and top stains.

One might also estimate the impact of academic critics on his own work (the Hamiltons, George Hunt and Donald Greiner) or Updike's prodigious reading, including works of contemporary poets and novelists (Ogden Nash, Vladimir Nabokov,* John Cheever,* J. D. Salinger* and Philip Roth*). Updike has looked for solutions to writing problems from contemporary writers throughout the world. One might also explore the impact of art,* cartooning* and film* on his inventiveness, as well as his keen awareness of popular culture,* newspaper and magazines, television* and radio. Of course, one might follow Updike's lead and connect his creative process to biographical facts—the birth of his children, life in New York,* his divorce* and remarriage, the deaths of his parents. Apart from such considerations, it is well to recall Updike's democratic opinion that "creativity" can show itself in any activity that is done with a "craftsmanly affection" for materials and the process itself, as well as a sense of wonder and the ability to "organize, predict and persevere."

Updike's personal agreement with Knopf to publish a novel every other year and volumes of essays, stories or poems (which sell less well) between novels prompted a major turn in his career. Owing Alfred Knopf a novel in 1970 and finding that his projected work about President James Buchanan* could not be made into a novel, he returned to his "old friend" Rabbit Angstrom, especially since many people had wanted to hear what happened to him after Rabbit left Ruth Leonard Byer.* Thus was produced—unplanned—*RRed*. This led Updike to decide to write two other books in the Rabbit saga in the next two decades, *RIR* and *RaR*. Not only did this create his most memorable character, but he later turned the Buchanan material into the play *BD* and found a place to recycle it in *MF*. Without his agreement with Knopf, Updike's career would have undoubtedly been different. *See* **Books of Updike**.

Bibliography: Updike, "Accuracy," "Why Write?" "One Big Interview" (*PP*); "On One's Own Oeuvre" (*HS*); "Getting the Words Out" (*SC*); "Literarily Personal"

(*OJ*); "Updike and I," "Remarks Delivered in Acceptance of the Howells Medal" (*MM*); Elizabeth A. Falsey, *The Art of Adding and the Art of Taking Away* (Cambridge, MA: Harvard College Library, 1987); Ristoff, *UA*.

Criticism by Updike. Updike has produced almost 4,000 pages of literary reviews and articles in five books of criticism published about a decade apart (*AP, PP, HS, OJ, MM*), two other books on art* and music (*JL, CC*) and a selection of essays and fiction taken from previous books on golf* (*GD*). Updike routinely revises his criticism and reviews before collecting them. Thus he updates remarks on politics written in 1993 to reflect the climate of 1999, and he scans work published by an author since his original review of that writer's book. Of course, he also makes stylistic revisions as well. The sheer labor involved in such revision makes one wonder how he also manages to produce a novel every other year, as well as volumes of stories and poetry.* Even without his creative work, Updike would still have stature in American letters for this output of reviews, articles and belles lettres. So it is peculiar that one so devoted to criticism has been largely ignored as a critic, particularly when professors like James Schiff have compared him to Henry James* and Edmund Wilson,* and James Wood has found him unmatched "in the range and responsiveness of his reading." Yet Updike insists that he is not a critic: "A critic I understand to be someone who devotes a major part of his life and publication to the appreciation and analysis of an art; I, instead, am merely willing now and then to read a book and give my opinion of it in public" (*MM*). The critical and popular success of his novels, the huge volume and breadth of his criticism and perhaps the fact that much is written for the *New Yorker** and similar journals may have caused some academic critics to feel that Updike cannot be considered a major critic. On the other hand, in a review Professor Larry Graver calls *PP* "a splendidly cluttered Italian museum where profane and sacred treasures, monuments and miniatures, make dizzying claims on our attention."

Though Updike is interested in critical theory, especially deconstruction since it upsets the relation of reader and writer, he has never been interested in developing an explicit theory of fiction. Yet never before has so important an American fictionalist been so thoroughly engaged as a critic. Schooled in the New Criticism, Updike has employed whatever approach seems likely to shed most light on his subject—biographical, historical, psychoanalytic, Marxist, feminist—but always he seeks, in his phrase, "readiness." Often he considers the entire sweep of the writer's career to buttress his evaluations. He seeks a writer's special structures and thoughts, usually through close reading and comparison to other work by that author. He always tries to find the originality of style and insight that provides the writer his personal voice. Updike's standard tactic is frequent quotation, permitting the author to speak for himself as much as possible. In a talk, "The Glittering City" (*MM*), Updike's quoting is incessant so that he can provide a mosaic of voices speaking about New York.* He applies a confident taste that concretely discriminates success from failure. As Updike says in *OJ*, he adopts the persona of the family lawyer. A very generous critic, he prefers not to review his fellow American writers since he is still learning from them, but when he does review even friends like John Cheever* and Philip Roth,* he does not lose sight of fairness in rendering judgments. His severe reviews, however, are few, as though he would rather repress a bad review than publish it. Generally, Updike looks to authors from other countries to reveal clues about directions in modern fiction. Updike's rules for book reviewing can be found in his foreword to *PP*, in which he advises the reviewer to attend to what a writer says, not what the reviewer wishes he had said, supply quotations that enable the reader to make his "impression," confirm a description of the book with quotation, and if the author is "deficient," draw from the writer's "*oeuvre*" for successful examples. He insists that the reviewer must free himself from all bias or else review something else.

Updike's explorations represent the stylish articulation of a lively mind, able to respond to Johann Sebastian Bach,* baseball, beer cans, Claude Bonnard, Jorge Luis Borges,* John Barth and Roland Barth with equal sympathy, enthusiasm and insight. Updike's commentary often provides clues about how his own creative work should be read. Thus, when he provides the information that he went to see Ted Williams as a fan, not as a reporter, he adopts the role of a friendly common reader. His first critical collection, *AP (1965)*, suggests that a reader of *RR* and *Couples* might well trace the sources of these books to works by Karl Barth* and Denis de Rougemont. One critic feels that the seventeen reviews in *AP* are effectively critical essays that take most writers to task for slovenly writing and a "paleontology of failure," creating a "sick literary situation." Yet Updike's tone is usually encouraging, and his early essays suggest prophetically that French antirealist fiction might refresh American writing. Updike's meticulous, socially conscious reviews help to establish his descendance from Edmund Wilson.

Updike's second collection of reviews and criticism (without parodies), *PP* (1975), offers an eclectic miscellany of comic pieces, various introductions, and reflections on writing, golf and religion,* but above all a series of reviews of major authors who were profound and acknowledged influences on his writing—James Joyce,* Marcel Proust,* Vladimir Nabokov* and Ernest Hemingway.* It also includes a thoughtful sampling from many interviews.*

Updike's third collection, *HS* (1983), shows why he called himself "a kind of bridge between national cultures." Like Edmund Wilson, Updike is committed to discovering the imaginative vision novelists communicate about mankind not only in his own backyard and France, England, Germany and Russia (once more he writes on Nabokov), but also in Eastern Europe, India and Africa. His creation of nonwhite characters apparently formed a loop, spurring his interest in Third World writers and causing him to explore his fictional black characters more fully in *RRed*, *Coup* and *B*. His concern about freedom for the artist, central to *BB*, *BIB* and *BaB*, may also have turned his attention to a writer like Milan Kundera who writes under the fear of political repression. It seems likely that Updike, after reading Jorge Luis Borges, Gabriel García Márquez and Maurice Blanchot, would be stimulated to use magic realism* in *W* and *B*. Also, Updike's essays on Ralph Waldo Emerson,* Walt Whitman,* Herman Melville,* Nathaniel Hawthorne* and William Dean Howells show Updike reviewing American literary history. He has written so substantially on American authors that he could provide a volume on the history of American literature.* Updike again completes the volume with an omnibus interview, "On One's Own Oeuvre."

Updike's fourth book of criticism, *OJ*, *(1991)* continues his interests in contemporary literature as well as Third World writers, and he adds many new interests like Finland, architecture, popular music* and television.* Besides a series of essays on Philip Roth, Updike provides sections called "Hyper-reality" centering on Umberto Eco, Italo Calvino, Mario Vargas Llosa and other postmodernists. *OJ* shows the process by which Updike continues to evolve as a writer and thinker.

Finally, Updike's fifth collection of reviews and criticism, *MM (1999)*, injects some new interests with essays on politics, science-fiction dialogue about the war between print and computers, and essays on New York. As usual, Updike offers a massive number of reviews about American and foreign writers. In many ways the collection seems more relaxed than the previous volumes, and Updike takes the occasion to speak with an authority that has been earned by the previous decades of critical reflection.

This substantial body of commentary on writers provides clues about Updike's own process of composition, since he has always used everything that comes his way for his fiction and poetry. His interest in Latin American writers and magic realism could be applied to *W* and *TE*. His concern for continental writers clearly supplies understanding of Henry Bech* (*BB*, *BIB*, *BaB*). Meanwhile, his rapacious curiosity about popular culture,* eroticism, science,* art, and religion evident in all his books of criticism supply a solid support for understanding all his characters* and themes.

Bibliography: Updike, "Remarks Delivered in Acceptance of the Elmer Holmes Bobst Award for Fiction" (*MM*); Greiner, *OJ*; Schiff, *JU*.

Crosby, Harry Lillis "Bing" (1904–1977). Harry Lillis "Bing" Crosby, an American romantic singer of the 1930s and 1940s, appeared in many films,* particularly with comedian Bob Hope. He won an Oscar in 1944 for his role as a priest in *Going My Way*. Crosby's "White Christmas" is the biggest-selling song ever recorded. "Bing" Crosby is mentioned by Mrs. Mary Robinson* as an example of an entertainer who grew rich on his talent, and also nostalgically by Isabel Leme's* uncle in *B*, who recalls Crosby as an unforgettable singer he heard in his youth. Such popular crooners are regularly pitted against rock stars throughout Updike's work to suggest the deterioration of music, musical taste, art* and America. *See* **Classical Music;** *Concerts at Castle Rock;* **Popular Culture; Popular Music**.

Cuban Missile Crisis. In October 1962 the United States learned that the Soviet Union had supplied Cuba with nuclear missiles. Although Soviet premier Nikita Khrushchev* said that no missiles were on Russian ships approaching Cuba, President John Kennedy* demanded the right to search them. After a blockade of Cuba, Khrushchev removed the weapons, and nuclear war was narrowly averted. When Piet Hanema* personalizes this global crisis as merely another "ominous" sign of trouble for his affair with Foxy Whitman,* he reveals a superstitious dread that the outside world will impinge upon the closed community of Tarbox and his idyllic love affair (*Couples*). Updike thus parallels the crisis of trust between nations as a larger version of the failure of trust within the family or between lovers. *See* **Presidents**.

Cummings, E(dward) E(stlin) (1894–1962). E. E. Cummings, an American experimental poet who employed unconventional punctuation, capitalization and visual appearance, satirized the middle class, as Updike does. Among Cummings's special targets were those pretending an interest in the arts, such as "The Cambridge Ladies," a poem alluded to in "Grandparenting" (*A*), a story that describes a reading by Cummings at Sanders Theatre, Harvard,* which Updike may have attended. Updike alludes to this reading again when Joan* and Richard the Maple* hear Cummings (*SC*). Both Updike and Cummings wrote both criticism and fiction, studied art,* lived in New York* and went to Harvard. *See* **American Literature; Poetry**.

Cunningham, Candace "Candy." Col. Félix Ellelloû's* American wife and his second wife in *Coup*, Candy Cunningham met him at McCarthy College, Wisconsin, and thus knew him before he became an Islamic Marxist. Voluptuous and shallow, Candy, even by her name, embodies America as described by Harry "Rabbit" Angstrom* (*RRed*) and Natsume Shimada,* (*RaR*). She nicknamed President Ellelloû, ironically, "Happy,"* her translation of his first name Felix, and though he may have been delighted to return to Kush with such a trophy as Candy, she embodied all that the conflicted Ellelloû detested in America, as well as all he desired.

D

Dakar. The capital of Senegal with nearly two million people on the westernmost point of Africa, Dakar is an important air and maritime center as well as a center for processing fish and peanut oil. It is mentioned in *Coup*.

Dalai Lama. The ruler of Tibet, the reincarnation of Buddha* and thus the spiritual leader of Tibetan Buddhism, Tenzin Gyatso, the fourteenth Dalai Lama, fled to India when the Chinese Communists overwhelmed Tibet. Harry "Rabbit" Angstrom* hears of his disappearance on his car radio while he is fleeing his wife and child (*RR*). He then roguishly links himself to the missing holy man because he "gives people life" and is on a quest for "the thing that wants him to find it." After his heart attack, Rabbit tells his mistress Thelma Harrison* that he "always kind of identified with" the Dalai Lama and has an inkling that "this'll be his year" (*RaR*). Updike and the Dalai Lama were born in 1932, Rabbit in 1933. *See* **Arhat (Arthur Steinmetz); *S*.**

Bibliography: Ristoff, *UA*.

D'Annunzio, Gabriele (1863–1938). An Italian novelist, poet and dramatist whose work exemplifies his flamboyant life, Gabriele D'Annunzio had an affair with the tempestuous actress Eleonora Duse, the model for the heroine of his novel *The Flame of Life*. His life and work ironically parallel those of George Allenson, who suppresses his wife in "George and Vivian: I, Aperto, Chiuso" (*A*). Harold little-Smith has some of D'Annunzio's books in *Couples*.

Dante Alighieri (1265–1321). The Italian epic poet Dante Alighieri was inspired to write his masterpiece *The Divine Comedy* (1307) after meeting Beatrice Portinari, a young noblewoman, in 1274 in Florence. Dante blended his passion for her with a complete conception of the human and divine order, buttressed by a vast scientific and humanistic knowledge. He became embroiled in the politics of Florence, and when he was exiled, Dante condemned numerous enemies to various places in his *Inferno*. His *Divine Comedy* describes his allegorical journey through hell, purgatory and heaven. Dante is guided through the Inferno and Purgatory by Virgil, the Roman voice of reason, and through heaven by Beatrice; each guide furthers his understanding of God's plan. The epic can be read on many levels and is unmatched in its depiction of human evil and human transcendence. It is also Dante's personal voyage toward wholeness.

Dante's images of transcendent love are referred to by Updike's Jerry Conant* and Piet Hanema.* When Jerry and his mistress Sally Matthias* fly into Washington, he sees her face, outlined by the "rose" formed by the city from the air, as so beautiful that Dante could not have dreamed it in creating his mystical Rose of Paradise (*Marry*). When Piet Hanema is with Foxy Whitman,* he thinks himself in the seventh circle of bliss in Paradise (*Couples*). The more disturbing elements of the epic suggest accommodation to death* and human grotesqueness. The Arhat* sees the journey of Kundalini as being like Dante's journey through heaven and hell (*S*.). In "The Journey to the Dead" images of Dante's descent into hell are coupled to similar visions to describe the distress of visiting a terminally ill friend (*TM*). Roger Lambert,* observing that midwestern coeds carry their breasts as though they were burdens, recalls, in Italian, that the condemned rolled "dead weights with full chest pushing square" in *Inferno* 7.27 (*RV*). (Professionally, Lambert cites the translator, Laurence Binyon.) Courtly Claudius* quotes Bertrand de Born,* whom Dante placed in Hell.

Also, Prosser tells his high-school students that only Dante presents a more complete image of life than Shakespeare ("Tomorrow, and Tomorrow and So Forth" [*SD*]), and, more personally, Henry Bech* metaphorically considers his seven books as "like fading trail-marks in a dark wood, *una selva oscura*" ("Bech and the Bounty of Sweden" [*BaB*]). Updike loosely imitates Dante's terza rima (rhyming *aba, bcb,* and so on) in the first section of "Midpoint" (*M*). In this way Updike suggests comparisons between Dante's personal appraisal at midlife and his own "midpoint." Updike's poem "Humanities Course" (*CH*) shows resentment for the way Harvard's* Professor Varder treats Dante with "wry respect," for, despite admiring his imagery, Varder knows that "it's all a lie," and in a note to this poem Updike acknowledges that the fashionable interest of the 1950s in the Middle Ages buttressed his own religious feelings. But another poem, "The Moons of Jupiter" (*FN*), records how the discovery of the motion of the moons by Galileo "let out all the air that Dante breathed" by helping to establish the heliocentric system and to refute the position of earth as the center of the universe, a scheme intrinsic to *The Divine Comedy*. In *S*. the Arhat calls

Dante's story of Heaven and Hell a lie, but a lie which, like other stories, burns away "other garbage." *See* **Religion; Science; Thomas Aquinas, St.**

Daughters of the American Revolution (DAR). The Daughters of the American Revolution (DAR) is a women's association admitting only persons descended from participants in the American Revolution. A ring belonging to a DAR woman is robbed by Tristâo Raposo* (*B*), who gives it to Isabel Leme* because he thinks that DAR spells the Portuguese word for "give." She accepts the gift, and their relationship begins with a blend of the amorous and the monetary, the spiritual and the stolen. The DAR perpetuates fighters for American independence, and as the lovers evade capture by Isabel's rich relations, they fight for their personal freedom. Isabel is compelled to barter the ring, however. *See* **Tristan and Isolde.**

Death. Though Updike said in an interview that he feels a tenderness toward his characters* "that forbids making violent use of them," violent death appears throughout his work, as well as death by accident and natural causes. Updike also employs what he called "false" death. Since death raises questions about the afterlife, those equipped with faith fare better than those without it. Updike's first novel (*PF*) uses as a collective protagonist elderly people on the edge of the next world whose faith helps them. A blind woman wonders if she will be able to see in heaven and is reassured that in heaven all are blind. John Hook,* age ninety-four, uses his traditional belief to ward off the atheistic prefect Stephen Conner.* As Conner burns the Lutheran magazine *Sweet Charity*, Hook tells a slave story that discredits the Quakers and later answers Conner's recital of experiments that disproved the soul, "There is no goodness without belief. . . . And if you have not believed, at the end of your life you shall know you have buried your talent in the ground of this world and have nothing saved, to take into the next."

Harry "Rabbit" Angstrom* and others lack such certainty. Rabbit fears that he may be merely matter the ground can swallow, or that he will become "first inside, then out, garbage." Even though he cannot understand why God would not lift the tub stopper that would have kept his baby from drowning, he nevertheless senses that his daughter has been taken to heaven (*RR*). Conversely, George Caldwell* has no faith to ward off his fear of cancer*; consequently, he says that nature* and farmers remind him of death (*C*). (Updike's father Wesley,* upon whom Caldwell was modeled, noted often the things that reminded him of death.) In his science* class Caldwell writes out the equation for the chemical conversion creating energy, life. When the equation stops, so does life, and you become "a worthless log of old chemicals." He tells his son Peter Caldwell* that the equation can be reversed with energy taken from the sun in photosynthesis, though someday the sun too must die. Peter must wrestle not with his fear of his own death but with his knowledge that his father must die. Peter faces this through prayer and, a dozen years later when he comes to tell the story that composes the novel, by mythologizing his father as the centaur Chiron* who accepts his death. Like Caldwell, the father of David Kern* in the story "Pigeon Feathers" (*PigF*) also thinks that man is only a collection of chemicals. When David feels his faith in Jesus undermined and thus his life and the world a "horror," his father tells him that "soil has no soul" and mocks the Bible.* David's faith is restored by a revelation of God's plan through the intricacy of pigeon feathers. Like Caldwell, Ben Turnbull* in *TE* fears cancer and has no religious faith, and he not only knows that the sun will die but, strangely enough, appears to witness its early stages of death.

Accidental death visits the Angstrom family in one of Updike's most powerful scenes, in which Janice Angstrom* accidentally drowns her baby (*RR*). Updike has said that the death of Jill Pendleton* in *RRed* "balances" the baby's death; as Janice was responsible for the drowning, so Rabbit is responsible for events leading to Jill's death. Accidental death claims Piet Hanema's* parents in *Couples* and throws him into illicit sex in a desperate effort to flee death. On the other hand, Rabbit's horror of the death of his baby has caused him to renounce sex with Janice for ten years from fear that he might impregnate her and thus produce another child who will die (*RRed*). Though Piet is religious and saves the Tarbox Congregational Church's weather vane from fire, he does not find that religion* staves off his fear of death as effectively as sex.* Though Piet tries to protect his daughters from death, a pet hamster dies from spite, and he cannot shield them from the upsetting fact of Jackie Kennedy's miscarriage. Also, the accidental opium overdose of Ann Coleman* haunts President James Buchanan* with guilt in *BD*, and historian Alf Clayton* becomes fixated upon the circumstances and meaning of her death (*MF*). We receive a dispassionate report in "The Music School" (*MuS*) that a stray bullet has accidentally killed a man while he dined, and this is never explained, but it fits the narrator's bewilderment at the strange turns his own life is taking. In "The Afterlife" (*A*) death may or may not have happened from a fall on a darkened staircase of an English country home. A man falls in front of a subway train, perhaps by accident in "Bech Noir" (*BaB*).

Updike commented that since he found it so hard to destroy characters he loved, many of his works contain "false deaths." Thus John F. Hook experiences an attack at the end of *PF* that is unresolved, and Mrs. Mary Robinson* at the end of *OF* has a heart attack, though it is unclear if it is life-threatening. Ruth Leonard Byer* threatens to abort her child in *RR*, but thirty years later, by the end of *RaR*, the reader is still uncertain if her child was aborted or not. Some readers assumed that George Caldwell, so closely identified with Chiron the centaur throughout the novel, dies at the end of *C* because Updike wrote, "Chiron accepted death." But Updike stressed in interviews* that Caldwell died only metaphorically by accepting his daily responsibilities. All these false deaths are symbolic. John Hook's and Mrs.

Mary Robinson's attacks result from what they feel is an injustice: Conner mistakenly accusing Hook of having led a rebellion against him, Mrs. Mary Robinson feeling that her son has defied her by marrying a woman she cannot approve and returning to a profession she thinks unworthy of him. Many readers remain unsure if Rabbit died at the end of *RaR* since, seconds from death, he speaks his last words with shocking clarity, and since they are within quotation marks they do not seem to be words merely thought but actually spoken. In *TE* Ben Turnbull* thinks that he may have killed his wife, but since she appears alive later, he decides that the murder may have occurred in some parallel universe.

Death often occurs offstage but reverberates for survivors as an absent presence, like the passing of Piet Hanema's parents, which causes him to seek sexual encounters to dispel death. In the hiatus between the narrative action of the Rabbit novels the parents of Rabbit and Janice Angstrom die, yet the deaths vibrate less than the passing of Skeeter,* whom Rabbit sees as "a certain light withdrawn," and Rabbit carries in his wallet a news story of Skeeter's apparent death. Aging, Rabbit reviews his dead as he jogs in *RaR*—his mother, Jill, two lovers and Marty Tothero—and throughout the novel he is haunted by the deaths of celebrities like John Wayne and Jimmie the Big Mousketeer,* as well as those in horrible airplane* crashes. Even the retirement of ballplayers strikes Rabbit as a kind of death.

Janice is the only one of Updike's characters to reap a reward from death by inheriting Springer Motors,* though Alf Clayton theorizes that the death of Ann Coleman propelled James Buchanan on a path leading to the White House (*MF*). Col. Félix Ellelloû* profits momentarily by beheading the king of Kush, but this encourages a coup against him (*Coup*). The witches satisfy their vengeance by murdering Jenny Gabriel, as her father Clyde Gabriel had by murdering her mother, Felicia Gabriel, but the witches lose their lover Darryl Van Horne* anyway, and Clyde's act precipitates his own suicide. Perhaps only Henry Bech* by cold-bloodedly murdering four hostile critics* enjoys his revenge; he only stops when his mistress threatens to tell the police ("Bech Noir" [*BaB*]). Claudius* protects himself and his mistress Queen Gertrude* by murdering her husband, but enjoys his safety less than a year (*GC*).

Survivors of their loved ones are always unhappy, whether they survive a husband, wife or lover, like Janice Angstrom, Bernadette Ong (*Couples*), the witches, Van Horne and Isabel Leme* (*B*), or parents, like Piet. Images of the loved one sometimes actively participate in life, as when Joey Robinson* wears his father's clothes, and when the photograph of Fred Springer* dominates the Springer home, along with his way of doing things as Bessie Springer* understands and transmits it. As Rabbit says, the dead "make room," but their presence continues, as when the ghost of Jill visits him one night. The overwhelming effect of President John Kennedy's* assassination reveals the futility of sex as a defense against death to Piet, just as his lover's abortion* of their child shows him that a love idyll can actually create death. The adultery of Claudius* and Gertrude* leads to their deaths and that of seven innocent people (*GC*). After their baby's death the Angstroms nearly succeed in surviving it, but thirty years later Janice makes the Freudian slip, saying that she wants to be sure that in her absence Rabbit, recovering from angioplasty, does not drown. Joey Robinson feels the persistence of his mother's force when he examines several photographs ("A Sandstone Farmhouse" [*A*]). The pain of memories, thankfully, dissolves.

Updike points out in his essay "Facing Death" that the nineteenth century saw the body as holy because it saw the body as "the person," even after death, but that in our time we worship instead "disembodied energy." There are no shields from death, though, as Updike continues, ritual and semiotic systems try to provide them. "The Music School" (*MuS*) introduces absurd death when a bullet crashes through a window and into the head of a man at breakfast; this leads Arnold Schweigen to try to write a novel about the dead computer specialist. *Couples* combines the themes of animal death, near death, absurd death and national deaths, all of which are ritualized. Piet Hanema cannot protect his daughter Ruth's hamster from being killed by a cat, yet a solemn burial is undertaken. Jackie Kennedy cannot circumvent a miscarriage, but the nation mourns with her, and JFK remarked that he could not stop a "madman with a rifle," but the nation was entranced in several days of national mourning. But, significantly, when Piet and Foxy choose to have an abortion and death enters their lives concretely, they treat it without ritual.

Only *B*, *W* and *IB* contain more images of death than *Couples*. In *B* violent deaths occur when the lovers must murder in self-defense to ward off capture, while in *W* death arises through murder, suicide, witchcraft (or cancer) and accident. *IB*, unlike the other novels, explodes in violence only at the end of the action as Updike stages a battle similar to the Branch Davidian confrontation of religious zealots and the authorities. When Clark DeMott* is killed after shooting the fanatic Jesse Smith,* Updike presents the only truly heroic death in his work. Finally, in *TE* Updike uses his greatest off-stage violence when Turnbull looks back with 20/20 hindsight on the Chinese-American atomic war, then apparently witnesses the violent end of the universe.

Politics can serve as an excuse for death. In *Coup* Colonel Ellelloû uses Marxist Muslimism to excuse his immolation of a U.S. government representative. He beheads the old king and allows his people to starve in the name of national autonomy. When the decapitated king's head speaks and becomes a theme-park attraction, the coup that removed Ellelloû brings a black-humor* image of death to Kush. Such murder occurs on a grander political scale in war. As Dilvo Ristoff contends, war is a major image throughout the Rabbit saga. The American Civil War is discussed in Updike's first novel *PF*, and nuclear war has occurred in his sixteenth, *TE*. In between, memories of World War II flash by in Mrs. Smith's recollections (*RR*) and the presence of a tank in the Brewer* square (*RRed*). Adolph Hitler's name recurs throughout Updike's books. Rabbit serves "Uncle" during the Korean War,* and Vietnam* haunts *RRed*, with Skeeter contributing highly graphic descriptions of the dead that are reinforced on nightly television, and a Vietnam veteran torching the Angstrom house as if it were a hooch. Skeeter believes that the war augurs a coming race war of world proportions. Rabbit reads Barbara Tuchman's grim study of the Revolutionary War, which highlights grisly atrocities, in *RaR*. Witchcraft is thought to be part of the vast killing ground of the Vietnam War, and the "honored dead" of Vietnam are political footballs in *W* since no one can agree if a Polish dead hero should be memorialized. Ed Parsley's* apparent death by one of his own war-protesting bombs shows the conviction at the heart of the idealistic effort to stop the Vietnam War's senseless killing. Clark DeMott ends the carnage created by Jesse Smith by killing him and dies a hero's death when authorities storm Smith's complex in *IB*. In contrast, Queen Gertrude* describes the carnage in Danish wars as resembling the innocent ways predators slaughter their prey (*GC*).

Such concentration on death reflects Updike's own crisis over the afterlife, shown in his autobiographical poem "Midpoint" (*M*), in which he concludes stoically, "Our Guilt inheres in sheer Existing, so / Forgive yourself your death and freely flow." This seems to be the meaning of Rabbit's stoic remark to Nelson* as he dies, "It isn't so bad": anyone can face death if it is accepted as a natural consequence of having lived (*RaR*). Such an insight may have occurred to Clark DeMott as he protected the children at the cost of his life (*IB*). Like Clark and like Chiron, sacrificing himself for mankind, Rabbit could forgive himself his death because he kept alive the vision of "first-ratedness" he had felt as a basketball* star, which had been transmitted first to his daughter Rebecca* and then to his granddaughter Judy* and possibly also to Annabelle Byer,* the daughter he has become convinced Ruth did not let die. Forgiveness of death would seem to require a vision of perfection that cancels death's harrowing finality. For Thelma Harrison,* Rabbit's dying mistress, that vision is her love of Rabbit's simple existence and his joy at being alive (*RaR*). Updike's own fear of death has also been developed fictionally in "Pigeon Feathers" (*PigF*) and "Bech Panics" (*BB*). See **Afterlife**.

Bibliography: Updike, "Facing Death" (*MM*); Taylor, *PA*; Hunt, *JU*; Greiner, *JU*.

De carne Christi. *See* **Tertullian**.

Deleon, Florida. The fictional town of Deleon on Florida's* west coast near Fort Myers was the place of retirement in the late 1980s of Harry "Rabbit" Angstrom* and his wife Janice Angstrom* (*RaR*). Deleon, named after Florida's discoverer Ponce de León,* is supposedly the spot where the explorer "was slain by Indian arrows"; Rabbit dies there. Deleon is pronounced "*Deel-yun*," as if the locals are "offering to deal you in." Rabbit's son Nelson Angstrom* and his family vacation with his parents at Christmas. Ponce de León was the hero of an unpublished novel by Linda Hoyer Updike.*

DeMott, Alma. *See* **Wilmott, Essie/Alma Demott.**

DeMott, Clark. Neglected because of the attention put on her film* career by his mother, Essie Wilmot/Alma DeMott,* Clark DeMott drifts until he is transformed by Colorado cult leader Jesse Smith,* who gives Clark the name Esau, founder of the Nation of Edom, alien to the Israelites. Jealous cult members call Clark "Slick." Brainwashed, Clark serves faithfully until he recovers his common sense during a battle and conflagration at the compound. He then realizes that Smith is crazy and shoots him, and he himself is killed. His heroism balances the sudden loss of faith of his great-grandfather, Clarence Wilmot.*

Diamond County. The Pennsylvania "Dutch" (meaning German, a corruption of *Deutsch*) county in which Reading*/Brewer* is located, Diamond County was modeled on Berks County, Pennsylvania. As Harry "Rabbit" Angstrom* observes, the south of the county is not as aggressively Dutch as the north, since the brick churches get "spiky" and the houses and barns are made of limestone, not sandstone (*RIR*). One afternoon Jill Pendleton* takes Skeeter,* Rabbit and his son Nelson Angstrom* for a drive through the county. They encounter slag heaps and a mysterious mansion belonging to a coal baron. Jill's car fails because of her neglect. *See* **Plowville, Shillington, Pennsylvania**.

Dien Bien Phu. In 1954 the French and the Vietnamese Communists (the Vietminh) fought a climactic battle at Dien Bien Phu that led to the division of Vietnam* and the surrender of French claims to Indochina. Col. Félix Ellelloû* rose rapidly through the ranks when he fought in this battle (*Coup*). Updike noted that the Vietnamese found that they could not trap American forces into such a disaster (*SC*). *See* **Kennedy, John F.**

Disney, Walt(er) Elias (1901–1966). Updike's plan to work as a cartoonist for the famous cartoon artist and animated film* producer Walt Disney spurred his creation of a great many drawings while in high school and college and stimulated him to emulate *New Yorker** artists like James Thurber.* Updike praises Disney in "Midpoint" (*M*), Janice Angstrom* and her husband Harry "Rabbit" Angstrom* watch the *Mickey Mouse Club* (*RR*), and Rabbit's sister Miriam "Mim" Angstrom* works at Disneyland, where she is a guide to its Mount Vernon replica. (Disneyland opened in 1955 in Anaheim, California.) Mim amuses her family by imitating the automatons of

George Washington and Abraham Lincoln.* This leads her father to observe that "Disney more than FDR kept the country from going under to the Commies in the Depression" (*RIR*). In *RaR* Rabbit's granddaughter Judy Angstrom* sings Disney songs while saving his life. Many Disney films are mentioned in Updike's work: *Mickey Mouse* (*IB*), *The Shaggy Dog* (*RR*), "Steamboat Willie," one of the first Mickey Mouse cartoons (*S.*), *Dumbo* (*RaR*), *Snow White* (*Couples*), *Pinocchio* (*SC*) and *Fantasia* ("Playing with Dynamite" [*A*]), which introduced classical music to a full-length animated film. *See* **Art; Cartooning; Drawing and Painting**.

The Divine Comedy. *See* **Dante Alighieri**.

Divorce. Divorce is a major subject throughout Updike's work, attesting to the fluidity of the characters of "middleness."* Alfred Schweigen, the narrator of the short story "The Music School" (*MuS*), asserts, "We are all pilgrims, faltering toward divorce," though few make it. For him, divorce is necessary if people are to go on loving. For the most part, Updike's male characters do not seek a divorce until they have been discovered in adultery.* Joey Robinson,* having chosen a cold artist for a wife, corrects this by having an affair and then marrying a woman who represents the very fecundity of his mother's farm (*OF*). Jerry Conant* finds Sally Mathias far more sensual than his wife, Ruth Conant*; though he strives to extricate himself from Ruth, the outcome is unclear (*Marry*). Piet Hanema* finds his wife Angela Hanema* an unapproachable angel and gravitates to the more spontaneously sensual Foxy Whitman.* Angela raises the question of divorce only after Piet asks her to help him arrange an abortion* for his mistress (*Couples*). Webb Murkett* simply divorces his women when they age, trading the formerly attractive Cindy Murkett* (*RIR*) for a twenty-year-old (*RaR*). Henry Bech* leaves his wife Bea Latchett* Bech for her sister Norma Latchett* when she has helped him through his writer's block (*BIB*). But in the most carefully delineated separation and divorce, *TF*, Updike shows that a decent person pays in guilt and physical stress to become a modern "pilgrim." Though divorce can be averted by having several wives concurrently, as Col. Félix Ellelloû,* a Muslim, does, his wives satisfy only some of his needs (*Coup*).

Women frequently falter toward divorce because their situations are unendurable. Foxy Whitman's husband Ken Whitman* is an aloof microbiologist in a dull career. Neglected, she finds herself in love with Piet Hanema (*Couples*). Essie Wilmot/Alma DeMott* divorces men who exploit her for drug money (*IB*). Though Sarah Worth's* husband Dr. Charles Worth is a womanizing snob and she begins legal action against him and thoroughly delineates the terrible situation of divorced women, she changes her mind when her friend Midge, whose husband is a boisterous drunk, tells her that she intends to marry Charles (*S.*). Since this intention is revealed in Sarah's last letter, Updike leaves the outcome of her marriage in doubt. Updike also describes marriages in which adultery can be tolerated by men and women without recourse to divorce (*RR, RRed, RIR, RaR, MF, RV, W, B, TE*).

Bibliography: Tallent, *MM*; Greiner, *Adultery*.

"The Dogwood Tree: A Boyhood." Updike's first autobiographical essay, "The Dogwood Tree: A Boyhood" (*AP*), was commissioned to show how his boyhood was representative of a creative person growing up in the 1940s. Rather than treating his life chronologically, Updike provides a mosaic of charged images and events, as he would do in his autobiographical poem "Midpoint" (*M*) and in the essays collected in *SC*. "The Dogwood Tree: A Boyhood" first establishes the personal connection to nature* with a dogwood tree planted in honor of his first birthday, measuring his days. Updike puts himself in "history" by explaining how he responded to his grandparents, who lived with him. Then he describes the great significance of "place," asserting that for him Shillington* was the center of the universe. But that "center" includes a poorhouse, which leads him to consider in the section "Democrats" the economic and political situation of the depression, which caused his grandparents to lose their Plowville* farm and his father to work for low wages. In "Environment" Updike explores the importance he felt as a schoolteacher's son, and how he felt his first slap and first love. Updike then turns to the significance of films* and the first recognitions of the mutability of friendship. Most of the essay then examines the "three great secret things," sex,* religion* and art.* Asking the ontological question, "Why was I I?" (a question that haunts Updike throughout his career), he explains how he found in art a way "to transcribe middleness* with all its grits, bumps and anonymities, in all its fullness of satisfaction and mystery." The personal consequence of such art would be to ride "a thin pencil line" out of Shillington into "an infinity of unseen and even unborn hearts." The image recalls Harry "Rabbit" Angstrom's* perfect golf* shot that confirms his sense that he "can do anything" (*RR*); but for Rabbit the golf shot is purely personal, while the use of the pencil for Updike is social. "The Dogwood Tree" provides valuable insight into the writing of such stories as "Pigeon Feathers," "Son" and "Flight" (*PigF*) and the novels *PF* and *C*. Critic George Hunt has explored much of Updike's work from the perspective of "the three great secret things."

Bibliography: Hunt, *JU*; Yerkes, *JU*.

Drawing and Painting. As a boy, Updike showed great interest in drawing, especially cartooning,* and this affected his writing. After his aunt gave him a subscription to the *New Yorker** in 1944, he modeled his drawings on those of James Thurber* and other cartoonists; at his request Thurber sent him a signed drawing that Updike afterward kept in his study. Updike dreamed of getting his work into the *New Yorker* and plotted a career as an animator for Walt Disney.* Perhaps for this reason, he always includes in the mini-biographies he appends to his books his year at the Ruskin School of Drawing and Fine Art,* Oxford,* England, 1954–55. Updike has mentioned that at that time he planned to become a painter and did several portraits of his wife and family. Painting had taught him, he said, how difficult it is to see things exactly as they are, and that the painting is "there" as a book is not.

The impact of drawing upon his poetry* is first seen in his "shaped poems," in which the poem's form resembles its subject. Shaped poetry interested Updike because it enabled him to use the printed page's space imaginatively, as in "Nutcracker," "Letter Slot," and "Pendulum" (*CH*). Jesting, Updike said that "Nutcracker" was in its way as good as the seventeenth-century poet George Herbert's "Angel's Wings." He even improved the three poems' appearances when they were reprinted in *HH* (1959), *V* (1965) and *CH* (1982). His long autobiographical poem "Midpoint" (*M*) gave the eye a "treat," as he said in an interview, not only by altering size and appearance of type, but also by including photographs enlarged so that the white and black dots comprising the pictures became part of the photo. As a result, the reader is acutely aware of the artificiality of the representation of the world and this creates what the speaker calls an "eye/I" pun, in which the viewpoint creates the world. Updike supplied a paragraph about the letter "V" as a companion to David Hockney's illustration of that letter (*Hockney's Alphabet*, NY: Random, 1991).

Even though Updike later gave up both light verse* and drawing, he insisted that all his novels have a visual design in them—for instance, *RR* a zigzag, *C* an "X." Settings also reveal a visual interest when Rev. Tom Marshfield's* motel is shaped like the Greek letter omega to recall Christ as the Alpha and Omega (*MS*), and the town of Eastwick* is shaped like an *L*, perhaps revealing its commitment to hell (*W*). The many poems alluding to painters and sculptors, like the stories "Kid Whistling" (*SD*) and "Museums and Women" (*MW*) and the novels *C* and *W*, show Updike connecting taste in drawing and art* with personal values. Peter Caldwell's* love of Jan Vermeer's* paintings indicates his precocious sense of the beauty of actuality, and his career as a painter of abstract art suggests the new perspective necessary to see the truth about his father. For Peter, "Art is the visible mirror of God's invisible glory" (*C*). Darryl Van Horne's* worship of pop art* indicates his demonic urge to parody reality. Such characters* disclose Updike's own aesthetic views, that in an "eye-oriented era" dominated by television* and film,* writers are naturally jealous that the rich and young have been captured by those arts, but writers must also rededicate themselves to exploring what language has to offer that graphic arts do not. *See* **Barbarella**.

Bibliography: Updike, "Verminous Pedestrians and Car Tormented Streets," "Funny Faces" (*MM*); Campbell, *UN*; Louis Menand, "The Complete Book of

Covers from *The New Yorker*, 1925–1989," *New Republic* 202 (26 Feb. 1990): 27; Malcolm O. Magaw, "From Vermeer to Bonnard: Updike's Interartistic Mode in 'Marry Me,' " *Midwest Quarterly* 33 (Winter 1992): 137; James Plath, "Verbal Vermeer," in Broer, *RT*.

The Dream of the Rood. *The Dream of the Rood* is a poem by an unidentified Anglo-Saxon poet of the eighth century. When Lee recounts his dream-vision of Marcel Proust,* along with his realization of how "the book will end," his wife Jane says, "It's like *The Dream of the Rood.*" Jane is being sarcastic because she is jealous of his nearly religious involvement with Proust, which has reduced his care of his family ("Incest" [*SD*]).

Dreams. Dreams permit deep access to the personal problems of many Updike characters.* Echoing Sigmund Freud,* Updike believes that the experience of dreaming permits people to "become Gods, creators and subjects at the same time . . . both author and character, God and Adam" (*Couples*). The content of dreams may expose the anxieties of the "American dream," revealing the subterranean suffering created in the attempt to get ahead. Updike fills his works with dreams, and an analysis of several from *RA* will disclose his methods and intentions.

Two of Harry "Rabbit" Angstrom's* dreams in *RR* suggest how Freud's insight can be used to explain the anxiety Rabbit has experienced in pursuing the American dream. The first dream occurs after Rabbit makes love to Ruth Leonard Byer.* He dreams that he is eating with his family, and his sister Miriam "Mim" Angstrom* opens the icebox and Rabbit's eyes fixate on the ice cake. Mim is then scolded while eating, and the words feel for Rabbit "like deep inner bleeding." His mother says, "Tart can't eat decently as a baby"; as Rabbit defends his sister, she dissolves into Rabbit's wife Janice Angstrom.* Since making a good marriage is part of the American dream, and Rabbit fears that his marriage was second-rate, his dream has brought him before a judge and jury in the form of his mother. The family strife in the dream has replicated Rabbit's guilt at leaving Janice. When her face dissolves in his hands despite his effort to hold it, Rabbit's "frozen marriage" in the form of the ice cake has now dissolved, and since Rabbit could not hold it together in his hands, he is responsible for its failure. Also, elements of his parents feeding his son Nelson Angstrom* before he drove south are assimilated by the dream. After waking, Rabbit cannot eat lunch at first because he remembers holding Janice's dripping face. Later that guilt is linked to Rabbit's stomach distress after he returns to Janice. Also, the blend of his sister with his wife reveals the way Rabbit's family love has stood between Janice and him.

In the second dream, after he has learned of the death* of his baby, Rebecca,* Rabbit sees two disks in the sky, one pale and one dense. When he hears a voice intone, *"The cowslip swallows up the elder,"* he knows that the disks are the sun and moon, and he understands that death has eclipsed life, and that he must go forth and found a new religion.* Metaphorically, these images are the dream of the American family, Rabbit's children, Nelson and the dead Becky. Since Rabbit feels certain that his daughter "has ascended to Heaven" at the cemetery, the dense disk might have been an image of his daughter, who was described as having a "moon" face when Rabbit saw her in the hospital, so deeply filled with promise that he thought that she would "know everything." Personally, Becky embodies the American dream for Rabbit, eclipsing the "sun" disk of Rabbit's son Nelson, paler than death and "eclipsed" in Rabbit's grief, as he had been in Rabbit's affection when he fled his family. Nelson is the reality that challenges the dream; the eclipse is momentary, and the "elder" child Nelson is all that Rabbit has as an heir. The "new religion" Rabbit might now found could be based on the knowledge of what it means to pass along a hope for perfection to your daughter who dies, and the need to live with the imperfect son. Such an understanding of Rabbit's dream might help to explain why he is so fixated on having a daughter throughout *RA*. The disk image of the cowslip Becky also recalls the golf* ball Rabbit struck perfectly, assuring him as it disappeared in the sky that such perfection could be attained. Since he was in the act of explaining the "thing" that wants him to find it, the disk/ball image reinforces the symbolic reading of Becky as Rabbit's personal dream of the American dream.

In *RRed* L-Dopa produces terrible dreams for Rabbit's Parkinson's-ridden mother Mary Angstrom.* In one dream her husband is overjoyed that persons are attached to tubes like televisions,* and in another she fears being buried alive. Both dreams indicate her sense of helplessness, and within the context of Rabbit's downward path in this novel, they illustrate his own further fall from his American dream. Later Mary dreams that a man is trapped in a refrigerator. Though L-Dopa may prompt the nightmares, they have not distorted the dour vision of America in *RRed*. The blend of personal and national "dreams" again appears in *RIR* when Rabbit dreams that he screams over the phone at Nelson at the car lot but hears no sound, his jaws frozen wide.

In *RaR* the automobile* as symbol of the modern dream decays into an old trolley in another dream. The trolley goes to an amusement park that then becomes the tunnel of love. The image of conveyance into a tunnel is an image of death, and the tunnel as a sexual symbol is apt to express the love of death that has become Rabbit's unconscious dream in his self-destructiveness. Later Rabbit dreams that he struggles with an unknown antagonist in an old railroad terminal or chapel, the dreams anticipating his death, and when the phone interrupts the dream, it is Janice telling him that she knows he has slept with their daughter-in-law Teresa "Pru" Angstrom,* leading to his flight to Florida* and eventual death. In Florida he dreams that he lies beside a man in black like a ventriloquist's dummy and in a bright basement like a cruise ship in which he meets his parents. The dream again foreshadows Rabbit's death in this surreal trip to the underworld; in Homer's *Odyssey* Odysseus reports having met his mother, Anticlea, there. In *RaR* Rabbit's Jewish golf partners consider him a "big pale uncircumcised hunk of the American dream. He in turn treasures their perspective." Rabbit tells them that he fears a heart bypass operation partly because he would be so anesthetized he wouldn't be able to dream. Considering his dreams, it is odd that he would want them, but this also indicates that he still hopes that he can capture the elusive dream of "the thing," the American dream that his friends feel he embodies. Perhaps the personal and national dreams merge in the refrain Rabbit recalls to a childhood song, "Life is but a dream" (*RaR*).

Elsewhere, Updike explores a variety of understandings of how the dreamer is both "creator and subject." In *Marry* Jerry Conant's* affair with Sally Mathias* creates violent dreams for his wife Ruth Conant.* She dreams that her father, a minister,* has crashed a black buggy, crushing an old lady from the *Babar* books. The dream may indicate how she sees herself in her relation to her father, and it anticipates her own car crash later. In "The Journal of a Leper" (*P*) the narrator dreams that the fluorescent tube used to cure his disease becomes his phallus. Symbolically he has recognized the relation between his potency and his disease; ironically, when he is cured, he loses his mistress and his ability to create great art. In "Incest" (*SD*) Lee tells Jane of his dream of a film* of Marcel Proust's* novel *Remembrance of Things Past*, and how he gave a backrub to a girl in the theater, then saw a huge image of Proust's young face and knows how the novel will end. Jane likens this to *The Dream of the Rood*,* perhaps indicating that the importance of Proust to Lee is like that of Christ to the *Rood* poet, and perhaps suggesting that the religious quality of dreaming persists even in the modern world. Concerning the woman and backrub, Lee protests that he cannot be accountable for everyone he meets in dreams, abdicating his role as godlike creator of the images of his dreams. *See* **Drugs; Jung, Carl Gustav**.

Dreiser, Theodore (1871–1945). The work of the American novelist Theodore Dreiser advanced the possibilities of realism by providing a new frankness in the treatment of women's sexual desire. As a result, he had difficulty publishing *Sister Carrie*, a landmark in the favorable presentation of a woman's rise to power in a man's world. Dreiser also advocated a social determinism, particularly in *Sister Carrie* and *An American Tragedy*, that saw man as a "will o' the wisp," destined to be the plaything of forces he could not understand. In a review of a Dreiser biography, Updike cites Dreiser's inability to evolve beyond realism. Significantly, Henry Bech,* Updike's Jewish novelist, found Dreiser an important antecedent, but neither novelist evolved artistically (*BB, BIB, BaB*), though Bech does publish a "blockbuster" novel and wins the Nobel Prize* by default. *See* **American Literature**.

Bibliography: Updike, "Not Quite Adult" (*MM*).

Drugs. Updike's characters* take drugs to combat pain, of course, but as personal stimulants, drugs are more significant and more adaptable to symbolic meaning. In *RA* Updike offers his fullest description of these uses of medical and "recreational" uses of drugs.

Drugs ease childbirth and terminal illness in *RA*. In *RR* Janice Angstrom* needs drugs to give birth to her daughter Rebecca Angstrom,* and the drugs cause her to feel that she has no legs; she forgives her husband, Harry "Rabbit" Angstrom,* for running away. A decade later, in *RRed*, Rabbit's mother, Mary Angstrom,* takes L-Dopa to combat Parkinson's disease; the drug produces nightmares and inappropriately increases her libido, thus appearing to mock sexual desire. Rabbit's wife's lover, Charlie Stavros,* needs nitroglycerin pills to combat a heart attack, but Janice Angstrom* mistakes Coricidin for them; despite the error, she helps him survive. In *RIR* only Thelma Harrison,* who has lupus, requires painkillers, but in *RaR* a wealth of medications appear: Lyle uses illegal AIDS* medicine bought with money Nelson Angstrom* embezzles from Springer Motors,* and Rabbit uses nitrosat for his heart condition. Ben Turnbull's medication eases the pain of his prostate cancer* (*TE*), but no drugs ease Jenny Gabriel's suffering as she dies of cancer (*W*).

Jill Pendleton* exhibits both the dangers of heroin addiction and the attractions of hallucinogens like mescaline in *RRed*; she is hooked on heroin by two different lovers, but through "mesc" she is able to see God. But because of this, Skeeter* makes her dependent on heroin so he can confirm that he is the chosen of God. Meanwhile, Rabbit, Jill and Skeeter spend several nights in a haze of marijuana during "consciousness-raising sessions." In *RIR* Nelson, Teresa "Pru" Angstrom* and others socialize with marijuana, their authority-defying alcohol substitute. In *RaR* Nelson, protesting that he uses cocaine "recreationally," embezzles from Springer Motors to support his habit and thus nearly ruins his parents' lives. The path from alcohol abuse (Janice, Marty Tothero*) to cocaine portrays the American middle class's increasing dependency on drugs, while life-enhancing drugs are discovered that postpone death.*

Alarmed by the drug culture of the 1960s, Updike drew attention in *RRed* to its dangers. Jill's addiction leaves her a helpless victim of violence as she burns to death. Middle-class Rabbit watches as Skeeter (*RRed*) and Nelson (*RaR*) seem able to control their addictions. They "turn on, tune in, and drop out," as Timothy Leary, the hippie* guru from Harvard,* advocated, but Rabbit still has too much of the athlete's regard for his body to want to tune in. Even socially acceptable addiction is dangerous when it is blended with conflicted values. In *RRed* drugs destroy Jill partly because she and Skeeter are unable to compromise their racism and class privilege as their part of the American dream. Skeeter dreams of becoming the Black Messiah; Jill has found her parents' life of the accumulation of wealth intolerable. Yet Rabbit believes that the L-Dopa–inspired horrors his mother dreams truly depict things as they are. He lives those nightmares in his bondage to Jill and Skeeter. With a further irony, heroin and L-Dopa are molecularly similar, though they create opposite results: the "frozen" Parkinson's victim is relieved of rigidity, but the heroin abuser becomes paralytic. The body's cellular response to drugs becomes a virtual symbol of the country's state in 1969. Life-destroying and life-sustaining drugs are again closely allied in *RaR*, when Nelson's cocaine dependency disturbs Rabbit's staid retirement. The drugs Nelson witnessed his father using a decade earlier have given Nelson an excuse to destroy himself and the family fortune.

Though Rabbit justly castigates Nelson for destroying the family business, he has failed to detect that for Rabbit food* has become a drug. His son's boast that he can control cocaine is the counterpart of Rabbit's assumption that he can control his diet. Ironically, though Nelson does overcome his addiction and finds in rehabilitation the God that Skeeter had sought through Jill's drug visions, Rabbit finds no way to stop destroying his heart. The failure and success of father and son suggest again the importance of character in handling any addiction; since Nelson is Rabbit's son, Rabbit has passed along the qualities of value needed to withstand an almost irresistible force.

Drugs thus symbolize America's self-destructiveness during the Vietnam* War. Not even the witches of Eastwick,* during the 1970s, can control drugs, since Darryl Van Horne* apparently uses them to aid in seducing the witches. As Jill's experiment with hallucinogens caused her to see God, attract Skeeter and become hooked on heroin, so Van Horne seduces the witches with rum and hallucinogens (*W*). Drugs introduce an element of disorder that can be withstood only with discipline. Natsume Shimada* the Toyota representative sent to cancel the Springer Motors Toyota franchise, lays the blame for Nelson's embezzlement on not just Nelson's but America's lack of discipline (*RaR*). Updike's interest in the death of President James Buchanan's* fiancée, Ann Coleman,* suggests a cultural continuity in America's inability either to control its use of drugs or to enjoy its liberation. Ann, confused about Buchanan's intentions and hysterical about his betrayal of her love, accidentally dies of a laudanum overdose (*BD*, *MF*), leaving Buchanan to social ostracism and guilt. His despair causes him to deflect his pain in the study of law and thus in a political career leading to the presidency. But since Nelson was able to overcome addiction, Updike shows that American history* is not deterministic but can change.

In his non-Puritanical Jewish writer Henry Bech,* Updike offers a comic view of drug use. Bech imagines that an adoring student intended to disorder his wits with drugs in order to steal his mistress. The situation clearly intensifies Bech's sense of insufficiency at a critical moment in his life ("Bech Takes Pot Luck" [*BIB*]). The same disorder occurs in another story, in which a son lies when he tells his father that the brownies he offers are not laced with hashish; the result is a series of misadventures leading to a loss of a lover ("Trust Me" [*TM*]). Though magical drugs are momentarily a positive force to keep Brazilian lovers from detection by transforming them into the opposite color, the result is tragic in *B*, partly because the change brings with it a careless arrogance in Tristâo Raposo that leads to his death. Roger Lambert* wonders if Verna Ekelof's* "recreational" use of cocaine might have contributed to her abuse of her child (*RV*). Finally, despite the wonder drug of the 1960s, "the pill," which inhibits contraception, paradise is not regained by Piet Hanema,* whose impregnation of his mistress and subsequent abortion* leads to an unraveling of their marriages (*Couples*). Surprisingly to some, Updike's view of America's abuse of drugs is thus severely critical and conservative. *See* **LSD; Pot**.

Dualisms. Like the American novelists he admires most, Nathaniel Hawthorne* and Herman Melville,* Updike uses dualism in theme, structure and character. Thematically, Updike often employs the "yes, but"* dualism: the clash between the desire to respond to instinct and the need for social restraint. His most thorough exploration of "yes, but" is in *RA*: Harry "Rabbit" Angstrom* distinguishes between the "right way and the good way" (*RR*)—his desire to flee the second-rate and his awareness that he should not neglect his family. In fact, he is quite willing to modify his personal needs to fit social forms: he makes love to Ruth Leonard Byer* "as he would his wife" and lives with her as he had lived with his wife Janice Angstrom.* Thirty years later Rabbit tells his granddaughter, "My instincts are always to do the opposite." Though he admits, "It's gotten me into a lot of trouble," he adds, "I've had a lot of fun." Yet when he reflects on that "fun," Rabbit can only make a list of the women he has slept with, most of whom had calamitous effects upon his life. He wanted to say yes to his "dwindling," as Updike calls it, but doing so only made him fear his instincts.

Structurally, the form of *C*, for example, shows a division between the world of men and that of gods, with some chapters given to ordinary people in Olinger and others to the gods in Olympus. Human beings are limited to a terrestrial boundary, as Updike's epigraph* from Karl Barth* states, though the narrator stresses the occasional blending of gods and men. Thematically, Updike's dualism of heaven and earth does not entirely prohibit commerce between the two. Thus the characters of *C* sometimes take on godly traits, but the narrator is aware of his divided self, since Peter Caldwell* acknowledges the strain of feeling exalted by Jan Vermeer* and depressed by Olinger bums. Another aspect of Peter's awareness is his reflection, at twenty-seven, of his struggles with his father when he was fifteen. Several sorts of dualistic division are thus used in *C*.

A quick survey of Updike's other works will show how thoroughly dualisms of all kinds proliferate in his work. Dualisms in Theme, structure, character and images are closely allied to subject, as seen in the separation of man from God, experienced by Tom Marshfield* (*MS*) and Clarence Wilmot* (*IB*); the separation of man from nature,* revealed in George Caldwell's* torment in "Old Man Winter's belly" versus the Arcadian myth of *C*; the separation of city and country when Joey Robinson* struggles with his mother's farm (*OF*) and Ben Turnbull* meticulously records arrivals of flowers and changes in the weather in his home far from congested, mercantile Boston* (*TE*); the contrast of pop art* and serious art in *W*; the separation of things crafted from the factory-made, seen in the love of old carpentry by Piet Hanema* versus the marketable prefabricated houses of his fellow contractor Terry Gallagher; the separation of man from what he produces, whether selling gadgets, cars or insurance (*RA*); the separation of man from the machines man has made, whether George Caldwell wrestling with autos (*C*) or Dale Kohler* hacking at the computer (*RV*); the separation of the individual from his fellow man through the regimentation of Stephen Conner* (*PF*) or Col. Félix Ellelloû* (*Coup*); the separation of writer from audience, shown through Henry Bech's* writer's block (*BB*), as well as writer from his characters (*BaB*); ministers* who lose touch with their congregations, like Tom Marshfield (*MS*) and Clarence Wilmot (*IB*); the confrontations between democracy and communism witnessed by Henry Bech (*BB*) and Colonel Ellelloû (*Coup*); the distance between the citizen and his nation, demonstrated in Skeeter's* Vietnam* experience (*RRed*) and Ben Turnbull's disconnectedness after atomic war (*TE*); the separation from one's personal past in Rabbit's nostalgia for his youth (*RA*) or another's past in Alf Clayton's* struggle with the hiatuses in the life of President James Buchanan* (*MF*); the antipathy of blacks and whites as Rabbit wrestles with black history (*RRed*); struggles with the Other, Indian or Asiatic (*RA*); the encounters between gays and straights in reality and fantasy (*RaR*); and the conflicts of men and women revealed throughout Updike's work, but especially in *Couples, Marry, MS, MuS, RV, TF* and *W*.

The dualistic conflict of protagonist versus antagonist is naturally necessary to all conflict and thus to all fiction, but Updike's treatment goes beyond aligning characters* in opposition like Stephen Conner and John Hook* in *PF* or Janice and Rabbit in *RA*. Instead, he links such oppositional characters to values and ideas, since this dualism, he explained in an interview,* exists throughout culture. Thus in *PF* Hook and Conner represent old age and youth, liberal and conservative, but Hook's reverence for handmade craft and Conner's acceptance of the factory productions separate them as do a realistic view of Abraham Lincoln* by history* teacher Hook and a mythologizing of him by organization man Conner, and Hook's individualistic empathy versus Conner's impersonal bureaucracy. Personal values are also expressed in oppositions in *OF* and *Couples*, in which Joey Robinson* and Piet Hanema reject women who represent the "angelic" and sexually unexciting for women who offer down-to-earth erotic appeal (a variation on the madonna/whore opposition). Often such values are in conflict within the individual character, as in Sarah Worth,* who seeks inner enlightenment through Buddhism but keeps a firm hold on her inherited silver and the latest beauty tips (*S.*). Such internal dualisms are most obvious in the many ministers who profess the faith but have trouble living it (*MS, RR, RV, S.*).

Updike offers symbolic ways out of such dualisms. Caldwell and his superior, Louis Zimmerman,* represent the perennial conflicts of teacher/administrator, order/chaos and heart/mind. Yet these oppositions are united in the figure of Chiron,* the mythical centaur, who can accept such oppositions, since he is both man and beast and has his head "afloat in the firmament" and his feet in the swamp (*C*). Comedy* can also help to resolve dualisms, as in *W*, in which an initial allegiance between Darryl Van Horne* and the "witches" becomes a manic opposition, and in *S.*, in which Sarah Worth's initial devotion to the Arhat* dissolves when he is unmasked as a dual figure. In *B* the love of Tristão Raposo* and Isabel Leme* overcomes the opposition of white/black, rich/poor, urban/country, literal/magical and brutal violence/poetic feeling. The erotic love of Piet Hanema for Foxy Whitman* nearly achieves the same, since love calls forth the radical sense of importance each person intuits about himself, destroying the opposition of self and other. Art* may also help to overcome the dualism, since Peter Caldwell is able to recapture his father in all his self-conflicts and celebrate him through the creation of a verbal montage, the novel *C*. Likewise, film star Essie Wilmot/Alma DeMott* is many things to many people as she assumes various roles in her films (*IB*). Updike thus suggests that the artist may rise above cultural dualisms by adopting guises that satisfy basic human needs that go beyond dualism. Wryly, Updike suggests that even the dualist Henry Bech can at last "enter Heaven," where all dualisms vanish (*BB*).

Bibliography: Taylor, *PA*: Hunt, *JU*: Neary, *SN*.

Du Pont. The Du Pont family was headed by Eleuthère Irénée Du Pont de Nemours (1771–1834), a student of Lavoisier in Paris, who by 1802 established E. I. du Pont de Nemours and Company, a gunpowder manufacturer. The name Du Pont became a symbol for the material promises of the American dream, a theme Updike uses in *RA* by creating suggestive parallels between young Irénée Du Pont and Harry "Rabbit" Angstrom.* They each travelled to a new place without money but with a belief in a new future. But unlike the Du Ponts, Rabbit turns back in confusion when he is travelling south in *RR*. As Rabbit drives near Wilmington, Delaware, he fantasizes that the Du Pont women are frigid nymphomaniacs. A decade later he meets the closest woman to a Du Pont he ever knows in *RRed* when Jill Pendleton* becomes his mistress. As he guessed, she is frigid and sexually liberated. Rabbit cannot love her, though he is absorbed by her effort to show him how empty her upper-class life has been. In *RRed*, despite Rabbit's hatred of the well-off doctors of Penn Park (he fantasizes blowing them up, perhaps with Du Pont explosives), he counters his father's claim that the Du Ponts were greedy monsters "doing this country in" by advising his father, "Don't get too radical, Pop." Rabbit becomes in *RIR* a kind of parody of a Du Pont when through marriage rather than personal effort he becomes part-owner of Springer Motors,* enabling him to admire his wife, Janice Angstrom,* for paying bills by signing her name, "just like a Du Pont." Like a Du Pont, Rabbit can afford to take her on a Caribbean vacation by investing in precious metals. When he drives toward Philadelphia in *RIR*, Rabbit accepts the truth that he will never sleep with a Du Pont woman. In his final trip south, Rabbit avoids Wilmington altogether, thinking that thirty years before he had made the mistake of heading south "too soon, toward . . . a vision of barefoot Du Pont women" (*RaR*). Rabbit therefore fails to possess the elusive world of materialistic value, a version of the American dream the Du Ponts represent.

E

Eagle. *See* **Reading Eagle**.

Eastwick, Rhode Island. The setting of *W*, the town of Eastwick is shaped like an *L*, hugging Narragansett Bay. It contains businesses along Dock Street, where Sukie Rougemont's* newspaper, the *Word*, is located. Dock Street also contains such trendy shops as the Yapping Fox and the Hungry Sheep—named from a phrase in John Milton's poem "Lycidas"—which stock Alexandra Spofford's* figurines, and Nemo's Restaurant, where Sukie Rougemont lunches, and where Darryl Van Horne's* servant Fidel picks up an Antiguan waitress. Big old homes sit at a right angle to Dock on Oak Street. At the south end of Dock Street is Landing Square, with its obelisk war memorial; some want to rename it Kazmierczak Square to honor a high-school football star who was killed in Vietnam.* Sukie lives in Eastwick's center, in a 1760 "saltbox" house on Hemlock Lane. On Cocumscusouc Way, off Elm Street, behind Oak Street, are a Greek-revival Unitarian church (1823), newspaper offices and a school. Streets named Benefit and Benevolent contain allusions to the Puritan past. Sukie trysts with Ed Parsley* at the Point Judith Lighthouse. Darryl Van Horne buys the Victorian gothic Lenox Mansion on the edge of town, fills it with pop art* and intends to extend his home into the wetlands. His property is connected to the town by a causeway that becomes flooded by tidal water. Jane Smart* lives in a ranch-style house in the Cove Homes development. A depressed town, Eastwick has many homes for sale, but farmland has been converted to a shopping mall and high-tech businesses. The name "Eastwick" contains both suggestions of "East of Eden" and "wicked," which may recall T. S. Eliot's* Mme. Sosostris and her "wicked" pack of tarot cards in *The Waste Land*.

Eating. The subject and motif of eating underline character and theme, whether through the kinds of food* eaten, the way food is prepared, or the occasions at which it is consumed. Dining is laden with psychic meaning for Harry "Rabbit" Angstrom* throughout *RA*. At the opening of *RR* Rabbit observes his son Nelson* being fed by his parents as they once fed him; feeling supplanted and unloved, he deserts his family. He meets Ruth Leonard Byer* at a Chinese restaurant and is delighted that they enjoy food that shows no obvious sign of coming from an animal that had been killed (*RR*). This gustatory compatibility helps create their sexual relationship, and Rabbit is delighted to learn that Ruth, unlike his wife Janice Angstrom,* is a good cook. These two "dining" scenes are transformed in a surreal dream* the night Rabbit sleeps with Ruth, in which he is eating with his mother and sister and gazes deep into a cake of ice within the icebox. When he awaits the birth of his child, Rabbit's guilt causes stomach cramps. After returning to Janice, Rabbit runs from her again after she has had problems breast-feeding her baby. *RR* ends when Rabbit, intending to buy food for a meal over which he plans to convince Ruth not to abort their child, runs past the delicatessen and out of her life instead.

In *RRed* Rabbit condemns himself to a decade with Janice in which he fears her sex* as if it were a "tiger's mouth." When the Angstroms accidentally dine with Janice's lover Charlie Stavros* at a Greek restaurant that Janice specifically chooses because of its associations with Charlie, the suspicious Rabbit draws Charlie into a quarrel over Vietnam,* in effect a spat about America as the primary consumer of the world's resources. Rabbit watches the lunar landing of *Apollo 11** while eating his mother's birthday cake, a cake that his bad humor had almost made fall. Jill Pendleton* supplies Rabbit with nutritious food in *RRed*; their bargain is sealed when she urges Rabbit to buy her a Cashewburger and offers him her body in payment. Her cooking turns uneatable as she succumbs to drugs.* In *RIR* and *RaR* Rabbit's preference for candy, nuts and cholesterol-laden food leads to his self-poisoning and eventual fatal heart attack at age fifty-six. In this Rabbit resembles America, according to Piet Hanema,* who calls it a nation of candy-eaters (*Couples*).

Eating also differentiates characters*: the "dog" group of *RA* is led by Janice Springer Angstrom's family ("Springer," a breed of dog), which favors roast meat. In contrast, Rabbit as rabbit prefers salads and fatty shoofly pie, cashews and scrapple. He finds a part-time ally in Melanie, a devotee of health food, in *RIR*, and in Teresa "Pru" Angstrom* in *RaR*, who understands nutrition. But neither woman can overcome Rabbit's dependency on food that turns his arteries to sludge. Updike contrasts the homes of Rev. Jack Eccles* and Rev. Fritz Kruppenbach* by noting that Kruppenbach inhabits a home in which roast beef seems to have been rubbed into the furniture like a varnish. The more domestic Eccles has a wife, Lucy Eccles,* who bakes a cake and resembles, to Rabbit, a "sharp vanilla cookie." Alice and Kenneth

Hamilton indicate an etymological relation between "vanilla" and "vagina," and eating may also involve aspects of lovemaking in which the lovers feast upon each other as a "form of knowing," as Updike has said, referring to Piet Hanema* and Foxy Whitman* (*Couples*). This theme blends with Rabbit's rabbit food when Jill indicates the similarity between his penis and a carrot, and the blend occurs again in *B* when Isabel Leme* thinks that her lover Tristâo Raposo's* penis is said to resemble cashews and yams.

Eating draws characters into conflict symbolically. In *RV*, for example, Esther Lambert* invites Dale Kohler* to dinner and makes a roast. Her husband, Roger Lambert,* clumsily cuts it, intuiting Esther's interest in Kohler before they become lovers. Dale and Esther even pass cryptic messages as she serves him pie. In *W* Darryl Van Horne's* sloppy eating habits underline his "devilish" character, as he invites people for drinks and drugs, not food. Similarly, Nelson Angstrom's ingestion of cocaine makes him a lout at the dinner table.

Bibliography: Charles Thomas Samuels, "The Art of Fiction XLII: John Updike," *Paris Review* 12 (Winter 1968): 84–117.

Eberhart, Richard (1904–   ). American poet Richard Eberhart's "The Groundhog," perhaps indebted to William Blake, is alluded to in "Ode to Rot," as Updike explains in a note: the woodchuck dies, but "leaves behind a poem." He quotes other lines in his appendix, admiring the way imaginative creation transcends both "love and loathing" (*FN*). Eberhart wrote thirty books of poetry, issuing his collected poems in 1986. Like Updike, Eberhart studied at Harvard,* often treats religious themes, won the National Book Award and lived in Boston.* *See* **Poetry**.

Eccles, Jack. The minister* of St. John's Episcopal Church, where the family of Fred Springer* worships in *RR*, Rev. Jack Eccles tries to persuade Harry "Rabbit" Angstrom* to return to his family, intercepts him at the Angstrom apartment and suggests that Rabbit is immature to think that God wants Janice Angstrom* to suffer. Rabbit replies that maturity is the same as death,* prompting Eccles's admission that he is also immature. Eccles grows to like Rabbit for his spontaneity, and he is instrumental in keeping Rabbit concerned about his family, so that when his love affair with Ruth Leonard Byer* turns sour and Janice gives birth, Rabbit returns to his family. Eccles, however, has problems with his own wife, Lucy Eccles,* and Updike includes a scene in *RA* within *RRed* that reveals that Eccles's marriage failed. Rabbit had an inkling of their problems when he witnessed an argument between Eccles and his wife about raising their daughter Joyce.

On the way to golf* in *RR*, Eccles confides to Rabbit how his father, in reaction to his "Darwinian Deist" grandfather, had become very orthodox. Rabbit in turn remarks that, as Eccles's grandfather had said, God was in the woods as well as in stained glass; for Rabbit, "somewhere behind all this" is "something" that wants him to find it. Having slyly forced this confession, Eccles then tries to show Rabbit that such intuition is misleading, but he underestimates the strength of Rabbit's conviction. Eccles gets Rabbit a job gardening, continues to meet him for golf and finds their "rapport" a "harmless ecstasy." Despite the criticism of Eccles by Rabbit's Lutheran minister Fritz Kruppenbach,* who insists that Eccles should "burn with Christ" rather than involve himself in the marital struggles of two immature persons, Eccles interviews the Springer and Angstrom parents, though to little effect. Yet his sermon* on Christ's conversation with the devil, whose theme, that suffering is an initiation for those who follow Christ, seems inspired by Kruppenbach. But Rabbit is bored by the sermon. Eccles blends his social and spiritual concerns by calling Rabbit when Janice goes into labor. He is satisfied that he has united them, but later he calls Rabbit to say that something tragic has happened to "us," in announcing the death of Rebecca Angstrom.* He officiates at the funeral of the baby, insisting that the tragedy will strengthen their marriage. As *RRed* shows (in the scene only in the *RA* edition), Eccles is wrong and thus ineffectual. His reappearance in this novel as a divorced ex-clergyman emphasizes the general failure of the ministry to provide spiritual aid. As Donald Greiner remarks, Eccles places "busyness" before belief. *See* **Religion**.

Bibliography: Hamilton and Hamilton, *EJ*; Greiner, *JU*.

Eccles, Lucy. The wife of Jack Eccles* in *RR*, Lucy Eccles opposes Jack's view of himself as a minister,* arguing with him about giving beast tales by Hilaire Belloc* to his daughter to read and goading him for lacking interest in difficult cases and wasting time with adolescents and their social problems. She ridicules his enjoyment of Harry "Rabbit" Angstrom's* cheerfulness, though she does not report Rabbit's patting her backside or his later rejecting what he construed as a pass, since she is apparently attracted to Rabbit. (Rabbit later uses this scene for a masturbation fantasy.) Lucy enjoys confusing unsophisticated Rabbit by alluding to Sigmund Freud* and Oedipalism, just as she forces Eccles to admit that his faith is weak. When Rabbit rejects Lucy's "pass," he precipitates a chain of events leading to his daughter Rebecca Angstrom's* death, and Lucy tells Eccles that "the worthless heel" killed his baby. When Rabbit calls in desperation after he runs from the cemetery and tries to reach Eccles, she slams the phone down. "Lucy" is, etymologically, "light," "Lucifer"; thus she is an arch–femme fatale.* *See* **Names**.

Bibliography: Hamilton and Hamilton, *EJ*; Greiner, *JU*.

Ego and Art in Walt Whitman. *See* **"Whitman's Egotheism"; Whitman, Walt**.

Ekelof, Paula. The mulatto daughter of Verna Ekelof,* Paula Ekelof is an illegitimate child of an unknown black father (*RV*). Her only utterances are "Da," perhaps a cry for her father and a pun on the Sanskrit word for sympathy, *da*, used by T. S. Eliot* in *The Waste Land*. Verna gives her little sympathy, calling her "pooper," abusing her and breaking her arm. Paula's irritable cries for her father recall Pearl, Nathaniel Hawthorne's* "imp-child," who helped Arthur Dimmesdale acknowledge that he was her father. Like Pearl, Paula has vaguely magical qualities: she is unhurt by eating glass that makes her feces shine like diamonds. *See* **Children**.

Ekelof, Verna. The half-niece of Roger Lambert's* sister, Verna Ekelof becomes Roger's lover. In the words of a song that runs throughout the narrative, Verna is a girl "who just wants to have fun." She has many lovers, and a child from one of them. Lambert tries to help her to a better life by giving her money so she will not prostitute herself, leading her away from drugs* and trying to convince her to go back to school. Verna resists his good intentions, however, and uses a tutorial in William Cullen Bryant's "Thanatopsis" to try to seduce Lambert. After she abuses her child, Lambert helps to cover the abuse up. She recognizes that Lambert was sexually interested in her mother and successfully seduces him with this knowledge (*RV*). *See* **Femmes Fatales**.

Eliot, T. S. (1888–1965). A Nobel* laureate (1948) and the most famous poet of the twentieth century, Thomas Sterns Eliot was a dominant force in literary and social criticism and is often mentioned in Updike's work. After graduating from Harvard,* Eliot met Ezra Pound* in England and began to consider changing modern poetry from romantic and didactic to imagistic and ironic, as is evident in *Prufrock and Other Observations* (1917). Suffering a moral and philosophical crisis, Eliot wrote *The Waste Land* (1922), which describes historical and national catastrophes and personal failures rooted in the estrangement of man and God. This poem's complex blend of erudition, radical metaphors, strange juxtapositions of images, contemporary observation and religious intensity set the tone for a generation of poets. As the editor of the *Criterion* (1922–39), Eliot influenced the literary taste of a generation, particularly by his imaginative and socially responsive literary criticism. He helped to establish the critical approach to literature called the New Criticism or Formalism, which examines a text unaided by historical or biographical information. Also, Eliot insisted that modern poetry should espouse the "tradition" created by Homer, Dante,* William Shakespeare and the French symbolists, particularly Charles Baudelaire and Jules Laforgue. Though many of his conservative positions in politics and religion* made him seem an "elder statesman," they clashed with his role as the chief experimental poet of his generation. "Ash Wednesday" (1929) described his conversion to Anglicanism, and *Four Quartets* (1944) revealed his religious meditations on faith in wartime.

Though Updike says that he first read *The Waste Land* when he was fifteen, he first responded to Eliot's irony and "fastidious ennui" (*SC*) at Harvard. Later Updike wittily attacked Kenneth Rexroth, Kenneth Patchen and Kenneth Fearing for their academic critiques of Eliot ("Kenneths" [*TP*]), and he lets the narrator of "Thoughts While Driving Home" mock himself when he says, "Eliot's ashes are dead" (*TP*). At Harvard, Updike said, "we worshipped [Eliot's] cool, detached, modern style. . . . That dryness is still part of me" (*SC*). In writing Eliot's obituary for the *New Yorker*,* Updike maintained that the world had lost a "cultural presence" who extended the tradition of the poet-critic into modern times, and that modern writing was adrift without a figure such as Eliot for guidance.

Not surprisingly, Updike's early fiction particularly reflects an imaginative use of Eliot, with failure and irony disclosing an Eliotic search for belief to forestall meaninglessness. Thus the desert of Kush (*Coup*) reflects Eliot's physical and spiritual waste lands. Eliot's famous paradoxical opening line of *The Waste Land*, "April is the cruelest month," may have suggested the ironic death of Rebecca June Angstrom* in late spring (*RR*) and the ironic time of divorce in "Separating" (*TF*), in which Joan* and Richard Maple* decide to separate on a "brilliant" June day that mocks their "internal misery with solid sunlight." Adultery* in *The Waste Land* is repeated in *Couples*, in which Updike evaluates those seeking to make sex* "the new religion" when the churches prove ineffectual. When Piet Hanema* considers asking Foxy Whitman* to abort his child, he thinks, "Pluck, Lord. Pluck me free" (*Couples*), an allusion to the third section of *The Waste Land*, which paraphrases St. Augustine, "Lord thou pluckest me out / burning." Since Eliot acknowledges St. Augustine's* *Confessions* as a source for this fire image, both he and Updike may have jointly used Zechariah 3.1–2 ("Joshua . . . a brand plucked out of the fire"). Piet makes this prayer shortly after the 1962 Cuban Missile Crisis* nearly started nuclear war. Eliot signified purification through fire to burn out concupiscence and used it as well in a poem written during the London Blitz, "Burnt Norton" from *Four Quartets*. Updike employs the image of fire as purification on several occasions, most notably when Harry "Rabbit" Angstrom's* house is burned (*RRed*) and in "Augustine's Concubine" (*P*). Eliot's surreal image of a woman with hair pulled back becomes Augustine's soul "pulled back taut, like the hair at the back of her skull."

Abortion,* dramatized in *The Waste Land*, appears in *RR*, *RIR*, *Couples* and *RV*. In a covert allusion to Mme. Sosostris and her "wicked" tarot cards of *The Waste Land*, Updike has Janice Angstrom* and Bessie Springer* deciding the fates of Rabbit and his son Nelson Angstrom* over a game of bridge. Bessie's hand is strong in diamonds, and Rabbit intones, "What power!" (*RIR*). Henry Bech,* who admires the modern writers like James Joyce,* admits, "I make a good Phoenician Sailor but I'm a poor Fisher King," alluding to two of the cards Mme. Sosostris deals. With a wit that glances at both James Joyce and Eliot's notes to *The Waste Land*, Updike supplied a "Mythological Index" to *C* and a Sanskrit glossary to *S*. His epigraph* from Martin Heidegger to *MF* resembles the multilayered epigraph of the Sibyl in *The Waste Land*. The hopelessness of the condition of J. Alfred Prufrock of Eliot's "The Love Song of J. Alfred Prufrock" is mocked, fittingly, by a witch in *W* when Jane Smart* quotes Prufrock's "Do I dare to eat a peach?" and the following two lines about walking on the beach. The quote is prophetic, for Alexandra Spofford* does indeed walk upon the beach and call upon her powers to chastise mocking Frisbee players; and upon the causeway to Darryl Van Horne's* house she not only rolls her trousers but doffs them in negotiating her way through the onrushing flood tide. *See* **Awards; Carthage; Poetry**.

Bibliography: Updike, "T. S. Eliot" (*AP*), "Updike Regnant," *Harvard Magazine* July–Aug. 1998: 67.

Ellelloû, Colonel Hakim Félix. The Marxist Muslim leader of Kush, an African country similar to Ethiopia, Col. Hakim Félix Ellelloû becomes president after leading a coup in 1968 against his old teacher, King Edumu. He has four wives, each representing something different to him; for example, his American wife Candace "Candy" Cunningham* reminds him of the voluptuous temptations of American capitalism. Ellelloû's name may derive from the great-grandfather of the prophet Samuel, Elihu, meaning "he is God" (Samuel 1.1). When Ellelloû is deposed by a right-wing coup in 1973, he is exiled to the Riviera, where he writes his memoirs (*Coup*). In an irony Updike might enjoy, a Nobel Peace Prize winner was named Elihu Root. *See* **Names**.

Bibliography: Detweiler, *JU*; Greiner, *JU*.

Ellora, India. Ellora in central India contains nineteen large Brahman, Buddhist and Jain temples (500–1300 A.D.). The Brahman Kailasa temple is 138 feet wide by 88 feet deep. In *S*. the Arhat* (Arthur Steinmetz) tells how instead of going to Vietnam* he went to India and after fifteen years founded an ashram at Ellora that attracted many Westerners. The caves figure significantly in E. M. Forster's *A Passage to India*, in which a woman is frightened by them and by her Indian guide, whom she falsely accuses of assaulting her—an ironic parallel to Updike's narrative, in which Steinmetz becomes Sarah Worth's* lover but loses her and her ashram funds when she leaves. *See* ***Bhagavad-Gita*; **Buddha, Gautama**.

Emerson, Ralph Waldo (1803–1882). The major American transcendentalist, Ralph Waldo Emerson was removed as a minister at Harvard* because he insisted that men should not pray to Christ but instead imitate Him. His exploration of philosophical, literary and social questions and his editing of the leading transcendentalist magazine, *The Dial*, brought him into contact with Henry David Thoreau,* whom he directly influenced, and Walt Whitman,* whom he championed. In "Emersonianism," Updike calls Emerson "the prophet of the new American religion"(*OJ*), and Updike's early work shows an appreciation for the "cosmic optimism" of Emerson, founded in a mystical connection to nature.* *RR* shows Updike's acceptance in part of Emerson's positive view of man in the universe; Harry "Rabbit" Angstrom* even believes that the universe is somehow created for him. In *C* Chiron's* creation myth, in which love sets the universe in motion, resembles Emerson's view of the "Oversoul" that interpenetrates all. Peter Caldwell's* more poetic view of nature seems intended to oppose the scientific view of his father, George Caldwell.* When Peter observes falling snowflakes, he resists his father's scientific view of them, for he thinks, "The stars are in fact falling gently through a cone of observation of which our earthly telescopes are the apex." Like Emerson, Peter sees that "the small universe both does and does not end." Encountering foreign nature, the urbanite Henry Bech,* becomes in "Bech Panics" (*BB*), an Emersonian "transparent eyeball," with, in Emersons' words, "dead eyes, cleansed of healthy egotism, discovered a startled tenderness, like a virgin's whisper, in every twig, cloud, brick, pebble, shoe, ankle, window mullion and bottle-glass tint of distant hill." But the new way of seeing things does not take root in Bech.

Updike said in "Emersonianism" that Emerson's "Divinity School Address," in predicating the collapse of modern Christianity from a failure of faith, is strikingly similar to Karl Barth's* crisis theology. Emerson noted that no religion* has taken up the slack left by the demise of Puritanism, and, for Updike, when Emerson "invokes" the soul as "redemption," he means "what Karl Barth warned against when he said, 'One can *not* speak of God by speaking of man in a loud voice' " (*HS*). Many of Updike's characters* make that mistake, notably Stephen Conner* (*PF*) and Dale Kohler* (*RV*). In *TE* Updike surprisingly expresses an Emersonian vision through Ben Turnbull,* who thinks, "*Our minds harry God from every covert, and yet he lives within.*" He is sure that the priests who "configured with stars and moons" persist with their "archaic language" despite all. *See* **American Literature; Unitarianism.**

"Emersonianism." "Emersonianism" originated as a talk given at the Davis campus of the University of California, October 25, 1983. It was revised for Updike's talk at the American Academy of Arts and Sciences in Cambridge, Massachusetts, November 9, 1983. Updike added details and quotations when including "Emersonianism" in *Ralph Waldo Emerson: Essays and Lectures*, Joel Porte, ed. (Library of America, 1983) and when publishing it in the *New Yorker*, June 4, 1984. The essay was also published in a signed, limited edition as *Emersonianism* (Cleveland, Ohio: Bits Press, 1984). Finally, "Emersonianism" was included in *OJ*, with notes. *See* **Emerson, Ralph Waldo**.

English Literature. Apart from various allusions to older English literature throughout his work, Updike employs William Shakespeare most extensively, particularly in *Couples*, in which Harold little-Smith obsessively quotes the Bard to the point of self-parody. Freddy Thorne* quotes lines describing Ophelia's death to express his horror about the submarine *Thresher*,* imploded in the deep sea with all hands. Frank Appleby quotes lines from *A Midsummer Night's Dream* to describe pregnancy and anticipate the pregnancy of Foxy Whitman.* Updike quotes Edmund Spenser in a review and selects the reading of his *Faerie Queene* as a great moment of reading bliss. He did his senior thesis at Harvard* on "Non-Horatian Elements in Robert Herrick's Imitations and Echoes of Horace." Larry Taylor has suggested that *C* may reflect the use of Milton's pastoral* elegy, and Updike's *Harvard Lampoon** poem "Reverie" parodied Book 9 of *Paradise Lost*. "Redux" may have been a word Updike discovered for *RRed* in John Dryden's *Astraea Redux*, which in turn was influenced by Shakespeare's *Henry V*, whose hero, like Harry "Rabbit" is Angstrom,* is also known as Harry. (Dryden perhaps influenced Anthony Trollope in his titling *Phineas Redux*.) In "Rhyming Max" (*AP*) Updike provides a brief history of English poetry from the viewpoint of rhyming and shows how a quatrain from Jonathan Swift's "Verses on the Death of Dr. Swift" can be written in a variety of different meters and forms. Updike quotes several lines from William Blake's *Jerusalem* that reveal Sir Isaac Newton to be a "beautiful angel measuring the world with compasses." In "A Constellation of Events" Jane Austen's* novel *Emma* becomes a go-between for lovers (*TM*).

Perhaps because Restoration, romantic and Victorian literatures were not fashionable when Updike went to Harvard, his work contains fewer mentions of writers from these periods. But Updike does quote from Percy Shelley's "England in 1819," extensively from George Gordon, Lord Byron's poetry, from William Wordsworth's "Ode on Intimations of Immortality" and knowingly from George Eliot's *Middlemarch*. Updike offers a religious perspective on Shakespeare and several modern English writers like Charles Dickens, Henry James* and Graham Greene in "Religion and Literature" (*MM*). The alarming fables of Hilaire Belloc* make a dramatic appearance in *RR* when a dispute arises between Rev. Jack Eccles* and his wife Lucy Eccles* about whether or not Belloc is appropriate bedtime reading for their children. Updike contributed a "Foreword for Young Readers" to fairy tales of Oscar Wilde.

Updike's reading in modern English writers has been nearly entirely in fiction, but he shows an enthusiasm for Samuel Beckett* and Harold Pinter in drama and W. H. Auden* and T. S. Eliot* in poetry, though Eliot is also considered an American poet. A. E. Housman's "To an Athlete Dying Young" has been offered as an interesting comparison to Updike's poem "Ex–Basketball Player" (*CH*). Updike has paid particular interest in his reviews to Anthony Burgess, Martin Amis, Muriel Spark and Iris Murdoch. It is unlikely that direct borrowings from such novels can be asserted, but Updike has professed that he learned much stylistically from Henry Green,* particularly using *Concluding* in the writing of *PF*. Irish writer James Joyce* was a very strong influence on his use of stream of consciousness in his early novels, and Updike has reviewed the correspondence of George Bernard Shaw. *See* **American Literature; Classical Literature; French Literature**.

Bibliography: Updike, "The Virtues of Playing Cricket on the Village Green" (*OJ*); "Religion and Literature," "Elusive Evil," "Shirley Temple Regina," "Introduction to *The First Picture Book*" (*MM*); Taylor, *PA*; Katherine L. Denman, "To Die at the Top: A Comparison of Housman and Updike," *English Journal* 74 (Feb. 1985): 74–75.

Epigrams. A trademark of Updike's style, the use of epigrams helps supply a pithiness to his writing that often counterpoints his lyrical style and his graphic realism. His sensitivity to epigrams may have been honed by his proverb-quoting family (*SC*). Sometimes epigrams are drawn from Pennsylvania Dutch proverbs: "Too soon dumb, too late smart" (*C*), "Some are born old, some die young" (*RR*), and "You take your own hide to market" (*SC*). In *RaR* Japanese supplies an epigram: "Things change is world's sad secret." Updike's *Coup* alters the stereotypical Arab penchant for quoting the Koran* to provide epigrams that are graphic if sometimes strained: "Freedom is like a blanket which, pulled up to the chin, uncovers the feet" (*Coup*). George Caldwell* takes personally "Time and the tide for no man wait" as he misquotes it, because he is obsessed with death* (*C*).

Often epigrams are converted proverbs: thinking of teaching, George Caldwell puns, "Another day, another dolor," and he puns further on considering a dental appointment, "Another day, another molar" (*C*). Epigrams provide authorial comments: "Nothing happens, then everything happens: cactus blooms, cancer* declares itself" (*Couples*) and "What is a teacher but a student grown old?" (*C*). The courtly tone sometimes supplies epigrams, as in *Couples*: "The loveless man is best armed" and "No act is so private it does not seek applause." Epigrams often supply philosophical pronouncements: "Truth is constantly being formed from the solidification of illusions" (*OF*); "Happiness has its sensual consolations; foolishness has none" (*Couples*); and "We are all exiles who need to bathe in the irrational" (*Couples*). The epigram often forces consideration of the weight of insights like these: "Our inner spaces warrant palaces" (*Marry*) and, from Jerry Conant* of *Marry*, "The world is composed of what we think it is; what we expect tends to happen; and what we expect is really what we desire." This last epigram has dramatic importance since, ironically, Conant surprises his mistress Sally Mathias* by returning to her, something unexpected. *See* **Style**.

Epigraphs. Updike's books nearly always contain epigraphs; one even has two epigraphs. Epigraphs suggest, sometimes cryptically, the author's intentions and are drawn from philosophers: Boethius* (*CH*), Blaise Pascal (*RR*), Jean-Jacques Rousseau (*MF*), Søren Kierkegaard* (*BD, RV*), Henri Bergson (*SD*), Friedrich Nietzsche (*W*), Jean-Paul Sartre (*OF*; given in French in *PP*) and Martin Heidegger (*MF*); essayists: Ralph Waldo Emerson* (*SC*), Frederick Douglass (*RaR*), Martin Gardner (*TE*) and Jacques Derrida (*MF*); politicians: John Quincy Adams (*BD*), James K. Polk (*BD*), Joseph Holt (*BD*); historian: Henry Adams (*BD*); playwright: William Shakespeare (*Couples*); novelists: Nathaniel Hawthorne* (*MS, S., RV*), Virginia Woolf (*SC*), Sinclair Lewis* (*RIR*), Ernest Hemingway* (*Emersonianism*), Franz Kafka* (*PF*), James Joyce* (*TT*) and Saul Bellow* (*SC*); poets: Robert Herrick (*Marry*), Walt Whitman* (*B*), Julia Ward Howe (*IB*), T. S. Eliot* (*SD, Emersonianism*), Wallace Stevens* (*MuS, RIR, BaB*), Alexander Blok (*Couples*), Charles Wright (*TE*) and Jane Miller (*RV*); theologians or religious works: the Bible (*SC* St. Paul quoted by Bishop Nicholas West), (*MW*, Ecclesiastes; *MS*, Psalm 45; *PF*, Luke), the Koran* (*Coup*), Karl Barth* (*C, RV*), and Paul Tillich* (*Couples, MS*) and NASA transmissions (*RRed*); *La Grande Encyclopédie* (*BIB*); accused witches (*W*); and Updike's own *RIR* (*RaR*). Epigraphs always appear in novels, sometimes as chapter headings (*RRed, W*). They seldom accompany collections of stories, essays or poems and are very rarely used in special editions.

A minor controversy swirls around Updike's epigraphs. Some critics think that they are subtle indications of the heart of the books, but to others they are pretentious, irrelevant and a literary affectation. For some, the epigraph from Pascal to *RR* merely demonstrates Updike's eclectic reading, but for others like critic Charles Berryman it reveals clues about how to read *RA*. Thus the key terms "hardness of heart," "circumstances" and "grace" characterize the selfishness of Harry "Rabbit" Angstrom,* the determinants within his society that cause him to be hard-hearted, and the opportunities of grace that he perceives and sometimes ignores. Updike's hostile critics* feel that the Sartre epigraph to *OF* inflates a slender novella by straining for an intertextual relation to the French existentialist and Nobel Prize* winner that the narrative does not support. But this and other epigraphs suggest that Updike sees his books as part of a dialogue with world culture. Thus *OF* may be only the story of how a second wife is introduced to a resistant mother, but the meaning of the confrontation could profitably be tested against Sartre's insights, which are not mere academic observations but living realities.

Updike has claimed that his early novels were intended to create a debate with the reader; the epigraphs provide the first propositions of that debate.

Perhaps for this reason Updike has noted that the epigraphs have a "quite important" (Plath, *CU*) place in his work. This is very clear in *MS* in which the epigraph is taken from Psalm 45.1, "My tongue is the pen of a ready writer," to preview what will be major themes in the novel: the psalmist's praise of the interconnection of sex,* faith and writing. Though one might puzzle over the pertinence of the epigraph to *RIR* from Wallace Stevens's* "A Rabbit as King of the Ghosts," the epigraph from Stevens's "To the One of Fictive Music" certainly helps the reader to explore themes concerning imagination in the story collection *MuS*. Updike uses epigraphs to talk to the reader, as when he employs in *MF* a remark by Jean-Jacques Rousseau about the writer's need to give the reader perhaps more information than the reader wants. This epigraph also suggests a narrative voice* of amusement and the self-involvement of Alf Clayton.* A second epigraph, also from *MF*, contains layers of interest since the comment by Martin Heidegger about being contains a footnote that, with academic parody, says that the quote is really not from Heidegger but from Derrida, who is quoting Heidegger. In addition, since the crucial word "being" is struck out, the reader would have to research the quote to know who struck it out and why. On the other hand, Updike is simply sharing his delight when he discovered a passage in Joyce's *Ulysses* containing the name of his wife, Martha (*TT*).

Bibliography: Hunt, *JU*; Campbell, *JN*; Newman, *JU*; Charles Berryman, "Updike Redux: A Series Retrospective," in Broer, *RT*.

Ernst, Max (1891–1976). A surrealist German artist mentioned in "The Other Side of the Street" (*A*), Max Ernst used strange human forms and bizarre creatures to populate carefully composed Renaissance worlds, searching for ways to render the dream world in two or three dimensions. Updike's reference provides a psychological dream impression when Rentschler revisits his neighborhood. *See* **Art**.

European Literature. The European writers who have most influenced Updike are Marcel Proust,* Vladimir Nabokov* and Franz Kafka.* Proust solidified for him the importance of time as a theme and consequently nostalgia as a tone, as well as the use of stream of consciousness in the mode of stories Updike called variously the "personal-abstract," "personal-meditative" and "fugal weave": "Leaves," "In Football Season," "The Music School" and "Harv Is Plowing Now" (*MuS*) and "The Sea's Green Sameness" (*MW*). Nabokov inspired Updike to use satire* and the grotesque, as well as eroticism, particularly involving an older man and a much younger woman (*TE*). From Nabokov Updike also received support for his interest in tragicomedy, like the murder of the four critics in "Bech Noir" (*BaB*). Kafka provided Updike with black humor* and surrealistic effects, especially in *C*, *Coup*, *W* and *TE*. Updike has written often on all three writers, but in addition, he has published reviews of a great many other writers who do not write in English, including Gustave Flaubert, Raymond Queneau, Günter Grass, Italo Calvino, and Jorge Luis Borges.* The range of Updike's acquaintance with non-English-writing authors is thus as wide as it is eclectic. *See* **French Literature; Literary Influences**.

Bibliography: James A. Schiff, "Updike Ignored: The Contemporary Independent Critic," *American Literature* 67 (Sept. 1995): 531–52.

Evers, Medgar (1925–1963). An African-American* civil rights leader, Medgar Evers organized voter registration of Mississippi blacks and boycotts of racist businesses. He is the subject of a discussion by conservative Harold little-Smith and liberal Irene Salz, whose passionate stand against the socially indifferent couples of Tarbox is tainted by her own moral smugness (*Couples*). Evers's murder by a Ku Klux Klan member on June 12, 1963, along with the assassination of President John F. Kennedy,* exacerbated Piet Hanema's* personal fear of death* (*Couples*).

Expertise. Updike's poetry,* fiction and nonfiction are noted for their use of a wide number of esoteric subjects, such as classical music,* witchcraft, computing, art* and Hindu religion.* His range of response to literature is vast, and he has also shown in-depth knowledge of popular subjects like golf,* film,* automobiles* and dance. Updike's encyclopedic knowledge of the texture of daily life—its songs, news items, magazine articles and television* shows—seems inexhaustible and appears most effectively in *RA*, in which Harry "Rabbit" Angstrom* listens to popular songs, reads *Playboy* and *Consumer Reports*, sees the movies *The Shaggy Dog* and *Funny Girl* and marches in a parade as Uncle Sam.* Also, Updike is comfortable in university settings and used-car lots, in printing houses and cult compounds, in Brazilian jungles, the Norfolk broads and Eastern European cafes. In his "casuals" for the *New Yorker** Updike was required to write about everything from dinosaur eggs to an eclipse. His five volumes of essays and reviews show him adroit at discussing baseball, politics, Finland and cosmology.

Updike's expertise in literature is everywhere apparent. To make a point about rhyme, he rewrites a Jonathan Swift stanza as prose, blank verse and heroic couplets ("Rhyming Max" [*AP*]). In his poem "Midpoint" (*M*) Updike uses the Spenserian stanza to describe polymers and their scientists and equations. In short fiction* he provides a wide variety of special knowledge: "Extinct Mammals" (*P*) peoples its narrative with the names and descriptions of dozens of Pliocene mammals; "Augustine's Concubine" (*P*) uses extracts from the saint's life to make intimate parallels between Augustine* and a modern adulterer; and "The Man Who Became a Soprano" (*A*) shows not only how to play various recorders but the compositions and sheet-music editions that would be used.

While other novelists like John Barth, Norman Mailer* and Thomas Pynchon have imported specialized information into their work about colonial Maryland, ancient Egypt and the V-2 rocket, few have blended such material as gracefully into their characters' lives as Updike. He works from "the inside" in using such subjects in his fiction as basketball* (*RR*), Greek myth* (*C*), physics, chemistry and astronomy (*RV*), President James Buchanan* (*BD, MF*), botany and carpentry (*Couples*), the pharmacology (*C*), pop art* (*W*), Latin palindromes (*W*), cello playing (*W*) and Brazilian magic (*B*). In *RV* he quotes from Tertullian* in Latin and writes about computers like a hacker, and in *IB* he quotes dozens of passages from the Bible,* cites many theological books and refers to over two hundred films* and film personalities. His knowledge of the Toyota car dealership (*RIR, RaR*) led Philip Roth* to lament that he could not write as well about the operation of his own Toyota. (Clearly not a slave to simple accuracy for its own sake, Updike retained in *RA* a historical inaccuracy concerning the meeting place of Harold Macmillan and Dwight D. Eisenhower because it suited fictional purposes.)

Though Updike says that he garnered his knowledge of Greek myth from an old book belonging to his first wife, Mary Updike,* he writes with easy familiarity about myth in *C*, incorporating the languages of myth, Greek and Latin, casually into his narrative. Such use of foreign languages* strengthens the authority of his special knowledge, as he demonstrates in using Portuguese (*B*), African languages (*Coup*), Hindi (*S.*) and Provençal (*GC*).

In his later novels Updike has carefully acknowledged a wide range of sources in creating his intimate knowledge of his particular subjects. His bibliography of works on Buchanan in *MF* contains sixteen entries, one of which, Updike's own *BD*, contains a seventy-nine-page "Afterword" with annotations on each entry. Updike gratefully acknowledges the experts he has consulted in writing *RV, B* and *IB*, such as MIT computer scientists. But no amount of research can explain how he weaves such information so gracefully into his narratives to provide the impression of the felt apprehension of life. *See* **Classical Literature; English Literature; Popular Culture; Science**.

Bibliography: Ristoff, *UA*; Ristoff, *JU*.

Ezana, Michaelis. Michaelis Ezana is Col. Félix Ellelloû's minister of the interior, who plots against him in *Coup*.

Ezekiel (597–571 B.C.). The supposed author of the chief book of Old Testament prophecy, Ezekiel was probably a priest before the fall of Jerusalem and a captive in Babylonia, events he had prophesied. On his return to Israel he became a major lawmaker. He also reveals his vision of God's chariot and describes man's fate as a valley of dry bones without the animating force and spiritual power of God. (This image, along with Ezekiel's phrase "Son of Man," was used in T. S. Eliot's* poem *The Waste Land,* a work Updike knew and used.) Ezekiel was the first prophet to stress obedience to God and to mention the Jewish sense of a religious heritage. Considering the close relation between language, eating* and sex* in *MS,* Updike would no doubt know that Ezekiel is said to have eaten a scroll on which words of prophecy were written in order to symbolize his appropriation of the message. Updike remarks that apart from Ezekiel's extensive measurements of heaven, the Bible* says little about heaven; thus men ought not to be too graphic in their depiction of their place in it when residing there forever. Updike is skeptical of such an afterlife ("On Being a Self Forever" [*SC*]). *See* **Religion**.

F

Facing Nature (New York: Knopf, 1985). Updike's sixth collection of poems, originally published in a great many magazines, *FN* offers "Sonnets," "Poems," "Seven Odes to Seven Natural Processes" and "Light Verse." As in his previous poetry* collections, Updike reveals his entertaining side, but here he also shows himself as a serious nature* poet, providing insights in odes about natural processes he would like the reader to "face." Thus the book's darker tone results from Updike's placing the odes at the heart of it, blending the diction of physics, biology and chemistry with the figurative language of poetry. Through this dual language the speaker faces nature directly and accommodates himself to the benign indifference of its marvelous processes.

The first section, "Sonnets," celebrates grace under pressure, exploring first the dignified dying of his *New Yorker** friend L. E. Sissman, whose work Updike had reviewed admiringly. (He would read Sissman's poetry at Harvard* in 1999 and publish an introduction to Sissman's poetry that year.) The sonnets record Sissman's bravery in facing Hodgkin's disease. Other sonnets depict birth and insanity, aging and cities that seem inhabited by ghosts (Poe in "Richmond," conquistadors in "L.A."). These poems oppose the static to the "natural" and "human" throughout the book. "To be alive is to be mad," he says in the nadir of one "Spanish Sonnet." Other sonnets confront self-obsession and the twin terrors of history* and insomnia.

The second section, "Poems," also contains meditations on death.* Several nature poems declare growth the slave of rot, summer "burdensome." Mountains of trash seem to reflect the perishable mountains we are. "Plow Cemetery" reviews Updike's ancestors and his own final rest, plotted there by his mother. His "life in time" will seal shut "like a scar." "Penumbrae," recalling Wallace Stevens's* "Sea Surface Full of Clouds," explores "gray on gray" to add to the grimness and ambiguity of these poems. Another nature poem seems to provide a code written on the window by the rain, but the rain may also be a "spy." Love, however, offers an antidote to fear: lovers cling together as if to a spar in a shipwreck. Yet a day alone brings its promises: a book is enjoyable, the failure to win a literary prize can be endured, and falling snow can supply entertainment. Several poems about painting rescue the speaker because art* defies time: a Jan Vermeer* portrait of a girl may outlive him. Meanwhile, things we eat turn into us with or without guilt ("Crab Crack"). Updike examines life in the air, akin to a bird in one poem, and in another poem, the terror of flight. Nature's air is inhospitable but must be travelled. This section ends by defying nature, travelling from earth to "The Moons of Jupiter" (continuing Updike's interest in science* in his early verse and "Dance of the Solids" [*M*]). Updike perceives in the moon's scarring and cratering "unforgiven wrongs." At the reaches of nature, then, may be "the man-made world of information," but the last "information," Io's volcano, symbolizes the human reptile brain's fear of death.

The third section, "Seven Odes to Seven Natural Processes," faces the reality of disintegration and entropy but in the end celebrates "healing" as a natural process too. "Ode to Rot" begins with *Gott* saying, "Let there be rot," a humorous echo of Genesis. Rot is a merciful "counterplot," and all processing is reprocessing. The rot of a groundhog, Updike observes, brought Richard Eberhart* a very fine poem ("The Groundhog"). In another ode evaporation acts as a counterforce to gravity, "carrying skyward," and Updike adds levity by noting that the same force evaporating oceans evaporates the poet's ink. An additional ode asks us, ironically, to rejoice in death as a natural progress of growth, itself a mystery. "Ode to Crystallization" celebrates positive ascent. The "Ode to Entropy" defines entropy as "nowhere in nature" but rather in human consciousness and equations, and thus not fearful. Such acceptance of death and entropy is new in Updike's work; he will explore it in novels like *RaR* and *TE*. Finally, the "Ode to Healing" identifies a scab as the body's "invisible motto: In God We Trust." (The motto is alluded to at the end of "Trust Me" [*TM*].) Thus "faith is health's requisite." The name of God acts as an enclosure for all natural processes in these odes—authoritative *Gott* in German in the first line, a benevolent *bon dieu* in French in the last.

The last section, "Light Verse," provides a humorous balm for the weighty themes in the previous sections, though some dark overtones linger. In one poem a comic literalness connects women to machines—a Swiftian close-up in a shaving mirror forces declarations of self-love—and a villanelle connects the indifferent consumption of energy to its inevitable depletion. No such fatigue, however, mars these passionately thoughtful poems. *See* **Light Verse**.

Bibliography: Updike, "A Foreword to the French Edition of *Facing Nature*" (*MM*); Lee Grove, "Facing Nature," *Boston Magazine* (Boston) June 1985: 84; Ralph C. Wood, "*Facing Nature*," *Christian Century* 103 (19 Feb. 1986): 180–81; "*Facing*

Nature," Poetry 148 (Mar. 1986): 297–98; Peter Forbes, "Master of Mimesis," *Poetry Review* (June 1987): 22–23.

Farnsworth, Hubert, or Hubert Johnson. *See* **Skeeter**.

Faulkner, William (1897–1962). An American novelist mentioned in "Bech in Rumania" (*BB*), William Faulkner is admired by Updike in a review as the American writer who created a "saga" in his cycle of novels and stories set in Yokapatawpha County, Mississippi. In a note explaining his own intentions in creating a series of novels about Brewer,* Updike said that only Faulkner followed the example of Honoré de Balzac in creating a "human comedy," a study of complex social systems laced with in-depth portraits of representatives of those systems. Both Updike and Faulkner stress the importance of an area's geography and history as determinants of behavior. In *HS* Updike clarifies the qualities of Robert Pinget and Heinrich Böll by pointing to Faulkner's habit of starting a chapter in the middle of a stream of consciousness. He compliments Joyce Carol Oates for being the first American writer since Faulkner to be "mesmerized" by "a field of imaginary material (*OJ*)." He detects the influence of Faulkner on Gabriel García Márquez in his devices of indirection, "class torpor, obsessive circling" (*OJ*). Like Updike, Faulkner wrote stories and poetry as well as novels and won the National Book Award and the Pulitzer Prize. Faulkner admired James Joyce* and Ernest Hemingway,* as does Updike. *See* **American Literature**.

Faute de mieux. *Faute de mieux* is a French term meaning "for want of something better." It is used in "Bluebeard in Ireland" (*A*).

Fauvism. Fauvism ("beastism") was a French art movement (1898–1908) that championed brilliant colors with harsh juxtapositions, typified by the vigor, intensity and drama of Georges Rouault, Raoul Dufy, Maurice de Vlaminck and its leader, Henri Matisse. Such artistic "violence" outraged some viewers. Alexandra Spofford's* awareness of fauvism is seen when she detects the clashed patches of red and green in the October leaves, a contrast to Darryl Van Horne's* immersion in pop art* (*W*). *See* **Art**.

The Federalist. *The Federalist* is the title of eighty-five essays written by Alexander Hamilton, James Madison and John Jay. Col. Félix Ellelloû* studied the essays in his Wisconsin college political science course (*Coup*). They supported ratification of the Constitution and assured merchants that they needed the protection of a strong federal government, two things opposed by Ellelloû's leftist regime. *See* **Presidents**.

Feminism. Feminism is treated rather ambiguously in Updike's work. This has provoked steady attacks from critics who find his women stereotypical and outmoded. Despite the powerful figure of the mother that dominates the early fiction, Updike has been accused of creating, in his own phrase in *OF*, often used against him, "dull, bovine" women who seek to pacify and entertain men, or, as Melanie calls them in *RIR*, "baby" males. Most critics draw their evidence from the attitudes of Harry "Rabbit" Angstrom.* His references to his wife Janice Angstrom* as "dumb" and "mutt" and his constant appraisal of every woman according to her desirability rather than intelligence or prowess provoke many readers. Thus when considering the deaths* of Rebecca Angstrom* and Jill Pendleton,* critic Mary O'Connell asserts that in Rabbit's world, women serve only as mistresses, then wives, then corpses. Rabbit's attitude of predatory disrespect and assumptions of superiority are those of the middle-class white American born into the privileged patriarchy who customarily sees women in supporting roles, not leading roles of importance. But contrary to O'Connell, even when they are acting their subordinate roles, Updike's women are indifferent wives and mothers. Thus the source should be considered in any evaluation of Rabbit's attitudes; similarly, Updike can hardly be faulted for being honest in his depiction of a male chauvinist. In fact, his accurate portrayal of Rabbit's assumptions of superiority can be construed as negative modeling. It might be overhasty to see Rabbit as Updike's spokesman.

Updike replied to such overstatements about his portrayal of women directly in his novels of the 1980s and 1990s: *W, S., IB* and *RaR*. In *W* Updike explores how women gain empowerment through their own resources rather than those allotted by men. The witches have dispatched their husbands and have united to form a "cone of power" that makes their sisterhood powerful enough to attract lovers and destroy their wives. These strong women seek success through careers, not husbands, and use men as casually as men have traditionally used women. The witches form strong, even erotic, bonds. But critics like Mary Allen note that the witches' dependence upon love makes them conventionally vulnerable to Darryl Van Horne's* aggressive and degrading lust and apparent sympathetic belief in their accomplishments. Their willingness to please him by altering the directions of their careers to fit his vision of them reveals their willingness to set aside their own concerns in order to please men. Their murder of Jenny Gabriel when Darryl marries her is a stereotypical jealousy set in motion by their dependency. Depicting women thus, some feminist critics argue, betrays Updike's unwillingness to create truly modern women.

In *S.* Sarah Worth's* letters describe an independent woman rebelling against her routine life as a wealthy eye doctor's wife. Though she still retains the pretensions of her privileged life, and though she clearly has not weaned herself from the love of exquisite objects, she learns at the ashram to curb her condescending attitude. Her modish enthusiasm, along with that of other bored housewives, for Eastern philosophy becomes a vocation and leads to the unmasking of a fake (male) religious leader and her clever absconding with the cult's funds. But feminists note that whether she is married or divorced, Sarah is still dependent upon men, and that her embezzlement simply shows her choosing to play by men's rules in order to succeed by using outmoded feminine wiles. Updike's use of self-reflexive irony, in which Sarah satirically incriminates herself without knowing so, undermines her serious interests in spiritual growth. Since Sarah is modeled on Nathaniel Hawthorne's* Hester Prynne, Updike has smeared one of the great feminist saints. The fact remains, however, that Updike has tried to create a woman's voice, since Sarah speaks only through her letters in this epistolary novel. Her letters enable us to hear her as a complete person.

The way to power for women, Updike thus seems to suggest, is still through powerful men, and this is certainly true of Essie Wilmot/Alma DeMott,* whose rise to film* stardom takes the familiar path, since she recognizes that the currency of Hollywood is sex (*IB*). First a male photographer exploits her as a sex* object, then important producers advance that exploitation, and finally she gains her visibility by securing screen roles opposite marquee-name actors. Yet Alma also plays by her own rules by keeping in mind an almost mystical involvement with her audience. She imagines her image on the rectangular screen as completing the "family rectangle" whose corner was torn when her grandfather, who introduced her to movies, died after failing as a minister.* Yet Alma's reliance upon men is hardly the same as that of Sarah Worth or the witches. Through her identification with her grandfather, Alma discovers an empowerment that is wholly her own, as much an aspect of her creative imagination as her intuitive ability to identify with a vast range of women characters. She embraces her ability to serve as a flexible symbol of so many women for so many different audiences, and she adjusts to the demands of new technology as she slips easily from the silver screen to the television* tube.

When feminists remarked that Updike's intentions were good, but his execution revealed him still stuck in a conventional way of presenting women, Updike offered a more self-reliant Janice Angstrom* than the first books of *RA* revealed. Her rise to power as a real estate sales representative permits her to extricate Springer Motors* from bankruptcy and support her son through drug* rehabilitation and her husband through angioplasty. She has also selected two lovers, saved one from death, and saved her marriage through strength of will. Yet Janice is a middle-class woman whose development seems less important to Updike's feminist critics than the depiction of professional women. Updike has answered, however, that he writes about what he knows and that such women are not available to him as literary characters.* He understands the conditions set for women by the patriarchal society, and that society is the material for his creative work. He will thus never be satisfying to feminists who refuse to grant him his subject and ignore his own increasing awareness and sympathy for women. Such sympathy was shown very early in his work. In *PF* he describes the artistic ability of Amy Mortis and of those who make quilts. In *RR* Updike provides sympathetic interior monologues of Ruth Leonard Byer and Janice Angstrom (the latter the most powerful writing in the novel) to take us directly into the world as they know it. In *Couples* he provides the letters of Foxy Whitman* to reveal her own sense of self through the language she selects. These few examples taken from Updike's early novels show that he did not suddenly come to some realization that he needed to be more balanced in his appraisal of women because feminists were uneasy with his portrayals. To miss this is to miss the sense of development in Updike's writing. *See* **Femmes Fatales**.

Bibliography: Updike, "A Woman's Burden" (*MM*); Mary Allen, "John Updike's Love of 'Dull Bovine Beauty,' " in *The Necessary Blankness: Women in Major American Fiction of the Sixties* (Urbana: University of Illinois Press, 1976), 97–132; Josephine Hendin, *Vulnerable People: A View of American Fiction since 1945* (New York: Oxford University Press, 1978), 88–99; Stacey Olster, " 'Unadorned Woman, Beauty's Home Image': Updike's *Rabbit, Run*," in *New Essays on Rabbit, Run*, ed. Stanley Trachtenberg (New York: Cambridge University Press, 1993), 95–117; O'Connell, *UP*.

Femmes Fatales. Women who are dangers to men and who may delight in embarrassing or destroying them—femmes fatales—appear throughout Updike's work, but particularly in *RA*. In *RR* Harry "Rabbit" Angstrom* runs because he finds his marriage second-rate. His wife Janice Angstrom* had trapped him by her premarital pregnancy, and her delivery of their second child returns him to her, with tragic results. Rabbit's lover Ruth Leonard Byer* traps him with a threat to abort their child if he does not divorce Janice. Lucy Eccles* leads Rabbit to believe that she is interested in him, and when he rejects what he thinks is an invitation, she refuses to help him contact her husband, Rev. Jack Eccles,* when he is distraught. Later she accuses him of "as good as" killing his daughter. When Janice leaves him in *RRed*, Rabbit takes a young runaway, Jill Pendleton,* for his lover, but her presence, along with that of a black criminal, Skeeter,* brings about the burning of his home. Janice also decides that Rabbit will not see Margaret Fosnacht, with whom he had spent the night as his house burned, to thwart Rabbit's interest in her. In *RIR* Rabbit is trapped by both Janice's inheritance of Springer Motors,* which makes him rich but lacking in authority, and her mother's disdain. Rabbit finds his early sense of transcendence engulfed by materialism. He also witnesses how his son Nelson Angstrom* is not only trapped, as he was, by a premarital pregnancy, but maneuvered into marriage by Janice. In addition, it is likely that Janice helped to arrange the spousal sharing, since she was interested in Webb Murkett"; afterward she insisted that they would no longer see Ronnie Harrison* and his wife Thelma Harrison* because Rabbit had slept with her during the wife swapping. Janice's support of Nelson in *RaR* pits father against son, nearly destroying the business; her neglect of Rabbit on his return from the hospital makes him vulnerable to the temptations of his daughter-in-law, precipitating admission of their one-night affair, Rabbit's flight to Florida* and his eventual death.* Also, Ruth Leonard, from spite, brings Rabbit a lifetime of frustration when she refuses to acknowledge if she aborted their child or not (*RaR*).

But the chief femme fatale for Rabbit, driving his entire life, may be his mother, Mary Angstrom.* She supplied him with a sense of what critic Joyce Markle calls "specialness," enabling him to excel as a basketball* player, which later became the source of his dissatisfaction, his lost first-ratedness. However, Mary Angstrom also taught him a hardness of heart toward women by advising him to leave Janice and his son in *RRed* during her affair. In *RRed* Jack Eccles had left Lucy, his children and the ministry, partly because her hectoring had forced him to admit that he loved only those who could not return love and was a failure at saving souls. Eccles thus mirrors Rabbit in the abuse he receives from women, but frees himself in a way Rabbit cannot.

In *RRed* another destructive woman, Margaret Fosnacht, lures Rabbit away from his live-in mistress Jill Pendleton, and his neglect costs Jill her life. Jill, the open, available woman, is an ambiguous femme fatale, ingenuously driving a wedge between Rabbit and Nelson, frustrating Janice's efforts at reconciliation, and helping to hide Skeeter from arrest, but making Skeeter more vulnerable in the process. In *RIR* Rabbit's attraction to Cindy Murkett* nearly leads to his death when he capsizes their Sunfish. In a parallel scene Updike suggests that even Rabbit's granddaughter Judy* endangers him when another Sunfish capsizes and Judy plays a prank that nearly kills him (*RaR*). Rabbit's daughter-in-law Teresa "Pru" Angstrom* entices him into sleeping with her in *RaR*, then betrays him to his family, irrevocably estranging him from them and contributing to his death. When Rabbit returns from angioplasty, Janice neglects him by attending a real-estate quiz, and while he is dying, she realizes that his obstruction to her plan to sell the house would be overcome by his death. Though another femme fatale, Thelma Harrison, establishes a ten-year affair with Rabbit, her willingness to please him only leads him to a discovery of death through sex* (*RIR*), and her confession of the affair to Ronnie Harrison accelerates a complete rupture between the old teammates (*RaR*).

Such sirens dominate Updike's presentation of women, from the interfering Rebecca Cune ("Snowing in Greenwich Village" [*SD*]) to Isabel Leme,* whose selection of Tristão Raposo* for her first lover brings on his death (*B*), from Vera Hummel, who puts George Caldwell's* job in jeopardy even though he resists her (*C*), to Ann Coleman,* whose hysteria and death put James Buchanan* in momentary disgrace (*BD*, *MF*), and from Foxy Whitman,* who not only ruins two marriages but exiles herself and her lover from Tarbox (*Couples*), to the woman who draws Richard Maple* from his wife and four children (*TF*). Yet, though these women often bring about disaster, they also serve to regenerate men whose ambitions would otherwise remain dormant, as Caldwell, St. Augustine,* President Buchanan and Claudius* show. Rev. Roger Lambert* seems to regain interest in his marriage after his affair with Verna Ekelof,* his half-sister's daughter, who had lured him with the knowledge that through her he might make love to his half-sister (*RV*). *See* **Sex**.

Bibliography: Markle, *FL*: O'Connell, *UP*.

Feng (also Fengon). *See* **Claudius**.

Film. Film references appear with great regularity throughout Updike's work. The experience of the movie theater itself for him was thrilling. Film plots, characters, actors and images immediately moved him, and in his writing he uses them to make his ideas concrete and his people more visual. Individual films often bring characters to illuminations, and they aid Updike himself to clarify the question, "Who am I?" Also, Updike has experimented with adopting film techniques to fiction.

In several works Updike recounts his thrill at attending movie theaters. They represent an exotic place that houses a world of excitement and wonder. In "The Old Movie Houses" (*MM*) he asserts that the elegant details and spaciousness of the old "theatres of dream" were "designed to inculcate a religious mood. . . . No wonder so many of the vacant theatres are now churches. We worshipped in those spaces." Critic Donald Greiner points out that in his poem "Movie House" (*TP*), Updike says that theaters "tell man's story best." But Harry "Rabbit" Angstrom* witnesses how the downward spiral of America carries the theaters with it. In one decade he sees that "the old Baghdad that used to show M-G-M" now is given over to pornography (*Sepia Follies, Honeymoon in Swapland*) (*RRed*). For Updike, the theater is a secular church, and the silver screen within it "captivates" and "hypnotizes." The huge images enable ordinary people to find their personal sense of importance objectified through expanded images of themselves. In *IB* he suggests that the rectangular screen resembles America's roughly rectangular shape; the screen gives back great images that awe, inspire and transport ordinary lives into something epic.

Since his Shillington* High School days, when he reviewed dozens of movies, Updike has employed film in his writings, sometimes just the titles, sometimes by a casual allusion to a film star. He has used all sorts of films—cartoons, comedies, tragedies, melodramas and costume epics, violent action films, pornography and love stories—in all his writing, fiction, poetry* and nonfiction. Of all his books, only *BD*, set in the nineteenth century, contains no film references. Alluding to hundreds of films from *Adam's Rib* to *Ziegfeld Girl*, Updike has also written nonfiction essays about Doris Day, Gene Kelly, Lana Turner and Goldie Hawn. He unfailingly records screen personalities throughout his work from Bud Abbott to Carl Zuckmayer, including directors, producers, writers and administrators. In *Marry* Jerry Conant* meets Marlene Dietrich in an airline terminal in Nice, France, and in "Ace in the Hole" (*SD*) Updike shows how the style of film stars has been adopted by the young married. In *IB* Updike creates a film star as his central figure, and Essie Wilmot/Alma DeMott* not only stars opposite film personalities like Paul Newman, she even has affairs with them. *IB* is certainly Updike's most vigorous exploration of everything related to movies, and Alma's dedication to the rectangular screen posits her intuition that she can supply a new spiritual leadership against her grandfather's loss of faith.

Individual films are often used to underline themes and offer methods of exploring character. *Bell, Book and Candle* in *RR*, for example, offers ironic views of Harry "Rabbit" Angstrom's quest for love. Critic Dilvo Ristoff has shown how *The Return of Martin Guerre* and *Working Girl* operate thematically and reveal character in *RaR*. After seeing *Working Girl*, Janice Angstrom* becomes convinced that she can become a real-estate seller; she does, and this leads her to neglect her husband Rabbit, while it proves to her that she has an objective worth never before tapped. Watching *The Return of Martin Guerre* on television, Rabbit considers the advantages of changing families every decade, forgetting that doing so cost Guerre his life. Janice has discovered a new life through film; Rabbit has imagined one, but his alternative is impossible, though ironically his liaison with Teresa "Pru" Angstrom* for one night suggests that he can find a better life than the one he leads (*RaR*).

But a single film in a novel may activate connections beyond character and theme. Stanley Kubrick's *2001: A Space Odyssey** in *RRed* supplies a form and controlling images to the novel and stimulates deeper understanding of the action. First, the movie brackets the action by appearing at the beginning and end of the novel, paralleling not only the circularity of the action but the possibility of reeducation by a review of the past. Second, *2001* contains a quest theme similar to that of the novel: the flights of Janice from her husband Harry "Rabbit" Angstrom, Jill Pendleton* from her parents' upper-class world and Skeeter* from the police and the history of white America all parallel the flight of the astronauts to the moon, since all have taken flight and are on a journey whose outcome is unknown. Third, since *2001*'s dark monolith appears to communicate some profound meaning, it resembles Skeeter, whose Vietnam* experience has provided him a new understanding of America, which he is certain will undergo a race war in which he will emerge as the Black Messiah. He communicates this to a bemused Rabbit, just as the monolith tries to communicate its mysterious meaning to mankind. Fourth, the image of the "Star Child" at the film's end touches Janice deeply, perhaps reconnecting her to Rebecca "Becky" Angstrom,* the baby she accidentally drowned in *RR*. The Star Child's enormous image indicates both the huge guilt Janice had carried and the great importance of the baby to her. Becky thus returns to her and facilitates Janice's acceptance of her death. But the film's image of the space station that looks like a "wheel" suggests autoerotic things to Janice and leads her to recall her encounter with her lover. Kubrick's imagery has penetrated Updike's characters* and has facilitated his own exploration of character.

Teased by the example of James Joyce* and others to apply cinematic devices to fiction, Updike tried, modestly, to create a cinematic montage in *PF* and, gaining confidence, originally called *Rabbit, Run*: A Movie and wrote the novel in the present tense to approximate the presentness of film. He employed another cinematic montage in a dream chapter of *C*. Then, after selling *Couples* to Hollywood, Updike hoped to write the script of his love story because the purchasers mistook it for a satire. The film was never made, and Updike, who once wanted to work for Walt Disney,* eventually became convinced that cinematic effects were poor vehicles for the ambiguity or introspection of character that were his fictional goals. His study of the French "new wave" cinema convinced him that too much was sacrificed when film devices were imported into fiction. Such novels lacked the concrete texture of life.

Finally, film has aided Updike's personal quest for meaning, since, as he said, George Sanders, Errol Flynn and others helped him form a code of conduct as an adolescent. Richard Maple* admits the same thing, that he took his "ideals of behavior" from film stars: "coolness" from Humphrey Bogart, "debonair recklessness" from Errol Flynn and "duality and deceit" from Superman ("Gesturing" [*TF*]). Updike's mature philosophy about the nature of being was later clarified for him by Peter Seller's performance as the man without identity, Chance Gardner, in *Being There*. Updike found in it a "philosophical allegory" in which " 'being there' = Heidegger's *Dasein*." (Updike had reviewed Jerzy Kosinski's novel *Being There*, the novel on which the film was based [*PP*]). It is "the first mystery that confronts us, 'Why me?' The next is 'Why here?' Shillington was my here" ("A Soft Spring Night in Shillington" [*SC*]). Film has occupied Updike at every level of his being. *See* **Art; Cartooning; Films Made from Updike's Works; Griffith, D. W.; Popular Culture**.

Bibliography: Updike, "One Big Interview" (*PP*); "Books into Media," "A Nameless Rose," "Suzie Creamcheese Speaks," "On One's Own Oeuvre" (*HS*); "Heavily Hyped Helga" (*JL*); "Overboard on *Overboard*" (*OJ*); "The Old Movie Houses," "*Samson and Delilah* and Me," "Legendary Lana," "Books into Film," "Genial, Kinetic Gene Kelly" (*MM*); Greiner, *OJ*; Newman, *JU*; Jack De Bellis, " 'The Awful Power': John Updike's Use of Kubrick's *2001: A Space Odyssey* in *Rabbit Redux*," *Literature/ Film Quarterly* 21.3 (1993): 209–17; Jack De Bellis, " 'It Captivates . . . It Hypnotizes': Updike Goes to the Movies, *Literature/Film Quarterly* 23.3 (1995): 169–87; Ristoff, *JU*.

Films Made from Updike's Works. Three full-length films have been made of Updike's works: the novels *RR* and *W* and a few stories from *TF* (a title created when the collection accompanied the film's release). Four short films were made from stories: "A & P" (*PigF*), "The Music School" (*MuS*), "The Christian Roommates" as *The Roommate* (*MuS*) and "Pigeon Feathers" (*PigF*). Dramatized scenes from *RA* are included in *The South Bank Show*, a British survey of the work after the release of *RaR*. Of these short films only "A & P" has not been shown on television.

RR, produced by Warner Brothers–Seven Arts in 1970, was directed by Jack Smight and starred James Caan as Harry "Rabbit" Angstrom,* Anjanette Comer as Ruth Leonard (Byer),* Carrie Snodgrass as Janice Angstrom* and Jack Albertson as Rev. Jack Eccles.* Updike had been interested in working for Walt Disney* when he was young, and he was eager to write the screenplay for *RR*, but he was not offered the chance. He wanted to write it particularly since he had employed present-tense narration in the novel to approximate the "presentness" of film and had originally called the book *Rabbit, Run: A Movie*. Updike was impressed by the film's ability to particularize physical facts of the Angstroms' life, and he felt that James Caan, if not a perfect Rabbit, moved like an athlete. He liked the actresses, though he felt that Comer was too slender for Ruth. Since the film was shot on location in Reading,* Pennsylvania, the film's setting was especially vivid to him, as were the uses of songs and the drowning of Rebecca Angstrom.* He must have liked Smight's displaying the Pascal epigraph* as well. But of course the language was lost, along with Rabbit's dreams and visions. Why, then, would he permit the novel to be transferred to an alien mode, so dependent upon multiple workers, money and intangibles like weather? Though he feared that this book would be lost in translation to the screen, as with *Couples* (sold but never produced) and *W*, Updike was willing to "let them do their own things, while my text, safe between covers, did its." He understood what film would do, that film "breaks upon us like a natural phenomenon—ungainsayable, immediate, stark, marvelous, and rather bullying." Though he made suggestions about the making of the film, Updike knew that "the inner story" could not be told. Finally, he found the enterprise "intensely embarrassing" (*PP*), yet when Rabbit saw *RR* being made in *RRed*—a postmodern touch—he was dazzled.

W, produced by Warner Brothers in 1987, was directed by George Miller and starred Jack Nicholson as Darryl Van Horne,* Cher as Alexandra Spofford,* Michelle Pfeiffer as Jane Smart* and Susan Sarandon as Sukie Rougemont.* George Miller took enormous liberties with the book, providing a surreal chase scene at the end, altering the plot so that the witches would not kill Jenny Gabriel, providing Jack Nicholson with opportunities for bravura acting, changing the religious thrust of Van Horne's attack on God to an attack on women, and eliminating Jane Smart's revelations about death. Above all, to Updike the women were not shown equal to men in evil, his major feminist thrust in the novel. The film was entertainment, not an exploration into evil. Updike's response was to acknowledge that film and fiction have different aesthetic goals: "The visceral simplicity of cinema embarrasses criticism" (*OJ*). Yet he did write his film agent to say that he enjoyed the "skating around in pink balloons," but "the less it resembled my book, the better I felt," since "successful movies tend to take off from the book, rather than take it seriously" (*OJ*). Updike recognizes that filmmakers "owe nothing to the authors of books they adapt except the money they have agreed to pay them," and the author owes only "a tactful silence" (*OJ*).

Updike stories from the 1960s and 1970s were made into films, primarily for use in high schools. "The Music School" (*MuS*), written with a weaving of images rather than straight narrative, would have seemed likely to make a good film. The story's most successful part, Updike thought, was the description of a novel of the future shot through pink filters. But Updike felt that the film made the hero's guilt "positively sodden." "The Christian Roommates" (*MuS*), a story often taught to freshmen at Harvard,* was reduced to *The Roommates* as a film and struck Updike as "lugubrious" because the roommates' jittery antipathy "turns downright pathological." Better were the standard treatments of the stories comprising *Too Far to Go*, selected from *TF*. Blythe Danner and Michael Moriarty give restrained performances that make the film touching. The same could be said of "Pigeon Feathers," the last of Updike's stories to be made into a film (1988). Since Updike is a remarkable stylist, he worried, correctly, that such "stubbornly verbal stories" as "The Music School" and "Pigeon Feathers" would not fare well as movies. Ultimately, he said, any film adaptations would seem, "to the author of the original, heavy on detail and light on coherence." Perhaps one of his characters spoke for him when he said, "The movies cannot show the precipitous, palpable slope you cling to within" (*P*). *See* **Film**.

Bibliography: Updike, "Embarrassed," *TV Guide* (December 6, 1986); Frank Gado, "Writer in the Middle," *Idol* 47 (Spring 1971): 3–32.

Firetown. Firetown in "Pigeon Feathers" (*PigF*) and other early stories, as well as the novel *C*, is the fictitious analogue of Plowville,* Pennsylvania. The Updike family moved to Plowville in 1945 when Linda Hoyer Updike* purchased her parents' farm. *See* **Alton; Brewer**.

The Fisherman and His Wife. *Texas Arts Journal*, Summer, 1977: 14–38. Uncollected. *The Fisherman and His Wife* is a children's opera adapted by Updike from a tale by the brothers Grimm, with music by Gunther Schuller. It was commissioned by the Junior League of Boston in 1967 as a gift to the children of Boston. The transformation theme (the wife catches a fish who is really a prince) is a recurrent motif in Updike, appearing in *C* (George Caldwell* is an analogue of Chiron* the centaur), *W* (ordinary housewives who are witches kill a woman through magic), *B* (black and white lovers exchange color) and *TE* (a deer metamorphoses into a woman, and Ben

Turnbull* branches into four different people in widely separate times and places). Just as Updike recognized points of connection between Chiron and Christ, in the Grimms' tale he discovered parallels between the fisherman's wife and Eve in their common desire to be godlike.

Flanagan, Edward Joseph, Father (1886–1948). The founder, in 1917, of Boys Town, an Omaha, Nebraska, home for homeless and troubled boys and, after 1979, girls, Father Edward Joseph Flanagan provided education and guidance and became known for his remark, "There's no such thing as a bad boy." Boys Town was made famous by the 1938 film* starring Spencer Tracy, for which he earned an Oscar. Since 1983 Boys Towns have sprouted around the country, and the related sites offer various family-centered counseling services. In "A Gift from the City" (*SD*), though James is sympathetic enough to contribute to Father Flanagan's cause, he is afraid to emulate Father Flanagan to an annoying Negro in need. James fears the Negro particularly since he comes to his apartment and coerces his wife. These requests for charity test his values after he moves to New York,* where he feels keenly that he may well be duped. *See* **African Americans**.

Bibliography: Jack De Bellis, "The Group and John Updike," *Sewanee Review* 72 (Summer 1964): 531–32; Greiner, *OJ*.

Florida. Symbolizing the fountain of youth in the four novels of *RA*, in each novel Florida gets progressively closer as Harry "Rabbit" Angstrom* ages. At first, Rabbit intends to drive south after his flight from his family to rest on the Gulf of Mexico's sands, but he never gets closer than West Virginia (*RR*). His rival Charlie Stavros* does get to Florida's west coast, though, when he seduces Melanie (*RIR*); Rabbit merely flies over the state on his way to a Caribbean vacation (*RIR*). In *RaR* Rabbit retires to Deleon,* on Florida's west coast, but his son Nelson* interrupts his rest by nearly destroying Springer Motors.* Later in the novel Rabbit runs to Florida for the last time after Teresa "Pru" Angstrom* reveals that they have slept together; he dies there. Florida may symbolize for Rabbit "the thing that wants me to find it," Eden, which becomes death.* Vietnam* is described by Skeeter* in *RRed* as Florida-like and Edenic, and the Brazilian interior that promises Tristâo Raposo* and Isabel Leme* freedom, love, protection and wealth becomes a place where they must kill to survive (*B*). Likewise, Florida, as the paradise of Ponce de León's* Fountain of Youth and a place of death, becomes Rabbit's ultimate hutch. Updike's mother, Linda Updike,* had planned a book on Ponce de León, and Updike named Deleon in her honor. *See* **Pastoral**.

Food. Throughout his work Updike pays attention to every appetite and what satisfies each, among them the appetite for food. Harry "Rabbit" Ang-

strom,* as befits a man nicknamed for a rabbit, repeatedly refers to his preference for rabbit food, food that shows no trace of having come from a
living animal. Fittingly, the MagiPeel Kitchen Peeler he demonstrates in *RR*
processes vegetables, but in his home he fixates on a television* commercial
for Tootsie Rolls. He connects sweets to sex* when he thinks of Lucy Eccles*
as a "sharp vanilla cookie." As a rabbit, he prefers nuts, Chinese food and
shoofly pie. A bad cook, Janice Angstrom* is immune to Rabbit's quip about
his MagiPeel Kitchen Peeler saving her drudgery in the kitchen (*RR*). Meanwhile, he thinks of Margaret Fosnacht's body as candy, "gumdrops," as he
makes love to her (*RRed*). A decade later Janice still buys TV dinners, partly
for the attractiveness of the picture on the box (*RIR*). Rabbit finds a kindred
spirit in Ruth Leonard Byer* when they realize that they both enjoy Chinese
food (*RR*), and a similar bond is established between Rabbit and Jill Pendleton* (*RRed*), Melanie (*RIR*) and Teresa "Pru" Angstrom,* though he
strays from their nutritional care when he is left to himself. In *RaR* we learn
that Rabbit, despite Janice's rather tepid insistence that he restrain his use
of sodium and other harmful items, has continued to poison himself, ironically from fears of death,* and clogs his arteries so that he has two heart
attacks, the second fatal.

Janice makes roasts for company, but in each case they are prompted by
interest in another person, for example, in matching her former lover Charlie
Stavros* with Melanie because she fears that Melanie will cause Nelson Angstrom* to stray from the woman he impregnated, Pru, and not follow
through with Janice's plan that he marry Pru (*RIR*). Like Janice, Esther
Lambert* also invites a guest, but this is a presumptive lover, Dale Kohler,*
and their conversation about pie becomes a code for their mutual interest
(*RV*). Alexandra "Lexa" Spofford* opens *W* by preparing spaghetti sauce to
use up a bumper crop of backyard tomatoes. She notes the similarity between
the sauce and her menstrual fluid, thus joining together the energy of the
natural world to her reproductive power while performing conventional domestic duties. Lexa feels that making the sauce may be a tribute to her Italian
lover, just as Janice takes her family to a Greek restaurant to bask in the
atmosphere of her Greek lover, Stavros (*RRed*). A decade later Rabbit buys
Jill Pendleton* a Cashewburger at Burger Bliss, knowing that she will pay
for the food later with sex. Jill explains, "I usually try to rise above food."
As Jill deteriorates through drug* addiction, so does her cuisine; her meals
become inedible. Ten years later, when Rabbit goes to the restaurant where
Melanie had waitressed, he selects one of the most destructive salads for his
meal while discussing with Stavros whether or not to have heart bypass
surgery (*RaR*). Darryl Van Horne* uses food imagery* to explain his quest
for a reversal of natural laws as only the effort to find "mayonnaise" for the
new "sandwich" he hopes to make of a mixture of undiscovered elements
(*W*). See **Eating**.

Ford, Gerald (1913–   ). As president of the United States (1974–76), after Richard Nixon resigned following the Watergate scandal, Gerald Ford's first words were, "Our long national nightmare is over," and a month later he pardoned Richard Nixon "for any crimes he committed or may have committed." The pardon contributed to Ford's lack of popularity and ineffectiveness as president. Ford presided over the collapse of American forces in Vietnam,* ordering the evacuation of the Saigon Embassy in April 1975. The Republican party moved further to the right during Ford's tenure, leading to the eventual challenge by Ronald Reagan in 1976. At the end of *MF*, Ford is a barely described "present absence," since Alf Clayton* can recall nearly nothing about Ford's administration. Instead, Clayton records that during Ford's time he had an adulterous affair and was unable to finish a book about an equally ignored but underrated president, James Buchanan.* *See* **Presidents**.

Franz Joseph I (1830–1916). Habsburg emperor of Austria (1848–1916) and king of Hungary (1867–1916), Franz Joseph I is mentioned in "Slippage" (*TM*). He became emperor during the revolution of 1848, but his stand on the Crimean War and the loss of Italian possessions weakened the empire, as did his disagreement with the Hungarian and German rulers over Slav independence after Austria and Hungary merged in 1867. His only son and heir, Archduke Rudolf, committed suicide (alluded to in T. S. Eliot's* *The Waste Land*), and his nephew, Francis Ferdinand, heir to the throne in 1914, was assassinated. The murder led to World War I and extinguished the Habsburg monarchy. In "Slippage" Professor Morrison, fearing that his masterwork will not be written, becomes preoccupied about the death of Franz Joseph as he falls asleep.

French literature. Of all French writers, Marcel Proust* has had the most enduring influence upon Updike's style* and point of view. Proust provided him with the great theme of time and the yearning to recapture the past, and also with a lyricism that enriched the theme. Updike's early and continuing interest in nostalgia and stream-of-consciousness writing shows his absorption in Proust, and he describes the impact of Proust on such novelists as Edith Wharton.

At Harvard* Updike read Jean-Paul Sartre and Albert Camus, and he provides the Marxist Col Félix Ellelloû* with similar existential reading in André Gide, Sartre and Jean Genet. The three existentialists are concerned with questions of freedom and responsibility, of great concern to Ellelloû as he tries to keep his people from being drawn into the spheres of either the Soviet Union or the United States. André Gide (1869–1951), like Sartre, focused upon the question of discovering identity through a "gratuitous act." His *Travels in the Congo* (1929) is said to have brought on reforms in French colonial law. At first an admirer of Russian communism, Gide published his disenchantment on returning from the USSR in 1936.

Jean-Paul Sartre (1905–1980) blended philosophical searches for authentic existence with a quest for the social role of the artist. As a philosophically but not politically committed Communist, he sought the merging of art* and politics to effect social change. Sartre's focus on freedom through individual responsibility is at variance with the political freedom with which Ellellô irresponsibly robs the natives of Kush of their authentic selves. Updike's epigraph* to OF quotes Sartre's realization that in seeking freedom for yourself, you must also want freedom for others. The epigraph directs the reader's attention to both the selfishness with which Mrs. Robinson* reacts to her son's search for happiness with his second wife, and her refusal to will his first wife's happiness. Perhaps Joey Robinson* also has problems in willing the freedom of his wife. The epigraph could stand for all of Updike's books.

Sartre wrote a biography of the novelist and playwright Jean Genet (1910–1986), who also was convinced of the need to rebel against convention to discover the true self, even to the point of murder. In The Blacks (1959), as in his novels, Genet used role playing to ridicule bourgeois values. His concern for "Negritude" in his play The Blacks appealed to Ellellô (Coup). The sexually curious Freddy Thorne* keeps Genet's Our Lady of the Flowers by his bedside and assumes the role of spokesman for modern couples (Couples). Elsewhere Updike notes that Albert Camus (1913–1960) wished to anatomize the "emotional emptiness of modern, Godless man." This ambition places Updike in the company of Camus. Updike has reviewed such French writers as Louis-Ferdinand Céline, Raymond Queneau, Robert Pinget and Nathalie Sarraute and in passing shows his familiarity with the history of French literature. See European Literature.

Bibliography: Updike, "Honest Horn" (AP); "A Foreword to the French Edition of Facing Nature" (MM).

Freud, Sigmund (1856–1939). An Austrian psychiatrist and founder of psychoanalysis (1896), Sigmund Freud is mentioned and quoted repeatedly in Updike's work to expand his treatment of sexuality in literature and to provide insights into character. Updike has said that Freud helped him as a writer and helped America cleanse itself of the Puritan view of sex.* Such convictions enabled Updike to champion a sexual frankness in his and others' writing, in the tradition of James Joyce,* Henry Miller,* Edmund Wilson* and D. H. Lawrence. Though Updike clearly employs many of Freud's theories throughout his work, he is also wary of Freud, sometimes attacking him obliquely through his characters.* Since Updike is concerned with "middleness,"* he might have connected this to Freud's concern for the ego, the midground in which demands of the id clash with the restraints of the superego in the battlefield of the ego.

In his early work Updike employed Freud's theory that all persons pass through the oral, anal and genital stages in forming the superego. Though one might see the concern for fellatio and cunnilingus as aspects of the oral stage (ages one to three) that has become an oral fixation in *RA* and *Couples*, Updike has said that oral attachment could be considered a kind of sacred feeding. Problems at the anal stage seem quite appropriate to "anal-retentive" types like Harry "Rabbit" Angstrom*; *RRed* contains a wealth of scatological imagery, and *RIR* connects feces with money: Nelson Angstrom,* Rabbit's son, says succinctly, "Money is shit."

Problems in sexual development may stem from difficulties at the genital stage, ages three to five. For men, complications include problems with authority figures and prolonged attachment to the mother. Oedipal problems for both men and women occur mainly in such early stories and novels as "Flight" (*PigF*), *RR, C, OF*, and *Couples*. In *RR* Lucy Eccles* states, "I think Freud is like God." Though Rabbit does not know who Freud is, he is shocked with her application of the Oedipal complex to her own children when she remarks that her three-year-old daughter Joyce is responding to "sexual antagonism" for her, shown in Joyce's desire to climb into bed with her husband, Rev. Jack Eccles.* Jack Eccles thinks that this is absurd and later explains to Rabbit, "Children are very sacred in psychology." (In *OJ* Updike says that Freud considers the infant "the fundamental stewpot.") This scene suggests Rabbit's larger problems in his resistance to his father and bond with his mother, who has the most "force." Rabbit's problem might have been encapsulated in Updike's remark in a review of Colette in which he notes "Freud's assertion that a mother's favorite keeps for life 'that confidence of success which often induces real success' " (*HS*). Updike shows Rabbit's high valuation of himself contributing to a hardness of heart, especially toward women, that grows harder throughout *RA*. Certainly, his unresolved problems interfere with his son Nelson's passage through his anal stage, since his drug* dependency nearly destroys Springer Motors,* and Nelson's passage through his Oedipal stage, since he fantasizes, "Why doesn't Dad just die?" (*RIR*). Also, the stories in *PigF*, the novel *C* and poems like "Leaving Church Early" (*TT*) describe fathers who are inept and embarrassing and who, in the son's eyes, stand between son and mother, as Peter Caldwell* of *C* states. In *OF* the dead father's son wears his clothes and, for a time, sides with his mother against his second wife.

In *Couples* Updike blends Freud's theory of the relation of sex and death* with the Tristan and Isolde* love affair of Piet Hanema* and Foxy Whitman.* Piet's wife reads *The Interpretation of Dreams*, and so does Freddy Thorne,* who also keeps by his bedside Freud's *Beyond the Pleasure Principle*, along with Richard von Krafft-Ebing (whose *Psychopathia Sexualis* concerns sexual deviation), Theodore Reik, a loyal early student of Freud who developed the theory of the psychology of love, Wilhelm Reich, Freud's early supporter and purveyor of the notorious theory of orgone energy, and Karl Menninger (of the Menninger Clinic, Topeka, Kansas). Freud and his followers seem guilty because they are admired by "lord of misrule" Freddy Thorne, who proposes that he and his friends are making sex the new religion since the church has failed to "humanize" them. This oblique attack on Freud by way of Thorne is repeated in the depiction of menacing Roger Lambert,* an ex-minister who is particularly attracted to Freud's view that sexual desire leads to death, which he calls "being screwed by God" (*RV*). In these and other novels Updike seems to agree with Freud's aphorism in *Civilization and Its Discontents*, "The more complex the society, the more neurotic its inhabitants." *RA* depicts a society growing increasingly complex, and Updike carefully depicts signs of its increasing disorder.

Though sympathetic to psychoanalytical theory, Updike views practical psychoanalysis critically. Sally Mathias hates "goddamn" analysis and thinks that she bore her children to satisfy her analyst. Her lover Jerry Conant* despises it too, but Richard Mathias affirms the importance of therapy and says that his wife's affair nearly drove him back to it (*Marry*). To Piet Hanema, his wife Angela Hanema's* therapy resembles witchcraft. Marcia Smith and Janet Appleby also see therapists as a result of their adulteries* with each other's husbands. The therapy of Janet and Angela focuses on their parents, and Janet becomes ridiculous as she brings her analyst's remarks to bear upon her relations with the couples (*Couples*). In his short fiction* Updike shows additional realism in his attitude toward psychoanalysis. In "The Fairy Godfathers" (*P*) lovers confide their therapists' attitudes and ideas to one another in comic counterpoint. Their psychiatrists' satiric names, Oz and Rhadamanthus (which pit a wizard against "read a man thus"), connote an inept ruler and a judge in the Underworld, yet they make their analysands feel that their lives exist to feed their therapy sessions. In "My Love Has Dirty Fingernails" (*TF*) Joan Maple* enters therapy because of the adultery of her husband, Richard Maple.* The abstract and theoretical response given to her by her analyst infuriates her, though she does not discontinue therapy.

Freud's question, What do women want? appears with regularity in the minds of Updike characters and is particularly distressing to Ben Turnbull,* who has spent much of his life puzzling over it (*TE*). Though women speak for themselves in first-person segments in *RR*, *Couples* and the epistolary *S.*, they do not settle the question. In a review of Freud's fellow Austrian, painter Egon Schiele, Updike uses as a guide Freud's observation from *Civilization and Its Discontents* that the love of beauty derives from sexual feeling; thus the love of beauty is "an impulse inhibited in its aim" ("Can the Genitals Be Beautiful?" uncollected). Dreams* could be thought to do the same, since dreams deflect the material of sexual desire or wish fulfillment into something else, mechanisms described in detail in Freud's *Outline of Psychoanalysis*.

Dream theory led Freud to his theories of infantile sexuality and the Oedipal complex, and Updike uses them to explore these and other psychic dimensions. *See* **Art; Jung, Carl Gustav; Sex.**

Bibliography: Updike, "Can the Genitals Be Beautiful?" *New York Review of Books* 44 (4 Dec. 1997): 10. Markle, *FL*; Robert Detweiler, "Updike's *A Month of Sundays* and the Language of the Unconscious," *Journal of the American Academy of Religion* 47 (Dec. 1979): 611–25; Hunt, *JU*; Detweiler, *JU*; Ancona, *WA*; Newman, *JU*; Jack De Bellis, "Oedipal Angstrom," *Wascana Review* 24 (1989): 45–59; Paula Buck, "The Mother Load," in Broer, *RT*, 150–69.

G

Games. Updike employs games to suggest the intellectual quality and tensions within his characters* and to reveal the social importance of games. Sometimes the games are personal creations, like the insomnia game that helps the hero sleep after a frustrating day ("Incest" [*SD*]) or Rafe's staving off boredom on the bus by matching house numbers to significant events in the history of art* and literature ("Toward Evening" [*SD*]). Sometimes the games are ritualized socializing, like card playing. When Harry "Rabbit" Angstrom* plays bridge with his wife Janice Angstrom* and her mother, Bessie Springer,* the game becomes a ritual of dominance counterpointing the assertion of their power against him. Board games once played by a family are tossed on the dump, and with them an entire segment of a life spent playing father ("Still of Some Use" [*TM*]). Board games serve to structure competitive energies that might otherwise be used for sexual encroachment ("Leaf Season" [*TM*]).

But the most interesting games in *Couples* link the couples ritualistically, appealing to their competitiveness, perceptiveness and personal bond to the group. At the Saltzes, after playing four games of Ghosts, two of Truth and three of Botticelli* (which in *SC* Updike recalls playing at Harvard*), they play Impressions. As a newcomer, Foxy Whitman* is initiated through the test of the "Who am I?" game Botticelli* in which she must discover the group's designation of her as Christine Keeler, a prostitute whose entanglement with British war minister John Profumo* and Soviet naval attaché Eugene Ivanov brought down the British government in 1963. (For legal reasons the British publication had to omit any reference to Keeler, making the end of the game rather incomplete.) When Foxy cries on realizing what the group thinks of her, they understand that she is having an affair with Piet Hanema.* The group's game has caught Foxy off-guard. The game brings an outsider into the fold where there are no secrets, under the cover of a formalized diversion. Freddy Thorne,* the Lord of Misrule, organizes games like Wonderful in which guests name their most wonderful thing. Each detail reveals the personal values of the responder whether he or she chooses to do so or not, thus exposing his or her vulnerabilities to the group and strengthening its cohesion (*Couples*). Beyond social games are metaphorical political "games" played during the oil shortage of 1979 by "Big Oil" (*RIR*), during the Civil War (*BD*) and during the Vietnam* War (*RRed*). *See* **Basketball; Golf; Sports.**

Bibliography: Hunt, *JU*; Newman, *JU*; Jack B. Moore, "Sports, Basketball and Fortunate Failure in the Rabbit Tetralogy," in Broer, *RT*.

Gertrude, Queen of Denmark (also Gerutha and Geruthe; for convenience she is called Gertrude in this entry). The mother of Prince Hamlet* in *GC*, Gertrude considers herself a female who must take what the world offers, so when she is forced by her father, Rorik, to marry King Horwendil without love, she complies. Rorik saw in her a blend of dark and light, since she united his Danish blood and his wife's Wend heritage. Gertrude willingly accepts her male exploitation so long as she gains male protection. Empty of purpose, she spends her life reading French romances and ornamenting her husband's court. But when Gertrude is nearly fifty years old she is pursued by Horwendil's brother Claudius* (earlier called Feng) who by appealing to her vanity awakens her as if she were a princess in a fable. Gertrude, however, prefers presents to Claudius's vision of her as holy wisdom. She rebukes him for attempting to make her into an abstract idea of love, when she simply wants to indulge her passion. After Claudius murders the king (now called Old Hamlet) who had discovered his brother's treachery, Gertrude marries Claudius unaware that he is the killer. Gertrude, feeling guilty for neglecting her son Hamlet, now craves a closer relation to him, but it is too late, and her vanity, founded in her romantic nature, has estranged them. Updike ends her story at this juncture, though readers of *Hamlet* know the aftermath. Although Gertrude is victimized by the patriarchal sexism and ruthless self-aggrandizement of a corrupt court, she failed to take seriously the possibility that she might indeed possess the holy wisdom Claudius had discovered in her. Thus Queen Gertrude recalls Jenny Gabriel of *W* who indulged her erotic desires with the witches and succumbed to Darryl Van Horne.* Like Darryl, Claudius had stirred Gertrude, "permitting her to *be*" (Plath, *CU*). Queen Gertrude is a rare portrait of a middle-aged woman in love, an odd sister to Thelma Harrison.* *See* **Adultery; English Literature; Feminism; Sex.**

Gertrude and Claudius (New York: Knopf, 2000). Updike deliberately modeled *GC* on historical and literary sources as he had done in the "*Scarlet Letter* trilogy"* (*MS, RV* and *S.*) and in *MF*. But while those narratives are set in the modern world, Updike places *GC* in sixteenth-century Denmark and creates a "prequel" to Shakespeare's *Hamlet*. In the novel's three parts, Updike reflects Shakespeare's sources and his play, using ideas from, in Part One, Saxo Grammaticus's *Historia Danica*, written in the twelfth century and translated into English in 1514; in Part Two, F. de Belleforest's *Histoires tragiques*, a sixteenth-century history; and in Part Three, *Hamlet*. Updike's adherence to these three sources presents a difficulty for the reader, since he uses three different names given to the protagonists by the two historians and Shakespeare: Amleth/Hamblet/Hamlet*; Horwendil/Horvendile/Old Hamlet; Gerutha/Geruthe/Gertrude; and Feng/Fengon/Claudius. For clarity, the familiar names from *Hamlet* are used in this entry and other entries related to the characters of *GC*. By employing these sources, Updike creates characters who appear to evolve from the Dark Ages to the Renaissance, and from barbarism to "subtlety," to use Queen Gertrude's* favorite word. Updike provides progressively intricate portraits of Old Hamlet, Gertrude, Hamlet* and Claudius,* while increasing the tension as the tragic knot tightens.

The narrative describes Gertrude's marriage against her will to Old Hamlet, her seduction by his brother Claudius after his return from Italy and Byzantium, his poisoning of Old Hamlet when their betrayal is discovered, and Claudius's marriage to Gertrude and crowning as king. Meanwhile Gertrude's son Hamlet becomes estranged from his mother and stepfather, and *GC* ends nearly where *Hamlet* begins, with rumors of a ghost patrolling the battlements. Updike's abrupt ending apparently intends to allow those familiar with *Hamlet* to savor the ironies of Gertrude's anticipation of Hamlet marrying Ophelia and Claudius's dream of a dynasty.

Deciding to disregard his usual practice of writing about contemporary America, Updike sets his story in sixteenth-century Denmark and creates several problems for him. First, he transfers his customary immersion in modern social problems (with its imagery of popular culture) to another era's unfamiliar political situation. Updike overcomes this difficulty by concentrating on his habitual themes of dysfunctional families, adultery,* revenge and violence, themes he had explored in such recent books as *RA, IB, TE* and *BaB*. Updike dresses these subjects in the imagery of medieval court and countryside, language made overly familiar by the vast number of historical romances and films. Second, Updike's decision to use sixteenth-century Denmark as his setting confines his language to approximations of the voices of Shakespeare and the chroniclers, employing words like "fornacatrice" and imitations of Shakespeare's representation of the verbosity of Polonius and the bombast of Claudius. While this tests Updike's prodigious talent as a novelist capable of creating any sort of character, it can lead to unintentional parody. Third, Updike's treatment of the queen's seduction risks self-parody by recalling his many adaptations of the legend of Tristan and Isolde* in his short fiction, *Marry, Couples* and *Brazil*. He also risks the banalities of the language of historical romance, since Updike uses the ancient love story without the restraint of irony imposed by his modern contexts.

One way in which Updike overcomes these self-imposed limitations of setting, theme, structure and language is through juxtaposing the mysteries of Byzantium to cold, practical Denmark, an opposition resembling that of northern and southern Diamond Country in *RA* and of India to America in *S*. Gertrude, in fact, seems to continue Sarah Worth's* journey from loveless upper-class privileges to unbridled passion and spiritual awakening. Gertrude's quest is prompted by Claudius's stories of his Byzantine adventures. Gertrude will discover, as Sarah Worth had, that her lover has not been entirely honest with her.

A more interesting way Updike surmounts the obstacles of his self-imposed limitations is through his presentation of Claudius as a *poèt maudit*, a sensitive, dangerous man. Claudius is an inventive, ardent lover who plies Gertrude with increasingly personal gifts, and he appeals to her sensual responsiveness and her repressed desire to act for herself rather than through her assigned roles as daughter, mother or wife. Thus Claudius entrances Gertrude with exotic stories of Byzantium, and he embellishes his Othello-like exploits with thirteenth-century love poetry that blends physical desire to spiritual longing in the image of "holy wisdom." Yet Claudius also arouses Gertrude's passion by introducing her to falconry, knowing she will find erotic excitement in controlling a wild bird who kills at her command. Through their use of the specialized language of falconry, Gertrude and Claudius divulge their secret desires. (This scene resembles the way in which Dale Kohler* and Esther Lambert* [*RV*] communicate their mutual attraction through computer language.) Finally, blending Claudius's poetic and dangerous natures enables Updike to develop his inquiry into evil from Stephen Conner* (*PF*) to the Arhat* (*S*.), Darryl Van Horne* (*W*), Jesse Smith* (*IB*) and Henry Bech* (*BaB*). Updike suggests that the sensitive men of the sixteenth century who might act with murderous impulses are reappearing in modern America. Like Claudius, such persons can dissociate their brutal inclinations from their spiritual aspirations without troubling their consciences.

Such separation of mind and feeling also characterizes Hamlet. As Updike implies in his "Afterword," Hamlet, the courtier and poet, was not entirely justified in bringing about the deaths of seven people and himself. However, with his dying breath Hamlet asks that his story be told, and Updike has obliged. By sympathetically foregrounding the incestuous* adultery and chivalric romance in the lives of Gertrude and Claudius, Updike has partly explained Hamlet's divided nature. Surprisingly, Hamlet and Claudius cause one to consider Harry "Rabbit" Angstrom* a fellow *poèt maudit* who like them has occasional transcendent insights and yet brings disorder when he is forced to smother his dream of finding something beyond the ordinary.

Updike's startling link of Hamlet and Rabbit helps bridge the distance between England and America, then and now, Shakespearian tragedy and the fiction of domestic disorder, power politics and suburban crises. *See* **English Literature**.

Bibliography: *Kirkus Reviews*, 19 Dec. 1999; Richard Eder, "Spoiled Rotten in Denmark," *New York Times Review*, 27 Feb. 2000: 9.

Geruthe (also Geruthia). *See* **Gertrude, Queen of Denmark**.

Golf. Golf has appeared throughout Updike's poetry,* fiction and essays since 1958, and in 1996 he collected many pieces for his anthology *GD*, illustrating the frustrations and thrills of the game, in which perfection is sought and rarely found. From the start, Updike has used the game of golf to provide pastoral* settings with underlying suggestions of Eden and innocence and to explore character. Updike traces his interest in the sport to the English novels he read as a boy, and he took up the sport when an aunt appeared one day with a set of clubs. He has been an avid golfer ever since. But Updike has recognized that the natural opposition of two golfers or two "twosomes" could form an ambiguous mixture of relaxation and confrontation. Such meetings are often the occasions for "deal-making," so in *RR* when Rev. Jack Eccles* and Harry "Rabbit" Angstrom* play golf, Eccles tries to force Rabbit to admit that he deludes himself if he thinks that he is on a spiritual quest for "the thing." Eccles scorns this as a rationalization for Rabbit's desire for sexual freedom. Rabbit demonstrates that the "thing" is real by dramatically stroking a perfect tee shot and saying, "That's it!" For Rabbit, the perfect drive is a release from the gravity-bound terrain into the spiritual home of the sky.

In *RIR* Rabbit enjoys not only more congenial company with Webb Murkett,* Ronnie Harrison* and others, but also the prestige of the Flying Eagle Tee and Racquet Club membership. Harrison's presence affords an opportunity for the old basketball* teammates to continue their smoldering resentments by other means. The rancor deepens as they play golf after swapping wives and a decade later coruscates in *RaR* during a match after Harrison's wife, Thelma Harrison,* dies, since she had been Rabbit's mistress. In *RaR* Rabbit also plays golf with Jewish friends in Florida* and uses the opportunity, as Eccles had, to gather information about the dangers of heart surgery.

Despite the sense of defeat inevitable for golfers, Updike keeps his sense of humor with comic essays on golf tips and the story "Farrell's Caddie." The leprechaun-like caddie somehow knows Farrell's intimate secrets and offers tips more useful than those concerning his backswing. As with all his other interests, Updike has explored his passion for golf with unrelenting zeal and acute sensitivity. His nonfiction golf writing includes portraits of

Tiger Woods, analyses of different courses and the joys of December golf. *See* **Sports**.

Bibliography: Updike, "Golf in the Land of the Free" (*MM*); James Dodson, "18 Holes with . . . John Updike," *Golf Magazine* 32 (July 1990): 108–14.

Golf Dreams (New York: Knopf, 1996). *GD*, a collection of articles, stories and poems, many first published in golf* magazines, contains observations on golf by Updike, a passionate amateur of the game since he began playing in his twenties. Included in the fiction section are excerpts from novels, particularly *RA*, stories and poetry. Updike supplies a revealing, witty "Preface" in which he notes how at midnight he jotted down tips like "Think *schwooo*." He focuses on his bafflement at the decline of his game. This is one of very few books by Updike to contain drawings, by Paul Szep. *See* **Games; Sports**.

Bibliography: Updike, *PP*; *HS*; *MM*.

Green, Henry (Henry Yorke) (1905–1973). "Henry Green" is the pseudonym of English novelist Henry Vincent Yorke, whose *Blindness* (1926), *Living* (1929), *Loving Back* (1946), *Concluding* (1948) and *Nothing* (1950) made a great impact on the writing of Updike's early fiction. Updike acknowledges that Green "taught me how to write." He notes how Green's first novel showed religious themes and "formal ambitiousness" in its "overt virtuosity," both qualities of Updike's fiction from *PF* to *OF*. Updike learned from Green how to have his characters* describe themselves through subtle indirection. Green shared with Updike the conviction that the details of the world contain mysterious beauty. In an interview* Updike remarked that he would gladly aspire to the "touch of truth" of this "saint of the mundane," praising Green's "verbal and psychological accuracy" and comparing him to Daniel Defoe. Updike has acknowledged the influence of Green's *Concluding* on *PF*, and critic James Schiff has traced Green's influence in setting, time frame, plot structure, characterization, unresolved ending, separation into three parts and impressionistic style. In addition, the blind woman in *PF*, Elizabeth Heinemann,* may have been influenced by Green's *Blindness*.

Updike noted that Green may have influenced *RR* through his employment of multiple points of view and daring symbolism,* along with his ability to see comedy,* excitement and beauty in impoverished lives. In "Sunday Teasing" (*SD*) Arthur's wife Macy wants her husband to stop reading Miguel de Unamuno and Søren Kierkegaard and try fiction; she is reading Jane Austen* and Green. Updike provided introductions to *Surviving* and a one-volume edition of *Loving, Living, Party Going*, along with a review of *Blindness* and a blurb for Green's *Pack My Bag*. In the *Surviving* introduction he said that Green "was a novelist of such rarity, such marvelous originality, intuition, sensuality and finish, that every fragment of his work is precious."

Updike elaborated on the influence of Green on R. M. Spackman in "Happiness, How Sad" (*MM*). Green and Updike shared Proust* as an "artistic hero." Jim Morrison, in a letter to me, notes that many of the stories in *TF* contain the "ing" ending in their titles, a trademark of Green's titling. *See* **English Literature**.

Bibliography: Updike, "An Introduction to Three Novels by Henry Green," in *HS*, 311–20; "Green Green," in *HS*, 321–29; *OJ*; "Introduction to *Surviving: The Uncollected Writings of Henry Green*" (*MM*); Schiff, *JU*.

Griffith, David Wark (1875–1948). One of the greatest of all film* directors, D. W. Griffith made such classics as *The Birth of a Nation* (1915) and *Intolerance* (1916). With Mary Pickford, Charlie Chaplin and Douglas Fairbanks, Griffith created United Artists studio in 1919. In *IB* Griffith is shown making the costume epic *The Call to Arms* in 1910, starring Pickford, who faints, exhausted by the New Jersey heat and cumbersome clothing. The film is mentioned only by the Paterson Chamber of Commerce handbook and does not appear in books about Griffith. The film is very useful to Updike in this novel. It establishes from the first scene the importance of film, emphasizes the "made-up" quality of film as an art, points to the illusory quality of the scene, which, while purporting to take place in Europe, is shot in Paterson, New Jersey, and, in Pickford's real swoon, describes the very real physical toll the movies take on their artists. Though Pickford swoons, Essie Wilmot/Alma DeMott,* who becomes established in the novel's third chapter, endures any hardship to succeed. She becomes a symbol of the modern artist and even the modern novelist. Since Pickford's faint occurs at precisely the moment that Rev. Clarence Wilmot* loses his faith, the juncture of the two lives stresses the way the movie house has replaced the church, a dominant theme in the novel. *See* **Film**; **Films of Updike's Work**.

H

Hamlet, Prince of Denmark (also named Amleth and Hamblet, but who for convenience is called Hamlet in this entry). Hamlet, the Prince of Denmark in *GC*, was born on the day of his father's greatest victory and named after ambiguous words from a war song. Born with a caul on his face, Hamlet as a baby constantly complains, to the consternation of his mother Gertrude,* who fears she lacks maternal feeling. As a youth he vacillates in his affection toward his mother and toward the king's counsellor's daughter, Ophelia, partly because he detects that neither woman felt loved enough by their fathers, but the source of his discontent is never clear. Nor is the reason why he comes to view the world as a joke. Hamlet becomes enraptured by his discovery of the "new learning," dependent on inductive rather than deductive logic, which seems to support his sense of the absurdity of life. When Hamlet is about thirty, Gertrude marries his uncle Claudius,* increasing his estrangement from her and the Danish court. At this point Updike's narrative stops, but those who know Shakespeare's *Hamlet* know that Hamlet's discontent will burst upon his puzzled mother. Through him Updike shows what happens when a person becomes estranged from his family and alienated from the goals of a warrior nation, despite of, or because of, his sensitivity to life and awareness of the supernatural. His attitude of bitter amusement toward life contrasts to the passionate and exotic adulterers Gertrude and Claudius. But in his ingenuity Hamlet represents a man willing to look beneath the surface of courtly placidity and pomp that conceal betrayal and murder. Hamlet resembles the restless Clark DeMott,* who is also dissatisfied with his mother and is swept into a vortex of violence in which his heroic actions stem the tide of evil (*IB*). Yet Updike's "Afterword" to *GC* points out that Hamlet "pulls to death" several people who are perhaps undeserving of such a fate. *See* **Adultery; Children; Death; English Literature**.

Hanema, Angela Hamilton. The thirty-four-year-old wife of Piet Hanema* in *Couples*, Angela Hanema is a competent mother of their two girls, but after nine years has become sexually unsatisfying to her husband because of her remoteness. Angela had been a schoolteacher and enjoyed astronomy, having been tutored by her uncle. She was from a "piratical New Bedford family," and so she wanted to move from their home to one closer to the sea, the "Robinson place." The images of stars and sea related her to the legendary Isolde of the Tristan and Isolde* myth. Meanwhile, a new couple, Foxy Whitman* and her husband Ken Whitman,* buy the place, and Piet is contracted to repair it. Angela represents what Updike called "the supernatural," so, abstracted, she tries to ignore Piet's numerous affairs, and when he reveals that he loves Foxy, Angela agrees almost at once to a divorce.* Five years of living in Tarbox have perhaps prepared her for this crisis, and the split between her and Piet has become wider since she does not profess a religion,* as he does, and takes little delight in their friends. Though voluptuous, Angela is seen by most as aloof, detached and unreachable, like the stars. Despite her therapy later, she remains unable to engage emotionally with the others.

Angela is so detached from her body that when she is asked to sleep with Freddy Thorne* as payment for Foxy's abortion,* she agrees without argument, and Thorne is impotent with her because of her frigidity. Piet rightly sees her as lacking the energy to grapple with life. Angela seems out of touch with terra firma, but she does help Piet identify the constellations, though he is more interested in astrology than astronomy. During therapy Angela begins to see that her parents may be the source of her problems, though Piet discredits her counselor and causes Angela to lose her conviction. The portrait of Angela continues Updike's depiction of marital failure as stemming from the wife's inability to provide sexual satisfaction and thus revisits the contrast, sometimes called "madonna and whore," between Ruth Leonard Byer* and Janice Angstrom* in *RR*, Joey Robinson's* first and second wives in *OF*, and Doreen and Gloria Turnbull* in *TE*. *See* **Adultery**.

Bibliography: Markle, *FL*; Detweiler, *JU*; Greiner, *JU*.

Hanema, Nancy. Piet* and Angela Hanema's* five-year-old daughter in *Couples*, Nancy is frightened by death,* first in the death of her sister Ruth's hamster, for which she was responsible, and then in Jackie Kennedy's miscarriage. She fuses this sense of an unpredictably hostile world antithetical to life with the decision of Jackie Kennedy's baby, who preferred, she concludes, to die rather than be born. Piet had constructed a hamster cage to protect the pet and to shield his daughters and himself from death brought into his own home. Ironically, Nancy leaves the hamster cage unlocked, enabling the family cat to kill it. Nancy thus mirrors Piet's own fear of death, particularly when she insists that in her "whole life" she will not die. She also resists growing up, thinking that this will stave off death too, and her resistance reflects Piet's unwillingness to "die" in his marriage and his determination to stay young in his affair with Foxy Whitman.* He discovers in marathon sex* with Foxy that he needs to push beyond it to find protection from death. *See* **Children**.

Hanema, Piet. The chief character of *Couples*, Piet Hanema is a minor contractor in Tarbox, Massachusetts, and has a craftsman's appreciation for the church's old wood carving. But this sensitivity also makes him aware of how life has declined since those old days. Piet has been married to Angela* for nine years and has two small daughters. When his parents, Marte and Jacobus Hanema, die in a car crash, Piet has numerous affairs to stave off his fear of death.* Caught up in the whirling social life of his friends, Piet falls in love with Foxy Whitman* while renovating her house. Piet is a thoughtful person, troubled by the failure of faith and family to sustain his need for spiritual sense validating his personal feeling of what critic Joyce Markle calls "specialness." His affair causes the social fabric to unravel: the Hanemas and Whitmans divorce, and Piet and Foxy remarry. Piet's new start brings to a conclusion Updike's concern with how existential crises are met in modern middle-class America, for Piet's concerns are similar to those of Harry "Rabbit" Angstrom,* David Kern* in "Pigeon Feathers" (*PigF*), Walter in "The Astronomer" (*PigF*), Peter Caldwell* (*C*) and Joey Robinson* (*OF*). In addition, critic Larry Taylor finds that the narrators of "In Football Season" and "The Music School" (*MuS*) are "precursors" of Piet Hanema because they are sensitive, adulterous, "nostalgically religious" and "preoccupied" with death.

Bibliography: Taylor, *PA*; Markle, *FL*.

Happy. The nickname "Happy" (derived from the Latin "felix") for Col. Felix Ellelloû* at McCarthy College was probably ironic since he was quite unhappy both with American society and the conventional leftist attitudes and ideas of his fellow students (*Coup*).

Harrison, Ronnie. Harry "Rabbit" Angstrom's* former teammate on the Mt. Judge* High School basketball* team, Ronnie Harrison appears in three of the novels in *RA*. He may be Rabbit's alter ego* ("Harry's son"), Rabbit's other self, the "enforcer" who fouled to protect Rabbit so he could be a star. Ronnie is thus the unwilling enabler of Rabbit's greatness. But he is also Rabbit's foul-mouthed intimidator, a relentless unmasker and "reality instructor" who punctures Rabbit's pretensions, spoils his jokes and steals his women. Harrison is responsible for a crucial event in *RR*. After explaining to Ruth Leonard Byer* during a double date that coach Marty Tothero* thought that Rabbit was no team player, he lets Rabbit know that he had once been Ruth's lover. Feeling retroactively betrayed, Rabbit demands that Ruth perform fellatio on him as she had on Harrison when she was a prostitute. Since her love for Rabbit had caused her to give up prostitution, she fears that such a "humbling" might kill his love for her, and though she is pregnant with Rabbit's child, it does. Harrison enjoys heckling Rabbit for having slept with Margaret Fosnacht one night (*RRed*) and continues the sexual rivalry between them in *RIR*. This competition becomes humiliating when Harrison sleeps with the girl of Rabbit's dreams, Cindy Murkett.* Ironically, Rabbit's night with Harrison's wife Thelma Harrison* leads to a ten-year affair that is satisfying to Rabbit because it is undemanding; he can accept her unconditional love without having to worry about returning it. Harrison has become a successful insurance salesman who regularly plays golf* with Rabbit at the Flying Eagle Tee and Racquet Club, and during a game of golf, when Harrison is Rabbit's guest on the links, he tells Rabbit that Thelma had confessed their affair shortly before dying and asked forgiveness (*RaR*). Still, Rabbit is aware at this point that Ronnie had always been "an aspect of himself he didn't want to face but now does." In a sense Ronnie has faced the same thing by finding that his wife has loved a person he never respected. This would seem to be Rabbit's unplanned, ultimate revenge.

Harrison, Thelma. The wife of Ronnie Harrison,* Thelma becomes Harry "Rabbit" Angstrom's* mistress at the end of *RIR*, having loved him for a long time. She had quietly supported his opinions whenever she had the chance, had laughed at his jokes and had bolstered his ego. Yet Rabbit ignored her for ten years because of her "school-teacher" demeanor and her need to cover herself against sunlight because of her lupus, which eventually kills her. Thelma expresses her love for him only when they accidentally sleep together during an episode of spouse sharing (*RIR*). That night the uninhibited Thelma initiates Rabbit into anal intercourse in order to make some aspect of their lovemaking unique. The act produces for him a realization of nothingness, and because of this or despite it, Rabbit's affair with Thelma continues for ten years. But they discontinue because Rabbit fears that his injured heart cannot stand it, and because he fears AIDS.* Though Thelma is on a dialysis machine, she is still willing to continue her adoration of Rabbit. He learns at her funeral that she had admitted their affair because she was Catholic and feared dying with the sin on her soul. When Ronnie Harrison confronts Rabbit with this fact and is indignant that Rabbit could not return Thelma's love, Rabbit can muster no real affection for her. Thelma is thus an example of a loving woman willing to accept Rabbit's hardness of heart. Rabbit ignores Thelma's good advice from the spouse-swapping night not to pursue voluptuous young women but instead to concentrate on mature women capable of appreciating his value. Rabbit's failure to heed her advice eventually brings him to a night with his daughter-in-law, Teresa "Pru" Angstrom,* which leads to exile from his family when she tells his wife and son about their lovemaking, and contributes to his death. No doubt Thelma had found her own sense of specialness with Rabbit, but he failed to recognize that she might have been "the thing" that wanted him to find it all along, for she offered him love unreservedly. *See* **Feminism; Sex**.

Harvard Lampoon. The *Harvard Lampoon*, a Harvard University* humor magazine, was a major recipient of Updike's apprentice* writing. He contributed poems, stories, articles and drawings from 1951 to 1954 and served as its editor, 1953–54. Updike's prime reason for going to Harvard rather than Cornell was his conviction that the *Lampoon* would best serve his goal to become an animator for Walt Disney.* What he termed his "romantic weakness for gags" (verbal as well as visual) found a welcome outlet at the magazine, which often published several pieces by him in one issue. Working on the magazine provided Updike, as he remarked, his metamorphosis from a caterpillar, since he was in the company of "true butterflies." Robert Benchley, the *New Yorker** writer who also worked for the *Lampoon*, was a formative influence, perhaps, in turning the *Lampoon* into an imitation *New Yorker*, easing Updike's transition from one sophisticated magazine to the other. In 1984 novelist Nicholson Baker met Updike at a *Lampoon* party and on the strength of that meeting and his awareness of a few Updike novels wrote his unusual novel-memoir *U and I*. *See* **Light Verse**.

Bibliography: Updike, "Introduction to *The Harvard Lampoon Centennial Celebration, 1876–1973*" (*PP*); Robert McCoy, "John Updike's Literary Apprenticeship on *The Harvard Lampoon*," *Modern Fiction Studies* 20 (Spring 1974): 3–12.

Harvard University. Because Updike's mother had read an anthology revealing that nearly all great writers of a particular year attended Harvard University, she encouraged him to apply. Updike finally chose Harvard over Cornell because he wanted to do cartoons for the *Harvard Lampoon*,* which became a vehicle for his graphic talents. Yet he also contributed poems, essays and commentary to the magazine, and when he became editor of it, he used the skills he had developed as editor of the Shillington* High School *Chatterbox*.* It has been said that Updike's failure to get into Archibald MacLeish's creative writing course three times made him turn his energies to the *Lampoon*. Updike entered Harvard in 1950, majored in English and graduated Phi Beta Kappa and summa cum laude in 1954. In "Cartoon Magic" Updike describes the "silence" of the dormitories and the faint Harvard radio station that brought him lectures of Adlai Stevenson and the Army-McCarthy hearings. As he said in *OJ*, Harvard Yard became and remains "the center of New England" for him. He "learned the right costume" and "the proper polite, ironical manner" there, but still felt "an outsider," which suited him because "a writer is an outsider" ("Two Answers to the Question of Why I Live in New England" [*MM*]). He shows what hard work studying was at Harvard in the story "The Christian Roommates," (*MuS*), and he himself admitted to exhaustion at the end of his Harvard years. He wrote his admittedly dull thesis on "Non-Horatian Elements in Robert Herrick's Imitations and Echoes of Horace" (*OJ*). The thesis foreshadows his impressive use of the classics throughout his work, as well as a lifelong dedication to poetry.* He would later call Harvard, with tongue in cheek, not a very good school for training practical artists, but "pretty good" for writers (like T. S. Eliot,* Robert Frost and Wallace Stevens*).

Harvard gave him "the liberating notion that now I could teach myself," an idea that peaked in his junior year. Apart from providing him with a thorough knowledge of literature, history* and philosophy that he would weave into his literary work, and giving him the opportunity to expand his omnivorous interests, Harvard was the place where Updike learned how to learn, as his studious research in Africa, Brazil, India, theology, computers and President James Buchanan* reveals. He found his years at Harvard "idyllic," since he heard writers like Carl Sandburg, Robert Frost, E. E. Cummings,* Wallace Stevens and T. S. Eliot. Guest writers like John Hawkes appeared in his creative writing course. Deftly Updike limns several instructors who escorted him through his English major. As he remarks in *OJ*, he enjoyed Hyder Rollins's romanticism course, Walter Jackson Bate's Johnson course, Roger Chapman's seminar in George Bernard Shaw and Kenneth Murdoch's course in the metaphysical poets. But of special importance may have been Harry Levin, who taught Shakespeare, Thomas Mann,* James Joyce* and Marcel Proust.* He never forgot Levin's remark in a Shakespeare course that fortified Updike's concern for average people: "Shakespeare's characters have no I.Qs." Updike reviewed Levin's "scholarly shotgun," *The Gates of Horn: A Study of Five French Realists*, finding it "the highest reach criticism can attain while remaining academic" (*AP*). Certainly, Levin's teaching was of fundamental importance to the development of Updike's understanding of modern literature. Though he earned a C+ in Edwin Honig's seminar on modern poetry, he read a great deal of Wallace Steven's poetry and learned to love his "rollicking vocabulary, the bearish delicacy, the tirelessness of the onrolling blank verse, and the rare glimpses of Berks County terrain" (*MM*). Another important faculty member, Kenneth Kempton, introduced Updike to J. D. Salinger's* work in his writing course (*OJ*). He may have met Edward Hoagland in such a class while he was writing his novel *Cat Man*; Updike later praised his nature* essays and said of Hoagland, "Like Thoreau,* he knows his cosmic place" (*OJ*). Decades later Updike recalled Professor Douglas Bush's course in which he was introduced to Edmund Spenser and dreamed of reading everything.

Updike met his first wife, Mary Pennington (Weatherall) Updike,* in a course in medieval art; they married on June 26, 1953, the summer before his senior year. Updike began to consider a career in drawing* or writing to support his wife; his first child arrived in April 1955. Despite teaching creative writing at Harvard in 1962, Updike, unlike many other writers, would never attach himself to a university, though he has given readings and talks, conducted classes and participated in workshops at a great many schools. Such trips have enabled him to write "from the inside" when using academic settings for his work.

Harvard forms the background of two stories and a few poems, but Updike refused, as he put it, to act as a Harvard panegyrist, particularly since he felt that he had been pacified at Harvard against his will and had perhaps even lost his "essential self." Certainly Harvard challenged his religious belief, as "Humanities Course" (1955) indicates (*CH*). There Updike satirizes "Professor Varder" as "the personification of Harvard" because, as he explains in a note in *CP*, "humanistic knowledge nibbled away at my Christian faith." Yet Updike wondered if Harvard's "high regard" for the Middle Ages may have helped him to "keep" his faith as well. Updike may have provided a witty allusion to the loss of the "essential self" at Harvard in the story "The Wallet," in which Fulham panics when he mislays his credit cards to "The Harvard 'Coop' " and "The Harvard Club" (*TM*). One of Updike's least likable characters, biologist Ken Whitman* (*Couples*), graduated from Harvard, and the heroine of that novel, Foxy Whitman,* studied at Radcliffe (like Updike's first wife, Mary; his second wife, Martha Bernhard,* graduated from Harvard with a master's degree in education, 1964). The only use of Harvard as a setting for his fiction may be "The Christian Roommates" (*MuS*), in which a midwesterner is frustrated by his unconventional roommate. Harvard often assigned this story to its incoming freshman. The divinity college in *RV* has been identified as based on Harvard Theological Seminary. Harvard was founded to teach the tenets of John Calvin's Puritanism.

If Updike was representative of the Harvard undergraduates studied in Kenneth Keniston's *The Uncommitted: Alienated Youth in American Society* (New York: Harcourt, Brace and World, 1961), he might have felt "rejection of the system" and "rebellion without a cause." Such feelings could have been transferred to his alter ego* Harry "Rabbit" Angstrom* (*RA*). Certainly Updike has looked on Harvard with affection, as his contributions to various Harvard anthologies attest, as well as a poignant description of Harvard Yard, with its "puritan aura" and "sacred atmosphere of books" (*OJ*). For his poem "Midpoint" (*M*), Updike selected photos from the *Harvard Register* depicting him as a freshman and senior. Later in the 1960s he attacked some of its professors who called for an end to the Vietnam* War, but in 1973 he contributed an introduction to *Harvard Lampoon* memorabilia and wrote the "Phi Beta Kappa" poem, published privately by Harvard, then published as "Apologies to Harvard" (*TT*). The poem acknowledges the continuing impact of Harvard since it "hatched" him, took him in raw, then "spit him out a gentleman." If he had "no regrets," he also felt "little gratitude." Though he reflects on math and Latin courses and his homesickness his first year, the poem mainly describes his meetings with his wife-to-be, Mary Pennington Updike. He knows that Harvard was not the world; no blacks or poor were there, and it set impossible standards from the nineteenth century.

Harvard privately published a poem translated from Latin by Updike in a 1986 anthology and a year later provided a handsome exhibition and catalogue of his work, with a black-tie reception. Also in 1987, Updike read "Howells as Anti-Novelist" at Harvard. After making continuous gifts of his manuscripts to Harvard since 1965, Updike formally deposited his literary papers in the Houghton Library in 1991. He received an honorary Doctor of Letters from Harvard in 1992. In May 1998, he became the fourth recipient of the Harvard Arts Medal, reading at Lowell House,* where he had lived on the fifth floor, and "A Shuffled Multitude of Hostile Strangers: Manuscripts and Drawings by John Updike, '54" was exhibited at Houghton Library at that time. Updike returned on March 2, 1999, to read the poetry of L. E. Sissman, an acknowledged influence on Updike's "Apologies to Harvard." In "Grandparenting" (*A*) Updike describes the reading he attended given by E. E. Cummings at Sanders Theatre. Since 1958 Updike has lived within one hundred miles of the university, and he was interviewed at Harvard's Houghton Library by Charlie Rose about *BaB* for PBS in 1998. He has reviewed the work of several instructors who were at Harvard when he was there, among them Edmund Wilson and Stephen Jay Gould. *See* **Academia**.

Bibliography: Updike, "Honest Horn" (*AP*); "The Industrious Drifter in Room 2," *Harvard Magazine* 76 (May 1974): 42–45, 51; "Foreword to *The Harvard Lampoon Centennial Celebration, 1876–1973*" (*PP*); "A Reminiscence for the *Harvard Gazette* on the Occasion of My Thirtieth Reunion in June of 1984" (*OJ*); "The Harvard Summer School Chorus," in *Concerts at Castle Hill* (Northridge: Lord John Press, 1993), 28–29; "Lost Art," "Two Answers to the Question of Why I Live in New England," "Five Remembered Moments of Utter Reading Bliss" (*MM*); Daniel Hoffman, ed., *Harvard Guide to Contemporary American Writing* (Cambridge, MA: Belknap Press, 1979), 145–48, 270–71; "John Updike to Receive Harvard Arts Medal," *Harvard University Gazette* 11 Mar. 1998: 11; "The Early Days of John Updike '54," *Harvard University Gazette* 30 Apr. 1998: 1, 4.

Hawthorne, Nathaniel (1804–1864). An important American Renaissance fictionalist whose symbolic novels criticize the past and the incursions of social and scientific change, Nathaniel Hawthorne was of great interest to Updike for his psychological insight, his exploration of Puritan mores, his sensitivity to feminist matters, his skeptical refusal to accept the bromides of Christianity and his serious exploration of evil. Updike mined Hawthorne to update the "Romance" genre, modeled three of his novels on *The Scarlet*

Letter, wrote a novel steeped in Hawthorne about witchery (*W*) and used allusions to Hawthorne's work to supply character insight.

Updike was interested in Hawthorne's understanding of the romance novel and subtitled *Marry* a romance as "my last romance." Hawthorne provided this famous definition of romance in the Preface to *The House of the Seven Gables*: "Romance . . . may not swerve aside from the truth of the human heart," but "has a right to present that truth under circumstances . . . of the writer's own choosing." Updike chose to set *Marry* during March–November 1962, the "Camelot"* years of John F. Kennedy's* presidency, identifying this as a time that "infused all of us with a romantic sense of ourselves that's gone." Updike modernizes Hawthorne's theory by offering the Camelot era as a parallel to Brook Farm* of *The Blithedale Romance*, which Hawthorne called "a dead society of a recent past," and he quotes Miles Coverdale's depressed realization that at Brook Farm field work does not encourage etherealization; rather, thoughts become "cloddish" (*OJ*). James Schiff argues that *The Blithedale Romance* is a chief source for *S*.

In *BB* Updike describes how Henry Bech* finds his dreams haunted by Hawthorne's "Roger Malvin's Burial," a story of bad conscience and guilt, principal themes of Hawthorne's *Scarlet Letter*, upon which Updike deliberately modeled three of his novels comprising the viewpoints of Arthur Dimmesdale (*MS*), Roger Chillingworth (*RV*) and Hester Prynne (*S*). Updike's Dimmesdale analogue, Rev. Thomas Marshfield,* purges himself by writing a thirty-day journal (complete with four sermons*) in which he explores his sexual delinquency and his spiritual despair. Updike uses his Chillingworth analogue, Roger Lambert,* to expose Lambert's diminishing libido: Lambert imagines that a research student, Dale Kohler,* has become his wife's lover, while the student (the Dimmesdale analogue in this novel) seeks "God's hand showing through his creation." Finally, the Hester Prynne parallel, Sarah Worth,* describes her quest for spiritual and sexual fulfillment at an ashram led by a charismatic leader, the Arhat* (another Dimmesdale analogue), only to find him a fraud. Updike not only uses Hawthorne in these works to contrast Hawthorne's Puritanism with the relativism of modern morality, but revises his own opinions about sex,* spirit and woman in the process.

Elsewhere, Updike uses the names of Hawthorne characters in *S*., wittily naming Sarah Worth's faithless best friend, Midge Hibbens, after Mistress Hibbens, the witch in *The Scarlet Letter*. In "More Stately Mansions" and "The Lovely Troubled Daughters of Our Old Crowd" (*TM*), Salem Street and the town of Mather are locales, their fossilized Puritan origins mute commentators on the continuance of Puritanism in modern America. Updike's stories "The Afterlife," "The Black Room" and "Farrell's Caddie" (*A*) may also show Hawthorne's influence in operating as "moral embodiments, rimmed in a flickering firelight of fantasy" (*OJ*), as Updike described the stories of John Cheever,* Updike's "poet of the poisoned" (*OJ*).

During his fifteen-year use of Hawthorne for his fictional purposes, Updike wrote and revised "Hawthorne's Religious Language," an essay eventually called "Hawthorne's Creed," which surveys Hawthorne's lifelong struggle with religion. Updike notes that Hawthorne was not a churchgoer, satirized Unitarianism,* was impatient with Melville's constant questioning of the hereafter and felt the Puritanism of his ancestors a personal menace. Hawthorne's creed becomes an opposition of earth and heaven in which man's spirit matters. As several critics have noted, Updike is more aware of ambiguity than of a polarizing of good and evil.

Though not derived from Hawthorne, *W*, as James Schiff remarks, "*feels like Hawthorne.*" The novel concerns three witches consorting with the devil in a town where "Puritania" is a chic decor. The hellfire sermon is parodied when Darryl Van Horne* delivers an attack on God's "Terrible Creation," and he also supplies a graphic, sympathetic description of witch-hunts. They all enjoy a hot-tub Walpurgisnacht on Halloween. Updike delights in naming the Eastwick newspaper *the Word*, sprinkling the exclamations "Jesus" and "Hell" throughout the narrative and empowering the witches to suspend tennis balls in the air and to commit murder through sympathetic magic. One might also connect the Puritan origins of Tarbox to the Hawthorne influence (*Couples*), as well as the friend who unwittingly interferes in the relationship of Sally Mathias* and Jerry Conant,* A. D. Wigglesworth, whose name recalls the author of the Puritan poem *The Day of Doom*, Michael Wigglesworth (1631–1705), a Harvard* graduate and pastor at Malden, Massachusetts. The initials "A. D." may refer to *anno domini*, but do they also allude to Arthur Dimmesdale? Updike reviewed, with subdued resistance, two critical works on Hawthorne. He found E. H. Miller's work "relentless" in its Freudianism and calls his biography "ghostly," as his work is treated as the equivalent of "an analysand's dream." *See* **Antinomianism**.

Bibliography: Updike, "Introduction," in *Soundings in Satanism*, ed. F. J. Sheed (New York: Sheed and Ward, 1972), vii–xii; "Hawthorne's Creed" (*HS*); "Emersonianism" (*OJ*); "Man of Secrets" (*MM*); Greiner, *JU*; Newman, *JU*; Schiff, *JU*.

Heinemann, Elizabeth. Blind since childhood, Elizabeth Heinemann wonders if she will have her sight restored in heaven. Updike describes with great clarity her perceptions as an aged blind person as she makes her way through the halls of the poorhouse (*PF*). She is comforted by the thought that in heaven all will be blind. The only blind person in Updike's work, she may have been a result of Updike's reading of Henry Green's* *Blindness*.

A Helpful Alphabet of Friendly Objects (New York: Knopf, 1995). Illustrated with photographs by Updike's son David Updike,* *HA* contains a poem for each letter of the alphabet (R is, aptly, "Rabbit"). *HA* is a companion to "A Cheerful Alphabet of Pleasant Objects" (*CH*, not included in *CP*), which

Updike had dedicated to David. The contrast between the two sequences of poems is interesting. "Cheerful" is a *tour de force* of visual and verbal playfulness. "Shaped poems" intended to resemble graphically the poem's subject ("Flower Pot," "Letter Slot," "Mirror," "Nutcracker," "Pendulum" and "Yardstick") would appeal to a child's eye. But the language of "A Cheerful Alphabet" might be difficult: X, for example, is for "Xyster," and "Trivet" contains a line in French. And sophisticated allusions abound, thus "Apple," which refers to Paul Cézanne and the Puritan religion, and "Yardstick," which alludes to John Milton. In contrast, the language of *HA* is simple in treating concrete things the child has experienced: cats, eggs, oatmeal, flowers. These poems are clearly intended to be read aloud, and Updike plays with the appearance of words to emphasize a speaking voice. Updike restrains the earlier portentousness of such poems as "Apple," "Nut" and "Vacuum" (*CH*), instead providing an occasional frisky metaphor, as when in "Cat" a cat's lips "smell blue of fish" (*HA*). As in *ChC*, each poem is accompanied by an illustration, and David Updike's photographs are also peppy and straightforward: a child smiles into a mirror, eats oatmeal or plays a xylophone. Two photos show Updike with a child, perhaps his grandsons, since Updike dedicated this book to Anoff, Kwame, Wesley, Trevor and Kai, "cousins all." Wesley is David's child, Anoff and Kwame are Updike's daughter Elizabeth Updike's* children, Trevor is Updike's son Michael Updike's* son and Kai is Updike's daughter Miranda Updike's* child. *HA* is filled with a grandfather's joy. *See* **Children**.

Hemingway, Ernest (1899–1961). An American novelist and story writer, winner of the Nobel Prize* (1954), Ernest Hemingway was one of the "moderns" whom Updike, in reviews, commended as a shaper of the style of modern fiction by his pristine observation and sharp ear for dialogue. At Harvard,* Theodore Morrison, as Updike recalled, "staid, tweedy," read Hemingway's "The Light of the World" as an example of consistent point of view successfully violated" (*MM*). Updike alludes to Hemingway's Nick Adams* fishing ("Big Two-Hearted River") in "Meditation on a News Item" (*TP*), in which "the tournament," Donald Greiner notes, "becomes Hemingway fiction." Updike may also have used Hemingway's career as a warning to the young writer who takes his public image too seriously, since Updike noted that Hemingway was "destroyed by his own persona and his huge name." Yet Updike feels that there is something "lovable" about Hemingway. His best-loved novel, *The Old Man and the Sea*, won the Pulitzer Prize in 1953; Updike has won the award* twice. *See* **American Literature**.

Bibliography: Updike, "Papa's Sad Testament" (*PP*); "The Sinister Sex "The Short Story and I" (*MM*); Greiner, *OJ*.

Hippies. "Hippies" was a general name for young liberals in the 1960s concerned with various social reforms like free speech, civil rights, women's rights, sexual freedom and gay rights, and with ecological and environmental issues, as well as an end to the Vietnam* War. Generally they advocated freer laws regarding sex* and drugs* and greater tolerance for differences of all kinds. They rejected capitalist values of business and technology and opposed materialism and "family values" for more personal expression and communal sharing. The only thread knitting such disparate groups was rock and folk music, particularly the groups the Rolling Stones, the Beatles and the Grateful Dead and singers Bob Dylan and Janis Joplin. Hippie style virtually required interest in the occult, smoking of marijuana, long hair and "counterculture" costume. Experimental in personal and social matters, hippies resisted anything that contaminated their sense of individuality, which they cultivated through drugs, usually marijuana but sometimes hallucinogens. They revered aspects of existentialism, Japanese and Indian thinking and Native American views of life. Hippies are sometimes credited with reviving beat literature, ending the Vietnam War, forcing President Lyndon Johnson* to decide against running for a second term, and making higher education socially accountable. Though they have been credited with helping to create a more liberal society, hippies often seem shortsighted dreamers, opposed to "the system" with little consideration about how to replace it. Hippie political naïveté is mocked by Col. Félix Ellelloû (*Coup*). Dale Kohler* (*RV*) offends Roger Lambert* by his hippie clothes and his acting like a "Jesus-freak," another characteristic of hippie style.

History. Apart from Updike's famous remark in the *Paris Review* interview that his fiction of everyday people "has more history in it than history books," his fiction and poetry* often incorporate historical events and personages, but tend to demythify historical heroes (Plath, *CU*). For example, in *PF* John Hook* and Stephen Conner* debate about Presidents James Buchanan* and Abraham Lincoln,* slavery and the welfare state. The same figures and ideas recur as well in *BD*, and *MF*, in which Buchanan is a central character. Updike has said that his novels take place during a specific presidency, and his characters reveal an interest and knowledge about Buchanan, Lincoln, Franklin Roosevelt,* John Kennedy,* Richard Nixon and Jimmy Carter. Even those indifferent to history like Harry "Rabbit" Angstrom* watch the moon landing, argue about Senator Teddy Kennedy's responsibility for the drowning of a Pennsylvania woman at Chappaquidick Island (*RRed*) and read Barbara Tuchman's book about the unheroic aspects of the American Revolution (*RaR*).

Updike has acknowledged that he used research to steep his books in verisimilitude* (*S.*, *B*, *RV* and *TE*). Updike's absorption of the literature of a great many countries involves him in the social and political histories of, for example, Brazil, Russia and Ethiopia. Critic Dilvo Ristoff has discussed how historical events infuse the characters of *RA*, virtually determining their lives. But Ristoff notes that sometimes Updike retains historical inaccuracies in his work, for example, when he writes in *RR* that President Dwight Eisenhower had a summit meeting at his Gettysburg farm, rather than at Camp David. Updike is, finally, a novelist, not a historian. By the 1990s Updike could write, "History . . . is anti-heroic" and a matter "for little anonymous lives, or market records and statistics, of life-styles and technology" (*MM*). But he concludes that it may be better this way, since "the times that breed heroes are generally grim times for the unheroic multitudes." See **American History; Presidents; Vietnam.**

Bibliography: Newman, *JU*; Ristoff, *UA*; Ristoff, *JU*.

Ho Chi Minh (1890–1969). The Vietnamese Communist president of North Vietnam (1954–69), Ho Chi Minh led the war against French and American forces. After he won a decisive battle against the French at Dien Bien Phu,* the Geneva peace treaty divided Vietnam,* and Ho Chi Minh was given only North Vietnam. He continued war against South Vietnam, assisted by China and the Soviet Union, whereas South Vietnam was backed by the United States. After Ho's death a cease-fire agreement was signed in 1973, but the North Vietnamese government gained control of all of Vietnam in 1975, changing Saigon's name to Ho Chi Minh City. Ho Chi Minh is mentioned in *Couples* as the solution to a word game, but domestic struggles mean more than civil wars to the egocentric Tarbox couples, indifferent to political games played on a global scale. Brenda Parsley* (*W*), though, does what the Tarboxes cannot do; she links witchcraft to Dwight Eisenhower's refusal to sign a truce with Ho Chi Minh, creating American involvement in Vietnam. See **Games.**

Holmes, Oliver Wendell (1809–1894). The genial wit of Boston poet and essayist Oliver Wendell Holmes in *The Autocrat of the Breakfast-Table* (1857) and *Atlantic Monthly* reviews earned him eminence among the cultivated Boston "Brahmins." His poem "The Chambered Nautilus" (1858) is the symbolic center in "More Stately Mansions" (*TM*), a shell supplying a "Proustian"* moment for the narrator involving a past affair in which the shell's speckling seemed to him the freckles on his mistress's face. She had bought the shell but had never given it to him. The poem's most famous line is used in the story's title and directs the reader to the narrator's epiphany: "We all have to *grow*." See **American Literature.**

Homosexuality. Updike's treatment of homosexuality reflects the changing social attitudes of the past four decades. Like America itself, Updike's characters* show a movement from conflict to accommodation. Updike's work in the 1950s and early 1960s, like "The Lens Factory," emphasizes the fear of being harassed by homosexual passes. In the story "At a Bar in Charlotte Amalie" (*SD*) a gay character is portrayed stereotypically as "camp," distressing vacationers, but in *PF* subtle hints of attraction between Stephen Conner* and his brother Buddy Conner suggest latent homosexuality. Practical necessities forced Polynesians who had no women to live on the uninhabited Fanning Island and so "made women of each other" ("The Blessed Man of Boston, My Grandmother's Thimble, and Fanning Island" [*PigF*]). In *C* Updike uses homosexuality twice, once when the goddess Venus tells Chiron* that Dionysus "made me perform as if I were another boy," and again when a "bum" (the god Hermes) accuses George Caldwell* of taking his son, Peter Caldwell,* to a hotel for immoral purposes. Updike ends *W* with a shocking revelation: Darryl Van Horne* eloped with Chris Gabriel—the devil is gay.

But when Harry "Rabbit" Angstrom* becomes aware of his coach's stare as he undresses, he becomes self-conscious, and Updike begins a long exploration of Rabbit (and America's) shifting view of homosexuality. In the approved manner of athletes, Rabbit and his rival Ronnie Harrison* trade sexually sadistic jokes in *RR*, and he often thinks of Harrison in terms of his friend's penis. In the 1970s Updike depicted in *RRed* the most overt homoerotic behavior when Skeeter* and Rabbit are drawn together through sharing Jill Pendleton,* and when Skeeter, being fellated by Jill, encourages Rabbit to enter her. The action suggests Skeeter's desire to communicate sexually through a female intermediary. Skeeter's masturbation in Rabbit's presence seems to Rabbit a homosexual invitation, and he panics. Rabbit may also have a concealed incestuous desire in fantasizing about sex* between his sister Miriam* and Charlie Stavros,* but he later masturbates while thinking about Stavros's phallus. In the 1980s Rabbit thinks in *RIR* that having shared Janice* with Stavros raised her value and brought the men closer. Now that homosexuals have become more visible in *RIR*, Updike alludes to lesbians for the first time. Rabbit remains conflicted, however, and can share a homophobic laugh with his son Nelson Angstrom* at the expense of the apparently homosexual minister, "Soupy" Campbell: Rabbit calls Soupy a "fag," and Nelson is obscenely satiric. More important, Nelson and Rabbit call each other "queer," and when Rabbit asks Nelson why he is not attracted to voluptuous Melanie, Nelson sneers, "I'm queer." (Ironically, Nelson and Melanie are already lovers.) Such sexual sparring underlines their Oedipal problems, since father and son seek to disqualify each other for the sexual favors of Janice Angstrom,* wife and mother. Rabbit seeks to neutralize, even castrate, his competitive son; accusing him of being "queer" is one way to do so.

For the first time, Updike describes a shift toward understanding of gays in *RIR* when Teresa "Pru" Angstrom* and Annabelle Byer* accept Lyle and Slim as simply expressing different sexual preferences. Although Janice and Rabbit are eager to use the politically correct language of the 1990s to attack one another's homophobia, their underlying bigotry makes their language merely cosmetic. Later in the 1980s Updike uses homosexuality more subtly. Updike rejected an early idea in *Couples* of using a homosexual attracted to a married man, but later employed it in "Beautiful Husbands" (*TM*), in which a woman's lover finds himself having the affair in part because of an attraction for her husband. The theme is repeated in *RIR* when Rabbit imagines that he is sexually engaged with both Cindy* and Webb Murkett.* Updike treats the subject with black humor* in *W*, using male homosexuality as a punch line as Darryl Van Horne* escapes the fury of three witches who had killed the woman he married, Jenny Gabriel; they discover that he married her only to disguise his interest in her brother, Chris, thus committing "near-incest"* as a consequence. Meanwhile, the witches initiate a newcomer into lesbianism in the cauldron of their hot tub. Roger Lambert* often wonders if Dale Kohler* may be homosexual and fantasizes about his wife fellating Dale (*RV*).

In the 1990s Lyle, dying of AIDS,* becomes Updike's first important gay character (*RaR*). Rabbit, fearing death* himself, sympathizes with Lyle, but without compassion. But, conflicted, Rabbit in his anger attributes the Springer Motors* bankruptcy to "pills for a queer." Perhaps Rabbit simply struggles against his own homosexual curiosity, since he admits that he cannot think of Thelma Harrison* without thinking of her husband Ronnie Harrison's penis. Rabbit considers that perhaps all men are "queer" and that penises are what men "care about." He earlier mused that vaginas are "homely" and nipples "scary" (*RIR*). In a scene added to *RaR* for *RA*, Rabbit, in a hellish locker room, is entranced by the "hairy column" of an old man's behind. Thus Rabbit is brought to seriously consider a subject lightly dismissed when homosexuals were stigmatized in Brewer* (*RaR*). Moreover, in the story "Cruise" (*A*) Updike considers the social repercussions of being falsely considered gay. *See* **Sex**.

Bibliography: Updike, "The Lens Factory," *Granta* (Fall 1989): 265–69. "A Same-Sex Idyll," *New Yorker* 31 May 1999: 113–14; Marshall Boswell, "The World and the Void: *Creatio ex Nihilo* and Homoeroticism in Updike's *Rabbit Is Rich*," in Yerkes, *JU*.

Hook, John. Modeled on Updike's maternal grandfather, John Franklin Hoyer, John Hook is a ninety-four-year-old retired history* teacher in *PF* who rebels against the treatment given him and others in the poorhouse by the new prefect Stephen Conner.* Hook's intellectual confrontations with Conner form the spine of ideas in the book, and Conner's subsequent misidentification of Hook as an instigator in Conner's stoning forms the novel's melancholy end. A patient, thoughtful and unconventional man, Hook maintains an appreciation for the ways of the past, including woodcrafting and quilting, religion* and more humanistic treatment of humans and animals alike. He fails to convince Conner that Conner's hope for a world without pain and waste is utterly misguided "busy-ness." Hook recognizes that Conner's world would dissolve religion, but Hook sees virtue "workable as wood."

The exchange of Hook and Conner foreshadows the confrontation of Rev. Jack Eccles* and Rev. Fritz Kruppenbach,* in which Eccles's concern for the psychological and social health of his congregation is rejected by Kruppenbach, who says, "There is nothing but Christ for us . . . all this . . . busyness, is nothing. It is Devil's work" (*RR*). Hook has a moment of understanding at the novel's end, prompted by his view of a quilt at the fair. The quilt brings together his personal and social insights, but in his advanced age he is unable to focus them. Similarly, the narrative closes with Hook searching for something he must tell Conner and failing to find it. His search makes a circular connection to the opening of the narrative, in which Hook asks, "What's this?" of newly tagged porch chairs.

Hoping for a Hoopoe (London: Gollancz, 1959). The title of this English edition of *CH*, *Hoping for a Hoopoe*, indicated to Updike something closer to the spirit of England than a "carpentered hen" since the hoopoe, a lark, is essentially Eurasian. Updike mentions it in a poem; no doubt he knew of its literary ancestry as Keats's skylark and Shakespeare's figurative lark of Sonnet 30, which "sings hymns at heaven's gate." In *C* Updike reminds us that Zeus first made love to Hera as a hoopoe. In myth* the hoopoe was the bird into which Tereus was transformed after Procne and Philomela had begged the gods for help after their murder of Itys; part of this myth is employed by T. S. Eliot* in *The Waste Land*. Perhaps because of this transformation, a hoopoe is considered good luck. Clearly, good luck followed Updike after this book. *See* **Light Verse; Poetry**.

Hostile Critics. As a critic himself, Updike seldom publishes a review of a book he has not liked and has generally avoided reviewing the work of his American contemporaries. In *PP* he offered his own principles for reviewing. He advised the critic never to review the author, only the book, and that the author never be used to settle scores with other critics. Among those who have followed these principles but have still written negative reviews of Updike's works are some of America's finest critics, like Frederick Crews and Michiko Kakutani. William Gass, Richard Aldridge and Richard Gilman allege that while Updike has a wonderful style,* he has nothing to say. Diana Trilling uttered what Updike called the "banshee cry of indignation" at the sex* in *Couples*. Dorothy Rabinowitz panned *MW*. Jonathan Yardley wrote a lone but impassioned dissent about the vulgarity of *RIR*. Frederick Crews objected to sexism in *RV* (as did Michiko Kakutani about *S.*,) and also found racism in *B* and cynicism in *TE*. Ralph Wood rebuked Updike for not being morally decisive in *IB*, and Gore Vidal attacked Updike for defending the Vietnam* War in *SC*.

But as one of America's foremost writers, Updike has offered an irresistible target for certain reviewers, some of whom sound more than the occasional "banshee cry." A few relentless critics who automatically reject Updike write for *Commentary*, which, Updike has felt, has a policy developed by its editor, Norman Podhoretz, of opposing him, not just his books. Even Harold Bloom, who edited a collection of essays on Updike, compares Updike to John P. Marquand, a writer Updike sees as a mere chronicler of the upper class. Updike has said about such comments, "One would rather hear something else," and generally does not read them. Yet in a Philip Roth* review, Updike remarked, "By the age of fifty a writer should have settled his old scores" (*OJ*). So he responded to Vidal, finding that he was severely limited by his "incredible rejection of the American lifestyle," that he created surprisingly stupid and angry characters, and that he lacked "the love one needs to write about something effective" (Plath, *CV*). Three years after Vidal's attack on *SC*, Updike reviewed a book on H. L. Mencken* with a "superfluous foreword" by Vidal in which his sneers at Mencken seemed "quite abstract, rooted in nothing less airy than a belief that sneering becomes him" (*MM*).

Updike once explained that he left New York* in 1957 partly because, paraphrasing Ernest Hemingway,* its literary society was composed of "tapeworms trying to feed on each other" (Plath, *CU*). Updike learned much later that writers at the *New Yorker** whom he idolized—John Cheever,* Ogden Nash and S. J. Perelman—confirmed Hemingway's insight. They had written spiteful letters concerning Updike's writing and public appearances; Updike chose to think this not only "chastening" but edifying. Perelman, Updike knew, objected to anyone's efforts to write graphically about sex, and he understood the insecurities that drove Cheever to undermine him. Updike realized that the literary scene "is a kind of *Medusa's* raft, small and sinking, and one's instinct when a newcomer tries to clamber aboard is to stamp on his fingers" (*OJ*). Another *New Yorker* contributor, Truman Capote, asserted in *Esquire* in 1972 that apart from the drowning of baby Becky in *RR*, the rest of the novel was "hooey." At a meeting in 1964, Capote said that Updike "thought I was crazy." Richard Gilman in *The Confusion of Realms* also assaulted Updike's style. John Gardner in *On Moral Fiction* expressed disappointment with Updike's titillating the bourgeois need for sexual perversion in *Couples*, but Updike simply replied that his work required graphic sex. He has stated his refusal to "placate hallucinatory critical voices," like those of Gardner and other hostile critics. Consequently, he has not replied to the outrageous remarks by Eugene Lyons, who attacked *RRed* for its "breathtaking ineptitude" and Skeeter's* "sentimental and self-contradictory blather."

Instead of replying directly to Norman Mailer's objections that his style smelled of stale garlic and that he has nothing to say, Updike answered him in his own fiction. In his "Foreword" to *BB* Updike's Jewish novelist Henry Bech* rails at "John"* for making him a man of "bravura narcissism" who sounds like a "gentlemanly Norman Mailer." Later Bech refers to himself as scribbling reviews and "impressionistic" journalism for *Esquire*, for which Mailer then wrote. Mailer changed his tone in 1998 by telling interviewer Charlie Rose that he would rank Updike among the top five American writers. In "Bech and the Bounty of Sweden" (*BaB*) Bech thought Mailer more worthy than he of the Nobel Prize.*

Updike's career-long serious influential opponents have been limited to Norman Podhoretz, John Aldridge, Harold Bloom, Dorothy Rabinowitz, Diana Trilling and Gore Vidal. In *PP* Updike instructed Aldridge and Podhoretz never to try to put an author "in his place" or make him a "pawn in the contest with other reviewers." Updike also sent Henry Bech after them. In Bech's "bibliography" to *BB*, Podhoretz and Aldridge are mocked by the very titles of their pieces on Bech. (Perhaps Updike refused to be what Michael Sragow called "the fall goy" for New York Jewish intellectuals like Podhoretz.) In "Bech Noir" (*BaB*) five critics die, one of whom, Lucas Mishner, may be modeled on Bloom. Bech reads about Mishner's natural death with glee because Mishner had written that "the American sublime" would "never touch his pages." Bloom's "Introduction" to a collection of essays on Updike in 1987 accuses Updike of being a major stylist who will never touch the "American sublime." The phrase was taken without attribution from Wallace Stevens.* In Updike's essay "Stevens as Dutchman" (*MM*), Updike showed that the remark stung. Stevens, he wrote, had been "hoisted into great esteem by such connoisseurs of the American sublime as Harold Bloom." Mishner's death gives Bech the idea of becoming the "Scourge of Gotham" and killing his old critics.

As for Bech's other victims, it is teasing to think that Aldie Cannon might be Aldridge and Debora Frueh might be Dorothy Rabinowitz or Diana Trilling. (In *RRed* Jill Pendleton's* mother's new married name is Aldridge; Jill's uttering her name brings tears. Of her husband, Harry "Rabbit" Angstrom* thinks, "The man remained blank for me.") In various interviews following *BaB*, Updike cited the reviewer Dorothy Rabinowitz's attack on *MW* as an effort to destroy him, not just his work and his career, by insisting that he applies "the same baroque effort to make much of little." Updike has not commented on the astonishing attack on *SC* by Fred Inglis.

Updike's remarks to his creature Henry Bech, if taken literally, show that even friendly critics can strike Updike painfully: "Even the on-cheering ones have read a different book than the one you wrote. All the little congruences and arabesques you prepared with such delicate anticipatory pleasure are gobbled up as if by pigs at a pastry cart." But Updike has generously responded to serious criticism, indicating works by Alfred Kazin, Alice and Kenneth Hamilton, Joyce Markle, George Hunt and the present writer as stimulating and perceptive. *See* **American Academy of Arts and Letters; Criticism by Updike**.

Bibliography: Updike, "Bech Meets Me" (*PP*); "On One's Own Oeuvre," in *HS*, 870–75; "Henry Bech Interviews John Updike" (*MM*); Norman Mailer, "Norman Mailer vs. Nine Writers," *Esquire* 60 (July 1963): 63–69, 105; Norman Podhoretz. "A Dissent on Updike," in *Doings and Undoings* (New York: Farrar, Straus, 1964), 251–57; John Aldridge, "The Private Vice of John Updike," in *Time to Murder and Create: The Contemporary Novel in Crisis* (New York: McKay, 1966), 164–71; Charles T. Samuels, "The Art of Fiction XLII: John Updike," *Paris Review* 12 (Winter 1968): 84–117; Eugene Lyons, "John Updike: The Beginning and the End," *Critique* 14 (1972): 44–58; Dorothy Rabinowitz, "Current Books in Short Compass," *World* 24 Oct. 1972: 52–53; Harold Bloom, "Introduction," in Bloom, *JU*; Scott Donaldson, *John Cheever: A Biography* (New York: Random House, 1988); Fred Inglis, "On Being a Dud," *Nation* 249 (10 July 1989): 59–61; John Cheever, *The Journals of John Cheever* (New York: Knopf, 1991).

Hoyer, John Franklin (1863–1953). Updike's maternal grandfather, John Franklin Hoyer, was born in Berks County just after the Battle of Gettysburg, of Pennsylvania Dutch Democrats who were involved in county politics. He and his wife Katherine Kramer Hoyer* lived with the Updikes in Shillington* and later in Plowville.* Updike described him as having "that old-fashioned way of talking as a kind of performance." Updike has said that he made an "oblique monument" to his grandfather in the "guise" of John F. Hook,* so one surmises that Hoyer's voice patterns became those of Hook, the retired teacher of *PF*. Also, Updike compared his grandfather to President James Buchanan": both were Masons, knew the Bible* well and "depended upon and distrusted women." Updike included in *PF* the only political story he recalls his grandfather telling, of the Quakers' exploitation of runaway slaves. He dedicated *CP* to "all" of his family, from John Hoyer to a recent grandson, and he leaves them with a proverb "ascribed" to John Hoyer: "You carry your own hides to market." Hoyer's father helped to build the steeple of Plow Church, as Updike notes in "Plow Cemetery" (*FN*). His daughter Linda Hoyer Updike* was born in the Hoyers' sandstone farmhouse in Plowville. Though her parents sold it during the depression and lived in Shillington with the Updikes, Linda Updike repurchased the home in 1945 and relocated her parents to the farm where each of them were to die. *See* **Epigrams**.

Bibliography: Updike, "The Blessed Man of Boston, My Grandmother's Thimble, and Fanning Island" (*PigF*).

Hoyer, Katherine Ziemer Kramer (1880?–1955). Updike's maternal grandmother and the youngest of a dozen children, Katherine Hoyer held him in 1935 when he was three years old and twenty years later, afflicted with Parkinson's disease and dying, held his daughter Elizabeth, then three months old. Married to a man much older than she, Katherine Hoyer gave birth to Linda Hoyer Updike* in their Plowville* farmhouse, to which the Updikes moved in 1945. Updike notes that the "image she projected" was "always serving" (*OJ*). In a nostalgic story he recalls how with adolescent gusto Updike had carried his little grandmother, "who had carried me," and how his mother remembered her mother as "always" doing things like lighting lamps. "Shaped like a sickle," as he saw her, "her life whipped through grasses of confusion," he wrote in "The Blessed Man of Boston," "My Grandmother's Thimble" and "Fanning Island" (*PigF*). This Proustian* work concerns his rediscovery of the thimble Katherine Hoyer had given him and his wife Mary* as a wedding present. Fighting a "long battle with Parkinson's disease," she is remembered in the disease afflicting Mary Angstrom* (*RRed*), and since he witnessed her strength when he was a child and her enfeeblement when he was an adult, Katherine Hoyer represents the physical unraveling of life, a dominant theme in Updike's work.

"Hub Fans Bid Kid Adieu." "Hub Fans Bid Kid Adieu," Updike's famous report of the last game played by baseball Hall of Famer Ted Williams, was undertaken on Updike's personal initiative in September 1960. First published in the *New Yorker*, the essay was collected in *AP* and has been reprinted frequently as one of the masterpieces of sports reportage, both for its lyricism and accuracy and for its clear understanding of the significance of the game in which Williams homered in his final at bat and then refused to answer the adoring ovation of his fans. As Updike realized, "Gods do not answer letters."

Bibliography: "Diamonds Are Forever," *Time* 130 (21 Dec. 1987): 66; Mimi Kramer, "Hub Fans Bid Kid Adieu," *New Yorker* 65 (13 Mar. 1989): 75.

Hugging the Shore (New York: Knopf, 1983). *HS*, Updike's third collection of essays, reviews and miscellaneous writing, continues the pattern of *PP*. The book is divided into two parts, "Persons and Places" and "Other People's Books," with a composite interview* "On One's Own Oeuvre." *HS* contains one hundred pieces from the *New Yorker*,* of which ninety-two are reviews. The title is oddly modest, asserting, as the "Foreword" reveals, that "hugging the shore" is the critic's choice, as he mediates between mind and mind. The artist strikes for the open sea and seeks a "fervent relation with the world."

In the "Foreword" Updike refers to his "improvised sub-career as a reviewer" for the *New Yorker*, as he had in *PP*, and alludes to his tactic of filling his reviews with quotations so that if a review was bad, the writer was condemned "out of his own mouth." Updike also indicates that some pieces in the book are "attempts at humor and fantasy, journalistic assignments," and thus should not be taken overly seriously. Proudly Updike counts 34,869 pages "specifically reviewed or introduced, all within the eight years since I wrapped up *Picked-up Pieces*." He had hoped for a "smaller heap"; this was larger, *OJ* would be larger still and *MM* as well.

In part one, "Persons and Places," Updike supplies amusing pieces on "eminent Americans" and his only piece of science fiction, "The Chaste Planet." Two pieces on golf* were later reprinted in *GD*. As if to serve notice that he is now a New Englander, Updike reprints five pieces on New England churches, baseball and beaches. The light tone of these pieces recalls the light-verse* sections of his early books of poetry, *CH* and *TP*.

Part two, "Other People's Books," ten times longer than part one, projects a serious engagement with Nathaniel Hawthorne,* Herman Melville* and Walt Whitman.* Hawthorne's* *Scarlet Letter* was particularly important since it directly influenced the writing of *MS, RV* and *S.*, the "*Scarlet Letter* Trilogy," and Whitman provided ideas that helped to shape *IB*; the impact of Melville on Updike's work is harder to trace. Updike follows these scholarly essays with several reviews of the correspondence of Gustave Flaubert, James Joyce,* Franz Kafka,* Ernest Hemingway* and E. B. White, all of whom were major influences on Updike. The seven reviews following and remembrances of Edmund Wilson* and Vladimir Nabokov* again focus on writers of lifelong concern to Updike. Updike then takes up reviews of contemporary American and British novelists, particularly the significant influence Henry Green,* and examines writers from Russia, Poland, India, China and Africa. The African reviews helped Updike in researching *Coup*, an example of how his fictional interests fed his reviewing. The extraordinary range of such reviews identifies Updike as a major critic of world literature, as he had been in *PP*. In addition, Updike reviews nonfiction in a biography of Doris Day, the criticism of Roland Barthes and the poetry of L. E. Sissman, Updike's Harvard* friend. He also reviews books about his fellow Reading* poet, Wallace Stevens,* and about W. H. Auden.*

As in *PP*, Updike furnishes a large omnibus interview, "On One's Own Oeuvre," which continues his publication of biographical information. The interview touches on his earliest reading (James Thurber*), life at Harvard, influences on *RR* and the evolution of the novel *Couples* from "Couples: A Short Story." Updike apparently decided that publishing such "insider" information would reduce the possibility of critics probing his biography and getting the facts wrong. He would continue to be forthcoming in *HS, SC, OJ* and *MM*.

Undoubtedly surprising to those who know Updike solely as a fictionalist are the many pages devoted to poetry.* He reprints several translations (adapted from literal translations) of poems by the Russian Yevgeny Yevtushenko. Updike also shows, side by side, the inaccuracies that occurred when two of his poems were translated into Russian from literal English versions. He points out the "less excusably propagandistic" damage done to one of his poems containing a stanza about the protest against the Vietnam* War. To illustrate his own sense of the importance of his poetry, Updike reprints in its entirety an interview concerning *TT*, and in a response to a query from a high-school magazine, he supplies a description of the inception of his poem "Seagulls." For scholars, Updike supplies an "Autobibliographical Note" to his sixteen sonnets published in a special edition.

After these pieces on poetry, Updike argues against government funding for the arts. His own creation, Henry Bech,* conducts a famous interview with him—Bech had appeared as interviewer in *PP* also—eliciting from Updike the admission that he does not want to write "gushers" but books that "unlock the traffic jam in everybody's head." Updike closes this section and *HS* with acceptance speeches for awards.* In his acceptance speech for the National Book Critics Circle Award for *RIR*, Updike thanks his characters* "for coming to life as best they could and for enduring in resilient style the indignities I had planned for them." For the same novel Updike accepted the American Book Award, remarking that prizes may produce more discomfort than joy since so many writers go unrewarded, and he tells the "prizeless" to have faith that society does need to know "what only you can tell it." *HS* won the National Book Critics Circle Award for nonfiction. *See* **Criticism by Updike.**

Bibliography: Schiff, *JU*.

I

ICBM. The acronym ICBM stands for intercontinental ballistic missile, a weapon capable of long-range destruction with a conventional or nuclear warhead. Kush has ICBMs in its arsenal, pointed at the Soviet Union and the United States (*Coup*).

I Love a Mystery. The radio program mentioned in *C*, *I Love a Mystery*, featured "Doc, Red, and Curly." The show aired in the 1940s, and Updike recalls it taking place in "a cave full of chirping monkeys." During this time Updike was reading, as he said, "hundreds" of mysteries by Agatha Christie,* Earl Stanley Gardner, Dashiell Hammett and many others; Ruth Leonard Byer* also reads mysteries in *RR*. Cosmic mystery and human mystery form the substance of *RV*, and one is tempted to see Roger Lambert,* his red-headed wife Esther Lambert* and Dale Kohler* as Doc, Red and Curly. Updike has said that he tries to inject mystery into everything he writes, and his ambiguous treatment of the death* of Harry "Rabbit" Angstrom* has left many readers mystified about whether or not Rabbit really died, just as readers of *C* were puzzled about George Caldwell's* death. *See* **"Murder Makes the Magazine."**

Bibliography: Updike, "Reflections on Radio" (*MM*).

Imagery. Precise, evocative images are a hallmark of Updike's style.* Updike takes great care in creating images that appeal concretely to the senses, particularly the visual senses (e.g., eye color). Some images that recur throughout Updike's fiction and poetry* are films,* food,* mirrors, drugs,* clothing and art.* Updike, as he has said, enjoys the challenge of creating a single dominant image that might take its place with Huckleberry Finn, and such an "image" is the character* Harry "Rabbit" Angstrom.* Updike also aspires, as he has said, to keep a mass of images moving forward throughout a novel in a coherent pattern. Thus in *RR* images of ascent/descent, doubleness, nets and traps, Peter Rabbit, food, water and circles are woven together to deepen the narrative and themes.

Images often form patterns related to themes and thus become motifs, like the motif of "congestion" that dominates *RA*, or of nature* in *TE*. Although a great many patterns of images form motifs in Updike's work, a few can be isolated for special attention. *PF* uses eye imagery to distinguish the opposition of John Hook* and Stephen Conner.* Eye images make a series of puns ("eye/I") in "Midpoint" (*M*). *RR* develops holes, ascent/descent, traps and images of color, clothes and indigestion derived from *The Tale of Peter Rabbit.** *RRed* uses images of the moon landing and Vietnam* as well as the radio serial *The Lone Ranger** and scatology. *RIR* uses money and energy images attached to the theme "running out of gas." *RaR* creates patterns of images of airplanes,* sports* figures and wars. *RA*, taken as a whole, uses images of sex, religion, art, food, clothes and films. *RV* employs images from computing, particularly I/O (input, output) and spatial imagery. *MS* utilizes typos as puns as an image pattern. *Couples, Marry, B* and *GC* employ images of courtly love connected to the story of Tristan and Isolde.*

Bibliography: Markle, *FL*.

Incest. In *PP* Updike remarked that "rape is the sexual sin of the mob, adultery* of the bourgeoisie, and incest of the aristocracy," and twenty-four years later he added that incest is "self-love turned heterosexual . . . the Romantics' ultimate daydream" ("Excellent Humbug" [*MM*]). Updike used this "ultimate daydream" frequently in his work to indicate a fantasy of subversive sex* or to symbolize psychological wholeness. In Updike's early work incest appears subversively in children* and adolescents passing through the Oedipal stage of psychic development, in which a son or daughter competes for the opposite parent's affection. Lucy Eccles,* who thinks Sigmund Freud* "God," draws Harry "Rabbit" Angstrom's* attention to the incestuous desire of three-year-old Joyce Eccles for her father, Jack Eccles,* to Rabbit's surprise (*RR*). The incest motif is revealed in *Couples* when Janet Appleby's Freudian analyst uncovers her incestuous desires as a child.

This complex can be prolonged if entanglements occur during passage, and thus incestual desire can remain. Peter Caldwell* in *C* actively wishes to replace his father, George Caldwell,* "That silly sad man whom I thought our romance had long since excluded." In his imagination he and his mother live in a "little intricate world . . . where my father was a fond strange joke." On the phone she speaks, to his ears, "incestuously." Peter, now in his second marriage, is transformed into Joey Robinson* in *OF*, a narrative, Updike said, that takes place "after the centaur has died." Joey dresses in his father's clothes and shares intimate secrets with his mother, partly designed to undermine his choice of a second wife (*OF*). Harry "Rabbit" Angstrom's Oedipal pattern continues throughout *RA* and facilitates his son Nelson's* own Oedipal entanglement. In *RR* Rabbit admits that his mother had the most "force" of anyone he had known, and he is indifferent to his father, Earl Angstrom.* After Rabbit leaves his wife Janice Angstrom,* Earl castigates his son as "the worst kind of Brewer bum." Janice tells him that his deep attachment to his mother drove her to adultery (*RRed*). Rabbit's unsuccessful Oedipal journey contributes to his son Nelson's wish that Rabbit would die, "then me and mom." Also, in "Eros Rampant" (*TF*) ten-year-old Richard Maple, Jr., is in love with his thirteen-year-old sister Judith. Elsewhere, men may metaphorically maternalize their wives, or wives paternalize their husbands. Richard Mathias assures his wife Sally Mathias that Jerry Conant* will not divorce her since men don't divorce their mothers (*Marry*). In "Incest" (*SD*) Lee fears that he may have married his mother-in-law, finding in his wife traits of her mother. Also, he dreams of an immense face of Marcel Proust,* whose fabled dependency on his mother is known to Lee and his wife Jane. Images associated with their daughter Jane and his mother-in-law seem to blend in a dream* Lee has.

Some men, however, feel that a psychological union with close kin may restore their sense of identity, though it is dangerous. To Charlie Stavros's* disgust, Rabbit expresses his desire for his daughter-in-law Teresa "Pru" Angstrom* (*RIR*), and Rabbit sleeps with her a decade later, discovering "Paradise" anew. But Pru's confession to Rabbit's son Nelson and Rabbit's wife Janice precipitates Rabbit's flight to Florida* and eventual death (*RaR*). In *RV* Roger Lambert* is more fortunate in his metaphorical return to innocence. As an adolescent, he had wanted to sleep with his half-sister Edna; years later, he sleeps with her daughter Verna Ekelof,* who, knowing his desire for her mother, urges him to transfer those feelings to her. Lambert does so only when desire and curiosity erode his scruples. Again, only after years and two divorces does Hank Arnold satisfy his infatuation for his wife's twin. This quasi-incest unites him with his lost self ("The Other" [*TM*]). In the town of Tarbox of *Couples*, friends become "family," so Piet Hanema* notes the incestual simplicity of making love with Georgene Thorne. Oedipal fantasy becomes adult action, but with painful consequences for Piet. Also, Claudius* waits more than twenty-five years before seducing his brother's wife (*GC*). The candid observations of Piet, like the deliberate actions of Hank Arnold, Roger Lambert and Rabbit, reveal men in moral turmoil during the sexual revolution. Amusingly, the gods in *C* dare incest, but Chiron,* attracted to his half-sister Venus, observes the ban and refuses her offer. *See* **Style**.

Bibliography: Greiner, *JU*.

Influenced Writers. Surprisingly, direct influence by Updike on other writers is not easy to trace. The most obvious case is that of Nicholson Baker in his autobiographical *U and I*. Updike's profound effect upon Baker as a writer and person is described, sometimes comically, as Baker records how subjects, themes, characters and images he wished to explore were in fact anticipated in Updike's fiction. Their lone meeting takes place at a *Harvard Lampoon** reception, and Baker is surprised to discover that Updike clearly recalls Baker's work, even a Baker story in the same issue of the *New Yorker* in which Updike appeared.* Although Baker's book could be one more experiment in his highly inventive career, he may well be speaking for other writers who felt anticipated by Updike.

Andrew Field's Nabokovian* novel *Fractions* (1969) includes a minor character named Dick Upjohn who has written *Rabbit, Run* and *The Centaur* as well as many stories in the Updike oeuvre. At times Field writes in superficially Updikean style, but his purpose is never entirely clear, despite the hero, Dick, ironically intending to write a critical book about Upjohn. Field's novel also resembles Vladimir Nabokov's *Pale Fire*, and in a "Foreword" by "Truman Forward," Field remarks that no one should confuse Upjohn with Updike, a disclaimer that suggests that celebrity writers are already perplexed about their identities, something Updike has shown in "Updike and I" (*MM*). The "foreword" resembles that of Henry Bech* to Updike in *BB*. Also, Updike has noted some similarities in style to *RR* of the sole instance of attributed influence, Kenzaburo Ohe's *The Personal Matter*. Updike disowns Martin Walser's *No Man's Land*, despite a blurb announcing, "The closest thing the Western Germans have to John Updike."

Bibliography: Nicholson Baker, *U and I* (New York: Random House, 1991).

Interviews. Despite his frequently stated aversion for interviews, Updike has consented to dozens in print and on radio, television* and the Internet, and he has enjoyed using the form, both satirically and seriously. Quite early, Updike discovered that the interview, a necessary evil for the successful author, could be turned into a crafted work, so he revised his written replies to questions before their publication, creating a more carefully articulated reply to the queries Updike chose to answer in, for example, the *Paris Review* interview (Plath, *CV*). This was also a way in which Updike might avoid being asked the same questions repeatedly. But he also overcame what he considered an "intrinsically phony" transaction, because the writer's art simply eludes description, and talking about it promotes an illusion that the craft of writing is a fully conscious endeavor, and also deflects attention from the work to the writer. Thus Updike declared in an interview (ironically) that the interview is a "half form, like maggots, and a form to be loathed." Words tossed off because of a prompt become equal in weight to words polished to precision for publication. Since Updike sometimes revises already published work when he is republishing, his concern for the spoken word's slipperiness must be all the more acute. Interviewers necessarily seek to reveal the "real Updike," but as he indicated in his essay "Updike and I" (*MM*) "Updike" the writer is a mystery to John Updike. One would not be able to guess these things, though, from the patient, charming, poised, witty and gracious interviews Updike has given, but his resistance shows clearly in his comic and serious treatments of interviews.

Updike satirizes and parodies the interview form throughout his work, from the early *New Yorker** amusements, ten of which were collected as *People One Knows* (Northridge, CA: Lord John Press, 1980) to "The Interview" (*TM*). But in Henry Bech's* painful seduction-interview by a parasitic London reporter ("Bech Swings") Updike provides a sympathetic portrait of the badgered writer-celebrity who fears that he will be abused but cannot contain his vanity. Turning Bech himself to satiric account, Updike has Bech interview him, his creator, about *RRed, RIR, MF* and *BaB*. Bech's approach is typically sardonic, supercilious and self-concerned. Updike's characters,* usually women, interview each other in *S.* and *W.* Sarah Worth* even conceals a tape recorder to question the Arhat* and gets a more personal tape than she anticipated. Sukie Rougemont* queries Darryl Van Horne* for her newspaper The *Word* as Van Horne insists on trying to improve her interviewing technique. Each interviewee is distinctly uncomfortable. A more excitable character instructs the questioner about what can and cannot be used while offering extraneous information that bores the reporter, as though the interview simply reveals that one person has a job to protect and another a job to do ("One More Interview" [*TM*]).

Bibliography: Updike, "Bech Meets Me," "One Big Interview" (*PP*); "Updike on Updike," *New York Times Book Review* 27 Sept. 1981: 1, 34, 38; "On One's Own Oeuvre," "Interviews with Insufficiently Famous Americans" (*HS*); "Literarily Personal" (*OJ*); "Introduction," *Writers at Work: The Paris Review Interviews, Seventh Series*, "Updike and I," "Henry Bech Interviews Updike" (*MM*); "Questions of Character: There's No Ego as Wounded as a Wounded Alter Ego," *New York Times* 1 Mar. 1999: E1, E7; Plath, *CU*.

In the Beauty of the Lilies (New York: Knopf, 1996). *IB* is the first Updike novel to treat the history of a family through several generations and through most of the twentieth century. The novel's four sections explore four members of the Wilmot family, each with spiritual problems. The book follows, as Updike has said, the "curve" of his own family, with Clarence Wilmot* clearly modeled on Updike's paternal grandfather, Hartley Updike,* and Wilmot's wife, Stella Wilmot, on his paternal grandmother. Like Hartley Updike, Wilmot has a throat problem that makes it impossible to preach; his wife delivers his sermons.* Updike connects the loss of voice to Wilmot's loss of faith, which, because he loses his job as a minister,* cripples his family. While Hartley sold insurance, Wilmot sells encyclopedias, and when business goes bad, Wilmot goes to the movies. After Wilmot's death, his son Ted Wilmot* rejects a chance to live a fast life in New York for the slow

Courtesy of Martha Updike

pace of a small Delaware town, where he works as a postman. Ted rejects God because God did not aid his father's crisis. Ted's daughter, Essie Wilmot,* becomes a film* star, Alma DeMott, instinctively feeling that she completes her grandfather's religious work. Her son Clark DeMott,* after wasting his life, dedicates himself to a religious cult and is killed when the fanatical leader, Jesse Smith,* confronts the authorities. The novel's structure thus places Essie/Alma's career between the loss of faith of Wilmot and Smith's religious fanaticism.

The novel is important for its direct treatment of the problem of spiritual disillusionment, something Updike's other ministers had suffered (see *RV* and *MS*) and for its demonstrated connection between the religious impulse and the attractions of the movies. When Reverend Wilmot suddenly recognizes that he cannot answer biblical debunkers or realistic modern religious thinkers, he rejects his ministry, and a year's enforced sabbatical (resembling that of Rev. Tom Marshfield* in *MS*), does not help Wilmot to retrieve his faith. He then sells encyclopedias, a virtual parody of ministers who spread "the Word": though he supplies millions of words, none help him to recover his faith. The encyclopedia, an authoritative and systematic organization of information, is a distraction from his loss of religious inspiration, and moviegoing substitutes for churchgoing and supplies a different sense of transcendence. Wilmot's failure to reclaim his faith leads, in the second chapter, to his son's rejection of religion,* since Ted feels that God preferred not to save his father by giving him the faith he craved. Yet Wilmot's faith is reborn in his granddaughter Essie, who becomes a film star, claiming a vast congregation of followers and completing the ministry begun by her grandmother, who spoke for Wilmot when he strangled on the words of the sermon he could no longer believe.

Alma's success is in proportion to Wilmot's failure. She is able to provide vast assemblies with magnified images they can relate to. But she pays a great price for her art when, in the fourth chapter, her son Clark, neglected by Alma while she pursued her career, finds spiritual commitment in Jesse Smith's apocalyptic interpretations of the Bible.* Only when Clark at last understands that such literal decoding of the Bible will result in outright murder does he recover his senses and kill the false prophet. Clark thus embodies Clarence Wilmot's need to pursue belief even to death,* Ted's dismissal of a God indifferent to human need and Alma's ability to satisfy the longing of filmgoers with her larger-than-life film portrayals. Like his mother, he becomes an example of the possibilities of making one's role in life something worthy of emulation, and like her he becomes a television* star.

Updike offers an unconventional description of how the movies have replaced the churches as respites for spiritual renewal by describing the appeal of film to the defeated Wilmot and showing how Alma's fixation with film stars led her to satisfy others in her screen roles. She unknowingly reiterates Wilmot's belief that the material and immaterial worlds could be linked. The need to believe is unbounded, accounting for both the stardom of Alma and the charisma of Jesse Smith. Smith appeals to the same need for transcendence, but unlike Alma, he relies on the language of Revelation to supply answers, as Skeeter* had in *RRed*. Smith divides the world into good and evil, but Alma inclusively accepts all roles she is given and adopts to new media like television as mankind alters its style of belief. Clark is the interface of the flexible Alma and the rigid Jessie. If film has replaced print media as a better method by which to transcend the everyday notion of the self, Clark's earning a moment on video news by killing a false prophet is an effective demonstration of the hazards of the new transcendence. The impact upon the video audience of his heroism may be no less dangerous to some than Wilmot's questioning of Christ's divinity, Alma's magnification on screen of a variety of human types, or Smith's fanatical encoding of the Bible. Yet the film and video world's direct presentation of images allows the congregation to accept or reject those images in accordance with its own construction of the world. Updike's various real and symbolic ministers thus extend his continual concern for the meaning of sustaining faith in the immaterial world while one is situated in the material one.

The novel also provides interesting connections to Updike's previous novels. In *IB*, for example, he lovingly re-creates Paterson, New Jersey, in the manner of his re-creations of Shillington* and Reading,* Pennsylvania, in *RA*. Clark's decision to stay or run echoes Harry "Rabbit" Angstrom's* celebrated flight and Alma's lengthier "run" from small-town values to a universally satisfying art. Insofar as the film world is a community and Smith's commune is a community, *IB* recalls Updike's other communities of *PF*, *Couples*, *S.* and *W*. The novel also exhibits Updike's love of expertise* with his generous quoting from the Bible and theological sources (shown in *MS* and *RV*), and his citing of dozens of films and film personalities continues his lifelong absorption in film. Updike has written about the postal service in "The Wallet" (*TM*). The sweeping time scheme recalls "Made in Heaven" (*TM*), which takes place from 1930 to 1980. Updike indicates that elements of his family history in the story "The Family Meadow" (*MuS*) resemble his family history in *IB*.

Bibliography: Updike, "Legendary Lana," "A 'Special Message' for *In the Beauty of the Lilies*" (*MM*); "*In the Beauty of the Lilies*," *Publisher's Weekly* 13 Nov. 1995: 48; Michiko Kakutani, "Seeking Salvation on the Silver Screen," *New York Times* 12 Jan. 1996: C1; A. O. Scott, "God Goes to the Movies," *Nation* 12 Feb. 1996: 25–28; George Steiner, "Supreme Fiction," *New Yorker* 11 Mar. 1996: 105–6; Ralph C. Wood, "Into the Void: Updike's Sloth and America's Religion," *Christian Century* 24 Apr. 1996: 452–55, 457.

Ipswich, Massachusetts. After marrying on June 26, 1953, John Updike and his wife Mary Pennington Updike* began their honeymoon three hours later in Ipswich, Massachusetts. After Updike left the *New Yorker* (April 1957), they returned to Ipswich, partly to avoid the distractions of the New York* literary life. Ipswich gave him the environment in which to concentrate his full resources, and it enabled Updike to raise his family and live as an ordinary person. Ipswich gave him "elbow room, writing room," but in a sense he was returning to Shillington,* Pennsylvania, the town of his boyhood. Eventually Updike wrote in a secluded poorly heated room over a restaurant in downtown Ipswich. He took part in the life of the town, writing the Ipswich pageant for "Seventeenth Century Day," along with joining the Congregational Church building committee, working on the Democratic town committee, joining a recorder group and reviewing concerts. Though he would later write that "Massachusetts is the Puritan superego of New England," in *SC* he wrote, "In my seventeen Ipswich years . . . I felt well located artistically, in a place out of harm's way. . . . Other places I have lived

(Cambridge, New York, Beverly Farms) have been too trafficked, too well cherished by others." In Ipswich he felt "enlisted in actual life."

Ipswich was imaginatively transformed into Tarbox of *Couples*, though Updike insisted that he "never confused" any Ipswich persons with his characters.* His concern for the city's history anticipated Updike's other interests in New England history (*RV, W*) and perhaps awakened his interest in Pennsylvania history (*BD, MF*). Updike remained at Ipswich until 1974, and moved to Beverly Farms, a few miles from Ipswich, in 1982. As he remarked, "A town begins by being anyplace and ends as the Only Place." Three novels (*RR, C, OF*) and a story collection (*MuS*) were published as "Ipswich editions."

Bibliography: Updike, *Three Texts from Early Ipswich: A Pageant* (Ipswich, MA: 17th Century Day Committee: 1968), *A Good Place: Being a Personal Account of Ipswich, Mass., Written on the Occasion of Its Seventeenth-Century Day, 1972, by a Resident, John Updike* (New York: Aloe Editions, 1973); "The Houses of Ipswich," *Architectural Digest* 47 (June 1990): 26, 32; *Concerts at Castle Hill* (Northridge, CA: Lord John Press, 1993); "Foreword to a Special Edition of the Story, 'The Women Who Got Away,' " "Two Answers to the Question of Why I Live in New England" (*MM*); Jonathan Schwartz, "Updike of Ipswich," *Boston* Aug. 1965: 35; "The Dilemma of Ipswich," *Ford Times* 65 (Autumn 1972): 8–15.

Iwo Jima. In *OF* Mrs. Robinson* confuses Iwo Jima with the Bikini Atoll when she misidentifies the bathing suit worn by her daughter-in-law, Peggy Robinson,* as an "Iwo Jima," not a bikini. Her ironic mistake may suggest an indifference to two monumental events in the Pacific during and after World War II. A bloody battle was fought on the Japanese island of Iwo Jima, memorialized in the famous statue erected in Arlington National Cemetery, *The Raising of the Flag on Mt. Suribachi.* In contrast, Bikini Atoll was the site of atomic bomb testing after the war intended to demonstrate American power to the Soviet Union. Peggy's son Richard reads science-fiction stories about the effects of those experiments, and in one all human life is destroyed except for one man. Updike traces the development of the image of the flag raising and its degeneration as it is used in an advertisement (*MM*).

Bibliography: Updike, "Descent of an Image" (*MM*).

J

James, Henry (1843–1916). Henry James was an American novelist whose realistic, psychological approach has formed one of the most important influences on modern writers who depict the mind's intricate workings. His analysis of states of feeling and thought can be detected in Updike's *OF*. James Schiff finds that *IB* "in its moderated sadness . . . seems . . . Jamesian." Updike also shared with James an interest in Nathaniel Hawthorne,* James focusing on craft in *The Scarlet Letter* in his book on Hawthorne, and Updike concentrating on Hawthorne's "creed" and Puritan view of love and modeling three novels on *The Scarlet Letter*. In quoting James's letter to Sarah Orne Jewett in which he warned her away from writing historical novels, Updike found support for his sense of discomfort in writing in Victorian style about James Buchanan.* Yet he experimented with the style in *BD, MF* and *IB*, perhaps taking a cue from James's admission that a "*visitable* past . . . may reach over to us." James explored the complex interactions of Americans in Europe (e.g., *The Ambassadors*, 1903) and Europeans in America (e.g., *The Europeans*, 1878). Updike's Henry Bech* (*BaB, BB, BIB*) may ironically use James's "American theme" by showing how the wily Bech resists various contaminations of foreign countries, while Col. Félix Ellelloû* (*Coup*) in his disdain for American culture may reveal aspects of James's European theme. Also, James's gothic horror fiction like *The Turn of the Screw*, which investigates the ambiguity of good and evil, can be compared to similar uses of the gothic in Updike's *W* and "The Afterlife" (*A*).

James raised short fiction* and criticism to art forms, which Updike has furthered in his constant concern for craft in short fiction and his reviews of fictionalists, both contemporary and canonical, like Herman Melville* and Marcel Proust.* Critic James Schiff has stated that James is the critic Updike most resembles "in his prolific output and astonishing range, his disappointment and disgust with the current state of American fiction, his use of criticism as a 'workshop and testing ground for his creative process,' his particular concern with the shape of a writer's oeuvre, and his 'impressionistic and lyrical' style." Updike uses comments from James's preface to *Roderick Hudson* to distinguish between literature and vulgarity in assessing Tom Wolfe's *A Man in Full*. *See* **American Literature**.

Bibliography: Updike, "How Does the Writer Imagine?" "Introduction to *Indian Summer* by William Dean Howells" (*OJ*); Greiner, *JU*; Schiff, *JU*.

JAP. In slang during the 1960s and 1970s a JAP was a "Jewish American princess," an anti-Semitic term alluding to the privileged position supposedly occupied by young Jewish women in America. A great many jokes were created called "JAP jokes." Ben Turnbull* simply identifies one of his companions in 1969 as "Hester, that flaxen-haired JAP," with indifferent bigotry (*TE*).

Jester's Dozen (Northridge, CA: Lord John Press, 1984). The limited edition *Jester's Dozen* contains twelve poems of forty Updike published in the *Harvard Lampoon** from 1951 to 1954, with eight illustrations by Updike. The book contains a "Foreword" and "Overheard in Widener," "How to Watch a Crew Race," "Professor Harlow Shapley Warbles the Praises of Natural Sciences 115," "Untitled," "Lines," "The Summer Reader," "Lines on the Passing of the *Jackolantern*," "Reverie," "I Like to Sing Also," "Ballade for Subway Sitters," "untitled" and "untitled." All contain Updike's typical witty light verse,* and none of them were reprinted in *CP*. Updike explains in the foreword that these poems contain "a parody of Milton, an exercise in the meter of Ogden Nash, an extended mock-ballad in the manner of Phyllis McGinley, a ballade such as Arthur Guiterman and Louis Untermeyer used to write, and a threnody of sorts" for the *Dartmouth Jackolantern*. *See* **Poetry**.

Jesuits. A Catholic religious order for men (also called the Society of Jesus), the Jesuit order was founded in 1534 by St. Ignatius of Loyola, who aimed to convert the Muslims. The Jesuits intended chiefly to educate the nobility and wealthy persons, most successfully in Paraguay. The order is mentioned in *B* by the bandits' captain to explain how Brazil had been exploited by the "black-robed traitors to their race and religion." Updike thus emphasizes the relation of colonialism and religion,* the context in which the lovers find themselves in attempting to cross class and racial boundaries.

Jimmie, the "Big Mouseketeer." The leader of the Mouseketeers in *The Mickey Mouse Club* Disney* television* program of 1955–59, Jimmie Dodd captures the attention of Harry "Rabbit" Angstrom* and his wife Janice Angstrom* when he offers proverbs from a "wise old Greek" who counseled, "Know thyself." But, as critic Larry Taylor observes, Jimmie equivocates by making this classical "proverb" synonymous with "be yourself." Jimmie also uses religious imagery to challenge his audience of children to express their individuality, since "God doesn't want a tree to be a waterfall." That bromide affects Rabbit, since he has lost his basketball*-star notoriety and has a sure sense of his importance. Ironically, Rabbit defends his interest in Jimmie by thinking of him as a salesman from whom he might learn. Instead, Rabbit sees in Jimmie's wink, which he mimics, "Fraud makes the world go round," that just as he lies about his MagiPeel Kitchen Peeler, so Jimmie lies about his proverb. Later Rabbit mirrors Jimmie when he uses the tree/waterfall idea to refute Rev. Jack Eccles's* arguments against his immature behavior in leaving his family; he is unprepared for Eccles's riposte, "No, but he wants a little tree to become a big tree." Rabbit replies that he would rather not grow up, since maturity is the same as death*; in other words, Rabbit would rather remain a little tree, a child. Jimmie's advice was therefore worthless to him. Eccles admits later that Jimmie's remark stymied him momentarily, perhaps because he shares Rabbit's fear of maturity. In *RRed* we discover that Eccles has left his wife and family, as though he emulates Rabbit. Jimmie is identified as a "guide" by critics Alice and Kenneth Hamilton, but Rabbit is a more trustworthy guide for children than Jimmie. Though each "instructs" children in self-improvement skills, Jimmie falsifies ancient truth and suggests that proverbs are not useful anyway, but Rabbit instructs kids playing basketball by his stellar example (*RR*). In *RaR* he tries to instruct Judy Angstrom* by telling her that he always followed his feelings, which may have gotten him in occasional trouble but brought him a lot of fun. His dying words are intended to help his son Nelson Angstrom,* but his statement—and the situation—are ambiguous. *See* **Cartooning; Classical Writing; Drawing and Painting; Epigrams; Literature**.

"John." Updike's first name is used by Henry Bech* in "his" letter to the author that Updike calls the "Foreword" to *BB*. This "Dear John" letter shows how Updike was willing to allow his alter ego* to evaluate his own motives for creating him, something that also bothers Bech in "Bech and the Bounty of Sweden" (*BaB*). He chides Updike for not really describing Bech as he truly is. Wittily acerbic, Bech warns Updike to produce a character* who really sounds like Bech, not Saul Bellow,* Norman Mailer* or I. B. Singer. Bech inveighs against the exploitation of writers, and he castigates Updike for his "goyishe brass" in asking him to write the "Foreword." Bech later turns the tables in his interviews about *RRed, RIR, MF* and *BaB*, disdainfully probing into his author's work and life. Updike is slyly described by Bech's "snaggle-tooth" reference in "Appendix A" (*BB*). Audaciously, he refers to the critic Orlando Cohen, whom Bech murdered in "Bech Noir" (*BaB*), as supporting his judgment that Updike knows nothing about "being Jewish" (Updike, "Questions of Character"). *See* **Updike, John, in His Work**.

Bibliography: Updike, "Bech Meets Me," "One Big Interview" (*PP*); "On One's Own Oeuvre" (*HS*); "Henry Bech Interviews John Updike" (*MM*); "Questions of Character: There's No Ego as Wounded as a Wounded Alter Ego," *New York Times* 1 Mar. 1999: E1, E7.

Johnson, Hubert. *See* **Skeeter.**

Johnson, Lyndon Baines (1908–1973). Lyndon Johnson, the thirty-sixth president of the United States, (1963–69); served in the House of Representatives (1937–42) and in the Senate (1948–60) and became noted as a powerful Democrat active in civil rights. He helped elect John Kennedy* president and became his vice president, then vigorously supported the space program. As JFK's successor he initiated a "war on poverty" and pursued Kennedy's civil rights bill. These social programs and his opposition to the Vietnam* War helped elect Johnson president in 1964, and he launched "the Great Society," composed of housing, education and Medicare bills. But when he expanded American involvement in Vietnam, committing over half a million men by 1968, antiwar protests dramatically reduced his effectiveness. Despite assurances by his aides that the war was being won, the Tet offensive in 1968 proved otherwise and caused Johnson two months later to reduce the war's intensity. The victories in the presidential primaries of Senator Eugene McCarthy forced Johnson out of the race. In *RRed* Johnson is supported by Harry "Rabbit" Angstrom,* who seems indifferent to his father's defense of Johnson while they have a beer after work, but vigorously defends Johnson against the antiwar Charlie Stavros.* Stavros tricks Rabbit in their argument into accepting responsibility for the genocide of Native Americans and being forced to see that the "Indians" in Vietnam are now taking their turn. Perhaps fueling Rabbit's violent rationalizations for the war is his awareness that Stavros has become the lover of his wife, Janice Angstrom.*

Updike replied to a questionnaire in 1966 that he supported the war if the Vietnamese could thereby determine their own future. He said in a follow-up letter to the *New York Times* that he credited Johnson with "good faith and some good sense," but he prophetically suggested that Johnson not seek another term. In Updike's final "Talk of the Town" column for the *New Yorker** he praised Johnson's decision not to run as a "victory of imagination" and declared that he was leaving "Talk of the Town" columns to "more leftish hands." Updike also resented the "snobbish dismissal" of Johnson by Harvard* professors, and the peace movement, declaring, "It was a citizen's plain duty to hold his breath and hope for the best, not parade around spouting pious unction and crocodile tears" (*SC*). *See* **Presidents.**

Bibliography: Updike, "An Untitled Statement", in *Authors Take Sides on Vietnam: Two Questions on the War in Vietnam Answered by the Authors of Several Nations*, ed. Cecil Woolf and John Bagguley (London: Peter Owen, 1967), 50–51.

Journalism. Updike's journalistic experience included submitting prose, poetry* and drawings* to the Shillington* High School *Chatterbox*,* working
for the *Reading* (Pennsylvania) *Eagle*,* editing the *Harvard Lampoon** and
writing reportage for the *New Yorker*.* He left the magazine because he felt
that in eighteen months he had mastered a form that called for impressions
of Central Park or observations of an eclipse. Updike presently edits his
collections, reading and making revisions in his novels, poems, stories, essays,
cartoons and reviews. Besides this activity, he has edited many collections
by others, including the drawings of David Levine (*Pens and Needles*), a symposium, *Reality and the Novel in Africa and America*, and a collection of *The
Best Stories of 1984*. He has also contributed dozens of prefaces, forewords
and introductions to his reprinted work and that of other writers, from Herman Melville* to Henry Green.*

Updike's reportage has included articles on American monuments, golf,*
Al Capp,* Lana Turner, Antigua and television.* He continues to admire
the men who put the *Reading Eagle* together, and he shows a lively journalistic concern for every aspect of bookmaking, from choice of paper to design
of dust jackets and from the selection of type to binding. He is even concerned with marketing of his books, from presentation in bookstore windows
to availability in crucial places like airport bookstores.

Newspapers and magazines are ubiquitous in Updike's novels, from the
punning Lutheran monthly *Sweet Charity* (*PF*) and the *Olinger Sun* (*C*) to
the description of the workings of the *Brewer** *Vat* (*RRed*) and the *Eastwick**
Word (*W*). Throughout, Updike's characters* peruse dozens of magazines
from the *Saturday Evening Post* to *Playboy* and from *Consumer Reports* to the
New Yorker, while Updike creates poems springing from items in *Life* and
Scientific American. He has been fascinated by a number of journalistic forms:
the interview* ("One More Interview" [*TM*] and four interviews with Henry
Bech*), obituaries (*C*), gossip columns (*BB* and *W*), sports* columns (*RIR*),
decrees of death* (*Coup*) and hard news set in print by Harry "Rabbit" Angstrom,* linotyper (*RRed*). These news stories dramatize Brewer's decaying
state while recording the passage from the more personal world of human
typesetting to the impersonal technology of offset printing. Updike also uses
Rabbit's trade to reveal Rabbit's crumbling hold on the actual world as personal problems intrude upon his job as a transcriber of fact. Consequently,
the newspaper provides the social setting for Rabbit's private confusion. (In
his dissertation David Cox has proposed that Updike uses the typography
of printing as a series of complex signs—the ampersand and mail box, e.g.—
that underline theme throughout *RRed*.) In *RIR* Rabbit carries in his wallet
for years a clipping from the *Vat* describing Skeeter's* death, probably sent
to him by Thelma Harrison,* who also may have sent the clipping of a
"shaggy goose joke." Updike satirically portrays a small-town reporter, Sukie
Rougemont,* who is taught by Darryl Van Horne* to restrain her tendency
to gush (*W*). In his lone description of a newspaper editor, Updike shows

Clyde Gabriel, editor of the *Word*, while hanging himself, seemingly proof-reading the galley of his last moment and shifting one letter from "blackness" to "blankness" as he expires.

Updike remarked in an interview that fiction is "journalism of a kind," since novelists are also "voyeurs." While he was writing *RR*, he deliberately injected precisely what he heard on his radio into Rabbit's car radio. (The manuscripts of *RR* show that Updike checked his work for accuracy.) Television reporters and newsmakers alike are shown throughout *RA* both documenting and manipulating social unrest to discredit the civil rights movement (*RRed*).

Apart from direct uses of newspapers and magazines to delineate the texture of daily events, Updike provides an ironic counterpoint between historical events recorded in the papers—images of coups, air crashes and the submarine *Thresher** sinking reveal the hazards and fragility of life outside insulated Tarbox—and the indifference of Tarbox readers (*Couples*). Updike's training in journalism may have reinforced his forty-year routine of reviewing books and art* shows, but his understanding of journalism's potential problems has been part of what has prompted him to write autobiographical essays to discourage inept scholars or journalists from writing his biography (*SC*). Despite his clear affection for journalism, Updike has said, "Fiction makes sociology look priggish, history problematical, the film media two dimensional and the *National Enquirer* as silly as last week's cereal box." *See* **Apprenticeship; Light Verse;** *Odd Jobs; Picked-up Pieces*.

Bibliography: Ristoff, *UA*: James Schiff, "Updike Ignored: The Contemporary Independent Critic," *American Literature* 67 (Sept. 1995): 531–52; Ristoff, *JU*.

Joyce, James (1882–1941). One of several modernists Updike frequently cites as a major influence on his creative consciousness, James Joyce developed the stream-of-consciousness technique and provided provocative links between myth and realism in his masterwork *Ulysses*, a modern version of Homer's *Odyssey*. The impact of Joyce's "montage" and stream of consciousness is shown at the end of *PF* and in the interior monologues of Janice Angstrom,* Ruth Leonard Byer* and Harry "Rabbit" Angstrom* (*RR*). In *RR* the disruptive child of Rev. Jack Eccles* is named Joyce, a sly comment on James Joyce's rebellion against the church, perhaps; Eccles Street appears in *Ulysses* as well.

Updike first read *Ulysses* when he was about fifteen, and he has said that Joyce was continually in mind when he was writing *C*, though he reversed Joyce's use of classical analogues by treating overtly the direct interpenetration of the world of classical gods. Critic Larry Taylor indicates that Joyce and Updike create heroes conspicuous by their ordinariness, and that both Leopold Bloom and George Caldwell* are survivors who know how to love. Taylor also notes that Peter Caldwell* resembles Joyce's Stephen Dedalus, "directly associating the artist in our time with the classical hero." Joyce may also have given Updike a model for his uses of the Latin and Greek languages in *C* and *RV*. Joyce, *Ulysses* and the film made from the novel (1967) are mentioned in *BB*, predictably, since Henry Bech* is a great admirer of the moderns (T. S. Eliot,* Paul Valery, and others). Updike, however, disliked the film. Something both Bech and Updike might trace to Joyce is their belief that trivial things can have mythic significance. Critics detect a connection between Joyce's "Araby" and Updike's stories "You'll Never Know, Dear, How Much I Love You" (*PigF*) and "A & P" (*PigF*). The comic brilliance of *Ulysses* is reflected in *Coup* and the Bech* books.

Updike scatters references to *Ulysses* profusely throughout his work. He opens the English edition of the book and is "appalled" by "the keen scent of death* the packed words gave off" ("My Uncle's Death" [*AP*]). He uses an extensive quotation from *Ulysses* in his dedication of *TT* to his second wife Martha,* perhaps because her name is used in the quotation. He quotes an onomatopoeic sentence about trolleys from the novel, and he notes that Joyce's "triumph was to move from the mind of Stephen Dedalus into that of Leopold Bloom—to put a dime-novel mentality in a narrative frame of Thomistic rigor and Homeric grandeur" (*OJ*). Updike approximates this when he places information about Dale Kohler* within the mind of Roger Lambert,* though it would seem impossible for Lambert to know such things (*RV*). Updike refers to the multiple voices at the end of *PF* as resembling the "Wandering Rocks" of Joyce's novel and suggests that "Bech Panics" (*BB*) derives from the "Lotus Eaters" section of *Ulysses*.

In his review of Joyce's *Giacomo Joyce* (*PP*) Updike reveals an intimate knowledge of Joyce's work and offers learned suggestions on Joyce's probable intentions in writing *Ulysses* while evaluating its importance in understanding Stephen Dedalus, and in reviewing a work by Italo Calvino, Updike explains the "intertwining schemata" of *Ulysses*, with its "huge apparatus of multiple significance," while observing how Joyce wed his "encyclopedic" ambitions to the daily petty grit (*OJ*). Updike also quotes Joyce in canto IV of "Midpoint" (*M*). James Schiff suggests that "Essie/Alma" section of *IB* resembles *A Portrait of the Artist as a Young Man*, since it traces the actress Essie Wilmot/Alma DeMott* from childhood. Hovering in the background of *RA*'s world of commercialism may be Joyce, who, Updike said, was the first to realize that "the texture of daily life for Western man has become predominantly commercial" (*OJ*). Thus Joyce was a general influence on much of Updike's work, and his review of Joyce's selected letters, showing detailed knowledge of *Finnegans Wake* reveals a scholar's concern for the creative development of the greatest of modern novelists (*HS*). *See* **Literary Influences; Thomas Aquinas, St.**

Bibliography: Updike, "Religion and Literature" (*MM*); Stanley Edgar Hyman, "Chiron at Olinger High," *New Leader* 46 (4 Feb. 1963): 20; Taylor, *PA*; Joyce Carol

Oates, "*The Coup* by John Updike," *New Republic* 180 (6 Jan. 1979): 32–35; Craig Werner, "Homer's Joyce: John Updike, Ronald Sukenick, Robert Coover, Toni Morrison," in *Paradoxical Resolutions: American Fiction since James Joyce* (Urbana: University of Illinois Press, 1982), 68–96; Detweiler, *JU*; Walter Wells, "John Updike's 'A & P': A Return Visit to Araby," *Studies in Short Fiction* 30 (Spring 1993): 127–33; Schiff, *JU*.

Jung, Carl Gustav (1875–1961). A follower of Sigmund Freud* until they differed on the makeup of the psyche, Jung saw neuroses as resulting from a failed quest for what he called "wholeness." This theory resulted from his training in biology and archaeology, as well as his interests in religion, shown in his *Psychology of the Unconscious* (1912), which delineated the similarities between myth* and psychotic fantasies. *Psychological Types* (1921) described personality types like extrovert and introvert. Jung also developed a theory of the collective unconscious composed of universal "archetypes," or images charged with meaning, related to birth, death* and initiations. As a therapist, Jung sought to unify components of personality he called persona, anima and shadow, which represent the social mask, the spiritual striving and the darker, evil self. Such integration of self produces individuation and wholeness.

Critic George Hunt interprets *OF* from a Jungian perspective and probes Joey Robinson's* dreams from this perspective, as he does the female archetype throughout this novel. Jung interprets libido more generally than Freud as containing all life processes, not simply sexuality. Hunt and other critics have identified Jungian "archetypes" related to such processes in *OF* and other novels. Some of these archetypes are the quest (*RA*); the mother (*OF, S.*); the hero (*C*); and the "shadow" (*W*). Robert Detweiler interprets *C* as related from the point of view of Peter Caldwell's* Jungian collective memory, and he treats the archetype of the femme fatale* or the Eve archetype in *OF*.

Bibliography: Hunt, *JU*; Detweiler, *JU*; Diana Staynskas Moran Steel, "An Archetypal Approach to John Updike's Rabbit Trilogy," Ph.D. Dissertation, 1987, Cleveland State University.

Just Looking (New York: Knopf, 1989). *JL*, a collection of essays on art* ranging from a medieval reliquary to pop art,* not only establishes Updike's interest in the visual arts but also accounts in part for his ability to translate his sensory experience into verbal imagery* throughout his fiction and poetry.* These essays, written, as Updike's literary essays had been, from the viewpoint of the common "reader," provide "impressions" (the British edition's title) that clearly establish the significance of point of view in the evaluation of art, something Updike's writing has relentlessly presented in forcing the reader into a "debate" with his work. As in the Henry Bech* books, Updike insists on the social and economic aspects of art, while he is alert to the fakery sometimes prompted by the artist's declining ability and media hype, as in the careers of Pierre-Auguste Renoir and Andrew Wyeth.

Updike's interest in art began as a child when he visited the Reading* Art Museum and modeled his drawings* on those of James Thurber.* Throughout high school he developed as an artist. He took up painting at Harvard* and spent a postgraduate year studying painting at the Ruskin School of Drawing and Fine Art,* doing portraits of family members. For the next several years he pursued what he called his "amateur" work. While working for the *New Yorker,** Updike often strolled to the Museum of Modern Art (which he first saw at age thirteen), looking to museums for examples he might translate into his writing, as he later remarked. Painters, like his favorite Jan Vermeer,* and sculptors, like fellow Pennsylvanians Alexander Calder* and George Segal, are integral to the appreciation of *C*, *MW* and *W*, respectively. Perhaps ironically, Norman Mailer* called Updike the Andrew Wyeth of American letters. As Updike remarked of Mailer, this assertion, though apparently wild, has a kernel of insight, because of Updike's exquisite care with details and ability to suffuse his emotion through them.

Bibliography: Updike, "Gaiety in the Galleries" (*HS*); "Art's Dawn" (*OJ*); "The Sistine Chapel Ceiling," "The Frick" (*MM*); Christopher Lehmann-Haupt, "A Man of Letters and the Pull of Visual Arts," *New York Times* 138 (9 Oct. 1989): C-18; Arthur C. Danto, "What MOMA Done Tole Him," *New York Times Book Review* 15 Oct. 1989: 12; Marjorie Welish, "Writers on Art—Reported Sightings: Art Chronicles," *Partisan Review* 58 (Fall 1991): 742–45; James Plath, "Verbal Vermeer: Updike's Middle-Class Portraiture," in Broer, *RT*.

K

Kafka, Franz (1883–1924). Franz Kafka was a Czech fictionalist whose allegorical and surreal stories had an immense impact on modernism. Kafka "epitomizes" modernism for Updike because he records unlocatable anxiety, "a sense of an infinite difficulty within things," and a need to record with acute sensitivity every pain he experienced (*OJ*). Updike mentioned in interviews* that "an essential chord" was struck when he first read Kafka in 1950. Updike clarified that "chord" by noting in his "Foreword" to Kafka's stories an astonishing technique and a "spiritual unrest" that linked him in Updike's mind to existentialists like Søren Kierkegaard.* Though direct influence of Kafka on Updike is hard to trace since Kafka affected so many writers Updike admired, the impact can be deduced in the surrealistic effects in *C*, *Coup* and *W*, and in stories in *MuS* and *A*. Updike also employs the ironic tone of Kafka through black humor.* To Henry Bech,* Kafka was his "suffering older brother," and Bech praises Kafka in "Rich in Russia" (*BB*) and particularly in "Bech in Czech" (*BaB*). Other Kafka ingredients include guilt (*B*), Oedipal problems (*RA*), grotesquerie ("From the Journal of a Leper" [*P*]) and fantasy (*TE*). *See* **European Literature; Literary Influences**.

Bibliography: Updike, "Introduction to *The Complete Stories*, by Franz Kafka" (*OJ*).

Kama Sutra. The Hindu book of the art of love that Freddy Thorne* keeps by his bedside in *Couples*, the *Kama Sutra* may be a marital aid for him, since Thorne might be impotent. No doubt Thorne would divorce sex from Hinduism, since he believes that "sex* is the last religion." Such erotic material reveals the fragile methods used by those in Tarbox to maintain their sophisticated hedonistic lives. *See* **Arhat; Buddha, Gautama; Religion**; *S.;* **Sex; Worth, Sarah.**

Keller, Helen (1880–1968). A deaf and blind Alabama child who learned to speak, write and read, Helen Keller became the author of numerous inspirational and influential books. Nine-year-old Ruth Hanema plays Helen Keller in her school play *The Miracle Worker*, by William Gibson (1959) (*Couples*). The role is apt, since Ruth's father Piet Hanema* tries to remain blind to the reality of death* but is eventually taught to "see." Keller's courage contrasts with the general moral weakness of the affluent residents of Tarbox. After her divorce, Angela Hanema* became a teacher of young girls, as Anne Sullivan had taught Helen Keller. Like Angela Hanema (and Updike's first wife, Mary Pennington Updike*), Keller graduated from Radcliffe College. In a review, Updike explores Keller's complex life, particularly her erotic life.

Bibliography: Updike, "Large for Her Years" (*MM*).

Kennedy, John F. (1917–1963). The administration of John F. Kennedy, the thirty-fifth president of the United States (1961–63), supplies the political background of *Marry* and *Couples*. The "honeymoon" period of JFK's first two years as president is reflected in the idyllic love affairs of Sally Mathias and Jerry Conant* in *Marry* and of Foxy Whitman* and Piet Hanema* in *Couples*. Kennedy saw his presidency as a new start for America, but *Couples* also includes JFK's last tragic year as president. The young, charming, confident Kennedy seemed a spiritual leader for Piet, offering hope in the place of his fear of death.* Yet JFK faced two crises: the Berlin blockade, which threatened a confrontation with the Soviet Union; and the Cuban missile crisis* in which the USSR supplied Cuba with the means to attack American cities. These events followed the fiasco of the Bay of Pigs invasion (1961), which was an attempt to overthrow Cuban president Fidel Castro; Kennedy regained his prestige in 1962 when he forced the Soviets to withdraw the missiles. His problems in foreign affairs ironically mirrored the struggle in Tarbox over the couples' disruptive affairs. Kennedy's wily commitment to Vietnam* appealed to the idealistic belief in self-improvement of suburbanites generally, and his decision to land a man on the moon directly affected Tarbox, funding scientists like Ben Saltz. Generally, though, political matters were of minor concern for Tarbox.

Yet Kennedy's ideal society, like the Camelot* he admired, was accompanied by domestic tragedy. Jackie Kennedy's miscarriage caused Piet's daughter Nancy Hanema* to panic and to mirror her father's dread of death. Piet's efforts to control this anxiety had partly led to his compulsive affairs. His lover Foxy learns of Kennedy's assassination while having a cavity filled by Freddy Thorne,* who will later arrange an abortion* for her: the national pain is reflected in local pain. Foxy calls JFK a martyr like Abraham Lincoln,* and his death casts a pall over the Tarbox hedonists who thought, in Piet's words, "News happened to other people." At the Thornes' party that night Piet imagines that they are dancing on Kennedy's grave, though others allege that he was only "a manufactured politician." Foxy suggests that JFK died because of Marina Oswald's sexual rejection of Lee Oswald; perhaps Foxy projects what she feels might happen if she divorces to marry Piet. The president's death signaled, as Updike pointed out in his 1963 *New Yorker** articles, that America had now irrevocably lost its innocence and perhaps its hope, reflected in Piet's sense that his "whole life seems just a long falling." Such insecurity throws Piet back to Foxy, and another death, the abortion of their child, restores her to Piet. Their union in another town insinuates that Kennedy's death brought regeneration, not defeat. *See* **Presidents.**

Bibliography: Newman, *JU*; Ristoff, *UA*; Ristoff, *JU*.

Kern, David. The youthful protagonist of Updike's important story "Pigeon Feathers" (*PigF*), David Kern has his religious foundation challenged when, at fourteen, he is upset by H. G. Wells's assertion that Christ was not divine. This leads him to anxiety concerning death* and questions about the immortality of his soul. Inquiries to his parents and minister* leave him unsatisfied; instead, he detects that the intricate design of a pigeon's feathers reveals that God would not deny him an afterlife. David is comforted by this "argument from design," which asserts that a watch found on the beach implies a watchmaker; so the universe, pigeon feathers and David had a maker. Though the argument was labeled invalid long ago, the solace David receives allays his fear of oblivion.

David, much older, reappears in "Packed Dirt, Churchgoing, a Dying Cat, a Traded Car" (*PigF*), connecting four elements of his life, from his parents' church habits to his mature fears of annihilation. To show how persistent this fear is to Updike, David's problem also affects Farrell in "The Wallet" (*TM*) as well as Dale Kohler* in *RV*. Also, David avoids a homosexual pass ("The Lens Factor," *Granta*, 1989) as he labors to find his sexual identification. David Kern thus supplied continuity for Updike's exploration of religious and sexual anxiety. The character is Updike's earliest representative of the developing youth who appears in his short stories as Ben, Sammy, Mark, Allen, Robert, William or John.

Bibliography: Burchard, *YS*; Greiner, *OJ*; Luscher, *JU*.

Kerouac, Jack (original name Jean-Louis Kerouac) (1922–1969). America's most famous beat-generation novelist of the 1950s, Jack Kerouac developed unusual writing methods to record spontaneously all that he felt about America and his friends, who included such beats as Allen Ginsberg, Gregory

Corso and William Burroughs. One such method was "automatic writing," in which Kerouac typed as rapidly as possible everything that came into his mind. His style mirrored his resistance to conventionality and traditional institutions, which he felt postwar America was determined to force upon everyone. His *On the Road* (1957), written in three weeks, became the key book of the beats because it provided an uninhibited description of the beat life, a world of drugs,* jazz and easy sex.* The first-person novel (a thinly veiled autobiography) traces Kerouac's trips back and forth across America pursuing the essence of the country. Henry Bech* actually crosses the country in "Bech Pleads Guilty" (*BaB*). Kerouac's book is mentioned in "Bech in Rumania" (*BB*), and Bech's travels around the world while waiting to be freed of his writer's block parallel but also parody Kerouac's quest (*BB, BIB* and *BaB*). Bech lectures, reads, judges poetry contests, meets dissident writers and endures interviewers and adulators, and his first novel, *Travel Light*, which concerns "continent-spanning motorcyclists," recalls Kerouac's subject matter. Updike has acknowledged his interest in Kerouac's questing characters, though he has expressed more concern about those left behind as "the social fabric unravels" when the quester follows his own impulses. Updike may have had in mind specifically Kerouac's friend Neal Cassady, who accompanied Kerouac on the road, leaving behind his wife and child, like Harry "Rabbit" Angstrom.* Updike admitted in an interview* that as a fledgling writer he was jealous of Kerouac's successful novel, but he caviled at "relatively privileged" persons running around the country "with no visible means of support." Updike's parody of *On the Road*, "On the Sidewalk" (*AP*), suggests that he found Kerouac's frenetic style and adolescent exaggerations to be pretentious and puerile.

Yet Updike has indicated that Kerouac's present-tense style in *On the Road* helped him create the form and conception of the flight of Rabbit (*RR*). But *RR* was written partly as a reply to *On the Road*. Like Kerouac's, Rabbit's drive is circular, leading him back to himself. In the other Rabbit novels, the road motif continues to surface. Grounded in *RRed*, Rabbit is nevertheless again on the road in Jill Pendleton's* Porsche, but the jaunt passes only slag heaps and an abandoned mansion; her car eventually "freezes up," signifying the end of an anti–road trip. In *RIR* Rabbit's road adventures are reduced to driving to Ruth Leonard Byer's* farm and spying on her. In *RaR*, in pursuit of his lost daughter, Annabelle Byer,* he drives to the farm and confronts Ruth about Annabelle. After he sleeps with his daughter-in-law, Teresa "Pru" Angstrom,* Rabbit's flight to Florida* causes his family to unravel, and rather than pull the threads together, he remains in Florida, where he dies. (In an apparent allusion to Kerouac, Updike refers to Rev. Fritz Kruppenbach's* son, who had roared through town on his motorcycle in *RR*. The biker was modeled on the son of Updike's minister, Rev. Victor Kroninger.

Other uses of the road symbol reveal society unraveling. George Caldwell* twice gets stuck in the snow trying to drive his son Peter Caldwell* to school; the second time, they abandon the car and stay in a hotel, where they are mistaken for homosexuals (*C*). In *Coup* President Félix Ellelloû's* fact-finding mission across the Kush desert leads to his government unraveling in a coup. Like Rabbit, Sarah Worth* flees west from a second-rate marriage only to be disillusioned by her lover, the Arhat.* Like Rabbit's drive south, her flight to Arizona is disillusioning (*S.*). Darryl Van Horne* seems to be the only one to have been happy in unraveling the social fabric when he leaves Eastwick* for New York* with Chris Gabriel. *See* **American Literature; Literary Influences.**

Bibliography: Updike, "On the Sidewalk" (*AP*).

Khrushchev, Nikita (1894–1971). The premier of the USSR from 1958 to 1964, Nikita Khrushchev is mentioned in *Couples* as creating the Cold War atmosphere as well as the hot war in Vietnam.* After the death of Joseph Stalin in 1953, Khrushchev became effectively the Communist party head, and in 1956 he accused Stalin of responsibility for mass murders and the German invasion in 1941. Though he advocated peaceful coexistence with the West, Khrushchev stockpiled nuclear weapons and in 1962 precipitated the Cuban missile crisis*; his subsequent humiliation by President John Kennedy* led to his being deposed in October 1964. Khrushchev's risk of provoking atomic war forms the backdrop to *Couples*, in which Piet Hanema* drops domestic bombs, betraying his wife, arranging an abortion* for his mistress and divorcing. As though responding to the threat of annihilation, the Tarbox couples try to make a religion* of sex. Harry "Rabbit" Angstrom* remarked that despite "nuclear blackmail," Cold War Americans lived with less ambiguity because they knew the enemy (*RRed*), an idea Updike seconds in *SC*. Updike traveled to the USSR in October 1964 and translated ten poems of Yevgeny Yevtushenko for that poet's *Stolen Apples* (1971). Updike presented his views on the post-Khrushchev USSR through Henry Bech* in "Rich in Russia" (*BB*), and "Appendix A" of *BB* is based on Updike's experiences in Russia from October 20 to December 6, 1964. *See* **Presidents.**

Kierkegaard, Søren (1813–1855). The foremost Danish philosopher and theologian Søren Kierkegaard was concerned with man's ambiguous condition, which produces angst* and guilt. Raised a Lutheran, like Updike, Kierkegaard came to use his own intuitive understandings and developed an existential stance that stressed the nonrational nature of life and the need for stringent self-examination. Updike began reading him extensively in his twenties, finding Kierkegaard's declaration that existence precedes essence "very liberating."

Updike found in Kierkegaard's *Fear and Trembling* and *The Sickness unto Death* (which he read in 1955 or 1956) books that changed his life by validating subjectivity and relieving his appalling fear of death* "For a time," Updike wrote, "I thought of all my actions as illustrations to Kierkegaard" (*OJ*). Kierkegaard's themes of guilt, anxiety and the fear of nothingness appear in Updike's early stories "Pigeon Feathers" and "The Astronomer" (*PigF*) and in his novels *RR* and *Couples*. Kierkegaard was among the first modern thinkers to associate sex,* guilt and fear of death; his exploration of the Adam and Eve story from this viewpoint may have influenced the Adam and Eve sermon* in *OF*. Harry "Rabbit" Angstrom's* surname suggests that angst is part of a natural inheritance. Piet Hanema* deals with his terror of death by making a religion* of sex, since he fears that God has turned His back on man (*Couples*). Like Rabbit's fear of falling in a quarry (*RR*), Piet's attempt to build a cage to protect his daughter's hamster testifies to an inability to fend off "nothingness." To Piet, sex may be the modern religion because it alone satisfies the need to validate personal worth in a hostile world, and because companionship is essential in facing human loneliness. But sex both underscores and palliates isolation: Piet's lover Foxy Whitman* remarks that sex intensifies the fear of nothingness, though it also provides companionship in facing it.

Kierkegaard's parable of the man who could see only distance with one eye and closeness with the other, and for whom everything was thus relative, had excited Updike when he read it in 1954 into contemplating writing a novel about such a character; the character became President James Buchanan,* who had similarly odd vision (*BD, MF*). Updike said that he found in Kierkegaard a sense of the problematic nature of life, the constant dilemma of "either/or." Such a dualism* may lie behind the computer language of "or/and/not" in *RV*. Updike used the same dialogue form Kierkegaard employed in *Either/Or* in his two humorous dialogues on print and fiction in *MM*.

Updike concludes his *Atlantic* "brief life" of Kierkegaard, perhaps self-reflexively, with the observation that Kierkegaard's life was "incarnated" in his books, which may have prompted Updike's epigram* "My art is that of which the residue, my life, is trash" (*PP*). Kierkegaard's fascination with nature* may also account for Updike's remarkably exact and passionate descriptions of nature throughout his work, particularly in *RA* and *TE*. Kierkegaard had a direct influence on many writers, and Updike thought that Franz Kafka* was the writer best able to develop Kierkegaard's ideas into "epic symbols." The dual impact of both Kierkegaard and Kafka can be detected in Updike's continuous pursuit of the ambiguity of human experience, the need for clarification of subjective responses to it and the sense that rules and philosophies must bow before the individual's personal evaluation of what gives life meaning.

Bibliography: Updike, "Søren Kierkegaard" in *Atlantic Brief Lives*, ed. Louis Kronenberger (Boston: Little, Brown, 1971), 429–31; "The Fork" (*PP*); "[A Book That

Changed Me]" (*OJ*); " 'Introduction' to *The Seducer's Diary*" (*MM*); Sue Mitchell Crowley, "The Rubble of Footnotes Bound into Kierkegaard," *Journal of the American Academy of Religion* 45.3 Supplement (1977): 1011–35; George W. Hunt, "Kierkegaardian Sensations into Real Fiction: John Updike's 'The Astronomer,' " *Christianity and Literature* 26 (1977): 3–17; Hunt, *JU*; Sue Mitchell Crowley, "John Updike and Kierkegaard's Negative Way: Irony and Indirect Communication in *A Month of Sundays*," *Soundings* 68 (Summer 1985): 212–28; Newman, *JU*.

King, William Lyon Mackenzie (1874–1950). A Canadian statesman, William Lyon Mackenzie King studied political science at Harvard,* particularly labor, and was elected prime minister and served during World War II. He chaired Canada's delegation to the United Nations. Updike's poem "The Visions of Mackenzie King" (*FN*) was based on articles in Toronto newspapers. In it King describes visions of luminaries he had known when he was head of state: Adolph Hitler, Franklin Roosevelt,* Winston Churchill* and others. King derives simple lessons from each of them, but is himself puzzled by the surreal quality of some of his dreams* in which the trivial (using his hat to hit a vole that had drunk from his decanter) overweighs the important (Churchill having a cigar and a drink while the servant is chastised). The visions embarrass King, yet they show that he was insecure "in those decades of demons of whom I was one." According to the Toronto papers, such visions were kept secret for thirty years. Updike is clearly amused at governments that keep such material confidential.

Kohler, Dale. A twenty-eight-year-old computer expert at a theological school, Dale Kohler seeks factual confirmation of God's existence by entering information from various sciences that apparently reveal "God's Hand" showing forth through the universe's mechanics. Although his distant relation and ostensible ally, Roger Lambert,* as a professor at the college, helps Dale secure funding, Lambert really expects Dale to fail and confirm his own feeling that God will remain hidden from man. Eventually Dale thinks that he sees images of God's face and hand on the computer monitor, but he cannot repeat his experiment, and when a scientist reveals that Dale's theory rested on false assumptions, he abandons his project. Meanwhile, Dale has an affair with Lambert's wife Esther Lambert* and loses her, but not before apparently impregnating her.

Updike attaches religious allusions to Dale: he flees the "devil" in Idaho, works at a lumberyard and composes a "Tree" in his computer program that he names "Deus." Blending Christic imagery with Søren Kierkegaard's *Either/Or*, Kohler teaches the Lamberts' son how the computer works with various "gates" made of "or/and/not." Ironically, the lesson comes to involve Esther, who uses the language to show Dale that she is attracted to him. Dale's "Argument from Design," that the complex mathematics of the universe proves a purposeful creation, resembles David Kern's* view of pigeon feathers ("Pigeon Feathers" [*PigF*]). Kohler is the name of a famous Pennsylvania plumbing company (*RV*), suggesting that he approaches an understanding of God as a plumber might explore a clogged drain. *See* **Hawthorne, Nathaniel; Religion**.

Bibliography: Schiff, *JU*.

The Koran. The sacred Islamic scripture (from "quaran," to read), recorded by Muhammad, the Koran is frequently quoted in *Coup*. Muhammad referred to each of the revelations he received from Allah in 114 suras (chapters) containing the Islamic religious and social codes, all asserted as absolute truth. Throughout his work Updike supplies abundant quotations from other sacred books—the Hindu Vedas (*S.*) and the New Testament (*IB*). *See* **Religion**.

Korean War. What began as a "police action," in President* Harry Truman's phrase, in 1948 became a war when North Korea invaded South Korea in 1950. General Douglas MacArthur eventually drove the invaders toward the Chinese border, where a large Chinese force crossed into Korea. After a two-year deadlock peace was established at the prewar boundary of the 38th parallel. The war cost 23,000 American lives and millions of civilian casualties. Harry "Rabbit" Angstrom* served in the army at the time of the Korean War but did not see service, to his eventual regret (*RA*). Two important things happened to him while he was serving in Texas: he was dropped by his high-school sweetheart, and he had sex* for the first time, with a prostitute. *See* **Vietnam**.

Bibliography: Ristoff, *UA*.

Krishna, Lord. In Hinduism Lord Krishna is the most popular of the nine incarnations of the god Vishnu and the teacher in the *Bhagavad-Gita*,* mentioned in "Bech Takes Pot Luck" (*BB*). Updike quotes extensively from the Hindu sacred texts in *S*. *See* **The Koran; Religion**.

Kroll's Department Store. The chief department store in Brewer,* Kroll's Department Store is the place where Harry "Rabbit" Angstrom,* unpacking crates, meets his future wife Janice Springer Angstrom,* who is selling nuts (*RR*). As a sign of change indicating an economic downturn and the weakening connection to the past, Kroll's closes in *RIR*.

Kroust, Mildred. Mildred Kroust is Fred Springer's* devoted bookkeeper at Springer Motors.* Her illness enables Janice Angstrom* to help balance the books, leading to her affair with Charlie Stavros* (*RRed*). The affair ultimately costs Jill Pendleton* her life and drives a deeper wedge between Rabbit and his son Nelson Angstrom.* Rabbit relies on Mildred when he takes over the business (*RIR*), but when Rabbit and Mildred retire, Nelson has the opportunity to embezzle from his parents' company. Nelson claimed that Kroust had not been able to adapt to the computer and should not have been retained past retirement. Ironically, this was Rabbit's situation in *RRed* when he was fired at Verity Press because his job was rendered obsolete (*RaR*). Though Rabbit brings Mildred out of retirement, this bulwark of Springer Motors cannot restore order, and Toyota accountants are called in to discover the extent to which Nelson and his friend Lyle have juggled the books. Her passing is one more indication to Rabbit of the downward spiral he sees everywhere, and she is one more woman who fails him, as he sees it, when he needs her most. Rabbit all his life has surrounded himself with protective women.

Kruppenbach, Fritz. Mt. Judge's* Lutheran minister* for twenty-seven years and the Angstroms' minister, Rev. Fritz Kruppenbach appears in only one scene in *RA*, in which he reprimands Rev. Jack Eccles* for getting involved in social problems, "Devil's work," to the detriment of his spiritual ministry (*RR*). As John Hook* (*PF*) chastised prefect Stephen Conner* for attending to the mere social welfare of the aged and neglecting their souls, Kruppenbach castigates Eccles for intervening in the lives of the immature young marrieds Harry "Rabbit" Angstrom* and his wife Janice Angstrom,* rather than making himself "an exemplar of the faith" for them. Kruppenbach's hectoring makes Eccles so mad that he refuses to pray with Kruppenbach. Imagery* reinforces the differences between the ministers: whereas Kruppenbach's home smells of roast beef, and he sweats from lawn work, Eccles has been desperately thirsty that afternoon and plays golf.* Despite this quarrel, Kruppenbach apparently never extends his help to the Angstroms. Updike thus balances the social and spiritual aspects of modern religion* and reveals each to be imperfect.

Throughout *RA* and in other works like "Pigeon Feathers" (*PigF*) and *C* Updike reveals the ineffectuality of ministers. Thus Kruppenbach asks too much when he demands that ministers be exemplars of Christ and give up their social "busyness." But Eccles admits that he commits fraud "with every schooled cadence of the service." Yet Kruppenbach may have affected Eccles, for Eccles's sermon* on Christ's forty days in the Wilderness (which has been compared to one by Karl Barth*) was based on the "*going through*" aspects of Christianity Kruppenbach would have extolled. However, Eccles's change in direction so bores Rabbit that he turns his attention from the sermon to Lucy Eccles.* This leads to her ambiguous "pass," Rabbit's forcing sex* with Janice, his flight after their quarrel, and Janice's drowning of their baby. Not even a blend of Eccles and Kruppenbach can challenge Rabbit's intuitive conviction about the "thing" that wants him to find it. Yet the "thing" is not totally different from Kruppenbach's insistence on grace; each expresses a belief in the "motions of grace." Kruppenbach was modeled on

Updike's reading of Karl Barth, and he called Kruppenbach "the touchstone of the novel . . . Barth in action." Kruppenbach was also modeled on Shillington's* Reverend Victor Kroninger, who baptized and confirmed Updike in Grace Lutheran Church.

Bibliography: Hunt, *JU*.

Kubitschek, Juscelino (1902–1976). The president of Brazil (1956–61) whose programs for material progress, especially building Brasilia, created inflation, Juscelino Kubitschek was deposed by a coup in 1964. Kubitschek is mentioned in *B* as partly responsible for the laxity of Brazilian morals.

Kutunda. Kutunda is one of Col. Félix Ellelloû's* mistresses and plots to depose him. Candace Cunningham* begs Ellelloû to divorce her and marry Kutunda (*Coup*).

L

Lambert, Edna. Edna Lambert is the half-sister of Roger Lambert,* whose incestuous longings for her are confirmed by her daughter Verna Ekelof.* Lambert's affair with Verna acts out this adolescent desire (*RV*). *See* **Incest**.

Lambert, Esther. Petite, redhaired, thirty-eight-year-old Esther Lambert grows restless in her marriage to theology professor Roger Lambert* (*RV*). She befriends Dale Kohler,* Lambert's distant relation who has requested his support for a grant at the theological college where Lambert teaches, and demonstrates a quick understanding of computers under Dale's tutelage. She invites him to tutor her son in the "New Math," and this leads to their affair; their feelings are first conveyed through New Math problems and computer lingo. Updike also suggests that Roger's graphic imagination may cause him to visualize the adultery, so Esther may not have been unfaithful. Since Esther was consciously employed as an analogue of Nathaniel Hawthorne's* Hester Prynne (*The Scarlet Letter*), her affair with Dale parallels that of Prynne with Arthur Dimmesdale and has led, as did Prynne's, to her pregnancy.

Lambert, Lillian. Roger Lambert's* first wife, Lillian Lambert, is repeatedly described by him as sterile and from a vulgar family, probable rationalizations for his having left her and his ministry for the more sensuous Esther Lambert* (*RV*).

Lambert, Roger. Roger Lambert is a fifty-two-year-old professor at a divinity school resembling Harvard's.* His specialty is the early church fathers and heresies (*RV*). In scenes reminiscent of the conflict of Rev. Jack Eccles* and Harry "Rabbit" Angstrom,* Lambert plays the devil's advocate to the ideas of Dale Kohler,* a distant relation who believes that he can discover

God by using the computer. Lambert wants him to fail, partly because the finite discovery of God offends him aesthetically and theologically, and partly because he suspects that his wife Esther Lambert* is sleeping with Dale. Lambert exhibits a form of extrasensory perception by witnessing their intimacies and imagining precisely what the lovers do. Meanwhile, though ostensibly helping his half-niece Verna Ekelof* shift her life from drugs* and promiscuity, Lambert has really transferred to her a youthful interest in her mother, his half-sister, Edna Lambert*; Verna and Roger have a brief affair.

Roger Lambert thus represents one of Updike's many fallible ministers* who struggle against rising desire and atrophying faith. So far has Lambert fallen that satanic images (smoking, telepathy, fear of having God made accessible) make him a true devil's advocate. Dale, by contrast, is described in Christic imagery.* Roger's relentless debonair cynicism radiates through everything he observes and thinks, a smudged lens blurring love and faith. Through this lens he even sees Fourth of July picnics as part of a "tedious tradition and the mummified past, that rural past when the stupid, sluggish, malingering earth spirits need periodic human cavorting to remind them to switch on the next season." Updike saw the patriotic holiday more favorably than Lambert did in two essays and a poem. *See* **Augustine, St**.

Bibliography: Updike, "Stones into Bread" (*MM*).

Languages. Although Updike has said that he is "grateful to have been born into English, with polyglot flexibility . . . its pliable grammar and abundant synonyms" (*PP*), he has used throughout his work modern and ancient languages to establish the reality of the setting, add to characterization and create atmosphere. The languages range from Berber (*Coup*) to Pennsylvania Dutch (*Couples, RA*) and include Czech ("Bech in Czech" [*BaB*]), French (*Couples, Marry*), German (*RA*), Hebrew (*Couples*), Hindi (*S.*), Japanese (*RaR*), Korean (*Couples*), Portuguese (*B*), (*GC*), Russian (*Coup*), modern and Old Spanish (*PF*) and Yiddish (*BIB, RIR*). He also uses the classical languages of Sanskrit (*S.*), Greek (*C*, "The Golf Course Owner" [*HS*]) and Latin (*MS, C, RV*). Also, Piet Hanema's* friends pun on the names of Vietnamese leaders in mock-Vietnamese (*Couples*). This reader has the impression that *B* was translated from archaic Portuguese.

Updike employs quotations from major books of various languages, often in the original: the Koran* from Arabic (Col. Félix Ellelloû* comments on the qualities of the dialects in which the Koran is spoken [*Coup*]); *The Kama Sutra** from Hindi; Virgil's *Aeneid*, Lucretius's *De rerum natura* and Tertullian's* *De resurrectione carnis* from Latin; myth* from Greek; Pascal's writings from French; and *The Good Soldier Schweik* of Jaroslav Hašek from Czech. Updike has translated ten poems by Yevgeny Yevtushenko from Russian and poems by Jorge Luis Borges* from Spanish and Joannes Secundus from Latin, the latter called a particularly fine translation by Professor Barbara

Pavlock in a letter to me. Updike blends his translations of two Anglo-Saxon poems to form the quatrain that is "Winter Ocean" (*TP*), and he uses seventeenth-century English in *W* and nineteenth-century "upholstered prose" in *BD*, *MF* and *IB*. Updike discriminates dialects of American English throughout *RA*, with prolonged attention to "Black English" in *RRed* through Skeeter,* and he does the same for English spoken in England, Australia and Canada (*BB*, *BIB*).

Though he supplies a glossary of Sanskrit and Hindi for *S.*, Updike's use of untranslated Greek at the end of *C* mystified many readers, and the un-translated Latin in *RV* and Czech in "Bech in Czech" would befuddle others. Such things enable the reader to sympathize with Peter Caldwell's* difficulty in translating a passage from Lucretius (*C*). Still, in the context Roger Lam-bert* provides enough translation to help us through Tertullian*; in fact, the reader's attention to the way he construes the passage draws the reader much closer to him. A check on English editions helps with the Czech. But the Greek in *C* remains a mystery, and the Latin phrase dropped casually into *W*, "Sator arepo tenet opera rotas,"* would certainly elude the common reader. Sukie Rougemont* uses the palindrome when she is turning milk into cream, but since the sentence when translated has no special significance ("Sower Arepo holds the wheels at his work"), the reader is only being asked to appreciate the ingenuity of the sentence as a cubist palindrome.

Updike's languages enable him to provide verisimilitude* of place while at the same time deepening the reality of his characters* and supplying oc-casional bilingual puns, something he enjoys in his light verse,* as in "Some Frenchmen," "Farewell to the Shopping District of Antibes" and "Exposé" (*M*). Updike also incorporates the alphabets of many languages—Arabic, Cyrillic, Greek and Latin—for verisimilitude and sometimes for special vi-sual effects, like the "S" on the cover of *S.*, which simultaneously represents Sarah Worth's* initial and the letter that forms "Kundalini," a Sanskrit vi-sualization of feminine sexual power. *See* **Translations**.

Bibliography: Updike, "A Foreword to the French Edition of *Facing Nature*" (*MM*).

Lanier Club. Henry Bech* speaks to the Lanier Club, a college club hon-oring Georgia poet Sidney Lanier (1842–1881), in "Bech Panics" (*BB*). La-nier's religious nature* poetry is the opposite from Bech's steamy naturalism, but it tests Bech's realistic attitude when he hears Lanier's "The Marshes of Glynn"* read. In it Lanier speculates about what may be hidden beneath the opaque marsh's surface, and Bech panics because he cannot see beneath the surface of existence. A similar poetic counterpoint occurs when Roger Lambert* teaches his niece Verna Ekelof* the meaning of William Cullen Bryant's "Thanatopsis" while she attempts to seduce him. *See* **American Literature**.

Latchett, Bea. Henry Bech's* wife in *BIB*, Bea Latchett is a source of discontent for him because she is a "suburban softy" and a Christian. Bech torments her on a junket to Israel and Scotland, ironically resenting her appreciation of the Holy Land, which he disdains. He somewhat maliciously shows enthusiasm for the atrocities of Protestantism, which he strains to connect to her Scottish ancestors. He seems to resent her efforts to love him. By enforcing greater discipline on Bech, Bea had enabled him to overcome his writer's block and produce a successful novel, *Travel Light*. But, as if in revenge because the novel offends Bea by showing gentiles slavishly in love with Jews, Bech divorces her. Soon after its publication he marries her sister Norma Latchett,* his former mistress.

Latchett, Norma. The mistress of Henry Bech,* Norma Latchett is mentioned in "Rich in Russia" and "Bech Takes Pot Luck," in which she is discarded for her sister Bea Latchett* *(BB)*. Her realistic attitude, which denigrates Bech's breakthrough novel, *Travel Light*, causes him to return to her shortly after his marriage to her sister because he secretly distrusts Bea's support and his own talent.

Lehigh University. Located in Bethlehem, Pennsylvania, Lehigh University is noted for its outstanding colleges of arts, business and engineering. Ronnie Harrison's* son Ron goes to Lehigh but withdraws after two years to become a hippie* *(RaR)*. *See* **Academia**.

Leme, Isabel. Daughter of a wealthy businessman, Isabel Leme selects her first lover, Tristão Raposo,* on Copacabana Beach and falls in love. She then defies her family and steals from it to finance running away with Tristão. When her uncle sends henchmen to retrieve them by force, she travels deeper into the jungle. Isabel never falters in her love, inviting other men to join their intimacies because she thinks this will excite Tristão and prostituting herself when they grow poor, even bearing children by other men. When she fears that she is losing Tristão, and to protect them from easy detection, she applies folk potions to change their skin color. She discovers that sex is not as exciting because of her transformation to a black concubine. Though Updike modeled the lovers on Tristan and Isolde,* unlike the legendary lovers, Isabel survives after Tristão is murdered. *See* **Sex**.

Leonard, Ruth. *See* **Byer, Ruth Leonard**.

Leonardo da Vinci (1452–1519). One of the three greatest Italian artists of the Renaissance (with Raphael and Michelangelo), particularly for his inventiveness and originality, as well as his mastery of science* and engineering principles, Leonardo da Vinci enjoyed pitting his genius against novel problems, as seen in his drawings for submarines and airplanes.* Leonardo's fresco *The Last Supper* seizes the dramatic moment when Christ announces that he has been betrayed. His celebrated painting, the *Mona Lisa*, with its ambiguous smile, has puzzled viewers for centuries. Leonardo's many drawings of war machines for Ludovico Sforza of Milan and Cesare Borgia (Machiavelli's* model for *The Prince*) show his knowledge of engineering, which he used in Florence's war against Pisa. He left unfinished a monumental painting of a major Florentine victory, as well as a monumental bronze horse in honor of Francesco Sforza. Rebecca Cune's pallor created by the weight of her eyelids and a "certain virtuosity" of her mouth suggest to Richard Maple* a face in a drawing by Leonardo. The ambiguous Rebecca, who has entranced Richard with her various exciting tales, may well have a "certain virtuosity" of her mouth, and her pallor may be a warning of what awaits Richard should he betray his wife ("Snowing in Greenwich Village" [*SD*]). *See* **Art**.

Leopold II (1835–1909). Leopold II was king of Belgium (1865–1909). Having financed Henry Stanley's 1872 Congo expedition (1884–85) and having acquired the territory in 1908, Leopold was criticized for exploiting the Congo's resources and its people. Col. Félix Ellelloû* uses the example of Leopold II to support his claim that colonialism is too expensive a policy to support (*Coup*).

Lewis, Sinclair (1885–1951). Sinclair Lewis was an American novelist and Nobel Prize* winner (1930) whose *Babbitt* (1922) satirized the world of salesman George Babbitt. Updike acknowledges this precursor of salesman Harry "Rabbit" Angstrom* in an epigraph,* thereby suggesting connections between *Babbitt* and *RIR*. Both books satirize social and personal ambitions as well as the American success myth, and each hero is at odds with his world. Like Rabbit, Babbitt is sensitive to nature* and fantasizes about a "fairy child." Babbitt never meets his, and Rabbit decides not to discover if Annabelle Byer* is really his child. In his pastoral* escape, Babbitt goes to Maine, but the trip is a failure, rather like Rabbit's drive to the cotton fields (*RR*) and his retirement to Florida.* Both men for a time leave their families for other women. Though critic Larry Taylor sees Rabbit's gardening for Mrs. Smith as "pathetically impotent," she does feel that Rabbit has given her life, and Rabbit loves making things bloom, "folding the hoed ridge of crumbs of soil over the seeds," despite his realization that once he has procreated, nature is finished with him, and he is just "flower stalks." Perhaps because Henry Bech* represents the realistic backlash against smug conventions, Updike has him speak admiringly of Lewis. Updike reviewed new editions of *Babbitt* and *Main Street* in 1993, and in his essay for *A Century of Arts and Letters*, "1938–1947: Decade of the Row," Updike reports that Lewis thought that the mission of the American Academy of Arts and Letters* should be to "serve as a Supreme Court to accept or reject novelties in the American vocabulary." In "The Key People" (*MM*) Updike notes the feminist ideas of *Main Street*, something perhaps of interest to him as he formulated female characters in the 1980s. He also speculates on the impact of James Joyce's* *Ulysses* on *Main Street*, while admiring Lewis's scholarly interest in details, a trait Updike shares with Lewis. See **Satire**.

Bibliography: Updike, "The Key People" (*MM*); Wayne Clinton, "The Novel of Disentanglement: A Thematic Study of Lewis's *Babbitt*, Bromfield's *Mr. Smith* and Updike's *Rabbit, Run;*" *Dissertation Abstracts* (1967): 2801A, University of Michigan; Taylor, *PA*.

Liberace (born Wladziu Valentino Liberace) (1919–1987). A flamboyant pianist-entertainer, Liberace gave stage performances and had a long-running television* program in the early 1950s, then performed at Las Vegas engagements in the 1960s, mentioned in "One More Interview" (*TM*). See **Popular Music**.

Licks of Love: Short Stories and a Sequel (New York: Knopf, 2000). *Licks of Love* contains twelve previously uncollected short stories written from 1994 to 1999, in the order of their publication. The sequel is a novella, *Rabbit Remembered*, that resumes the Rabbit Saga* nine years after *RaR*. The title *LL* reflects Updike's penchant for naming story collections after a key story.

None of the stories is experimental, and all demonstrate Updike's expert ear for dialogue and matchless precision of observation. Nearly all of them involve a deliberate or spontaneous meditation on the past. Five of the stories concern Updike's signature theme of adultery* ("The Women Who Got Away," "New York Girl," "Natural Color," "Licks of Love in the Heart of the Cold War" and "His Oeuvre"). "His Oeuvre" treats his alter ego* Henry Bech.* Four stories are based on elements of his own life ("Lunch Hour," "My Father on the Verge of Disgrace," "The Cats" and "How Was it, Really?"). Four stories focus on characters that are departures for Updike ("Oliver's Evolution," "Scenes from the Fifties," "Licks of Love in the Heart of the Cold War" and "Metamorphosis").

Three stories rely on Updike's personal past: "Lunch Hour" about a class reunion, apparently at Shillington High School; "My Father on the Verge of Disgrace," based on his father Wesley Updike*; and "The Cats," recounting the aftermath of Updike's mother's death. "Lunch Hour" returns to a character from Updike's early stories, Allen Dow, who attends a high-school class reunion in the town he was happy to escape and realizes that reunions only reveal "that keenly felt structure of implacable discriminations to have been a poor predictor of adult performance." He comes to see that he had learned self-acceptance from Julia Reidenhauser who recognized the man he would become, and he instinctively introduces her to his wife, realizing they are each women, not just "growing girls." The story is a tribute to those who helped him achieve what he only guessed he might become. "My Father on the Verge of Disgrace," is a touching character sketch based on Updike's life from 1940 to 1950. Updike's narrator, whom his father calls "young America," has an adolescent fear that his father will topple his family from the ledge of respectability. He recalls three potentially "toppling" episodes: when his father's fellow teacher Otto Werner had his father pass affectionate notes to a student, when his father borrowed money from high-school sports receipts and when his father kissed a male teacher when playing Pyramus to his Thisbe in a school production of *A Midsummer Night's Dream*. Yet the narrator changed his attitude when he came to know his father better during their daily commute after the family moved to a farm in 1945 and saw that his father's trust of strangers put his father "at the mercy of the world." By 1950 and his graduation from high school, the narrator's pity and love for his father gave him the courage to see that "part of being human is being on the verge of disgrace." "My Father on the Verge of Disgrace" is an interesting footnote to similar revelations in *C.* Finally, "The Cats," can be linked to stories in *A* based on Updike's mother. "Working like a man," she had moved her family to an isolated farm and attacked its renovation with vigor, but when she dies her son Frank must attend to a "mewing puddle" of "half-feral" cats she had befriended to curb their appetites for the birds she loved. The narrator had always thought the farm a trap from which "my clear duty was to escape." The cats impede his escape, just as they represented how "nature kept getting ahead of her." Guilty at selling the house, he sees her ghost and wants to scream "in shame and helplessness." When he returns for the last time, assuming the cats have been trapped and given to the Boone Township Humane Society as his mother directed, he finds instead that the cats, thinking that he is his mother, have returned. As "nature kept getting ahead of her," so it also gets the best of him. Though the cats represent visceral need and dependency reflecting the child that still inhabits the narrator, the cats also symbolize his mother's indomitable spirit transferred to her son. "The Cats" thus has a relation to "Pigeon Feathers" (*PigF*) written decades before, revealing the intricate relation of nature to man and his own slow recognition of the magical trust binding all sentient life.

Several stories continue the tone of Proustian* nostalgia demonstrated in *A*, but are concerned almost exclusively with attempts to discover the precise value of a love affair. The heroes of "His Oeuvre," "The Women Who Got Away," "New York Girl" and "Natural Color" struggle to recapture the significance of a former love. In "His Oeuvre" Henry Bech* is convinced that a woman who arrives late at his public reading resembles a woman with whom he had had an adulterous affair. Though his "forty-year old prose poems" may seem as he reads them "fatally mannered, as well as badly dated," his lover remains untouched by time. He comes to recognize that those women of his past are his real "masterpieces." Like several of these stories set at the end of the Vietnam* War, "The Women Who Got Away" looks back nostalgically on the "high moral value of copulation," and Martin the hero reflects on women he had not made love to, perhaps perceiving this to be a moral failure. One such woman is a "piece of the cosmic puzzle" that never fits his piece. Another "got away" because she didn't have the requisite "innocence." Martin's wife Jeanne also "got away," since his affairs and subsequently hers ended their marriage. Martin rationalizes his loss of two other women, Audrey and Winifred, when he observes them holding hands, apparently happier together than with him. The failure, he apparently imagines, is not in himself but in the women. But in "New York Girl," a rare story about New York, Stan recollects precisely an adulterous affair with Jane fifteen years before that had produced a "camaraderie of New Yorkers" who found a "genial way" of "folding" adultery into its "round-the-clock hustle." Given the chance to be "somebody else," Stan finds taking Jane to the Automat resembled "entering a Hopper with a Petty girl on my arm." Stan's New York girl is "tucked" into his consciousness "like a candy after dinner." In memory he can revisit Jane's apartment as if it were "the city itself, the universe of anonymous lights." Stan, now married to his second wife, meets Jane fifteen years later and discovers that she hated New York. Perhaps his affair with Jane had given him the courage to leave his first wife, for his New York girl provided an illusion that he could place his women in convenient venues in his life. Another character who maintains an illusion about a past affair is Frank of "Natural Color." His chance encounter after twenty years leads him to recall why his affair with Maggie Chase led to her divorce but not his. He chose to remain "the beautiful prisoner" of his marriage for his marriage "fattened" on it: his wife Ann exhibited passionate jealousy, and she admired him for his spectacular conquest of a woman whose hair was "done up in a burnished, glistening twist," though she was certain it was not natural but dyed. Her claim makes Frank the victim of an illusion about Maggie, but Frank's view of Maggie's "flash of red hair" produced not only a willingness to accept illusion over reality but the bitter realization about Maggie that as long as he loved her, he must also hate her. Evidently to keep his marriage "fat," Frank must let the natural color of his lover blaze in his memory. In contrast, Ed Franklin, the narrator of "How Was It Really?" is frightened by how little he can remember with certainty, dimly recalling "being in love with one or another man's wife."

"Metamorphosis" counters the trend of the stories of nostalgia and loss with transformation, prompted by a woman. Anderson seeks cosmetic surgery for a cancerous growth and becomes so infatuated with the Asian doctor's "perfectly natural, assimilated American English" that he likens her voice to a "moon buggy determinedly proceeding across uneroded terrain, in conditions of weak gravity." He is that weak gravity, and he succumbs in his "bliss of secure helplessness" that he asks her to make his eyelids like hers. His face becomes "lunar" under her attentions, and in the spring "his own healing emerges into beauty." His growth finds parallels in Dr. Kim's two pregnancies. Under her genius his face becomes "Oriental in its smoothness and impassive expression." Anderson has metamorphosed into something from her "perfect world." Updike has used a favorite theme, the return to Eden, but without sexuality as part of the transformation. Another metamorphosis takes place in "Oliver's Evolution." After his parents thoughtlessly mistreat him and fail to detect his "sleepy eye" and divorce while he is at a vulnerable age, Oliver makes bad grades, crashes cars, abandons jobs and marries a drug addict. Yet his wife adores him, and he becomes a "protector of the weak" because "What we expect of others, they try to provide." The assistance of a woman very different from Dr. Kim has led Oliver to transform despite his parent's apathy. Oliver bears a kinship to Nelson Angstrom* of "Rabbit Remembered," who was destructive when young but a caregiver when mature.

"Licks of Love in the Heart of the Cold War" recounts adventures in pre-Vietnam Russia told by an unusual Updike narrator, Eddie Chester, a Virginia banjo-player, whose flippant tone recalls Henry Bech* of "Rich in Russia" (*BB*). Imogene Frye calls him "my god," and shows a passionate interest in banjo-playing, giving Updike a chance to reveal his expertise* of the banjo. After Chester makes love to Imogene and discards her, she sends love letters to Russia where he gives concerts for the State Department. He becomes disgusted by her infatuation. In control in America, he becomes progressively muddled in Russia, as he discovers Russians more interested in American racism than in his encyclopedic knowledge of banjo styles and visits a monastery in which a monk appears to be a Russian agent. When Chester's wife discovers his affair, he consoles himself with, "you can't blame a person for thinking you're a god." His arrogance ironically undermines his position as representative of the world's greatest democracy. In his irresponsibility he has blurred the distinction between freedom and license. Given the freedom to develop as an artist, he accepts adulation from those he mistreats. Chester continues Updike's exploration of the artist as public representative of his country begun with "The Bulgarian Poetess" (*BB*).

Updike's continuing interest in homosexuality* is displayed in "Scenes from the Fifties." The narrator recalls how, when his "Manhattan ambitions" and marriage were "not happening," he was homosexually propositioned. He feels this "assault" "threatened the very meaning" of his life. Though he confides the experience to his friend Brian who tells him that homosexuals are harmless and cultivated people, the narrator keeps it a secret from his wife. A few years later he leaves her for Brian. Apparently, this conversion to homosexuality creates no threat to the meaning of his life. "Scenes from the Fifties" is far more sympathetic to unconventional sexual preference than previous depictions of it in *W, RIR* and *RaR*.

"Rabbit Remembered" is Updike's final word on Harry "Rabbit" Angstrom. Those who thought the ambiguous ending of *RaR* suggested that Rabbit survived his heart attack now know for certain that he died in Florida and was cremated. But like the phoenix he seems to rise from the flames and lives in the thoughts and emotions of everyone who knew him years after his death. The narrative describes how Annabelle Byer,* Rabbit's daughter by Ruth Leonard Byer,* seeks a place in the Angstrom household after Ruth dies. Annabelle is confronted inhospitably, however, by the former Janice Angstrom* who is now married to Ronnie Harrison.* Annabelle has inadvertently rekindled Janice's outrage at Rabbit for his affair with Ruth, and Harrison is still bitter that Rabbit impregnated Ruth, his onetime sexual partner, as well as having had an affair with his wife Thelma Harrison.* At Janice's Thanksgiving dinner Annabelle is gratuitously insulted by Harrison who calls her a whore's bastard. However, Annabelle finds a protector in Nelson Angstrom* who has continued in his career as a counselor begun in *RaR*. After defending her, Nelson vacates Janice's home; thus Annabelle helps him to become independent. The narrative then focuses on Nelson's delight in finding he has a sister, the secret Rabbit had tried to confide as he lay dying in *RaR*. Nelson helps reconcile Harrison and Annabelle, and on the eve of the millennium Nelson introduces her to his friend Billy Fosnacht, who presumably proposes to Annabelle as the narrative ends.

Rabbit forms an absent presence in the narrative. Each character still bears the imprint of his actions and personality. Janice hates him for having deserted her. Ron is embittered both for having impregnated Ruth and for cuckolding him with Thelma. Pru still carries the imprint of her night with Rabbit; it even colors her view of President Bill Clinton. But Nelson and Annabelle are the living embodiment of Rabbit's masculine and feminine sides, and they are a positive legacy. They also continue Rabbit's search for something beyond himself, since much of the narrative reveals Nelson's effort to help manic-depressives and schizophrenics, divided persons, and even though Nelson feels he has failed when one client kills himself, he doesn't lose faith in therapy. As a nurse, Annabelle is also a caregiver. Balancing Harrison's unprovoked hatred of Annabelle, Nelson, in the name of love, forces Annabelle to admit that Ruth's husband, Frank Byer, had abused her. Her admission will apparently free her to accept a mature relationship. Though Updike appears to flirt with incest* in the love between Nelson and Annabelle, incidental details reveal that they are each joined in Rabbit. Each supports President Bill Clinton during a discussion of his impeachment as Rabbit had defended President Lyndon Johnson* during the Vietnam War in *RRed*. They also share similar empathic responses to the characters in the film *American Beauty*. Such maturity in Nelson may surprise some readers, but his growth is a continuation of Rabbit's spiritual development. In Nelson and Annabelle the most vulnerable and most caregiving aspects of Rabbit's dual nature have continued to live. Rabbit, therefore, is "remembered" not just through anecdotes and images and recollected quotations but in his personal continuation. The question of Rabbit's "death" has been answered with a definitive yes and no. Nelson, because he has forgiven if not understood his father's ambiguity, has become free to promote harmony rather than discord. In caring for his step-sister Nelson has also discovered his father's other identity. Updike suggests that what had been divisive between father and son for so long has been made, at last, whole. *See* **Rabbit Angstrom**; **Updike, John, in His Work**.

Light Verse. Updike's light verse defines the form: it provides sportive treatments of everyday events, sometimes using parody or burlesquing the difference between a serious model and the playful style treating that material. Rhyme and other musical devices are often used for surprise, and the verse always demonstrates the poet's wit. Updike described light verses stemming from the man-made world of information (*CP*). Updike began writing light verse at fourteen, using such models as *New Yorker** writers Phyllis McGinley, Arthur Guiterman, Robert Service, Ogden Nash, Morris Bishop, Franklin P. Adams and James Thurber,* who is mentioned in "Bech Enters Heaven" (*BB*). By 1982, in a "Foreword" to the Knopf edition of *CH*, Updike announced he would no longer write light verse, leading Brad Leithauser to label Updike the "last prolific writer of light verse in America" ("Light Verse Dead but Remarkably Robust"). As a contributor to the *Harvard Lampoon*,* Updike was influenced by the metric wit of *Punch*, the model for the Harvard magazine. Though Updike has described his light verse as cartooning* in print, he has insisted that his light-verse science* poems are also serious because they reveal the gap between what science shows the universe to be and the evidence of our own senses. He demonstrated his mastery of light verse in his first two poetry collections, *CH* and *TP*. Although he has said that light verse began to disappear about the time "when it no longer seemed even the littlest bit wonderful to make two words rhyme" (Plath, *CU*), Updike has continued to write it because, as he noted, light verse satisfies a need for "an exercise of the word not entirely lacking Promethean resonance." Updike has incorporated light verse in his novels, particularly *Couples*, *BB*, *W* and *S*. *See* **Collected Poems, 1953–1993**; **Poetry**.

Bibliography: Updike, "Rhyming Max" *AP*; "Foreword" 1982 reissue of *CH*; Greiner, *OJ*; Brad Leithauser, "Light Verse: Dead But Remarkably Robust," *New York Times Book Review* 7 June 1987: 1, 26–27.

Lincoln, Abraham (1809–1865). Abraham Lincoln was the sixteenth president of the United States (1861–65) and kept the Union from dissolving by his determination to win the Civil War. His best-remembered single act was the Emancipation Proclamation, which, though it freed no slaves, since the Confederacy did not recognize Northern laws and Northern blacks were not slaves, made Lincoln a moral icon. His assassination in 1865 assured Lincoln of saintly status among presidents,* but John Hook* takes exception to this, saying that Lincoln was "no lover of morals" and in private "an atheist." Hook also connects Lincoln to the corruption of the administration of President Ulysses Grant; to Hook they were "Baal and Mammon" (*PF*).

Literary Influences. Updike has spoken often of influences on his poetry* and fiction, and his readers have been active in suggesting others. Updike has acknowledged the impact of *New Yorker** poets Ogden Nash and Phyllis McGinley on his light verse*; critics have suggested such influences as Richard Armour, E. B. White, Morris Bishop, Peter De Vries, Dame Edith Sitwell and John Betjeman. Influence on Updike's serious poetry is less easy to trace. His experimental poems like "Nut" (*CH*) and "Midpoint" and "Love Sonnet" (*M*) may reflect his reading of George Herbert and E. E. Cummings* at Harvard.* Updike's fondness for writing sonnets was surely abetted by the example of fellow *New Yorker* poet L. E. Sissman, a reviewer of *M*. In introducing Sissman's poems, Updike acknowledged the influence of Sissman on "Apologies to Harvard," praising his "prodigious festive way with the English language." His "odes" show the admitted influence of Richard Eberhart's* "The Groundhog." Updike consciously used Dante's* terza rima and some structural ideas from *The Divine Comedy* in "I: Introduction" from "Midpoint," and Updike clearly relies on Edmund Spenser's stanza form in "III: The Dance of the Solids" from "Midpoint" (*M*). "Midpoint" also incorporates quotations from Walt Whitman,* Ezra Pound* and Theodore Roethke and the practices of Pound and T. S. Eliot.* Updike has frequently alluded to, quoted, parodied and written about Wallace Stevens,* and "The Sea's Green Sameness" shows Updike's reading of Stevens's "Sea-Surface Full of Clouds." Some readers have detected similarities to W. H. Auden.*

Influences upon Updike's fiction are marked by differences rather than similarities. His primary sources of inspiration were Vladimir Nabokov,* James Joyce,* Marcel Proust,* Henry Green* and J. D. Salinger.* Updike's most often acknowledged mentor was Nabokov, best known for having depicted the love of a mature intellectual for a "nymphet," Lolita, in his novel *Lolita* (1955). Updike may have depicted similar lovers in *TE*, and *RR* contains images and situations that parallel *Lolita* in the long drive of Rabbit and his jealousy over a previous lover. Nabokov affected the writing of *Coup*, according to Joyce Carol Oates, who was perhaps thinking of *Invitation to a Beheading*. Also, Nabokov's concern for the craft of fiction provided Updike an example of dedication to style.* Like Nabokov, Updike sought to move, as he said, a "mass of images" forward, but his review of Nabokov's stylistically obscure *Ada* shows an unwillingness to follow his mentor uncritically. Nabokov represented a supreme example of the dedicated craftsman, something Updike notes in his many reviews and memorials to Nabokov.

Updike has explained in interviews* the influence of James Joyce's use of myth* and stream of consciousness on *PF*, *C* and *RR*. In *PF* he supplies a montage of voices based on the "Wandering Rocks" segment of *Ulysses*. In a late chapter of *C*, mindful of Joyce's method, Updike uses the fevered imagination of Peter Caldwell* to create a dreamlike fluidity in which Updike moves from Peter's realistic situation to myth and symbol. In *RR* Updike adopted the interior monologue of Joyce's Molly Bloom to the streams of consciousness of Rabbit Angstrom,* his wife Janice Angstrom* and Ruth Leonard Byer.* Updike also uses Joyce as a model for a new freedom in writing about sex.* In Rabbit's mind, as in Leopold and Molly Bloom's, erotic images arise that caused *RR* and *Ulysses* to be censored for a time.

The impact of Proust is mostly seen in Updike's concern for the beauty of detail and metaphor, the blend of his personal life with imagined narratives, and his constant interest in the past, as in *C*, *MF*, and *RA* and stories in *PigF* and *MuS*. Proust is at the heart of Updike's "abstract-personal" or "lyric-personal" style in short fiction* such as "Leaves" and "The Music School" (MuS). The play *BD* is Proustian in its presentation of an incapacitated man trying to understand events in his past life. Updike's interest in Proust is certainly connected to the nostalgia of characters like Harry "Rabbit" Angstrom (*RR*) and Alf Clayton* (*MF*). Proust's satiric view of society emerges in *Couples* and *RIR*.

The impact of Henry Green has been described by Updike as impelling his use of shifting viewpoints and tones in *PF*, *RR* and *C*, as well as giving him empathy for the outsider. Updike has delineated at length the impact of Henry Green's *Concluding* on *PF* and notes that Green affected the decision to write *RR* in the present tense. Green's brilliant style, compressing language and imagery,* also influenced Updike's early work.

J. D. Salinger was introduced to Updike in a Harvard creative writing course, and Salinger's image of a young man unable to accept his place in society is revealed in such Updike stories as "Ace in the Hole," "Who Made Yellow Roses Yellow?" and "The Alligators" (*SD*) and "A & P" (*PigF*), as well as in the novel *RR*, which developed from "Ace in the Hole." Rabbit could be considered a grown-up Holden Caulfield (*The Catcher in the Rye*), more frustrated in rebellion. Like Holden, Rabbit sees maturity as "the same thing as being dead." Also, Salinger's religious concerns may have supported Updike's use of religious crises in stories like "The Astronomer" and "Pigeon Feathers" (*PigF*). Nabokov, Proust, Joyce, Green and Salinger abetted Updike's willingness to develop a flexible style that would use slice-of-life realism but incorporate an originality of imagery and particularity of voice, hallmarks of Updike's style.

Among other writers who have influenced Updike's fiction, no doubt Updike's friend for many years, John Cheever,* also contributed to his style as well as his psychological penetration into submerged sexual needs. Cheever and Updike were so close in their treatment of suburbia and domestic crises that they were sometimes confused with each other. Also, Updike shares with Philip Roth,* a near contemporary, many themes—the constrictions of convention, the pressure of desire versus middle-class values, and the writer's need to employ fantasy. A book-length comparison of Roth and Updike reveals interesting parallels. Like Nabokov, Joyce Cary is detectable in Updike's *Coup* because Cary also wrote about Africa, and Updike acknowledged that Cary's use of the present tense in *The Horse's Mouth* influenced the "cinematic" present tense of *RR*. Cary's trilogy about the artist Gully Jimson may also have stimulated Updike's interest in writing his trilogies (*BB, BIB* and *BaB* about Henry Bech*; *MS, RV* and *S.* based on *The Scarlet Letter*) as well as his tetralogy *RA*. Possibly Cary's trilogy also fortified Updike's interest in writing a trio of related novels (*RR, C, OF*). Nathaniel Hawthorne* was certainly a major influence, and Updike has written an essay concerning Hawthorne's themes and artistry. Yet even though Updike modeled *MS, RV* and *S.* on characters from *The Scarlet Letter*, he was not affected by Hawthorne's style, point of view or Puritanism. Critic James Schiff sees *W* as resulting from Updike's long interest in Hawthorne. Surprisingly, Updike says that Robert Pinget provided him with the courage to write *W* through his use of "malicious chit-chat, in the permutability of events as they are reflected and refracted in a community." Updike also admired William Styron's The *Confessions of Nat Turner* for its evangelical tone (Plath *CU*); the voice of Nat Turner may have helped Updike create Skeeter* (*RRed*). Considering Updike's enormous reading in modern and contemporary writers of many countries, his ability to sustain his own particular voices from work to work may be more significant than any individual influence, though Updike often pays tribute to Ernest Hemingway's* style, and its impact can be detected in Updike's dialogue.

Jack Kerouac's* *On the Road* was admired to some degree, since, as Updike says, Kerouac "attempted to grab it all" and wrote *On the Road* to answer "man's disquiet." Updike wrote *RR* partly because he saw that despite the attraction of taking to the road, "there are all these other people who seem to get hurt." Thus *On the Road* is a negative model for *RR*, though Updike delineates the need to run to overcome "inward dwindling." Updike's *C* is a counterattack on Kerouac, illustrating the virtues of shouldering responsibility and staying in one place. This may explain Updike's parody "On the Sidewalk," one of his few parodies of a living American writer. The vibrancy of Kerouac's style may have influenced the present-tense style of *RR*.

Among many suggestive connections between Thomas Mann* and Updike's fiction, one may list their interest in the opposition of reality and artifice (*W*); the exploration of several generations of certain cultural impacts (*IB, RA*); each uses the modern artist as a hero (*BB, BIB, BaB*); and each dramatizes, sometimes through debates, conflicts of science* and religion* (*RV*).

Updike has noted that his single play, *BD*, was influenced by Samuel Beckett.* It bears some relation to *Krapp's Last Tape*, since both plays are concerned with the memories of an incapacitated man, and *BD* moves fluidly from present time to past memories. At least one commentator has found that as a critic Updike resembles Henry James* for his breadth of interest in literature and his engagement with the craft of fiction. James wrote his famous prefaces to his New York edition; Updike has supplied copious introductions, notes and "special messages" to many of his novels and individual poems, stories and essays. *See* **The Novel; Sex**.

Bibliography: Schiff, *JU*.

Lone Ranger. A program about the old West that ran on the radio from 1933 to the mid-1950s and in a television* show from 1949 to 1957, *The Lone Ranger* followed the story of the lone survivor of an outlaw ambush who is saved by an Indian, Tonto. Wearing a mask, the Lone Ranger helps establish frontier justice. His silver bullets, his friendship with Tonto and his "Hearty Heigh-Ho Silver" as he called to his horse were parodied in a skit on *The Carol Burnett Show* watched by Harry "Rabbit" Angstrom* and his son Nelson Angstrom* in *RRed*. Rabbit tries to explain mysterious aspects of the Lone Ranger to his resistant son, such as Tonto's name for him, "Kemo Sabe." Images of the skit recur when Rabbit, arguing with Charlie Stavros,* makes an analogy between the Vietcong and American Indians (*RRed*). In *RIR* the purchase of scrap silver for investment recalls the Lone Ranger's silver bullets, while in *RaR* Rabbit plays golf* with Ed Silberstein and Joe Gold, references to his investments in gold as well as silver. Ed sends Rabbit to his son, who has changed his name to Greg Silvers, in order to rent a Sunfish. Greg helps resuscitate Rabbit when he suffers a heart attack. *See* ***I Love a Mystery*; Popular Culture; Vietnam**.

Bibliography: Andrew S. Horton, "Ken Kesey, John Updike and the Lone Ranger," *Journal of Popular Culture* 8 (Winter 1974): 570–78.

Lowell House. When Updike was a sophomore at Harvard* in 1951, he was assigned for the next three years to Lowell House, apparently named for James Russell Lowell, which was especially created for those majoring in English and related subjects. It is one of eleven undergraduate residence halls, each housing about 350, in which students sleep, eat and recreate. The houses also contain libraries. Professors and graduate students, who act as advisors, live in each house, mingling socially with undergraduates. In Updike's time, each house had a unique character, because each was student selected; now students are chosen for the house at random. In Updike's junior year he lived on the fifth floor. His marriage in the summer before his senior year ended his stay at Lowell House.

Bibliography: Updike, "The Industrious Drifter in Room 2," *Harvard Magazine* 76 (May 1974): 42–45, 51; "The Early Days of John Updike '54," *Harvard University Gazette* (30 Apr. 1998): 1, 4.

LSD. Lysergic acid diethylamide (LSD) is a psychedelic drug that induces hallucinations. It was popular in the 1960s primarily among college students and was championed by Professor Timothy Leary of Harvard* as a sacred drug. He urged students to use it in order to "turn on, tune in, drop out." Jill Pendleton* thinks that she has seen God while taking LSD. Skeeter's* conviction that Jill can see God through the use of heroin creates her addiction to it and her eventual death (*RRed*). *See* **Drugs**.

M

Machiavelli, Niccolò (1469–1527). Niccolò Machiavelli was an Italian politician and philosopher who is mentioned in *Marry* when Jerry Conant* accuses his wife Ruth Conant* of being devious in her refusal to name her lover, in order to maintain power over her husband; she never tells him that her lover was his mistress's husband. Machiavelli was an advisor to Cesare Borgia, possibly Machiavelli's model prince in *The Prince*, a manual for getting and keeping power.

Magic Realism. Although magic realism is grounded in realism, it admits antirealistic elements of the supernatural, myth,* dream* and fantasy. The technique is associated with expressionism, surrealism and black humor.* Although magic realism is chiefly associated with Latin American writers like Jorge Luis Borges* and Gabriel García Márquez (the term was coined by Cuban novelist Alejo Carpentier), some critics consider even Homer a magic realist. Magic realism has been used by American fictionalists Nathaniel Hawthorne,* Herman Melville* and Mark Twain for macabre and comic purposes. Modern magic realism was developed by James Joyce* and Vladimir Nabokov* and has been employed by the expressionistic American dramatists Eugene O'Neill and Thornton Wilder, who were both indebted to the European magic realist August Strindberg. Magic realism has become a staple of film* directors Federico Fellini and Ingmar Bergman, and black-humor writers like John Barth and Thomas Pynchon have used it extensively. Reviewing stories by Gabriel García Márquez in 1985, Updike was surprised that his magic realism was "blacker" than expected (*OJ*), and in reviewing Adolfo Bioy Casares, Updike traces the "pedigree" of magic realism to "Borges, back through the fantasy of Chesterton and Stevenson . . . clear to Hawthorne and Poe" (*OJ*). In another place he considers magic realism basically a method of nostalgia: "The past—personal, familial, and national—weathers

into fabulous shapes in memory without surrendering its fundamental truth
... Fantasy [for Latin writers] is a higher level of honesty" (*OJ*).

Updike employs magic realism for various effects. In *C* mythical figures
take on human presence and vice versa. In *BB* Henry Bech* apparently goes
to "heaven" in the last chapter and visits great authors, some of whom are
dead. *Coup* employs African folk tales to expand realism into magic, as when
the king's decapitated head speaks. *W* asks the reader to accept the reality
of modern suburban witches who can really inflict death, suspend natural
laws and read minds. Roger Lambert* (*RV*) apparently has telepathic powers. *B* uses the world of Indian folklore and myth to account for how black
and white protagonists exchange colors. *TE* moves abruptly into widely different time zones and intimates that the hero's wife changes into a deer and
back again. Updike uses magic realism throughout to allow him to shift tones
into comedy and irony, thus injecting new vitality into realism. Thus, Updike
said, it "gave a kind of spriteliness" to *W*. *See* **Magritte, René; The Novel**.

Bibliography: Updike, "The Other American" (*OJ*).

Magritte, René-François-Ghislain (1898–1967). A Belgian surrealist artist,
René Magritte juxtaposed commonplace objects with odd contexts to jar the
observer into unexpected views of reality. The result is called fantasy or
magic realism.* His parody of the portrait of Madame Récamier by Jacques-
Louis David replaces the sumptuous woman with a coffin, forcing the observer to consider simultaneously erotic and morbid images. Similarly, in the
story "Slippage" (*TM*) Professor Morison thinks of his daughter as "a pea
suspended in the center of an empty cube, waiting to be found"; an image
that "had the sadness of a Magritte." That sadness perhaps impels Morison
to think, before falling asleep later, of Emperor Franz Joseph* in his coffin.

Mailer, Norman (1923–   ). An American novelist who has explored violence in such novels as *The Naked and the Dead*, which made him an instant
success, and *The Executioner's Song* and in reportage such as *The Armies of
the Night* (which won a Pulitzer Prize), Norman Mailer has said that Updike's style* smelled like garlic and that his apprenticeship* under *New
Yorker** writers kept him from having anything to say. Updike wrote (in an
unpublished book note) of Mailer's account of war protestors' march on the
Pentagon, *The Armies of the Night*, "fascinating, if hysterically high-flown,"
with his sociological analysis of the event going from "the farcical to the
brilliant" and giving it "a decent, sensual complexity" (*PP*). Updike wittily
caricatured Mailer in his "Foreword" to *BB* by having Henry Bech* rail at
"John"* for making him a man of "bravura narcissism" who sounds like a
"gentlemanly Norman Mailer." Later Bech refers to himself as scribbling
reviews and "impressionistic" journalism for *Esquire*, a magazine Mailer contributed to at the time. Mailer did insist that Updike would be preferable to

him as a reporter-astronaut, should the moon be visited again, but they were on opposite sides about the Vietnam* War: Mailer opposed the war; Updike favored it. In a 1995 interview Mailer altered his earlier view of Updike when he said that Updike was extremely substantial, wonderful and poetic and "extraordinarily good at what he does." Meanwhile, Updike remarked that "one of Mailer's irrepressible strengths has been his ability to become interested, and then quickly expert, in almost anything," though he admits of Mailer's *The Gospel According to the Son* that his "first-person voice only fitfully convinces us that we are occupying Jesus's psychological center. To do more would have indeed been a miracle" (*MM*). *See* **American Literature; Hostile Critics;** *Self-Consciousness*.

Bibliography: Updike, "Stones into Bread" (*MM*); Norman Mailer, "Some Children of the Goddess," in *Cannibals and Christians* (New York: Dell, 1966), 120–21; Joyce M. Flint, "In Search of Meaning: Bernard Malamud, Norman Mailer, John Updike," *Dissertation Abstracts International* 30 (1969): 3006A Washington State University; Robert Joseph Nadon, "Urban Values in Recent American Fiction: A Study of the City in the Fiction of Saul Bellow, John Updike, Philip Roth, Bernard Malamud, and Norman Mailer," *Dissertation Abstracts International* 30 (1969): 2543A.

Manichaeanism. The most successful heretical sect to challenge Catholicism, *Manichaeanism* was created by the Persian sage Mani (c. 216–276), whose visions told him that he was a prophet. Having been accused of offending Zoroastrianism, Mani said that he was the last in a line of prophets starting with Jesus and including Zoroaster. *Manichaeanism* advocates that good and evil have equal power. They were originally separated, but evil infiltrated goodness, resulting in the human race. Humans are likewise dualistic; the soul struggles against the trap of the body. To solve the problem, one must know the sacred teachings of the prophets: Jesus, Buddha,* Zoroaster and Mani. In time, goodness would triumph, and evil would again be separated from good. By the fourth century *Manichaeanism* had reached Africa, where St. Augustine* professed it for nine years until he was converted to Catholicism. *Manichaeanism* lasted into the Middle Ages, attracting Albigensians, among others. Roger Lambert* is an expert in early church heresies and scans his class notes on *Manichaeanism* while, ironically, Dale Kohler* asks for his support in order to prove the factual existence of God (*RV*). In "Elusive Evil" (*MM*) Updike reviews four books about the nature of evil, one of which traces St. Mark's demonizing of the Jews, thus creating a "cosmic war" between light and darkness, Semites and anti-Semite Christians. This *Manichaean* "image" became culturally absorbed as detecting "evil" in "the other," whoever was designated as "other." St. Mark returns in *TE*; he debates with St. Paul about the efficacy of spreading the word of Christ. *See* **Antinomianism; Marcion; Thomas Aquinas, St.**

Bibliography: Updike, "Elusive Evil" (*MM*).

Mann, Thomas (1875–1955). The German novelist, critic and Nobel* laureate Thomas Mann examined the individual within society, often in the family, as in *Buddenbrooks* (1901), his first novel. Both Updike and Mann work a good deal with oppositions, contrasts and dualisms* and treat discrepancies between reality and dream, romance and actuality, and artifice and truth (compare Mann's "Tonio Kröger" and *The Magic Mountain* with *PF, C, MS, RV, B* and *W*). *Buddenbrooks*, like *RA*, explores the social determinants that form individuals and shape their minor rebellions and search for spiritual values. Like Mann, Updike has always been concerned with a self-transcendence that gives life meaning (*Couples, RA, IB*), and just as Mann in *Death in Venice* depicted a writer giving his life for such a vision, so does Updike when Henry Bech* nearly dies while giving a reading of his work in "Bech Panics" (*BB*). As Mann explored creative genius in *Dr. Faustus*, so Updike examines the writer Bech and a film actress (*IB*). As Mann's magnum opus may be his tetralogy based on the biblical tale of Joseph, *Joseph and His Brothers* (1934–44), so Updike's may be *RA*, the story of an ordinary Everyman. The Bech books, like *B*, also reflect the picaresque spirit of Mann's *Confessions of Felix Krull, Confidence Man* (1922; English Translation, 1954). Mann and Updike are masters of accuracy in detail and psychological insight, and each focuses keenly on middle-class life, in which unimportant people face spiritual crises. Another connection could be drawn between Mann's novel of ideas, *The Magic Mountain* (1924), and Updike's dramatization of the conflict between religion* and science* in *RV*. Mann and Updike brought the novel* and short-fiction* genres to new levels, and each wrote essays of pivotal importance as well as highly personal memoirs. As Mann exiled himself from Germany after 1933, so Updike left New York* to avoid an environment inhospitable to the best writing.

Bibliography: Updike, *HS, OJ*.

Maple, Joan. A college-educated artist and wife of Richard Maple* in *TF* and in "Grandparenting" (*A*), Joan Maple is first presented as a newlywed living in Greenwich Village ("Snowing in Greenwich Village" [*TF*]). The stories sweep through the 1960s and 1970s, depicting episodes that illustrate her effort to save her marriage in the face of Richard's growing discontent with her. "Snowing in Greenwich Village" reveals Joan's ingenuousness in inviting a former girlfriend to their apartment; she never suspects Richard's growing inclination toward adultery.* Joan's sympathies with the civil rights movement seem artificial to Richard ("Marching through Boston"), and their four children fail to bring them together. When a second honeymoon in Rome fails ("Twin Beds in Rome"), Richard is determined to leave, and after they see other people when Joan agrees to an "open marriage," another, more sensual woman eases his exit. Their similar educations, attitudes and love of their children make Richard's departure excruciating, but Joan tries to retain the integrity of the family after Richard leaves her and the four children ("Separating"). When they meet years later in "Grandparenting," their previous warmth kindles jealousy toward the people they have since married.

Maple, Richard. Husband of Joan Maple* in *TF* and "Grandparenting" (*A*), Richard Maple is torn between the requirements of his wife and family and his need for other sexual partners, which arises partly in rebellion against what he perceives as Joan's remoteness. In the early story "Snowing in Greenwich Village" he senses that adultery* is a possibility, and though he takes Joan to Rome to reconcile, his image of the Coliseum as being like a rotting wedding cake shows that he has soured on their marriage. When Joan marches for civil rights, Richard ridicules her and mimics the black speaker they listen to ("Marching through Boston"). Experimenting with an open marriage, Richard envies her ability to attract more lovers than he can ("Your Lover Just Called"). When he eventually finds a way out of the marriage, Richard's anxiety and pain infect the entire family, despite his close alliance with Joan ("Separating"). Conflicted over his need to be free and his fear of unraveling his marriage, Richard resembles Harry "Rabbit" Angstrom.* Both men rebel against stale marriages, but neither anticipates the importance of marriage as an institution for him. "Grandparenting," however, shows that despite remarriage, Richard still cannot extricate himself from his first marriage; he is as jealous of Joan's second husband as he had been of her lovers.

Marcel, Gabriel (1889–1973). Gabriel Marcel was a French philosopher who is read by Jerry Conant* in *Marry*. Marcel thought that morality was contextual and that moral meaning was established during "secondary reflection." Thus Updike might consider Marcel as supporting adultery* since it brings a kind of wisdom through action, as Ruth Conant* thinks. *See* **Religion**.

Marcion (c. 100–160). The son of a bishop, Marcion left his native Turkey for Rome, broke with the established church and founded his own, second only in power to the Catholic church. His church preached asceticism and kept the sacraments, but opposed the crucial concepts of the Incarnation and the Resurrection. Instead, he advocated that God is both the Old Testament God of Justice and the New Testament Jesus Christ. Marcionism survived until it was absorbed by Manichaeanism,* a heretical doctrine that saw good and evil as equal in power. Tertullian* led one of the most famous attacks on Marcionism. As Dale Kohler* tries to convince Roger Lambert* that he can provide a factual basis for belief in God, Lambert glances at his notes on Marcion, who, in Roger's opinion, plausibly saw the Old and New Testament Gods as different. He muses that Marcion "had a case" for scorning the God who created evil and copulation, a major reason for his denial of the Incarnation. Lambert's thoughts become ironic since he not only conspires behind the scenes to destroy Kohler, but fantasizes about his wife's adultery* with Kohler while drifting toward quasi-incest with his stepniece (*RV*). See **Antinomianism; Augustine, St**.

Marcus Aurelius (full name, Marcus Aurelius Antoninus) (121–180). Marcus Aurelius was emperor of Rome (161–180) and a philosopher whose reign was marked by enacting social reforms, reducing taxes, improving the lives of slaves and building hospitals. His *Meditations* counsels a life of Stoic detachment from emotional bondage that alone leads to peace and justice through the precept of moderation. The modern-day analogue of St. Augustine* in "Augustine's Concubine" (*P*) is named Aurelius to draw attention to the ironic distance between Augustine's earlier turbulent life and his later pursuit of moral truth and peace. See **Classical Literature**.

Marry Me: A Romance (New York: Knopf, 1976). In one respect the novel *Marry*, begun three or four years after *RR*, resembles that novel, since a planned abortion* brings a relationship to a head. In *Marry* Ruth Conant* threatens her husband Jerry* with an abortion, as Ruth Leonard Byer* had threatened Harry "Rabbit" Angstrom.* Between *C*, about a couple enduring marital tension, and *OF*, in which the hero brings his second wife home for his mother's approval, Updike had written the short story "Couples" about infidelity. As Updike noted, many details of the story were used in *Marry*. Like the characters* of *Couples*, the characters of *Marry* are college educated, upper-middle-class suburbanites. The time and place of *Marry* (Greenwood, Connecticut, 1961) mirrors that of *Couples* (Tarbox, Massachusetts, 1963), and in both novels President John Kennedy's* administration provides the political background. Jerry Conant and Sally Mathias, like Piet Hanema* and Foxy Whitman,* conceive of themselves as having found their ideal mates. Their spouses, Ruth Conant* and Richard Mathias, resemble Angela Hanema* and Ken Whitman.* Ruth is an aloof artist who has failed to nurture Jerry's erotic life, and Richard is impersonal, realistic and atheistic. Belying his conviction that he had found his ideal mate, Jerry, a cartoonist for television* commercials, falls in love with Sally. Ruth at the same time has an affair with Richard, and Jerry insists that this will liberate Ruth to become the painter she wanted to be when they met in college. When Jerry asks Ruth for a divorce,* Ruth makes him promise not to see Sally until the summer's end, but Jerry breaks his promise. In the fall Sally tells her husband of the affair, and he forces Jerry to affirm his intentions; when Jerry seems willing to marry Sally, Richard prepares to divorce her. However, Jerry's love of his three children and of Ruth makes him reluctant to leave. The novel ends with three scenes showing Jerry in Wyoming with Sally, with

Ruth and his children in France, and alone on the island of St. Croix, having an imaginary conversation with Sally.

Often considered Updike's weakest novel because the characters are not as complex as in his other fiction, because the almost entirely scenic novel seldom showcases Updike's lyricism, and because its subtitle *A Romance* and its ending confuse readers, *Marry* is also one of Updike's more subtly experimental novels. Using four separate viewpoints in its four chapters, it interweaves the male and female viewpoints within those chapters. Also, Updike's three alternative endings ask the reader to decide about the fate of the characters and thus whether or not the book ends happily. Though Updike said in an interview* that the Conants really went to France and St. Croix, the ending suggests that Jerry and Sally may have found a life together. *Marry* represents another of Updike's efforts to define what he calls "the twilight of the old morality," uncoincidentally at the end of America's innocence, the "Camelot"* years of John Kennedy's presidency. Like *Couples*, *Marry* uses the ancient story of adulterous love, Tristan and Isolde,* adjusting imagery* and setting to provide a specifically artistic and ethereal setting for his tale of extramarital sex: Jerry sees Sally as a more beautiful rose window than Dante* ever saw, and the narrator refers to Jerry as Adam from a medieval sculpture tympanum and as Michelangelo's David. Jerry thinks in the lyric style of a courtier and, like Piet Hanema,* is obsessed with death,* a fear partly eased by reading existential writers such as Gabriel Marcel,* but mostly relieved by his love of Sally. Sally to Jerry is his ideal self, his spiritual self, but in the end he apparently returns to Ruth and his family.

Like *Couples*, *Marry* exhibits some of the elements of the pastoral* tradition in its idyllic opening chapters depicting escape from the city and in the possible escape to Wyoming at the end. Just as in *Couples*, the pastoral world proves illusory. Updike probably called his novel *A Romance* because he wanted to draw attention to the idyllic nature of the love affair and to suggest multiple views of it. So Updike uses painting, particularly modern art, more than in other novels to force us to think about how perspective and subjectivity govern meaning in love. Updike's view of romantic love is not reassuring if he had in mind Clara Reeve's remark in her 1785 *The Progress of Romance*: "Romance . . . describes what has never happened nor is likely to." Critic Larry Taylor similarly defines "pastoral" as an Eden or Arcadia returned to only briefly, never entirely.

Bibliography: Taylor, *PA*; Alfred Kazin, "Alfred Kazin on Fiction," *New Republic* 175 (27 Nov. 1976): 22–23; Greiner, *JU*; Margaret Hallissy, "Marriage, Morality and Maturity in Updike's *Marry Me*," *Renascence* 37 (1985): 96–106; Newman, *JU*; Barbara Leckie, " 'The Adulterous Society': John Updike's *Marry Me*," *Modern Fiction Studies* 37 (Spring 1991): 61–79.

"The Marshes of Glynn." "The Marshes of Glynn" is a loose ode by Sidney Lanier in which the marshes near Brunswick, Georgia, symbolize both the restorative power of nature* and its transcendental reflection of God. Near the poem's end, in a passage Henry Bech* quotes, Lanier remarks that no one can know what terrors may swim beneath the beautiful surface of the marshes ("Bech Panics" [*BB*]). The lines reflect upon Bech, who, despite his fierce psychological self-probing, does not understand his relation to women, the reason behind his writer's block, nor the connection between women and his block. The lines also suggest that the urban Bech has much to learn from nature, but that he resists such knowledge. *See* **Lanier Club.**

Bibliography: Jack De Bellis, *Sidney Lanier* (New York: Twayne, 1972); Jack De Bellis, *Sidney Lanier: Poet of the Marshes* (Atlanta: Georgia Humanities Council, 1988).

Marshfield, Reverend Thomas. The hero of *MS*, Rev. Thomas Marshfield is sent to a retreat in Arizona, where he must record his daily reflections on his sexual misconduct in order to become a useful minister* again. At first he mocks this penance by writing entries that are blasphemous and pornographic and self-consciously comment on his own writing style and typing errors. He amuses himself by re-creating erotic scenes, but admits that they may be fantasies. Gradually the spiritual disaffiliation and erotic need that led to his adulteries are brought under control through his recovery of the past and his meditations upon it in his journal. Yet Marshfield's apparent seduction of the motel manager Ms. Prynne* suggests that his erotic delinquencies are not yet mastered, leading to questions of Marshfield's sincerity concerning his recovery of faith. Some argue, however, that the seduction proves the power of the word, and thus the power of his reunification of spirit, since his diary entries mirror the spiritual changes he has undergone. The seduction may also indicate the link between spiritual wholeness and sexual health, a theme Updike uses in *Couples*. *See* **Religion.**

Bibliography: Detweiler, *JU*; Greiner, *JU*.

Marx, Karl (1818–1883). An enormously influential German political philosopher who is credited with founding communism, Karl Marx adopted revolutionary ideas similar to those of Friedrich Engels. Together they devised the principles of communism, founded an international working-class movement and coauthored *The Communist Manifesto*, the first full description of Communist theories. The *Manifesto*'s most famous proposition is that history is a political struggle between rulers and oppressed, making inevitable a successful revolution by the oppressed and leading to a classless, leaderless society. This book became the most important text for revolutionary movements throughout the world. In other books Marx argued for armed revolt to destroy capitalism. He wrote for the *New York Tribune* (1852–61), whose editor, Horace Greeley, fiercely opposed President Abraham Lincoln.* Marx is mentioned by Brad Schaeffer in "Made in Heaven" (*TM*) as saying that God is dead, a quote originated by Friedrich Nietzsche, suggesting by the misidentification the indifference of the leisure class to Marx. In "Leaf Season" (*TM*) Josh thinks of Marx's phrase "rural idiocy" to refer to chores like chopping wood, and from Marx's viewpoint such trivializing of his concept would be a typical bourgeois indifference in the face of exploitation.

Updike's novels frequently explore what he called the search for meaningful work, but most of his people suffer from meaningless labor, best exemplified by Harry "Rabbit" Angstrom's* demonstrating a marginally useful gadget, a food peeler. Such work makes him realize that "fraud makes the world go round," but instead of rebelling, Rabbit glides easily into life as a car salesman, with its occupational prevarication. For a while he finds work as a typesetter, but virtually withdraws into the machine itself (*RRed*), which is characterized as both mother and child to him. Updike covers a great many kinds of work and questions their value, from writing by Henry Bech* to acting by Essie Wilmot/Alma DeMott,* and from advertising by Joey Robinson* to journalism,* teaching and ministering.

Bibliography: Newman, *JU*; Wesley Kort, "Learning to Die: Work as Religious Discipline in Updike's Fiction," in Yerkes, *JU*.

Masochism. This psychological term *masochism* identifies the desire to experience pain, especially through humiliation during sex.* In popular parlance the term has been used to designate the endurance of a painful situation that one lacks the will to change. It is taken from the surname of Austrian novelist Leopold von Sacher-Masoch, whose characters got sexual satisfaction from being whipped. In *Marry* Richard Mathias, who had undergone psychoanalysis, accuses his mistress Ruth Conant* of being a masochist in maintaining her marriage to Jerry Conant.* *See* **Freud, Sigmund**.

McLuhan, (Herbert) Marshall (1911–1980). A Canadian professor of literature, Marshall McLuhan argued in his influential *Understanding Media: The Extensions of Man* (1964) that all vehicles of information, from the printing press to television,* are extensions of the human sensorium and are freighted with symbolic implications about how each culture is understood. His slogan "The medium is the message" became a watchword in the 1960s and increased the suspicion that technology was robbing people of freedom of choice because the particular media in a place and time determine how that culture views the world. Manipulation of those media would therefore operate as a control on that culture. McLuhan theorized that the world could be connected electronically as a "global village," as the World Wide Web has proven. Updike notes that the "media has swamped the message" of astronauts walking on the moon ("Seven New Ways of Looking at the Moon" [*TT*]). Yet the media garble the message when Harry "Rabbit" Angstrom* cannot understand what Neil Armstrong says as he steps on the moon (*RRed*). Rabbit does, however, understand the message of the media: television has manipulated his attention, and the lunar landing has failed to "lift him." As a linotyper, Rabbit is a "Gutenberg man" who thinks in quantitative terms, literally in black and white, up and down, left to right. This underlines a series of implied hierarchies by which he lives, the foremost being his leadership in his family and his significance as an individual, first on the basketball* court, now as a person with a special destiny. His wife Janice Angstrom,* however, shows an affinity for the electronic age by responding to the film* *2001: A Space Odyssey** (*RRed*). That film presents her with images that challenge linear time and conventional space, and it brings her, through the "Star-child," an enlarged image of the baby she had drowned and symbolic forgiveness. In addition, Janice seeks unconventional patterns of thinking to enrich her sex* life. In *RRed* she takes a lover who enables her to explore her sexual power for its own sake, not for its reproductive value or for its use in entrapping a lover into marriage. In *RIR* Janice rejects the sexual exclusivity of conventional marriage when she helps arrange an interlude of spousal sharing. In *RaR* Janice uses imaginative financing to save Springer Motors* from bankruptcy and her son from prison. Her notion of her work as a real-estate salesperson is nonlinear, since she sees property not as an extension of her personal importance but as something to be used; thus she can sell even her own home without emotional attachment.

Bibliography: Newman, *JU*; O'Connell, *UP*.

Melville, Herman (1819–1891). A nineteenth-century American fictionalist, Herman Melville is mentioned in stories involving Henry Bech,* as well as in "The Lovely Troubled Daughters of Our Old Crowd" (*TM*). To Bech (and Updike), Melville is a precursor of modernism and a writer unappreciated in his lifetime. Just as Bech was unable to write fiction for a time because of writer's block, so too Melville gave up writing fiction after 1857 (except for the late "Billy Budd"), not because of a writer's block, but because he had grown disenchanted with the ability of fiction to alleviate the despair of what he termed the "post-Christian age." Updike maintains that Melville's *Pierre* (1852), mentioned in "Bech in Rumania" (*BB*), was a complete failure because Melville's exploration of domestic problems was not his strength. Yet the novel broke new ground by treating incest,* a subject of concern to Updike in *RV* and *RaR*. In a talk given in 1981, "Melville's Withdrawal," Updike emphasized Melville's discovery of his inability to supersede the cosmic vision of *Moby-Dick* and concluded that he was correct to withdraw as a novelist. Unlike Melville, Updike has maintained a vast readership and an enthusiastic critical interest that have enabled him to follow his own intuition about what his novels might be. Fayaway, a character from Melville's *Typee*, is referred to in "Heading for Nandi," and a description of her is quoted extensively in Updike's notes to that poem (*TT*). *See* **American Literature; The Novel.**

Bibliography: Updike, "Melville's Withdrawal" (*HS*); "Introduction" to *The Complete Shorter Fiction of Herman Melville* (*MM*).

Memories of the Ford Administration (New York: Knopf, 1992). Updike's novel *MF* could be called "Buchanan Redux" since it reworks material concerning President James Buchanan* from his closet drama *BD*, a play that resulted from Updike's inability to convert his research into fiction. But the novel also shows Updike bringing to fruition several projects that had been unresolved in the past.

In *MF* Alfred Clayton,* professor of history at Wayward Junior College, is asked by the Northern New England Association of American Historians (NNEAAH) for his "Memories and Impressions of the Administration of Gerald R. Ford." Since at the time of the Ford administration Clayton was considering leaving his wife, Norma, for Genevieve Mueller, the wife of a history colleague, Brent Mueller, his "memories" concern his personal life and do not concern President Ford.* Also at that time, about 1975, Clayton was researching the life and career of Buchanan. Clayton, reflecting on each of these things, blends them in his mind. He uses the "memories" to review his theory about how Buchanan's ill-fated love for Ann Coleman* led to his political career and hence America's course toward Civil War. Since Clayton claims that the "Ford Era" was marked by sexual liberation, he graphically discloses his affair with the mother of a student. When Genevieve learns of this affair, she discards Clayton, forcing him to return to his family. His domestic and scholarly obsessions have made him ill equipped, he admits at the end of his letter to the NNEAAH, to remember anything about the Ford administration.

The novel expands a debate about Buchanan presented in *PF* while bringing to fruition a scheme Updike had set for his first four novels. In *PF* John Hook* named Buchanan "a very unfairly estimated man . . . last of the presidents who truly represented the entire country." Updike took up this proposition in *BD*, but only after relinquishing his scheme to follow *PF*, *RR* and *C* with a novel written in the historical past. Updike explained in 1965 that he had planned to cap a Pennsylvania tetralogy with a historical novel about Pennsylvania's only president. But the material proved intractable, since Updike intended to write a historical novel to complete the "present" *RR*, the "past" *C* and the "future" *PF*. However, Updike came to agree with Henry James* that the past cannot be truly evoked in fiction when he discovered that he could not write the standard historical fiction with its "upholstered prose." Although he undertook the Buchanan project after he had published *Couples*, Updike had to publish *RRed* before he used the Buchanan material in a play, *BD*. Perhaps he was prompted by parallels between the Civil War and the Vietnam* War, which was an intrinsic subject in *RRed*. In using his research, Updike decided on a "Beckettian* tone," converting the inherent problems of historical fiction to benefits by reenvisioning the research material in a drama, *BD*. In this way, Updike completed the project begun with *PF*, but not quite, since he had yet to write a Buchanan novel. In *MF* Updike saw a way to recycle the old material into a novel, using two frames: one in the present (1991), in which Clayton is contacted for information about Ford; the other in the remembered past, in which Clayton meditates on his lost love, which also brings him to think about Buchanan, the subject of his 1970s research. Clayton thus has another chance to make sense of Buchanan, just as Updike has.

MF has drawn together several threads from Updike's early novels and fiction. The love and marriage conflict of *MF* resembles the marital crisis of Richard Maple* and his wife Joan Maple* in *TF*, though the Clayton marriage survives. In *MF* Updike settled with Buchanan, completing his "Pennsylvania tetralogy," and revised the Maples' crisis. In addition, Updike continued his interest in an academic setting, shown in *C*, and in doing so made use of the critical theory called deconstruction. *MF* also reexamines the problem of writer's block explored in *BB* and *BIB*.

MF shows why Clayton was blocked by Buchanan. Throughout the narrative Alf Clayton explains important passages of his "memories and impressions" for the editor of *Triquarterly*, the proposed publisher of the Ford symposium, and though he offers the editors the right to "chasten" his prose, Clayton fears a loss of control over his work, apparently convinced that his 339-page "memories" would be printed. This is unlikely since the editors would surely blue-pencil the irrelevance of his memories to both Ford and Buchanan, the erotic character of those recollections and the pedantic footnotes of footnotes Clayton feels obliged to use in his search for truth. Clayton's professional interest in Buchanan may have been to pardon him for not ending slavery, but Clayton also reveals the necessary involvement of the writer's life with his research and thus the inevitable contamination of history by the historian who himself creates from an unstable text his own unreliable book.

Finally, by using an academic historian who himself is a historical figure since Clayton writes about himself as he was in the past during the Ford administration, Updike can playfully explore the complications that arise when a modern historian employs the literary approach called deconstruction, essentially a demythologizing of authors and an awareness of the instability of texts. With a playfulness similar to that of *W* and *S.*, Updike "deconstructs" his own work. He draws attention to deconstruction by using a history professor, Brent Mueller, who teaches the method and who shepherds Clayton in the approach. But despite his apparent interest, Clayton secretly hates the method because it exposes the author's tricks, and he parodies it when he writes: "My hysteria—my h(i)st(o)ria, the deconstructionist might say . . . if their anti-life con(tra)ceptions were not now becoming at last passé and universally de(r)rided." The last word plays on the name of deconstructionism's founder, Jacques Derrida.

Clayton's own instinct is to "poeticize" and "*construct*," and Updike acknowledged that in *MF* he used "the new boldness that Latin American magic realism* had introduced," with a fictional person shouldering "all the difficulties I had encountered in my travails of reconstruction." Clayton also combats Brent's "ghost" (and thus deconstructionism) through his wife Norma, Brent's mistress. Though Clayton ultimately reconstructs his marriage and Buchanan so far as he is able, in effect he deconstructs both since neither the president nor Clayton's marriage reveals a complete commitment. Though he insists that he wants to "reconstruct" Buchanan, he calls this "modern fiction," since "it thrives only in showing what is *not* there," acting on the principle that "life must now and then be allowed to take precedence over history—else there will be no new history." Similarly, President Ford, an "absent presence" in the novel—as a deconstructionist would say—"thrives" by not being part of the narrative but being constantly in the background of the reader's mind.

Clayton "reconstructs" Buchanan's abortive love affair, adding imagined scenes, and lines from George Gordon, Lord Byron's "Epistle to Augusta," passages from Thomas De Quincey that he himself thinks stray from fact, and he provides new elements superior to the actual record of President Andrew Jackson's conversation with Buchanan. Updike's book of "memories" thus deconstructs the Buchanan book he had begun in 1964 and ironically finishes it because it demonstrates how life takes precedence over history in order to create "new" history. Though deconstruction points to the difficulty of ever finding the facts from history or memory, Clayton works studiously with Buchanan's corrupt or ambiguous texts until his own work becomes a compilation at the end of the book of those texts and thus a "superambiguous text." For example, who wrote Ann Coleman's obituary? What were Buchanan's destroyed "relics"? Clayton searches unsuccessfully for answers to such questions, but ambiguous texts thwart him—yet theories about them proliferate in his own text, his letter to NNEAAH. Clayton himself is, metaphorically, a "corrupt text" since he feels that the most important thing about history is neither texts nor "relics" but guilt: "If you deconstruct history you take away its reality, its guilt." But, to deconstruct Clayton, how serious is he, personally, about wanting to preserve guilt? He describes his guilt when during the "Ford Era" he tried to free himself from "disempowering" Norma to find happiness with Genevieve. His guilt was partly aroused by his "infidelity" with his own wife (as Gen sees it) and his fling with his student's mother, Ann Arthrop. That affair was partly occasioned by his fantasy that he was making love to Ann Coleman, thus rescuing Ann and Buchanan from Buchanan's guilt over her death.* Ironically, the failure of his effort with Gen resembles the failure of Buchanan with Ann

Coleman (Updike remarked that *BD* and *MF* are linked not by "and" but by "Ann"). Buchanan's ambiguous political career mirrors the uncertain achievement of Clayton's academic efforts to finish the Buchanan study under the ruse of his letter concerning Ford. Thus Updike's novel about Ford reduces to a novel about Buchanan that deconstructs to a novel about marital problems. Clayton deconstructs himself in the process as well, since he includes intimate details of his life during his 1974 crisis while writing about Buchanan in response to questions about Ford. He also offers a connection between the past of public figures and the present of his private distress.

As in *C*, Updike once more contrasts contemporary life with the legendary and remembered past. But since Buchanan is historically regarded as a failure, not a hero like Chiron in *C*, the contrast deflates the importance of the comparison of the academic world to the historical personage. In addition, Updike's apparent satire* of academia* deconstructs to a consideration of how unstable Updike's own created text, *MF*, is. By drawing such attention to the immersion of Clayton in his history of Buchanan, Updike "deconstructs" his novel. For example, he inserts his own play *BD* into Alf Clayton's bibliography and includes authors he has reviewed, with perhaps a sly allusion to his own *MF*. Also, Updike has Clayton refer to page numbers in this novel, numbers Clayton should have no access to since this is Updike's book, not Clayton's. Such things deconstruct the opposition of character and author and remind us of the artifice of narrative and reality. If Clayton's Buchanan history "never quite jells," Updike's novel may, since "history, unlike fiction . . . never quite jells; it is an armature of rather randomly preserved verbal and physical remains upon which historians slap wads of supposition in hopes of the lumpy statue's coming to life." In the best deconstructionist tradition, Updike's final word on Buchanan demonstrates the futility of historical and textual reliability, while at the same time he satirizes, as in *RV*, the pedantry of college professors. *MF* is a multifaceted demonstration of Updike as a playful postmodernist, turning deconstruction on its head in order to show that, as he said in a review, deconstruction's "fatiguing premise" is that "art has no health in it, it is all cultural pathology" (*OJ*). Perhaps he shows a subtle attack on the critics who said that he had never done anything important, since neither had Buchanan, Clayton or Ford, but Updike's witty defense of Buchanan reveals him to be quite worthy of attention.

Bibliography: Updike, "Henry Bech Interviews Updike apropos of His Fifteenth Novel," "A Special Message for the Franklin Library Edition of *Memories of the Ford Administration*" (*MM*); Christopher Lehmann-Haupt, "A Heroic Then, a Realistic Now," *New York Times* 22 Oct. 1992: C-25; Lee Lescaze, "Musings on a Much-mocked President," *Wall Street Journal* 28 Oct. 1992: A-16; Alfred Kazin, "The Middle Way," *New York Review of Books* 17 Dec. 1992: 45–46; Ned Balfe, "John Updike: Originality and Sin," *Sunday Times Books* 28 Feb. 1993: 3.

Mencken, H(enry) L(ouis) (1880–1956). The American journalist and essayist H. L. Mencken, like the novelist Theodore Dreiser* and Sinclair Lewis,* whom he championed in his newspaper columns, attacked middle-class vulgarities and pretensions in his political and social essays in the *Baltimore Sun*, the *Smart Set* and the *American Mercury*. Mencken's lifelong impatience with pretension and hypocrisy in language and thought appears in *The American Language* (1919 to 1963, with supplements) and in his autobiographies *Happy Days* (1940), *Newspaper Days* (1941) and *Heathen Days* (1943). His wit would be congenial to Updike's own satiric view of some aspects of middle-class life, but Mencken's stinging attacks on President Franklin Roosevelt* and on marriage would not be, since Updike came from a family of FDR Democrats and has been empathetic to women and marriage. Nor is Updike comfortable with Mencken's savage attacks on fundamentalists aroused by the Scopes "Monkey Trial" (1925). (In an essay on caricatures, Updike notes how Mencken's lips always appeared ready to curl into a "dangerous" sneer.) Updike observes that despite his cultivation, Mencken was not a "more complex organism than those still in the grip of Christianity's rococo doctrines." In regard to Updike's works, Mencken may be behind the characterization of Brad Schaeffer in "Made in Heaven" (*TM*), who assumes that God is dead, as Mencken, a lifelong atheist, had asserted, particularly in his iconoclastic "Memorial Service" (*Prejudices: Third Series*). In regard to his own experience, Updike attributed to his father's generation "a Menckenesque contempt for politicians" (*BD*). Updike also reviewed works about Mencken and contributed to an anthology to which Mencken provided the introduction. *See* **American Literature; Religion**.

Bibliography: Updike, "Laughter from the Yokels," "Funny Faces" (*MM*).

Middleness. What Updike has called his major subject, his interest in "middleness," was perhaps generated from having lived in a small town, Shillington,* and his personal sense of "having been stuck in the middle," which "reveals people and societies in tension." In "The Dogwood Tree: A Boyhood"* he described his mission: "to transcribe middleness with all its grits, bumps, and anonymities, in its fullness of satisfaction and mystery." For him, this is "the still center of the world." That "center," however, is not only social but psychological, fraught with anxiety and conflict, so it is naturally appealing to a writer. Updike provides a philosophical view of middleness in the middle of his life in "Midpoint" (*M*), and he dramatizes this condition in *RR* when he depicts Harry "Rabbit" Angstrom* running from "second-ratedness" toward "the thing that wants me to find it." Updike shows in *C* that man himself is a kind of centaur, a creature in the middle, with his feet in the swamp and his head "afloat in the firmament." The theme appears repeatedly. In the "*Scarlet Letter* trilogy," for example, Rev. Tom Marshfield* is pulled between desire and spirit (*MS*), Roger Lambert* between complacent spiritual certainty and theological curiosity (*RV*) and Sarah Worth* between security and asceticism (*S.*). In *IB* Essie Wilmot/Alma DeMott,* as a film* actress, mediates between the commonplace and the transcendent. Updike's early experience of middleness may explain the lack of melodrama in his writing, since he shows constant attention to the complexity and ambiguity of being pulled in two different directions and imparts sympathy toward both. For these reasons, Updike shows special sensitivity in the depiction of middle age. *See* **Dualisms; Ministers**.

Bibliography: D. Keith Mano, "Doughy Middleness," *National Review* 26 (30 Aug. 1974): 987–88; Margaret Gullette, "John Updike: Rabbit Angstrom Grows Up," in *Safe at Last in the Middle Years* (Berkeley: University of California Press, 1988), 59–84; Alfred Kazin, "The Middle Way," *New York Review of Books* 17 Dec. 1992: 45–46.

Midpoint and Other Poems (New York: Knopf, 1969). *M*, Updike's third collection of poems, is divided into four sections: "Midpoint," "Poems," "Love Poems" and "Light Verse." The poems are more personal than those in the previous volumes, and the title poem contains confessional aspects resembling beat* poet Allen Ginsberg and confessional poet Robert Lowell.

"Midpoint" was conceived in 1959, as Updike said, as a "series of meditations." Those meditations range from the deeply serious to the witty. Updike's longest poem, it contains five cantos: "I. Introduction"; "II. The Photographs"; "III. The Dance of the Solids"; "IV. The Play of Memory"; and "V. Conclusion." Updike has said that the presentation of his personal philosophy in canto I revealed to him that writers should be interesting to their readers only through "empathy and image-arranging," not through conscious philosophizing. That the poem is Updike's *Divine Comedy* is made clear in his labeling the five divisions "cantos" and by the following: in canto I by his use of Dante's* terza rima ("Notes" [*CP*]); by his inclusion of photos of the Updike family in canto II; by the witty incorporation of information taken from a *Scientific American* essay on polymers in canto III; by frank descriptions of his sexual life (guided in part by quotes from Walt Whitman*) in canto IV; and by providing a homage to mentors like Walt Disney* and Søren Kierkegaard* in canto V. By enlarging the black and white dots comprising the photos in canto II, Updike forces the reader to recognize the reader's part in making sense of reality, while signaling the important eye/I pun that forms the basis of knowledge. This shows that Updike's *Divine Comedy* must frankly reveal how what he sees has been bound by what he is, and vice versa. "Midpoint" reveals a stage of personal awareness begun with "The Dogwood Tree: A Boyhood"* (*AP*) and brought to closure in *SC*. Updike's subject in "Midpoint," the unflinching recovery of the meaning of life at a specific point in time, is related to his stories, particularly "Pigeon Feathers" (*PigF*), and his novels *RA*, *C*, *MS*, *BD* and *MF*. Yet Updike sensed an "unease" in "Midpoint" detected in odd self-mockery, though the poem expressed that meaning had been found in gratitude for simply existing, just as ordinary people, ministers* and presidents* all seek the meaning of their lives.

Section two of *Midpoint*, called "Poems," concerns daily things like films,* fireworks and a pet's death. The best of these, "Dog's Death," is a moving celebration of the dog's fidelity even while dying. Updike has said that the primary reason to have pets* may be to bring death* into the house (*CP*, notes), and the poem thus parallels the deaths of the hamster in *Couples*, but seen through adult sensibility. Among the poems in this section are those about Roman art in which Updike praises writers of the past, while acknowledging the mutability of art.*

Section three, "Love Poems," provides a minimalist wit in "Love Sonnet," which is composed only of letters of the alphabet that "spell out" erotic meaning reminiscent of E. E. Cummings.* "Fellatio" provides a shock for philosophical rather than prurient reasons. Section four, "Light Verse," offers tours de force in French-English rhymes, touching descriptions of toes and the Amish and a clever parody of Marianne Moore. *See* **Light Verse; Poetry**.

Bibliography: Updike, "Notes to Midpoint (*CP*); L. E. Sissman, "John Updike: Midpoint and After," *Atlantic* 226 (Aug. 1970): 102–4; Alice Hamilton and Kenneth Hamilton, "Theme and Technique in John Updike's *Midpoint*," *Mosaic* 4.1 (Fall 1970): 79–106; Elisabeth R. Wayland, "John Updike's Philosophy as Revealed in His Poem 'MidPoint,' " M.A. thesis, Campbell, *UN*; Shippensburg State College, 1978.

Millay, Edna St. Vincent (1892–1950). An American lyric poet and Provincetown Players playwright, Edna St. Vincent Millay expressed concern for feminist themes in conventional sonnets (*Collected Sonnets*, 1941). She wrote about love from a feminist viewpoint of "free love" of the 1920s, so it is ironically appropriate that Richard Mathias should quote the sonnet "Euclid Alone Hath Looked on Beauty Bare" in order to mock the romantic love espoused by Jerry Conant,* his wife's lover (*Marry*). *See* **American Literature**.

Miller, Esmerelda. An African-American* Communist at McCarthy College, Wisconsin, Esmerelda Miller cannot persuade Col. Félix Ellelloû* to accept communism; instead, he sees Charles de Gaulle's liberation of Algeria as the start of revolution across Africa. Esmerelda suggests that he stop dating white girls, but he marries one instead (*Coup*). Her name may derive from Esmerelda, the feisty Gypsy of Victor Hugo's *Hunchback of Notre Dame*.

Miller, Henry (1891–1980). An American novelist who dedicated himself to freeing American writing from Puritan restrictions, Henry Miller knew that he would face social and legal reactions. *Tropic of Cancer* (1934) and *Tropic of Capricorn* (1939) were so sexually forthright that they were prohibited from publication or importation into the United States on grounds of obscenity until 1964. Updike acknowledged Miller, James Joyce,* Edmund Wilson* and D. H. Lawrence as his precursors in the fight for greater artistic frankness for writers. He wrote approvingly of Miller's "slurping, comically physical concreteness." Updike's earliest adherence to this principle was *RR*, but Alfred Knopf, fearing obscenity charges, required him to expurgate certain passages. Updike then published his original version in England, and that edition was only published in the United States after the Supreme Court overturned obscenity charges against Miller. Miller's comical and philosophical approaches to sex are echoed by Updike in *Couples*, *RIR* and *S*. Freddy Thorne* keeps copies of Miller's books in his bedroom, apparently to fan his waning libido (*Couples*), but not even these can make him potent when sleeping with his wife or Angela Hanema.* Thanks to Miller, Updike moved coitus from the bedroom to the parlor, as he said he was determined to do in the *Paris Review* interview (Plath, *CU*). See **Sex**.

Bibliography: Josephine Hendin, *Vulnerable People: A View of American Fiction since 1945* (New York: Oxford University Press, 1978), 88–99.

Ministers. In 1997 Updike received the Campion Award for being "a distinguished Christian person of letters," yet Updike refused the label "Christian writer" in order to be "absolved from any duty to provide orthodox morals and consolations in my fiction." In short, he declared himself a writer, not a minister, and in a 1996 essay* he observed that modern Christian novelists like Graham Greene, Muriel Spark, Evelyn Waugh, Flannery O'Connor, François Mauriac, and Georges Bernanos also offer small comfort to modern Christians (*MM*). Like them, Updike describes a fallen world seldom aided by the Bible* or clergy. In *C* Peter Caldwell* agrees that a concerned writer who is also Christian can offer little spiritual help, but he also asserts that neither can ministers whose devolution began long ago. To Peter, a "classic degeneration" has devolved from priest (Peter's grandfather Kramer) to teacher (George Caldwell*) to artist (Peter).

Despite his high regard for the enormous difficulty ministers face for speaking what Harry "Rabbit" Angstrom* calls "the words the dead know," Updike's portraits of ministers generally emphasize their inadequacy. Yet in 1966 Updike expressed his admiration for ministers who "invest their entire lives in doing something that seems to be quite invisible," though they seem increasingly concerned with social and moral matters. Thus in "Pigeon Feathers" (*PigF*) Reverend Dobson's failure to help David Kern* understand the afterlife precipitates an identity crisis. In *C* Reverend March has no interest in helping George Caldwell with his questions about death* and eternity; instead, he blandly insists that Calvinism is as "Christocentric" as Lutheranism.

Repeatedly Updike reveals how the minister is ill equipped for life's realities and supplies platitudes or spiritual double-talk in place of sincere help. This view governs his vision of ministers from first to last and is aptly illustrated in *IB* (1996), where he places the successful career of an actress who provides audiences with something that transcends them between the stories of a minister who loses his faith and a zealot whose faith leads him to slaughter his flock. Between *C* and *IB* Updike describes the deterioration of ministers. In *Couples* the skeletal Rev. Horace Pedrick laces his sermons with money imagery.* Updike's "*Scarlet Letter* trilogy" (*MS, RV, S.*) describes in detail the stress placed on modern ministers, from sexual temptation to professional jealousy. In *MS*, for sexual and spiritual delinquency, Rev. Tom Marshfield* is penalized by being forced to leave his ministry and rusticate in an Arizona motel where he must write daily journal entries. These punishments return him to God, though without forsaking the flesh. The second novel of the trilogy, *RV*, examines Roger Lambert,* an ex-minister who has left his vocation to teach in a divinity school. His specialty in the early church fathers, like his cynicism and guile, suggests only a nominal interest in moral problems. For Lambert, Dale Kohler's* effort to prove God's existence by using the computer is a theoretical problem, only made interesting for him by his patrician desire to destroy the student. His esoteric arguments test Kohler's determination and knowledge, but he is aesthetically offended by a God who would make Himself known. Though Lambert aligns himself with Karl Barth* in this notion of a hidden God, in some respects his attitude is personal: Lambert's God reflects his own wish to be mysterious, unknowable. The last novel of the trilogy, *S.*, satirizes the fatuous efforts of liberated Sarah Worth* to explore her spirituality in an Arizona ashram; her unmasking of the cult leader, the Arhat* (Arthur Steinmetz), a Jewish student of Indian religions, reveals the state of the modern soul, since people are desperate for any minister to direct their spiritual craving. Despite the obvious good that the Arhat performed for Sarah, she exposes him because he is not the minister she wanted. The modern minister may assume many guises, but the laity is unwilling to adjust to a new kind of "minister."

RA, which spans nearly Updike's entire career, charts the gradual disappearance of the minister from the tetralogy, and thus from American life. In *RR* the quarrel between Rev. Fritz Kruppenbach* and Rev. Jack Eccles* demonstrates how Eccles forgot to practice the imitation of Christ, which Kruppenbach insists is the only job of a minister, because he found it more comfortable to immerse himself in the social problems of adolescents or young marrieds like the Angstroms. Updike never again depicts a minster of such conviction as Kruppenbach, who was modeled on the major influence of his early work, Karl Barth,* as well as the minister who confirmed him in Grace Lutheran Church in Shillington.* *RRed* drops Eccles from the narrative (an added scene in *RA* shows that he has quit the clergy and has been divorced) to focus on how Skeeter* intends to fill the vacuum left by the socialized ministers. He proposes not only to imitate Christ but to become the Black Messiah returned with a sword, fired in the kiln of Vietnam.* *RIR* introduces a gay minister, "Soupy" Campbell, a virtual caricature of the "soft" minister, who is ridiculed by the Angstroms and never perceives how he is seen. Behind his back the Angstroms laugh at the obscene jokes Nelson Angstrom* makes about the man who is about to marry him. In *RaR* ministers appear only as disembodied evangelists, voices on the radio, two-dimensional images on television.* While asking prayers for wayward husbands, they offer no direction to the wayward Rabbit. Clearly embittered at the failure of the ministry, Rabbit cynically witnesses Nelson's gravitation toward a quasi-religious counseling vocation. Updike has admitted that his own disappointment with the ministry has made ministers seem increasingly like failures and clowns.

A major problem for ministers, as for many Updike heroes, is man's situation midway between flesh and spirit. The "*Scarlet Letter* trilogy" records similar conflicts of flesh and spirit: Reverend Marshfield's four sermons* move him from a jocose defense of adultery* to a resurrection of the body and spirit (*MS*); ex-Reverend Lambert's religious contemplation is interrupted by shocking fantasies of his wife's adultery (*RV*); and the Arhat deludes young women seeking spiritual truth to gain their sexual favors (*S.*). Jesse Smith* does the same as a cult leader in *IB*; only he of all men in the commune has the right to intercourse, and with any woman of his choosing. In *W* Unitarian minister Ed Parsley* leaves his wife for a teenager in order to protest the Vietnam War and is "succeeded" by his wife Brenda Parsley,* who stands in for him (as Clarence Wilmot's* wife Stella Wilmot does in *IB*) and delivers a sermon that attacks the witches. Though the witches stifle her by filling her mouth with insects, Brenda cries "Pray" as she is led away, gagging. Jenny Van Horne perceives a link between local witchcraft and the demonism in the atom bomb and Vietnam. Women have begun to take up the vacuum left by the failure of male ministers.

Yet positive ministers can be found in Updike's early work, like the young unnamed minister in *OF* whose moving sermon on the creation of woman repairs the shredded feelings of Joey Robinson* and his mother, Mrs. Robinson.* Also, although Rabbit does not enjoy it, Reverend Eccles's "Christ's Forty Days in the Wilderness" sermon supplies a vivid *going through* style of muscular Christianity for him to consider. Despite his penchant for adultery, Marshfield does create a worthy sermon in the eyes of Ms. Prynne.* Perhaps Updike's depictions of ministers reveal his own hit-or-miss experiences with them. If so, he may share the plight of Brad Schaeffer, who takes his intended to Copley Methodist Church for services and discovers that the sermons are "pathetic." Yet when he is later active in the Episcopal church, he finds more congenial the new rector's "honey-smooth," "melodious" sermons ("Made in Heaven" [*TM*]). Updike has said that he admires ministers for trying to maintain the "impossible" and admits that his holding them to higher standards may have stemmed from being haunted by his grandfather's failure as a clergyman (dramatized in the collapse of Rev. Clarence Wilmot in *IB*, who reversed Søren Kierkegaard's* famous leap into faith by making a leap into nonfaith).

Updike has said that the laity may offer hope of salvation no longer possible for the clergy. But when secular persons assume the office of minister, the results can be perilous. Eccles in *RR* had warned Rabbit that men on spiritual quests were not pursuing God but chasing skirts, and Rabbit's insistence on this "religious" pursuit (he is called "Christ" and imagines himself the Dalai Lama*) creates tragedy. What is condemned by Eccles is elevated by Freddy Thorne,* a kind of blasphemous mock minister, into "the new religion." Thorne, however, is a poor convert, since he is impotent and is deeply wounded by finding that his wife has slept with Piet Hanema* (*Couples*). The hero of "Lifeguard" (*PigF*) as a "savior" of the drowning may be Christ or Antichrist, but Skeeter actually proclaims himself the "Black Messiah," promising to destroy all whites to establish heaven on earth (*RRed*). Skeeter tries to convert Rabbit to make him a disciple and hopes to appropriate Jill Pendleton's* drug-induced vision of God, but he precipitates the destruction of Rabbit's home and the death of Jill. New Yorker Darryl Van Horne,* seducer of three Eastwick* "witches" and embittered by the death of his wife, sermonizes on "terrible creation" to a congregation unaffected even by the Antichrist in their midst. Finally, the zeal of Jesse Smith destroys his congregation (*IB*). Secular ministers do not heal the soul as often as they contaminate it, it seems, but Updike agrees with Wallace Stevens* that perhaps writers are trying to offer ministerial leadership, so he also holds himself to very high standards, though he is wary of using artists as such leaders. Updike himself has assisted in writing the sermons of a Beverly Farms, Massachusetts, minister, although he insists that his role is minimal. Yet his female alter ego,* Essie Wilmot/Alma DeMott,* may suggest the symbolic role the laity may play, offering transcendence through art* that approximates what ministers had offered. In this way, the laity might help reverse the "classic degeneration" of the priest-teacher-artist (*C*).

Bibliography: Hamilton and Hamilton, *EJ*; James P. Wind, "Clergy Lives: Portraits from Modern Fiction," *Christian Century* 108 (4 Sept. 1991): 805–10.

Monroe, Marilyn (1926–1962). Marilyn Monroe was a famous film* star noted for her sensuality. Her death at thirty-six has been attributed to her frustrations as a serious actress. Her frequent casting in the role of the "dumb blond" (*Gentlemen Prefer Blonds*, e.g.), despite her effort at serious drama in films like *The Misfits*, impeded Monroe's progress as a thoughtful actress. Her death does not inhibit sexist Freddy Thorne's* corruption of her name to "Moronrow" (*Couples*). Thorne's need to keep women in stereotypical roles may account for his anger at his wife's adultery* with Piet Hanema* and his impotence with Angela Hanema.* He refuses to see his wife Georgene Thorne as unfaithful or the celestial Angela as sexually approachable. Monroe represented another case of the artist caught in social definitions that weaken and destroy her or him. Driven as a female to capitalize on her attractiveness, she herself was a commodity to be exploited, like any other artist, as Henry Bech* shows very well in his effort to provide the blockbuster demanded of him. Essie Wilmot/Alma DeMott,* Updike's composite film actress, contains aspects of Monroe, but Alma is stronger, more aware and luckier (*IB*). *See* **Sex**.

Bibliography: Updike, "M. M. in Brief" (*MM*).

A Month of Sundays (New York: Knopf, 1975). After Updike's research about President James Buchanan* failed to produce a novel on the president, he wrote *MS* in two months in order to fulfill his contractual requirement with Knopf. Steeped in theology at the time, Updike intended the novel to be what he called a critique of Karl Barth's* theology, with the hero, Rev. Thomas Marshfield,* being a Barthian whose great effort to stand as a model for others caused him to lose his faith in salvation by good works. Updike also expressed indebtedness to Martin Buber's "I/Thou" formulation, with Marshfield/Ms. Prynne,* the writer/reader and the novel/reader forming links. Since this was Updike's first important work since his separation from his wife Mary Pennington Updike* in September 1974, the novel may suggest Updike's personal effort to reclaim himself while in "exile."

Because of sexual "distractions," Marshfield has been ordered to go to a motel in Arizona and to keep a one-month journal in which he is to explore his soul in order to rediscover his faith. The motel is shaped like the Greek letter omega, symbolic of Christ as "Alpha and Omega," but the omega also suggests the female sexual organ. However, omega is symbolic of fire and apocalypse, as the letter alpha symbolizes the compass and thus God's creation. At first Marshfield mocks the journal idea, evoking "puppets" from his erotic memory in order to fictionalize scenes of his adulteries* with the organist Alicia and his wife's adultery with his assistant Bork. The journal entries are complicated by Marshfield's conscious and unconscious puns (*semon*, a blend of "sermon" and "semen") and parodies; for instance, in a Sunday sermon* in which he insists that adultery is biblically recommended. Marshfield's writing errors and wordplays are celebrated by him in comical footnotes because they represent his instinctual self that will not be suppressed by the penance of a formal journal. Additionally, the distance between his sense of self and the words that record that self supplies an additional "I/Thou" dualism* that parallels the ultimate opposition of self/God. Through his puns and parodies Marshfield attempts to keep the journal purely personal, but his delight in them and his explanations show that he clearly has a reader in mind from the start. In short, he assumes that his personal writing is a public document. As a minister,* he understands that God can be reached only through language.

The four sermons written on his four Sundays of incarceration chart the course of his self-renewal. The first sermon, on adultery, is "blasphemous," since it argues that marriage is a sacrament only because it makes adultery possible; that is, it creates a state in which love can continue, since with marriage it withers. The second sermon is defiant, the third begins to become more orthodox, and the last is "a sermon that could be preached," in the opinion of house manager Ms. Prynne. Updike remarked that this "parody" of the writer-reader relationship demonstrates the way in which Marshfield intends to seduce Ms. Prynne, just as all writers systematically seduce their readers with words. Ms. Prynne represents both the unseen reader and the unseen God, and the journal entry describing the copulation between them on Marshfield's last night suggests the union of writer and reader and of the erotic and the spiritual. This ending dissatisfies most readers, who expect the conventional "conversion" of Marshfield to entirely spiritual matters, having learned to abjure the flesh. But Updike intends to shock the reader into recognizing that a man may find his spiritual way without forgetting that his body is made for love as well.

Another aspect of the novel's "doubleness" is its resemblance to Nathaniel Hawthorne's* *Scarlet Letter*, a deliberate "parody or a variation in the musical sense of the term" (Plath, *CU*), as Updike described it, intended to review the themes of adultery and religion* in modern times. Like Hawthorne's Rev. Arthur Dimmesdale, Reverend Marshfield must reconcile the demands of the flesh with the needs of the spirit. If Dimmesdale is plunged into guilt and spiritual despair by his sexual infractions with Hester Prynne, Marshfield's despair is not quite linked to his sexual wandering. Nor is Ms. Prynne a figure capable of lifting him into action; rather, she is an invisible presence toward whom he bends both his seductive powers of writing and his sexual desire. Updike has noted that Marshfield's salvation comes essentially through his ability to restore his interest in others, a further contrast to Dimmesdale. *See* **Sex**.

Bibliography: Updike, "Lust," "Religion and Literature" (*MM*); George Hunt, "Updike's Omega-shaped Shelter: Structure and Psyche in *A Month of Sundays*," *Critique* 19.3 (1978): 47–60; Robert Detweiler, "Updike's *A Month of Sundays* and the Language of the Unconscious," *Journal of the American Academy of Religion* 47 (Dec. 1979): 611–25; Gary Waller, "Stylus Dei or the Open-Endedness of Debate? Success and Failure in *A Month of Sundays*," in Macnaughton, *CE*, 269–80; Donald Greiner, "Body and Soul: John Updike and *The Scarlet Letter*," *Journal of Modern Literature* 15 (Spring 1989): 475–95; Schiff, *UV*.

More Matter (New York: Knopf, 1999). *MM*, Updike's fifth book of literary criticism, provides an allusion to Shakespeare's *Hamlet* in the title: Polonius is asked by Queen Gertrude to provide "more matter, with less art." Updike's allusion is typically modest and amusing, since he provides a great deal of material that is more than mere matter, and he does so with his customary artistic delight and imagination. The idea of Updike being chided as though he were merely an attendant lord wittily understates the quality of his observations on his art, himself and world literature.

The "Preface" explains that in response to a more fact-inclined age, Updike has dutifully turned out much factual prose. For the first time he offers a glimpse of his journeyman work at the *New Yorker,** and he admits that he set out to be a wordsmith, but he also reveals the "quiet joys of the scholar" when he writes on such a figure as Herman Melville.* The book is divided into four parts: "Large Matters" (including matters of state, gender and religion*); "Matter under Review" (containing ten Updike introductions, comments on "past masters" and reviews of fiction, biography and popular culture*); "Visible Matter" (containing comments on film,* photography and art*); and the largest segment, "Personal Matters" (composed of forewords and "special messages" about various special editions of his work, acceptance speeches and comments on everything from his bibliography to his cartooning*). The sheer bulk of such an intimidating compilation of essays and reviews defies all but the most cursory description. As in *PP*, *HS* and *OJ*, the immense range of Updike's interest and the stylistic brilliance of his writing are evident everywhere.

In the first part, "Large Matters," the reader is immediately arrested by the depth of Updike's political engagement as he examines in detail the meaning of freedom and equality in America. In answer to a question posed by *Forbes* about why Americans feel so bad when they have it so good, Updike details his own disillusionment since the 1950s, and he appends to this essay remarks of 1998 on "the atmosphere of scandal . . . to the point of national demoralization" from a "relentless rain of tawdriness" during the (unnamed) Clinton-Lewinsky imbroglio. Rarely has Updike been so clearly disturbed about the downward spin of America. In a piece for *Newsweek* "The Fifties," he lovingly delineates for "Baby Boomers" the decade that had a clear idea of American values, thanks to the Cold War. Topical pieces provide amusing personal comments on dancing and suntanning, which Updike applauds as exercises in *carpe diem*. Among lighter "Large Matters," Updike writes an alternate ending to *Romeo and Juliet* in iambic pentameter. Since sex* and religion* are twin passions of Updike, he includes essays about lust and a learned introduction to the Song of Solomon emphasizing how it humanizes and "completes" the Bible* The essay "Religion and Literature" offers a view of ancient and classical epics and tragedies, tracing the vacillations in religious belief. "Large Matters" also includes two witty dialogues in the manner of Søren Kierkegaard's* *Either/Or*. "Fiction" opposes an alien and a defender of fiction, and "Print" pits Bill Gates against Johann Gutenberg in arguing the merits of computers versus print. Updike offers an extensive tour de force of literary pastiche to describe the joys and stresses of New York* in "The Glittering City," and he includes, among the many humorous essays written for the *New Yorker*, "Paranoid Packaging," the most popular article Updike ever wrote. Some humorous pieces, such as "Hostile Haircuts," which charts changing hair styles, suggest the realistic novelist at work. Updike's pieces show a personal enjoyment of the peculiarities of New York, the "terrors" of Christmas and a zany fantasy that explains how to emulate James Joyce* and T. S. Eliot* as easily as lip-synching Madonna.

In the second part of *MM*, "Matter under Review," Updike offers seventy reviews, all but nine of which were published in the *New Yorker*; they present an array of ideas about a great many writers. His ten introductions supply workmanlike biographical and historical information, and he offers sharply perceived preparatory comments to a book about writers who were interviewed by the *Paris Review*, writers photographed by Jill Krementz and writers writing about writers. His introduction to *Heroes and Anti-Heroes* examines the photographs of everyone from Chairman Mao to Dr. Spock with the steady eye he elsewhere directs at painters, Mickey Mouse or "Li'l Abner." In the subsection "American Past Masters," Updike offers an especially expansive description of Edith Wharton's works and films made from them. Then he startles the reader by proclaiming H. L. Mencken* a yokel. In other pieces Updike recalls his Harvard* reading of Wallace Stevens,* identifies Edmund Wilson's* combat with eros and thanatos at his life's end, endeavors to restore the reputation of 1920s writer Dawn Powell and praises the collected short fiction of a mentor, Vladimir Nabokov.* Updike finds distasteful the mixture of "a spectacular splash of bile and melancholy, of clean style and magical impressionability" in the journals of his friend John Cheever.* Of a novel of another friend, Philip Roth's* *Operation Shylock*, Updike notes that his oeuvre "presents an ever more intricately ramifying and transparent pseudo-autobiography." With characteristic vividness Updike says that Roth's characters "seem to be on speed, up at all hours and talking until their mouths bleed." Ever alert for talented younger writers, Updike remarks that Thomas Mallon is "one of the most interesting American novelists at work."

In this section Updike also shows why he is the most prominent writer in English concerned with the writing of countries often bypassed by other reviewers. He finds that Orhan Pamuk of Turkey "suggests Proust,"* observes that African writers like Sony Labou Tansi readily embrace surrealism and detects that the Caribbean "awakens Homeric analogies in its bards." Tracing the influence of American literature on the Indian novelist Arundhati Roy, Updike discovers in her novel *The God of Small Things* "one more example of William Faulkner's* powerful influence upon Third World writers; his method of torturing a story—mangling it, coming at it roundabout after portentous detours and delays." One of the most interesting reviews of American writers, Updike's appreciation of Norman Mailer's* near "miracle" in writing in the voice of Jesus in *The Gospel According to the Son*, shows Updike's ability to take an apparent disrespect for Jesus and find artistic exactitude.

As always in gathering his reviews, Updike provides remarks that update his knowledge about writers like Marguerite Yourcenar or Alain de Botton. In addition, Updike's review of over a thousand pages of V. S. Pritchett's essays is a primer for reviewers: Updike compares the book to previous collections of Pritchett's work, selects pertinent quotations, advances deft judgments concerning style and tone and offers arresting remarks that illustrate Updike's catholicity of reading, such as his pronouncement that Tobias Smollett, Ouida and Thomas Hood "may have received from him the last intelligent consideration that they will ever get." Updike applauds Pritchett's book as "encyclopedic wealth," demonstrating that "love of literature and love of life are indistinguishable," undoubtedly a hallmark of Updike's commitment to writing.

On the other hand, Updike is disarmingly honest when he admits, with pain, of Martin Amis's *Night Train*, "I wanted very much to like this book, and the fact that I wound up hating it amounts to a painful personal failure." Updike turns a clever phrase often, but never at the expense of the reviewed writer, as when he remarks of a novel by Vargas Llosa, "*Death in the Andes* is rich fare, hastily and confusingly served. Half as many dishes, more slowly cooked, would have made a better novel." Sensitive to the language of non-Western writers, Updike compiles an extensive list of "recondite terms," such as "bromliad," in *Mating*, by Norman Rush, and he discovers a full page of *z*'s in Tibor Fischer's *Thought Gang*.

In one of his longest nonliterary reviews, "Elusive Evil," Updike investigates the genetic side of evil while remarking on earlier rationalizations for evil as simply compatibility with the reality of nature,* noting that Auschwitz refuses to satisfy our "curiosity" about evil. Pursuing the problem of evil, Updike sees David Koresh, the model for Jesse Smith* in *IB*, as "less comprehensible" than those who follow him, and he indicates in a footnote a source suggesting that followers in fact "create the leader" as "an excuse for extreme behavior." Updike further observes that the "cultural emphasis on individual freedom makes choosing evil a lively option." Updike is persuaded by *The Origin of Satan*, by Elaine Pagels, that St. Mark may carry the "ultimate blame" for much of modern evil, since he set the story of Jesus in the context of cosmic war "between good and evil in the universe" and thus helped create Christian anti-Semitism. Updike concludes this key review-essay by noting that although the word "evil" is dead as a noun, "it remains an adjective."

Updike's reviews of biographies show a fear of what he calls, in a review of Robert Benchley, "the remorseless all-baring" that threatens to deflect interest from a writer's work to unsavory aspects of the writer's life. Updike detects this error in biographies of Nathaniel Hawthorne,* Theodore Dreiser,* F. Scott Fitzgerald, Dorothy Parker, Graham Greene and others. From this section of reviews, the reader might construe Updike's understanding of fiction. Thus in one place he remarks, "The fiction writer's life is his basic instrument of perception—that only the imagery we have personally gathered and unconsciously internalized possesses the color, warmth, intimate contour, and weight of authenticity the discriminating fiction reader demands." This sentence explains in part why Updike is suspicious of biography's tendency to rob the author of his uniqueness by making unappealing aspects of his life visible at the expense of the "basic instrument of perception."

In part three, "Visible Matter," Updike supplies essays about film, art and photography, and the number of them will surprise the average reader who knows Updike mainly through *New Yorker* literary reviews; these twenty-two reviews were printed in eleven different magazines and reveal Updike the artist and researcher. These immersions in graphic media are directly related to Updike's constant emphasis on observed actuality in his work. Thus what he enjoys about actresses like Lana Turner and Marilyn Monroe* are the subtle gestures and the minute adjustments that create responses in the viewer. Photography, whether by his mother, Linda Updike,* or by Jill Krementz, proves that the person photographed is "inarguably there," whether the person holds a "Big Little Book" or, like Saul Bellow,* is seated at his desk. The writer and the photographer are similar: both see the visual world as an opportunity for "wonder and study." Those interested in Updike's emphasis upon entropy in his work will recognize the importance of his view of photography (and, by extension, writing) as a "nullification of time's blurring, eroding progress."

Another key idea of Updike the writer is that of ambiguity, and he reveals its appearance in pop artist* Roy Lichtenstein when he observes in the painter's work "the multidetermination of the artistic impulse; it can satirize and memorialize at the same time, reconcile scorn with affection." Of Claes Oldenburg's use of irony in constructing a monumental clothespin, Updike notes, perhaps thinking of his own writing, "Irony is a way of having one's cake while appearing to eat it." Updike the researcher is evident in his probing the relation of Daniel Webster and the artist Sarah Goodrich, whose revealing likeness Webster carried in a miniature.

The fourth part of *MM* contains more evidence about Updike's work than he has ever confided in print. Instead of the omnibus interviews* of *PP*, *HS* and *OJ*, Updike reprints notes on several stories, many remarks on his cartooning, reminiscences about his childhood, the foreword to a major bibliography of his work, and a great many acceptances for prestigious awards.* Updike even describes his involvement with the project "Murder Makes the Magazine"* and includes unsigned "Talk of the Town" *New Yorker* pieces.

He offers his opinions on celebrity women, homes in New England, radio and his reading, and he presents his own list of the ten best books of the last thousand years. The overwhelmed reader finds that Updike has not only "tidied his desk," as he has remarked, but has offered the fullest description of his life as an author thus far. The acceptance speeches are a gracious acknowledgment of his importance to modern letters. *MM* is a stunning summing up of Updike's literary life since *OJ*.

The essays and interviews in the fourth part provide arresting evidence of Updike's lively wit and thoughtful understanding of his discipline, which selected quotation can only suggest. For example, in "Updike and I" he questions the dual nature of his existence as writer with celebrity status and ordinary person with ordinary human needs. The "I" finds that "Updike" is now "the monster of whom my boyhood dreamed." He recounts requests to sign his books purchased at a church sale where he does "duty" and concludes that "the fetish of the signature is surely one of the more pathetic features of contemporary religion," something bound to disturb the serious Updike collector. Writing about his short fiction,* Updike says unexpectedly that, more perfectly than his poems or novels, they hold "my life's incidents, predicaments, crises, joys." He admits that the *New Yorker* returned his Maples stories because his depiction of their marriage had become "too bilaterally and carefreely betrayed." He describes his excitement in a book factory and "the angelic beauty of human engineering." With a telling image Updike characterizes his *New Yorker* editor William Shawn: "His adamancy of taste had been hardened in a buried moral fire." He generously attributes to a bibliographer of his work an "eagle eye." Writing a self-portrait, Updike paints a multidimensional picture. He describes his "lower lip sagging" in his concentration. The recollection for him is so strong that he now dislikes doing drawings because memories of his former enjoyment clash with his sense that now his drawing is "inferiorly done." Also, he vividly recovers a childhood transgression when he made a rut with his bicycle wheels on the spring mud of a baseball diamond. He notes how at Harvard* he adopted the "proper polite, ironical manner." Writing of his own role, he astutely detects a danger in writing criticism since his "inner ear" might become corrupted by "the too-comfortable cadences and jargon of the critical voice."

Writing of the Rabbit saga for a special edition, he quickly sketches his personal feeling as he worked, his biographical circumstances and his effort to be faithful to the setting of Berks County, "a land fertile for even the absentee farmer," where he could fashion a book about "an American citizen." Describing the writing of *MF* for his character Henry Bech,* Updike admits that he realized that "everything I did was . . . a sequel to something I had done earlier," which he calls a "sound conservation policy." Remarkably, he recounts an adolescent dream that was, in effect, the Tristan and Isolde* story that would be transformed into *B*. He admits that in *IB* a major pleasure for him was to be "in imagination, a young woman," Essie Wilmot/

Alma DeMott.* Updike describes his creation of Ben Turnbull* in *TE* as an endeavor to create character according to the expectations of Karl Barth,* who said, "Show me man as he always is in the man of today." As if to underline the centrality of reading for a committed writer, Updike ends this book with a series of pieces explaining what books were his most powerful reading experiences. In accepting the Campion Award as a "distinguished Christian person of letters," he states that Christianity has made him aware that "truth-telling" is a "noble and useful profession." *MM* shows that whatever Updike writes about, he strives to be a professional truth-teller. *See* **Criticism by Updike**.

Bibliography: Michiko Kakutani, "Making a Thing Real by Pinning it Down in Words." *New York Times* 21 Sept. 1999: Late Edition-Final, Section E; Column 3; 8; William H. Pritchard, "His Own School of Criticism." *New York Times Book Review* 26 Sept. 1999, Sunday, Late Edition-Final, Section 7:7. George Scialabba, "The Fertile Continental Shelf of John Updike." *Boston Globe* 3 Oct. 1999, Sunday, City Edition, Books; C3.

Mortality and Immortality. The question of mortality and immortality is a major theme throughout Updike's work. Updike offers no single response to it, but instead provides a mosaic of reactions through a wide variety of characters.* In his first novel he confronts the question directly, but provides a traditional answer: mortality is no problem for those of strong religious conviction. But as his work gets further from such belief, the terror of mortality requires other responses. Mortality takes center stage in *PF* because elderly persons, clearly, are closer to the end, but John Hook* and the other poor can face the end stoically, and Hook can also reveal to the social humanist Stephen Conner* the emptiness of his vision of a universe without God.

The next four novels (*RR, C, OF, Couples*) question the purpose of life and display the terror of its extinction. The old people of *PF* have the solace of traditional faith, but George Caldwell,* in *C*, who fears that he is dying of cancer,* finds his consolations in science* (as Stephen Conner* had in *PF*) when he teaches his science class that the volvox, by fashioning cooperation of many cells, ended single-cell immortality and thus imported death* into biological evolution. Death is therefore part of a cooperative project that places the individual life within a vast context, but this cannot deliver Caldwell from his anxiety over the medical tests. Caldwell transmits this anxiety to his son Peter,* who realizes twelve years later that his father died daily but willingly in doing a thankless job for the sake of his family. Caldwell's mythical analogue, Chiron,* rejected immortality in order to save Prometheus and advance human understanding, and for this, Chiron was made into the constellation Sagittarius. Death was thus once assuaged by the gods, who could confer immortality; now Caldwell gains a human immortality by his son's memories turned into the retrospective narrative. Peter's elegiac story eases his own fear of death, already palpable in a skin disease that warns him of the corruption of the flesh to come.

In *OF* Joey Robinson* seems to replicate his dead father's life during his visit to his mother when he wears his father's clothes and echoes his mannerisms, but he does so not to venerate the dead but to supplant the father. His return to his mother with his new wife nearly kills his mother, but he does not let this interfere with how his life must be lived. Piet Hanema* in *Couples* uses sex* to ward off his fear of death, but he cannot even protect his daughter's hamster from being killed by a cat any more than he could have kept his parents from being killed in a car accident. Piet's idyllic affair with Foxy Whitman* leads to his decision to abort their baby. President John Kennedy* is assassinated, and a friend of Piet's dies as well, showing that no matter how well insulated, no community can wall out death, and that sexual satisfaction only momentarily numbs its sting (*Couples*) and may itself introduce death.

RA traces from *RR* through *RaR* Harry "Rabbit" Angstrom's* steady descent toward death and his conscious reflections on it; his fears are reflected in physical and social entropy in the devolution of Brewer* and America. Rabbit feels life slipping away and recognizes that nature* has fooled him by giving him a sexual desire whose end, procreation, will render him useless and an impediment to the generation he fathered. He will become, as he realizes when he is gardening, "garbage." So his daughter's birth provides a sense that his ego will continue in her after he is gone, but her drowning makes him fear sex, for in giving life he also gives death. Ironically, Rabbit does produce life one time, in the child Ruth Leonard Byer* claims to carry, but she tells him that the penalty for his not divorcing his wife Janice* and marrying her is the death of her child. The image of the child is perhaps connected in his mind to the "thing" that wants him to find it, the first-ratedness he imagines he can return to that will produce a sense of transcendence capable of conquering death (*RR*). Avoidance of death-giving sex in *RRed* proves an untenable solution, and sex permits death to enter his house when runaway Jill Pendleton* dies when his home is burned. Meanwhile, the Vietnam* War body count rises, and the black militant, Skeeter,* Rabbit befriended promises Armageddon to the whites. Skeeter, however, is convinced that he is immortal, the Black Messiah. Rabbit's mother is dying of Parkinson's disease and advises him to escape his family, but like Caldwell, he stays, works and makes some effort to clarify the confusion in his personal life and in America (*RRed*).

In *RIR* Rabbit has finally insulated himself from death through money and has yoked sexuality to riches; he seems to have warded off fears, and for the first time he renews his interest in parentage, convinced that his supposed daughter by Ruth lives. The concept of a "daughter" has been a fixation of Rabbit's, perhaps because a daughter represents reproductive immortality for him. His son Nelson Angstrom* provides him a granddaughter to replace the drowned baby, Rebecca Angstrom,* but Rabbit's problems with Nelson interfere with the adoption of Judy Angstrom* as a substitute for his loss. Being a person of little empathy or abstract reasoning, Rabbit must learn through his senses how to stave off dissolution; to the limits of his ability, he does. Yet he has inklings that Nelson is right, that money is waste, and he glimpses the truth: "To be rich is to be poor." He also realizes that to live, other living things must die; he feels children "crowd" and knows that, like Fred Springer,* the dead "make room," as someday he must. Intuitively he combats his son, who must naturally supersede him. Even as he jogs to strengthen himself for the fight, he recalls his personal dead, his mother's voice seemingly beckoning him. Taking a lover who adores him, Thelma Harrison,* Rabbit experiences anal intercourse, emptying his potency in a conduit of waste, yet Rabbit's confrontation with "nothingness" makes him "lighter," capable of realizing that everyone carries a "blackness" within. But as a result of this realization he feels "freer, more in love" with life. When Rabbit's enlarged athlete's heart gives him a great scare in *RaR*, he intuits that an airplane* falling from the sky over Lockerbie, Scotland, prefigures his death. Thelma, like the mother who provided unconditional love, is dying of lupus throughout their decade-long *Liebestod*, daily proof that no love can withstand death. In a last effort to drive out the fear of death, Rabbit sleeps with his daughter-in-law, Teresa "Pru" Angstrom,* but the action leads to his death. Though the effort to overcome mortality proves futile, Rabbit can only die on his own terms, winning one last basketball* game. To the end he has not discovered a faith that can enable him to accept death, but possibly in his final decision to die as he had lived, he has maintained some belief in being first-rate that combats death with the only tools he has.

Other works face mortality directly, with few illusions. Updike explores the last year of President James Buchanan* and imagines him trying and perhaps failing to understand the key moment in his life, when his fiancée killed herself over what she felt was his betrayal (*BD*). She is tragically mistaken, but on the terms she understands, life is not worth living. Similarly, *IB* reveals the downward spiral and death of Rev. Clarence Wilmot,* whose sudden leap into nonfaith was caused, like David Kern's* ("Pigeon Feathers" [*PigF*]), in part by his reading books that questioned Christ's divinity. Wilmot refused to compromise his faith, even though his adamant behavior jeopardized his family as well as his soul. He drifts, sells encyclopedias, watches movies and slowly dies of tuberculosis. Jesse Smith,* the mirror image of Wilmot, is a true believer who is convinced that once "launched," that is, murdered, in a Waco-style battle, his followers will achieve immortality (*IB*). Updike's memoir "On Being a Self Forever" (*SC*) explores unflinchingly his personal extinction and rejects the survival of his personality. Unlike David Kern, Updike has come to accept this, while retaining his religious faith.

In the late 1980s and the 1990s Updike seems to have prepared himself for the mortal conclusion of his career by completing his *"Scarlet Letter* trilogy" (1988), writing his memoirs (1989), gathering together his essays on music (1993), collecting his poetry (1993), writing the finis to Rabbit Angstrom (1995), assembling pieces on golf* (1996), completing the escapades of Henry Bech* (1998), issuing a last collection of critical pieces and collecting his short fiction.* This is what he called, speaking of Edmund Wilson,* "tidying up his desk." As he commented when tracing the decline in *RaR* of his most famous character, Rabbit Angstrom, the chest pains he suffered while his character suffered angina proved sympathetic reminders of his mortality. His oeuvre has supplied such reminders throughout his career, but they assure him an artist's immortality. As he remarked, "My life is in a sense trash; my life is only that of which the residue is my writing" (*PP*). *See* **Pets**.

Mt. Judge. A fictional suburb of Brewer,* Pennsylvania, in *RA*, Mt. Judge is modeled on the actual Mt. Penn,* just as Brewer is modeled on the actual Reading,* Pennsylvania. Mt. Penn is situated on the east face of the mountain whose west face overlooks Brewer, fifty miles northwest of Philadelphia. Harry "Rabbit" Angstrom* goes to Mt. Judge High School and becomes a basketball* star there. (At the end of *RRed* he wears his old Mt. Judge jacket.) His wife Janice Angstrom* also attended that school, and they live together at 447 Wilbur Street, on the third floor, apartment #5, Mt. Judge. Updike provides a scenic tour of Mt. Judge when Rabbit runs home after playing basketball with kids, and then when he goes to pick up his car at his mother-in-law's house and his son Nelson Angstrom* at his parents' home. Updike provides a meticulous description of Rabbit's walk along Wilbur Street to Potter Avenue, past the ice plant and down Kegerise Street, past a box factory and a beer outlet, past a boarded-up old sandstone farmhouse and the Sunshine Athletic Association. In reality, many of these places are modeled on actual places in Shillington*; therefore Mt. Judge is a composite locale, embracing both Shillington and Mt. Penn. The farmhouse might allude to the farmhouse in Plowville* where Updike lived after 1945. Rabbit, with his mistress Ruth Leonard Byer,* hikes to the Pinnacle Hotel (Mt. Penn's Pagoda Hotel) on Palm Sunday and, when examining Brewer, the "flower pot city," from there, Rabbit strains to see the "cancer-blackened soul of an old man mount through the blue" (*RR*). As critic Joyce Markle points out, the image of ascent/descent of the basketball in *RR* is a controlling image for that novel. Rabbit's run home is an ascent, just as his flight from Janice is a descent. Thus the selection of Mt. Judge for the home of the Angstroms links to the controlling image and reinforces it.

Mt. Penn. The eastern suburb of Reading, Pennsylvania,* Mt. Penn, named by the sons of William Penn (1644–1718), is used as the fictional Mt. Judge* in *RA*. Mt. Judge provides Updike with "downward descent" as Rabbit runs at the start of *RR*, an important image throughout the tetralogy. The Pinnacle Hotel in Mt. Judge is modeled on the Pagoda Hotel (erected 1906–1908) in Mt. Penn, a peculiar Chinese structure, landmark and trysting spot.

"Murder Makes the Magazine." Updike began the story "Murder Makes the Magazine" about the *New Yorker** in 1960 and then gave it to the "Virtual Bookstore," Amazon.com* on the World Wide Web, to encourage participation by other writers. With this composition Updike entered the cyberspace marketplace by inviting writers to supply daily paragraphs that would advance the story from Updike's initial paragraph of 293 words. Updike described the enterprise as "sticking my head in the mouth of the electronic lion." Each day for the forty-three days of the contest an addition was selected to carry the story forward; each daily contributor received $1,000. On the forty-fourth day, September 12, 1997, Amazon.com awarded $100,000 to a sweepstakes winner, not necessarily a person who had written a continuing paragraph. Although Updike was identified as one of the "judges" for the daily award, his exact participation in the contest as a judge is unclear.

The contest, essentially a "chain story," had antecedents like *Naked Came the Stranger* and Nicholson Baker's story "The Remedy," finished by Robert Phillips. Updike's story represents an unusually commercial enterprise for him (he was paid about $5,000) as well as his first public appearance on the Internet, despite serious reservations he had expressed about the conflict between the computer and the print media, amusingly written as a dialogue in "Print" (*MM*). The work should be seen within the context of Updike's other publication ventures. For example, he has published many of his works in "first printings before publication" by about two dozen publishers* besides his trade publisher Knopf (which has also published many of his books in signed special editions).

Updike's contribution to "Murder Makes the Magazine" presents Miss Tasso Polk, forty-three, sensitive, reserved and dedicated. When she arrives at "The Magazine," apparently to work as an editor, she senses something strange. So ends Updike's opening. Then forty-odd participants continued the story until September 12, 1997, when Updike finished it by adding 547 words that tied loose ends by accusing the Internet of having been the villain because those who once read the magazine's "scrupulously edited, fact-packed pages . . . now cruise the Internet, communicating interactively with a world of electronic buddies. Print has become a mug's game." Miss Polk is made editor (an allusion to Tina Brown's assuming the editorship of the *New Yorker?*), and the future of the magazine is assured. "Murder Makes the Magazine" marks Updike's first foray into the murder-mystery genre since, when young, he had tried to write several mysteries and abandoned them; he then tried one, in 1960, set at the *New Yorker*.

Though Updike says that this particular story was written in 1960, "Murder Makes the Magazine" has much in common with an abortive 1946 murder mystery published in *First Words* (1993). Thriftily, Updike managed to recycle both projects. He uses the same name, Merriweather, in both works, and his exotic Spanish private eye in the 1946 story apparently changed to a female investigator with an Italian-sounding first name, Tasso Polk. In both "Murder Makes the Magazine" and the 1946 story the letter *M* has a conspicuous presence: the three *M*s of the title, when seen upside-down, mimic the "www" designation of "World Wide Web," and Updike might have noticed that he began his story with a capital "M," and a crucial note identifies the murderer as "M . . ." but breaks off. By bringing out of retirement an abortive story begun many years ago and using it in 1997 for this contest, Updike shows once more a conscious effort to draw together the beginning and ending of his career. Updike had already done this by publishing his collected poems in 1993, publishing *RA* in 1995 and bringing the stories of Henry Bech* to apparent closure in 1998. A sense of closure has also been achieved by linking his first novel, *PF*, and the 1996 *IB*. Each portrays characters* based on Updike's maternal and paternal grandfathers, respectively. *PF* also resembles 1997's *TE*, since both are set in the near future, and each uses a retiree as the hero.

Bibliography: Updike, Self-interview (*MM*); Mel Gussow, "John Updike, Impresario of Fictional Relay Race," *New York Times* 2 Aug. 1997: A11, 16; *New York Times* 18 Aug. 1997: sec. 6, 38; Noah Robischon, "Updike.com: A Novel Effort," *Entertainment Weekly* 10 Oct. 1997: 100.

Murkett, Lucinda "Cindy" or "Cin." The wife of Webb Murkett,* Cindy Murkett is Harry "Rabbit" Angstrom's* love object. The voluptuous Cindy is introduced in a swimming suit at the Flying Eagle Tee and Racquet Club pool, and Rabbit is entranced. But she is never more than friendly, even after she saves his life when Rabbit capsizes their Sunfish as he tries to flirt with her (*RIR*). When Cindy confides her Catholic feelings about contraception, she remains unaware about Rabbit's smoldering interest, little realizing that Rabbit had desired a woman like her for many years, "a little Catholic" (*RR*), but to Rabbit at that time "Catholic" meant flowerlike, dumb and shabby.

Cindy is very different. While snooping in the Murketts' bedroom, Rabbit discovers intimate Polaroids of them that cause him to denigrate Cindy. But Rabbit assumes that he has at last captured her when the Murketts, Harrisons and Angstroms decide to swap spouses while vacationing. But apparently the women had made their selections earlier, and his detested rival Ronnie Harrison* gets Cindy, the recognized "treasure" of the women. Rabbit's partner and later mistress, Thelma Harrison,* admonishes him to forget Cindy since she is too young and shallow to value him properly. Ten years later, at Thelma's funeral, Rabbit meets Cindy, whom Murkett had divorced for a much younger woman, perhaps because Cindy had grown fat. Rabbit's desire for her vanishes (*RaR*). The reversal of Rabbit's fortunes underlines his lack of aggressiveness in sex,* despite his notoriety as a Don Juan. Ironically, the swapping seems to have been engineered by Janice Angstrom,* who not only gets her dream man, Webb Murkett,* but has great sex. Rabbit experiences reversals such as this in *RIR* and *RaR* as he loses control of Janice, his son Nelson Angstrom* takes charge of the car lot, his mistress dies, and his pursuit of his daughter goes unresolved. he is even reversed after death, since Janice is then free to sell their home, something he had opposed. Cindy represents Rabbit's "fairy girl," reminiscent of Sinclair Lewis's* image in *Babbitt* of the fairy girl that Babbitt thinks of as he falls asleep, but for Rabbit she may also represent something of the feminine principle that mystifies him and remains ever elusive.

Bibliography: Detweiler, *JU*; Greiner, *JU*.

Murkett, Webb. The contractor in *RIR* whom Harry "Rabbit" Angstrom* respects for his knowledge about woodworking, where to buy clothes and how to invest money, Webb Murkett acts as Rabbit's materialistic mentor. Although Rabbit is irritated when Murkett takes another golf* partner because Rabbit must attend his son Nelson's* wedding, Webb's success with women makes him Rabbit's ego ideal. Murkett not only has a beautiful, much younger wife, Cindy Murkett,* the object of Rabbit's sexual fantasies, but he discards her ten years later for an even younger woman when Cindy grows fat. After the women initiate the idea, Murkett sets the rules for the spousal sharing that enables him to provide Janice Angstrom* a thrilling night. Rabbit's failure to sleep with Cindy Murkett not only hinders his own plans, but the lack of reciprocity also makes Rabbit all the more subordinate to Murkett, particularly when Janice admits that he is also a better lover than Rabbit. A negative guide, Murkett represents an incarnation of Rabbit's coach Marty Tothero*: each seems to be a guide to first-ratedness, but each impresses Rabbit with the wrong values, particularly when Murkett tells Rabbit to invest in gold and then to sell the gold and invest in silver. In both cases Rabbit's investments are successful, but since he already knows that money is waste and that "to be rich is to be poor," what good was Murkett's advice except to lead Rabbit further into false values (*RIR*)? *See* **Characters.**

Museums and Women and Other Stories (New York: Knopf, 1972). Updike's collection of stories in *MW* is a transitional volume bringing together twelve years' work that sums up previous concerns and techniques. The loss of innocence in the guiltless 1950s is reflected upon nostalgically in "When Everyone Was Pregnant." The story may mark a turn toward maturity in

Updike's fiction because it specifies the division between hopefulness (symbolized by pregnancy) and the failure of belief and the increase of waste and aimlessness of that generation. "The Sea's Green Sameness" (significantly placed in the second section, "Other Modes") provides variations on mutability recalling "Sea-Surface Full of Clouds" by Updike's fellow Pennsylvanian, poet Wallace Stevens.* William Young, who discovered love and its loss in "A Sense of Shelter" (*PigF*), now finds love and loss punctuating his life in "Museums and Women," though he has not relinquished his quest for "radiance" in women or art.* Section three contains stories concerning Joan* and Richard Maple's* marital tensions, eventually collected with others to form *TF*. Critics generally feel that *MW* lacks the vitality and ingenuity of earlier collections.

Bibliography: Alice and Kenneth Hamilton, "John Updike's *Museums and Women and Other Stories*," *Thought* 49 (Mar. 1974): 56–71; Alfred F. Rosa, "The Psycholinguistics of Updike's 'Museums and Women,' " *Modern Fiction Studies* 20 (Spring 1974): 107–11; Greiner, *OJ*; Detweiler, *JU*; Luscher, *JU*.

The Music School (New York: Knopf, 1966). Updike's collection of stories in *MuS* continues his dominant realistic mode, which for some readers epitomized the *New Yorker** style, and which has been compared to that of F. Scott Fitzgerald. But the stories also provide more experimental directions. With an unsentimental retrospective of his Harvard* years, Updike explores the development of spiritual impulses in an unconventional student in "The Christian Roommates." In the same vein of frank detachment, Updike examines the problems of Richard* and Joan Maple* in the stories "Giving Blood" and "Twin Beds in Rome," later collected in *TF*. He applies a more satiric style to the award-winning "The Bulgarian Poetess," in which he introduces an alter ego,* writer Henry Bech,* for the first time making the writer's life the subject of his fiction. A rather new lyricism appears in "Leaves" (which Updike later called his "best story"), "Harv Is Plowing Now," and "The Music School." The latter two show Updike's new capabilities for interweaving startling images with quotidian episodes of the fragility of life. In "The Music School" Updike also introduces a major theme he would develop in *Marry, Couples* and *MS*: "We are all pilgrims faltering toward divorce." This story provides a mosaic of seemingly unrelated incidents and images that suggest the narrator's inner struggle with his infidelity. The unusual form of the story foreshadows a demonstration of the artifice of fiction in *MS* and *Coup*. "The Music School" was made into a film* for the Public Broadcasting System.

Bibliography: Taylor, *PA*; Joyce B. Markle, "On John Updike and 'The Music School,' " in *The American Short Story*, ed. Calvin Skaggs (New York: Dell, 1977), 389–93; George Hunt, "Reality, Imagination and Art: The Significance of Updike's

'Best Story,' " *Studies in Short Fiction* 16 (Summer 1979): 219–29; Greiner, *OJ*; Detweiler, *JU*; Luscher, *JU*.

Myth. Though Updike is usually classified as a realist, his awareness of myth and symbolism* frequently challenges such a label. Updike was eager to remind an early interviewer that he had worked myth into his first several novels, using the story of St. Stephen's stoning in *PF*, *The Tale of Peter Rabbit** in *RR*, and many mythic analogues in *C*: Olinger becomes Olympus, and exact reference is made to mythic figures. One mythic chapter, apparently, is derived entirely from Robert Grave's *The Greek Myths I*. In each of these novels Updike has supplied a surprise in his treatment of myth—futurism and melodrama in *PF*, comic counterpointing in *RR* and tragicomedy in *C*.

Sometimes Updike uses several myths within one work. Although he remarked that in *Couples* Piet Hanema* is Lot fleeing Sodom, the more apparent myth embracing the story of adulterous lovers is the Tristan and Isolde* legend, reused in the stories "Four Sides of One Story" (*MuS*) and "Tristan and Iseult" (*A*), for a deliberate narrative underpinning in *B*, and possibly in *Marry*. *Couples* may also bear traces of the Don Juan story. Updike also interlaces a modern narrative with extracts taken from other books, as if they were a mythic resource, as in his use of *The Confessions* of St. Augustine* in his story "Augustine's Concubine" (*P*). Critic James Schiff contends that Updike's use of earlier stories may be called a "mythic mode," a "salient" feature of his fiction.

Rollo May's *Cry for Myth* (1991) offers useful mythic paradigms for considering extent and patterns in Updike's employment of myth. Thus Updike's early story "Flight" (*PigF*) describes the struggle for resolution of the Oedipal complex. The struggle is intensified in *C*, *OF* and the four novels of *RA*. Love and marriage archetypes underlie most of Updike's work, including *RA*, *Couples*, *TF*, and *Marry* and the "*Scarlet Letter* trilogy" (*MS*, *RV* and *S*.), as well as *MF*, *B*, *IB* and *TE*. The archetype of work with its accompanying figure of Sisyphus, who was condemned by the gods to do the useless work of endlessly rolling a rock up a hill, only to have it roll back down again, operates in *RA* and *C*. The archetype of approaching death,* accompanied by descents into the underworld of Odysseus and Dante,* appears in the poem "Midpoint" (*M*), the stories "Bech Panics" (*BIB*), "Journey to the Dead" (*A*) and "Cruise" (*A*), the play *BD*, and the novels *PF*, *C*, *Coup*, *MF*, *B*, *W* and *TE* and the first section of *IB*. This pattern is incorporated in the so-called heroic myth, in which the hero descends into hell, rediscovers himself and emerges renewed, the pattern of *C*, *MS* and *Coup* and perhaps *MF*, *S*., *TE* and *IB*. (in which Essie Wilmot/Alma DeMott* renews what Rev. Clarence Wilmot* lost, and in which Clark DeMott* dies during his regeneration).

Other myths appear in Updike's work, the most important of these being the quest, in which the archetype is Hermes, the trickster god (*RA*, *C*, *Coup and B*); the myth of Narcissus (*RA*); the "Arcadian myth" treated directly in *C* and *TE*, as well as in pastoral* scenes of golfing (*RA*, *GD*), and related to the Edenic myth (OF); the "rags-to-riches" myth in *IB*; and the mythical Babel of languages* (*MS*, *RV*). The narrative of *OF* can be found in Joseph Campbell's description of the hero's relation to women, according to critic George Hunt.

It would be a mistake, however, to think that Updike's use of myth is entirely intellectual. He considers mythmaking natural to children, who see, as Peter Caldwell* says, "myth-size," with people looking especially mysterious and fraught with meaning (*C*); so, in reconstructing the story of the life of his father, George Caldwell,* Peter adjusts his vision to re-create how his father for him had the mythic reality of Chiron.* The other mythic figures are likewise embodied in every detail of life, or "around the corner," as Peter says. Allegorizing by nicknames shows the natural need to inflate the ordinary—"Rabbit" for Harry Angstrom,* "Pumpkin Eater" for Peter Caldwell, "Mr. Spoil-Sport" for Nelson Angstrom.* Art* sustains this natural mythmaking by making of realistic characteristics a representation of larger qualities, as Tarzan becomes a symbol of the natural man, or Rabbit Angstrom a symbol of America or Everyman. At the same time, Rabbit is rooted in Beatrix Potter's* *Tale of Peter Rabbit*. Perhaps this is why Updike remarked, "I always have some sort of mythological referent in mind when I write." *See* **Freud, Sigmund; Jung, Carl Gustav.**

Bibliography: John J. White, *Mythology in the Modern Novel: A Study of Prefigurative Techniques* (Princeton: PUP, 1971), 5, 53, 70, 87a, 113, 123, 133, 135; Vargo, *REF*; John B. Vickery, "*The Centaur*: Myth, History and Narrative," *Modern Fiction Studies* 20 (Spring 1974): 29–43; Hunt, *JU*; David Malone, "Updike 2020; Fantasy, Mythology and Faith in *Toward the End of Time*" in Yerkes, *JU*. Jack De Bellis, "Oedipal Angstrom," *Wascana Review* 24 (1989): 45–59; Jack Branscomb, "Chiron's Two Deaths: Updike's Use of Variant Mythic Accounts in 'The Centaur,'" *English Language Notes* 28 (Sept. 1990): 62–66; Schiff, *JU*.

N

Nabokov, Vladimir (1899–1977). The premier Russian-American novelist, Vladimir Nabokov emigrated from Russia in 1919 and came to the United States in 1940. Though he began as a poet, after 1926 he wrote essentially fiction, and though he wrote his early fiction in Russian, he composed in English after 1941. His novels have been praised for brilliant style and for inventiveness including parody, particularly *Pale Fire* (1962), composed of a long poem and a series of footnotes, the interplay between poem and notes creating a subtle narrative. Edmund Wilson* befriended Nabokov on his arrival in America. He taught at Cornell University (where Martha Updike,* Updike's second wife, took a course from him and was called a "genius" by Nabokov) until he published—abroad—the erotic *Lolita* (1955), the success of which relieved him forever of teaching. This novel affected Updike's view of the content of fiction, and other Nabokov ideas would emerge in Updike's story collections and the form of specific stories. One wonders what the impact upon Updike might have been had he not passed up the chance to take Nabokov's humanities course at Harvard.*

Lolita gave Updike an important model of a serious artist who could incorporate sexual explicitness in fiction, influencing the explicit writing of *RR*. Updike would not use the relationship of an older man and a nymphet until *TE* (Ben Turnbull's* intimacies with a thirteen-year-old girl stop short of intercourse). Updike gathered ideas about form as well as content from Nabokov, asserting that from Nabokov's *Pnin* he got the idea of creating a "half novel of short stories about a single character," Henry Bech.* Since *Pnin* is about Nabokov's life in America and the character Pnin is his alter ego,* it is fitting that Updike's book based on *Pnin* should be about his alter ego Henry Bech. "Bech Panics" (*BB*) shows a specific influence of Nabokov in Updike's use of the device of the slide show. Chapter 8 of Nabokov's autobiography, *Speak, Memory* (1951), begins, "I am going to show a few slides," and the "slides" become a narrative device. Updike's frequent use of a series of photographs as a narrative control may derive from this, as "A Sandstone Farmhouse" (*A*) suggests. Finally, in Bech, Updike found a guiltless murderer like Nabokov's Humbert Humbert of *Lolita* when Bech rids "Gotham" of four hostile critics* before settling down to wife and baby—a virtual parody of the end of Nabokov's novel ("Bech Noir" [*BaB*]). Possibly the appearance of *Speak, Memory* in the *New Yorker** (1948–50) provided the impetus for Updike to write his autobiographical essay "The Dogwood Tree: A Boyhood"* and the similar memoirs that comprise *SC*.

Nabokov left his mark on two other works by Updike, *Coup* and a short story. Both Nabokov and Updike also seemed to have agreed on a basic aesthetic point. Updike said that in *Coup* he wished to create a "Nabokovian unreality" in his effort to create a country and to write Nabokov's "spectacular English!" Joyce Carol Oates perceived a relation between *Coup* and Nabokov's *Pale Fire*, and critic Joyce Markle observes that Col. Félix Elleloû* is saved by his aide Sirin, whose name is Nabokov's pen name. The decapitation of the king in *Coup* may have its source in Nabokov's *Invitation to a Beheading*. In the short story "George and Vivian II: 'Bluebeard in Ireland' " (*A*) the Nabokov connection appears when *Pale Fire* is mentioned as a point of common interest between George and Vivian Allenson, but Nabokov's novel of deception and betrayal makes an ironic comment on their troubled relationship. Nabokov's view of art* expressed in *Speak, Memory* may be close to Updike's. In chapter 8 Nabokov remarks: "The world is a kind of delicate meeting place between imagination and knowledge, a point arrived at by diminishing large things and enlarging small ones that is intrinsically artistic." This resembles Updike's oft-quoted remark that "details are the giant's fingers" ("The Blessed Man of Boston, My Grandmother's Thimble, and Fanning Island" [*PigF*]). Updike has been occupied with Nabokov in his nonfiction as well, recalling that James Buchanan* shared Nabokov's birthday date (*BD*), declaring that Nabokov's death was "an ugly footnote to a shimmering text, reality's thumbprint on the rainbow" in his memorial (*HS*), and squelching the rumor that M. Ageyev's *Novel with Cocaine* was written by Nabokov (*OJ*). See **Chess; Literary Influences; Miller, Henry; Sex**.

Bibliography: Updike, "Grandmaster Nabokov" (*AP*); the section "Nabokov" contains seven pieces (*PP*); "In Memoriam," in *In Memoriam Vladimir Nabokov, 1899–1977* (New York: McGraw-Hill, 1977), 27–38; "*Selected Letters, 1940–1977*" (*OJ*); "Introduction," in *Lectures on Literature*, by Vladimir Nabokov (*HS*); "Sirin's Sixty-Five Shimmering Short Stories," "On Cervantes' *Don Quixote*" (*MM*); George Steiner, *Reporter* 28 (14 Mar. 1963): 52; Charles W. Pomeroy, "Soviet Russian Criticism 1960–1969 of Seven Twentieth Century American Novelists," *Dissertation Abstracts International* 32 (1972): 449A, University of Southern California.

Names. Updike's wit and sensitivity to language are apparent in his playful and clever selection of names, which he called "the hidden dimension" of his work. His most famous character, Harry "Rabbit" Angstrom,* is given his nickname to identify vaguely rabbitlike facial features, but Updike includes a great many rabbitlike activities that underline the nickname, such as his appetite for vegetables and goobers, his aimless running and his search for symbolic burrows. The nickname is given literary resonance when it is combined with allusions to Beatrix Potter's* *Tale of Peter Rabbit.** Rabbit's surname suggests his anxiety: *Angst** is a vortex; *strom* comes from the German *Strom*, meaning "stream." Also, an *angstrom* is one ten-billionth of a meter, used to measure light waves and thus the tiniest bit of illumination that can provide "enlightenment"—apt ways to suggest both Rabbit's ordinariness and his inner "illumination" that some thing wants him to find it. Rabbit's daughter, Rebecca June Angstrom,* is named for the month in which spring changes to summer, but since the baby dies in June before summer begins, her name is ironic. The name of Rabbit's wife, Janice Angstrom,* suggests the two-faced god Janus for whom January is named and thus her coldness to Rabbit, her ability to look both ways in accepting his affair with Ruth Leonard Byer* and her ability to start things, like the reclamation of Springer Motors,* as January initiates the year. Since rabbits are associated with fertility and thus with spring, the spring/winter opposition of Rabbit and Janice suggests their incompatibility. This is also indicated by Janice Springer Angstrom's maiden name, which suggests a species antagonism between husband and wife (rabbit versus dog) that is supported by incident and imagery* throughout *RA*.

The name of Rabbit's alter ego,* Ronnie Harrison,* is apt (Harry/son, "son of Harry"); they are rivals, as Rabbit is with his own son Nelson Angstrom,* and Harrison is in a sense Rabbit's second, baser self. Temptress Lucy Eccles's* given name is related to "Lucifer," recalling the fallen angel. (In *RIR* the object of Rabbit's interest is Lucinda "Cindy" Murkett*—"Lucinda" relating her to Lucy Eccles—shortened by Rabbit to the punning "Cin.") Another name for the morning star, Lucifer, is Venus, goddess of love, as well as light, again representing "illumination," which Rabbit always associates with women; perhaps, like Venus the planet, Lucy is also a general symbol of women for Rabbit—distant, shining, beckoning, unreachable. Lucy's married name is associated with pastry, Eccles cake, as well as with Eccles Street in Dublin, the home of passionate Molly Bloom in James Joyce's* *Ulysses*. When her husband, Rev. Jack Eccles,* is considered, the association suggested is Ecclesiastes; coincidentally, Updike acknowledges the aid of Sir John Eccles, an Australian neurophysiologist and Nobel laureate (1963), in *RV*. Shrewdly, Updike has made Rabbit's coach Marty Tothero's* name divisible (tot/hero) suggesting Rabbit's hero worship. But Updike's presentation of the coach as a deteriorating, drunken whoremonger suggests another division of his name, created by circularizing it: to/the/rot.

Such visual punning is characteristic of Updike's poems in "A Cheerful Alphabet of Pleasant Objects" (*CH*).

In *Couples* the narrator notes that Piet Hanema's* given name recalls "peat," alluding to his earthiness, and "pious," with his spiritual longings. His surname echoes "anima" and "a man" and "amen": Piet is a man caught, like George Caldwell,* between mud and heaven. The "mud" association converts Hanema to "enema," according to scatological, demythologizing Freddy Thorne,* whose wife Georgene Thorne is Piet's mistress. Since Georgene tells Piet's wife Angela Hanema* about Piet's affair with the earthy Foxy Whitman,* her name aptly resembles "gorgon." Piet's wife and mistress correspond to his piety and earthiness: Angela Hanema, Foxy Whitman. Similarly, in a later novel the first name of Alma DeMott (the professional name of Essie Wilmot*), a screen star who plays larger-than-life figures, is "soul" in Spanish (*IB*).

Updike plays with mythical, fictional and historical characters' names in several novels. He uses so many mythic analogues throughout *C* that he helped his readers (and amused himself) by supplying a "Mythological Index." George Caldwell's* given name recalls the *Georgics* of Virgil and relates him to the pastoral* world of Chiron* the centaur. His surname suggests that he is one "called well" to his job and his sacrifice. His son Peter's* given name recalls that Peter means "rock" in Greek and refers the reader to the rock on which Prometheus, Peter's analogue, had been fastened. The principal of George Caldwell's Olinger (Olympus) High School is Louis Zimmerman* (Zeus), and Doc Appleton* is Apollo. Caldwell's father-in-law Pop Kramer, who is capable of "throwing an atmosphere," is Kronos. In *B* Tristâo Raposo* and Isabel Leme* reflect in their names, as well as in their story, the myth of Tristan and Isolde.*

Throughout his "*Scarlet Letter* trilogy" Updike adapts Nathaniel Hawthorne's* characters' names: Arthur Dimmesdale becomes both Thomas Marshfield* (*MS*) ("doubting Thomas," and "dale" converts to "marsh") and Dale Kohler* (*RV*), whose surname refers both to a plumbing magnate and to Kaufmann Kohler, a theologian of Reform Judaism, as critic James Schiff notes. Arthur Steinmetz's first name and his title "Arhat"* echo Arthur Dimmesdale's first name (*S.*). Steinmetz explains that his last name refers to the electrical engineer Charles Proteus Steinmetz, a genius who was misunderstood and exploited by General Electric; Arthur Steinmetz is a religious "engineer" and a master of disguises. Roger Chillingworth becomes both Roger Lambert* (*RV*) and Charles Worth* (*S.*), as well as Marshfield's father-in-law, Professor Wesley Chillingworth, a Unitarian minister in *MS*, whose given name refers to the founder of Methodism, John Wesley. Lambert's surname derives from German physicist Johann Lambert, who named the measurement of the brightness of light called the "lambert." Hester Prynne changes to Ms. Prynne,* a name capable of puns like "Ms. Print" (*MS*), to Esther Lambert* (*RV*) and to Sarah Worth* (*S.*). A mistress of

Marshfield's, Alicia, draws a disclaimer about her name in a footnote in which Marshfield swears that "it is not contrived to fit Wonderland" (*MS*).

Other works besides those from *RA* and the Hawthorne trilogy show Updike's tireless ingenuity with names. In *MF* the narrator, Alfred L. Clayton, was named Alf by his parents in honor of Alf Landon (*MF*). As a prank, Updike has Henry Bech* include the names of real, mostly hostile, critics* in his bibliography (*BIB*), and Updike gives names derived from two critics to two witches (Phoebe-Lou Adams and Rhoda Koenig as Phoebe Koenig and Rhoda Adams) (*W*), while assigning to Sarah Worth's* dentist the name Podhoretz, one of Updike's fiercest opponents, Norman Podhoretz. Hostile to everyone is Darryl Van Horne,* whose first name chimes with devil, and whose surname supplies the image of the horned Satan, suggestive of sexual potency (*W*). "Horne" is also embedded in the surname of Freddy Thorne, the Lord of Misrule in *Couples*. The witch Sukie Rougemont's* last name recalls Denis de Rougemont, the writer on love whose books Updike had used as the background for *Couples* (*W*). Also in *W* Updike names two characters Abigail and Lovecraft, alluding to Arthur Miller's Abigail, who started the witch hysteria in *The Crucible*, and H. P. Lovecraft, an American horror writer, who lived in Providence, Rhode Island, near the fictional Eastwick.* Scattered throughout this novel are various names taken from Hawthorne's works, just as names of streets (Potter, Warne) scattered through *RR* derive from the name of the author and the publisher of *The Tale of Peter Rabbit*. Updike even creates an acronym of the title *MS* (*A Month of Sundays*) when he names a character "Amos." The "extra dimension" has supplied Updike's ready sense of multileveled meaning, and he looks into that dimension when, for example, he examines Umberto Eco's use of the name "Casaubon" (*OJ*).

Bibliography: Hamilton and Hamilton, *EJ*; Taylor, *PA*; Jack De Bellis, "The 'Extra Dimension': Character Names in Updike's 'Rabbit' Trilogy," *Names* 36 (Mar.–June 1988): 29–42; Schiff, *JU*.

Narrative Voice. A discussion of narrative voice in Updike's work involves considering such questions as these: How sympathetic is the narrator to the protagonist? What tactics has the narrator employed to conceal his own voice? Does the detectable voice alter a reading of the text? To the question of sympathetic narrative voice, one notes that Updike has remarked that in his early novels he "sought to present both sides of an unresolvable tension," and this seems to typify his weaving in and out of sympathy for his hero in *RA*. Thus, when Harry "Rabbit" Angstrom* strikes a golf* ball well, the narrator notes that he felt "aggrandizement," which is not a word within Rabbit's vocabulary. Here the narrator seems to supply a word Rabbit might use if he were more linguistically sensitive than he is. But when the narrator deliberately enters the mind of characters like Ruth Leonard Byer* and Rabbit's wife, Janice Angstrom,* the narrator conceals his own voice, to take up the second question, and allows us to witness without the filter of an intervening voice. To conceal his own voice, Updike sometimes employs unusual tactics of "conversing" with his characters. In *RRed* for example, a dialogue seems to take place that suggests a homogeneity of narrator and Rabbit: the apparent narrator thinks at one point, "Time is our element, not a mistaken invader," but the next line shows it to be Rabbit's idea: "How stupid, it has taken him thirty-six years to begin to believe that." The same is true in *RIR*, in which the narrator offers summary aphoristic remarks that suggest the presence of a narrator: "Our tears are always young," but the narrator calls the idea Rabbit's "idiotic thought." As Rabbit ages, he seems to grow into the voice of the narrator as he thinks, "To live is to kill," "To be rich is to be poor," and "We are cruel enough without meaning to be." The result is intimacy with Rabbit but sufficient distance to generalize or provide stylistic punch. Updike allows himself the latitude to lyrically interpret the feelings of his ordinary people; the lyricism separates the narrator from them and brings us closer to what they might feel if they had his articulation.

In works like *W* Updike is more deliberate, drawing attention to how the events are related "gropingly . . . reluctantly," and in the last paragraph the narrative voice seems to be that of the Eastwick* community: "We were just an interval in their lives, and they in ours." The reader suddenly realizes that the narrative has been presented through a "choric" voice, a reminder to Eastwickians that the monstrous and mysterious are always in their midst. Updike thus generally permits the narrative to tell its own story without overt intrusion by the narrative voice, but when he wishes, he permits himself an intimate relationship to his hero and allows himself a kind of "summing up." At times, as in *C, Coup, MF, MS* and *S.*, he uses a first-person viewpoint that effaces the narrative voice completely and keeps his voice nonjudgmental; yet self-reflexive irony undermines the narrator, for example, when Alf Clayton* does not understand how foolish he is in imagining that his editor will actually print hundreds of pages blending his personal life with that of his quandary over President James Buchanan.* A narrator need not comment; the irony does the work of such a voice.

Two other examples shed light on the flexibility of narrative voice. Updike remarked that the film version of "The Music School" (*MuS*) failed because it could not reproduce "the leaps of the narrator's voice," showing the flexibility and variation possible to the technique even in short fiction.* An unusual voice is that of *B*, which is stilted, as if it is intentionally antiquated to give the impression that the speaker is from another age, thus heightening the sense that the novel's tale of lovers takes its place with the medieval myth of Tristan and Isolde.* *See* **The Novel**.

Nature. Updike has been praised for his ability to record nature with meticulous detail and affection. He identifies flowers and trees by name, often with a lyricism that invests them with wonder. This is a signature of Updike's style* and at first, in *PF* and *RR*, caused some critics to cavil at the alleged waste of his remarkable talent describing sunsets or snowflakes. But through *RA* and *TE* he continues to intertwine nature and man. In *RaR*, for example, Harry "Rabbit" Angstrom* regains his sense of the beauty of life after his heart attack by intensely seeing Bradford pear trees in bloom that bring him to tears at the simple miracle of the turning seasons. Those seasons are recorded with great care throughout *TE* by Ben Turnbull,* despite an atomic war's denuding much of America and cancer* cells threatening to waste his life. He starts virtually each day, week and month with careful depictions, in the manner of Henry David Thoreau,* of which blossoms are late, which blooms are early. Updike's pastoralism repeatedly connects women to the earth and to flowers (*C*), as Rabbit, gardening, can smell the flowers on a Catholic girl he fantasizes about. Nature is not sentimentalized: the Edenic world of Florida* is so effulgent it is nearly threatening (*RaR*), and the "seethe" of nature brings the witches power (*W*), while the green jewel of Vietnam* hides in its lushness sickening forms of death (*RRed*). *See* **Pastoral**.

New York. The largest city in population in the United States, New York contains important centers of theater, art,* finance, sports,* shipping, music and commerce. When Katharine and E. B. White met Updike in Oxford* and hired him to write for the *New Yorker*,* Updike, excited that the Whites thought him a writer of great promise and thrilled to live in a city he "really loved" (Plath, *CU*), thought that he had reached the fulfillment of his dreams. He moved at once in August 1955, with his wife Mary* and four-month-old Elizabeth* to West Eighty-fifth Street and Riverside Drive, a sixth-floor apartment that faced away from the city. His obligatory legwork for his *New Yorker* pieces enabled Updike to visit art in the nearby Museum of Modern Art on his lunch hour. He also got to know New York from Central Park to Yankee Stadium. New York was used as the setting of "The Lucid Eye in Silver Town" (*AP*), which recounts a disillusioning effort to see the paintings of Jan Vermeer.* Living in New York impelled Updike to use the city in several stories in *SD*, but his novels did not use New York. Instead he wrote a 600-page novel *Home*. It has not been published (Plath, *CU*). New York reappears only when Updike creates a New York writer, Henry Bech,* but he places him in New York in only four stories, "Bech in Heaven" (*BB*), "White on White" (*BIB*) and "Bech Presides" and "Bech Noir" (*BaB*). In April 1957 Updike left New York, saying that he was unlikely to get beyond the form of the "Talk of the Town" pieces he was filing. Fearlessly, he took his wife and two children to Ipswich,* Massachusetts, set aside a novel that had preoccupied him, and began writing *PF*.

Updike's decision to leave New York resulted from his conviction that it was no place for a serious writer. The plethora of agents, writers and "participants" interfered with his concentration and recalled to him Ernest Hemingway's* description of literary New York as filled with tapeworms feeding on one another. In a review of a biography of Dorothy Parker thirty years later, Updike said that what made this book enjoyable was "its deglamorized depiction of the literary and cultural world that hatched and to an extent smothered Dorothy Parker," and he derided the "Algonquinists' " "blithe misuses of their time" and "quick-fix approach to literary production." Other writers like Ross Lockridge testified to the damage inflicted by New York, and Norman Mailer,* very nearly ruined by publicity, congratulated Updike on this "withdrawal." Updike must have been impressed by fellow *New Yorker* writer J. D. Salinger's* protection of his privacy, as he later would be of Thomas Pynchon's. However exciting New York was, he knew that it was no place, as he said, "to hatch" books about small-town Americans so different from New Yorkers. Fittingly, New York has never been the subject of one of Updike's long works. Henry Bech, an Updike alter ego,* is an example of what might have happened to Updike had he remained in New York. In "Bech Noir" Henry Bech is so responsive to New York critics that he systematically murders four of them. Updike visualized as his ideal reader an ordinary person living somewhere near Kansas, not a New York sophisticate like Darryl Van Horne,* whose materialistic vulgarity and egocentric deviltry allow Updike to satirize The City as he never ridiculed middle America (*W*). Besides these reasons for his departure from New York for Ipswich, Updike had found that his psoriasis improved with sunbathing, so relocating near a beach seemed a good idea. Perhaps he undertook the change because he was a small-town boy who thought that Shillington* was the center of his world ("The Dogwood Tree: A Boyhood"* [*AP*]).

Updike's departure suggests similarities to that of his mother's relocation in 1945 of her parents, husband and son from Shillington to Plowville,* and her later urging her son to leave Pennsylvania for Harvard.* The improvement of Updike's life was a crucial determinant in each case. Yet Updike did not reject New York, any more than he rejected Shillington once he moved to Plowville and Ipswich.* Updike keeps a New York office to confer with his Knopf editor Judith Jones and her assistant Ken Schneider, to discuss his writing for the *New Yorker*, to attend professional meetings like those of the American Academy of Arts and Letters,* to lecture at the Morgan Library, to read his work at many locations and to write about art openings at the Metropolitan Museum of Art, the Museum of Modern Art and other museums. Leaving New York enabled him to balance his cosmopolitan interests and his need for privacy. It also enabled him to move on from depictions of the lost pastoral* world to a surer hold on the realism he often counterpoised to the pastoral. As critic Larry Taylor says, Updike moved "from Pastoral Olinger to anti-pastoral Manhattan," enabling him to "delve into the most fundamental themes and issues of Modern American life" (Taylor, *PA*, 135). As Updike remarked thirty years after leaving The City, New York has "constant usefulness; it makes you glad you live somewhere else." In fact, "New York takes so much energy as to leave none for any other kind of being" (*OJ*). *See* **Scenes from the Fifties**.

Bibliography: Updike, "Is New York Inhabitable?" (*OJ*); "The Glittering City," "One Big Bauble" (*MM*); Taylor, *PA*.

The *New Yorker*. A magazine of New York* happenings, the *New Yorker* was started by Harold Ross in 1925 as a weekly of sharp observation and Big City attitudes. The *New Yorker* style has been described by Roderick Cook in a review of *MuS* as "poetical, comical, tragical, pastoral, metropolitan." Its fiction has been drolly defined as having no beginning, no ending and an undistributed middle.

In 1944 Updike's aunt, Mary Updike,* gave his family a Christmas subscription to the magazine, and he was immediately captivated by its format— the signature at the end of each piece rather than on a contents page, and the title font, evoking, as he said, "the twenties and Persia and the future all at once." Everything about the *New Yorker* was "very cool" (Plath, *CU*). It "knew best, *was* best, and . . . its pages were far above all other possible display cases" (*OJ*). It became, as he said in a tribute to an editor there, "the object of my fantasies and aspirations." Yet, Updike allowed, the *New Yorker* stories might be "just a new kind of slick" ("The Short Story and *MM*"). At Updike's request James Thurber* sent him a drawing of a dog that still hangs in his study as a "talisman." Later, the *New Yorker*'s writers and cartoonists, particularly Thurber, Robert Benchley, Ogden Nash and Morris Bishop, influenced Updike's cartoons, fiction and light verse* that he published in his Shillington* High School newspaper, the *Chatterbox*,* and in the *Harvard Lampoon*.* Like his mother, Linda Hoyer Updike,* whose stories were regularly rejected by the *New Yorker* for a while, Updike sent cartoons, stories and poems that were rejected. For instance, "The Lucid Eye in Silver Town" (*AP*) was carefully dismissed: "Stories about visitors to New York City made [William Shawn] nervous" ("The Short Story and I *MM*").

But when the magazine published Updike's poem "Duet with Muffled Brake Drums" in June 1954, Updike was launched on what he calls his "professional career" and was invited inside the offices of the magazine before leaving for Oxford,* England, that year. The story "Friends from Philadelphia" (published on October 30, 1954) showed *New Yorker* editor Katharine White that he had great promise, and when they met in Oxford that summer she offered him a job writing for the "Talk of the Town" section. He contributed items like "Central Park," "Beer Can" and "Eclipse," joining fellow contributors Dorothy Parker, Thurber, Eudora Welty, Edmund Wilson,* John O'Hara, John Cheever,* J. D. Salinger* and Vladimir Nabokov.* (Updike remarked that Nabokov had called its pseudonym, *The Beau and the Butterfly*, "the kindest magazine in the world.") Parker and Thurber, along with Benchley and Alexander Woollcott, occupied the Algonquin Round Table of wits, "a teen-age fascination" for Updike (*OJ*), but he was not attracted to the magazine for its literary society, perhaps because, as he discovered, "civilization and its discontents was the overall topic." Though he left the magazine in April 1957, a fortunate change in editors enabled him to write about the last game played by Ted Williams, "Hub Fans Bid Kid Adieu,"* an often-reprinted classic of sports* reportage and perhaps his best work in that genre.

Updike's relation to the *New Yorker*'s editors reveals his admiration, respect and understanding of its goals. He has praised the magazine's fiction editors as well as poetry editors Howard Moss and Alice Quinn, and he has written a spirited review of a biography of Katharine White. In "Three *New Yorker* Stalwarts" Updike wrote touching remembrances of two editors who had recently passed away, William Shawn and William Maxwell. For Shawn, Updike wrote, "you wanted to produce" what he called "the real thing." William Maxwell, we learn, found that real thing when he spotted, in Updike's lunch chat, a story, which Updike then wrote; "The Alligators" was then printed. Updike also explains how Maxwell extracted from a "killed" story of thirty pages six or seven that were publishable. He supplies a deft, celebratory portrait of another editor, Brendan Gill. No doubt his respect for such editors caused him to accept requests for changes to the end of the story "Trust Me" (*TM*) and the poem "Earthworm" (*TP*; *CP*, "Notes"), even though the poem's original draft contained what he called "his philosophy."

Updike has continued to publish hundreds of poems, stories, reviews and articles and a few drawings in the *New Yorker*. The writers Updike indicates as his current favorites are often writers from this magazine—Jorge Luis Borges,* Donald Barthelme, Saul Bellow,* Ann Beattie, Alice Munro, Anne Tyler and Nicholson Baker among them. The magazine revived in him a desire to write a mystery story in 1960, "Murder Makes the Magazine."* Despite changes of ownership in 1994 and of editors, prompting shifts in viewpoint and format, Updike continues to appear in its pages with regularity. He feels that the new *New Yorker* is "more highly colored, and very legitimately they're looking for stories that reflect how people live now." Though Updike is sometimes criticized for reflecting the style of the magazine too perfectly, his career indicates that the magazine's style is but one of many he has brought to perfection.

Updike wrote an introduction to *The New Yorker Book of Covers*. He mentions the *New Yorker* in *Couples* and describes an Edward Koren cartoon in *RV* and a Charles Addams* cover from the magazine in *IB*. Addams included a caricature of Updike for his dust jacket of Brendan Gill's reminiscence of the magazine, *Here at The New Yorker*. The foremost *New Yorker* photographer, Richard Avedon, has photographed Updike. The weekly was satirized in *Snooze*, with a parody of Updike's mythic style from *C*.

Bibliography: Updike, *Talk from the Fifties* (Northridge, CA: Lord John Press, 1979); "Talk of a Tired Town" (*PP*); "The Glittering City," "The Short Story and I," "Three *New Yorker* Stalwarts," "Smiling Bob," "Verminous Pedestrians and Car Tormented Streets," "Self Interview" (*MM*); James Thurber, *The Years with Ross* (Boston: Little, Brown and Company, 1959); Roderick Cook, "*The Music School*," *Harper's* 233 (Sept. 1966): 113; Brendan Gill, *Here at the New Yorker* (New York: Random House, 1975); Brian James Nerney, "Katharine S. White, 'New Yorker' Editor: Her Influence on the 'New Yorker' and on American Literature," *Dissertation Abstracts International* 43/11A (1982): 3637, University of Minnesota.

Ngo Dinh Diem (1901–1963). Ngo Dinh Diem, the president of South Vietnam* (1955–1963), was supported by the United States in order to check the incursion of Ho Chi Minh* after the division of Vietnam into two countries in 1954. Diem drew U.S. ire when he refused to hold free elections, as agreed upon by the Geneva Treaty. He was assassinated by a 1963 coup, possibly American inspired. Ngo and the coup are mentioned during a parlor game in *Couples* when Foxy Whitman* uses his name, playfully declining, "Diem. *Dies. Diei, diei, diem.*" Such reduction of crucial historical persons reveals the insular egotism of the Tarbox couples. Updike felt a personal need to support the South Vietnamese leaders from Diem to Nguyen Cao Ky to Nguyen Van Thieu, like them or not (*SC*). See **Kennedy, John F.**

Ninety-ninth and Riverside. The New York* residence of Henry Bech* at Ninety-ninth and Riverside is mentioned in "Bech Takes Pot Luck" (*BB*). Updike lived south of his alter ego* at Eighty-fifth Street and Riverside Drive from 1955 to 1957 while working for the *New Yorker,* but Bech moved south of Updike's address when Bech moved to West Seventy-second Street after leaving Westchester and his wife Bea Latchett* ("White on White" [*BIB*]). See **Updike, John, Residences.**

Ninotchka. Ninotchka is a 1939 film* by Ernst Lubitsch (1892–1947) starring Greta Garbo. In "The Wallet" (*TM*) Fulham watches it on television* with his granddaughter when he misplaces his wallet and, for a time, his identity. The film's plot concerns a romance between an American and a Russian woman and her seduction by American capitalism during the depression. It thus recalls "Bech in Russia" and "The Bulgarian Poetess" (*BB*). The movie was remade as the musical *Silk Stockings*, with Fred Astaire and Cyd Charisse (1957).

Nobel Prize in Literature. The Nobel Prize in Literature is given annually from the fund of Swedish inventor and philanthropist Alfred Nobel, whose will stipulated that the literature award should belong to the most outstanding work of an "idealistic tendency." Certainly Updike is a writer of "idealistic tendency" because of his continual concern with spiritual matters (he won the Campion Award in 1997, given for outstanding cultural contributions by a Christian writer), passionate dedication to his art, and sensitive portrayals of a great many persons from car salesmen to African dictators, from modern-day witches to ministers* and Jewish novelists. Since several American novelists have been recipients of the Nobel Prize (Sinclair Lewis,* Pearl Buck, William Faulkner,* Ernest Hemingway,* John Steinbeck, Toni Morrison and Saul Bellow*), Updike seems a logical contender. He has been mentioned as a candidate since about 1988, when Truman Capote, asked if Updike might win, casually said, "He probably will." Though Updike has said in an Internet interview, "I'm 66 and Nobel Laureates tend to be in their early 60's," in "Updike and I" he remarked, thinking of his "writer self," "I treasure his few prizes." Yet he has said, "I try to console myself for not winning by describing the hell of exposure that accompanies winning it," the exposure of Henry Bech.*

During the awards month, October 1998, Updike caused a stir with the publication of "Bech and the Bounty of Sweden" in *BaB*, in which Henry Bech receives the Nobel Prize for Literature for 1999 by default. This seemed to be Updike's response for not having won, and some, apparently forgetting that Bech was hardly Updike's spokesman, interpreted Bech's attitude toward the "celebrity of prizes" as Updike's attempt to demean the Nobel's importance. In interviews* Updike remarked that he was not a real candidate because he is male, white and past the prime age of most winners. He elaborated, "It's a prize I didn't think much about until my mid 50's." At that time a German critic assured him that he would win because he "created character." Considering Updike's fondness for awards* he has won and his dedication to daily, uninterrupted work, he may be conflicted about winning the Nobel.

The "exposure" of which Updike has spoken is deftly described in "Bech and the Bounty of Sweden" (*BaB*). Bech at first is shocked that he has been selected for the Nobel Prize because he considered Norman Mailer* and Philip Roth* as more worthy. The media consider him an unknown. Bech is at least able to remark that "the Nobel Prize has become so big, such a celebrity among prizes, that no one is worthy to win it, and the embarrassed winner can shelter his unworthiness behind the unworthiness of everyone else." His ironic acceptance speech, "The Nature of Human Existence," is "given" by his baby daughter Golda, who says "Hi!" to the notables, moves her bowels and waves goodbye. Its brevity, simplicity and directness make it a very powerful statement, which some have taken to be Updike's rejection of the Nobel Prize. Yet the story does reveal the fact that the Nobel laureate becomes an instant celebrity and instantly accountable for his ascension, as well as his way of spending the prize. In a whirligig of interviews, Bech recognizes that his own dedication to writing is of little concern to anyone; only his prominence matters. When he learns that he was not the committee's first choice, he is chastened. When he learns that one Swedish luminary prefers to read him in French, he is perplexed. However, since Bech makes a serious effort to produce the required speech, he does not take the prize lightly; the speech he and Golda deliver is certainly a summary of the meaning of life in the manner of Lucky from *Waiting for Godot*, by former laureate Samuel Beckett.* The reader of "Bech Noir" (*BaB*) understands, as the Swedish Academy cannot, that it has, ironically, given the prize to a writer who has murdered four of his hostile critics.*

Bibliography: Updike, "Updike and I" (*MM*); Michael Skube, "Updike Has Moved beyond the Nobel, Work by Work," *Atlanta Constitution* 27 Sept. 1998; Ethan Bronner, "John Updike Returns to His Source," *New York Times* 6 Nov. 1998: A-14.

The Novel. Updike has described himself as "a conservative realist writer" because, as he says, "there's a kind of feedback from the world in general that I need to feel." Though he originally devoted much of his time to writing short fiction,* the novel has become increasingly his mode of choice because it allows him the world's feedback through numerous characters* and subjects. Above all, such feedback enables Updike to act as a witness of what he called "God's fingerprints." As he put it, "A novel begins with a wish to make a statement of a fairly large order about the society." For example, he realized that the presence of ex–basketball* stars littering Shillington* said something about American society, and *RR* gave him the breadth to discover what that was. Another statement occurs in *IB*, in which Updike wishes to comment on the changing style of religious faith in America. The great flexibility of the novel is a constant source of pleasure for Updike, enabling him to apply whatever content he chooses through whatever form he can devise.

Updike, as he related, once asked a literary critic if he, Updike, was a postmodern novelist. "In which work?" asked the critic. The answer pointed to Updike's ability to adopt other orientations toward the novel besides that of a conservative realist. Thus in *C* he can integrate myth* and realism, in *B* write in a narrative voice* that sounds as if it is translated from older Portuguese, and in MF integrate (and undermine) the literary theory of deconstruction into a modern academic novel, a near-past story of domestic crisis, and aspects of the life of President James Buchanan.*

To examine content first, since for Updike everything observed testifies to God's creation, fiction provides, through the microcosmic depiction of the smallest detail and the subtlest analysis of human feelings, a record that becomes a form of praise. As Updike has said, "It's my intention to describe the world as the Psalmists did" (Plath *CU*). His minute observations of nature* testify to this, making him a kind of modern Henry David Thoreau* (*TE*). But as he indicated in *PP*, a streetcar is as worthy as a rose of a writer's attention. His concern for the specific details of daily living has enabled him to explore a huge gallery of people. In *Couples* he treats ten families, and in *IB* an immense assortment of characters. At the same time, the novel offers Updike greater space for extended analysis of character development and change, as in the growth to stardom of Essie Wilmot/Alma DeMott* (*IB*) or the continual revelations concerning Alf Clayton* (*MF*), not to mention the development through four novels of Harry "Rabbit" Angstrom.* His comprehensive exploration of institutions, from college to church and from car lot to farm, has shown how human beings organize their energy and how they create waste. Situating his characters within historical events as palpable as the daily paper enables Updike to understand how the management of human life has been achieved over time (*PF*, *Couples*, *Coup*, *MS*, *IB*, *RA* and *RV*). As a consequence of this immersion in daily life, Updike creates maps and calendars* of events that fix his people in the here and now, and that often reveal how human beings and what they create steadily wind down, like the universe. Sometimes the power of history* is so strong—he has said that each of his works takes place during an inferable presidential adminis-tration—that history threatens to determine the course of his characters' lives, as Dilvo Ristoff has argued. Yet the attention to placement of his characters in time and space also produces attention to repeated actions of special importance that gives them the force of ritual. Efforts to ritualize ordinary experience through social situations, sports* and sex are never en-tirely satisfying. Despite their efforts to believe in what Rabbit calls "the thing that wants me to find it" (*RR*), his people often find their secularized religious strivings unsatisfying. This might take place over decades, as with Rabbit, or in a flash, as with Clarence Wilmot.*

The form of an Updike novel is unpredictable, making the appearance of one a source of surprise and discovery. From the beginning Updike has shown an interest in expanding the novel's form, and he has referred to his enjoyment in probing its limits. However, he could not be called an exper-imentalist, constantly looking for novelty for its own sake. His first novel, *PF*, set its narrative in the near future and concerned the impersonal treat-ment of the very old. Updike later called it his science-fiction* novel. After nearly forty years Updike produced another novel with science-fiction fea-tures, *TE*. Yet no one could have guessed that the young novelist making his living entirely from his pen would follow the success of *PF* with a novel that investigated how the frustrations of an ex–basketball star led to domestic tragedy (*RR*). Nor would anyone anticipate that his third novel would blend mythical figures to ordinary high-school figures. Though *C* won the Na-tional Book Award, Updike had no interest in repeating this device either. Instead, his next novel, *OF*, provided a Jamesian* analysis of a family.

One might have expected that the next novel in the Rabbit saga, *RRed*, would be in the mode of *RR*, realistic and would contain a wealth of material from popular culture* and contemporary history, but few foresaw that the writer who specialized in domestic tension would fill *RRed* with a lunar landing, violent sex, drug* addiction, the Vietnam* War and racial hatred. Beyond such surprising content was also a thorough demonstration of how Updike could keep a "mass of images moving forward," one of his major ambitions in writing novels. The imagery* of the moon and of Vietnam propels dozens of tropes forming solid strands that bind the novel together. The third and fourth novels of the Rabbit saga are equally surprising in the "buoyancy," to use Updike's word, of *RIR* and the unremitting tension and black humor* of *RaR*. Few novelists would dare to take so many different directions in their early work, and fewer would revisit their characters at ten-year intervals (RA), update Nathaniel Hawthorne's* *Scarlet Letter* in three novels (*MS, RV, S.*) or write about a writer utterly unlike himself in two dozen pieces (*BB, BIB, BaB*) that have the continuity of a novel, or "quasi-novels," as Updike called them, borrowing a term from Vladimir Nabokov.*

Updike's other interests in the form of fiction include what he termed a "romance" (*Marry*), a work of magic realism* (*B*), a novel about a country resembling Ethiopia in the voice of its black leader (*Coup*), a novel enclosing the life of President James Buchanan (*MF*), a family saga (*IB*), a gothic satire (*W*) and, within the "*Scarlet Letter* trilogy," *MS*, a series of journal entries, and *S.*, each replete with esoteric religious information. The concluding novel of this trilogy, *RV*, features a narrator apparently capable of extrasensory perception. *TE* uses science fiction and myth, while *GC* is set in sixteenth-century Denmark. Finally, Updike made a novel from a short story (*Couples*) and turned his research for a novel into a play about President Buchanan, later recycled as *MF*.

Updike's choice of point of view, narrative voice and structure are thus all dependent upon the specific requirements of the individual work, and this makes generalization about his conception of the novel very difficult. It seems, however, that he relies upon dualisms* to dramatize oppositions. For example, in *RV*, he opposes an amateur scientist, Dale Kohler,* and a religion professor, Roger Lambert,* yet the scientist uses his talent to discover God, while the ex-minister prefers a God who will not reveal Himself. Thus Updike's characters are often "centaurs" like Rabbit, rooted in the here and now but longing for ultimate truth. Since they frequently think that the ecstasy of sex provides an analogy to spiritual intuition, Updike's dualistic people, generally men, are balanced between "groin and brain pan."

Updike is sometimes criticized for having problems with plotting. Defenders say that this is an aspect of his training as a *New Yorker** writer, particularly in leaving his plots open-ended. But since plot and character are interrelated, questions of plot often appear to be questions of character motivation and resolution. Readers were perplexed by such things as Stephen Connor's* assumption that John Hook* and not the more obvious Gregg was responsible for instigating Conner's stoning. Did George Caldwell* die at the end of *C*? Did Rabbit return to his wife Janice Angstrom* because his humbling of Ruth Leonard Byer* had destroyed their affair, or because he was concerned about the birth of his child, and to where does he run at the end of *RR*? Who organized the wife swapping in *RIR*? Janice? Thelma Harrison*? Was Rabbit's pursuit of his child by Ruth a red-herring plot, since he apparently refused Ruth's statement that she had had the abortion* and evaded conclusive evidence of Annabelle Byer's* paternity at the end of *RaR* after wondering about it for twenty years? Why the ambiguous pronoun "our" at the end of *OF*? Read one way, it shows resolution of Joey Robinson's* problem with his mother, but read another way, it intensifies it. Why does Angela Hanema* follow Piet Hanema's* direction and sleep with Freddy Thorne* (*Couples*)? Did Jerry Conant* in fact return to his wife or not? Which of the three endings we are given is the preferred one in *Marry*? Why does Rev. Tom Marshfield* apparently contradict his own conversion by reverting to his promiscuous ways in sleeping with Ms. Prynne* (*MS*)? How can the witches turn from conventional living to murder and back again so easily, and was Ed Parsley's* girlfriend, Dawn Polanski, a witch? Was Jenny Gabriel (*W*)? Is Esther Lambert* pregnant by Roger or Dale at the end of *RV*? Why was Dale so crushed by Kriegman's rebuttal to his "Deus" project? Were Dale and Esther lovers, or was this Lambert's fantasy (*RV*)? How is it that the change in color of Isabel Leme* and Tristâo Raposo* is never really apparent to her uncle (*B*)? Why did Clarence Wilmot lose his faith, and why did Clark DeMott* take so long to realize the madness of Jesse Smith* (*IB*)? Did Ben Turnbull* actually kill his wife, or did she transform into a deer? Were Deirdre and Doreen somehow the same person (*TE*)? Such questions stimulate understanding of the total meaning of each work, but they indicate Updike's penchant for mystification of motivation and complication of plot. As he remarked, a novel is a kind of game that has its secrets, and a mystery stands at the center of most of his fiction (Plath, *CU*).

Updike's generally impartial narrative voice has prompted critics like Ralph Wood to accuse him of failing to take moral stands. Updike seems aware of this when he characterizes himself as a writer "disoriented" by the social unrest of the 1960s (*RA*, Introduction). Yet if his novels do not fan the flames of social protest, they clearly criticize human behavior and modern institutions. Consider the stinging descriptions in his novels of religious hypocrisy (*S.*, *RV*, *B*), religion* (*Couples*, *MS*, *RV*, *S.*, *IB*), art* (*W*), business (*RIR*, *RaR*, *TE*), academia* (*C*, *MF*, *RV*), politics (*Coup*, *RRed*, *BD*, *MF*, *GC*), medicine (*RRed*, *RaR*), journalism* (*RRed*, *W*), the film* industry (*IB*), the welfare state (*PF*), upper classes (*B*), sports* ethics (*RR*), the literary life (*BB*, *BIB*, *BaB*), war (*RRed*, *W*, *TE*), sexual experimentation (*Couples*, *RRed*, *RIR*, *W*), family life (*RA*) and adultery* (*Couples*, *RA*, *Marry*, *BB*, *MF*, *MS*, *RV*, *S.*, *B*, *W*, *TE*, *GC*). A great many stories, articles and poems could also be placed in these categories. Updike's protest voice is there. More direct statements of Updike's views are to be found, naturally, in his essays and reviews, particularly *SC*.

But the novel is also used to indicate possible moral reform through re-
spect for the past and craftsmanship (*PF, Couples, RR*), through love (*Marry,
OF, Couples*) and through honoring the mythic in the mundane (*C, Couples,
RR*) and the spiritual in the commonplace (*PF, RV*) and in nature (*TE*).
Sometimes such things are seen more clearly in the stories like "Pigeon
Feathers" (*PigF*), "Harv Is Plowing Now" (*MuS*), "When Everyone Was
Pregnant" (*MW*), "The Music School" (*MuS*) and *TF*. It might be unwise
to separate the novels from the short fiction* for a fuller understanding of
Updike's middle ground between satire* and protest. Updike's major "reform" might lie in his insistence on looking at the world with such care that
it seems in spite of all not beyond salvaging, its intricate beauty always there,
as in *TE*, to reassure attentive perception. For the writer whose art seeks to
replicate such intricacy, novels may be, as "Updike" told Henry Bech, "crystallizations of visceral hopefulness exuded as a slow paste which in the glitter
of print regains something of the original, absolute gaiety" (Plath, *CU*). His
advice to future American novelists is to avoid becoming "slaves to the autobiographical," because the American novel "must force its imagination outward, try to stretch it as much as possible without losing that urgency of the
person writing it" while realizing that "the Gutenbergian age is in its twilight" (Plath, *CU*).

Bibliography: Updike, "Bech Meets Me," "The Future of the Novel" (*PP*); "The
Importance of Fiction" (*OJ*); "Fiction: A Dialogue" (*MM*); Ralph C. Wood, "Into
the Void: Updike's Sloth and America's Religion," *Christian Century* 24 Apr. 1996:
452–55, 457.

O

Odd Jobs: Essays and Criticism (New York: Knopf, 1991). *OJ*, Updike's fourth book of reviews and criticism, is divided, like *PP*, into two parts: "Fairly Personal," with several essays and a playlet; and "Mostly Literary," several times as long as the first part, containing tributes to Edmund Wilson* and John Cheever,* speeches and introductions, several pieces on Philip Roth,* criticism of writing in English, French, Russian and other languages, criticism of avant-garde writing under the heading "Hyperreality" and several reviews of biographies. As in *PP*, Updike offers remarks on his life and work in an appendix, "Literarily Personal," half the size of the first part. It does not include interview segments, as in *PP* and *HS*, but instead is a composite of responses to questions, prefaces and two unsigned "Talk of the Town" pieces. The book's form is thus "from the fairly personal into the wide heavens of other people's books and then back to the grassy earth of the personal again" (*OJ*).

In his "Preface" Updike calls his title *OJ* "honest labeling" and describes how his vocation as a writer caused him to answer requests for "a few paragraphs" on subjects from the Gospels to golf.* He thus styles himself as a journeyman writer who enjoys testing himself against unusual entreaties, enjoying the "frequent reassurance of proofs coming and going, of postage and phoning, of input and output." He calculates that his life spent reviewing has constituted "ninety-two five-day weeks." He styles his reviewer's persona as that of a "lawyer in the family." Having apparently well earned it, Updike eschews the title "man of letters" given him by reviewer Michiko Kakutani because it seems to him that "men of letters live in limbo."

The first part of *OJ*, "Fairly Personal," describes Updike's trip to Finland, followed by a fictionalized account of his agonized marching in a parade. In the fictionalized "First Wives and Trolley Cars" William Farnham, like Peter Caldwell,* looks back on himself at age eleven or twelve delivering movie circulars in Wenrich's Corner (Shillington*) and blends his thoughts on first wives with memories of a trolley ride with his mother. Updike transformed his story "Your Lover Just Called" into a playlet given for friends. Essays on being on television* reveal how delicious it is to be "multiplied." Updike shares his enthusiasm for a Goldie Hawn film, and he tells us what a novelist means by "lived-in space." He also describes American monuments as not immune to time's ravages. Updike views his continuous absorptions in baseball and popular culture.* He thinks that popular culture cannot be fully distinguished from high art in literature, but high art detached from popular culture would be sterile. "Reviews" explores mainly books "from across the Atlantic or south of the border," but begins Updike's American literary tributes with Edmund Wilson, the polymath critic, a precursor of Updike, whom he praises as the "most civilized voice" of the "global literary scene." Updike also pays tribute to his friend John Cheever, whose passing had led to several public and private reflections. Updike calls Cheever a man of "remarkable work" and a "celebrant." He asks in one speech for the government to cease funding the arts. In another he reflects on Herman Melville's* "war" with his audience's expectations and then explores the relation of creative imagination to the modern audience. Updike turns amusing epigrams* within a lecture that contradict his performance: "Asking a writer to lecture is like asking a knife to turn a screw." He surprises himself by admiring the "catalytic" Ralph Waldo Emerson,* whose trust in feeling seems to ignore the damage done to the social fabric (Emerson thus resembles Harry "Rabbit" Angstrom*), but he finds Emerson "immensely right" in suggesting that ego must be optimistic. He notes that William Dean Howells put his finger on fashioning literature from "common, crude material . . . the right American stuff."

In the "Introductions" Updike revisits two important interests, Franz Kafka* and Karl Barth.* He explains which of Kafka's works created the adjective "Kafkaesque," why Kafka wished his work to be destroyed, and why Kafka's letter to his father was the turning point in his career and hence in literary modernism. Updike's "Introduction" to fellow Pennsylvanian John O'Hara's *Appointment in Samarra* locates the determinants in Gibbsville that made Julian English what he was, the relationship of place to protagonist that is of deep concern to Updike in *RA*.

The section "Moralists" reveals the scholarly and insightful side of Updike, so-called Professor Updike. He treats the Gospel of Matthew with care for the text and its commentators. Perhaps surprisingly, he also includes Benjamin Franklin in the "Moralists" segment, partly because details of his life have "passed into American mythology." He finds that the "image" of Franklin "is with us still" and particularly enjoyed Franklin's scientific spoof that proposed making flatulence sweet smelling. Franklin was "a release into the Enlightenment of the energies cramped under Puritanism." For Updike, Tolstoy is the opposite kind of moralist, his journals revealing self-mortification "and a dandyish *Weltschmerz*," and Updike, always a generous critic, is uncomfortable with Tolstoy's "downright dismissive comments on other writers."

The reviews of "Americans" open with homage to Sherwood Anderson, whose notion of Americans as "twisted apples" strikes a familiar note to small-town Updike. Anderson pursued "the mystery" in "meagre lives," which suggests that he is a precursor of Updike. Of Ernest Hemingway,* Updike remarks that he was hobbled by the need to have a hero "who always acts right and looks good." He notes how Peter Taylor can find "Southern social history" in a hat, and he perceives that Kurt Vonnegut's moral outrage has become "a fireside glow." He finds in Donald Barthelme's *King* "a dazzlement of style both minimal and musical." He wonders if Joyce Carol Oates was born too late for the readership worthy of "her tireless gift of self-enthrallment" and finds that her descriptions of boxing in *You Must Remember This* make Norman Mailer's* "mere sports journalism." Among reviews of other women writers, Updike praises Cathleen Schine for her ability to depict pain and Elizabeth Thomas's creation of a lovable heroine. In Updike's reviews of books by Philip Roth he finds Roth an "exquisitist" (the word is typical of Updike's occasional daring), expending on his themes in *Zuckerman Unbound* "ever more expertness and care," making the "comic diatribes" more "finely tuned." But though Roth's *Anatomy Lesson* is "heartfelt," ultimately Updike decides that Nathan Zuckerman's inability to rise above hostile critics* weakens the novel. He also remains unpersuaded by Roth's effort in *Zuckerman Bound* to relate the hero to wider suffering and gently chides Roth for not offering more full-blooded women. Of *The Counterlife*, Updike asserts with an inventive metaphor that "reading a Roth novel becomes like riding in an overheated club car, jostled this way and that," eventually discovering that "we already *were* in this station" as Roth pushes "confessional fiction into metafiction."

Updike offers thirty pages of commentary on French writers, noting that Raymond Queneau is "Mozartian," "the least depressing of the moderns." He remarks upon the stunning power of Emmanuel Carrère's *Moustache*. In a segment on Iris Murdoch and others, Updike explains why Umberto Eco's semiotics change the way he approaches historical fiction. Iris Murdoch is "the happiest imaginer in the English-speaking world." Of Penelope Mortimer, he remarks, "I don't know when I have last read fiction that gave me such an exhilarating sensation of being scoured by the brisk, bleak truth of our human condition." He is surprised by a blacker magic realism* than expected from Gabriel García Márquez, and in reviewing Adolfo Bioy Casares he establishes the "pedigree" of magic realism. Updike's detecting "adolescent terror turned outward" suggests a gloss on "Pigeon Feathers" (*PigF*). He unveils the impact of Vladimir Nabokov* on Mario Vargas Llosa. In passing, Updike notes that detective stories, favored by Latin American writers, are the most bookish form of fiction. In the segment on "The Evil

Empire" he finds that Milan Kundera has "the reach of greatness" in *The Joke* because it supplies "geography amplified by history." Of his acquaintance Yevgeny Yevtushenko, Updike observes his "trick of self-echo," causing repetitions, and, in passing, he indicates the absurdities in the translation.

With his customary boldness and concern, Updike reviews work from "Other Countries Heard From" in another segment of "Reviews." He finds in an Albanian novelist "superb balance and unforced amplitude," but he considers an Arabic novelist "insufficiently westernized to produce a narrative that feels much like what we call a novel." However, a novel in Hebrew "shows no lack of sophistication in the ways of the literary West." He elucidates the meaning of narrative voice* in discussing a Nigerian novelist. Updike's catholicity of taste and his endless interests take him to China, Japan, Sweden, Chile and Israel as he charts the changing conceptions of what makes a novel. He pays respect to favorites: "Borges* reveals himself as a treasure"; "the Nabokov estate continues to come up with treasures," though some of Nabokov's letters reveal a tone of "offended hauteur." Throughout many reviews Updike worries the term "postmodernism" wittily, wondering if there is such a thing.

In his "Biographies" reviews Updike assumes the role of the common reader, wondering why he had trouble reading a book that had provocative facts and insights (*Cleopatra*, by Lucy Hughes-Hallet) and why he enjoyed a book with a sour subject (*Dorothy Parker* by Marion Meade). Updike reveals his own rules for writing biography, as he had offered his rules for reviewing in *PP*: the biographer should not adopt a hectoring voice and insist on cause and effect (*The Nightmare of Reason: A Life of Franz Kafka*, by Ernst Pawel); should be allowed free access to holders of material when the subject is safely dead (*T. S. Eliot: A Life*, by Peter Ackroyd); should not criticize the subject unduly (*Onward and Upward: A Biography of Katharine S. White*, by Linda H. Davis); should avoid sour tones or sneers (*Dorothy Parker: What Fresh Hell Is This?* by Marion Meade and *Artful Partners: Bernard Berenson and Joseph Duveen* by Colin Simpson); and should avoid using deconstruction as a methodology (*Cleopatra*, by Lucy Hughes-Hallet).

In the "Hard Facts" reviews Updike queries the forces of utility and play in mankind, examining the apparently trivial pencil and the stupendously original prehistoric painting. The essays echo his decision as a young artist to ride "a thin pencil point" into "unborn hearts" ("The Dogwood Tree: A Boyhood"*). He expresses wonder that science* has so easily provided acceptable myths about so much in our modern belief systems, and he reviews works on biology and the computer that clearly developed from his concerns in *RV*.

Finally, "Literarily Personal" provides a description of his life at Harvard,* his taste in reading, his response to bad reviews and the modern writers he most enjoys, like John Barth, Philip Roth, Cynthia Ozick, Joyce Carol Oates and Thomas Pynchon. He also describes how "obscenities" were excised from *RR*, provides inside remarks on the inceptions of *W*, *RV*, *S*. and *RA*, lists the favorite novels of his own oeuvre (*C, Coup, RV* and *S.*) and provides a touching re-creation of the aftermath of his mother's death. *See Assorted Prose;* **Criticism by Updike;** *Hugging the Shore; Just Looking; More Matter; Picked-Up Pieces.*

Bibliography: Schiff, *JU.*

Oedipal Complex. *See* **Freud, Sigmund.**

Of the Farm (New York: Knopf, 1965). Updike's novel *OF* completes his expressed desire to write a series of novels based on his family and set in Pennsylvania. *PF* concerned a character modeled on his maternal grandfather, John Hoyer*; *C* used an analogue for his father, Wesley Updike; and *OF,* which Updike has called a "sequel" to *C* in *MM,* focused upon his mother, Linda Updike.* As Updike observed, *OF* is set in the same world as that of *C,* "but after the centaur died." (One might squeeze *RR* into this list of family-based novels, since it uses an alter ego* of Updike.)

OF is a subtle investigation of three generations, of a protracted struggle for freedom from emotional bondage and of the philosophical meaning of the relation of men and women. The novel contains few dramatic moments and thus resembles in tone *PF* rather than *C* or *RR,* though like them the essential conflict focuses on the hero's need to free himself from Oedipal bondage. Its closure arrives oddly, with a sermon* at the novel's end concerning Adam and Eve. Updike had originally written this sermon for publication in the *Ladies' Home Journal* in 1964. When it wasn't published, Updike explained, "I used the novel as a mounting for it."

The narrative concerns advertising man Joey Robinson,* thirty-five, who, after leaving his wife and three children, visits his mother's farm in order to introduce his new bride, Peggy* and her eleven-year-old son, Richard. Although she had never liked Joey's first wife, Joan Robinson, Mrs. Mary Robinson* acts as though she had, and so the visit becomes a psychological conflict, with Joey torn between his mother and Peggy. Mrs. Robinson subtly undermines Peggy and leads her son into traps of old affection based on family "myth." Richard's question as they arrive at the farm—"What's the point of a farm nobody farms?"—is answered obliquely through the psychological conflict: to keep alive the myth Mrs. Robinson had created about how she saved her family by leading an exodus from city distractions to a pastoral* world where Joey could become a poet. But from her viewpoint, his life is tragic because he rejected her myth by not becoming a poet and by going to New York,* where, she asserts, God cannot live. Mrs. Robinson takes Joey's action as a rebuke of her own way of life, and she thinks that he is now forcing her to accept his myth of the good life—advertising, New York and Peggy. Accepting Peggy would defeat Mrs. Robinson's ideals. Since she realizes that Joey's need for Peggy is as powerful as her need for the farm, giving in to his love for Peggy will cause her to metaphorically lose the farm.

Because of his bond to his mother, Joey aligns himself with her myth for a while. He betrays Peggy by agreeing with his mother that Peggy is "stupid," and, prompted by the insecurity his mother makes him feel with Peggy, he constructs a myth of Peggy's sexual promiscuity. Though Joey does resist his mother's family myths, which are connected to her many photos of Joey, at the same time, he takes on the image of his father by dressing in his clothes. Joey's father is the novel's absent presence. Despite his hatred of farming, Joey mows the farm, as his father would do, but he mows as if plowing nature* sexually, while Mrs. Robinson embraces the land delicately.

But Joey's action demonstrates to his mother what he cannot discuss, his physical response to Peggy and its diminishment with Joan. He realizes that his mother's effort to intensify his guilt over leaving his family is a disguise for her own manipulation of him. Thus Updike creates a centripetal pull toward mother and guilt and a centrifugal push toward freedom and Peggy. Joey and his mother come to realize that though the past must be honored, change is the rule of life, just as change of seasons rules the farm. Gradually, after reminiscences over photos, a discussion of how Mrs. Robinson sacrificed herself for her husband's freedom and an analysis of Mrs. Robinson's tantrum, Mrs. Robinson accomodates herself to Joey's choices. Yet these accommodations are so difficult that she has a heart attack as Joey leaves.

Nevertheless, the narrative ends with some sense of resolution. Joey is now more comfortable with Peggy, who is convinced that Mrs. Robinson has resigned herself to their marriage. Yet Joey and his mother retain differences of opinion that are stated obliquely through their discussion of a Sunday sermon they attend concerning Adam and Eve. This sermon, derived from Karl Barth,* teaches that man seeks immortality abstractly, while woman's fertility incarnates the future concretely. Theologically, these ideas are embodied in Christ's Incarnation, spirit and body in one being. Thus men and women have a spiritual, as well as physical, need for one another, though the sermon argues that love is a struggle since men and women do not always see this. The biblical story seems to transcend the mother's myth and the son's resolution. Each has come closer to unifying her or his feminine and masculine selves during the weekend on the farm.

OF incorporates many of the themes of Updike's three previous novels. As John Hook* (PF) found his freedom cramped by the strictures of the welfare state, so Joey finds himself pressed to discover himself by reformulating his position within the community of the farm. Joey Robinson's life appears to be an alternative for young Peter Caldwell's.* At the end of *C*, George Caldwell* had tried to align Peter with a friend who had promised to get him a job in advertising; Peter rejected this (Caldwell infers that his silence means "Go to hell"), and at the end of the novel Peter is seen to be instead an artist living in New York with a mistress. Peter's life thus appears to be what Mrs. Robinson wished for Joey. As Peter after many years re-discovered his love for his father by creating a mythology about him, so Joey discovers that some ties to his mother warp him, but others wrap remarkable presents. As Harry "Rabbit" Angstrom* sought something first-rate that or-dinary life denied, Joey discovers in that ordinary life something capable of helping him define himself and understand women and his relation to their power. If Rev. Jack Eccles* condemns Rabbit's hypocrisy for elevating sexual desire into a spiritual pursuit, Joey seeks in sexuality a personal liberation, and he finds biblical support for this.

Updike's first four novels created a four-sided vision of the context of self-definition: within the traditional and modern community (PF); through in-tuitions of excellence that run counter to diminished social expectations (RR); through a child's vision of the adult world as containing larger-than-life mys-teries that he understands only upon exploration as a mature person (*C*); and through challenging myths, Joey's own as well as his mother's (OF). The four novels contrast a tawdry material world against striving for immaterial values, and each context expresses hope, however subdued, of the possible triumph of spirit over matter, freedom over coercion. Updike has suggested that these characters learn how to bless one another, and he has explained that the epigraph* from Jean-Paul Sartre indicates the novel's central theme: desiring your own freedom requires that you desire everyone else's. *OF* re-veals the painful process of learning how to do this. For Joey, clarifying the Oedipal bonds that entangle him and recognizing the diminishment he has created for the women in his life begin his education in freedom. If Joey was an alter ego for Updike, as Rabbit and Peter Caldwell were, one could understand why Updike disclosed that he felt "embarrassed" about *OF* and never read it again. This novella, however, remains one of his most suc-cessful and absorbing works, worthy of "best" ranking by critic Donald Greiner.

Bibliography: Taylor, *PA*; Alison Lurie, "Witches and Fairies: Fitzgerald to Up-dike," *New York Review of Books* 17 (2 Dec. 1971): 6, 8–11; Markle, *FL*; Hunt, *JU*; Detweiler, *JU*; Greiner, *JU*; Schiff, *JU*.

Olinger Stories (New York: Vintage, 1964). Ten of these eleven stories of *OS*, set in fictional Olinger, Pennsylvania, had been previously collected in *SD* and *PigF*; one story, "In Football Season," was later collected in *MuS*. Olinger was modeled on Shillington, Pennsylvania,* Updike's home town, which is transformed into a pastoral* world that asks you to stay; Updike explains in the "Foreword" that the name should be pronounced "O-linger," emphasizing the lost past, a pastoral view applied to a suburban town in his early fiction. Updike has arranged the stories as a chronology for a "collec-tive hero" from adolescence to marriage. The organization had a personal meaning for Updike: when the stories were included in the English Penguin edition, he admitted that he arranged them to dimly echo "the shape of my life." Updike further notes that his implied theme is "We are rewarded unexpectedly," and the selected stories show how those rewards have a place in God's plan in "Pigeon Feathers," express realizations of the need to break from the family in "Flight," address the complications of adult life just beyond adolescence in "A Sense of Shelter," describe the joy of being useful to others in "The Happiest I've Been," evoke nostalgia for lost innocence in "The Persistence of Desire" and reveal how to accept birth and death* in "Packed Dirt, Churchgoing, a Dying Cat, a Traded Car." Formally, the stories move from realism to semiautobiography and folk history ("The Blessed Man of Boston, My Grandmother's Thimble, and Fanning Island") and the lyrical and Proustian* ("In Football Season"). Olinger was also used as the setting of *C*, in which the students spell out the letters of the word, emphasizing the "L" as "Hell," "a school tradition," a contrast to the narrator's nostalgia for a lost world.

Bibliography: Taylor, *PA*; Richard Michael Ready, " 'Not Only'—An Examination of Abstraction in the Writings of John Updike, with a Particular Emphasis on the Olinger Narratives," *Dissertation Abstracts International* 36/11A (1975): 7415, New York University; Jerome Klinkowitz, "John Updike's America," *North American Review* 265 (Sept. 1980): 229–39; Robert M. Luscher, "John Updike's Olinger Stories: New Light among the Shadows," *Journal of the Short Story in English* 11 (Autumn 1988): 99–117.

Ollenbach, Elvira. A sales representative at Springer Motors,* Elvira Ollenbach has been hired by Harry "Rabbit" Angstrom* because he knows that female buyers might prefer doing business with a woman. Young and attractive, Elvira shows little romantic interest in Rabbit, but he wonders if she is his son Nelson Angstrom's* lover. Elvira is knowledgeable about baseball, to Rabbit's displeasure, particularly when she rejects his idolizing attitude toward Phillies star home-run hitter and future Hall of Famer Mike Schmidt. To Rabbit, Mike Schmidt's retirement has the class of a champion, something he clearly wishes to emulate (and later does). Elvira sees his retirement only as weakening the team. Their conversation thus shows the conflict of the old individualism and the new corporate emphasis on team play. Toyota's representative Natsume Shimada* flirts with Elvira by asking her questions about tennis and ultimately lures her away from Rabbit's troubled Springer Motors (*RaR*). Elvira represents the kind of "working girl" Janice Angstrom* aspires to be. *See* **Femmes Fatales**.

On Literary Biography (Columbia: University of South Carolina Press, 1999). This revision of "One Cheer for Literary Biography" (*New York Review of Books* [4 Feb. 1999]) gives one "cheer" for literary biography if it advances the reader's understanding of the author's work. Updike makes clear, however, that the current trend in biography takes readers sharply

Courtesy of Mary Weatherall

away from such understanding, often toward a prurient interest in salacious facts. In his Appendix Updike comments on an exhibit of his work collected by Professor Donald Greiner of the University of South Carolina, remarking that it would be "disingenuous" not to be grateful to the four collectors in the country who have taken a "keen interest in assembling my published work." *See* **Collecting Updike**.

Ovaltine. Ovaltine is an imitation chocolate drink given to Col. Félix El-lelloû* in *Coup*. It disgusts him because the Ovaltine cans littering his cell as he awaits trial represent an incursion of U.S. goods into his Marxist-Islamic state of Kush.

Oxford, England. Updike studied in Oxford at the Ruskin School of Drawing and Fine Art* as a Knox Fellow in 1954–55. This was his last "lap around the park" as a painter (Plath, *CV*). He noted that he was very "frightened" that year and in Oxford read a great deal of Karl Barth* in seeking spiritual comfort. Also, for the first time he read Vladimir Nabokov,* who was to become a literary mentor. E. B. White and his wife, Katharine White, fiction editor of the *New Yorker*,* met Updike in Oxford and offered him a job writing for the "Talk of the Town" column, a major turn in Updike's career. Oxford also appears in several of Updike's works. The story "A Trillion Feet of Gas" (*SD*) concerns a party in Oxford with a mixture of Oxford residents and Americans. "A Dying Cat," an episode included within "Packed Dirt, Churchgoing, a Dying Cat, a Traded Car" (*PigF*), describes an event that took place in Oxford. Updike's "March: A Birthday Poem" commemorated the birth of his first child, Elizabeth Pennington Updike,* born in Oxford on April 1, 1955, to the chagrin of the poet, who had expected her birth on March 31 (*CH; CP*, "Notes"). *See* **English Literature**.

Bibliography: Updike, "March" (*CH, CP*), "Notes of a Temporary Resident" (*PP*); "A Response" (*MM*).

P

Paine, Thomas (1737–1809). Col. Félix Ellelloû* studied the American political writer Thomas Paine to supplement his Marxist stance while attending a Wisconsin college (*Coup*). Paine propagandized for the American Revolution and was thus of interest to the future Kush revolutionary. In *Common Sense* Paine urged independence from England as a matter of common sense; to Ellelloû, rejecting Western interest in Kush was also common sense. Paine's *American Crisis* rallied soldiers against the British so effectively that it started his political career. He later held office in France, the country to which Ellelloû was exiled. But like Ellelloû, Paine had problems: In England he was indicted for treason while en route to France; in France he was imprisoned by Maximilien Robespierre for opposing the death of King Louis XVI; and when he returned to America, he was miscalled an atheist and died in disgrace.

Pandemonium. Pandemonium is the domain of Satan in Milton's *Paradise Lost*, mentioned in "The Happiest I've Been" (*SD*) when John Nordholm considers Alton* a suburb of some larger city, like Pandemonium or Paradise. *See* **Brewer; Reading, Pennsylvania**.

Paraclete. "Paraclete" literally means "defending counsel," as opposed to the accuser or "diabolos" (devil). The term is interchangeable with Holy Spirit, but also refers to the spirit within Jesus, who, according to the Gospel of John, extends the range of Jesus' teaching, advances the disciples' understanding of truth identical to that of Jesus, will be permanent, unlike Jesus, and will be invisible. At a Thanksgiving dinner to which Esther Lambert* and her husband Roger Lambert* have invited Dale Kohler* and Verna Ekelof,* Updike employs a subtle irony when Roger Lambert struggles to carve the turkey, which he calls the "Paraclete." He thus dissects the Holy Spirit in the presence of the "accuser," the diabolic Dale, who, from Lambert's viewpoint, refuses to accept the reality of Christ through faith delivered through the Holy Spirit. Since Abélard, of Héloïse and Abélard fame, set up a monastery called the Paraclete, which he later gave to Héloïse, the term also conveys the romantic attachment of the medieval lovers, and so of Dale and Esther (*RV*). *See* **Ministers; Religion**.

Park, Mungo (1771–1806). Mungo Park was a Scottish explorer of the Niger River and its source. To Col. Félix Ellelloû,* he was a colonial invader who was treated too well by the Africans he tried to enslave (*Coup*). Park is also an ironic foreshadowing of capitalism's seduction of Kush.

Parsley, Brenda. The wife of Unitarian minister* Ed Parsley* who guesses that witchcraft is being practiced in Eastwick,* Brenda Parsley becomes a minister after her husband dies (cf. Stella Wilmot [*IB*]) and gives a sermon* linking witchcraft to Parsley's death. She later delivers a sermon indicting ecological ravages caused by technology and the Vietnam* War for creating the environment that has made witches emerge into the modern world. But she is so liberal that she permits anyone to give a sermon, even Darryl Van Horne,* who speaks in the Unitarian church against God's creation (*W*). *See* **Religion; Unitarianism**.

Parsley, Ed. A Unitarian minister* who, prompted by the Vietnam* War, becomes a political activist. He alerts his congregation to what he calls the marriage of Mammon and U.S. corporations responsible for the war. Sukie Rougemont* finds him "all causes and no respect for actual people." Parsley runs away with young Dawn Polanski (who may be a witch), joins the war-protesting terrorists, the Weathermen, and is blown up when making a bomb. His wife, Brenda Parsley,* assumes his position as minister and locates "evil," as he might have done, in technological interference with nature,* political brinkmanship leading to the Vietnam War and emerging witches who gain empowerment by misusing nature. *See* **Religion; Unitarianism**.

Pastoral. Pastoral is a tradition in literature that assumes a nostalgic view of a past time that was bucolic, uncomplicated and happy. Eden is the basic Judeo-Christian image of the pastoral, but before that it was a Greek mythical world inhabited by shepherds, nymphs and satyrs, celebrated first in songs paying homage to pastoral gods such as Ceres. Classical pastoral poetry stemmed from these folk songs. Pastoral dominated the work of Theocritus (c. third century B.C.), whose *Idylls* in turn influenced Virgil (*Bucolics*, *Georgics*), then Sir Philip Sidney's *Arcadia*, the first pastoral romance, and through it Shakespeare's* *As You Like It*. The pastoral elegy emerged in John Milton's "Lycidas," Percy Shelley's "Adonais" and Walt Whitman's* "When Lilacs Last in the Dooryard Bloom'd." Typically, the values of country life are shown to be superior to the contrasting town life, and the contrast has dominated much American fiction, such as Mark Twain's *Huckleberry Finn* and Ernest Hemingway's* *Green Hills of Africa*. But the link to realism, as in Twain's novel, usually creates a critique of pastoral themes; such antipastoralism has become a dominant mode in American fiction and has been a component of nearly all of Updike's fiction.

The pastoral appears in Updike's *C*, with its mixture of pure pastoralism in the chapters involving mythical figures in an Arcadian setting and lyric evocations of nature,* as in Peter Caldwell's* vision of a snowfall. *C* is also a pastoral elegy commemorating the (metaphorical) death of Peter's father, George Caldwell.* Pastoralism is rejected in the realistic sections of Updike's novel, which take place in winter. Caldwell (whose given name, George, may refer to the *Georgics*), the science* teacher and "shepherd" to his students, ironically declares, "I hate nature." In *OF* pastoral images are used by Joey Robinson* to describe his wife Peggy,* creating what Anthony Burgess called "genuine pastoral" in "Language, Myth and Mr. Updike." At one point Joey says, "My wife is a field." She is a "metaphorical farm," but the pastoral centers on Mrs. Robinson's* real farm and her fierce attempt to use its mythic past to hold her son to the land; his preference for the city and its values forms the tension of the narrative. *RR* also includes pastoral elements in the hero's nickname "Rabbit," suggestive of *The Tale of Peter Rabbit.* The children's pastoral fable with a moral resonates in *RR* in Rabbit's proposed flight from the "trap" of the city to Southern cotton fields and in his gardening for Mrs. Smith, who says that he "gave her life." Rabbit's apparent rejection of city values makes him seek that "thing" he once possessed in his "Golden Age" on the basketball* court. In *RRed* the pastoral is denied when Rabbit's excursion in Jill Pendleton's* Porsche only leads him to slag heaps, and Skeeter* describes idyllic Vietnam* as a paradise turned into a "black hole." But in *RIR* the pastoral continues in Rabbit's search for his daughter at Ruth Leonard Byer's* farm (Updike originally intended to call *RIR Rural Rabbit*), in his love of golf* and in his sensitivity to nature. In *RaR* his heart attack forces Rabbit from his Florida* retirement paradise back to Brewer,* and when he has sex* with his daughter-in-law, a jaded "swain," he thinks of her as "Paradise." But the return to Pennsylvania and Eden kills him when she makes their secret known.

Other novels also undercut the pastoral. The pastoral setting of a college lures Henry Bech,* but he has an anxiety attack in "Bech Panics" (*BB*); the lovers in *B* experience great hardship in their flight into nature, and the return brings Tristão Raposo's* death; in *W* the witches are empowered by nature but use their power to murder, and Darryl Van Horne* hopes to find a loophole in the law of entropy; and in *TE* Ben Turnbull* records a Thoreauvian* love of the turning seasons in the aftermath of atomic war.

As critic Larry Taylor has remarked, Updike initially uses the pastoral nostalgically, then employs the antipastoral increasingly, as though bitter that the pastoral promise could not last. Taylor indicates that the pastoral-antipastoral cover drawings of the *New Yorker** suggest how the sophisticated urban magazine patronizes the pastoral values of simplicity and return to nature. Taylor detects the "metaphoric boldness" in pastoral not only in the blend of George Caldwell with Chiron,* but also in the metamorphosis of Gloria Turnbull* into a deer, and the deer into Deirdre (*TE*). Unlike Henry David Thoreau, Turnbull is marooned in his own "walled-in" estate. Thoreau's withdrawal also seems a worthy withdrawal from the Polk administration's war policies, but Turnbull is hardly concerned with the atomic war that destroyed much of America and perhaps brings on his own cancer.* *See* **Classical Literature**.

Bibliography: Anthony Burgess, "Language, Myth and Mr. Updike," *Commonweal* 83 (Feb. 1966): 557–59; Taylor, *PA*.

Paul VI, Pope (1897–1978). Pope Paul VI (1963–78) guided the Catholic church through changes at the Second Vatican Council, reconciled the Greek Orthodox church to the Roman Catholic church and travelled extensively, seeking further reconciliation with other religions. He decided to increase the use of the vernacular in the Mass in 1963, visited Communist countries and the United States, and beginning in 1967 held many meetings to discuss problems of social and religious concern. He also continued the traditional conservative policies of past popes by opposing birth control. Since the pope was speaking in Philadelphia, his conservative measures were discussed at a party given by Cindy Murkett* and her husband Webb Murkett,* with Harry "Rabbit" Angstrom* using the contraception debate to gain more intimacy with Cindy, while Margaret Fosnacht, his former mistress, ranted about the pope's interference in abortion.* Rabbit proposed to his son Nelson Angstrom* that he would fund an abortion to keep Nelson from being forced into marriage (*RIR*).

Pendleton, Jill. A runaway eighteen-year-old from Stonington, Connecticut, Jill Pendleton left her prosperous family to protest its materialistic values, as Sarah Worth* would do in *S*. A "flower child" in the pattern of many upper-class 1960s runaways, Jill becomes Skeeter's* lover in Brewer.* But because she is conspicuously white and his fellow African Americans* fear facing charges of assault or kidnapping, Skeeter and others encourage Harry "Rabbit" Angstrom* to take her in when he visits Jimbo's Friendly Lounge. Jill dresses in white and accepts every experience, no matter how degrading, without protest. Perhaps Rabbit lets Jill stay in his home because he recognizes himself in her unwillingness to put up with the second-rate, or perhaps because he wants to take revenge on the upper classes or repay his wife Janice Angstrom* for having left him. But Jill causes him to risk breaking the law because she draws Skeeter, a fugitive, to his home also. Skeeter is interested in Jill because she had once seen God while taking the hallucinogen LSD,* and he thinks of himself as the Black Messiah. So Skeeter reasons that if Jill could see God again, it might confirm him as the leader of an apocalyptic race war; to that end he hooks her on heroin. Rabbit's acceptance of Jill and Skeeter eventually brings on the wrath of his neighbors and precipitates her accidental death. Rabbit had felt that through their encounters he could overcome his hostility to Janice, reestablish his sexual identity and provide Jill with a chance to solve her emotional problems. But his son Nelson Angstrom's* attachment to her complicates Rabbit's plans, and a rivalry develops between Nelson and Rabbit while Jill takes Nelson shopping. She also teaches him to panhandle, which so infuriates Rabbit that he beats her. Afterward, when he is penitent, she exacts a sexual penance.

Jill continues to share herself with Rabbit and Skeeter, and she hopes to alter Rabbit's racist, bourgeois arrogance by helping to educate him in American history* from a Marxist viewpoint. Jill's participation in nightly oral readings from authors such as Frederick Douglass changes Rabbit only slightly, but these evenings show why Jill, like Rabbit in *RR*, had fled the trap of middle-class values. She is especially bothered by Rabbit's fear of waste, even applied to the structure of the solar system, but she counters his notion that Jupiter might harbor life by proposing that the planets were created to teach men to count, a thought that echoes John Hook's* idea that the stars were placed there to give adornment to the night (*PF*). She attempts to wean Nelson from materialism, and in her "talking blues" autobiographical song she shows him the mistakes she has made, possibly as an example for him. (Since Nelson becomes a cocaine addict in *RaR*, Jill's lesson goes unheeded.) In the end, despite Nelson's awareness of Skeeter's abuse and Rabbit's weakness, he cannot save her when Rabbit's neighbors, angry when Jill's intimacies with Skeeter become too visible, burn the house.

Jill was crushed by the forces she wished to resist and the counterculture she wished to join. Rabbit and Janice recognize later that Rabbit's part in her death balanced Janice's accidental drowning of their daughter a decade before (*RR*), and she urges him to remember, "Not everything is your fault." When Rabbit senses that Jill's ghost has visited him, he feels absolved. But Nelson comes to believe that Rabbit was fully responsible for Jill's death, and she continues as an "absent presence" in the hostility between father and son. Coupled to Rabbit's earlier abandonment of him, Jill's death focuses Nelson's hatred of his father. *See* **Drugs**.

Pets. Pets, both Updike's own and those of characters* in his novels, appear in his writings. Two of Updike's pet dogs are memorialized in his poetry. In "Dog's Death" (*M*) Updike provides an unflinching but sentiment-filled description of his dog Polly's succumbing in 1965. She was a good dog, even to the point of crawling to use the newspaper as she died. The dog died, as many must, "surrounded by the love that would have upheld her" (*M*). In

the note to this poem, Updike wrote, "Sometimes it seems the whole purpose of pets is to bring death* into the house" (*CP*, "Notes"). Interestingly,
this thought reverberates through other texts. If Polly's demise brought
death into the house, the passing of another dog takes death out of it. Eleven
years after the death of Polly, Updike commemorated his golden retriever,
Helen, in "Another Dog's Death." A companion to the first poem, it is also
written in five quatrains. Helen sits by the grave as her master digs it: "I
carved her a safe place while she protected me." After she is euthanized, he
wheels her to the grave and detects that her fur "took the sun." Updike's
poems about his dogs reveal a profound bond between master and pet. Not
so with Updike's cats, who are presented differently in his writing. In *SC*
Updike reveals that while he was undergoing a crisis in 1974, his cats increased his distress by precipitating asthma attacks that made him feel as if
he were suffocating.

Updike also attaches pets to characters in his novels. In *Couples* Piet Hanema* attempts to protect his daughter Ruth's pet hamster by building it a
cage, but Hanema's younger daughter Nancy accidentally leaves the cage
door ajar, and the pet cat kills it. The cat's action leads Piet to the recognition that there is no real defense against death. Just as his parents had been
killed in an auto accident, the hamster dies by "accident," and death enters
the house. In *RRed* Margaret Fosnacht's dog intrudes into her lovemaking
with Harry "Rabbit" Angstrom* by nuzzling their feet. The situation is
comic, but perhaps also alludes to the fabled prophetic ability of dogs to
alert their masters: the dog may have tried to warn Rabbit that his home is
being attacked by arsonists, and his lover Jill Pendleton* is in danger of dying
in the house. This dog who interferes with Rabbit's pleasure may be a distant
relation to the pet dog of the Springers in *RR* who frightens Nelson Angstrom.* A dog-versus-rabbit conflict metaphorically attended the marriage
of Rabbit and Janice Angstrom,* née Springer; her parents' home contains
pictures of dogs; and Rabbit is aware that the Springers want to make a
Springer of Nelson, that is, figuratively, a dog from a rabbit. Thus the fictional pets play out the sentiments Updike has revealed about his own pets.

Bibliography: Updike, "The Hidden Life of Dogs" (*MM*).

Picked-up Pieces (New York: Knopf, 1975). *PP*, Updike's second book of
criticism, with essays and reviews from twenty-four sources, mainly the *New
Yorker*,* is divided into "Views" and "Reviews." "Views" contains introductions, speeches, notes and pieces on golf,* and "Reviews" contains several
sections devoted to James Joyce,* Marcel Proust,* Jorge Luis Borges* and
Vladimir Nabokov,* as well as reviews of lesser-known writers grouped under "Europe," "Africa," and "The Avant Garde" and a section, about 10
percent of the book, concerning nonfiction. In the last part of the book
Updike supplies a generous compilation of excerpts from many interviews*

called "One Big Interview." The book's great volume and scope show the distance Updike had travelled as a critic since *AP*, though *PP* contains a similar plan, starting with light pieces and moving to more serious ones. Updike's inclusion of an omnibus interview also shows that since *AP* he had become a writer who had attracted much attention. The interviews thus answer many questions for the inquisitive reader, answers presented in the final form of print rather than the extemporary form of improvised responses to questions.

In his "Foreword" Updike explains his brashness in accepting the role of book reviewer for the *New Yorker* in 1960 and his "youthful traumas" at the receiving end of critical opinion that led him to create rules for reviewing. Those five rules are eminently fair: (1) "Try to understand what the author wished to do, and do not blame him for not achieving what he did not attempt"; (2) "Give enough direct quotations so the reader can form his own impression"; (3) "Confirm your description of the book with quotation from the book"; (4) "Go easy on plot summary"; (5) "If the book is judged deficient, cite a successful example along the same lines, from the author's *oeuvre*." Updike adds a "vaguer" sixth rule, "Do not accept for review a book you are predisposed to dislike, or committed by friendship to like." He specifically instructs two of his hostile critics,* John Aldridge and Norman Podhoretz, not to "try to put the author 'in his place,' making of him a pawn in a contest with other reviewers. Review the book, not the reputation." Typically, Updike then indicates reviews that show how he himself has fallen short of his own rules.

The first part of *PP*, "Views," provides varied remarks about fiction in various essays and introductions. In the daring self-interview by his character Henry Bech,* Updike defines novels as "crystallizations of visceral hopefulness." In his acceptance speech for the National Book Award for *C*, he indicates the importance of accuracy by insisting that "fiction is a tissue of literal lies that refreshes and informs our sense of actuality." In "The Future of the Novel" he describes the novel* as about "living and loving," or "coitus and conversation." He predicts a "wonderful freedom" for the novel in which the field of the page will become a ground of experimentation. To the question "Why Write?" he answers, because it is a way of "adding to the world," rather than rearranging what is already there, and because it is a way of making connections. Other "views" include travel pieces about London and Anguilla,* introductions to books of caricatures by David Levine and a fond reminiscence of the *Harvard Lampoon.* More interesting are Updike's introduction to the Czech edition of *OF* and to *Soundings in Satan*. On *OF* Updike offers an explanation of the troubling preposition in that title and draws connections to *C*, and about *Soundings in Satan* Updike affirms his belief in hell. The essay forms a transition to the religious concerns of part two, "Reviews."

"Reviews" first examines the journals of Søren Kierkegaard* in "The

Fork," a seminal essay that testifies to Updike's deep commitment to the philosopher-theologian who had rescued him from the religious crisis of his post-Harvard* years. Kierkegaard's idea that anxiety was the root of human existence is in part embodied by Harry "Rabbit" Angstrom* (*RA*), whose very name is rooted in angst,* German for "anxiety." As the essay-review "Love in the Western World" (*AP*) of Denis de Rougemont's two books on love looked forward to uses of the Tristan and Isolde* legend, so "The Fork" looks backward upon Updike's crisis and forward to his other uses of religious crises in *MS, RV* and *IB*. Kierkegaard's journals also reveal to Updike Kierkegaard's relation to his own father and his musings on the paradox of God the Father who is also a victim of God. These ideas would appear in Updike's use of the Oedipal complex in his early work, as well as in *RA*, in which, Updike has said, the father-son relation is the major theme. Various other religious notes recall Updike's interests in the theologians reviewed in *AP*, Paul Tillich* and, above all, Karl Barth.* Updike notes the "exceptional compactness and pertinence of expression" of Barth's *Deliverance to the Captives*, and he probably had these qualities in mind when he created the Barthian sermons* of Rev. Tom Marshfield.*

Apart from such religious concerns, Updike explores a great many writers, particularly James Joyce and Marcel Proust. Updike shows his scholarly side as he probes an edition of Joyce's *Giacomo Joyce* and concludes that since it was "personal therapy and private communication," it was "too personal" to print. With Proust, Updike relies on his tactic of extended quotation to show how the images of Proust's *Remembrance of Things Past* connect "microcosmically." He also asserts that "macrocosmically" there are thrilling leaps of "far-flung continuations." Elsewhere, a writer Updike helped American readers to discover, Jorge Luis Borges, is described as proposing an "essential revision in literature itself." Updike examines this postmodernist's strange art, composed of mystery, the tracing of hidden resemblances, artifice and intertextual obsessions.

A major influence, Vladimir Nabokov, is the subject of seven pieces. In them Updike says of his mentor that he finds that Nabokov's "almost impossible style" met in America, to which he had emigrated, an equally "ungainly" "affluence." Yet Updike chides Nabokov's style in *Ada* for "garlicky puns, bearish parentheses, and ogreish winks" and wrestles with the obscurities and artifice in Nabokov to conclude that he is not a modern artist-priest, but a more ancient magician who has "harlequinized the world and tweaked the chessboard of reality awry." But in a birthday tribute to Nabokov, Updike defends him as a writer with not only art but "access to European vaults of sentiment sealed to Americans."

Other Updike reviews recognize a great many writers from England, France, Germany, Poland, and Africa. He thus reveals a catholicity of taste that for the first time suggests that he might well be the heir apparent to the literary chronicler Edmund Wilson.* Like Wilson, he is also engaged with poetry,* here a volume of W. H. Auden* in which Updike detects excremental imagery, there a biography of T. S. Eliot* that makes him wince at the critic's "faintly bellicose" style. For one of the first times Updike in print asserts that biography may detract from a writer's true accomplishment, his work. Also of interest for Updike's development as a novelist are his explorations of the French novelist Alain Robbe-Grillet, a writer of the *nouvelle vague* avant-garde style. Updike saw similarities between Robbe-Grillet's techniques and those of cinema, and, intrigued since *RR* by applying film* devices to fiction, Updike was naturally interested in the "new wave." He finds Robbe-Grillet's fiction "almost exclusively cinematic": it employs "the full syntax of splicing, blurring, stop-action, enlargement, panning and fade-out." Updike quips that Robbe-Grillet needs only "camera tracks and a union member operating the dolly" and concludes that these seem "mannered devices intended to give unsubstantial materials an interesting surface." Updike's own experiments in adopting cinematic techniques were now ended, because he understood how little they offered the working novelist.

Among Updike's reviews of modern American writers, he praises Erica Jong's *Fear of Flying*: having "all the cracked eggs of the feminist litany, her soufflé rises with a poet's afflatus." Appositely, in one of Updike's severest reviews, which he later thought might have exhausted patience, he scores James Gould Cozzens for having developed a style "unique in its mannered ugliness," composed of "Best Remembered Quotations," "The Lame Echo," "The False Precision," "The Infatuated Sonority," and so on. Endeavoring to be fair, Updike rereads Cozzens's first novel and finds that it was better than the work under review, then suggests what went wrong. He is no less judicious with his friend John Cheever's* *Bullet Park*; he asserts that the speed of events "almost" redeems it from "implausibility," but that Cheever's use of "the fantastic" is not a weakness since it contributes to "the accents of a visionary." Updike's reviews of nonfiction show him equally as comfortable with erotic art as with the lives of the cell.

The last part of *PP*, "One Big Interview," a composite of many interviews, ends the book in a novel way and sets the pattern for Updike's next two books of criticism, *HS* and *OJ*. Updike relies mainly on the interview by Charles T. Samuels for the *Paris Review* in 1968, which Updike revised. Though Updike had called interviews "a half-form like maggots," he gathered them for "the morbidly curious, or academically compelled." Updike comments on his early years and declares that his early novels were in some ways experimental and mythic, and that he strives to start his novels with a "solid coherent image, some notion of the shape of the book." He asserts that his fiction has "more history* in it than history books," and that his books "are all meant to be moral debates with the reader." He also explains the oral-genital contact in *Couples* and describes the evolution of *BB*. Updike clarifies many of his ideas about President James Buchanan* and caps this segment, and the book, by reprinting "Sayings," from a *Life* interview, the most provoking of which is "My life is, in a sense, trash; my life is only that of which the residue is my writing." *PP* has produced a remarkable "residue." *See* **Criticism by Updike**.

Bibliography: Lawrence Graver, "Even the Footnotes Sparkle," *New York Times Book Review* 30 Nov. 1975: 39; Martin Amis, "Life Class," *New Statesman* 91 (19 Mar. 1976): 368; Schiff, *JU*.

Pigeon Feathers (New York: Knopf, 1962). Updike's collection of short fiction* in *PigF* marks a steady growth in maturity. The nineteen stories, collected with no attempt to establish a theme or pattern since they appear more or less according to their date of original publication, predominately in the *New Yorker*, show a mastery of delineating the complex simplicity within ordinary incidents and Updike's deepening exploration of adolescent characters. Updike also shows a fine sense for irony and ambiguity, and he explores new directions in short fiction by creating mosaics that encourage a dynamic participation by the reader in construing the sum of the parts.

The title story treats David Kern's* crisis of faith when he viscerally experiences the meaning of extinction and at the same time feels that his lifeline to hope, his belief in Jesus, has been undermined by H. G. Wells's skeptical treatment of Christ. Updike has remarked that he himself had undergone what he recorded as David's despair when his desperate questions to his Lutheran minister* about immortality received perfunctory answers. A factual reality alone can satisfy David's spiritual craving: he must know if he will survive his death* as more than an idea in someone's memory. Ironically, through killing a pigeon and examining its feathers, David finds proof for his immortality. The orderly beauty of the feathers, so commonplace and easily overlooked, brings him the clue that design does exist in the universe and thus his immortality is assured, for if God takes such care of so trivial a thing as a pigeon feather, his promise to redeem man must also be true. Naïve though this "argument from design" might be (a watch found on a beach implies a watchmaker; thus the perfection in the feather implies a benevolent feather maker and immortality giver), it satisfies David emotionally and enables him to overcome his crisis.

Updike's most anthologized story, "A & P," treats the opposite side of adolescence in Sammy, the wisecracking, cynical supermarket checker who feels trapped in his job and constricted by rules. Sammy finds perfection in Queenie, who defies the supermarket rules by shopping in a bathing suit. Her chastisement from manager Lengel prompts Sammy to a quixotic defense of her that, though unnoticed by Queenie, leads to his quitting his job. When he seeks the girl in the parking lot, she has disappeared, and Sammy realizes that he is destined for other conflicts between his personal ideals and the rigid world. If David Kern finds an assurance for his spiritual doubts, Sammy finds a doubtful future ahead in a world of inflexible rules. Updike's wife, Mary Pennington Updike,* thought that "A & P" sounded rather too much like J. D. Salinger,* and Updike remarked that as an "idiomatic monologue," it was not his "usual style." In 1998 the story, in Japanese translation, was censored for Japanese high-school students by the Japanese Ministry of Education, which feared that it would cause "significant exasperation" in classes. Updike was even asked to produce a revised version by American textbook companies; he refused. Taken together, the two revelatory stories reveal the power of everyday situations. They are among Updike's best stories.

"The Astronomer" and "The Persistence of Desire" resemble "Pigeon Feathers" and "A & P," as if the heroes of these stories have grown up but not grown out of their problems of identity. "The Astronomer" charts how the narrator, suffering from spiritual trauma, has begun to find his way thanks to Plato* and Søren Kierkegaard.* He limply fends off the condescension of his astronomer friend Bela and is surprised when Bela in an unguarded moment reveals his own terror at the vast void of space, aroused by a trip to New Mexico. Though Bela's defenseless fear is not a pigeon feather fraught with metaphysical meaning, it reassures the narrator that philosophy can heal him. The hero of "The Persistence of Desire" seems arrested in his development, clinging to old girlfriends though he professes to love his wife "incredibly much." He meets his former flame during an eye exam in which he learns that he must wear glasses, but his insight is also failing since he is willing to disrupt two families to scratch the itch of youth. It is as though Sammy continued to search for a ruleless world after he himself had agreed to abide by the rules of marriage.

Other stories treat the clash between mother and son. In "Flight" Allen Dow's interest in a small-town girl counters his mother's ambition to get him safely into a college where his talents can blossom. The story parallels Updike's treatment of Oedipal entanglements in *RR*, *C* and *OF*. The story "Should Wizard Hit Mommy?" shows a child intuitively grasping the tensions between her parents and revealing that knowledge in the child's response to her father's bedtime story. Updike remarked that it had been his habit to create bedtime stories for his daughter Elizabeth Updike* in which, usually, an animal in trouble seeks help from a wizard who only makes things worse. The story within "Should Wizard Hit Mommy?" unwittingly aggravates the child's fears of abandonment.

These stories would be enough to secure Updike's reputation as a skilled short-fiction writer, but he breaks new ground with the lyrical, autobiographically based "Packed Dirt, Churchgoing, a Dying Cat, a Traded Car" and "The Blessed Man of Boston, My Grandmother's Thimble, and Fanning Island." As the titles suggest, these works are mosaics of seemingly unrelated incidents and Proustian* recollections. In the former, David Kern, now mature, discovers a relation between dirt packed by children's feet and God. He then considers how churchgoing, like voting, reminds you of your uniqueness and he further recounts how he helped a sick cat die on the night his wife gave birth to their first child. Since the cat story contains elements of Updike's experience in Oxford,* the four segments blend fiction to autobiography. The last segment recounts how, on the night before his birthday, the narrator tells his wife of his fear of obliteration only to discover the next day that his father has a life-threatening heart condition; death is coming closer. The four segments thus suggest that David has not put aside his spiritual crisis or his fear of death, as he had in "Pigeon Feathers." The lyrical insight about packed dirt gives way to religious doubt. Yet each is given equal weight in this single story. This experiment in form shows Updike's effort to move away from the conventional realistic story for greater expressiveness and a heightened sense of actuality.

Updike's delicate touch, exactness of detail, tape-recorder precision in dialogue and respect for the reader's intelligence are everywhere apparent in this collection. It established him as one of the great practitioners of the short-story form at a period in his career when he was essentially earning his living from his stories, but poised to become recognized as one of America's great novelists.

Bibliography: Stanley Edgar Hyman, "The Artist as a Young Man," *New Leader* 45 (19 Mar. 1962): 22; Robert H. Sykes, "A Commentary on Updike's 'Astronomer,' " *Studies in Short Fiction* 8 (Fall 1971): 575–79; Albert J. Griffith, "Updike's Artist's Dilemma: 'Should Wizard Hit Mommy?' " *Modern Fiction Studies* 20 (Spring 1974): 111–15; George W. Hunt, "Kierkegaardian Sensations into Real Fiction: John Updike's 'The Astronomer,' " *Christianity and Literature* 26 (1977): 3–17; William H. Shurr, "The Lutheran Experience in John Updike's 'Pigeon Feathers,' " *Studies in Short Fiction* 14 (Fall 1977): 329–35; Greiner, *OJ*; Detweiler, *JU*; Luscher, *JU*.

Plato (427–347 B.C.). A Greek philosopher famous for his dialogues that show how to establish truth through systematic reason, Plato held that what we perceive as real is only a shadow of ideal essence, which is the true reality. Some of his notions, like that of the soul, have been appropriated by religion, and others, like the search for a perfect society, have become staples of democracy and communism. Updike's knowledge of Plato is wielded according to the needs and understandings of his characters.* Thus Plato's thoughts are so much a part of modern thinking that even the popular art of a children's show finds Jimmie the Big Mouseketeer,* quoting a "wise old" Greek's "proverb," "Know thyself," but in keeping with the debasement of Greek thought, the admonition is converted into a socially useful bromide, "Be yourself" (*RR*). Plato's allegory of the cave from *The Republic* is offered to David Kern* by his concerned mother as a way of understanding life after death,* but it only makes the afterlife unreal for him. Harry "Rabbit" Angstrom* tends to idealize nature* and becomes affronted, for example, with the Amish, who at first are thought to be leading "the good life" but later are "fanatics" who "worship manure." Piet Hanema* finds that he is "more platonic than he imagined, missing friendship not friends," yet his meditation on the death of his daughter's pet hamster reveals that he cannot accept that "the idea of a hamster persists, eternal. Plato." The narrator remarks, "Piet was an Aristotelian" (*Couples*). Another who has problems with Plato is Mrs. Robinson,* who recounts the story of the division of the round, unified being into male and female from *The Symposium*, but finds that the fable does not bridge the gap between her son Joey* and her (*OF*). Mrs. Robinson also had a bucolic Republic dream in which she turned her farm into a retreat where people could become "round" again, but Joey dismisses it as fantasy.

The same problem of the real and the ideal persists in other stories. Brad Schaeffer's wife Jeanette asks if he loves her or "some idea" of her ("Made in Heaven" [*TM*]), and the hero in "The Other" (*TM*) seems to answer her: he is a Platonist more in love with the ideal woman than the one before him. This predicament is also considered in "Museums and Women" (*MW*), in which the aesthetic, perfect, unattainable woman clashes with the very real woman as lover. Updike says that he selected a Paul Tillich* remark about the soul's ambiguity as an epigraph for *MS* because it is "a very neo-Platonic . . . notion." Very Platonic notions are basic to Roger Lambert's* meditations on Tertullian* in whom he detects that "the Heavenly mystery of the Logos was made to descend by means of a Platonic scaffolding of degrees of ideality, down into reality" through sex* (*RV*). Updike notes that Iris Murdoch's novels are suffused with Platonism, her characters "half in a solidly realized England and half in a translucent realm of immaterial passions and ideas"; she had published a scholarly work on Plato, and her *Acastos* is two Platonic dialogues. Updike compares Plato's time, when "truth was thought to be attainable," to our own time "of built-in indeterminacy and ambiguity" (*OJ*). *See* **Atlantis; Classical Literature**.

Bibliography: Hunt, *JU*.

Plays. Updike wrote plays in high school such as "Murder at Blandings" (1950?), and later created a children's opera, "The Fisherman and His Wife"* (1967), and "Three Pieces from Ipswich" (1973), a pageant that excerpts the work of prominent early American writers. Updike's one full-length published play, *BD*,* is an anomaly. He had decided to write about Pennsylvania's only president, James Buchanan,* in 1968 to fulfill a promise to himself to complete a quartet of Pennsylvania novels begun with *PF, C, OF*. But after several years Updike discovered that writing a historical novel was repellant since it forced him to use an "upholstered style." He came to see that casting the novel as a play would enable him to avoid "scene-painting" by using his research in what he called a "verbal ballet." Yet in 1968 Updike had said he "never much enjoyed going to plays," and was bothered by "the unreality of painted people standing on a platform saying things they've said to each other for months" (Plath, *CU*). He had said that "A play's capacity for mimesis is a fraction of a novel's" (Plath, *CU*), yet in 1974 Updike published his "closet play," *BD*, and he offered the director suggestions in 1976 when he attended its San Diego production. Unsure that he was able to put into *BD* what he wanted to say, seventeen years later Updike incorporated much of the play into *MF*.

From his short story "Your Lover Just Called" (*TF*), Updike created in 1989 what he termed "a Playlet" as part of an evening of fifteen-minute plays (*OJ*). He has recently published two "dialogues" about the nature of fiction and the merits of print versus the computer (*MM*), perhaps modeled on dialogues in Søren Kierkegaard's* *Either/Or*. For amusement, Updike has written "A Different Ending," a parody of *Romeo and Juliet* (*MM*). Surprisingly, Updike has had nothing to say about plays in his reviews and criticism.

Bibliography: Greiner, *OJ*.

Plowville, Pennsylvania. A small town twelve miles south of Reading,* Pennsylvania, Plowville was the site of Linda Hoyer Updike's* birth. In 1945 she purchased the farm and farmhouse her parents had sold in 1922, and she and her husband Wesley Updike,* their son John Updike, age thirteen, and Linda Updike's parents, John Hoyer* and his wife Katherine Kramer Hoyer,* moved from Shillington* to Plowville on Halloween. Updike remarked that his mother had been moved by E. B. White's essays on Maine; thus, "It is one of the few authenticated cases of literature influencing life" (*PP*). The move to the sandstone farmhouse, built in 1812 by the Gordons, with eighty acres and a barn, enforced Updike's isolation.

Though the name Plowville sometimes embarrassed him, Updike often said that the move there marked his turning point, for it led him to read, draw and write more seriously than before, despite his farm chores. Updike records the reluctance of characters on a similar farm to do such chores in "Pigeon Feathers" (*PigF*) and *OF*. But in "Pigeon Feathers" David Kern* gains something positive in doing the hated chores: from disposing of messy pigeons he learns about immortality as he could not in church. In *OF* Joey Robinson,* a New York advertising man who always hated the farm, mows the field in order to help his mother. Updike shows that Joey's method of mowing reveals his attitude toward nature,* specifically sex;* we understand him better because of this. Also, Joey, in wearing his father's clothes to do the chore, aligns himself as well with his father's distaste for farming.

Linda Updike chose to stay in Plowville after her husband Wesley Updike died in 1972, and though Updike urged her to join him in Beverly Farms, Massachusetts, she died in the sandstone farmhouse kitchen in 1989. Updike returned to see her many times, of course, and he suggested that Harry "Rabbit" Angstrom's* covert visits to Ruth Leonard Byer's* farm in *RIR* were literary uses of his "spying" on his mother (*RA* "Introduction"). Updike's story "A Sandstone Farmhouse" fictionalizes the last days of Linda Updike.

Bibliography: Updike, "The Dogwood Tree: A Boyhood" (*AP*); "Plow Cemetery" (*FN*); "The Solitary Pond," "Leaving Church Early" (*TT*).

Poe, Edgar Allan (1809–1849). An American poet, story writer and essayist, Edgar Allan Poe was a master of emotional manipulation. In *Couples* "The Pit and the Pendulum" and "The Fall of the House of Usher" are mentioned during a discussion of how a woman's *National Geographic* collection had grown so large she was walled in and squeezed by the magazines. In another discussion of those stories Ken Whitman* says that the author is "I. M. Flat, a survivor in two dimensions." Ken's witticism is typical of the way the couples in this novel spar verbally, but this image of constricted space and death* obsesses Piet Hanema.* The narratives of these stories resemble the end of Piet's life: in the "The Pit and the Pendulum" a man is saved after feeling constricted, as Piet feels constrained and then saved by his lover, Foxy Whitman,* and in "The Fall of the House of Usher" Roderick Usher, like Piet, fears death to the point of neurasthenia. In an odd parallel to Piet, Poe was orphaned and spent his years learning his craft in Massachusetts; the death of Piet's parents scars him emotionally, and he, living in Massachusetts, struggles to maintain the high level of his own craft—refurbishing houses—in the face of his partner's sacrifice of quality. *See* **American Literature**.

Poetry. Although Updike is best known as a writer of novels and short stories and is probably most familiar to the general reader for his reviews in the *New Yorker*,* he has shown a lifelong interest in poetry as well. Critics have only just begun to consider the importance of Updike as a critic, and perhaps in the future he will be taken more seriously as a poet, since some of his volumes, *FN* in particular, are remarkable.

   To Updike, the impulses for poetry and fiction are similar, to bring forth "something live that surfaces out of language [that] brings a formal element without which nothing happens, nothing is *made*" (Plath, *CU*). His early creative impulse was a "connecting impulse," a link to a "kindred human urge . . . toward the exhaustive." The impulse is the same one that caused him to fasten on the simple actualities of the world—telephone poles, darning eggs, evaporation or the morning mail. This link to his fiction suggests that in his creative imagination the wellsprings of poetry and fiction are very much the same. The pages of pure lyricism in his fiction suggest that he draws upon his poetry resources to deepen and intensify the experience as his fiction writing dictates, whether it concerns an urban landscape in *RA* or pillow talk in *Couples*. For Updike, the genres of fiction and poetry touch in the "crystallizations of visceral hopefulness extruded as a slow paste which in the glitter of print" regains something of the original, absolute gaiety" (Plath *CU*). But he has said that when a poem begins to crystallize, he sets aside his fiction to enable the poem to form.

Critics, of course, are well aware that Updike devoted a good deal of energy to writing poetry while he was in Shillington* High School and while he was working for the *Harvard Lampoon** and the *New Yorker*, but they may be surprised to know that Updike's first poetry was similar to the making of cartoons; in fact, he called his light verse* "cartooning* in print." At Harvard,* though, his thorough reading of English and American poets deepened his appreciation for serious poetry; his thesis concerned non-Horatian elements in Robert Herrick's poetry. In his early essays Updike shows a keen awareness of the history of poetry. In "Rhyming Max" (*AP*) he provides a brief history of English rhyming and decides that rhyme is really the exception rather than the rule, and that those preferring to rhyme do so without "glorying" in it as John Skelton had. Additionally, he does a tour de force transformation of a stanza by Jonathan Swift into prose, blank verse and heroic couplets. Since then Updike has commented upon poetry in "Whitman's* Egotheism" (*HS*), in the occasional introductions to his poetry and in notes to *CP* and in a homage to Karl Shapiro. In *RV* he provides a tutorial on William Cullen Bryant's "Thanatopsis," and he uses a poem of Emily Dickinson's in *TE*.

Very briefly, Updike's poetry has failed to achieve the critical or general readership it deserves for four reasons. First, since Updike has been an extraordinarily productive writer of novels and stories, he is generally thought to compose poetry with his left hand, so to speak, unlike writers dedicated exclusively to poetry, such as Sylvia Plath or Robert Lowell. In addition, he writes parodies of famous poets like Marianne Moore ("Miss Moore at Assembly" [*M*]). Second, Updike's light verse was his first poetry to attract attention (he counted the start of his career as a professional writer with a light-verse poem in the *New Yorker*), so his philosophical poem "Midpoint" (*M*) brought little attention, to his disappointment, since it was prompted by requests that he articulate his personal philosophy. No doubt some poets and critics would rather praise Updike for being stuck in an outmoded form like light verse (which Updike long ago considered passé) than have to admit that a writer capable of winning the highest critical praise (and prizes) for short fiction* and the novel* could also be adept at serious verse. Third, Updike has written in forms like odes and sonnets, which many poets consider anachronistic. Updike has written "experimental" poetry, though almost entirely light verse, but he has attempted to do much of his serious work in "diffuse" forms like the ode or the modern sonnet. Finally, Updike has reviewed poetry sparingly, yet in *HS* he included seven essays on poetry and poets: three on Wallace Stevens* and others on Randall Jarrell, W. H. Auden,* *The New Oxford Book of Christian Verse* and the Russian Yevgeny Yevtushenko. In fact, he has translated ten poems by Yevtushenko, and he has translated poems from Bulgarian, Spanish and Latin as well. Updike has also praised Sylvia Plath, naming her "the best—the most exciting and influential, the most ruthlessly original—poet of her generation," and in his poem "Upon Looking into Sylvia Plath's *Letters Home*," he wrote, "We feel twins" (*CP*). Stevens and L. E. Sissman, a friend and colleague at the *New Yorker*, most concern him. Sissman reviewed Updike's collection *M*, but this review was left out of the collected essays of Sissman that Updike edited; yet such self-disqualification is not unusual when Updike edits work in which he might be included. He disqualified himself, for example, when he edited *The Best Short Stories of 1984*. He and Sissman have dedicated poems to each other, and Updike gave a reading of Sissman's poetry at Harvard on March 2, 1999. Updike nearly always reads only his own work, and he always includes his poetry. "Poetry," he remarked, has "a completeness that composes well" (Plath, *CU*). Updike has left poetry criticism to professional poetry critics more from humility than from lack of interest in the form. Yet scattered throughout his work, his remarks on Stevens, Robert Frost, Ezra Pound,* T. S. Eliot,* Walt Whitman, Dickinson and the symbolist poets show a rich knowledge of poetry. In short, the critical neglect of Updike's poetry rests on unsteady ground. See the individual entries on Updike's books of poetry for commentary that suggests how Updike's poetry might be better appreciated. He considered it "a good use of a life" to publish "one beautiful book" of poetry (Plath, *CU*).

Bibliography: Updike, "Autobibliographical Note" (*HS*); Karl Shapiro" (*MM*); Elizabeth Matson, "A Chinese Paradox, but Not Much of One: John Updike in His Poetry," *Minnesota Review* 7 (1967): 157–67; Greiner, *OJ*; Donald J. Greiner, "John Updike," in *American Poets since World War II* (Detroit: Gale, 1980), 327–34.

Ponce de León, Juan (1460–1521). A Spanish explorer who sailed with Columbus on his second voyage, Ponce de León conquered Puerto Rico (1508–11), then went to Florida,* seeking the "fountain of youth" (a now discredited legend) before dying in Cuba of an arrow wound inflicted in Florida. In *RaR* Harry "Rabbit" Angstrom* lives in the Florida town of Deleon,* named for the explorer, though the locals have long since apparently forgotten the origin of the name, pronouncing it "*Deely*un." (Compare Updike's preferred pronunciation of "Olinger" as the command "O-linger.") The mural in the Deleon Community General Hospital depicts an "explorer" about to be killed by an Indian with a bow and arrow, a foreshadowing of Rabbit's death. The image is a variation on the Lone Ranger* image of *RRed* that is repeated throughout *RA*.

The Poorhouse Fair (New York: Knopf, 1959). Updike remarked that he intended to write four novels, each treating a different aspect of time: the future (*PF*), the present (*RR*), the past (*C*) and the historical past (*BD*). *PF*,

Updike's first novel, was undertaken to memorialize his grandfather, John F. Hoyer,* a failed minister,* who had died in 1953. Perhaps placing him in a novel in the future was a way of having John Hoyer continue his presence beyond the present in the person of John Hook,* ninety-four and a former teacher. The autobiographical impulse that provoked the creation of *PF* produced a novel surprising for its confidence, compassion and craftsmanship. In depicting life in the Diamond County* Home for the Aged, near Newark, New Jersey, in the near future, Updike shows remarkable empathy for the very old, as well as great care in keeping the book from becoming sentimental. Critic Larry Taylor suggests that the elderly and the young of *PF* share challenges to religious faith. The old collectively support one another in their traditional faith against a new order that threatens to wrench it from them.

The action, conveyed through many vignettes, takes place on the day the poor have their craft fair, an August Wednesday in 1978, that is, in terms of when the novel was written, twenty years in the future. The poor of a state-run rest home have felt minor irritations at the impersonality of the so-called prefect, Stephen Conner.* Eventually frustrated by rain that threatened to spoil the fair and by Conner's clumsy efforts to befriend them, they grow restless under his hyperefficiency and indifference to their beliefs. Fueling their resentment is Conner's dispatching of a sickly cat, an outwardly humane act but one that suggests the probable fate of the poor when they grow enfeebled. Their indignation smolders, and when rain interrupts the fair preparations, they reminisce about the previous manager's more religious and benevolent ways. Trying to be companionable, Conner engages in their conversation, but turns it toward his own scientific and agnostic views, creating a quarrel with John Hook, who tells Conner that his progressive attitudes are the devil's work. Their debate is marred, as Updike notes in his 1977 "Introduction" (the twentieth anniversary of the book's inception), because, not understanding Conner's thirty-year-old mind, he failed to give Conner's humanist position its due. Probably Updike's personal feeling for his grandfather intruded. Later in the novel, with small provocation, the poor cast stones at Conner. Mistaking Hook as the instigator, Conner exacts petty revenge on him when the fair ends. As the fairgoers and antique hunters leave, laden with crafts sold for a small percentage of their worth, their fragmented, suggestive remarks create a vortex of confusion around the poor. Despite being penalized by Conner, Hook, perhaps feeling the onset of illness, forgets the advice he wished to give Conner.

The conflict between Hook and Conner creates what Updike later called a "debate with the reader" about the nature of goodness. Conner is not a bad person, but his abstract goals and heartless administration are lacking in charity. The poor contrast him to the previous prefect, caring and sympathetic Mendelssohn, who was also realistic about the poor's situation and eventual deaths. At the start, Updike depicts how the elderly are being robbed of their sense of individuality by showing how Conner has thought-lessly tagged the chairs they generally sit in with their names. They are affronted by such regimentation, and Gregg, usually irascible, feels that Con-ner has treated them as if they were dogs. Though Conner intends to pro-vide personal identities for them, he does not see his action through their eyes. The novel's opening line, "What's this?" asks not only about the new tag policy but about the new way in which the poor are conceived. With a structure Updike will often employ, he ends the book with ambiguity, and the last line is "What was it?" What was it that brought things to be this way? Updike asks the reader to ponder. How do good intentions have bad results?

But although his good intentions are defective, Conner is not bad. He means well, but when he fantasizes about receiving the Nobel Prize* for discovering a cure for cancer,* he reveals that his altruism is tainted. He really hates waste more than he loves people. Conner's aims are generally respectable, but the realities of sick cats and poor people are too specific for him. Updike has said that Conner's stoning contained the subtext of the stoning of St. Stephen, the first martyr, who created hostility by eloquent proselytizing. But while St. Stephen had been martyred for a religion* based on love, Stephen Conner's stoning is intended to drive away insensibility.

A secular humanist, Conner does alleviate pain when he has Gregg's pain-ful ear cleansed. But Hook reminds Conner, as Rev. Fritz Kruppenbach* will remind Rev. Jack Eccles* in *RR*, that pain is not evil but only an evil. As a scientist, Conner considers the poor a flaw, a symptom of the environ-ment he intends to cleanse. He imagines that by changing the environment, he will change mankind. Hook and the more traditional poor believe that man is much more, just as they believe that evil is more than pain. Conner's overt congeniality cloaks the pessimistic fear that human beings will not live up to his ideals. Neither can he, for while he secretly hates old people, he forgets that aging is a natural process of all life and dreams of a planet without the elderly.

Although Updike often cited his placing the novel in the near future as working with "experimental form," his experiment needed correction and clarification on its reissue in 1977, so Updike supplied an "Introduction" to that edition. He explained that he had had problems with Hook's dates (as he later would with the chronology of *RA*) of historical events, and he noted the anachronism of saying that all assassinated presidents* had been Repub-licans (from the point of view of 1978). He had made corrections in 1965 when the book was paired with *RR* by Modern Library, but Updike was now determined, with his passion for precision, to get the details right.

The novel is very modest science fiction. Updike set *PF* about twenty years into the future partly because he admired the sly way George Orwell commented on his own time in his novel *1984*. Since Orwell reversed the date of his publication year, 1948, Updike decided to do the same, but the date of publication of *PF*, 1959, would have been too obviously imitative if it had been inverted to 1995. Yet Updike needed to speculate on the trend of the American welfare state as President Dwight D. Eisenhower envisioned it; he knew, as he said in his "Introduction," that "the present is the future of the past." Bettering Orwell, Updike intended to make *PF* a modestly experimental novel that would incorporate elements of the French antinovel and even use an experimental punctuation and syntax. Such an ambition reflected his reading of Marcel Proust,* Vladimir Nabokov,* Henry Green,* H. G. Wells and James Joyce.* Updike in his "Introduction" also prided himself on the "phantasm" of the last dozen pages, which he likened to passages from *Ulysses*. Although hostile critics* Norman Podhoretz and John Aldridge claimed that despite his brilliant style Updike had nothing to say, in *PF* Updike set out to say something important about man's casual inhumanity to man, and he blends conventional realism with incisive characterization, lyrical style* (partly derived from his reading of Henry Green) and experimentalism in form. These would be characteristics of all the novels to follow.

The epigraph* from the Gospel of Luke ("If they do this when the wood is green, what will happen when the wood is dry?") points to the relationship of morality to craftsmanship, a theme Updike will use often. Amy Mortis's homespun quilt, for example, represents not only a craft but a body of traditions Conner's modern welfare state disowns. However, Hook finds himself entranced, staring into an intricately woven quilt's kaleidoscope images, which he identifies as part of the imagery* of his life and of America. The novel itself is like the quilt, a patchwork of entrancing images, and as the quilt's border contains the designs, the novel's unities of time, place and action provide a firm boundary for its images and scenes. The quilt remains as a reminder of how values were once sewn into a pleasing and useful object, but the quiltmakers, for Conner, have grown expendable—the "wood," the elderly, has grown dry. The importance of their work is admitted in the marketplace since their art commands high prices, but this speaks for the rarity of such art and the rarity of such values. But the pattern of the quilt, like its making, Updike suggests, is only meaningful for persons of another age, or for those sensitive enough to provide it the attention it deserves. Updike undoubtedly provided such attention to his grandparents, with whom he lived for eighteen years. Playfully, Updike faithfully records on the dust jacket of the novel's 1977 edition the praise of Henry Bech*: "*Poorhouse Fair*, surely his masterpiece."

Bibliography: Updike, "Introduction," in *The Poorhouse Fair* (New York: Knopf, 1977), vii–xx; *The Poorhouse Fair* (London: Penguin, 1994), vii–xvii; Taylor, *PA*; Markle, *FL*; George J. Searles, "*The Poorhouse Fair*: Updike's Thesis Statement," in Macnaughton, *CE*, 231–36; Hunt, *JU*; Detweiler, *JU*; Greiner, *JU*; Schiff, *JU*.

Pop Art. Pop art, a New York* graphic art movement (1953–80?), took for its content the commercial and vulgar consumer items of America and England. Its chief advocates were Robert Rauschenberg, Jasper Johns, Roy Lichtenstein, Claes Oldenburg and Andy Warhol. Their stance toward popular culture* was ironic and comic, serious and detached. Updike said that as a former cartoonist pop art "made sense to me and amused me." But pop art is treated with great seriousness by Darryl Van Horne,* who transplants his New York sophistication to Eastwick,* garnishing his house with Oldenburg hamburgers, Warhol multiple images and Lichtenstein truncated comic-strip panels (*W*). Since Van Horne exalts in the elaboration of the obvious and banal, he makes the creative imagination of God's creatures look absurd. To Van Horne, the best pop art—whether beer cans or copulating couples in cars—is that which most degrades mankind by stripping it of its soul. But despite his passion for what he calls junk, Van Horne admits that he has collected pop art only as an investment, so it is merely a means to an end. Pop art thus suits the devil. But he fails to make Alexandra Spofford* the next Niki de Saint-Phalle; she has neither the desire nor the talent to imitate the pop art sculptor. Updike noted that by the time Van Horne began collecting it, pop art already had "dust" gathering on the movement, and that "dustiness" is a way of saying that "not all is as it seems." Updike has reviewed shows of Johns and Lichtenstein and has written about Oldenburg, and his poem "In Memoriam Felis Felis" was illustrated by the British expressionist pop artist R. B. Kitaj. Pop art is mentioned in "Bech Panics" (*BB*). See **Art; Drawing and Painting;** *Just Looking*.

Bibliography: Updike, "Big, Bright and Bendayed," "Fast Art," "A Case of Monumentality" (*MM*); "Floor Plans," *House and Garden* Sept. 1996: 12, 126, 128.

Popeye. A creation of E. C. Segar in 1929, the cartoon character Popeye, a variation on the fighting sailor, is in love with Olive Oyl and combats her suitor, the malicious Bluto. Popeye can only defeat him by eating a can of spinach. In *RIR* Harry "Rabbit" Angstrom* observes that Webb Murkett* uses toilet paper decorated with images of Popeye, leading him to think about what the sailor now must eat, one of many scatological images in *RIR*. Popeye is one of many images from popular culture,* like the Lone Ranger,* that has deteriorated in meaning. See **Cartooning**.

Popular Culture. Updike remarks in *OJ* that he caught the bug of popular culture in "coloring books, animated cartoons, comic books, songs on the radio, radio drama and comedy, the so-called slick magazines, and the movies." Everywhere apparent in Updike's work, popular culture provides bedrock actuality. Updike's interest in the media fixes his work to specific places and times with plentiful specific uses of newspapers and magazines, radio and television,* popular music,* commercial artists like Norman Rockwell, cartooning,* and movies. He explores how a printer produces the local paper as well as the impact of television in *RRed* and describes the effort of a typical newspaper reporter in *W*. In *RA* and *Couples* he is scrupulously exact about the lyrics of popular songs; Updike noted that he typed into his manuscript names of songs he heard over the radio so that they could become part of Rabbit's trip south in *RR*, and his manuscripts show that he then checked them for accuracy before publication. In *IB* hundreds of films* and film stars are listed, and the plots are sometimes summarized and actors characterized. Of particular importance as symbolic reference points are the films *The Shaggy Dog* (*RR*) and *2001: A Space Odyssey** (*RRed*) and the television program *The Lone Ranger** in *RRed*. Oddly, Updike cites "the triumph of American popular culture" as a reason for the failure of the American writer to use America as a subject, since it "coats the individual, whom the writer would hold up to cultural study, in an impervious skin of cultural cliche" (*MM*). See **Drawing and Painting; Journalism**.

Bibliography: Updike, "The Fifties," "Remarks in Acceptance of the National Book Critics Circle Award for Fiction," "Women Dancing," "The Flamingo-Pink Decade" (*MM*); Andrew S. Horton, "Ken Kesey, John Updike and the Lone Ranger," *Journal of Popular Culture* 8 (Winter 1974): 570–78; Newman, *JU*; Ristoff, *UA*; George R. Bodmer, "Rabbit to Roger: Updike's Rockin' Version," *Journal of Popular Culture* 22 (Winter 1988): 111–17; Ristoff, *JU*.

Popular Music. Throughout his work Updike uses popular music to evoke character and emphasize themes. A song accompanies a shift in plot in *PF* when a driver delivering refreshments to the poorhouse is distracted by a Spanish song and backs into a wall, precipitating the smoldering indignation of the poor and their stoning of the prefect. In evoking character by way of music, few works are as effective as *RA*. In *RR* Harry "Rabbit" Angstrom* listens to the radio on his trip south, and many of the song arrangements recall the idyllic days of high-school dances, but some of the lyrics have ironic connotations: "The Man Who Ran Away" has direct reference to Rabbit on the run, while "Secret Love" refers to his high-school sweetheart Mary Ann, and "Autumn Leaves" anticipates the death* of his daughter Rebecca.* Such "music to cook by" reminds Rabbit of his wife Janice Angstrom,* a terrible cook, but this provokes memories and thus guilt; later a song predicts the outcome of his flight, "I Ran All the Way Home Just to Say I'm Sorry," but others punctuate his need for freedom: the punning "Happy Organ" and "Turn Me Loose." Music is thus associated with his premarriage freedom as a rural "rabbit." In *RRed* Rabbit hears the songs of Broadway played by a black pianist, Babe, in Jimbo's Friendly Lounge while African Americans* give him drinks and drugs* to make him more willing to accept from them a young white runaway. Babe, a fortune-teller, accurately describes in music Rabbit's condition: "Yesterday" and "I Can't Get Started," which together suggest why he is mired in guilt and inertia. He later listens to Jill Pendleton's* life story as she accompanies herself on the guitar to her "talking blues" (*RRed*). In *RIR* Rabbit listens to Donna Summer as he spies on Ruth Leonard Byer,* whom he had deserted at the end of *RR* as he ran down Summer Street. Meanwhile the songs are interspersed with commercials that urge Rabbit to purchase plastic car-seat covers and television* sets, while the news offers evidence that people do get rich quick and that religious leaders like the Dalai Lama* (to whom Rabbit compares himself) have gone into hiding.

Elsewhere, songs underline the weakness of ideology when the importation of American popular music into Kush in *Coup* reveals the confusion of underlying resistance to Islamic-Marxist ideologies. President Félix Ellelloû* drives through the desert to find his lost love Kutunda,* listening to "Love Letters in the Sand." Ellelloû knows that "freedom like music went straight to the heart." In *Couples*, to signal the inability of suburbanites to understand tragedy, the dance music at Freddy Thorne's* after President John Kennedy's* assassination emphasizes the delusory effort of the couples to link themselves to unearthly realms: they dance to "It Must Have Been Moonglow" and "Wrap Your Troubles in Moonbeams." To suggest the impossibility of such persons finding relief from their root anxieties, Piet Hanema,* in the aftermath of his separation from both wife and mistress, scoffs at the Bob Dylan lyrics heard from afar, "The Answer Is Blowing in the Wind." He thinks, perhaps cynically, that folk music is "out" and "love and peace are in." Another prophecy is offered in *Marry* by the song "Born to Lose," which predicts that Jerry Conant* will eventually lose his mistress Sally Mathias. Updike uses a song as a motif in *RV* when Cyndi Lauper's "Girls Just Want to Have Fun" refers to the promiscuity of Verna Ekelof* and the adulterous affair of Roger's wife Esther Lambert.* Lauper loses out to the more popular Madonna as Esther's affair dissolves, she becomes pregnant, and Verna abuses her own daughter. Updike provides a personal recollection of songs he heard throughout his life in "Popular Music" (*OJ*). *See* **Popular Culture.**

Pot. Pot is a slang term for marijuana, the Indian hemp, *Cannabis sativa*, a narcotic that is smoked, though the word is sometimes used for other drugs.* Updike shows his deepest concern about drugs in *RA* when he explores the dangers of heroin addiction in *RRed*, which leads to public sexuality, arson and death,* and when he reveals that Nelson Angstrom* nearly bankrupts his parents' business to satisfy his cocaine habit in *RaR*. In *RRed* pot and other drugs are introduced into the Angstrom household by Skeeter,* a psychopathic Vietnam* War veteran, and Jill Pendleton,* a runaway rich girl. She previously has had disturbing visions of God while using hallucinogenic drugs, and Skeeter is anxious to have her repeat those visions while using heroin so he can somehow confirm his self-appointed position as the "Black Messiah." Conservative Harry "Rabbit" Angstrom* impassively watches this while smoking pot to soothe the pain of being left by his wife. But after these experiences are over, Rabbit never again uses pot. In *RIR* Rabbit's son Nelson Angstrom uses pot when he goes dancing with his wife, Teresa "Pru" Angstrom,* and though she is pregnant, she also smokes marijuana. In *RaR* Nelson uses cocaine because of his anxiety about being an unsuccessful car salesman, husband and father, convinced that he can control his "recreational" use. Nelson later gives up drugs and becomes a counselor to addicts. Updike treats drugs comically in "Trust Me" (*TM*) when a son convinces his father that the brownies he offers are not laced with hashish, though they are. Updike reverses the situation when Henry Bech* thinks that his former student has given him LSD* though he has not ("Bech Takes Pot Luck" [*BIB*]). Darryl Van Horne* uses pot and hallucinogens to ease the seduction of the witches (*W*), as if in answer to *New Yorker** poet Ogden Nash's famous amended poem, "Candy is dandy / But liquor is quicker. / Pot is not."

Potter, Beatrix (1866–1943). After unsuccessfully trying to publish watercolors of fungi, Beatrix Potter wrote and illustrated *The Tale of Peter Rabbit** (1900), one of many such animal stories she would eventually publish. She also wrote and illustrated books about such animal characters as Jemima Puddle-Duck and Mrs. Tiggy-Winkle. *The Tale of Peter Rabbit* had a profound effect upon Updike and formed a subtext for *RR*. He paid homage to Potter in his poem "Agatha Christie and Beatrix Potter" for her care in providing an original kind of whimsy about "cozy" chases "that end with innocence acquitted / Except for Cotton-tail, who did it" (*TP*). Potter may have given Updike inspiration for writing children's books and telling children's stories.

Pound, Ezra (1885–1972). An American poet who, with T. S. Eliot,* changed the course of poetry toward imagism and away from didacticism, Ezra Pound established the principles of modern poetry as editor of *Poetry*, the *Little Review* and the *Dial*, and through essays and reviews as well as his own original poetry. He supported William Butler Yeats and James Joyce* and knew Ernest Hemingway* and Gertrude Stein. Pound's famous command from *ABC of Reading* to "make it new" may have influenced Updike's constant innovations in fiction and poetry. Pound's *Cantos*, his greatest work, incorporated classical, Renaissance, eighteenth-century and Chinese sources into a history of modern experience. Updike quotes from Canto LXXXI in "Midpoint" (*M*). Pound's Canto I is alluded to indirectly in "The Journey to the Dead" (*A*) when Martin Fredericks thinks that the dead inhabit a different world and recalls the section of Homer's *Odyssey* in which Odysseus visits his dead mother Anticlea. Pound's canto translates the same passage from Homer, but from a Renaissance Latin translation. Fredericks then compares the passage to the underworlds of *Gilgamesh*, Virgil and Dante.*

In a review of a Pound-translation, Updike compliments Pound for promoting James Joyce's *Ulysses* and T. S. Eliot's *Waste Land*. Updike describes vividly how the American Academy of Arts and Letters* accepted Pound as a member, then suffered his abuse and his anti-Americanism during the war. *See* **Poetry**.

Bibliography: Updike, "1938–1947: Decade of the Row," in *A Century of Arts and Letters* (New York: Cambridge University Press, 1998).

Powers, Francis Gary (1929–1977). Francis Gary Powers was a pilot who on May 1, 1960, flew a U-2 spy plane that was brought down inside the USSR. His imprisonment precipitated a serious Cold War confrontation between the United States and the Soviet Union. Powers is mentioned in *Couples*, the image of a plane crash haunts Piet Hanema's* dreams, and spying and betrayal characterize his affair with Foxy Whitman.* *See* **Airplanes**.

Presidents. Throughout Updike's work he refers to presidents and their administrations in order to provide a firm sense of historical time to his narratives and a forum for ideas sometimes also expressed in autobiographical essays. Updike has asserted that in his early novels "a precise year is given and a President reigns." With few exceptions, this is true of all his novels. His use of presidents helps to support his assertion that his novels have more history* than most history books. A lifelong Democrat, Updike reveals his favoritism while exploring both Republican and Democratic presidents, particularly James Buchanan,* Franklin Roosevelt,* John Kennedy,* Lyndon Johnson* and Richard Nixon. He even indicates that a president rules Kush, Col. Félix Ellelloû* (*Coup*); he creates a Jewish president, Lowenstein, for *PF*; and he names President Gerald Ford in the title of a book, though Ford appears in it for only one page (*MF*). Updike has expressed his pride at having mentioned all U.S. presidents in *MF*.

Updike mostly ignores the Founding Fathers: Washington appears, somberly, in the poem "February 22" (*TP*)—he "fathered" the country "without great joy"—and he and Abraham Lincoln* are parodied when Miriam Angstrom* demonstrates Walt Disney's* automatons (*RRed*). Updike marks the end of "the heroic age of politics" when presidents could be photographed, warts and all. His portrait of James Buchanan* of Pennsylvania receives the same treatment from Updike, yet he is also "the drowned-out voice of careful, fussy reasonableness." Updike reveals in *PF*, *BD* and *MF* how intertwined were the personal and political knots of Buchanan's life, and how maligned he became thanks to the Lincoln mythmakers. John Hook,* an ex–history teacher, maintains that Lincoln had economic, not humanitarian, reasons for freeing the slaves and calls Lincoln an "atheist," while Stephen Conner,* the prefect and Hook's nemesis, names Lincoln a Unitarian in religion.* But Hook's defense demonstrates Hook's individualism and thus refutes the welfare state's error of enshrining leaders to the point of abstractions (*PF*). Nearly four decades later Updike reviewed a biography of Lincoln and quoted his anti-Negro sentiments from the fourth debate with Stephen Douglas, but he arrived at a more judicious appraisal of Lincoln than Hook had (*MM*). *MF* looks at Buchanan from the perspective of an obsessed professor, Alf Clayton,* who also describes a meeting of Buchanan with Andrew Jackson to contrast the former's subtlety with the latter's ruthlessness. But the contrast also suggests that Clayton is self-absorbed, as Buchanan was; had Clayton been more fearless, like Jackson, he might have left his wife.

Many presidents in office after Buchanan are also referred to in Updike's prose. In *RRed* Skeeter* gives an overview of the mistreatment of blacks during Reconstruction by asserting that Democrat Samuel Tilden, who attacked New York City corruption, was cheated out of the presidency of 1876 by Rutherford B. Hayes. John Hook offers a capsule version of presidents Grover Cleveland, who turned out the muckrakers and had a tumor removed without anesthetic, and William McKinley, who sank Spanish ships "for show" (*PF*). The impact of the Franklin Roosevelt tenure is described in Updike's autobiographical "The Dogwood Tree: A Boyhood"* (*AP*). Updike explains how his parents were greatly affected during the depression by FDR. Consequently, the administration and death of Franklin Roosevelt impressed Updike while he was growing up and made him a confirmed, if, as he said, an unreflective, Democrat. Translating these feeling to *C*, he has George Caldwell* recount how FDR saved America, and his son Peter Caldwell* fends off attacks on FDR's Yalta* policies. In a story about the quest for religious faith written years later, Updike described how Brad Schaeffer converts to Episcopalianism as FDR's promise that the country would survive the depression comes true ("Made in Heaven" [*TM*]). (The story is unusual in that, like *IB*, it spans the administrations of Dwight Eisenhower, John Kennedy and Richard Nixon.)

Other works treat the general tone of various presidencies. Updike has said that he worked to make *C* distinctly a Harry Truman book, and the atmosphere of fright permeating *C* is attributable to Cold War tension between Truman and Joseph Stalin. Updike called *RR* an Eisenhower novel, probably because of the bland conformity of the "Silent Generation" of that administration, which seemed to curb individualism. Updike characterized his own view of politics at this time as "ironic detachment from social issues." Ironically, in *RRed* he links Eisenhower to liberal Charlie Stavros,* who lives at 1204 Eisenhower Avenue. Charlie is a critic of Lyndon Johnson's conduct of the Vietnam* War, which Eisenhower had struggled to avoid, though eventually he sent American "advisors" at Richard Nixon's advice. The sense of a new start in the John Kennedy administration, of what JFK called "Camelot,"* provides the tone of the postpill paradise of Tarbox (*Couples*). JFK's politics and personal life are discussed by nearly every character in that novel.

Piet Hanema's* seduction of Foxy Whitman* is partly motivated by the death of the Kennedy infant; their reconciliation occurs after the assassination, an event about which Updike wrote for the *New Yorker*.*

Updike's "On Not Being a Dove" (*SC*) provides his personal opinions about the Vietnam War, and his support of Johnson's policies was used in *RRed* when Harry "Rabbit" Angstrom* quarrels with Charlie Stavros, but Rabbit does not dismiss the antiwar comments of Skeeter* and Jill Pendleton,* so he is open to change. Updike's public support of Johnson's escalation of the Vietnam War brought such disapproval from his friends that he left the country for a while, astonished at what he called the savagery of the attacks on Johnson. Updike used the disasters of Johnson's administration as ironic counterpoint to a story of adultery, "More Stately Mansions" (*TM*). *RIR* also finds Rabbit rich during the Jimmy Carter administration, thanks to the administration's policy of gas rationing. Rabbit's success in trading gold and silver is likewise a function of Carter's effort to rescue American hostages, so his successful life is bound to his president's tactics, but, naturally, a different president with other policies might render Rabbit poor. Carter's policies only confirm Col. Félix Ellelloû's hatred of "the land of white devils" (*Coup*). Though Updike has said that he could not understand why no one liked Carter, and that he, like Rabbit, was trying to put his finger on what was wrong, in *RIR* Rabbit seems far more interested in seducing Cindy Murkett* or discovering if Annabelle Byer* is the daughter Ruth Leonard Byer* had by him than he is in exploring Carter's public relations problems. Nixon, praised by Fred Springer* in *RRed*, is angrily attacked in the same novel by Rabbit's Democratic father, and it has been suggested that Tom Marshfield's* disgrace resembles that of Nixon after the Watergate scandal forced him from office (*MS*). Rabbit muses that the Watergate scandal implicating Nixon helped to kill Janice's Republican father (*RaR*). The years under Ronald Reagan and Reaganomics are for Rabbit "a little dreamlike," with Reagan "spending money that wasn't his," exactly what Rabbit's son Nelson Angstrom* does in stealing from Springer Motors* (*RaR*). Though he has yet to include President Bill Clinton in his fiction, Updike has said in interviews that he admires his policies, but in a footnote to "The State of the Union, as of March, 1992" Updike wrote, "Had I written these impression in 1998 . . . I would have felt compelled to mention . . . the President who, though exemplary in many respects . . . has shrouded the White House . . . in an atmosphere of scandal and rumor, evasion and counterspin, to the point of national demoralization. . . . Our great Republic deserves better from above than this relentless rain of tawdriness" (*MM*). When Rabbit's neighbors were casting the role of Uncle Sam* for the July Fourth parade, they selected him as this symbol of America (*RaR*). Uncle Sam had been impersonated by both Updike's father ("How to Be Uncle Sam" [*TP*], [*CP*, "Notes"]) and himself ("The Parade" [*OJ*]).

Bibliography: Updike, "Such a Sucker as Me," "A Special Message for the Franklin Library Edition of *Memories of the Ford* Administration" (*MM*); Newman, *JU*; Ristoff, *UA*; Ristoff, *JU*.

Problems and Other Stories (New York: Knopf, 1979). The collection of stories in *P* pursues the subject of extramarital problems, sometimes with humor, but more often with poignant melancholy. Updike continues to follow the failure of the marriage of Joan Maple* and her husband Richard Maple* in several stories, especially in the anthology favorite, the prize-winning "Separating," perhaps Updike's most touching story. Balancing this serious fiction are several comic stories of domestic predicaments, notably "Problems," which uses elementary-school math puzzles to fashion the deepest emotional subjects; what begins as comic incongruity becomes melancholy insight as variables overwhelm the problems and prohibit solutions. "Problems" invites us to speculate upon the efficacy of therapy to help unravel the triangles of life, and we are asked to sympathize with the frenzied attempts to square guilt with desire. In a story in another experimental mode, "Augustine's Concubine," Updike describes St. Augustine's* life with his concubine and his desertion of her to pursue his religious vocation. By intercutting extracts from Augustine's *Confessions* with modern narrative parallels, Updike discloses that the same conflict between lust and spirituality that troubled the saint torments us still. The narrator, surprisingly, identifies Augustine's concubine as the true saint, since she made it possible for modern man to hate the flesh and thus sublimate desire. Obliquely, Updike has revealed a personal acceptance of Sigmund Freud's* insight that art* (or sainthood) is produced by sublimation created by neurosis.

In "The Egg Race" Updike introduces an older protagonist, Fergusson, who will appear in other stories later. Fergusson is an archaeologist who attends a class reunion and discovers the relentless sweep of the past despite his effort at "digging" into it. The story may fictionalize the experience Updike records in "A Soft Spring Night in Shillington" (*SC*), but unlike Updike, Fergusson is not alone with his memories; he feels that he has in some way failed his father and mentor. Completely different in mood is "Transaction," in which an arch tone is created by Ed's allusions to William Blake's *Auguries of Innocence*, and cosmic imagery* accompanying his tryst with a prostitute imports a wry view of sex.* Like "Augustine's Concubine," "Transaction" contrasts lust with spirit. This ironic use of literature resembles other uses of literature as go-between in *C*, *RV* and "A Constellation of Events" (*TM*).

Bibliography: George W. Hunt, "The Problems of John Updike," *America* 142 (8 Mar. 1980): 187–88; George Garrett, "Technics and Pyrotechnics," *Sewanee Review* 88 (Summer 1980): 412–23; Greiner, *OJ*; Detweiler, *JU*; Luscher, *JU*.

Profumo, John (1915–   ). John Profumo was a British official involved in a sex scandal with Christine Keeler in October 1963. Keeler is the person to be identified by Foxy Whitman* in *Couples* by asking, "Who am I?" in the guessing game* Botticelli.* Since the group is trying to discover if she is having an affair, Foxy is expected to discover her alter ego.* Her tears when she realizes this identify to all but Angela Hanema* that she is Piet Hanema's* mistress. For legal reasons Updike was not permitted to refer to Profumo or Keeler in the British edition.

Proust, Marcel (1871–1922). A French writer best known for his masterly exploration of French life, Marcel Proust was the author of the multivolume *À la recherche du temps perdu (Remembrance of Things Past)*. Other French novelists such as Honoré de Balzac and Émile Zola were equally adept at dissecting society, but Proust's style diverged from their slice-of-life technique to provide a sensuous, poetic evocation of internal states through the use of first-person interior monologue. As Updike remarked in selecting this as one of five moments of "utter reading bliss": "What shimmering Arcadian vistas of illusion and disillusion! This is *prose*." For Proust, the present exists primarily in relation to the past, and only by the sensual recovery of the past is the mind fully participating in experience. Although much of his work is concerned with the effort to reclaim a lost moment of love, its central subject is time.

Updike first read Proust in 1955 and commented in *Horizon* in 1966 that Proust, above all other nineteenth-century writers, "penetrated more deeply into the nature of things, their inter-relations and tones." Updike admitted that he later tried to imitate his language and tone "in the last two stories of *Pigeon Feathers* and *Of the Farm*." Thus, the last story of *PigF*, "The Blessed Man of Boston, My Grandmother's Thimble, and Fanning Island," uses in a "farraginous narrative" a Proustian montage. Like Proust, narrator David Kern* seeks "connections between unlike things." Originally Kern hoped to write a big book about the "Blessed Man," "thousands of pages . . . defiantly dull," so he searches for a way to tell the story of his grandmother's thimble, passed on to his wife and him on their wedding. This leads Kern to recount an incident of his grandmother's odd response to his grandfather's death and to conclude that language is not adequate to "the gestures of nature." But years later, when he recalls light verse* he had written when keeping his grandmother company, the words release such minute images as the features of her nose. From this he concludes, "We learn our desire by turning our backs on it." This becomes the point of the survival story about Fanning Island. From these episodes the narrator has learned how to select details of life that have the greatest resonance, as Albrecht Dürer selects lines in his engravings. This metafiction (a fiction that self-reflexively comments on the making of fiction) reveals how Updike tried to teach himself how to evolve as an artist through a religious adherence to details. Such selection of images would lead him to God's way in the world, or, as he says in "Fanning Island," to "the giant's fingers." The narrator has learned to seek a "Proustian moment" that fully recovers the past in all its meaning, something Updike explores at much greater length in *C*.

Updike nearly parodies this quest in *MF* when he has his hero speculate not on his personal past but the past of President James Buchanan,* in the longest recapturing of the past by any Updike narrator. A later story more in keeping with the discoveries of the early tales is "More Stately Mansions" (*TM*), in which a student's "show and tell" chambered nautilus causes a teacher to retrieve a meaningful love affair from his past. An ambitious Proustian recovery of nature* is demonstrated by Ben Turnbull's* effort to record every alteration in nature throughout the year (*TE*). To illustrate the impact of reading Proust, Updike shows how a character in a story dreams of Proust and suddenly realizes that he knows how *Remembrance of Things Past* will end ("Incest" [*SD*]). Updike can speak wryly of Proust's poignant exploration of time when he writes of the years of *temps perdu* playing golf (*GD*).*

Bibliography: Updike, "Remembrance of Things Past," *Horizon* 14 (Autumn 1972): 102–5; "Pinter's Unproduced Proust Printed" (*HS*); "Should Writers Give Lectures?" (*OJ*); "Proust Died for You," "Five Remembered Moments of Utter Reading Bliss" (*MM*); Hunt, *JU*.

Prynne, Ms. Ms. Prynne is the manager of the motel where Rev. Tom Marshfield* goes to rusticate in *MS*. When Marshfield surmises that she may have been reading his journal, he undertakes a seduction of her that succeeds the night before he leaves. This ending has created controversy, since it seems to nullify Marshfield's monthlong struggle to regain spiritual wholeness. If he commits adultery* with her, the argument runs, then he has not been redeemed, so he is at the least hypocritical and at the most a devil. Defenders say that Marshfield had never seen adultery as jeopardizing his soul, and that this union with Prynne brings him to the fullest concentration of soul and body. *MS* is the first of three novels modeled on *The Scarlet Letter*, by Nathaniel Hawthorne*; Ms. Prynne's name is meant to recall Hester Prynne, and thus the novel describes Updike's modern version of the seduction of Hester by Rev. Arthur Dimmesdale. Marshfield spins many puns on her name, including "Ms. Print." *See* **Ministers; Sex.**

Publishers. While Updike was publishing in the Shillington* High School *Chatterbox** and later the *Harvard Lampoon*,* he sent out many drawings and poems to various magazines, including the *New Yorker*.* When that magazine took three poems and a short story in June 1954, he knew that he had arrived as a professional writer. In 1958 Updike published his first book with Harper's, a collection mostly of light verse* that had originally appeared in the

New Yorker. When Harper's disagreed about the ending of *PF* the following year, Updike showed it to Alfred Knopf, who published it. Since then Knopf has been Updike's exclusive publisher of trade books. (Of course, Updike's introductions, forewords and the like have appeared in books not published by Knopf.) Knopf and Updike have had a happy relationship, with Updike agreeing to publish a novel every other year and Knopf publishing collections of essays, poems or stories in between. The pattern was interrupted in 1973, the only year in which Updike published no books, and in 1996–97 when the novel *TE* followed the novel *IB*. In addition, Knopf has published signed special editions of *BB*, *BIB*, *Coup*, *GD*, *HS*, *JL*, *M*, *Marry*, *MS*, *MW*, *OJ*, *P*, *PP*, *RaR*, *RIR*, *RV*, *S.*, *SC* and *TM*. Knopf has permitted Updike to help select the dust-jacket design and the cover color and even to write the blurbs. Knopf also created an Updike "standard edition," in which the format of the spines and covers does not vary, nor does the typeface, Janson, designed by Nicholas Kris; Updike has invariably published nearly the same brief biography and the same "A Note on the Type" in every Knopf book.

In addition to his professional relationship with Knopf, Updike has been published by Modern Library (*RR* and *PF* in one volume) and Random House/Everyman (*RA*). Updike's paperback publisher has been Fawcett Crest since *PF*. Updike has had many private special editions produced by a variety of over two dozen publishers. Foremost, and praised by Updike, are Lord John Press (Northridge, California) and William Ewert (Concord, New Hampshire). Among his two dozen publishers abroad have been these: in England, Deutsch, Hamish Hamilton and, for paperbacks, Penguin; in France, Gallimard and Seuil; in Germany, Rowohlt; in Italy, Feltrinelli and Mondadori; and in Spain, TusQuets.

Bibliography: Updike, "A Reminiscence of Alfred A. Knopf and Myself" (*OJ*).

Pygmalion. The mythical Greek sculptor Pygmalion's statue of Galatea was brought to life by Aphrodite at his urging. Galatea bore him a son, for whom the city sacred to Aphrodite, Paphos, was named. Updike's story "Pygmalion" (*TM*) treats the irony of a man exchanging one wife for another, only to find that his second wife resembles the first. *See* **Classical Literature**.

Q

Quakers. Originally known as the Religious Society of Friends, the Quakers were founded in the 1640s by George Fox. They espoused the "inner light" as their guide to meaning and so were persecuted by Protestants, but they were protected by William Penn in Pennsylvania. Plain and pacifist, they were progressive in their dealings with Indians and in their intolerance for slavery. Yet John Hook* in *PF* feels that the Quakers were hypocrites and recounts a story told to him by his mentor Rafe Beam. Beam relates that the Quakers willingly accepted runaway slaves, but only so that they would work their farms; they then turned the slaves out in winter to fend for themselves. Hook does consider that this may have been a fabricated story created by Beam's religious intolerance. *See* **Religion**.

Quantum Physics. Max Planck (1858–1947), the German physicist and Nobel laureate who formulated quantum theory, proved that energy is radiated in units he named quanta, and that a universal constant (Planck's constant) is related to quanta. Planck's law states that the energy of each quantum equals the frequency of the radiation multiplied by the universal constant. His discoveries created "quantum mechanics," which theorizes that electromagnetic radiation contains, paradoxically, the characteristics of both waves and particles. Thus subatomic particles act in ways that are counterintuitive; that is, particles can both exist and not exist simultaneously or in two different places at once. Cause may follow effect, and events may be created by the observer, leading to each observer's "creation" of his own universe. Such discoveries have thus challenged customary conceptions of nature* and of man himself. Yet quantum physics does describe the basic operations of nature.

In *RV* Dale Kohler* intends to show that such "madness" is in fact God's fingerprint, and he believes that when such information is installed in a computer, he will be able to force God to reveal himself and end all doubt about whether or not God exists. Kohler believes, with Einstein, that God "does not play dice with the universe," that He would not create a universe man could not understand. In the end, however, Dale is refuted when Myron Kriegman, a biology professor, explains that just as Kohler's logical explanation of how modern physics helps to reveal God, so other possibilities likewise exist which he and others reject because, although possible, they are counter intuitive. Other scientists have seen quantum physics as indicating that everything is connected by a "seamless whole," in which there is a wholeness in time, if not in space. Such an idea may be implied in Ben Turnbull's* meditations on "branching" and the various alter egos* he creates by it. According to "the multiuniverse" theory, which Kriegman had used to trip up Dale, the "branches" may be part of other universes. This leads Updike to employ the "many universes" theory in *TE*, in which Ben Turnbull shifts into four other persons and his wife becomes a deer. Quantum mechanics has been extensively used by science-fiction writers and novelists such as Thomas Pynchon to indicate that unpredictability at the microcosmic level shows that the universe is indeed absurd, a concept that opposes Dale's understanding, but one with which Turnbull seems comfortable. *See* **Science**.

Bibliography: David Malone, "Updike 2020: Fantasy, Mythology and Faith *Toward the End of Time*," in Yerkes, *JU*.

Quattrocentro. The Italian word *quattrocentro* literally means "the fourteen hundreds" and thus the fifteenth century. The word is used in *B* to characterize the aesthetic world of Isabel Leme's* uncle and ironically to comment on the almost medieval devotion of the modern Tristan and Isolde,* Tristâo Raposo* and Isabel Leme.

Queen of Sheba. In the tenth century B.C. the Queen of Sheba ruled an empire where Yemen is today and colonized Ethiopia. Because of its trade in spices, precious metals and stones, her country, Saba, was prosperous. Her celebrated visit to Solomon was partly made to test his reputation as a wise man, and thus it had a political purpose, intending to certify the wide-ranging importance of Solomon. But the story gradually gained a romantic luster, and their supposed son founded the Ethiopian empire. Col. Félix Ellelloû's* fourth wife is named Sheba; she is the only one of his four wives shorter than he, indicating, perhaps, that he is a modern Solomon (*Coup*). The Queen of Sheba is a nickname given to Marge Tremayne in "Leaf Season" (*TM*). *See* **Bible**.

R

"Rabbit" Angstrom. *See* **Angstrom, Harry "Rabbit."**

Rabbit Angstrom (New York: Knopf Everyman, 1995) *RA*, the definitive edition of the Rabbit saga, contains the four "Rabbit" novels (*RR*, 1960; *RRed*, 1971; *RIR*, 1981; *RaR*, 1990). The four novels collectively describe thirty years of American history,* and Rabbit's actions and reactions suggest a general view of the temper of the times as felt by an American Everyman. The title of the saga underlines the significance of its hero as Updike understood his achievement, for he has said that the highest aim of a writer is to create a character* who becomes of enduring importance, an image of national importance, like Tarzan. Rabbit thus fits into the American literary mythology of "American Adams," in R.W.B. Lewis's phrase in *The American Adam*, and joins Natty Bumpo, Huckleberry Finn, Billy Budd, Jay Gatsby and Holden Caulfield, in the estimation of critic Donald Greiner. Also, critic James Schiff in *John Updike Revisited* suggests that *RA* has epic qualities "in the tradition of Whitman's* *Leaves of Grass*." Akin to Walt Whitman's speaker, Rabbit is a common man who is sensual and prone to error, but who wonders about the universe and his place in it, and like other Americans, he is created in part by his nation's history, whether through large events, such as the moon landing, or minor ones, such as a ballplayer's retirement. Updike carefully restricts his point of view so that the reader witnesses the "felt apprehension of life" in all its ambiguity and creates his own conclusions about Rabbit and America, rather than being instructed about their meaning. For Updike, Rabbit was, as he said, "a way in, into the matter of America," (*RA*, "Introduction").

Updike supplied an "Introduction" to *RA*, and editors provided a chronology and bibliography, which was updated in the second printing to cite Jack De Bellis's bibliography of works by and about Updike to 1993. In his

"Introduction" Updike supplies information about the inception of each novel, and elsewhere he explains that Rabbit, "like every stimulating alter ego,* was many things the author was not: a natural athlete, a blue-eyed Swede, sexually magnetic, taller than six feet, impulsive, and urban." Despite this effort to bring the four novels together as a consecutive story, Updike stresses the individual problems attached to the inception and composition of each novel as a discrete work of art. Since Updike used this opportunity to review the novels collectively, he has amended inconsistencies, corrected a few errors, especially in the characters' chronologies, and added a scene with Rev. Jack Eccles* in *RRed* and a locker-room scene in *RaR* approximating the ambience of hell. Also, Updike establishes a timetable for each book.

The four novels appeared at nearly ten-year intervals, but instead of having each novel resume the narrative where the previous one left off, Updike captures events in "real time," as they happen now. This creates problems, since the reader needs to fill in the gaps, but Updike minimizes the inconvenience by supplying clues that the attentive reader will notice. Because he picks up each novel after the passage of time, the reader needs to be sure that the characters are the same ones he recalls, and also that they have experienced change. Like our own lives, theirs must offer a sense of continuity but also a sense of alteration. Part of the joy of reading the four novels consecutively is that we participate in Rabbit's recall. Thus when he reflects on a key image or line of dialogue, the reader does as well; the result is a greater identification with Rabbit and a more profound sense that he is like us, remembering images and events and putting them into the brain's inventory. This multileveled process creates Rabbit's identity, as it does ours. Thus the reader forges a very firm bond to Updike's hero. Since Updike has published a decade's worth of fiction, poetry and essays in between each of the Rabbit novels, his treatment of Rabbit alters as he matures as a novelist and undergoes his own evolution. As Updike ages, so does Rabbit, and so do we if we have read the novels at their times of publication. Not to have done so obviously creates a very different reading experience. To have been privileged to read them as they were published provides an experience that can never be repeated.

To give a sense of coherence to the four books, Updike not only supplies general consistency of characters and diversity within similarity, but he creates webs of images,* motifs and symbols* that bind the books together as muscle to tendon to bone. Thus the circular image related to the basketball* hoop in *RR* links to the circular moon in *RRed* and Krugerrands and silver coins of *RIR* and the central circular desk in the intensive care unit in *RaR*. The four books are circularized in Rabbit's run south at the start of *RR* and his run south at the end of *RaR*. Further, these circular images become motifs of entrapment underlining Rabbit's running in *RR*, jogging in *RIR*, and running in *RaR*. They are allied to a great many related images, like the golf* ball and cup, and above all the vagina, Rabbit's ultimate trap. Rabbit's own actions thus are circular: he ends where he began. Critics like Schiff and Charles Berryman have described the connections of other motifs across the novels; part of the reader's fun in perusing the novels is the personal discovery of such connections. The result, however, is unsettling, since the tightness of the many strands of images and symbols not only binds the books together as one and makes a lasting aesthetic and emotional experience, but also suggests a vast net pulled tighter around Rabbit as his narrative continues, an increasing constraint on his freedom. Updike has said that the title of the first novel, *RR*, should be read as an imperative for Rabbit— Rabbit, *run!*—who wishes to follow his inner light, but that imperative has challenged a social fabric made of many cords that are much stronger than he. Updike wondered if in following his urge Rabbit would make the social fabric unravel, but Updike's knot of images suggests that the social fabric is far stronger than Rabbit and in the end entangles him. *See* **Angstrom, Earl; Angstrom, Mary; Angstrom, Teresa "Pru."**

Bibliography: Updike, "Introduction," in *Rabbit Angstrom: A Tetralogy* (New York: Knopf, 1995); "Introduction to the Easton Press Edition of the Rabbit Novels," "Remarks in Acceptance of the National Book Critics Circle Award for Fiction" (*MM*); Schiff, *JU*; Charles Berryman, "Updike Redux:" "A Series Retrospective," in Broer, *RT*; Jeff H. Campbell, " 'Middling, Hidden, Troubled America': John Updike's Rabbit Tetralogy," in Broer, *RT*; Donald Greiner, "Rabbit as Adamic Hero," in Broer, *RT*.

Rabbit at Rest (New York: Knopf, 1990). The fourth and concluding novel of the "Rabbit saga," *RaR* chronicles the life of Harry "Rabbit" Angstrom* from his retirement to his death.* Occasionally humorous, the novel is essentially a somber farewell that particularizes gathering illness, unsatisfied longings, disillusionment with children and dissatisfaction with the changes in the world. Yet Updike provides a powerful series of images that reveal how Rabbit lived life on his own terms, in response to his intuition when he was twenty-six that some "thing" wanted him to find it. The "thing" now seems to be his sense of uniqueness, something everyone feels.

The narrative opens with Rabbit and Janice Angstrom* awaiting the Christmas visit of their son Nelson Angstrom* and his wife Teresa "Pru" Angstrom* and their children, eight-year-old Judy Angstrom* and four-year-old Roy Angstrom.* Rabbit does his best to entertain them, but when he takes them to Jungle Gardens, he accidentally eats parrot food, and when he takes Judy sailing in a Sunfish, the boat capsizes, and because Judy pretends to be in danger, Rabbit's strenuous effort to rescue her leads to his heart attack. Rabbit recovers in Florida,* then returns to Brewer* and eventually undergoes angioplasty, having rejected bypass surgery. He then discovers that Nelson has been stealing from Springer Motors* ("cooking the books") to finance his cocaine addiction, and though Rabbit moves swiftly to reorganize and to confront the Toyota representative, Natsume Shimada,* Janice and Nelson through imaginative financing save the company. Nelson successfully rehabilitates and becomes involved with social work, but Rabbit remains skeptical and quietly resents Janice's attempt to become a realtor. The night he returns from the hospital after angioplasty, Rabbit and his daughter-in-law make love, but when Pru reveals their tryst to Janice and Nelson, perhaps to ruin Janice's plan that they all move in together, Rabbit runs to a Florida retirement condominium and alternates between guarding his health and eating recklessly. Before he can reconcile with his family, Rabbit has a massive heart attack while playing a basketball* game and dies in the hospital as his wife and son watch.

Updike had two visions of Rabbit's adventures: one, of a four-volume set of Rabbit novels; and the second, of sending his hero out in style. He explained to shocked readers why Rabbit had to "go" and that *RaR* would have no sequel. For his first vision, Updike was not content to simply track the last year of Rabbit's life. He decided to provide parallels to *RR* so that the last book of the series would balance the first as a kind of bookend. Such counterpoising enables the reader to match Rabbit's start with his finish and gains an increased poignancy for his departure; the bookends also help to give a sense of circularity that completely encloses the hero. Nothing more remains to be said. Since each book is steeped in American history,* linking *RR* to *RaR* produces a review of the major political and social determinants in American life and raises the importance of Rabbit by enforcing his symbolic representation of America.

Like *RR*, *RaR* is divided into three parts, and in both books Rabbit runs south to flee domestic predicaments; but in *RaR* Rabbit makes it all the way south as he had wished to do thirty years earlier, to Valhalla, the symbolic name of his condominium community. Other incidents link the books: as Rabbit was responsible for the death of his daughter Rebecca Angstrom* in *RR*, his saving Judy rights the balance; Judy's part in saving Rabbit also cancels his sense, at the end of *RIR*, that she was "another nail in the coffin." Events draw *RR* and *RaR* together: desertion of his family in the first book becomes self-exile in the fourth; Janice's alcohol dependency in *RR* becomes Nelson's addiction, but with rehabilitation, in *RaR*. Characters from *RR* come to resemble those in *RaR*: Ruth Leonard Byer* transforms into his mistress Thelma Harrison,* who also evolves from Mrs. Smith, who said that Rabbit gave her life. Advice-giving Jimmie the Big Mouseketeer* and coach Marty Tothero* transform into three retired Jewish golfers; Tothero also appears as the dying Lyle. The golf* game with Rev. Jack Eccles* in *RR* becomes the bitter match with Ronnie Harrison.* Rabbit's hostile father in *RR* becomes Rabbit as father scolding his son in *RaR*. Bessie Springer's* money acumen restates itself in Janice's real-estate cunning in *RaR*. As the golf ball rose in Rabbit's perfect shot in *RR*, his urge toward ascent is brought crashing to earth in *RaR*, manifested in his fear that the plane carrying his family will crash to earth. That fear is also a foreshadowing of his crashing to the ground after making his last basketball shot. Entertaining fantasy films* with relevant messages occur in each novel: in *RR*, *Bell, Book and Candle*, a film about a man who loves a witch, has its counterpart in *RaR* in the movie *The Return of Martin Guerre*, about a man who impersonates a dead soldier and is burned for living the lie. Even images like the block of ice in *RR* become in *RaR* the colossal image of Antarctica. In short, Updike binds together these two books in numerous ways, mainly by developing elements of the original image. Thus what Updike called "interesting formal things" (Plath, *CU*) to be found linking *RR* and *RRed* can be discovered connecting all four novels, and that is part of the enjoyment of the accumulative power of the four books.

Rabbit is the most important of these structures, and the most mysterious. The reader, alternately sympathetic and critical of him, admires his determination to be himself but opposes his selfish misuse of others. Because he is a representative of America, if not of Americans, these oppositions are understandable. Even with a failing heart, Rabbit agrees to lead the July Fourth parade as a lurching Uncle Sam,* who, when he is asked for directions, realizes that he cannot tell anyone anything. His mask nearly peels from his face; some bystanders remember him as Rabbit, and this leads to his generality that America is the happiest country ever created. But that country, in his image, is staggering and ignorant. Rabbit's decade-long affair with Thelma Harrison no doubt produces the dual happiness of sex* with no emotional attachment and of cuckolding his enemy Ronnie. But after Thelma dies, Ronnie castigates Rabbit not because he has been told by her of the affair, but because Rabbit did not love her. This is a sudden edification from an unexpected source. Thelma's unconditional love has been wasted. Rabbit also seems to sleepwalk through his marriage, not only dependent on Janice since she effectively owns the business, but also unable to see the world through her eyes. We can sympathize with his irritation at her faults, but we tend to bristle at his continuous inability to recognize her strengths. As if learning a degree of tolerance, Rabbit sympathizes somewhat with the dying homosexual Lyle, even though Lyle has helped Nelson embezzle money from the family business in order to underwrite AIDS* medication. But Rabbit's sympathy is short-lived and essentially prompted by his own fear of death. Such oscillations in and out of sympathy are analogous to his weaving in and out of consciousness as he dies.

Though both *RR* and *RaR* are novels written in the present tense, *RaR* is necessarily more retrospective, as Rabbit recalls his early life with Ruth Leonard and again tries to find their daughter, convinced that Ruth did not abort her. Yet when it seems possible that the nurse who is helping him recover from his heart problem might in fact be his and Ruth's child, Rabbit rejects her offer to arrange a meeting with her mother. Rabbit takes to his grave this unfinished business so that he might live with the hope of spring, associated not only with the time of his affair with Ruth but with the Bradford pear trees bursting into bloom. "Tell your mother," Rabbit tells Annabelle Byer,* "we'll meet some other time," thinking, "Under the pear trees, in paradise." He thinks in the same images that were in his mind when Pru offered herself to him; thus Ruth and Pru in his mind are one. At the end of *RR* Rabbit runs off ambiguously; at the end of *RaR* he dies ambiguously, seemingly unable to speak, drifting in and out of consciousness in a way similar to that in the first novel when he wavered between "the conscience" of "the right way and the good way." Though Rabbit "says" to Nelson, "All I can tell you is, it isn't so bad," it seems unlikely he could speak so articulately. His last words are in his mind, without quotation marks, "Maybe. Enough." Perhaps the separation of the two words into sentences signals the onset of death. But we have no definitive statement such as "Rabbit died." Because we do not, Rabbit's consciousness appears not to have ended; the narrative voice* has refused to separate itself from him. Or it dies with him.

Updike has admitted in his "Introduction" to drawing together in *RaR* the three items of the *RR* epigraph*: "grace," "external circumstances" and "hardness of heart." In *RaR* "grace" may be shown through Rabbit's victory against extreme odds in basketball; "external circumstances" in the traps of Nelson's embezzlement and perhaps Pru's entrapment in "incest"*; and "hardness of heart" in Rabbit's break with his family and the literal scarring of his "athlete's heart." As Updike explains, "The hardened heart becomes no longer a metaphor, but an actual physical thing" (Plath, *CU*). Though some readers find Rabbit's incest with Pru detestable, their union does exhibit one last spontaneous effort at sex-as-healing. Facing death, he faces life, just as Pru, feeling worthless, is provided a slender sense of worth. Yet Updike is realistic enough to show that love hardly enters Rabbit's relations with Thelma, Pru and Janice. Rabbit lacks the confidence to love the custodians of the mystery of birth that so captivates him. He may also lack, as Nelson asserts, the courage to love since Rabbit is "afraid of it, it would tie you down."

For Updike, his hero's end was personal. When he researched cardiovascular problems (much like those that afflicted and killed his mother as he was finishing *RaR*), Updike experienced pains resembling those of Rabbit. He found himself physically tied to his alter ego.* Rabbit's finish felt like his own, Updike said, and at the end he admired Rabbit's arrogance in seizing life.

Bibliography: Updike, "Why Rabbit Had to Go," *New York Times Book Review* 5 Aug. 1990: 1, 24–25; "Introduction," in *Rabbit Angstrom: A Tetralogy* (New York: Knopf, 1995); Joyce Carol Oates, "So Young!" *New York Times Book Review* 30 Sept. 1990: 1, 43; Ralph C. Wood, "Rabbit Runs Down," *Christian Century* 107 (21 Nov. 1990): 1098–1101; Stacey Olster, "Rabbit Rerun: Updike's Replay of Popular Culture in *Rabbit at Rest*," *Modern Fiction Studies* 37 (Spring 1991): 45–59; Judie Newman,

"*Rabbit at Rest*: The Return of the Work Ethic," in Broer, *RT*; Edward Vargo, "Corn Chips, Catheters, Toyotas: The Making of History in *Rabbit at Rest*," in Broer, *RT*.

Rabbit Is Rich (New York: Knopf, 1981). *RIR*, the third novel of the tetralogy about Harry "Rabbit" Angstrom,* continues to explore the restless need Rabbit feels for something more than material success. The most humorous—Updike calls it "buoyant"—book of the quartet, *RIR* shifts attention toward Rabbit's son Nelson Angstrom* and his wedding, and toward Rabbit and his wife Janice Angstrom's* taking advantage of their money and leisure.

As the head of the Toyota agency partly inherited at Fred Springer's* death, and with the rising price of gasoline making gas-stingy Toyotas popular, Rabbit is rich. His money has bought him country-club membership, Caribbean vacations, investments in gold and silver with discretionary income and, eventually, a new home. Unlike the upheavals in America in *RRed* that had penalized Rabbit by destroying his home, the national gasoline shortage has brought him prosperity. The only flaw in this cozy life is Nelson, who mysteriously returns from Kent State with Melanie, a friend of Teresa "Pru" Lubell (Angstrom*), a secretary at Kent State whom Nelson had impregnated. Pru has sent Melanie with him to keep him from seeing other women, but ironically, Melanie and Nelson become casual lovers. Though Janice keeps Pru's pregnancy a secret from Rabbit, when Pru arrives, he divines that she is pregnant. Rabbit feels attracted to her, but not to the more available Melanie, who eventually has an affair with Charlie Stavros,* Janice's former lover and a Springer Motors* salesman. Rabbit fears that Nelson has been trapped, as he had been, by an unplanned pregnancy and tries to get Nelson to cancel the wedding. Nelson resents his father's interference and goes through with the wedding, though he whines to Janice about his father and makes obscene jokes at the expense of minister* Archie "Soupy" Campbell.

Rabbit gets richer by speculating in gold and silver at Webb Murkett's* recommendation. Three comic scenes underline the absurdity of Rabbit's riches: in one he sprinkles Krugerrands over Janice's nude body before intercourse; in another the Angstroms hustle the wealth (now converted to silver coins) to their safe-deposit box, Janice looking as if she is pregnant, Rabbit sweating as he never did for the money, and while they are in the vault, they consider having sex*; in the third scene talk of buying a new house accompanies their foreplay.

Since 51 percent of the car agency has remained in the hands of Janice and her mother Bessie Springer,* they install the newly married Nelson in Charlie Stavros's position as a car salesman, despite Rabbit's strenuous objections. Nelson had been involved in Oedipal rivalry with his father for both Janice and Jill Pendleton's* affections in *RRed*; working for Rabbit only aggravates the situation. Nelson even tells his mother that he wants Rabbit to die. However, Nelson disgraces himself, to Rabbit's delight, by buying convertibles and snowmobiles when the lot is entrusted to him during the Angstroms' brief vacation in the Poconos. But to Rabbit's dismay, the convertibles sell and Nelson is vindicated.

Meanwhile, Rabbit suspects that Ruth Leonard Byer* did not abort his child, as she had threatened (*RR*). He guesses in the first chapter that a young woman, Annabelle Byer,* might be his daughter, and so he spies on Ruth's farm (her husband is now deceased) looking for some evidence. He cannot confront Ruth about Annabelle, though, until he has settled with three other women in his life—Cindy Murkett,* Thelma Harrison* and Janice. Young and sexy, Cindy has been attractive to him for some time, but also because she is the wife of Webb Murkett,* his mentor, her acquisition would draw him closer to Webb. A disastrous attempt to flirt on a Sunfish with her makes the craft capsize, and Rabbit never declares his feelings to her. Rabbit's hopes really capsize when the Murketts and Thelma Harrison and her husband Ronnie Harrison* vacation with the Angstroms. The couples agree to exchange spouses, and Cindy goes to his archrival Ronnie. Deprived for one more night, Rabbit must settle for Ronnie's wife Thelma. Nelson's desertion of Pru the next day forces the Angstroms to return to Brewer,* destroying Rabbit's last chance to sleep with Cindy. However, he and Janice have reaped rewards. With Webb, Janice has had the best erotic time of her life, what Rabbit had hoped for himself. Thelma, who had "adored" Rabbit for years, has provided him a night of unforgettable playful, loving sex. Countering Webb's guideline that the affairs not be extended after the rotation of lovers, Thelma and Rabbit continue their relationship for ten years, even though he never loves her. Thelma's initiation of Rabbit to anal intercourse purges him of his fear of death* and his interest in Cindy.

When Nelson's desertion of his family forces Janice and Rabbit to return to Brewer, Rabbit concentrates his attention on discovering the truth about Annabelle from Ruth, but he finds only further ambiguity since Ruth has been embittered not only by his desertion twenty years before but also by his continuing indifference to her life. Although she insists that she aborted their child, Rabbit remains unconvinced, apparently still hoping to replace the daughter drowned accidentally in *RR*. As compensation, though, after he has established himself in his new home and freed himself from the tyranny of his mother-in-law, Bessie Springer, Pru presents him with his granddaughter Judy.* Judy now becomes Rabbit's real riches, but also concrete evidence of his irrelevance and coming death.

Updike's careful rereading of his previous two books provides close continuity to *RIR*, and the third novel of the series advances many of the images, motifs and themes of the previous two Rabbit novels. The image of Harry as a "rabbit" continues in his "running"—he even takes up jogging in the Poconos—his appetite for soft food* and his eating a kohlrabi raw, as well as, of course, in his sexual desire. The images of the drowned baby and the dead runaway Jill merge in Rabbit's capsizing the Sunfish. He is saved by a woman, as Janice has saved Stavros from a heart attack (*RRed*). Jill and Melanie have each had problems with their fathers; both are upper class and guiltless about sex and drugs,* but Jill succumbed to the dangers of the 1960s, while Melanie survived the 1970s. Janice has also evolved from subservience to action and from desperation to greater control. Still reliant on feminine subterfuge, Janice becomes more assertive by helping to get Nelson married, possibly arranging the wife swapping and screening Thelma, she thinks, from Rabbit afterward, as she had ended his affair with Margaret Fosnacht at the end of *RRed*.

The many active and clever women help to give the novel its buoyancy and humor. Since one characteristic of comedy* is that women win, the novel is primarily comic. Rabbit himself is often comical: the women keep him guessing about the reason for Nelson's return and Melanie's appearance; he tries to amuse the Flying Eagle crowd with a joke about a goose and becomes instead the butt of a joke; Ruth's bitch Fritzie is thwarted by Rabbit, who takes pleasure in feeling he outsmarted a dog; and his expectations are reversed when he fails to get Cindy, probably because of Janice's connivance. Finally, he fumes impotently as women install Nelson over his objections, but when he is potent, he makes love to an unconscious wife or purchases her cooperation with a shower of Krugerrands. He is overturned in the bed swap by the backstage machinations of the women. Above all, he finds that the wife he thought a dumb mutt is now his real treasure, but even so, he meekly allows Janice to feed him a frozen-food dinner because the picture on the package appealed to her.

Yet Rabbit is more than comic. As Ruth pronounced in *RR*, he is "still trying," and he tries nothing less than the reconciliation of his religious impulses to the tawdry reality he so willingly inhabits and the vulgar materialism that gives him his good life. He still seeks in the Sunday supplements evidence that God may yet have the last word, perhaps through quasars, and he keeps hoping that his daughter was not aborted, that out of his body he had created a woman. (Ironically, Nelson has performed that act of metamorphosis in creating Judy.) Rabbit's realism is not sentimentalized in the face of such hope and reconciliation: he still recognizes that as he is carried forward into the future by his grandchild, his life is nearly over. He may be running out of gas, but he is still a man in motion. The forces of growth have been with him: as he worked his own way toward accommodations with women and his son, his grandchild was gestating within Pru's body, as Becky had been within Janice in *RR*. But now he, not Janice, holds the future in his hands, or so he thinks.

Bibliography: Updike [Henry Bech], "Updike on Updike" (*HS*); Roger Sale, "Rabbit Returns," *New York Times Book Review* 27 Sept. 1981: 1, 32–34; Thomas R. Edwards, "Updike's Rabbit Trilogy," *Atlantic* 248 (Oct. 1981): 94, 96, 100–1; George

W. Hunt, "Updike's Rabbit Returns," *America* 145 (21 Nov. 1981): 321–22; Margaret Gullette, "John Updike: Rabbit Angstrom Grows Up," in *Safe at Last in the Middle Years* (Berkeley: University of California Press, 1988), 59–84; Ristoff, *UA*; Victor K. Lasseter, "*Rabbit Is Rich* as a Naturalistic Novel," *American Literature* 61 (Oct. 1989): 429–45; Schiff, *JU*.

Rabbit Redux (New York: Knopf, 1971). Updike has said that he had no intention of writing a sequel to *RR*, but that frequent inquiries about what happened at the end of *RR* led him to revisit his "old friend." Rather than simply continuing Harry "Rabbit" Angstrom's* situation from the point where he ended in *RR*, Updike decided on the more adventurous project of picking him up as if Rabbit had had a continuous existence since 1960. Thus Updike would replicate his own experience of writing the book from immediate experience. This "real-time" reentry of Rabbit would force readers to fill in the hiatus and wonder how and why Rabbit had changed since *RR*, intensifying the reading experience, since Rabbit and the reader would simultaneously be tested to recall what had happened in the previous book. To facilitate such recall, Updike devised many parallels to make *RRed* "Symmetric" with *RR* (*RA*, "Introduction"). Situating Rabbit in the 1960s also enabled Updike to make him the focus and embodiment of the excitement and confusion of that decade. Rabbit not only witnesses but experiences aspects of the Vietnam* War, the women's movement, the moon flight, civil rights protests, Black Power and drug* abuse. Since Rabbit is Updike's alter ego,* Updike shared Rabbit's defense of the Vietnam War and his conflicted feelings about women and African Americans.* As Updike noted, Rabbit was a "receptacle for my disquiet and resentments, which would sit more becomingly on him than on me." Rabbit responds, as critic James Schiff notes, suffering, marveling, listening and enduring, and in this he is like America of the 1960s. Updike's odd title draws attention to the need to bring Rabbit back to health. Only the upheavals of the 1960s would provide enough energy to spring him loose.

At the end of *RR*, Rabbit returns to his family after attempting to abandon them; in *RRed* the reader learns that he has been living a life-in-death since then. Sex* with his wife Janice Angstrom* is nearly nonexistent because he fears impregnating her again, associating their having a child with the death* of their daughter (as recorded in *RR*) and possibly bringing death back into his life. Apathetic to his personal extension into the future, he is also indifferent to the history* he witnesses daily while working alongside his father setting type at Verity Press. As *Apollo 11** takes men to the moon in the first chapter of the novel, Rabbit reluctantly celebrates the birthday of his mother, Mary Angstrom,* who warns him, like an oracle, that his wife, Janice, has taken a lover. When Janice admits that she loves Charlie Stavros,* Rabbit refuses to fight for her, and she leaves.

Rabbit then drifts into the counterculture, first by visiting an African-

American bar, then by sleeping with a runaway, Jill Pendleton,* foisted off on him so the blacks can avoid racially motivated attacks, then by hosting Skeeter,* a Vietnam veteran and drug* dealer. Rabbit indifferently accepts it all. Apathetic but curious, Rabbit allows Skeeter to stay, though this jeopardizes his son Nelson Angstrom.* In Updike's words, Rabbit's house "becomes America suddenly playing host to a runaway and black radical." Janice's frantic objections have no effect, and Rabbit drifts into evenings designed by Jill and Skeeter as "Teach-ins," which, as Updike reminds us in an introduction to *RA*, were intended to reveal to him how he has thoughtlessly supported an oppressive political system. Obviously Rabbit identifies so thoroughly with such American values that he feels no threat from the ideas of Jill and Skeeter. With them Rabbit smokes pot,* unaware that Skeeter intends to hook Jill on heroin so that she will envision God as she had when a previous lover gave her hallucinogens. Skeeter needs God's assurance that he will be the Black Messiah, destined to lead a revolution of which the Vietnam War is the first battle. Skeeter thus parodies Rabbit's ambition in *RR* to find "the thing." Skeeter lures Jill not only into addiction but also into sexual bondage, and during one of their liaisons local youths spy through the window while Jill fellates Skeeter. The aroused citizens, led by a Vietnam veteran, burn Rabbit's home; Jill dies in the fire. (Historically, a biracial couple were similarly burnt out in Reading*; as Updike reported, "The black man had attended my high school" [*SC*]). In the vacuum left by Janice's desertion, Nelson had created a close relationship with Jill, which Rabbit suspected was also sexual. Jill's death was Rabbit's fault, Nelson says, and her death forms a wound that will not heal.

Meanwhile, Janice has unleashed her rediscovered sexuality on Charlie Stavros, and since Charlie finds long-term sex with her likely to damage his weak heart, he tries to return her to Rabbit. But Rabbit has disliked Charlie for being Greek and a car salesman and resents his objection to the Vietnam War. Rabbit's trust in Lyndon Johnson's* policies resembles Updike's ideas as he expressed them in "On Not Being a Dove" (*SC*). Eventually, Janice leaves Charlie, but only after their strenuous sex induces his heart attack and Rabbit's sister Miriam "Mim" Angstrom,* now a Las Vegas call girl, helps Rabbit by seducing Charlie. Mim's intervention, the death of Jill and the flight of Skeeter enable the Angstroms to reconcile. Since the same technology that had put a man on the moon renders Rabbit's typesetting job obsolete, he cannot reject Fred Springer's* offer to sell cars at Springer Motors.* Rabbit's guilt over Jill's inadvertent death has canceled Janice's guilt over Rebecca's* accidental drowning, and Rabbit has been led a bit closer to health.

RRed came into existence not only because Updike's readers had begged to know what happened to Rabbit after *RR*, but because Updike could not turn his research about President James Buchanan* into a novel he had promised Knopf, so he returned to Rabbit. This was the most fortuitous writer's block of Updike's career, since critics would later hail *RRed* as Updike's "big book," with mighty themes and political ideas. Some thought that Updike's daring to create a black revolutionary in the wake of the furor over William Styron's *Confessions of Nat Turner* had produced the best black character ever created by a white writer. They would also come to hail the Rabbit saga as Updike's finest accomplishment, and several would begin to consider Rabbit Angstrom a modern Everyman. In tribute to the failed Buchanan project, in *RRed* Updike gave the name Buchanan to the character who introduces Rabbit to Jill. (James Buchanan was obliquely involved in the death of a young woman as well.)

As a continuation of *RR*, *RRed* is surprising. It does not seem to be written by Updike, since during the socially conscious 1960s he had been dismissed by many critics as politically disengaged. True to his material, rather than responding to his critics, Updike used Rabbit as a reactor rather than a "proactive" figure. As Rabbit said, the "inner light trip" he had once taken had resulted in his daughter Becky's death; he is wrong, though, to think that inaction will not also lead to death. His decision to leave the Vietnam War to President Johnson is personalized when he allows Hubert Johnson (alias Skeeter) to invade his home and corrupt his ally, Jill. He passively watches the film* *2001: A Space Odyssey** without seeing that his mechanical existence resembles that of the computer HAL who destroys astronauts attempting to resolve a cosmic mystery. Rabbit is a witness to the 1960s, but his malaise had been created by his return to Janice in June 1959.

The malaise is startling in its thoroughness. For example, when Rabbit is consoled by his mother about Janice's desertion, and while they each take part in history by watching the first moon walk, Rabbit admits that he feels nothing about *Apollo 11* or Janice's flight. When Jill arrives in his home, he merely sees her as offering sex in exchange for room and board and ignores the consequences for Nelson. If Janice was serious about trying to seek a "valid identity" (however, the phrase sounds like television* psychobabble), Rabbit's willingness to allow Skeeter as well as Jill to live in his home shows a desire for revenge on Janice and protection of an "invalid identity," a species of death wish. Rabbit responds to Jill's frank eroticism and openness with revenge on women, love and sex. He is unmoved by Skeeter's account of American history* in which blacks were left out of the Industrial Revolution to keep them enslaved. Rabbit is also not convinced by Skeeter's notion that by being marginalized, black Americans became "technology's nightmare," enabling them to overthrow white culture. Rabbit has so nursed his own suffering that he refuses any responsibility for black suffering.

Yet Janice does force him to reconsider his situation, Jill does enable him to humble himself to her, Nelson does remind him of his nurturing role, and Skeeter does wring from him the admission that had he the power, he would destroy the doctor who had callously treated his mother. His conscience, if not raised, has been revived. The late appearance of his sister

Mim has provided challenges to his views of sex, Vietnam and God. The first two challenges cause him to reformulate his attitudes, but the last causes retrenchment. Mim thinks that "God died on the trail" and advises Rabbit to beware the new generation in the West that understands that God is dead, since its members have developed a "cockroach philosophy" that has made them utterly unreceptive to compassion. Rabbit, however, resists this, still looks for God, senses that Jill's ghost has returned, and accepts Janice's observation that "not everything" is his fault. Rabbit's malaise has left him ill equipped to ward off alone the maladies of the 1960s, but his guides, despite their private agendas, have enabled him to learn something about self-healing. Some may see him, as critic Robert Detweiler does, as having undergone an education, but Rabbit is, as his creator says, "a somewhat slow learner." *See* **Science**.

Bibliography: Richard Locke, "Rabbit Returns: Updike Was Always There—It's Time We Noticed," *New York Times Book Review* 14 Nov. 1971: 1–2, 12–16, 20–21; Wayne Falke, *"Rabbit Redux*: Time/Order/God," *Modern Fiction Studies* 20 (Spring 1974): 59–75; Detweiler, *JU*; Jack De Bellis, " 'The Awful Power': John Updike's Use of Kubrick's *2001: A Space Odyssey* in *Rabbit Redux," Literature/Film Quarterly* 21.3 (1993): 209–17; Schiff, *JU*.

Rabbit, Run (New York: Knopf, 1960). *RR*, the first of four novels concerning Harry "Rabbit" Angstrom,* who would come to be known as an American Everyman, is Updike's most widely known book. The inception of the book occurred when Updike remarked that he was struck that so many ex-athletes seemed to litter Reading.* He thought this "statement" "worth somehow embodying" (Plath, *CU*) in a novel. An ex–basketball* player whose sports* success has left him unfit for the "second-rate" life of working and raising a family, Rabbit retains his inner need for first-ratedness, or what critic Joyce Markle calls "specialness." His belief that "something" wants him to find it questions the values of his time, though Updike does not offer Rabbit as either savior or martyr. Rabbit is a rich and complex character, but neither his striving for the "first-rate" nor his position as critic of his time earns Updike's endorsement.

Running home after work demonstrating the MagiPeel kitchen gadget, Rabbit intrudes himself into a boys' basketball game and is fired by the memory of how he set records as a high-school basketball star. He returns to his cramped apartment to find his pregnant wife Janice Angstrom* drinking a highball and watching *The Mickey Mouse Club*. She has left their son Nelson Angstrom* at his mother's and their car at hers, but when Rabbit fetches Nelson, he sees his parents so enraptured by feeding his boy that he feels no longer needed by his family. Life is second-rate, and to reclaim his first-ratedness he drives south toward the cotton fields, but after getting lost in West Virginia, he returns to Mt. Judge.* He finds shelter with Marty Tothero,* his former basketball coach, who taught him that success on the

Courtesy of Alfred Knopf

court would mean success in life, yet Tothero drinks, consorts adulterously with prostitutes and virtually pimps for Rabbit. After his night with Ruth Leonard Byer,* a part-time hooker, Rabbit moves in with her.

Meanwhile, Janice has asked her minister,* Rev. Jack Eccles,* to persuade Rabbit to return. Eccles, during a golf* game, undermines Rabbit's quest for the "first-rate" by urging him to admit that the "thing" he pursues cannot be touched or seen, and that his quest excuses the pursuit of his instincts. But when Rabbit hits a perfect tee shot, his spirit lifts with the ball, and he knows that his instinct can be followed. Sex* with Ruth also helps Rabbit confirm his first-ratedness, but when he discovers that his old teammate and rival Ronnie Harrison* had once been Ruth's lover, to erase her contaminating past, he compels her to perform the same action on him that she performed on Harrison, fellatio. She accepts this "humbling," but that night Eccles calls to inform Rabbit that Janice is in labor. Rabbit runs to the hospital, determined to end his flight of "cruelty, obscenity and deceit." He sees in his baby, Rebecca,* a confirmation that his own specialness has been passed on to her because "she knows she's good." But after she returns home with the baby, Janice resists Rabbit's sexual advances, so he decides to roam Mt. Judge all night. While he is gone, Janice gets drunk and accidentally drowns Becky while bathing her. Rabbit is devastated by the news, but he feels that his daughter has gone to heaven, so when he stands at the grave site feeling unfairly accused of her death,* he reminds everyone that Janice, not he, was guilty. Since everyone appears to feel that had he stayed home, Janice would not have become drunk and the baby would not have died, he clambers back to Ruth. But Ruth reveals that Rabbit has impregnated her and intends to abort his child if he does not leave Janice. Because Rabbit is unwilling to contribute to the death of a second baby, but is also unwilling to desert Janice, and because he cannot return to a family that unjustly accuses him of the death of Becky, he runs. Neither choice would return him to first-ratedness.

In *RR*, an experimental novel for its day, Updike used the present tense (as he would in the other Rabbit novels as well) to give a sense of immediacy, establish the primacy of instinctual feeling and action and create a cinematographic flow of scenes. (In fact, Updike originally called the novel *A Movie*; it was one of only two of his novels to be made into a film.*) Although Updike's narrative voice* constantly interprets Rabbit's feelings, it does not judge them, and his use of stream of consciousness with Rabbit, Ruth, Janice and Jack Eccles's wife, Lucy Eccles,* exposes thoughts without evaluating them. This strategy resembles the nondidactic mode of film. Judgment is left entirely to the reader. Updike has said that his early books were deliberately fashioned as debates with the reader about what goodness is, or what a good man is. The reader is forced to consider: should one insist on his "inner light" or extinguish it to become a good family man? The dilemma is what Updike calls the "yes, but"* problem: "yes to our dearest inner strivings, but the social fabric unravels."

Along with Rabbit's vague but real "inner strivings," Updike makes the social fabric concrete through a vivid use of Americana—songs, films, jokes and, above all, basketball, which, as Updike remarked, embodied for him the meaning of what it is to be an American. (He has confessed that he idolized basketball heroes and often pretended that he was one, never having made it past an "aborted year" in junior varsity.) Critic Joyce Markle observes that the images of basketball radiate throughout the novel, from the basketball net's circularity to the rectangular space in which to run and the ascent/descent of the ball. Critic Dilvo Ristoff has pointed out that Rabbit cannot really rend the social fabric, just fray it a bit, since he is so much a part of it. He does not reject marriage, just marriage to Janice. He does not resist religion,* just religion of certain kinds. He wants things to be as they were; he does not want things destroyed. But his "inner strivings" can only be expressed with guilt; Rabbit faces becoming an accomplice in the death of his baby Becky and the abortion* of Ruth's fetus.

Reverend Eccles ridicules Rabbit for not having a good-enough reason for deserting Janice and rending the social fabric, yet Eccles is criticized by Rabbit's Lutheran minister Fritz Kruppenbach* for plunging himself into the social fabric, to the neglect of his duty to serve as a model of Christ. Eccles has forgotten the spiritual embodiment of "first-ratedness." For the first time in his novels, Updike reveals the delinquency of ministers for failing to tend with adequate spiritual rigor to the souls of people, and Updike has insisted that all his early work in some way treats this as a serious religious problem. Eccles ridicules Rabbit for having a woman attached to his "inner light trip," but Ruth praises Rabbit for refusing to quit, and Mrs. Smith, for whom he gardens, says unequivocally, "You give people life." Rabbit attends one of Eccles's sermons,* and because it manifests a darker theological earnestness than Eccles had previously shown, Rabbit grows bored, and his eyes "glance toward the light," light reflected from Eccles's wife Lucy.

Updike thus fashions a problem that recurs in many of his characters*: how can one who aspires to self-perfection create such trouble? The reader feels forced to choose sides and uses the responses of various characters to Rabbit in framing an answer. Rabbit's parents are divided. His father Earl Angstrom* thinks him "the worst kind of Brewer* bum," but Rabbit's mother Mary Angstrom* blames Janice for trapping him with a premarital pregnancy. Janice's mother Bessie Springer* accuses Mary Angstrom of having inflated Rabbit's self-importance. Janice's father Fred Springer* nearly calls the police, but when Rabbit returns to Janice, Springer gives him a job selling cars at his lot, apparently so he can keep an eye on him. Rabbit's teammate Ronnie reminds him that he always let others do his dirty work on the court so he could keep from fouling out and score lots of points. Even Rabbit admits to Ruth that if you have "the guts to be yourself, others will pay your price." Yet in the end the price of rending the social fabric must be paid, and ironically too, since at the grave site Rabbit is accused of the death of Becky when his actions were only contributing factors. Rabbit's culpability becomes family myth.

What the social order does not perceive, though, is Rabbit's subjectivity. For instance, when he and Ruth look out over Brewer from Mt. Judge, he stretches his hands toward the city and empathizes with someone he imagines may be dying of cancer.* In a moment of intense observation of his newborn daughter, Rabbit knows that when her eyes open, "She will see everything and know everything." In a dream* he realizes that his daughter is safely in God's hands, and Nelson as well, and that he must found a new religion. These images suggest that Rabbit's "inner strivings" are not separate from his own desire to keep the social order intact through comforting the ill and seeking divine help in the face of personal tragedy. Rabbit is no saint, but his inner strivings cannot be ignored.

But because no one but Rabbit knows these things, his actions ostracize him. This is underlined by the children's story, Beatrix Potter's* *Tale of Peter Rabbit*.* Introduced in *RR*, but forming a spine through images and motifs throughout *RA*, the story forms an allegorical background that includes, naturally, Rabbit's name and physical traits, dozens of rabbit-related images throughout *RA* from clothes to food,* and a moral. Rabbit's face, body and movements suggest a rabbit, as do his "hopping" and seeking security in various "burrows." Like a rabbit, he runs, sometimes aimlessly, often from fear. We are told when he eats at the Chinese restaurant that Rabbit loves food, and that his appetite shows no sign of the carnivore's but is more like a rabbit's. His blue jacket, like Peter's, is caught on a fence when he runs from the cemetery. Rabbit walks on Potter and Warren streets, which recall Beatrix Potter and the rabbit's dwelling. Brewer's color resembles that of a flowerpot, which Updike noted is the color of the pot with which Mr. McGregor tried to trap Rabbit. Both the trap and McGregor images recur often. In playing basketball, Rabbit was able to elude traps by passing or shooting. Janice traps Rabbit into marriage, and Ruth traps him into a dilemma. The network of roads trap and return him to Mt. Judge. Rabbit strays literally and metaphorically into forbidden "gardens" when he strays into adultery,* though Mrs. Smith's garden provides Rabbit a safe haven, and she is kinder than Ruth as Mr. McGregor. The episode of Rabbit's run from the cemetery to Ruth and the proposed abortion contains the elements of Peter's invasion of the garden and his flight and near capture by Mr. McGregor. Rabbit complains of a stomachache after Becky's death, as Peter did after his escapade in the garden. Potter's moral may caution children to play safe, but adults, like the pastoral* Rabbit looking back upon his Edenic basketball life, need to test other gardens or face inner dwindling.

In the end, the reader must decide if Rabbit's risk in seeking his ideal self at the possible expense of others is worth the reward. The reader cannot be sure as Rabbit runs down Summer Street if Rabbit will try another garden, return to Janice or, like Peter Rabbit, go back to his mother. But at the novel's end the imagery* on Summer Street of darkened churches, dirt roads and cinders suggests that Rabbit may be running into a psychological breakdown from the effort to maintain a balance between conformism and his inner craving for his potentialities. One might conclude, like critic Larry Taylor, that the Peter Rabbit imagery makes Rabbit allegorical, but Updike's art of particularity makes Rabbit his most complex and controversial character.

Updike has said that he wanted to provide a sense of a "rejoining of [Rabbit's] animal self" (Plath, *CU*) at the end of the novel, as if only running could enable Rabbit to cope with angst.* It seems doubtful, though, that running overcomes Rabbit's angst, for when we encounter him in the sequel, *RRed*, like Peter Rabbit, Rabbit has returned home, and he has continued for ten years to resist the temptation of the gardens of inner striving. He even avoids the garden of sex not only in adultery but with his own wife.

He has returned to society and supported his family, but the angst remains. *See* **Freud, Sigmund; Sex**.

Bibliography: Taylor, *PA*; Markle, *FL*. Jack De Bellis, "Oedipal Angstrom," *Wascana Review* 24 (1989): 45–59; Neary, *SN*; Matthew Wilson, "The Rabbit Tetralogy: From Solitude to Society to Solitude Again," *Modern Fiction Studies* 37 (Spring 1991): 3–24; Derek Wright, "Mapless Motion: Form and Space in Updike's *Rabbit, Run*," *Modern Fiction Studies* 37 (Spring 1991): 35–44; O'Connell, *UP*.

Radio Play that had frightened everybody in New Jersey. Orson Welles's *Mercury Theatre* dramatized a landing of Martians in New Jersey on Halloween Eve, 1938. The realistic depiction of Martians decimating the population terrified those who tuned to the station without having heard the introduction explaining that the broadcast was fictitious. The play fits the mystery of the black room, mentioned in "The Black Room" (*A*). *See* **Popular Culture**.

Raposo, Tristão. A poor, black thief from Copacabana, Tristão Raposo is selected by Isabel Leme* to be her sexual initiator in *B*. He and his friends live by stealing from the rich at the resort, and his cunning makes their escape from Isabel's uncle possible. His own family rejects her because they suspect that she endangers him, as white Jill Pendleton* endangered the blacks of Brewer* (*RRed*). Deeply in love, Tristão takes Isabel into the jungle, kills henchmen sent to bring them back, endures her prostituting herself to keep them alive and kills to protect the gold he discovers. Although he complies with the magic she uses to keep them from discovery, Tristão, like Rabbit Angstrom,* grows restless, and he is killed when he goads a poor black thief, Tristão's mirror image. Tristão and Isabel are modeled on Tristan and Isolde* of medieval romance. *See* **African Americans; Pastoral; Skeeter**.

Bibliography: Schiff, *JU*.

Reader's Digest. The most widely read magazine in the world, the *Reader's Digest* is a monthly digest of articles mainly from other magazines and other sources. Founded in 1922 by DeWitt and Lila Acheson Wallace, it now sells in the millions and is published in many foreign languages. Its articles and anecdotes are mainly uplifting and homely. Peter Caldwell* reads several articles from various issues of the magazine, each seemingly related to him, from the typically hopeful "Miracle Cure for Cancer*?" which he immediately relates to his father's apparent condition, to "Ten Proofs That There Is a God," which, listing problems and solutions, promises far more than it delivers. Peter feels "more than disappointed, overwhelmed . . . by the smart rattle of the prose and encyclopedic pretense of the trim double-columns." Instead of hope, the *Digest* produces panic (*C*). Yet it must have been hope that dominated when Updike wrote an essay about his mother that echoed the title of a *Digest* department, "The Most Unforgettable Character I've Met."

Bibliography: Updike: "The Most Unforgettable Character I've Met," *Vogue* 174 (Nov. 1984): 441.

Reading, Pennsylvania. Reading, Pennsylvania, thirty-five miles northwest of Philadelphia, was named for the birthplace of William Penn (1644–1718), Reading, England. Reading was the model for Alton* of early Updike stories like "The Happiest I've Been" (*SD*) and "Packed Dirt, Churchgoing, a Dying Cat, a Traded Car" (*PigF*), and for Brewer* of *RA*. Mt. Penn* fictional Mt. Judge,* overlooks Reading from the east. Updike's hometown, Shillington,* is an eastern suburb, and Plowville,* where Updike lived after age thirteen, is about ten miles south of Reading. Reading, Shillington, Mt. Penn and Plowville appear in novels (*RA*, *C* and *OF*), in stories (*OS*, *A*), several poems ("Leaving Church Early" [*TT*], "Midpoint" [*M*]), memoirs ("The Dogwood Tree: A Boyhood"* [*AP*] and *SC*, particularly "A Soft Spring Night in Shillington") and the notes to *CP*. Updike has remarked that the writer's first work comes directly from his early experiences, so these pieces reveal how intense and particular those experiences were. His work as a "gofer" at the *Reading Eagle** is detailed in *SC*.

Updike said that he found Reading "grand" because it was a place that made things like costly textiles (*SC*). It is a "city of factories and railroad yards set squarely among exiguous but tidy and decorated solid brick row houses . . . between the gritty Schuylkill and the looming profile of Mt. Penn (*SC*). This "beautiful" (Plath, *CU*) city "was life" (*MM*)." Growing up, Updike took stacks of books from the Reading library, whose balconies seemed "cosmically mysterious." He read T. S. Eliot* there and wrote a college paper on Héloïse and Abélard (*OJ*).

Though Updike left Reading in 1950, he repeatedly returned for what he has called a "tonic" and a replenishing of his sense of Brewer. He has said that the working writer needs to have setting in mind first, and that from a setting like Brewer comes a conservatism, a hard-working mentality and the love of athletics so important to Harry "Rabbit" Angstrom.* About altering Reading to Brewer, Updike remarked that "Reading was an ominous great city; its geography consisted of scattered eminences and glimpses, and . . . I twisted its orientation by ninety degrees, making what was east north, and jumbled real route numbers like 422 with unreal ones like 111" (*OJ*). Updike's frequent trips to Reading to visit his parents helped him not only to resee the city as it changed but also to revisit what he called "its landscape and overall mortal mood." Reading thus focuses the steady erosion of time, a major theme throughout Updike's work.

Though Updike said several times that his move to Massachusetts meant the opening of new subjects after Pennsylvania had been thoroughly mined, the fact that the Reading area-based Rabbit saga continued to occupy him for decades after he left Pennsylvania attests to the vividness of the image of Reading. Updike said that he was always "excited by returning to those rather pedestrian streets." He still found the area "a muscular, semi-tough kind of place," but he adds that its changes were a downward spiral.

Once Updike read Reading's most famous poet, Wallace Stevens,* at Harvard,* he never forgot him, and he not only reviewed Stevens's posthumous work but imitated his style in both poetry* and fiction. Updike remarked, perhaps ironically, that although Reading never quite acknowledged the existence of Wallace Stevens, it did boast the successful novelist Mildred Jordan, author of a novel set during the French Revolution, *Asylum for the Queen*.

Bibliography: Updike, "Him and Who?" (*MM*); Robert F. Zissa, "Updike Discusses Reading," Reading (Pennsylvania) *Eagle* 3 Apr. 1977; "Updike Recreates Berks County in His Writings," *Easton* (Pennsylvania) *Express* 20 Dec. 1981; Susan Beth Hartman, "The Role of the Berks County Setting in the Novels of John Updike," *Dissertation Abstracts International* 48/08A (1987): 2062, University of Pittsburgh.

Reading Eagle, Reading Times. The *Eagle* and the *Times* were the newspapers of Reading,* Pennsylvania, which were united as the *Reading Times-Eagle*. During the three summers of 1951–53 Updike worked at the *Reading Eagle* as a copy boy. He used his spare time to write, and a few of his poems were published in the *Eagle*. Updike clearly picked up information there on typesetting and reporting that he would later use in *RRed* and *W*. Probably the daily contact with Reading gave Updike more concrete information for the creation of Brewer* in *RA*. Updike was succeeded in his job at the newspaper by a former Shillington* High School classmate, Don Van Liew. *See Self-Consciousness*.

Bibliography: Updike, "A Reminiscence" (*MM*).

Religion. The subject of religion is of utmost importance to Updike, appearing throughout his fiction and poetry* and often accounting for his greatest power. Updike's mother's father was a minister* and he was raised a Lutheran. Updike married the daughter of a Unitarian* minister, joined the Congregational church and is now active in St. Johns Episcopal Church of Beverly Farms, Massachusetts. He remarked that *Marry* was intended to present through its four major characters* "four different doctrinal positions," atheist, Unitarian, lapsed Catholic and professing Protestant. Such religion typing of his characters shows Updike's determination to provide them with spiritual resonance while testing their action against their convictions. Such convictions are presented in the form of a debate in Updike's first novel, *PF*, about religion and science* between John Hook* and Stephen Conner,* and the opposition is explored again in *RA, C, RV, W* and *TE.*

Updike was baptized and confirmed by Rev. Victor Kroninger, upon whom the character Rev. Fritz Kruppenbach* is based. In *RR* Kruppenbach refuses to accept Rev. Jack Eccles's* socially based Episcopalianism, insisting that ministers must burn for Christ, not try to mend broken marriages. Thus a debate about a minister's integrity is created. Eccles fails to unite Harry "Rabbit" Angstrom* and his wife Janice Angstrom,* and he himself feels his faith slipping. Meanwhile, Rabbit wonders why God could not save his daughter from drowning and numbly takes a job selling cars, though he knows that there is more to life than defrauding old people at Springer Motors.* Like the heroes of the novels from *PF* to *Couples*, Rabbit has religious faith, but he struggles to find the link between belief and moral action. Updike's characters typically look within themselves rather than to the church, the Bible* or a minister for personal truth.

Updike's first five novels treat death,* the afterlife and the difficulty of finding a safe religious harbor in a materialistic world, an indifferent universe and an absent God. *RA* and the stories "Pigeon Feathers" (*PigF*), Lifeguard" (*PigF*), "The Astronomer" (*PigF*) and "The Music School" (*MuS*) consider the deterioration of religious institutions that have grown more socialized. Personal spiritual crises are explored in books of the 1960s, 1970s and 1980s, *MuS, MS* and *S.*, as are the struggles within marriage between a serious believer and one who is religiously indifferent (*RA, C, Couples, RV* and *B* and the story "The Holy Land" [*BIB*]). Only in the marriages of Ed Parsley* and his wife Brenda Parsley* (*W*) and Clarence Wilmot* and Stella Wilmot (*IB*) does Updike portray a marriage of true believers, but when Ed Parsley's faith becomes politicized, he diverges from his wife's quieter faith, and when Clarence Wilmot's belief disappears, his wife preaches, for a time, in his place.

These contrasts of science/religion, material/spiritual and belief/nonbelief apparently stem from Updike's Lutheranism, which, he observed, contains a "rich ambivalence toward the world" and relishes paradox. Lutheranism also embraces "ambiguities" of a "radical otherworldly emphasis" while advocating faith rather than work. Such aspects form the central tension of his treatment of religion in his characters. His ministers, for example, are often consumed with "ambivalence toward the world" while they are occupied with the next world. In Updike's novels of the 1990s like *IB* and *TE*, he seems to feel that ministers have capitulated to the world, and that those questing for belief must go elsewhere for support, to the movies, for example, like Clarence Wilmot, or to quantum physics,* like "Jesus freak" and quasi-minister Dale Kohler* (*RV*).

Updike's shift from Lutheranism to Episcopalianism would seem to mimic the contrast between the Lutheran and Episcopal ministers in *RR*, yet Updike has never been as radical a Lutheran as Kruppenbach nor as social as

Rev. Jack Eccles. Updike has retained his faith because, as he remarked, "without lacking faith and charity I think I am truly hopeful." Hope, another ingredient of Lutheranism, is part of his writer's equipment, since he has remarked, "When you write, you do feel you're functioning by laws that aren't entirely human" (Plath, *CU*). Updike's sympathy for his characters—he said in *PP* that a writer should never satirize them but only love them—may be a response to Christ, who "advised us to empathize." His lyrical description of the world is meant to be "an act of praise," part of "the Old Testament injunction to give praise" (Plath, *CU*) by describing the world as perfectly as possible since it is God's creation.

The characters Updike sympathizes with in *RR* represent, as he said, "a fairly deliberate attempt to examine the human predicament from a theological standpoint (Plath, *CU*)." Rabbit's attachment to the world, especially through sex,* is a confirmation of his own concrete existence and his sense that there is "something beyond that can be reached." Updike insists that this is no paradox, for "religion and sex are traditionally linked in the United States" (Plath, *CU*), though the problem for modern Americans is the clash between modern sexual mores and biblical law.

Updike's knowledge of the Bible* and related writing is obvious throughout his work. He supplied an informed commentary on the Gospel of Matthew in a review, observing that from the parable of the talents he learned to "dare to take chances, lest you leave your talent buried in the ground" (*OJ*). Many of his characters are adept at biblical quotation, such as John Hook* (*PF*), Tom Marshfield* (*MS*) and, above all, the voluble Jesse Smith* (*IB*), who, like the devil, quotes Scripture to his own advantage. Updike supplies comments on the church fathers in his review of Norman Mailer's *Gospel According to the Son*, and he lists St. Thomas Aquinas's* *Summa Theologica* as one of the ten most important books of the last thousand years for its demonstration of the compatibility of faith and reason and because "without it Dante* could not have written the *Divine Comedy* or James Joyce* *Ulysses*." Updike read Thomas Aquinas and several other religious writers when he was seeking to overcome his spiritual crises of 1955–62. Of the other writers—Paul Tillich,* Hilaire Belloc* and Karl Barth*—only Barth remains a continuing influence on Updike. In reviewing *The New Oxford Book of Christian Verse*, Updike remarked that religious poetry leads language "toward an edge where words dim" (*HS*), which is the case with Rabbit when he demonstrates his belief in something beyond him with a perfect tee shot instead of the definition Eccles requires. In accepting the Campion Medal as a "distinguished Christian person of letters," Updike said of his faith that it "has given me comfort in my life and . . . courage in my work. For it tells us that truth is holy, and truth-telling a noble and useful profession; that the reality around us is created and worth celebrating; that men and women are radically imperfect and radically valuable."

Bibliography: Updike, "Stand Fast It Must" (*HS*); "Stones into Bread," "The Ten Greatest Works of Literature, 1001–2000," "Accepting the Campion Medal," "Remarks on Religion and Contemporary American Literature" (*MM*); Hamilton and Hamilton, *EJ*; Ralph Wood, *The Comedy of Redemption: Christian Faith and Comic Vision in Four American Novelists* (South Bend, IN: University of Notre Dame Press, 1988); William Scott Green and Jacob Neusner, eds., "Religion and Literature," in *The Religion Factor: An Introduction to How Religion Matters* (Louisville: Westminster John Knox Press, 1996), 227–41; Ralph Wood, "Into the Void: Updike's Sloth and America's Religion," *Christian Century* 24 Apr. 1996: 452–55, 457; Yerkes, *JU*.

The Ring (New York: Knopf, 1964). A retelling for children of Richard Wagner's "Ring" operas (*The Ring of the Niebelung*, comprised of *Das Rheingold, Die Walküre, Siegfried* and *Die Götterdämmerung*), *The Ring* demonstrates Updike's empathy for children's responses to difficult masterpieces as he retells the German epic on which Wagner based his operas. He has also retold Shakespeare's *Midsummer Night's Dream* and Mozart's *Magic Flute*. *See* **Children;** *A Child's Calendar;* **Pigeon Feathers ("Should Wizard Hit Mommy?").**

Bibliography: Thomas Lask, *New York Times Book Review* 1 Nov. 1964: 63.

Ripley's Believe It or Not. A newspaper feature created by cartoonist Robert Ripley (1893–1947) in 1918, *Ripley's Believe It or Not* ran in three hundred newspapers and two different television* series. The famous collection of odd facts and strange stories is alluded to by Jerry Conant* (*Marry*) when he notes that he read in the feature that the "Our Father" had been written on the edge of a knife. Thus he suggestively draws a connection between the image of the sword used for symbolic marriage in Tristan and Isolde* and the confluence of violence and religion* in an otherwise innocent sexual idyll. *Believe It or Not*, which Updike read avidly in the *Philadelphia Bulletin*, is a source for the "magic cube palindrome" used in *W*. It is magic because when each word is written directly below the other the letters created up and down create the words of the sentence. It appears totally self-contained. *See* **Classical Literature; Languages**.

Robinson, Joey. Thirty-five-year-old advertising writer Joey Robinson returns to his mother and her farm in *OF*. With him is his new wife Peggy Robinson* and her eleven-year-old son Richard by a previous marriage. Joey's father had died the year before, and while Joey is at the farm, a place he dislikes as much as his father had, he takes on some of his father's qualities, wearing his father's clothes and mowing the meadow. Since Joey's mother Mrs. Robinson* did not approve of his divorce and feels that he wasted his poetic talent on advertising, the visit is tension-laden. Because he is accustomed to acceding to his mother's force, Joey sides with her against his wife for a while, but he later reestablishes his loyalty to Peggy because of his powerful desire for her, and because he rejects his mother's family mythologies concerning his life. Meanwhile, Joey comes to discover that Peggy is a force of nature to him as much as the farm is to his mother. Understanding this gives him the strength to defy his mother, though when he leaves her, she is on the verge of a heart attack.

Joey Robinson returns in a short story, "A Sandstone Farmhouse" (*A*), in which he settles his mother's estate after her death and reexplores her vitality through a series of photographs. Since Mrs. Robinson was based partly on Updike's mother, Joey may be an alter ego* of Updike. The story was awarded the O. Henry First Prize and was included in *The Best Short Stories of 1991*.

Bibliography: Taylor, *PA*; Alison Lurie, "Witches and Fairies: Fitzgerald to Updike," *New York Review of Books* 17 (2 Dec. 1971): 6, 8–11; Markle, *FL*; Detweiler, *JU*; Greiner, *JU*.

Robinson, Mrs. Mary. Joey Robinson's* mother in *OF* has lost her husband the year before her son Joey returns to introduce his new wife Peggy* to her. Accustomed to dominating men, she interferes with her son's new marriage by hypocritically defending Joey's first wife, whom she never liked, drawing Joey into admitting that Peggy is stupid and dramatically forcing each situation into an emotional confrontation. Mrs. Robinson by her charm, cajoling, tantrums and frank reviews of family history tries to bring her son to recognize that his place in history* cannot be dissolved by his own desire for a career and a wife she never sanctioned. She also tells Peggy's son Richard her plan for a "people sanctuary," where those people ruined by the city can be made whole again by retreating to the farm's pastoral* world. This may be a covert way of suggesting how her son can yet be saved by returning to her farm and its myths. But eventually she recognizes her son's need for freedom and learns to accept it grudgingly when he insists that he can no longer accept her confining ideas of how he should live. They attend church together and hear a sermon* about Adam and Eve that causes her to reflect that the young minister* is wrong to ask women to accept a biblically supported burden of pain; Joey tepidly disagrees. When he prepares to drive back to New York, Mrs. Robinson has an apparent heart attack. Despite her evident pain, Joey leaves, and in their last words they contend about who really owns the farm.

Updike has said that he used his mother as the model for Mrs. Robinson, but the difference in her presentation is striking when compared to his presentation of other characters modeled after other family members. He presented his maternal grandfather John Hoyer* from an omniscient point of view (*PF*). Updike's father was seen through the retrospective first-person account of Peter Caldwell,* son of George Caldwell* (*C*). But in *OF* Updike restricts his view of Mrs. Robinson to Joey's immediate first-person account, the least reliable point of view. The story "A Sandstone Farmhouse" (*A*) provides a retrospective view of Mrs. Robinson through a series of images her son recalls while settling her affairs after her death.

Bibliography: Updike, "Introduction to the Czech Edition of *Of the Farm*" (*PP*); Taylor, *PA*; Alison Lurie, "Witches and Fairies: Fitzgerald to Updike," *New York Review of Books* 17 (2 Dec. 1971): 6, 8–11; Markle, *FL*; Detweiler, *JU*; Greiner, *JU*.

Robinson, Peggy. Joey Robinson's* second wife in *OF*, Peggy Robinson represents for him a complete departure from his first wife Joan, since she is earthy rather than artistic, erotic rather than spiritualized, direct rather than aloof. Recognizing that her mother-in-law, Mrs. Robinson,* dislikes her, Peggy skirts direct conflict until she is forced to confront Mrs. Robinson. Then Peggy insists that Joey defend her and loses faith in him when she overhears him apparently conspiring against her with Mrs. Robinson and calling her stupid. But Joey's sexual need for Peggy restores him to her, giving Peggy the confidence to explain to Mrs. Robinson that she alone allowed Joey to become a man by becoming the sexual field he could plow unself-consciously. Peggy also thwarts Mrs. Robinson's effort to seduce Peggy's son Richard into her fantasy of a "people sanctuary." Peggy's realistic attitude helps to reclaim him. The lively, inquisitive and sensible Richard is indirect evidence of what a good mother Peggy had been. Her husband had died the year before.

Bibliography: Taylor, *PA*; Alison Lurie, "Witches and Fairies: Fitzgerald to Updike," *New York Review of Books* 17 (2 Dec. 1971): 6, 8–11; Markle, *FL*; Detweiler, *JU*; Greiner, *JU*.

Rodin, Auguste (1840–1917). Generally regarded as the greatest French sculptor, Auguste Rodin was noted for reviving Michelangelo's grandiose treatments of the human body, though he worked almost exclusively in bronze rather than marble. Rodin's texturing created multiple planes that generated distortions of realism for the sake of psychological truth, as in the larger-than-life passion, pride and heroism of *The Burghers of Calais*. His frank depictions of nudes, particularly female sexual organs, shocked the French middle class. His most famous statues are *The Kiss* and *The Thinker*, a cast of which stands before the Rodin Museum in Philadelphia, Pennsylvania. His unfinished masterpiece, *The Gates of Hell*, was based on imagery* from Dante's* *Divine Comedy*. Col. Felix Ellelloû* in *Coup* is disgusted when the president of Zanji, Komomo, has a statue made that imitates Rodin's *Balzac* in order to glorify himself. Ellelloû had been outraged by Kush's Haussmann street plan, since Rodin and Georges Haussmann, the premiere French town planner of the nineteenth century, represent colonial French culture in Kush. However, like Rodin, Ellelloû is a revolutionary who tells the truth, though with some distortion, and his style can be likened to Rodin's with its rough form and its polished surface of elegant metaphors.

When Ellelloû proposes marriage to Kutunda,* she rejects him because the new Islamic Marxism will reject "muddled" images like Rodin's *Kiss*, preferring "frontal heroic statues in limestone of the Pharaoh and his sister-bride." Alexandra Spofford* refers to Rodin's *Balzac* to describe Dutch elm disease (*W*).

Roger's Version (New York: Knopf, 1986). *RV* is the second novel of a trilogy based on Nathaniel Hawthorne's* *Scarlet Letter*, begun with *MS* eleven years before. The novel employs the most extensive treatment of science* in Updike's work, and Updike described the inception of the novel as occurring when the "scrambled numbers" (*OJ*) on his computer monitor conveyed a message to his superstitious mind. His "superstition" transformed into Dale Kohler's* effort to force the computer to deliver cosmic messages and into the unusual psychic powers of the narrator, Roger Lambert.* The narrative contains difficulties for most readers because it deals with intricate problems in physics, cosmology and neo-Darwinism.

Lambert, a professor at a theological school of a university like the Theological Seminary at Harvard,* is approached by computer whiz Kohler, who seeks funding for a computer project in which he plans to discover the factual existence of God. Kohler intends to insert into a computer program recent scientific data. He theorizes that science has gotten to the fundamental building blocks of matter, the basic laws by which God created the universe. He expects to see some images of "God's hand" once the computer digests all of the information. Though Lambert recognizes the danger of Kohler's "Deus" program, both to the moral life of society and his own cozy sinecure, he agrees to help him because he is sure that Kohler will fail, and that faith will remain the only way in which God can be known. Kohler wins the grant and works obsessively. Eventually Kohler sees fleeting images resembling the hand and face of God, but he cannot print them or reproduce the commands that caused them to appear. His dejection turns to total defeat when a faculty member challenges his project by referring to an article in a popular science magazine.

Meanwhile, Kohler has had an affair with Lambert's wife Esther,* but since we learn of this through Lambert's first-person narration and there is no other evidence besides his testimony, we cannot be sure that the affair occurred. Even though Esther is pregnant, it is possible that Roger, not Kohler, is the father. Meanwhile, Roger is attracted to Verna Ekelof,* a friend of Kohler's, who lives by her wits in a seamy part of town with Paula,* her mulatto daughter. While Roger tutors Verna in literature, hoping that she will return to school and improve herself, she seduces him. After he helps her avoid arrest over her abuse of Paula, Roger extricates himself from the affair.

Updike has remarked that the bulk of the novel is "in the form of debates" (Plath, *CU*), much like the debates in Thomas Mann's* *Magic Mountain*, and so *RV* is related to *PF*, *RR* and *C*, which also debate with the reader the question "What is a good man?" Is Dale good because he wants to settle the question of God's existence and end the anxiety the question has caused mankind? Or is Roger good because he wants to reserve the God question for faith alone, not give it to science to answer, since science is in the constant process of redefining itself? Updike considers these issues in books as dissimilar as *RaR*, *Coup* and *TE*. Perhaps the debate concerns Updike because it is rooted in the conflict he detected in his family between his mother's belief that the "soil has soul" and his father's respect for facts as the real truth.

Hawthorne's brilliant scientist Roger Chillingworth, Lambert's analogue in *The Scarlet Letter*, has explored both European alchemy and Native American folk medicine, as well as psychology. Chillingworth marshals these with his Calvinist ideas of predestination in order to invade Rev. Arthur Dimmesdale's soul. Chillingworth assumes that Arthur had publicly humiliated him by fathering Pearl, the child of his wife Hester. Lambert, a modern Chillingworth, is conversant with the church fathers, as well as the latest scientific developments, and so he is a foil for the "Jesus addict," as he labels Kohler, who has amassed an enormous number of contradictions in modern cosmological and evolutionary theory that question the authority of science. Where Dimmesdale spoke as a "Tongue of Flame" to melt the heart of his congregation, Kohler passionately defends his viewpoint that atomic-particle theory and gene analysis reveal the very basis of reality, and thus God. Like Chillingworth, Lambert had married his "Hester," Esther, out of passion, giving up his first wife and his ministry to do so, but now the Lamberts only relate through their son. Like Hester, Esther has powerful feelings and a strong will that lead her, evidently, into her affair with Kohler. But she also shows Hester's aesthetic-intellectual prowess in grasping how the computer works. In fact, she is so adroit that, as critic Judie Newman shows, she is able to trade puns with Kohler referring to "gates" and "bytes," which also contain what Harry "Rabbit" Angstrom* called "codes for the deepest meanings," and unlike Hawthorne, Updike presents the intimacies of the lovers in graphic detail, though it is possible that Roger imagines the affair through his powerful empathy with Kohler. Unlike Dimmesdale, Kohler feels no guilt for the affair. Dimmesdale died after his "revelation of the scarlet letter," as Hawthorne ambiguously put it. Kohler is defeated after God's face is revealed on the computer screen. Updike would seem to side against Kohler, for, as he wrote in reviewing a collection of Christian poetry, "a concrete and manifest God would be an absolute tyrant with no place in His universe for free-willed men." Yet this does not imply that Updike sides with Lambert, since Lambert's use of free will is tyrannical.

Updike may offer an ironic version of Dimmesdale and Hester in the affair of Lambert and Verna. Like Hester, Lambert's half-sister's daughter Verna is a sensual and strong-willed woman. His effort to tutor her through William Cullen Bryant's "Thanatopsis" (a romantic poet's transformation of Calvinist themes of death* and the afterlife) approximates Dimmesdale's "Tongue of Flame" sermons* that must have ignited Hester. Just as Hester responded to Dimmesdale's sermons, so Verna quickly grasps the meaning of "Thanatopsis," but she uses the situation to arouse Lambert. That he resists Verna for a while may suggest Updike's reading of Hawthorne's novel: since Hester is the more aggressive, she may have seduced Dimmesdale. Updike uses Verna's daughter Paula as the analogue to Pearl. This strange child is given, like Pearl, to asking Verna who her father is and to unusual spontaneous pronouncements that seem to inquire about her parentage. Paula's "Da" is both baby talk and an expression of her almost obsessive need to find her physical and metaphysical fathers: she says "Da" to both Kohler and Lambert. Updike seems to use Verna's abuse of Paula as a parallel to Hester's threat to lock Pearl in a closet when she asks too many questions about her father.

But Updike does not merely draw parallels between his characters* and Hawthorne's. The characters contain elements of each other. Consequently, although Lambert, like Chillingworth, is a person of profound, nearly telepathic, powers of mind, which Dimmesdale identifies in Chillingworth as "interference with the human heart," he also coheres so thoroughly to Kohler that he can sense what Kohler sees and imaginatively walk in Kohler's shoes through the streets. Thus he seems to share Dimmesdale's power of feeling the truth in others' hearts. This enables Lambert to glide easily from a page of Tertullian's* Latin about the flesh/soul dualism* to erotically evoke Esther's performing fellatio on Kohler. (However, the affair may be imaginary; Esther's pregnancy could be explained by Lambert's sex* with her once he discarded Verna.) If Hawthorne's Dimmesdale is a person of profound theological understanding, Updike grants to Kohler the power of Chillingworth's scientific intellect. Kohler's need to know God resembles Chillingworth's Faustian commitment to knowledge.

Yet Updike separates Lambert and Kohler by returning to the conventional satanic and Christic imagery* implied by Hawthorne. Kohler resembles Christ by working in a lumberyard, by resisting Lambert's acting the devil's advocate in his computer project and by teaching Lambert's son Richard computer language. Fire and smoke images associate Lambert with Satan (as they had Stephen Conner* in *PF*). Kohler's failure to be able to reproduce images of God's face on his computer may punningly reveal that Jesus does not always save.

If *RV* is difficult because of its immersion in abstruse arguments of the church fathers, as well as in scientific subjects, the novel compensates with vigorous eroticism, a gritty portrayal of ghetto life, as in *RRed*, and a wicked satire* of academic affairs. The school has a professor of "holocaustics," pretentious and hypocritical faculty and docile students like those in *MF*. This is the battleground on which the modern conflict between heart and mind takes place, and Updike leaves it to us to decide the outcome of the struggle.

Like the other books in the *Scarlet Letter* trilogy, *RV* is written in the first person and forces the reader into Lambert's world view. Through him the reader sees eroticism, urban decay, spiritual longing and scientific realities, and all cloak everything with an unrelenting sardonic vision. Lambert is thus a challenge to those who would argue that the decay of the modern spirit can be averted. Through him we receive Kohler's failure to detect God's plan, simply confirming what Lambert already knew. Oddly enough, Kohler is shown to lack Lambert's intuitive belief in God's existence; Kohler, by contrast, is a doubting Thomas who demands ocular proof. He is thus another version of Rev. Jack Eccles,* who demanded that Rabbit tell him what the "thing" was that wanted Rabbit to find it. Eccles insists that such antinomianism* as Rabbit's was settled "in the heresies of the early church" (*RR*) and demands that Rabbit tell him if his vision "has polka dots." Perhaps Kohler's lack of faith makes him serve as a negative example of such belief in an "inner light": Kohler thus represents a warning to those who wish for conclusive signs of God's existence. As Rev. Fritz Kruppenbach* explained to Eccles in *RR*, if God wanted to end such doubt, He would declare His kingdom now. Perhaps this is why Eccles leaves the ministry, as we learn in a scene inserted in *RRed* in *RA*. Lambert is not the best candidate for belief because of his ironic attitude, so Updike does not necessarily leave us in Lambert's camp after Kohler has been run out of town. Nor do any of the other characters express real spirituality, which Updike defined as "the ability to make one's way among the unseen currents, to arrive at the truth while bypassing induction and deduction" (*OJ*). *See* **Marcion; Religion.**

Bibliography: Updike: "Spirituality," "A 'Special Message' for the Franklin Library's First Edition Society Printing of *Roger's Version*" (*OJ*); "Print: A Dialogue," "Stones into Bread," "At the Hairy Edge of the Possible" (*MM*); David Lodge, "Chasing after God and Sex," *New York Times Book Review* 31 Aug. 1986: 1, 15; Newman, *JU*; Donald J. Greiner, "Body and Soul: John Updike and *The Scarlet Letter*," *Journal of Modern Literature* 15 (Spring 1989): 475–95; Raymond Wilson III, "*Roger's Version*: Updike's Negative-Solid Model of *The Scarlet Letter*," *Modern Fiction Studies* 35 (Summer 1989): 241–50; John N. Duvall, "The Pleasure of Textual/Sexual Wrestling: Pornography and Heresy in *Roger's Version*," *Modern Fiction Studies* 37 (Spring 1991): 81–95; Schiff, *UV*.

Roosevelt, Franklin Delano (1882–1945). Franklin Delano Roosevelt was the thirty-second president of the United States (1933–45). His "New Deal" took America from distress to greatness, leading the country from depression to victory in World War II. Having saved America twice, Roosevelt, for the ordinary American, was a spokesman for "the little man." In *SC* Updike describes his paternal grandfather's holding office as a Democrat, and in "The Dogwood Tree: A Boyhood"* (*AP*) he discusses his parents' profound admiration for the president and the Democratic party. Characters such as Earl Angstrom* (*RR*) and George Caldwell* (*C*) express great belief in Roosevelt. Updike chose to name Alf Clayton,* the history professor and specialist in the life of President James Buchanan,* after Alf Landon, who was defeated by Roosevelt in 1936 (*MF*). *See* **Presidents.**

Roth, Philip (1933–   ). An American novelist famous for his analysis of the situation of American Jews, Philip Roth is mentioned by Henry Bech* as a reasonable candidate for the Nobel Prize* in "Bech and the Bounty of Sweden" (*BaB*) and by Updike in *SC* when he describes their opposed views on the Vietnam* War, about which, to Roth, Updike was the most aggressive person in the discussion. Updike and Roth share so much personally and professionally that a book by George J. Searles compares the two authors. They were born a year and a day apart, published their first novels in 1959 and won the National Book Awards in their first few years of publishing and most major awards* as their careers progressed. The chief subjects of Roth and Updike concern the family and the search for identity, usually within the context of middle-class ethnicity, WASP and Jewish. Roth's *Portnoy's Complaint* (1969) comically examines the life of a young man struggling with his Jewish identity and sexual life; like Harry "Rabbit" Angstrom,* he feels that his personal dreams were stymied by his parents and the larger cultural context. As Updike described the predicament of the modern Jewish novelist with a writer's block in *BB*, *BIB* and *BaB*, so Roth explored a similar writer, Nathan Zuckerman, who has a sensational success followed by a painful block in *The Ghost Writer* (1979), *Zuckerman Unbound* (1981) and *The Anatomy Lesson* (1983). Updike and Roth have explored sports,* particularly baseball, and although Roth is the more experimental in form, Updike has pushed the boundaries of realism (*PF, C, MF, B, TE*). Each has written memoirs and used his life as a subject, but Roth is the more self-referential. Both authors have a profound regard for non-American writers like Franz Kafka,* who may have influenced the writing of Updike's "Bech in Czech" and Roth's *Ghost Writer*. Though he is averse to reviewing contemporary American writers, Updike reviewed Roth's Zuckerman trilogy (*OJ*), and his review of *Operation Shylock* (*MM*) was alleged by Roth's first wife Claire Bloom to have discomfited Roth, proving that Updike would not let friendship interfere with truth as he saw it.

Bibliography: Updike, "Philip Roth" (*OJ*); "Recruiting Raw Nerves" (*MM*); Searles, *FP*; Charles B. Harris, "Updike and Roth: The Limits of Representationalism," *Contemporary Literature* 27 (Summer 1986): 279–84; George J. Searles, "The Mouths of Babes: Childhood Epiphany in Roth's 'Conversion of the Jews' and Updike's 'Pigeon Feathers,' " *Studies in Short Fiction* 24 (Winter 1987): 59–62.

Rougemont, Sukie. A reporter for the Eastwick* newspaper the *Word*, Sukie Rougemont enjoys minor witchery, turning milk into cream, freezing in air the tennis balls of her fellow witch Alexandra "Lexa" Spofford* and casting the spell that brings together Lexa and Darryl Van Horne* (*W*). Young, sexy and recently divorced (she has either literally or figuratively turned her ex-husband into a place mat), Sukie says that women have gone from "bitchery to witchery," thus linking her "powers" to the feminist movement. She numbers among her lovers the Unitarian minister* Ed Parsley,* her editor Clyde Gabriel and art collector Darryl Van Horne, who urges her to quit writing obituaries and interviews for the *Word* and start writing novels. However, her interview with him only reveals her limitations as a writer. Sukie forms a "cone of power" with Lexa and Jane Smart,* thus increasing her potency. The three witches force Clyde Gabriel's wife Felicia to spew tacks and dust balls in revenge for the wretched life she imposes on Clyde. Sukie becomes jealous when Van Horne turns his attention to Jenny Gabriel, Clyde Gabriel's daughter, and Sukie urges Lexa to make a witch doll of Jenny. Their spell kills Jenny. After Sukie is fired from the *Word*, she sells real estate (like Janice Angstrom* in *RaR*) and writes romances. Her name may be derived from that of Denis de Rougemont, whose books about love, *Love in the Western World* and *Love Declared*, were reviewed by Updike and helped form the structure of *Couples* and *B*. De Rougemont argues that romantic love was a late and somewhat destructive cultural invention, best illustrated by the romance of Tristan and Isolde.* Sukie's surname is thus appropriate for a woman emerging into liberation after having dispatched her husband and having become the most promiscuous of the Eastwick witches. *See* **Sex**.

Bibliography: Updike, "More Love in the Western World" (*AP*).

The Ruskin School of Drawing and Fine Art. After Updike graduated from Harvard,* he unexpectedly received a Knox Fellowship to study anything in the British Commonwealth. He chose art* and was admitted to the Ruskin School of Drawing and Fine Art, attached to the Ashmolean Museum in Oxford,* England. From the summer of 1954 to August 1955, he studied painting from a teacher who stressed the style of Paul Cézanne. Studying at the Ruskin School was to be, as Updike said, "one last run around the park" (Plath, *CU*) for his effort at serious art. Updike has noted, however, that painting helped to make him a writer, since, as Joseph Conrad had insisted, what is not seen is not rendered, and what is not rendered is not art. Updike has unfailingly noted his attendance at the Ruskin School in the biographies included with his books, and he remarked, "I'm Proud" for having studied art (Plath, *CU*). (Updike's first choice, the Slade School in London, had been unable to admit him.) *See* **Drawing and Painting**; *Just Looking*.

S

S. (New York: Knopf, 1988). Updike's only epistolary novel, *S*. flows entirely from the letters and audio tapes of Sarah Price Worth.* A rare upper-class character for Updike, Sarah divorces her wealthy husband Charles Worth, rejects their material world and seeks spiritual fulfillment in a Hindu ashram in Arizona. Her very confident, spirited and reflective responses to her adventure provide both a description of the modern woman's self-sufficiency and a satire* of American earthly excesses. At the same time, her infatuation with the ashram's spiritual leader, the Arhat,* to whom she gives substantial monetary gifts and her talents as a forklift operator and secretary, also provides Updike with a chance to explore the hypocrisies of modern American love and faith. Sarah, too, is a focus of such satire because she records American excess and because she herself is part of what she denounces. Her self-deception is sometimes comic and causes her to resemble Janet Appleby (*Couples*), Jill Pendleton* (*RRed*), Melanie (*RIR*) and Teresa "Pru" Angstrom* (*RaR*). Fortified by Sanskrit words that attest to Sarah's commitment to change her previously bored suburban life by dabbling in the religions of India, she explores the physiological and mythological meanings of her adopted religion. Gradually, she becomes aware of the hypocrisy of the Arhat and others, unmasks the fake and absconds with embezzled funds. The protests of the local community of the nearby town of Forrest provide another area of satire lodged against American gullibility. As a faithful if ingenuous narrator, Sarah Worth is a fine device by which to examine modern American mores while enabling Updike for the first time to write exclusively in a woman's voice.

Written in part to answer claims by feminists that he had never created "strong" or "professional" women (Plath, *CU*), *S*. particularizes Sarah Worth's life in elaborate detail. First, Updike mimics her voice, a dangerous tactic, as Updike has remarked in a review in *OJ*. Her language incorporates stiletto precision in skewering her psychiatrist, wily indignation with her German ashram lover, girlish chumminess with her confidante Midge and polished aloofness in defending the Arhat from snooping journalists. Second, Updike recounts her prescriptions for preventing the heirloom silver from tarnishing and relates her recognition of what men seek in women sexually. Sarah pays careful attention to the effects of vitamin A on the skin and knows how to bring credit as the "doctor's wife" by looking like an attractive ornament at parties. Besides supplying a wide range to Sarah's style, Updike also demonstrates that through will, ability and imagination, a woman disadvantaged by her advantages can make her way in a man's world. Rejecting her imprisoning conventions, Sarah shows that a woman can seize her life, no matter how desperate it might seem.

Apart from deliberately describing a strong woman in her own voice, *S.* is also the last of a trio of novels based on Nathaniel Hawthorne's* *Scarlet Letter.* Since the previous two novels were devoted to the first-person viewpoints of Tom Marshfield* in *MS* (Arthur Dimmesdale) and Roger Lambert* in *RV* (Roger Chillingworth), Updike now writes in Hester Prynne's voice and gives Hester Prynne the last word. Updike casts her narrative in letters to achieve five things related to Hawthorne's novel: (1) the letters approximate the form of Marshfield's diary entries, linking the lovers Hester and Dimmesdale, and her social letters balance his subjective journal entries; (2) the letters and diary entries reach across the barrier erected by the probing mind of Lambert/Chillingworth; (3) the letters provide a cinematographic "presentness" created by Sarah's writing spontaneously in the present tense, while differentiating her from the self-consciousness of Marshfield and Lambert; (4) the letters connect Sarah by way of a seldom-used literary form to the period of Hester Prynne, roughly the era when the epistolary novel was in vogue; and (5) the letters also form a refutation of Hester's scarlet letter of sexual shame, since the "S" symbolizes the seat of Sarah's passion in the Hindu image of Kundalini. They are also Sarah's epistles to the sisterhood of would-be liberated women, something that Hawthorne predicts will happen when a woman brings peace to the battle of the sexes. By using the letter *S* as his title, Updike gives the impression that this narrative is Sarah Worth's Dickinsonian "letter to the world," her "red-letter day."

Updike has included letters in his fiction from *PF* to "Bech Noir" (*BaB*), most extensively in *Couples*, in which Foxy Whitman* writes to her lover Piet Hanema,* but at such length that critics such as James Schiff feel that the letters retard the narrative. Updike has also used the letter form in short fiction,* for example, "Four Sides of One Story" (*MuS*), which treats the legend of Tristan and Isolde.*

Bibliography: Updike, "Unsolicited Thoughts on *S.*" (*OJ*); Anatole Broyard, "Letters from the Ashram," *New York Times Book Review* 13 Mar. 1988: 7: Alison Lurie, "The Woman Who Rode Away," *New York Review of Books* 35 (12 May 1988): 3–4;

Donald Greiner, "Body and Soul: John Updike and *The Scarlet Letter*," *Journal of Modern Literature* 15 (Spring 1989): 475–95; Schiff, *UV*; Judie Newman, "Guru Industries, Ltd.: Red-Letter Religion in Updike's *S*." in Yerkes, *JU*.

Salinger, J[erome] D[avid] (1919–   ). An American fictionalist, best known for his enormously successful novel *The Catcher in the Rye*, mentioned by Henry Bech* ("Foreword" [*BB*]), J. D. Salinger was an acknowledged source for Updike. Updike listed Salinger as one of the most appealing of his fellow *New Yorker** writers. Updike first encountered Salinger in the Harvard* writing course of Kenneth Kempton, who read some of Salinger's stories aloud to the class. Updike found in them a "refreshing formlessness," recognized that they said something to him "about the energies of people and the ways they encounter each other" and discovered those stories "open to tender invasions." Further, Updike realized then that "a good story could be ambiguous, the better to contain the ambiguity of the world." This seemed like a real advance in possibility over "the crisp, wised-up, decisively downbeat stories of Dorothy Parker and John O'Hara" ("The Short Story and I"). In an introduction Updike remarked that "A & P" (*PigF*) was written in an "idiomatic monologue, not my usual style," and his first wife, Mary Pennington Updike,* said that it reminded her "too much" of J. D. Salinger. The impact may be traced in Harry "Rabbit" Angstrom,* who shares with Holden Caulfield, the hero of *The Catcher in the Rye*, a suspicion that adulthood equals phoniness. Rabbit's voice sounds very close to Holden's when he tells Rev. Jack Eccles* that maturity means "the same thing as being dead" (*RR*). In *Couples* the aloof Angela Hanema* reads Salinger's *Raise High the Roof Beam, Carpenters*, forming an ironic comment on Piet Hanema's* job as a contractor, since while he is restoring Foxy Whitman's* home, he has an affair with her that leads to divorce and the "collapse" of his own "house." *See* **American Literature**.

Bibliography: Updike, "Franny and Zooey" (*AP*); "The Short Story and I" (*MM*); Jonathan Schwartz, "Updike of Ipswich," *Boston* Aug. 1965: 35; David D. Galloway, "The Absurd Hero as Saint" in *The Absurd Hero in American Fiction* (Austin: University of Texas Press, rev. ed., 1981); Howard M. Harper, *Desperate Faith: A Study of Bellow, Salinger, Mailer, Baldwin and Updike* (Chapel Hill: University of North Carolina Press, 1967); Ian Hamilton, "Redeemable Bad Guy," *London Review of Books* 23 Apr. 1998: 21–22.

The Same Door (New York: Knopf, 1959). *SD*, Updike's first collection of stories (all first published in the *New Yorker**), traces his transition from Pennsylvania to New York.* Mostly realistic, the stories include Updike's lyrical mode ("Toward Evening"). Also, the collection introduces alter egos* Fred "Ace" Anderson, the prototype for Harry "Rabbit" Angstrom* (*RA*) and Richard Maple,* featured in several stories (*TF*). Several interchangeable young men appear here who form a collective hero in the stories in *OS*.*

The stories of *SD* range widely from small-town hypocrisy ("Friends from Philadelphia") to big-town self-deception ("Snowing in Greenwich Village"). "Sunday Teasing" contains an insight by the hero that could represent the collection's theme: the "perceptive man caged in his own weak character"—a dominant trait of most of Updike's men. Perceptiveness and weakness are both shown in this story, in which Arthur, who prefers reading St. Paul and Søren Kierkegaard,* is asked by his wife Macy (who, like Updike, enjoys reading Henry Green*) to read a French story concerning star-crossed lovers. She feels that the man who left acted badly, but Arthur is moved by the hero's effort to act nobly though he is trapped. Like the hero, Arthur is perceptive about the tragic nature of human life, but weak so that he cannot end what they both realize is a failing relationship. Perceptiveness is also shown in "Toward Evening," in which Rafe buys a mobile made of birds for his baby's delight, amuses himself by matching the house numbers seen from a bus with cultural dates, is captivated by a beautiful woman whose dress is filled with *V*s and encounters frustration in his wife he cannot alter when she is dissatisfied by the mobile and their life. Weakness is also shown without perception, as in "Snowing in Greenwich Village," the first of the stories about Joan* and Richard Maple (*TF*), which shows the frailty of fidelity, "His Finest Hour," "A Trillion Feet of Gas," "Who Made Yellow Roses Yellow?" "Incest" and "A Gift from the City." Other stories reveal instinct as a recourse of poor perceptiveness, such as "Ace in the Hole" and "The Alligators," which dramatizes conflicted feelings of love and hate in elementary school. "The Happiest I've Been" quietly reveals a modest amount of strength and understanding when John Nordholm drives a sleeping friend to Chicago after a New Year's Eve party in a snow storm, pleased that he had earned two persons' trust that night.

If the men are mainly perceptive but weak, the women, whether wives, mothers, mothers-in-law, teenagers or children,* are often instigators of trouble because they are emotional or bored, as in "The Kid's Whistling," "A Gift from the City," "His Finest Hour," "Sunday Teasing," "The Alligators," "Incest," "Tomorrow and Tomorrow and So Forth" and "Snowing in Greenwich Village." Women interrupt Arabic lessons and phone the office ("A Gift from the City"), overreact to literature ("Toward Evening") or behave possessively ("The Happiest I've Been").

As in *RR* and *C*, *SD* reveals the problems of "middleness"* through the characters'* limited range of understanding. Often they are characterized through their attachment to film* ("Ace in the Hole," "A Gift from the City," "Sunday Teasing"), popular music* ("Ace in the Hole," "Tomorrow and Tomorrow and So Forth," "The Kid's Whistling"), religious ideas ("Dentistry and Doubt") and their attempts at artistic expression ("The Kid's Whistling," "Ace in the Hole," "Incest," "Toward Evening," "Intercession"). But whether they are architects ("A Gift from the City"), admen ("Who Made Yellow Roses Yellow?") or teachers ("Tomorrow and Tomorrow and

So Forth"), they feel stifled. The religious life produces stale theological thoughts without visions of truth ("Dentistry and Doubt"), and though the characters sometimes have revelations ("Toward Evening," "Sunday Teasing," "The Alligators," "The Happiest I've Been"), they are sometimes ironically undercut ("Dentistry and Doubt," "Tomorrow and Tomorrow and So Forth," "Snowing in Greenwhich Village"). Some stories suggest "metafictions" about how fiction itself comes to be ("Incest," "The Kid's Whistling," "Intercession").

The stories all reveal remarkable attention to detail and an authoritative use of high and low culture. Updike's eye is intensely accurate in rendering the proper way to make—and break—a Toyland sign ("The Kid's Whistling"), or the way a neon Spry sign was put in place ("Sunday Teasing"). Updike's ear is attentive to bohemian conversation ("Snowing in Greenwich Village"), high-school banter ("Tomorrow and Tomorrow and so Forth") and collegiate wit ("Who Made Yellow Roses Yellow?"). Such facility reveals the impact of Updike's reading, as in the subtle Proustian* psychological insight of "Toward Evening." Popular culture,* like film, is used to define character ("Ace in the Hole," "Toward Evening," "His Finest Hour"). Many of the characters in *SD* will be developed more fully in Updike's fiction, particularly the dissatisfied young marrieds of "Ace in the Hole," who become the Angstroms. The use of literary texts in "Sunday Teasing" and "Tomorrow and Tomorrow and So Forth" forecasts similar important uses in *RRed*, *MS*, *RV*, *MF* and *IB*. "Intercession" shows Updike's passion for golf,* a subject in *RA*. Articles, poems and stories on golf were collected in *GD*.

Bibliography: Greiner, *OJ*; Detweiler, *JU*; Albert E. Wilhelm, "Three Versions of Updike's 'Snowing in Greenwich Village,'" *American Notes and Queries* 22 (Jan.–Feb. 1984): 80–82; Luscher, *JU*.

Satire. Though Updike remarked in a 1968 interview, "I'm not conscious of any piece of fiction of mine which has even the slightest taint of satirical attempt" (Plath, *CU*), more than an attempt at satire can be found in his work, before and after 1968. Updike's adolescent writing and cartooning* show the usual exuberant debunking and lampooning directed at authority and institutions, so by the time he began publishing light verse* in the *New Yorker*,* noted for its satiric verse and prose by James Thurber,* Robert Benchley, Dorothy Parker and Ogden Nash, Updike had already established himself as a satirist. Light verse is often a vehicle for his satiric poetry. "Humanities Course" (*CH*), for example, satirizes how the great minds of Western thinking are misrepresented in Harvard's* humanities course. As Updike remarked, "I resented the way that humanistic knowledge nibbled away at my Christian faith" (*CP*, "Notes"). His depiction of scientists ("V. B. Nimble, V. B. Quick" [*TP*], "The Descent of Mr. Aldez" [*CH*]), self-styled wits ("Thoughts While Driving Home" [*TP*]) and literary critics ("A

Vision" [CP]) show a deft satiric touch. So do his parodies of the styles of Edgar Guest ("Publius Vergilius Maro, the Madison Avenue Hick [CH]"), Marianne Moore ("Miss Moore at Assembly"[M]) and Jack Kerouac* ("On the Sidewalk" [AP]).

Updike's science-fiction story "The Chaste Planet" (1975; collected in HS) satirizes not only sex* and rock music but science fiction too. Like most satire, this story calls for a return to traditional values by warning that "more is less." Satire directs the reader to the values of home and hearth, "sanity," conventional behavior and traditional institutions—the values of middle-ness,* which Updike made it his job to explore, as he announced in "The Dogwood Tree: A Boyhood"* (AP). Updike explores such values (marriage and the family, "decent" morality, the sacredness of sports*) in RR, and he uses Beatrix Potter's* Tale of Peter Rabbit,* a descendant of the satiric beast-fable genre, to undercut Harry "Rabbit" Angstrom* throughout RR. Like Peter, Harry disobeys because he wants to explore forbidden terrain and pays for it by becoming ill with a ten-year guilt. Harry himself supports the values he flaunts; he simply wants to return to the time when they were operational, when he was a young sports star. Since in an epigraph* to RIR Updike acknowledges Sinclair Lewis's* Babbitt, it is unsurprising that Updike throughout RA satirizes businessmen (Fred Springer,* Webb Murkett,* Nat-sume Shimada*), flower children (Melanie) and ministers* ("Soupy" Camp-bell).

In C Updike uses the disparity between classical and ordinary figures to produce comedy* that is often satiric, as in principal Louis Zimmerman,* who runs amuck as Zeus in George Caldwell's* class, or Vera Hummel as Venus rising from the sea in the steam of the girl's locker room. Couples clearly satirizes Janet Appleby and Harold little-Smith when they tumble into sex on a pile of dirty laundry. Updike uses Henry Bech* to satirize literary critics who had panned Updike's work (BB, BIB, BaB), Sarah Worth* to satirize society women seeking spiritual enlightenment (S.), Darryl Van Horne* to exhibit the quintessence of bad taste in art,* and Alf Clayton* (MF) and Roger Lambert* (RV) to satirize jargon and moral dishonesty in universities. These instances show that Updike does satirize his fictional characters,* but it would be a mistake to see them only as two-dimensional types. As Updike concluded about creating characters: "They're your crea-tures. You must only love them" (Plath, CU). No doubt Updike's characters have endured because he does love them, though he satirizes them too.

Bibliography: Taylor, PA; Newman, JU.

Sator arepo tenet opera rotas. The Latin sentence "Sator arepo tenet opera rotas" may be translated, "Sower Arepo holds the wheels at his work." Sukie Rougemont* uses this bit of "white magic" to change milk into cream (W). The words of the sentence create a "magic cube" palindrome when they are arranged one word beneath the next by the consecutive order of letters, forward and reverse in each row and each column. Thus the words spell up as well as down when the reader begins with the last letters and reads upward. Some believed in the Middle Ages that this magic cube was sacred, a linguistic symbol of God as alpha and omega, since it was thought to be an anagram for "Pater Nostra AO." Sukie's use of it is therefore blasphemous, and the computer building in *RV* called the cube might, by allusion to the magic cube, be similarly blasphemous. *See* **Classical Literature**.

***The Scarlet Letter* Trilogy.** *See A Month of Sundays; Roger's Version; S.*

Scenes from the Fifties (London: Penguin, 1995). In Updike's short story *Scenes from the Fifties*, first published in 1995, the hero Howard relates, in retrospect, how he had come to discover in 1959 that New York,* his marriage, his art* career and an incipient love had not "happened" for him. The story recalls "The Lens Factory" (*Granta*, 1989) and "Museums and Women" (*MW*).

Science. Updike's interest in science is prodigious. Everything fascinates him, from the new math to quantum physics,* and from microbiology to cosmology. Whether through a young boy asking his father if he is composed only of carbon atoms that are destined to decay or of a spirit that will live forever ("Pigeon Feathers" [*PigF*]), a computer expert seeking God's face (*RV*), a biologist working with chlorophyll (*Couples*) or an astronomer discovering a white dwarf star ("White Dwarf" [*TP*]), Updike enthusiastically explores the facts and theories composing reality.

Updike uses biology, chemistry, mathematics, astronomy and physics to clarify existential questions about who we are, and he puts to science a question principal Louis Zimmerman* claims George Caldwell* failed to address in his general science class: "What are the humanistic values implicit in the physical sciences?" When challenged to answer this himself, Zimmerman is evasive. But Caldwell has in fact given a very dramatic demonstration of how cosmological and biological evolution had ultimately produced in man a "death-foreseeing" "tragic animal" (*C*). Updike's heroes typically attempt to make human sense of the bewildering data science has amassed, but they often find that they (1) cannot understand what science tells them; (2) cannot articulate what they find; and (3) cannot keep their explanations from being misunderstood or rejected. Updike's heroes, however, show a great range of responses, from Dale Kohler's* passionate computer analysis of the latest discoveries in physics and microbiology (*RV*) to Ben Turnbull's* sober queries about quantum physics (*TE*). Updike's heroes are absorbed by the ways science prompts them to speculate about the questions Updike called fundamental: "Who am I?" "Why am I here?" Since science inquires into the "who" and the "here," it can help the "I" clarify the condition in which it puts the questions.

What clarifications are offered by these sciences? Astronomy and its bastard brother astrology relate man immediately to the sky and questions about the universe's origin. In Updike's light-verse* poem "White Dwarf" the narrator can patronize the newborn star (and disguise his fear) by modeling his poem on the nursery rhyme "Twinkle, Twinkle, Little Star." The unbelievably dense gravity of a white dwarf inspires fear that such a thing can exist. But such a new discovery forms an antidote to "cosmic fright" by forcing accommodation to new wonders. "White Dwarf" partly explains the story "The Astronomer" (*PigF*), in which Bela, a visiting friend and astronomer, mocks his host for reading Plato* and Søren Kierkegaard* to stem his anxiety. But Bela confides later that he was terrified driving through New Mexico since its vast emptiness mimicked the nothingness of outer space. Bela's cosmic fright is a companion to his friend's inner fright, and neither can use modern astronomy as an antidote. "The Astronomer" also marks a serious treatment of the scientist who is otherwise spoofed as a caricature in poetry* ("V. B. Nimble, V. B. Quick" [*TP*]) or a secondary figure in fiction (Ken Whitman* in *Couples*; Myron Kriegman in *RV*). We never know Angela Hanema's* uncle Lansing Gibbs (whom she identifies as famous for the "Gibbs Effect"), but as an astronomer he left his mark on her. Angela passes along her knowledge of the faint Andromeda galaxy*—companion to our Milky Way galaxy—to her husband Piet Hanema.* Dwarfed by questions of time and eternity, Piet cannot achieve the sense of wonder Angela captures from the faint island universe.

More meaningful to Piet is the astrological sign of the constellation Andromeda, the "chained lady" whom the hero Perseus frees after killing a gorgon (Georgene Thorne?). For him, the galaxy and astronomy are as remote as Angela, who cannot be freed by him. Another star configuration provides a similar clue to the future of his love affair, for after making love to Foxy Whitman,* Piet stares at the constellation Orion and thinks superstitiously, "The future is in the sky after all," realizing that he will now love Foxy less, perhaps because he recalls that Orion was blinded for having desired one woman and killed for wanting another (*Couples*).

If the sky offers different meanings for the Hanemas, Peter Caldwell* treats it from Piet's viewpoint in *C* when he explains at the end of his narrative of his father that Chiron,* whom his father embodied, was transformed into the constellation Sagittarius because Zeus loved his "old friend." (George Caldwell, apparently a Sagittarian, bears traits associated with his constellation: friendliness and a love of teaching.) Piet's insight is correct when it is applied to George Caldwell: his future is in the sky. Caldwell's dull student Judy Lengel had wrongly answered in the science class that the star at the center of the solar system is Venus. The wrong answer in a science class becomes the right answer in Chiron's academy, as chapter 3 shows.

For myth,* as for ordinary people, love does indeed make the world go round. Ben Salz also directed his energy toward Venus by building miniature parts for the Mariner spaceship to Venus, but all Tarboxians in *Couples* follow Venus in believing that love is "the new religion."

Like Piet Hanema, Col. Félix Ellelloû* knows that the vastness of space means that "we are less than dust" as he steers by Venus in the desert (*Coup*). Piet Hanema is not impressed when minister* Horace Pedrick tells him to think of God as electromagnetic waves, and, like Piet, Harry "Rabbit" Angstrom* sees the sky as offering no answers in *RRed* when *Apollo 11*'s* launch does not lift him up and the spaceship merely hits a big "nothing." But like Ellelloû, Rabbit thinks that "God may have the last word yet" when he reads, a decade later, about quasars, galaxies several billion light years away that emit such powerful energy that they were at first mistaken for stars (*RIR*). More satisfying is Brad Schaeffer's realization that the stars viewed from his aircraft carrier require him to witness them; this provides the religious experience that makes him a believer ("Made in Heaven" [*TM*]). But for Ben Turnbull at the end of his life, and perhaps speaking near the end of time, the days when clusters of stars formed "godlike creatures—a centaur" are past, and he now asks, "Where are the stars?" and reviews five possible theories for the stars' disappearance, none of them compelling (*TE*).

While George Caldwell can see man as nothing but chemicals (*C*), Updike in "The Dance of the Solids" (canto III of "Midpoint" [*M*]) matches the intricacies of modern polymer science and its investigators against the complexities of Spenserian stanzas. This poetic tour de force is impressive and the factual accuracy assured, since the poem was based on an article in *Scientific American*, and Updike's poem was published there. Updike's attitude toward the sciences is thus somewhat different from that of his characters,* approximating that of Roger Lambert, who is amused but not compelled by Dale Kohler's* description of the "finely adjusted constants" that keep the universe working and make human life possible (*RV*). Like Henry Palamountain (whose name recalls Palomar Mountain, California, seat of the 200-inch Hale Telescope) of "The Christian Roommates" (*PigF*), Roger sees no reason to become disturbed by scientific quarrels, since science is by its nature in a constant process of revision. Neither Lambert nor Palamountain would overlook the aesthetic and ethical discomfort of inquiring into those cosmological constants in order to see how "God is breaking through" (*RV*).

Like astronomy, physics takes Updike's characters to the basic questions about existence, but unlike astronomy, physics treats forces that have little impact on the senses and are thus more mysterious. In his light-verse poems Updike could smile at the sassy neutrinos that pass right through the bodies of lovers ("Cosmic Gall" [*TP*]) or the cloud physicist who seems to "dissipate" in his research ("The Descent of Mr. Aldez" [*TP*]). But the complexities of subatomic physics intrigue many of his characters with a promise of final understanding, what Dale Kohler mocks in American physicists' quest for the Grand Unified Theory that will answer all micro- and macrocosmic questions. For Dale, physicists are ignoring the truth that discrepancies in theories appear because God wants it that way.

One of God's most befuddling creations is quantum mechanics, a branch of physics that examines the behavior of subatomic particles. The experiments of Max Planck revealed that particles do not operate according to logic but according to probability. Dale Kohler shows the ingenuity modern physics uses in trying to explain quantum physics, giving the example of what happens when an electron strikes a proton. The electron divides as a result, but the divided unmeasured wave seems to disappear, or it somehow communicates with the other wave. Dale laughs at the physicists who conceive that the untraceable divided wave went into another universe, and he scoffs at this "infinite branching out of quantum-theory indeterminacy" (*RV*). But this theory is used thematically and structurally in *TE*. Ben Turnbull suddenly within the narrative, by branching, becomes, among others, a grave robber, St. Mark and a voice from millions of years in the future who speculates that the universe has reached a point of equilibrium in its expansion from the Big Bang and has now begun to collapse. His wife Gloria also "branches" into a prostitute, Deirdre, and into a deer. In *RA* Rabbit had thought that "time is our element," but in *TE* time, viewed through quantum mechanics, is more paradoxical than Rabbit could have dreamed.

More positively, Updike uses biology to stress the interconnectedness of the world. To George Caldwell, the volvox is not only a remarkable case of the first multicelled organism, but also a metaphor for sacrifice. Without giving themselves up to specialization, the cells comprising the volvox theoretically could have lived forever. The volvox contains symbolic meaning applied to Caldwell, relating to his sacrifice of his own life, metaphorically, for the good of the larger organism, society (*C*). The couples of *Couples* are a kind of parody of the volvox: in their Tarbox they sacrifice nothing in creating an "organism" greater than the sum of the parts. Piet and Foxy are able to leave this "organism" in the end, as Foxy leaves her biologist husband, but in becoming "another couple" they shift to another community of "cells."

Updike majored in mathematics in his freshman year, and he uses it in *P* to show how problems of love and adultery* do not compute as easily as high-school algebra conundrums whose answers reside in the back of the book. In *Marry* Jerry Conant* sees his extramarital affair with Sally Mathias as "like one of those equations with all variables." Since there are too many "unknowns," he returns to his wife. Roger Lambert's son has problems with new math that are as simple as pie for Dale Kohler, who, after he teaches the boy about computer circuitry, uses computer language to pass coded messages of "in" "and" "not" to Esther Lambert,* who, slicing the Thanksgiving pie, catches on, reciprocates the code and initiates their affair. *See* **Science Fiction**.

Bibliography: Robert Nadeau, "John Updike," in *Readings from the New Book on Nature: Physics and Metaphysics in the Modern Novel* (Amherst: University of Massachusetts Press, 1981), 95–120.

Science Fiction. As an adolescent, Updike read widely in science-fiction writers, from Isaac Asimov to H. G. Wells, appreciating most those who showed a solid knowledge of science.* Such reading ended when he went to Harvard,* and when he included science fiction in his work, it took the customary form of either dystopia or humor. Science fiction appears in his first novel, *PF* (1959), and again nearly forty years later in *TE* (1997).

In "Pigeon Feathers" (*PigF*) David Kern's* interest in H. G. Wells's *War of the Worlds* leads him, ironically, to trust Wells's credibility, so that reading what David feels is Wells's blasphemous account of Jesus in *The Outline of History* contributes to David's spiritual crisis. Updike has expressed pride in the science fiction in *PF*, though the effort is quite modest: he places the narrative in the near future as George Orwell did in *1984*. (When Updike recognized inconsistencies for a later edition, he changed the "future" to 1978.) In this enlightened time racism and anti-Semitism have ended, and a Hispanic presence is pronounced. But Updike's future also shows the triumph of the welfare state and secular humanism, which in the name of the abstraction "Mankind" ignores the past, substitutes cheap goods for craftsmanship, suppresses individualism and represses spiritual impulses. In two debates between ninety-four-year-old John Hook* and the prefect Stephen Conner,* Updike dramatizes the richness of the past that the future has repudiated.

Updike's droll use of science fiction appears in "The Chaste Planet" (1975), a work selected for a science-fiction anthology, though Updike has not included it in any story collection; it was placed in *HS*, a collection of reviews and essays. Again the story takes place in the near future, 1999, as the Sino-American Space Agency explorers visit Minerva, a planet within the atmosphere of Jupiter. (In *RRed* Harry "Rabbit" Angstrom* speculates about life existing in just such an environment.) The Minervans, who reproduce by "budding," find the notion of "love" stupefying and die by overdosing on music, which also renders them impotent. This amusing little satire* suggests that colonization of the solar system might be destructive and stresses a conservative view about the erotic life through the metaphor of music, that "more is less." "The Chaste Planet" was selected for *SF:75*, Updike's second selection for a science-fiction anthology, and these recognitions pleased him, since, he was thus considered a writer of science fiction "however miniscu-lely" (*The Chaste Planet*, "Foreword" [Metacom, 1980]).

Updike's only other science-fiction work, the dystopian *TE*, updates as-

pects of *PF*. *TE* deals with ordinary events in the near future, A.D. 2020—
the punning year suggests that 20/20 hindsight awaits us, or that the next
generation will have a sharper view of things. Though atomic war has dec-
imated the Midwest, Updike again is playful: FedEx has taken over governmental operations because its infrastructure is viable. The narrative mainly
concerns efforts to keep domestic peace in the home of a retired businessman, Ben Turnbull.* But several things disturb him: (1) the failure of law
and order permits gangs of murdering adolescents to demand protection
money; (2) sinister new forms of life, "metallobioforms" (which live either
on electricity or on grease and oil), have appeared; (3) space exploration has
failed, attested to by an orbiting space station with dead astronauts; and (4)
the narrator shifts into other persons when quantum "branching" affects him
spontaneously. Perhaps more important than such futuristic devices is the
way in which science fiction enables Updike to speak about time and its end.
He can explore quantum physics* in form and content, transforming a deer
into Deirdre, a prostitute, or converting Ben into a monk, a prisoner, St.
Mark and a lonely witness to the end of the universe. Science fiction in *TE*
thus permits Updike to expand the novel* as a form. Updike's meticulous
review of *The World Treasury of Science Fiction* lists omitted writers and works,
particularly ones by Vladimir Nabokov* and George Orwell's *1984*, and
poses answers to his own question, "What keeps science fiction a minor
genre?"

Bibliography: Updike: "The Chaste Planet" (*HS*); "Print: A Dialogue" (*MM*);
David Malone, "Updike 2020: Fantasy, Mythology and Faith in *Toward The End of
Time*," in Yerkes, *JU*.

Self-Consciousness (New York: Knopf, 1989). *SC*, Updike's only book of
memoirs, is a closure, like his collected poetry, his stories about Henry Bech*
and the completion of the Rabbit saga. Updike is not merely "tidying up his
desk," as he has often said of his works of the 1990s, but tidying up his life.
SC contains six chapters considering "self-consciousness" as personal discomfort and "self-consciousness" as consciousness of self, a quality of being.
Updike first examines his place in space and time by taking a Proustian* tour
of his hometown, Shillington,* and recalling his life there through age thirteen. Frequent footnotes draw connections between Shillington and the fictional Olinger. The next two chapters describe how Updike lived with
psoriasis and stuttering. The fourth chapter justifies his defense of the Vietnam* War, and in the fifth he passes on his knowledge of his forebears to
his grandchildren. The last chapter considers the continuation of the self
after death. The chapters thus progress from intensely personal revelations
of the physical self through various social personas to meditations about the
possible continuation of the self after death. The book forms Updike's first
comments, apart from interviews,* on the interrelation of his life with his

work, and Updike includes a plentitude of quotations from his novels, stories, poems and essays as footnotes to actual details of his life, something anticipated in the "Afterword" to *BD*, in which he quotes from *PF*. In *MF* Updike lists *BD* in the bibliography. (In *TE* some personal anecdotes related in *SC* are reused, but without footnoting.) Updike uses two themes to guide the reader: the impossibility of staying out of harm's way, and the impossibility of getting something for nothing.

The first chapter, "A Soft Spring Night in Shillington," could be called an "urban pastoral,"* since it describes Shillington as Edenic, a world of promise. As he strolls through the town, Updike looks back more than forty years, recalls the variety store where he bought Halloween masks and Big Little Books, and reflects on his talent for identifying upside-down every cartoon in *Collier's*. Above all, Updike revisits his home, which refused to give up its mystery despite being used so often as the setting that helped create "John Updike" the writer. After his stroll, Updike recounts that but for his mother's dream of his destiny and her pressure to force him to relinquish a high-school sweetheart, he might never have left Shillington. Updike discovers that Shillington is a product of his consciousness, and thus no different from the way billions of other consciousnesses have seized their places as theirs. (In "One More Interview" [*TM*] a similar fictional sojourn reveals an actor's excitement in the face of an indifferent interviewer.)

"At War with My Skin" recounts Updike's long battle against psoriasis, which produced endless self-examination and a feeling that the skin he showed the world was not "really" him. His sensitivity to the disease formed a surprising "narcissism" that made him wish to marry the first woman to forgive his condition. More important, psoriasis determined his closeted writer's discipline and accounted for major turns in his life: having children while young to surround himself with clean-skinned people; leaving the *New Yorker** because his skin suffered without the sun in urban shadows; and moving to Ipswich* because its beach could provide sunbathing that would restore his skin. Ipswich also made Updike more social as he took part in clubs, meetings and group activities that made him feel "part of the herd . . . human." In his search for sunny places like Anguilla,* Updike began to gain an admiration for African Americans.* His "war" with his skin also teaches him to forgive himself by learning that he is the victim, not the author, of the disease, and Updike, with remarkable humility, finds his skin metaphorical: his "relentless need to produce" could be a "parody" of his skin's "embarrassing overproduction."

In his third memoir, "Getting the Words Out," Updike examines his stuttering, claustrophobia, asthmatic attacks and other problems related to getting the air that gets the words out, but these are all metaphors, he comes to feel, for his self-consciousness about his prodigious volume of work. Updike finds that his stuttering is reduced when he is speaking to people who know "who I am," so with refined people his vocal cords apologize for being poor, and worse, for having nothing to say, "as a memorable early review of one of my books put it." Since Henry Bech* murders one of Updike's early critics in "Bech Noir" (*BaB*) by depriving him of oxygen as poetic justice for that critic having done the same, figuratively, to him, this chapter could be a gloss on the story. Stuttering, Updike discovers, reflects a shame at expressing yourself. Attacks of claustrophobia and asthma led Updike to realize that he wanted to leave his first wife, which permitted him to get more words out.

The longest chapter, "On Not Being a Dove," arose from Updike's response to a query given to writers worldwide about the Vietnam* War; it gave him the opportunity to explain his own proadministration stance. Since writers like Robert Lowell and Norman Mailer* advocated ending the war, Updike felt "out of step" with some writer friends, despite his otherwise liberal attitudes. Some of those attitudes were shown in his rather bohemian life in Ipswich, in which he "licked" the "sugar" of the counterculture. Updike was shocked that the same persons enjoying such liberty wanted to see America humiliated, and he acknowledges that power is dirty business with a slogan that appears also in *RRed*, "To be alive is to be a killer."

In "A Letter to My Grandsons" Updike offers his baby grandchildren of "mixed blood" a full report on the Updikes, from their European origins to their American accomplishments, revealing again Updike's ability as a research scholar. He also tells the children that black America has contributed "style and usefulness no purely white country has." He recognizes that their self-consciousness will be consciousness of color, but the name "Updike" connects them to place and people, illustrated dramatically in the frontispiece photo of the assembled Updikes in 1909. But the photo and chapter show a vanished time, as do old houses long gone or altered. (Updike provided fictional portraits of these children in *TE*.)

"On Being a Self Forever," perhaps the closest Updike has come to writing a sermon,* explains the "bedrock self" comprised of such things as scraps of memory and one's signature, but the afterlife is the opposite of such selfish impulses. So, Updike argues, we really yearn for a continuation of this world in the next because we acknowledge that being is good and the world a gift. Since experience of the self produces "an ecstasy," intuition tells us that "the world is good" and encourages belief in God. The recognition of a dominating subjectivity and of Ralph Waldo Emerson's* sense, as Updike acknowledges, that "a thread runs through all things" is the foundation of Updike's conception of the self. For Updike, truth is in the quotidian, the anecdotal, such things as those described in the first chapter in *SC*. Like David Kern* in "Pigeon Feathers" (*PigF*), Updike wants "this poor 'I' that I am and I feel myself to be here and now" to live forever.

Updike's many footnotes from his own work demonstrate his "self" and suggest a parallel life to the one he reveals that also contains his self but about which he cannot comment directly. Although these chapters were undertaken, according to Updike, to forestall any possible unauthorized biography, it will be a treasured resource for future biographers, since *SC* provides the chief resource for investigating Updike's many selves. His honesty and humility should also serve as a model for those future biographers.

Bibliography: Updike, "The Dogwood Tree: A Boyhood" (*AP*); "One Big Interview" (*PP*); "On One's Own Oeuvre" (*HS*); "Footnotes to *SC*," "Literarily Personal" (*OJ*); Denis Donoghue, " 'I Have Preened, I Have Lived,' " *New York Times Book Review* 5 Mar. 1989: 7, Christopher Lehmann-Haupt, "Why Updike Writes and What He Writes About," *New York Times* 9 Mar. 1989: C-25. Elizabeth Hardwick, "Citizen Updike," *New York Review of Books* 36 (18 May 1989): 3, 4, 6, 8; David Denby, "A Life of Sundays," *New Republic* 200 (22 May 1989): 29–33.

Sermons. Updike's interest in religion* is everywhere apparent in his work, and sermons enrich his treatment of the subject. In *RR* Rev. Jack Eccles* delivers a sermon in June on "Christ's Conversation with the Devil." The sermon seems odd, coming from a socially oriented Episcopal minister,* and would perhaps be more expected from Rev. Fritz Kruppenbach,* whose Lutheran perspective insists that a Christian should burn for Christ. Eccles's sermon, however, does not function as part of the narrative since it comes to us through the resistant reflections of Harry "Rabbit" Angstrom,* who does not like the "dark, tangled, visceral aspect of Christianity, the *going through* quality of it, the passage *into* death* and suffering that redeems and inverts these things, like an umbrella blowing inside out. He lacks the mindful will to walk the straight line of a paradox." Nor does Rabbit enjoy Eccles's "sinister" "performance." Since Rabbit's eyes always glance toward "light," his attention wanders to Lucy Eccles,* whose name, ironically, derives not only from "light" but from "Lucifer." Rabbit's conversation with this devil occurs later, however, when he thinks that Lucy's invitation to stop at the Eccles's home is "code" for a sexual invitation. His rejection of Lucy appears to be what Eccles called being initiated into following Christ. Yet Lucy's supposed overture drives Rabbit's lust toward Janice Angstrom,* Janice's understandable reluctance to have sex,* Rabbit's flight from her, and Janice's accidental drowning of their baby. No other sermons are delivered in *RA*, though during the wedding of his son Nelson* Rabbit thinks that he must hear the words the dead have spoken.

The sermon on the creation of Eve in *OF* is Updike's most complete sermon. Joey Robinson* and his mother, Mrs. Robinson,* listen to what has been called Updike's most "Barthian sermon," and they take away different opinions about it. Though the "young minister" who delivers the sermon quotes Karl Barth,* he does not reveal that his sermon relies upon Barth's "Man and Woman" from *Church Dogmatics: A Selection.* The sermon explains that woman is less than man and so is dependent on his "kindness," but she is also "superior" to him because "her motherhood answers concretely what men would answer abstractly." Afterward Joey Robinson's mother asserts that such a sermon is a way a man excuses himself from woman's pain; Joey, who had put his mother through pain with his divorce,* does not reply. Updike had originally written this sermon for publication in *Ladies' Home Journal* in 1964. When it was not published, Updike explained, "I used the novel as a mounting for it."

In *Couples* Rev. Horace Pedrick offers a virtual self-parody sermon mixing the diction and images of money into his prayer, a vivid contrast to a 1795 sermon Piet Hanema* picks up after fire destroys the Tarbox Congregational Church. That sermon stated that America has failed its duty to God and has given in to corruption. The couples in Tarbox represent that failure, but Updike said of this holocaust, "What are we to do when God burns our churches?"

In his most extended and varied use of sermons, *MS*, Updike offers a variety of responses to his own question. Rev. Thomas Marshfield,* forced to write a daily journal that might return him to spiritual health, creates four sermons that progress from spiritual fragmentation to spiritual wholeness. The first sermon, a parody, states blasphemously that the sacrament of marriage exists only for the sake of adultery,* making continuous love possible. The second sermon, an argument, seeks a way of overcoming the "severing with Christ" in recounting His miracles but assumes, with Barth, that God is "wholly other." The third sermon of Christ in the wilderness allegorically depicts Marshfield's view of himself (and shows him following the directions given by Eccles's sermon in *RR*). The fourth sermon, which Ms. Prynne* says "could be preached," is taken from St. Paul: "We are of all men most miserable." Man would indeed be miserable if the resurrection of the dead were only a horror show, he argues, but the fact of being here and not there in time answers the mystery of death with the fact of resurrection. Timed seven days (or "entries") apart, the sermons comment as well on the previous experiences Marshfield has described: they become continuing guides about the nature of his healing. They are also love letters for Ms. Prynne, the motel manager, whom Marshfield seeks to seduce. Though the sermons may have ambiguous results for Marshfield's spiritual reentry, they do effect the seduction of Ms. Prynne.

Elsewhere, Updike describes other kinds of sermons: the aborted sermon, the pseudosermon and the antisermon. In *PF* elements of the sermon survive in memories of the former prefect Mendelssohn ministering to the poor with singing and prayer and discussions of death and the afterlife. Clarence Wilmot* aborts his sermon on the parable of the tares when he is so stunned by his loss of faith that he cannot speak. In *RRed* Skeeter's* consciousness-raising sessions are really pseudosermons designed to impress his view of America's racist history upon Rabbit. They reveal Skeeter's understanding of his place in the future as the Black Messiah and blend with behavior that demonstrates his will to carry his understanding into action, even if it means hooking Jill Pendleton* on heroin. He takes as his text *The Autobiography of*

Frederick Douglass. Finally, Darryl Van Horne* produces an antisermon when he argues against "terrible creation," using the dictionary as his text to reveal the horrors of parasites (*W*).

Many of the ideas in the last sermon of *MS* reappear in Updike's "On Being a Self Forever" (*SC*). The essay has the same form as the sermons of *IB*, *RRed* and *W*, being divided into three parts related to memory, understanding and will. Because it is intended to reveal the speaker rather than ask the congregation or reader to apply the sermon to himself, Updike offers some personal signs of his own "self," like his signature, and he discovers in his first impressions as a child the source of his self. Following this "remembering" comes "understanding," a definition first of "self" concluding that there are many selves and a realization of how good the self is, how wonderful it is for it to continue. Then Updike explains the relation of his self to God, and how that requires from him the will to continue as a writer to "praise" God's creation and to praise being. He contrasts this to his mother's will at the end of her life, his own will in his "marketable self" reviewing books and writing novels, and his will to follow his instinctual self in order to find rapport with the "giant, cosmic other."

Bibliography: Hunt, *JU*; Robert Detweiler, "John Updike's Sermons," in *Breaking the Fall: Religious Readings of Contemporary Fiction* (New York: Harper, 1989), 91–121.

Sex. Updike's work reveals his conviction, as stated in the *Paris Review* interview (Plath, *CU*), that sex must be taken "out of the closet and off the altar and put [in] the continuum of human behavior." Updike has asserted that because the Puritan inheritance has harmed America, sex needs to be demythologized and desanctified. Since sexual experience most closely approximates religious experience, acts of love are in a sense religious acts. Also, Updike is convinced that a writer should be able to write frankly about sex since God knows everything and nothing written about His creation can be shocking or shameful to Him. Sex had been identified by Updike in "The Dogwood Tree"* as one of the "three great secret things," along with religion* and art,* and to critic George Hunt, sex encloses the other two and, unlike religion and art, is what most readers are aware of.

Unquestionably, sex is an Updike trademark. He explores erotica freely, examining such things as male and female masturbation (*RR*, *RRed*); fetishism ("The Other" [*TM*]); the making of a pornographic film ("Brother Grasshopper" [*A*]); and sex among the clergy (*MS*, *W*, *RV*, S.), among college students (*MF*, *RIR*), between races (*RIR*, *B*), between gays and lesbians (*RIR*, *RaR*, *W*, *B*, *IB*), among wife swappers (*RIR*), between an older man and a pubescent girl (*TE*), with a third person (*B*) and with prostitutes (*RR*, "Transaction" [*P*]). The poetry adds witty explorations of intercourse and genitalia ("Sonnet," "Midpoint," "Cunts," "Fellatio," "Klimt and Schiele

Confront the Cunt" [*CP*]) and porno theaters ("In Memoriam Felis Felis" [*CP*]). It would be hasty, however, to think that Updike endorses without qualifications the sex he describes without qualification. For one thing, he encourages us to see his exploration as part of a historical survey of America's changing attitudes toward sex.

As with his other themes, Updike supplies in his work a virtual history of the shifting ideas of sex in the past forty years. He begins with the 1950s, when sexual favors were parceled out so carefully, as in *RR*, that, as Updike remarked at a lecture, marrying a woman seemed the best tactic for sleeping with her. Though writers like James Joyce,* Henry Miller,* Edmund Wilson,* and D. H. Lawrence had launched assaults on sexual repression and were read clandestinely by Updike and many others in the 1950s, their effect had not yet changed the established patterns of sexual behavior. Updike charts how, in the 1960s, sexual restraints were lifted and what was shyly requested in the 1950s was freely given a decade later. Censorship laws were lifted, and Joyce, Miller and Lawrence, as well as the Kinsey report on the sexual behavior of men and women, were widely read. *Playboy* magazine, begun in the mid-1950s, included a multipart "philosophy" making healthy sex part of the sophisticated modern person's education. As censorship in film* and television* and popular culture* in general receded, homosexuality* received spokesmen and spokeswomen, and "the pill," limned in *Couples*, began to free women from reproductive worries and allowed them to reclaim their bodies, a crucial idea of the 1960s women's liberation movement. The pill and abortion* became essential to women's freedom (*Couples*), along with a more stringent treatment of rape and more relaxed attitudes toward promiscuity and group sex (*RRed*). Women sought to reclaim their bodies in all ways and fled the patriarchal Sigmund Freud,* whose theories they perceived as hostile to women, for the more spiritualized works of Carl Jung.* This freed sex in part from patriarchal models and relieved sex of its heavy moral burden. Virginity was a male value women became anxious to discard. Masturbation (*RR*) adultery* and open marriage (*TF*) gained acceptance, along with gay, lesbian and bisexual experience. Such liberalizing placed pressure upon church, government and family, and while the coming of virulent sexually transmitted diseases and AIDS* in the 1980s made erotic adventure dangerous, as *RaR* shows, it hardly slowed the tendency toward multiple sexual partners.

Despite its liberating message for women, Updike's use of erotica remains, arguably, the greatest obstacle for many female readers, since his adoption of frank language and his graphic sexual scenes seem, to them, unnecessarily demeaning, while the great attention given to the penis, especially in *RV* and *TE*, strikes women as boring. Yet his critics must admit that Updike has charted with accuracy the shifting sexual mores from 1960 to the present, and such mapping has not been undertaken to celebrate this change or to condemn it. Unlike God, Updike has said, he does not create the world; he describes creation. Updike maintained from the start that the requirements of absolute fidelity to the actual world demanded total honesty in sexual matters, since, as he said, the writer justifies his frankness when he describes "sexual transactions" with all their complexity and resonance. When Alfred Knopf feared that *RR* would be charged with obscenity lawsuits in 1959, Updike reluctantly agreed, as he said, to trim the obscenity "to the point where the book might slide past the notice of hypothetical backwoods sheriffs vigilant against smut" (*OJ*). Relaxed British laws enabled him to reinstate the original words for the English publication in 1961, and with the Supreme Court's overturning of censorship restrictions, subsequent American editions have restored the troublesome passages. Not only does *RR* describe sex frankly, but it also makes sex the center of a conflict of values; the narrative turns on Harry "Rabbit" Angstrom's* sexual demands, first in converting Ruth Leonard Byer* from pseudowife back to prostitute when he demands that she perform oral sex, and then when he makes distressing sexual demands on his postpartum wife Janice Angstrom.*

Updike found an interesting way to handle eroticism in *C*, since the most graphic sexual scenes take place between the gods, in the encounter of Chiron* and Venus, who are unlikely to create the same reader response as mortals might. Besides, the gods are also religious personages. At the same time, 1964, Updike inspected, in the story "The Music School," the necessity of adultery and divorce,* and then, in *Couples*, the possibility of "sex as the emergent religion." Consistent with the idea of sex and religion, Georgene Thorne, who betrays both her husband and lover, calls Tarbox "the post-pill paradise," and her husband Freddy Thorne* keeps *The Kama Sutra*,* a sacred book of eroticism, by their bed. Although Updike considers the love affair of Piet Hanema* and Foxy Whitman* a modern version of Tristan and Isolde,* he graphically describes their lovemaking, particularly oral sex, in order to show how sex makes them feel "radically confirmed" in the high valuation they place upon themselves. The tactic is shockingly reversed by Updike two decades later in *RV* when Roger Lambert,* a former minister,* interrupts his translating of Tertullian* from Latin to contemplate vividly his wife administering fellatio to a rival. His voyeurism has nothing to do with erotic self-confirmation, and the conjunction of a "church father" like Tertullian and oral sex is startling. By emphasizing Lambert's detached voyeurism, Updike establishes the sanctity of sex from a different perspective.

Updike also explores the complex meaning of sex in middle-class society, in which, for some, sex is an "emergent religion." In 1971 in *RRed* Updike explored the value-laden sexual affair of Jill Pendleton* and Rabbit. As part of her rebellion against her affluent parents and middle-class values, Jill attaches no importance to sex other than as a woman's coin of exchange for protection, food and shelter (with Rabbit) or heroin (with Skeeter*). As Rabbit's sexual freedom with Ruth contributed to the death* of his daughter, Jill's valueless sex leads her to addiction and death when she forgets that the middle class of Penn Villas demands that sex be kept private and out of sight. Updike had urged that sex be taken from the bedroom and put in the parlor, but the result of Jill's exhibitionism with Skeeter in Rabbit's parlor brings on her death. Though this appears to be a restatement of older Puritan attitudes toward sex, Updike condemns the indulgences of Skeeter and Jill because they are exploitative and not life-affirming, not because they violate traditional mores. Updike also reveals how Janice Angstrom's affair in *RRed* awakens her neglected passion and restores her confidence in life. Yet her rediscoveries are so powerful that she nearly kills her lover. Updike suggests that though destructive eroticism cannot be condoned, the writer is obliged to examine it in such detail that it may be understood. For example, as *MS* shows, Updike does not find adultery in itself reprehensible. Although one of Rev. Tom Marshfield's* sermons* praises adultery as part of a phase on his journey to redemption, in the end he commits adultery again. But this action is the capstone of his affirmation of life, not an act intended to injure or shame. His adultery does not cancel his regeneration.

Updike also defends sex as play, what Norman O. Brown in *Life against Death* called "polymorphous perversity." Thus, although oral sex is associated with prostitution in *RR*, it also had been part of the sex exploration of Rabbit and his high-school girlfriend Mary Ann in *RR*, as *RaR* makes clear. In *Couples* oral sex becomes what Updike calls a way of knowing, like eating the apple of knowledge in Eden. Since Updike had also remarked that the ways lovers attach to one another is instructive, he has Foxy Whitman suckle Piet Hanema. (Updike actually reduced the sex in *Couples* at his wife's request and said in 1978 that he would have deemphasized sex if he had been writing *Couples* at that time rather than in 1968 [Plath, *CU*]). In *RIR* anal sex and infantile sex play bring Rabbit a knowledge of emptiness and death that paradoxically makes him feel "light," free of death's terror. Rabbit's quasi-incest with his daughter-in-law Teresa "Pru" Angstrom* brings him a knowledge of what he calls "Paradise," akin to the vision of eternal beauty he experienced with Brewer's* Bradford pear trees. Unacceptable to many, the sex between them occurs from mutual need and mutual respect at a time when they feel disowned. (Critic Judie Newman has advanced the clever idea that Pru actually instigates the action in order to protect her own nest, but this seems rather too cunning.) Rabbit had also enjoyed sex without love with Thelma Harrison* for ten years, but her husband Ronnie Harrison,* a spokesman for middle-class values, castigates Rabbit for never returning her love.

Updike's depiction of homosexual men throughout his work traces the shifting attitudes toward homosexuality just as he had traced shifting attitudes toward heterosexual attitudes: resistance in the 1950s by his characters (the stories "Scenes from the Fifties" (uncollected) and "The Lens Factory" [*LL*]); a distancing satire stemming from fear in the 1960s and 1970s, particularly by Rabbit (*RRed*, *RIR*), and wary accommodation (*RaR*, *IB*) coupled with continuing societal sanctions in the 1980s ("The Rumor" [*A*]). The pattern coincides with America's gradual reduction in homophobia as homosexuals moved out of the closet and into American life.

The *Coup* and *S.* show that other cultures' erotic permissiveness is an antidote to both the American repression that prompted Ann Coleman's* hysteria (*BD*, *MF*) and the Angstroms' neurotic link between sex and death. Col. Félix Ellelloû's* need for four wives arises not from a sexual master-slave relationship but from Islamic custom and his need to discover parts of his own psyche in multiple women. Although the Arhat* is a fraud, he instructs Sarah Worth* carefully in the art of sex according to *The Kama Sutra*, a spiritualizing activity.

On the other hand, the Western Puritanism infecting New England in *W* shows what happens when sexual restraints simply disappear: sport sex becomes selfish and does not stem jealousy. The witches may explore one another and Jenny Gabriel in the hot tub, but when they sense that she has been preferred by Darryl Van Horne,* they kill her. In *RV* Roger Lambert tells his stepniece Verna Ekelof* that after sex she made him ready for death. Alone, Henry Bech* contemplates his phallus and finds it a symbol of man as both substance and illusion, death and life (*BB*). Updike's various approaches to erotic material develop his conviction that a fearless exploration of sex uncovers a good deal Americans need to know about themselves.

Bibliography: Updike, "Foreword: What Is Female Sexuality?" "An Interesting Emendation," "Coffee-Table Books for High Coffee Tables" (*PP*); "Women," "The Female Body" (*OJ*); "The Disposable Rocket," "MM in Brief," "The Vargas Girl," "Lust" (*MM*), "Is Sex Necessary?" *New Yorker* 21 and 28 February 2000: 280–82, 285–86, 289–90; Markle, *FL*; Francis L. Kunkel, "John Updike: Between Heaven and Earth," in *Passion and the Passion: Sex and Religion in Modern Literature* (Philadelphia: Westminster P, 1975), 75–98, 170–71; Tallent, *MM*; Detweiler, *JU*; John N. Duvall, "The Pleasure of Textual/Sexual Wrestling: Pornography and Heresy in *Roger's Version*," *Modern Fiction Studies* 37 (Spring 1991): 81–95; Judie Newman, "*Rabbit at Rest*: The Return of the Work Ethic," in Broer, *RT*.

Shepard, Sam (1943–   ). American actor and playwright (Pulitzer Prize for *Buried Child*, 1979) Sam Shepard's realistic, family-centered plays reveal his interest in strange characters and plots, verbal dexterity, and blending of popular culture* and distortion. Shepard shares with Updike a concern for forces weakening the American spirit. All of these traits appear in "The Wallet" (*TM*), in which Shepard is mentioned.

Shillington, Pennsylvania. Updike's residence (1932–45), Shillington, a town of 5,000, is a suburb of Reading,* Pennsylvania. (Updike was born in West Reading Hospital.) It has been lovingly described in two essays, "The Dogwood Tree: A Boyhood"* and "A Soft Spring Night in Shillington" (*SC*). Fictionally, Shillington is used as the setting for the novel *C*, as well as for many stories collected in *OS* and *A*. Updike went to Shillington High School, where he began his apprenticeship* as a writer, contributing dozens of poems, drawings and reviews to the *Chatterbox*.* Critic James Schiff suggests that the "middle-class quotidian life" of Shillington was also present in Ipswich* and thus made Ipswich attractive to Updike. In his fiction, the town of Basingstoke, Delaware, closely resembles Shillington and is rendered with affectionate care (*IB*). Shillington is called Wenrich's Corner in "First Wives and Trolley Cars" (*OJ*). In *SC* Updike acknowledges his schoolmate Barry Nelson and other Shillingtonians with whom he has kept in close contact for half a century. *See* **Brewer, Pennsylvania; Updike, Linda; Updike, Wesley**.

Bibliography: Updike, "Foreword" (*OS*); Edward R. Ducharme, "Close Reading and Teaching," *English Journal* 59 (Oct. 1970): 938–42; Susan Beth Hartman, "The Role of the Berks County Setting in the Novels of John Updike," *Dissertation Abstracts International* 48/08A (1987): 2062, University of Pittsburgh.

Shimada, Natsume. A Japanese representative from Toyota Motors, Natsume Shimada instructs Harry "Rabbit" Angstrom* in the reasons why his son Nelson Angstrom* stole money from Springer Motors.* In a tirade, Shimada insists that America has lacked discipline since winning the war against Germany and Japan, and he accuses Rabbit of not understanding the economic war between the countries that followed. He asserts that America's quest for freedom has gone awry, providing freedom for dogs to defecate on streets, but ignoring freedom from violence. He also explains that Rabbit's personal quest for leisure in retirement is typical of how American parents have betrayed their obligations to discipline their children. Shimada revokes the Toyota franchise and imposes financial penalties, which Janice Angstrom's* creative financing overcomes. Shimada also lures away Rabbit's only female sales representative, Elvira Ollenbach,* to another Toyota franchise after flirting with her by accepting her tennis tips. Shimada is the only Japanese character in Updike's work.

Bibliography: Ristoff, *JU*.

Sholokhov, Mikhail (1905–1984). While toasting the Soviets, Col. Félix Ellelloû* astutely guesses which of his Soviet friends expect him to praise Mikhail Sholokhov and denounce Aleksandr Solzhenitsyn (*Coup*). Ellelloû* knows that Sholokhov was a more acceptable person because the Soviet Nobel* laureate novelist (1965) wrote about village life in the lower Don and was a proponent of Soviet realism, receiving the Stalin Prize (1941) and the Lenin Prize (1960). Solzhenitsyn (1918–   ) was a winner of the Nobel Prize as well (1970), but unlike Sholokhov, he was prevented from receiving his award because he had been imprisoned for anti-Stalinist remarks and in 1969 had been expelled from the Soviet Writers Union for opposing censorship of his writings. After being deprived of Russian citizenship in 1974, he lived for a while in the United States. Solzhenitsyn's *Gulag Archipelago* (1974) exposed how Stalin terrorized his people. Though Ellelloû,* an Islamic Marxist, would probably have favored Sholokhov, ironically, he found himself exiled, like Solzhenitsyn.

Short Fiction. Updike is one of very few novelists to have distinguished himself as a writer of short fiction, garnering a great many awards* for individual stories, several of which are widely used in high-school and college courses, and critical praise for his collections. Updike dates the start of his career as a professional fictionalist to the publication of "Friends from Philadelphia" in October 1954, in the *New Yorker*,* a magazine that would publish nearly two hundred Updike stories. Although he has published short fiction in a great many other magazines, Updike's forty-five-year association with the *New Yorker* has led readers to identify him almost exclusively with the urbane, sophisticated characters and stylistically graceful writing that characterizes fiction in that magazine. Updike's brilliant use of detail and metaphor, his array of upper-middle-class characters* and his general unconcern for plot certainly show a congruence with the *New Yorker*'s trademark story, which has been wittily characterized as having no beginning, no ending and "an undistributed middle," that is, a fiction concerned primarily with character and tone and little with plot. Updike, as he has said, began writing with the periodical in mind and learned his apprenticeship* in part from *New Yorker* writers such as James Thurber,* John O'Hara, John Cheever* and J. D. Salinger.* Consequently, Updike's stories and the *New Yorker* are indelibly linked in the reader's mind.

Updike's allegiance to this subgenre of the American short story has kept pace with his concern for the novel,* though he has admitted that the writing of stories financed his work on novels in his early years. But the stories cannot be considered a means to an end; they are fully realized artistic works in their own right. Each collection deserves the attention it has been given in the separate entries of this encyclopedia, and viewed together, the collections allow the reader to trace the direction and development of Updike as a craftsman and the emergence and relationships of characters and themes as they appear in his stories.

Though Updike has evolved as a story writer, his essential methods were formulated in his first volumes. In *SD* the dominant mode of realism is announced, with the heroes close to Updike and his New York* world and domestic life. He would always work closely to his own experience, but, as Updike explained, with a twist: "The short stories are probably the most me, the most autobiographical. . . . you slightly exaggerate . . . you often combine experiences you had with ones you didn't have" (Plath, *CU*). In *SD* Updike's heroes face a revelation showing their limits as lovers ("Snowing in Greenwich Village"), husbands ("Toward Evening," "Sunday Teasing") and fathers ("Incest").

In *PigF* Updike returns to his own youth, most notably in "Pigeon Feathers" and "Flight." "Pigeon Feathers" depicts thirteen-year-old David Kern's* shattering fear of oblivion and his eventual realization that God will grant him an afterlife. To Updike, short fiction particularly requires that its meaning be delivered through images, and the image of pigeon feathers at the end assures David Kern that such beauty and variety must attest to a benevolent God. The story builds on Updike's own experiences in moving from Shillington* to Plowville* and alludes to his own existential anguish from 1945 to 1962. Another story apparently anchored in Updike's life is "Flight," which recounts the conflicted relation of a son and his mother and her ambitions for him. Imagery* has been sacrificed a bit to dramatize the Oedipal struggle. "A & P," Updike's most anthologized story, blends elements of the two previous stories. But Sammy does not quite understand his quixotic effort to defend an attractive girl who violates store policy by wearing a bathing suit in the A & P. The story, told in his own flippant adolescent voice—perhaps borrowed from J. D. Salinger,* as Updike's wife Mary Pennington Updike* suggested—reveals a sensitivity beneath Sammy's jaded surface. Unlike the previous stories, "A & P" ends ambiguously, as does "The Astronomer," in which a New York adult faces the same crises David Kern had. He finds in works of Plato* and Søren Kierkegaard* some protection from dread, but he is mainly bolstered by his astronomer friend, who has been terrified not by outer space but by the emptiness of the New Mexico landscape. Misery welcomes company, but the narrator must still face his problem. The last three stories of *PigF* are also more daring than those of *SD*. "Lifeguard" presents an ambiguous sermon*-monologue delivered either by a Christ or a Devil figure, while "The Blessed Man of Boston, My Grandmother's Thimble, and Fanning Island" as well as "Packed Dirt, Churchgoing, a Dying Cat, a Traded Car" supply mosaics of very different events held together through interweaving images, a technique developed in *MuS*.

Updike collected the stories situated in Olinger (fictionalized Shillington) as *OS*, thus focusing attention not on plot or character but rather on setting and tone. Updike instructs the reader to pronounce the town as "O-linger."

"Leaves," "The Music School" and "Harv Is Plowing Now" from *MuS* usher in a further evolution in Updike's craft with his "abstract-personal" mode. This method enabled him to construct fiction that depended upon networks of imagery and complex interweaving of themes, what Updike called a "fugal weave." The stories also show a more daring interlacing of scientific, religious and artistic images than he had used before. In "Twin Beds in Rome" Updike returns to Richard Maple* and his wife Joan Maple,* introduced in "Snowing in Greenwich Village" (*SD*), to reveal their now-disintegrating marriage. Thus Updike begins to create character continuity in his short fiction; seventeen Maples stories eventually appeared as *TF*. In introducing the blocked Jewish novelist Henry Bech,* Updike begins an even more extensive continuity. Bech, Updike's alter ego,* would concern Updike for the next thirty-five years and be the protagonist of *BB*, *BIB* and *BaB*, collections that Updike made into a series of connected stories that he sometimes called "quasi-novels." The *MuS* collection is surely pivotal in Updike's exploration of the possibilities of the short story.

MW builds on the experiments in *MuS* by adding five Maples stories and contributing another of the Olinger tales ("When Everyone Was Pregnant") and an "abstract-personal" fiction in "The Sea's Green Sameness." Updike, in a section called "Other Modes," also injects more humor into his work in stories that are often fantastical. *P* supplies more Maples stories, the best of which is the often-anthologized "Separating." "Ethiopia" anticipates *Coup* and continues the "fantasies" of *MuS* while working in a straight realistic manner that Updike had long since perfected. Such realistic fiction dominates *TM*, but with a modulated tone of loss that resonates through the collection. Humor, fantasy and the "abstract-personal" mode have been set aside; the result is a volume unified in tone and with cumulative power.

A again supplies a great diversity of approaches, from the magic realism* of "The Afterlife" to the fable of "Brother Grasshopper" and the suburban sex* comedy of "The Man Who Became a Soprano." "Short Easter" introduces religious ideas Updike had not presented in short fiction since "The Music School," and "Grandparenting" picks up the Maples after a hiatus of nearly twenty years. The most important stories, however, are those in the personal mode of *PigF* set in a town like Olinger/Shillington and concerning characters resembling Updike and his mother. The best of these, "A Sandstone Farmhouse," reaches back to the autobiographically disguised characters of Joey Robinson* and his mother from *OF*. The story is composed of a series of images, some of these photographs, that slowly acquaint Joey with the richness of his now-deceased mother. It is a masterpiece of restrained power and a study in the distinction between sentiment and sentimentality.

Updike's last collection (*LL*) continues the lines already developed. "Cats" also concerns a woman resembling Updike's mother, while "My Father on the Verge of Disgrace" seems to reach back to *C* and anecdotes from *SC*. In his effort to redefine the genre of the short story, Updike sometimes blurs the line between fiction and reportage. Are "Lucid Eye in Silver Town" or "My Father on the Verge of Disgrace" stories, as Updike says, or reminiscences? Updike himself blurs the distinction when he says, "To give myself confessional room there is a small but necessary remove of invention: my real father taught algebra and not chemistry." But he admits that "Museums and Women" was "possibly too much of an essay" (*MM*). The recent story "His Oeuvre" (*New Yorker*, 25 Jan. 1999, 74, 76–81), continues to follow the adventures of Henry Bech, and several stories, like Bech's, treat memories of past affairs. All are told in the realistic manner, with no recourse to the other modes. Updike has certainly brought great credit to a genre he has called a "running letter to mankind about my inner adventures" (Plath, *CU*).

This survey of Updike's short fiction has sketched his techniques and developments, but Updike's remarks on the short story describe his own sense of its aesthetic form as he explains his choices as a judge of first-rate stories or reveals his intentions in his own work. Weak stories Updike calls "hard-breathing," with a "tossing-it-all-in style of portentous flashbacks and parenthetical urgencies" ("Introduction," *The Best American Short Stories 1984*). The story should offer, instead, "facts, words I can picture. I want stories to startle and engage me within the first few sentences, and in their middle to widen or deepen or sharpen my knowledge of human activity, and to end by giving me a sensation of completed statement. The ending is where the reader discovers whether he has been reading the same story the writer thought he was writing." Updike wants stories to begin "energetically and end intelligibly" and to provide "a sense of deep entry" (*MM*) into life, not by skill but by passion. Finally, Updike reads stories for "a glimpse into another country: an occasion for surprise, an excuse for wisdom, an argument for charity." Updike notes that his own stories are of first importance to him: "More closely than my novels, more circumstantially than my poems, these efforts of a few thousand words each hold my life's incidents, predicaments, crises, joys. Further, they made my life possible, for I depended when young upon their sale to supply my livelihood." They are "situated somewhere between the novel and the poem, and capable of giving us the pleasures of both, the form also has the peculiar intimacy of an essay, wherein a voice confides its most intricate and important secrets to our ear." Finally, he says, "The voice of fiction speaks in images, and I find mine when the images come abundantly, and interweave to make a continuous music."

Bibliography: Updike, "The Short Story and I," "Introduction to *Self-selected Stories of John Updike*," "Foreword to *Love Factories*," "Note on 'Separating,' " "Introduction" to *The Best American Short Stories 1984*," "Note on 'My Father on the Verge of Disgrace' " (*MM*); "Introduction," in *The Best American Short Stories of the Century*, ed. John Updike, Katrina Kenison (Boston: Houghton Mifflin, 1999); Greiner, *OJ*; Luscher, *JU*.

Simpson, O[renthal] J. (1947–). A college and professional football player for the University of Southern California and the Buffalo Bills, O. J. Simpson was involved in the "murder trial of the century" but found not guilty of his wife's killing. In *Coup* an American public relations officer who does not think that he addresses Col. Félix Ellelloû* sarcastically suggests that Ellelloû* is Simpson. *See* **Sports**.

Skeeter, alias of Hubert Johnson or Hubert Farnsworth. The Vietnam* veteran and Black Power advocate in *RRed*, Skeeter meets Harry "Rabbit"

Angstrom* in Jimbo's Friendly Lounge. Since he knows that the bar is about to be raided, Skeeter forces his way into Rabbit's home and endures a beating, but is permitted to stay. At Jimbo's, Skeeter had slept with the white runaway Jill Pendleton,* and after Rabbit takes him in, they each share Jill. Skeeter provides Rabbit nightly with views of his African-American* reading of American history* to vent his anger and to educate Rabbit. By having the three of them participate in a "psychodrama" intended to reduce Rabbit's indifference to blacks, Skeeter reverses roles and has Rabbit play the part of a slave, and Skeeter plays a slaveowner who rapes Jill, a slave. Skeeter also describes his experience in Vietnam, which led to his belief that he is the "Black Messiah," destined to lead an apocalyptic race war. Skeeter's prediction of things to come barely impresses Rabbit until Rabbit discovers his own desire to kill the hard-hearted doctor who had treated his mother indifferently.

Skeeter knows that Jill has taken heroin and hallucinogens and has seen God while "tripping," so he hooks her on heroin so she will see Him again and verify Skeeter's godlike conception of himself and his mission. When Skeeter is about to be implicated in the burning of Rabbit's home and Jill's death, Rabbit gives him thirty dollars and a ride out of town. In April 1979 Rabbit learns of Skeeter's apparent death during the Philadelphia police's attack on the "MOVE" headquarters. Rabbit keeps the clipping in his wallet and later thinks that he has seen "Skeeter Lives" written on a wall. For Rabbit, Skeeter was a man of force; in a sense he was a combination of the two persons—Marty Tothero* and his mother—that Rabbit proclaimed in *RR* had the most force in his life. Skeeter is also Rabbit's "shadow" self, a warning of what happens when self-centered egotism goes uncontrolled.

Yet Skeeter is also a parody of Rabbit as a visionary, racist, outlaw and misogynist. Like Rabbit, Skeeter also believes that a "thing" wants him to find it, and he certainly has, as Rabbit phrased it in *RR*, the "guts" to be himself, so that others will "pay his price." Also, both are curious about the other as "Other," and though neither learns what the other wants to teach, they feel homosexual attractions, partly fueled by Skeeter's desire for white women and Rabbit's fantasies of black women. In sharing Jill, they symbolically communicate sexually with each other. Skeeter's strange praise shows that he has seen the same smoldering anger in Rabbit that he feels when he states, "As a white man you don't amount to much, but niggerwise you groove." Some have called Skeeter the most original African American in modern American fiction; others have said that he is a type and a caricature. Yet as a speaker of jeremiads, Skeeter remains one of Updike's most daring, most complex characters.

Bibliography: Bernard Oldsey, "Rabbit Run to Earth," *Nation* 214 (10 Jan. 1972): 54, 56; David Lodge, "The Lost American Dream," *Tablet* 15 Apr. 1972: 349–50.

Smart, Jane. Jane Smart is the most intellectual, the wittiest and the most committed to demonism of the three witches of Eastwick.* A feminist skeptical of male motives, Jane suspects that Darryl Van Horne* sympathizes with women's liberation merely to seduce her and her sister witches, Alexandra Spofford* and Sukie Rougemont.* Yet Jane takes Van Horne as a lover and under his influence becomes a cello virtuoso. She discovers in playing a Bach suite that men had kept the meaning of death* to themselves, and she leads the other witches in killing Jenny Gabriel, Darryl's bride. But Jane later realizes that Van Horne married Jenny so that he could seduce Jenny's brother, Chris Gabriel. After Van Horne leaves Eastwick, Jane casts a spell on a rich man. Jane Smart gives Updike a chance to exhibit his wit, as when she describes bad genes as "D'naughty DNA" (the first three letters spell DNA) and uses an ancient "magic cube" palindrome to change milk into cream. *See* **Classical Literature; Religion**.

Smith, Adam (1723–1790). Scottish economist Adam Smith is mentioned as one of the economists Col. Félix Ellelloû* studied (*Coup*). A member of the physiocratic school, Smith believed in the supremacy of natural law. His *Wealth of Nations* explored the nature of money and the historical development of commerce. He may have been the first economist to separate economics from political science and law. Since Smith supported laissez-faire, Ellelloû would reject Smith for providing the foundation for exploitative capitalism.

Smith, Jesse. A charismatic fundamentalist religious leader, Jesse Smith precipitates a confrontation with authorities that resembles the Waco, Texas, tragedy (*IB*). Smith provides his followers, particularly Clark DeMott,* a sense of mission and an alternative to the money-and-drugs* subculture into which Clark has drifted. As a Bible*-quoting patriarch, Smith coerces his cult, takes the commune women as his "wives" and plans an Armageddon that will send his followers directly to heaven. Smith fits the pattern of Updike's other ministers*: those who are not ineffectual, like Jack Eccles,* Rev. Tom Marshfield* and Clarence Wilmot,* are dangerous, like Skeeter,* Rev. Horace Pendrick and Roger Lambert.* Smith most closely resembles Skeeter (*RRed*), the self-proclaimed Black Messiah, whose holy war would erase the evils of white culture. But Smith's rigid society shares a kinship with that of Stephen Conner* and Darryl Van Horne.* Smith's rigid cult recalls the austere welfare state in which Conner acts as poorhouse prefect, while Smith's charisma, like Van Horne's, makes him devastating to women. Smith provokes an assault on his cult complex in order to eradicate the ills of a consumer-driven society, as Skeeter foresees his leading a race war that will destroy white culture. Like Wilmot, Smith falls into despair when he receives no sign from God. Smith expresses both the desperate need for faith and the danger of trying to bring heaven on earth into existence through human means.

Solzhenitsyn, Aleksandr (1918–   ). *See* **Sholokhov, Mikhail**.

Space. From the tagging of porch chairs in *PF* and the congestion of Rabbit's house in *RR* to the cramped quarters of the movie screen in *IB* and the claustrophobia of chambers within a pyramid in *TE*, Updike treats space throughout his work as a metaphor for obstruction. Even when Harry "Rabbit" Angstrom* plays basketball* with kids, he feels that they "crowd" him, and when he drives to Florida,* he still feels trapped by a "net" of highways (*RR*). In *Couples* images from Edgar Allan Poe's* story "The Pit and the Pendulum" reflect upon Piet Hanema's* fear of enclosure. Tom Marshfield* lives in an "omega"-shaped motel, whose image is both the last letter of Christ's description of himself as alpha to omega, or first to last, and the female sex* organ: Marshfield brought problems with both Christ and sex to the motel (*MS*). Rabbit thinks that the moon (like omega?) is a "big nothing" (*RRed*), and his body crowds him from within as his athlete's enlarged heart swells and becomes an "alien" in his chest (*RaR*). In his hospital bed Rabbit fixates on open spaces like Antarctica and vast reaches of outer space.

Updike's houses are often physically and psychologically constrictive spaces. To cite examples from *RA*, Rabbit finds his apartment locked in RR, and the television* is precariously teetering when he opens a closet door. In *RIR* his parents' sheltering maple trees, which provided a "religious" experience for Rabbit, are cut down. His own mock-Tudor home in Penn Villas really has no vista except for television antennas and houses like his, and the sewers are sluggish. The view is similarly obscured in Valhalla Village in Deleon,* Florida, where Rabbit has retired (*RaR*). Rabbit works within a printing machine that acts alternately like a smothering mother or a demanding baby (*RRed*). After their home burns in *RRed*, the Angstroms live for years with Bessie Springer.* Her radio accompanies their lovemaking, and her storeroom with dress dummies becomes Rabbit's bedroom (and the site of his sex with his daughter-in-law) when he returns from angioplasty in *RaR*. Though Rabbit's retirement to Florida supplies vistas and room and Valhalla Village promises open heavenly spaces, Rabbit feels that "we're being developed to death." Even when Rabbit spies on Ruth Leonard Byer's* farm, he has to flee the open space to the confinement of his Toyota to protect himself from her guard dog (*RIR*). In *RaR* Rabbit is trapped under the sails of his overturned Sunfish and suffers a heart attack. His space shrinks to a hospital bed, and while he recovers from angioplasty, his visitors interfere with his enjoyment of television, disturb his oxygen tubes and thoughtlessly inflict pain. Rabbit feels his son Nelson's* face press toward his face as he dies.

In *TE* atomic war has made the vast midwestern space uninhabitable, and Ben Turnbull* pays protection money to keep his property safe. Ben slips in and out of branches of quantum space/time, but the branches lead to prisons and pyramid crypts. In the end he witnesses (or imagines) space shrinking as the universe begins to contract. Only Roger Lambert* (*RV*), Darryl Van Horne* (*W*) and Updike himself are comfortable in space. Lambert can project his imagination into the cramped attic trysting place of Dale Kohler* and Esther Lambert,* or he can extricate himself from a complicated mistress at a high-rise restaurant while enjoying the 360° view as the city revolves beneath him. In *W* Darryl Van Horne is comfortable in a crowded hot tub and refurbishes an old mansion complete with laboratory, using it to seek a "loophole" in the law of the conservation of matter, the ultimate refutation of boundaries. Updike himself pursues the symbol of space when in "The Dogwood Tree: A Boyhood"* he dreams of "riding a thin pencil line out of Shillington* . . . into unborn hearts" (*AP*). In "A Soft Spring Night in Shillington" he lovingly describes the specific place in which his sense of self was formed (*SC*), showing that though he left, as he says in his poem "Shillington," "the having and leaving go on together" (*TP*). *See* **Reading, Pennsylvania.**

Bibliography: Markle, *FL*; Raymond Wilson III, "*Roger's Version*: Updike's Negative-Solid Model of *The Scarlet Letter*," *Modern Fiction Studies* 35 (Summer 1989): 241–50; Derek Wright, "Mapless Motion: Form and Space in Updike's *Rabbit, Run*," *Modern Fiction Studies* 37 (Spring 1991): 35–44.

Spofford, Alexandra Sorenson "Lexa." One of the three witches of Eastwick* (*W*), Alexandra Spofford is the most elusive of Darryl Van Horne's* mistresses, but her ability to create storms or freeze tennis balls in the air cannot defend her from Van Horne's diabolic charm. He convinces her that she can be a commercial success by making her small-scale dolls as large as those of pop art* sculptor Niki de Saint-Phalle. Though she does create a "mock-Calder*/Moore," her work never achieves the notoriety Van Horne had promised. Scorned by his marriage to Jenny Gabriel, Lexa perverts her craft by creating a witch doll and with the other witches gives Jenny cancer,* the disease Lexa had feared contracting. After Van Horne returns to New York,* Lexa meets a ceramicist and goes to Taos, New Mexico, with him. *See* **Hawthorne, Nathaniel; Sex.**

Sports. Updike has written about basketball,* golf,* baseball and football throughout his career, and sports energize all aspects of his characters'* lives, from sex* to spiritual longing. Though often related to personal transcendence, sports are also closely allied to death.*

In response to his plan to provide a different controlling "letter" for each of his projected twenty-six novels, Updike chose "B" for basketball in identifying the principal sport of *RR*. He had previously used basketball in the poem "Ex–Basketball Player" (*CH*) and in the story "Ace in the Hole" (*SD*), a work that foreshadowed the character of Harry "Rabbit" Angstrom.* All three works describe a past glory, a troubling present and an unpromising future. The scope of the novel and the other three connected novels about Rabbit (*RA*) allowed Updike to explore how Rabbit's passion for basketball discloses major aspects of his character. For example, in *RR* Rabbit tries to relive his past greatness by elbowing his way into a pickup game. This remembrance of his former "specialness" enables him, over dinner with coach Marty Tothero,* to re-create his feelings of first-ratedness when playing a game eight years earlier. Rabbit's memories when he is fleeing from his family show his link between sex and transcendence in basketball through his remembrance of how his girlfriend Mary Ann permitted cunnilingus because he came to her a "winner," enabling Rabbit to associate the basketball net with her sex, the ladylike swish of the ball through the skirt of the net. A connection thus forms in Rabbit's mind between sex as reward and basketball as sex. Additional transcendence is created in the game itself, as the arc of the ball toward the basket becomes for him a metaphor for his soul's ascent. Since Rabbit fears that he has been dragged into a second-rate life with Janice Angstrom* and their son Nelson Angstrom,* he runs from them before mediocrity obliterates his sense that he is destined for fine things in life approximating his greatness on the court. If he cannot continue to be first-rate, was he lied to about what his coach called the "sacredness of achievement," or have American institutions failed to keep pace with his dream? He had been given contradictory roles: on the one hand, as a star others defended so he could shoot; on the other, as a player denounced by his own coach as selfish, not a team player. What did America want from him, a leader or a joiner?

In *RRed* Rabbit's irritation at the new style of basketball stars (especially African Americans*) leaves him longing all the more for the past. In *RIR* his fame is embalmed in snakeskinlike clippings in a tomblike showcase, and yet he is remembered vaguely by Annabelle Byer* as a former sports star. But Rabbit is no longer known by his nickname. His former teammate Ronnie Harrison* is a constant reminder of how Rabbit had set records at the expense of Ronnie's rough protection. Their testy relationship is continued in their golf matches in *RIR* and *RaR*. In *RaR* Rabbit is remembered as a sports hero when he marches as Uncle Sam,* and his love of the game and the ideal it represented for him cause him to risk his life in a game of one-on-one, signifying his commitment to his youthful dream. This last basketball game mirrors the first scene in *RR*, as though what was reborn has flowered and died. Such "sacredness of achievement"—for Rabbit—was worth dying for.

Golf provides a forum in which Rabbit and Harrison can continue their competitiveness, each encounter marked by Rabbit's delinquency, as though

Harrison is his double or conscience. The meeting with Harrison at the Castanet Club in *RR* is marked by Rabbit's rage over his sister's premature dating and his realization that Harrison had been a client of Ruth Leonard Byer.* Rabbit's failed dream of swapping his wife for Cindy Murkett* is punctured doubly when Harrison gets Cindy and Rabbit must be content with Thelma Harrison.* The morning after the wife swapping the touchy men play golf (*RIR*). Rabbit's farewell to his undervalued mistress, Thelma (*RaR*), is followed by a last game of golf at the Flying Eagle in which the intrusion of smoldering resentments spoils their golf and parodies their friendship. Nothing has changed between them in the shift from basketball to golf. Relaxation after golf often finds Ronnie interfering with Rabbit's joke or squelching his personal confessions.

Updike has written so much about golf that his selected essays and stories on the sport were collected in *GD*. The essential tone of these works is, appropriately, playful, as in Updike's amused, if ardent, golf tips. Since golf is a sport Updike has played since 1957, when he was twenty-five (breaking eighty only once), he can write an insider's study of its joys and frustrations. Thus the ecstasy of the perfect drive in *RR* (Rabbit shouts, "That's it!") is a graphic metaphor for Rabbit's belief that his past greatness can be found again. The ball climbs into the clouds, echoing his wish for spiritual ascent and confirming the reality of flight his soul craves. As Rabbit's own ambitions shrink with time, so does his golf game trace a downward path throughout *RA*, from the ecstasy of RR to country-club socializing (*RIR*) and a foursome with Jewish retirees (*RaR*). While most golfers seek tips from other players, Rabbit seeks the secret of death from the retirees. They tell stories about bypass surgery that scare him so much that he decides to forgo the bypass for angioplasty. After the procedure Janice urges Rabbit to exercise by playing golf, though she later scoffs that the old men he plays are no challenge. Golf had been associated with death, from Rabbit's rage while golfing with Rev. Jack Eccles* in which he symbolically beat his wife with his clubs (*RR*) to a discussion of the Tibetan Book of the Dead after golf (*RIR*) to golf after Thelma's death (*RaR*) that ends Rabbit's friendship with Ronnie, and that is his last golf game and foreshadows his last basketball game and his death.

But golf is less dire outside *RA*. The story "Intercession" (*SD*) shows why competition leads to cheating, and "Farrell's Caddie" (*A*) provides a magical caddie who not only advises about clubs and swings, but also about stock options and love. Since Updike notes how his golf language is often religious or mystical, it is natural that Rev. Tom Marshfield* should play golf (*MS*). When he rusticates in the West, his exile has placed him in a kind of hell; Updike remarks that golf "faithfully" answers Dante's* description of the Inferno. The pastoral* golf course takes Marshfield closer to the spiritual feeling he had lost, as it had supplied Rabbit Angstrom with a place to hide from entrapment while seeking his "thing" (*RR*). Updike has often remarked that had he not played golf, he would have published more, yet golf and writing are not entirely different, since each involves perseverance in the face of nearly sure disappointment, and each is a craft that demands constant fine-tuning and often provides private delight.

Baseball is also connected with dissolution and death. In *RRed* Fred Springer,* the stereotypical American grandfather, takes Rabbit and Nelson to a local ball game. But the national pastime reflects the violence of the time, as baseball's pastoral realm has become a racist killing field with fans shouting, "Kill that black bastard." Also, the game seems to lose something when it is seen directly rather than through the intermediary of television* and its chatty announcers and commercial interruptions. Yet Rabbit's naïve idealism still emerges later when he thinks, "Where any game is being played, there is a hedge against fury." Though Rabbit follows the Phillies throughout *RA*, Ronnie Harrison enjoys pronouncing, "The Phillies are D.E.A.D." Underlining this, baseball's esteemed commissioner Bart Giamatti has a fatal heart attack (*RaR*). Ironically, a female sales representative, Elvira Ollenbach,* in *RaR* is the only person as interested in the Phillies as Rabbit, but she rejects Rabbit's sentimental view of the comeback effort of the future Hall of Famer, Phillie Mike Schmidt. Rabbit had linked Schmidt to the Phillie Whiz Kids of 1950 who were hot when he was a basketball star, so Schmidt's retirement, "on his own nickel," Rabbit says approvingly, foreshadows his own death. It is curious, in this context, to realize that Updike's famous sports reportage, "Hub Fans Bid Kid Adieu," described the famous exit by Ted Williams at Boston's Fenway Park. Updike had been there to see a hero enter baseball immortality, and Williams homered in his last at bat. Williams, also exiting "on his own nickel," refused to acknowledge the fans' applause because "gods do not answer letters." But Mike Schmidt returns later to act as judge in a beauty contest, as if assuring Rabbit that "death" by retirement is not real death. Rabbit thinks, "Schmidt judges. Skeeter* lives." Rabbit wants to believe that his heroes defy time.

Though some men might hope that their sons would carry on their love of sports, Rabbit knows that this is unlikely since Nelson has "little Springer hands," as Mary Angstrom* pronounces, and seems too short for basketball or baseball. Certainly Nelson could not play football. Football provides Piet Hanema* the chance to wreak revenge on his nemesis Freddy Thorne* by breaking Freddy's finger during a touch football game. Ironically, Freddy will later have Piet in the palm of his hand when Piet seeks an abortion* for his mistress Foxy Whitman* (*Couples*). Super Bowl 1980 is also linked to death. As Rabbit is presented with his first grandchild during the game, he thinks, "Another nail in his coffin." The Super Bowl seems to have supplanted religious feast days, and its grandiose halftime show salutes the 1940s and celebrates energy. Rabbit, a product of the 1940s and 1950s who made his money on people running out of gas in the 1970s, faces the loss of his energy in the 1980s (*RIR*), though his granddaughter's energy will propel her through the 1990s. Football heroes seem to be gods already installed in Valhalla as Rabbit watches the Bears and Eagles play on television in a dense fog (*RaR*) that obscures even "Neon" Deion Sanders. Sanders's other nickname, "Prime Time," also mocks Rabbit, who is running out of time. In *RaR* basketball, golf, baseball and football, along with Rabbit, take "curtain calls" as they all wind down. *See* **Games**.

Bibliography: Updike, "The Boston Red Sox, as of 1986" (*OJ*); "Bodies Beautiful" (*MM*); Robert W. Lewis, "Sport and the Fiction of John Updike and Philip Roth," *Dissertation Abstracts International* 34/11A (1973): 7028, Ohio State University; Wiley Lee Umphlett, "The Agony of Rabbit Angstrom: The Search for a Secure Self," in *The Sporting Myth and the American Experience* (Lewisburg, PA: Bucknell University Press, 1975), 145–56; Edward A. Kopper, Jr., "A Note on Updike's 'Ex–Basketball Player,'" *Notes on Contemporary Literature* 21.5 (Nov. 1991): 6; Jack B. Moore, "Sports, Basketball and Fortunate Failure in the Rabbit Tetralogy," in Broer, *RT*.

Springer, Bessie (dies June 22, 1982). The mother of Janice Springer Angstrom* and wife of Fred Springer,* Bessie Springer is a foil for Harry "Rabbit" Angstrom.* She resents her daughter's marrying beneath her and frustrates Rabbit's efforts to assume the leadership of Springer Motors.* In addition, she draws the son of Janice and Rabbit, Nelson Angstrom,* away from Rabbit, making him more of a Springer. Mary Angstrom* detects this when she wickedly explains to Rabbit that Nelson will never be a basketball player because of his "little Springer hands." In *RR* Bessie tells Rev. Jack Eccles* that Rabbit's mother (whom she considers a descendant of dirt farmers) had given Rabbit inflated notions of his self-importance, though his stardom was behind him and he had no real future. She tells Eccles that she would have brought in the police when Rabbit deserted Janice. Clearly, though, Janice is frightened when Mrs. Springer threatens to come to the Angstrom home when Janice is drunk; this fear might contribute to Janice's drowning of her baby Rebecca.* After Fred Springer's death, Mrs. Springer and Janice inherit 51 percent of Springer Motors. Imitating what she thinks Fred would have done, Mrs. Springer shows a business acumen that surprises Rabbit, particularly when she stymies his effort to keep Nelson from becoming a sales representative. Her efforts to install Nelson in the firm continue the rabbit-dog antagonism between the two families. She outmaneuvers Rabbit when Nelson becomes a salesman, misunderstanding how this will intensify the competition between Rabbit and Nelson and lead to Nelson's nearly ruining the firm. Mrs. Springer also keeps Rabbit subordinate by having the Angstroms live in her home after theirs is destroyed (*RRed*). She meets their plan to buy a new house with self-pity and intimidation. In *RaR*, though Bessie has passed on, her power is still exerted through Janice and Nelson, further isolating Rabbit and exacerbating antagonisms within the family. *See* **Feminism**.

Springer, Fred (dies 1974?). The father of Janice Springer Angstrom* and husband of Bessie Springer* in *RA*, Fred Springer is a successful businessman who builds a struggling used-car lot into Springer Motors,* a Toyota franchise. Since Springer feels socially superior to the Angstroms, as his wife does, he is outraged when Harry "Rabbit" Angstrom* deserts Janice and Nelson* (*RR*), and he only refrains from calling the police because of business considerations. But when Rabbit returns to Janice after their baby is born, Springer, whom Rabbit considers a "jerk," makes him a salesman, a job that Rabbit calls "cheating." Fred may have offered Rabbit the job in order to have him where he could watch him. With a businessman's language he tells Rabbit after Rebecca Angstrom* drowns that they must try to "cut the losses." In *RRed* Rabbit no longer works for him, but Springer takes Rabbit and Nelson to a ball game, criticizes Democratic presidents since Franklin Roosevelt,* and attacks Senator Ted Kennedy for his part in the death of a woman found in his submerged car. The situation parallels Rabbit's desertion of his wife and drowning of his baby, so Springer's raising the topic is either insensitive or cunning. Self-contradictory, Springer insists that American institutions are based on trust, yet his profession is based on deception. Dying in the period between *RRed* and *RIR*, Springer becomes an "absent presence" since his wife Bessie tries to run the agency as he would have done, and he clearly protects Janice by making her independent, should Rabbit again desert her. Springer's widow, Bessie, installs Nelson as chief sales representative. Bessie venerates Springer's memory by repeating his anecdotes or sayings, which to her contain nuggets of moral wisdom and business sense. Like an icon, his photograph dominates the Springer home, and the shrine oppresses Rabbit. However, Springer's death* for Rabbit means that "the dead make room," and that he now for the first time, by having married the boss's daughter, has the chance to succeed in business. He realizes, however, that as Fred Springer died and was supplanted, so will he be. *See* **Characters.**

Springer Motors. The Toyota firm of Springer Motors had been built from a small used-car lot by Fred Springer* as he participated in the American dream. Harry "Rabbit" Angstrom* is given a job at the car agency when he returns to his wife, Janice Angstrom,* at the end of *RR*, but to Rabbit, selling cars is more deceitful than hustling kitchen gadgets (*RRed*). Rabbit's youthful idealism decays as he sells. But Janice discovers a talent for business when she helps her father balance the books in *RRed*, and her place in the company enables her to stray from her family in an affair that unleashes her sexuality (*RRed*). After Springer's death his will gives control of the company to his wife, Bessie Springer,* and Janice, though as chief sales representative, Rabbit maintains the illusion that he is the star. Archconservative Springer had ironically converted his company into a Toyota franchise, and the company prospers when the energy crisis makes America vulnerable. Ironically, the weakness of America is directly responsible for Rabbit's achieving his "American dream." Nelson Angstrom* succeeds Rabbit on his retirement and nearly bankrupts Springer Motors, but the company rebounds, like many American companies during the recession of the late 1980s. Though Rabbit successfully confronts a Japanese investigator, he is less effective than Janice, whose shrewd tactics save Springer Motors, though the Toyota franchise is lost.

Updike provides impressive information about the sometimes dishonest financial operations of car dealers, as well as amusing scenes of the daily operations of a car agency. The rise and near demise of Springer Motors reflect automotive history from 1950 to 1990 as the original market for used cars gave way to gas guzzlers during affluence, trim imports during the gas crisis, sports cars when the gas crises ebbed and luxury cars and recreational vehicles such as jet-skis when affluence returned. Like America's progress from 1950 to 1990, Springer Motors' growth shows how hard work and ingenuity, mixed with shady business practices, produce the rise of the Springer and Angstrom families. Since the company both rises and falls because of circumstances beyond its control (the energy crisis), the American dream that it represents is partly rooted in luck. *See* **Automobiles**.

Stavros, Charlie. The second-in-command to Fred Springer* at Springer Motors* since 1963, the Greek Charlie Stavros provokes Janice Angstrom* and her husband Harry "Rabbit" Angstrom* into the presentation of their best and worst selves. He becomes Janice Angstrom's lover in *RRed* after Harry "Rabbit" Angstrom's* guilt over the death of his baby has left Rabbit afraid to have relations with Janice, since she might give birth to another child that will die. Charlie becomes afraid that Janice's sexual passion might affect his ailing heart, so he offers to return her to Rabbit, who refuses. Charlie's weak heart nearly fails during sex* with her, but Janice saves him by sheer force of will. Rabbit's sister Miriam "Mim" Angstrom* seduces Charlie and helps bring an end to his affair with Janice.

Charlie's liberal attitudes, especially toward the Vietnam* War, provoke Rabbit's fierce defense of the war and America. Yet in *RIR* Stavros and Rabbit can work side by side at Springer Motors because Charlie has taught Rabbit to appreciate Janice and because Charlie has also released Rabbit's sexual fears. Rabbit, watching Charlie seduce Melanie, the friend of the Angstroms' son, Nelson Angstrom,* admires Charlie's sexual prowess, despite their differing taste in women. When Bessie Springer* and Nelson conspire to place Nelson in Springer Motors, Charlie is fired. (He is rehired when Nelson goes through drug rehabilitation.) Rabbit objects to this on the false grounds that they are best friends, but Charlie quietly accepts this turn of events as he had his luck with Janice, Mim and Melanie. In *RaR* Charlie helps Rabbit at the lot after Nelson nearly destroys the firm, and he tells Rabbit to have a heart bypass as he had had, rather than angioplasty. Typically, Rabbit ignores Charlie's lifesaving advice.

Steinmetz, Arthur. *See* **Arhat**.

Stevens, Wallace (1879–1955). A foremost American poet, Wallace Stevens was born in Reading,* Pennsylvania. Updike was thrilled as an adolescent to discover that a "great modern poet had been born and raised in the heart of the city, on North Fifth Street" (*MM*). Noted for the extraordinary sensuality of his imagery and rhythms as well as his sometimes perplexing yoking of metaphors and his plunges into metaphysics as a poetic subject, Stevens was identified by Updike as having "eclipsed" the other stars of the Harvard* poetry seminar he attended—"[E. E.] Cummings,* William Carlos Williams, [Marianne] Moore, [Robert] Frost, even [T.S.] Eliot."* Stevens read at Harvard while Updike studied there. Although he worked all his life for the Hartford Accident and Indemnity Company, Stevens brought total dedication and polished craftsmanship to his art. Such respect for art* and duty to discipline out of the limelight were reflected in Updike's own attitudes and practices. Updike is especially sensitive to Stevens's use of Reading, his "Dutch" earthiness and the lush verse of "Sunday Morning," in which Stevens "bids farewell to faith with a Lutheran gravity" ("Stevens as Dutchman"). Yet Stevens's philosophical poems did not move Updike because Updike was "still too Dutch to believe" in the later poetry's "relentless essentialism."

Updike used a few lines from Stevens's "A Rabbit as King of the Ghosts" for his epigraph* to *RIR*. The rather elegiac lines suggest that Harry "Rabbit" Angstrom* is now poised to turn toward "the end of day." Updike's epigraph to *MuS* from Stevens's "To the One of Fictive Music" pays homage to a poem about pure creation; the stories show how such creation is frustrated by human predicaments. Critic George Hunt thinks that the epigraph is a key to understanding *MuS*, and he connects Updike's new mode of "the abstract personal" to the style of Stevens. Thus the stories resemble the "metaphor-centered" novels of *RA*, as well as others like *TE*. The epigraph to *BaB* is drawn from Steven's preface to the *Collected Poems, 1921–1931* of William Carlos Williams: "Something of the unreal is necessary to fecundate the real." The thought may characterize both Franz Kafka's* art and the unreality of Prague in "Bech in Czech" (*BaB*), or it may refer to Henry Bech's* tortured thought that he may not be real but a created character, or to the unreality of the Nobel Prize* stimulating Bech to new inventions. The epigraph may also refer to the reader's grasp of the real through the unreality of fiction.

Stevens's wit appears in Updike's playfulness in titles* like *CH, OF, MuS, MS, RRed* and *TE* and in his interest in philosophical subjects, sometimes approached esoterically. Critic Larry Taylor suggests that "Stevens is to modern poetry what Updike is to modern prose, writers concerned with idyls and irony, singers of love songs and chanters of dirges, poets and parodists—mixing 'fictive music' with 'possum and tatters and sop' to arrive at and re-create what Updike has called 'the mixed stuff of human existence.' " Taylor labels Updike's "In Football Season" "a piece of 'fictive music' " (*MuS*).

Another short story showing evidence of Stevens is "Bech Noir" (*BaB*), in which Henry Bech murders four of his critics. Commentator Jim Morrison, in private correspondence, has identified Harold Bloom as the murdered critic Lucas Mishner. Since Bloom borrowed a remark from Stevens in explaining that Updike would never capture the "American sublime," Bloom's use of Stevens must have been doubly stinging to Updike, since it suggested that Updike failed the standard set by a writer he admired. But in "Stevens as Dutchman" Updike had the last word by remarking that Stevens had been "hoisted into great esteem by such connoisseurs of the American sublime as Harold Bloom."

There are a number of other ties to Stevens. As Stevens used the form of his poem "The Death of a Soldier" to produce the graphic image of a gun, so Updike made a news story in the Brewer* *Vat* resemble a handgun to emphasize the relation of language to violence (*RRed*). The title of Updike's poem "Seven New Ways of Looking at the Moon" (*TI*) and his essay "Thirteen Ways of Looking at the Masters" (*HS*) may echo Stevens's "Thirteen Ways of Looking at a Blackbird", and "Sea-Surface Full of Clouds" may be a source for "The Sea's Green Sameness" (*MW*). Moreover, in "Bech Presides" (*BaB*) Bech alludes to Stevens's "The Worms at Heaven's Gate." *See* **Poetry**.

Bibliography: Updike, "Religion and Literature," "Stevens as Dutchman" (*MM*); Taylor, *PA*; Hunt, *JU*; Harold Bloom, "Introduction," in Bloom, *JU*.

Stevenson, Adlai (1900–1965). A U.S. statesman and liberal idealist, Adlai Stevenson had reformed education and health while he was governor of Illinois. A "Stevenson Democrat" was considered so liberal that Senator Joseph McCarthy was able to help Dwight Eisenhower win the presidency by smearing Stevenson as a Communist sympathizer. Richard Mathias in *Marry* claims that he voted for Stevenson for president in 1952, but considering Richard's conservative attitudes, he probably did not. *See* **Presidents**.

Style. All readers of Updike recognize his gifts for precise, sense-laden observation and endlessly inventive metaphors. He has always been the most punctilious of writers, shaving distinctions between words and fashioning punctuation with great deliberation. He was criticized early by hostile critics* such as Norman Podhoretz for having a wonderful style but nothing to say, but critics since have discounted this opinion because Updike's figures and images have an integral relation to theme and character. Richard Gilman, perhaps looking for the spareness of realistic writing from Updike, attacked his "moving from event to embroidery, from drama to coy detail." Others accused him of "lace-making," and his style in *C* was lampooned in *Snooze*, a parody of the *New Yorker*.* Updike himself has been accused of self-parody in such works as *TE*. Some have objected that in *RA* Updike's style often seems beyond what is appropriate to a middle-class salesman when, for example, he hits a golf drive. Yet Updike's style in *RA* is the product of the omniscient narrator's generous interpretation of all his characters,* permitting him to modulate from flat realism to subjective lyricism in interpreting his characters' interior worlds. Without alleviating the dullness or coarseness of their vernacular, the narrative voice* can provide figures and images in the deeper recesses of the characters and beyond their own ability to articulate. This is not so different from Shakespeare's treatment of Othello: in one moment Shakespeare has him speak as a poet, in the next as a brutal soldier. V. S. Pritchett said of *RIR* that Updike could make the Sears, Roebuck catalogue "sound like a chant from the Book of Psalms." Such unexpected lyricism is related to the stylistic device in *C* of magnifying the importance of ordinary people by relating them to mythic figures. A hallmark of Updike's style is his ability to keep, as he said, "a mass of images moving forward," usually through subtle, interconnected patterns. In *RA* this means that a great many images bind together each novel individually and the entire four books as well, making a coherent structure of each book and a unified reading experience of the entire tetralogy. Finally, Updike has said that the creation of a single, powerful image like *Huckleberry Finn* or *Don Quixote* is a chief goal of a novelist. With Harry "Rabbit" Angstrom,* Updike's Everyman, he may have achieved this. *See* **The Novel; Short Fiction**.

Bibliography: Updike, "Fine Points" (*MM*); Richard Gilman, *The Confusion of Realms* (New York: Random House, 1969); Philip Stevick, "The Full Range of Updike's Prose," in *New Essays on Rabbit, Run*, ed. Stanley Trachtenberg (New York: Cambridge UP, 1993), 31–52.

Sunshine Athletic Association. The Sunshine Athletic Association is a Brewer* men's club where Marty Tothero* lives in *RR*. Harry "Rabbit" Angstrom* goes there when he returns to Brewer after his abortive flight south, and Tothero takes him in. Rabbit sees that the club is a seedy place that smells of vice, something that also characterizes Tothero and Brewer.

Symbolism. Since Updike is a master of precise sensory details and original figures of speech, his images often rise, by repetition or strategic location, to symbols. Virtually all details in Updike's work contain implications that raise them to symbolic levels, whatever their origin. Some of the most important of these "charged images," as they are sometimes called, are related to categories like nature,* science,* religion,* popular culture* and the body.

Recurrent images within these groups include those related to costume, light, color, animals, space,* art,* automobiles,* names,* the days of the calendar* and the stars and constellations. Such images may rise to symbolic level in one scene, or they may form a pattern that recurs in several scenes, or they may operate as a dominant symbol for the entire work. Such images can retain traditional or assigned meaning, as in the symbol of the cross, or become ambiguous and capable of multiple signification, like the "S" of *S*. Updike frequently takes images directly from popular culture, such as the television* program *The Lone Ranger*,* to explore their symbolic possibilities; on the other hand, he may use an artistic or literary allusion with symbolic force, such as images derived from Vermeer* in *C* and Tristan and Isolde* in *B*.

In *PF*, for example, the natural image of rain threatens the fair. But rain in this novel also provides the means by which a symbolic difference of values between John Hook* and Stephen Conner* can be explored. Hook believes in reading the signs of nature to predict a coming storm; Conner relies on weather reports to forecast precipitation. The weather is seen from two perspectives and identifies a difference between the traditional man attached to the concrete particulars of his world and the modern man who transfers the basis for such evaluations from his own senses to technological measurements. Other natural images such as a season carry symbolic meaning through conventional associations. Thus in *RR* when Harry "Rabbit" Angstrom* runs from his family on March 20, the deliberate selection of the date forces the reader to see the first day of spring as symbolically connected to a rebirth of life in Rabbit. Yet when his daughter Rebecca June Angstrom* dies in June, we feel a reversal of the customary image, as the season of birth has become ironically the time of death.* (An additional irony arises, of course, when we consider that rabbits are usually associated with fertility, not death.) Likewise, the gestation of life takes nine months, but the nine months that pass in Rabbit's life in *RaR* represent the last months of his life: he is "born to death," or perhaps he is spiritually reborn in his last moments when he wins his last basketball* game.

Apart from natural images, man-made images take symbolic meaning as well. The weathercock atop the Tarbox Congregational Church in *Couples* looks down on the town as a traditional religious image suggestive both of Christ, associated with the dawn, and of Peter's betrayal, signified by Christ's prediction that he would betray Him three times before the cock crowed. Considering that it is a barnyard bird of procreative proclivity, the cock also represents sexual indulgence. Thematically, the meaning of the novel rests partly in the search for a new religion,* and Freddy Thorne* pronounces that new religion as based on sex.* The cock is thus also the symbol of a new religion, and it is all that survives the burning of the church after it is struck by lightning, a circumstance perhaps symbolizing God's abandonment of man.

A simpler man-made image is that of the Arizona motel to which Rev. Tom Marshfield* is forcibly rusticated in *MS*. It is shaped like an "omega," Marshfield notes, and the description automatically provides a graphic depiction of the building. But the omega shape also inevitably suggests, because of the religious context of the action, the "alpha and omega" of God. For Marshfield, it is perhaps the "last word" or letter signifying God's existence. But since Marshfield has been sent to the desert because of his sexual delinquency with the organist (a punning symbol), the omega also suggests the vagina. Marshfield has been cast into the very image that has driven him from God. The omega-shaped motel is thus an ironic sexual symbol. Spiritually or sexually the symbolic meaning of the motel's shape represents the larger action of the narrative. By the novel's end the reader comes to recognize a paradoxical relationship between sex and spiritual rebirth.

Events, too, take on symbolic meaning, as in *PF* when Updike uses the soda truck backing into the wall for a symbolic comment on how the modern welfare state walls in the aged with stones that can be turned against it when the scattered rocks are used to assault prefect Stephen Conner.* The event contains mythical symbolic meaning if one accepts Updike's explanation that the assault recalls the stoning of St. Stephen, and his selection of the name "Stephen" for Conner underlines that symbolism. Certainly, name symbolism is a modest form of signification that Updike usually relies on. Harry "Rabbit" Angstrom's nickname directly links meaning to image, and his surname conveys suggestions of smallness, storms and angst.*

RR illustrates how Updike uses patterns of images to create symbolic meaning. From the fact that basketball is played with a net to the connotation that a net is also a trap, Updike uses various kinds of nets and traps to suggest how Rabbit has trapped himself before and during marriage. From the parallels of Rabbit's mouth and blue eyes resembling a rabbit's, Updike draws into the pattern related images: thus Rabbit "hops," eats kohlrabi raw and fears predators like dogs. Rabbit also lives in a town with a street named Potter, so the intertextual allusion to Beatrix Potter's* *Tale of Peter Rabbit** supplies a symbolic story underlying Rabbit's narrative. Knowledge of the Potter tale urges the reader to be more attentive to the implications of details in the narrative that resemble those in the story—and to see symbolic meaning in deviations from Potter's pattern.

Other symbols in Updike's stories are original and ambiguous. Thus in *C*, not only does Chiron* function as a symbol of George Caldwell's* transcendent self, but also, as Updike remarked, "Chiron" might chime with "Christ" and thus draw together in one symbol images of classical and Christian meaning. But in the same novel Peter Caldwell,* the symbolic analogue for Prometheus, also takes on the symbolic qualities of Chiron, while George Caldwell sometimes suggests those of Prometheus.

Clearly some Updike symbols persist from novel to novel, like the images connected to Rabbit. They sometimes comment on one another, as the "horse" symbol of *C* is meant to contrast to the "rabbit" symbol of *RR*. From incidental images such as the names of newspapers or films* to the complexity of the moon landing or quantum physics,* Updike is constantly alert to symbols that represent meaning and deliver it with startling force. *See* **Imagery**.

Bibliography: Hamilton and Hamilton, *EJ*; Markle, *FL*; Robert A. Regan, "Updike's Symbol of the Center," *Modern Fiction Studies* 20 (Spring 1974): 77–96; Schiff, *UV*.

T

The Tale of Peter Rabbit. *The Tale of Peter Rabbit*, a story by Beatrix Potter,*
forms a spine of imagery* and contributes to theme in *RR*, and, to a lesser
degree, in other novels. Apart from the images connecting Harry "Rabbit"
Angstrom* himself to Peter Rabbit (each figure runs to a proscribed territory, is pursued by an authority figure, wears a blue jacket and suffers afterward), both books contain a similar moral. As Updike noted, Peter had been
instructed not to go into Mr. McGregor's garden and deliberately disobeyed
in order to satisfy his appetite and curiosity. Peter's penalties are terror
during his pursuit by the farmer and illness for having overeaten, resulting
in isolation from his siblings and mother. Rabbit's penalties are remorse,
guilt and self-imposed abstention from sex* for ten years. Though critic
James Schiff maintains that Updike provides no moral to "placate" the
reader, and that *RR* is thus "far less reassuring" than the tale, the two works
seem to share the message of the Garden of Eden story: play safe and obey
authorities. Of course, the moral of Potter's tale contrasts with the sophistication and intricacy of *RR*'s epigraph* from Blaise Pascal about "grace,"
"hardness of heart" and "circumstances." Few writers besides Updike would
risk joining together two such different intertexts into a story about "middleness."*

Updike has said that when one feels a "dwindling" of the self, it is natural
to want to listen to one's innermost "stirrings," what he called "the rabbitlike" thing within us that is "irresponsible" (Plath," *CU*). This is the "yes"
part of what Updike called the "yes, but"* problem. But he acknowledges
the "but" side too: following natural inclinations unravels the social fabric.
To underline the living presence of the Potter tale in *RR*, Updike names
one street "Potter" and another "Warren." ("Warren" is the name of a rabbit's burrow, but it may also refer to "Warne," Potter's publisher.) The
simplicity of the child's story contrasts with the complexity of Rabbit's need

to return to the time when he was first-rate. Ruth Leonard Byer* recognizes this craving, but having suffered because of it, rebukes him: "Run along, Rabbit. You've had your day in the cabbage patch" (*RIR*).

Updike acknowledged that he had been "traumatized" by Peter's being trapped in the flowerpot, and in 1968 he said that he recognized that his flowerpot red town of Brewer was Mr. McGregor's flowerpot, and that Rabbit is trapped like Peter. Clearly, part of the complexity of *RR* comes through Updike's sympathetic yet cautionary attitude toward Rabbit, which operates throughout *RA*. This is why Rabbit plays both Peter and McGregor in the four novels. In *RRed* Rabbit invades the forbidden territories of Black Power and sexual revolution represented by Skeeter* and Jill Pendleton,* who thinks that his penis looks like a carrot. In *RIR* Rabbit acts like Peter when he goes to Ruth's farm to find out if his daughter lived, and later when he goes to the garden of a Caribbean island for wife swapping. When he again visits Ruth's farm, he acts like McGregor invading the burrow in which Ruth's daughter Annabelle Byer* now becomes Peter Rabbit (*RaR*). Rabbit faces the forbidden territory of the sea and nearly dies for his effort when his attempted flirtation with Cindy Murkett* nearly results in tragedy in *RIR;* his effort at boating with his granddaughter Judy Angstrom* in *RaR* nearly costs them their lives. In *RaR* Rabbit also explores the figurative garden of incest* and the territory of black basketball* players and death* in Edenic Florida.* The Potter tale also underlines the plots of *RV, S., B* and *W. See* **Symbolism**.

Bibliography: Schiff, *JU*.

Telephone. The telephone is used repeatedly in *Marry* and *W* to provide a sense of disembodied communication. In *Marry* the phone conversations emphasize the isolation of the lovers as they attempt to keep lines open and the "ethereal" quality of their affair, as if their spiritual selves were really communicating. *W* opens with phone talk, as the witches keep each other informed this way. For them, the phone is a form of mind reading. Updike pointed out that the telephone is an "erotic instrument" because of "the sanitary distance it imposes, while permitting mouth-to-earth intimacy." In *RRed*, however, calls from Janice Angstrom* to Harry "Rabbit" Angstrom* often disturb him at work by reminding him of his neglect of their son Nelson Angstrom.*

Bibliography: Updike, "The Vargas Girl" (*MM*).

Telephone Poles (New York: Knopf, 1963). *TP*, Updike's second book of poetry* displays the same acuity for light verse* as *CH* (the two books were published together in paperback as *Verse*), but shows Updike anxious to be read as a serious poet with many poised and sophisticated poems. But the organization, with light verse in section one and serious poems in section two, may have countered his intention. In later volumes Updike relegates light verse to the last section (*M*, *CP*) and the middle section (*TT*). The title, alluding to the central poem, stresses the communicative link of poetic voice and reader/auditor.

The light verse shows nimble wit and surprising approaches. He finds "jagged apocalypse" in the ordinary clothes washer and "gall" in the way neutrinos pass through even the lover and lass. Updike parodies "Twinkle, Twinkle, Little Star" to describe a white dwarf star, as if it were a "tiny pill" to ward off "cosmic fright," though the existence of such a remarkably dense object is a very heavy matter. Elsewhere he builds a poem around "Kenneths," as he had a poem about "Jacks" in *CH*. He inspects local headlines for evidence of the silliness of how things are reported, for example, using a snatch of dialogue between Hemingway and Fidel Castro or a passing comment in the *Encyclopaedia Britannica* about animals whose hearts are far from the ground. He offers a "found poem" made from Dr. Johnson's notes on the Versailles zoo and takes a cue from Suetonius for a poem on "Caligula." Naturally, Updike delights in poems that are built of wordplay: "Recital," "I Missed His Book, but I Read His Name" and "Upon Learning That a Bird Exists Called the Turnstone." Others make clever allusions to other poems—Keats's "Ode to a Nightingale" in "Party Knee," John Donne's "The Flea" in "Mosquito." His cleverly ironic "Thoughts While Driving Home" lances the bubble of the witty speaker as he wonders, perhaps to his wife, how he performed at a recent party. "Was I wise? Was I wan? Was I fun?" The light-verse poems are all of these, what Updike called "cartooning* in print" (Plath, *CU*).

The longer second half of the book applies a more serious attitude toward the complex subject of the commonplace. "Telephone Poles" conceives of the poles as giants equipped with the power to "stun us to stone," "unnatural" trees that do not remind us of autumn's tragic "casting off." In another poem Updike records how his father "became Uncle Sam" marching in a parade and, mistaken for the real thing by an outraged taxpayer, was nearly punched. The poem thus demonstrates the seductions of artifice. (Updike used his own parade appearance in the story "The Parade" [*OJ*] and had Harry "Rabbit" Angstrom* march, so disguised, in a July Fourth parade [*RaR*]). In a valedictory to "Shillington,"* Updike notes that "the having and leaving go on together," a palliative of the inevitable mutability of time. The most interesting poems are those that show Updike paying homage to men who deeply influenced his thinking. He celebrates in "Les Saints Nouveaux" his personal gods such as Marcel Proust,* Paul Cézanne and Constantin Brancusi (whose art Updike would select for the jacket of his fourth volume of poetry, *TT*). They treated the subject of death,* they created an art* that seems a natural force, and they found in their art "theologies of vision." The companion poem, "Die Neuen Heiligen," celebrates other key writers who influenced early Updike: Søren Kierkegaard,* whose wit "slashed the Ideal /

and himself to bits"; Franz Kafka,* who found the world "defendants / all guilty of Fate"; and Karl Barth,* who "rooted" in utter despair / the Credo that Culture / left up in the air." Elsewhere he coins "Erotic Epigrams" that employ his favored myth of Tristan and Isolde* and offer meticulous discriminations about love. Other poems show a feeling for the arresting metaphor ("Flirt": "The flirt is an antelope of flame") and the archaic ("Winter Ocean": "portly pusher of waves, wind-slave"). "Seven Stanzas at Easter," probably Updike's most religious poem, has often been used in neoorthodox sermons, according to Updike, but critic Donald Greiner urges recognition of the conditional quality of the faith lodged in the first word, "If." The poem declares, "Let us not mock God with metaphor"; perhaps Dale Kohler* of RV should have listened. "Earthworm" also contains what Updike called his philosophy, that worship must take place in the human-bound factual world; it formed the epigraph to Yerkes, JU. The earthworm as metaphor appears in a sermon in OF. In Greiner's opinion, this collection of poems shows a "homage to the world in which small things are infinitely fine and the daily cycle is forever." Critic André Le Vot suggests that "The Stunt Flier" and "February 22" could be typographically rendered as prose paragraphs; conversely, passages from the novels* could be reassembled as poems. This suggests the close alliance between Updike's poetry and prose.

Bibliography: "Rustic and Urbane," *Times Literary Supplement* 20 Aug. 1964: 748; André Le Vot, "Updike Poet, ou le mythe d'Antée," *Langues modernes* 59 (Nov–Dec. 1965): 50–55; Elizabeth Matson, "A Chinese Paradox, But Not Much of One: John Updike in His Poetry," *Minnesota Review* 1 (1967): 157–67; Edward R. Ducharme "Close Reading and Teaching," *English Journal* 59 (Oct. 1970): 938–42; Greiner, *OJ*.

Television. Since Updike provides an exacting portrait of the middle class and popular culture,* television is omnipresent in his work. His general view of television is negative both for what it reports and for what it does to the viewers. A scene in *RR* illustrates both problems. Janice Angstrom* is watching a children's show, *The Mickey Mouse Club*, as Harry "Rabbit" Angstrom* returns from work, and though she disgusts him for watching and Rabbit has seen it dozens of times, he grudgingly admits to himself that it is cute. The show supplies not merely diversion but education. Jimmie, the "Big Mouseketeer,"* in his "Proverbs for Little Mouseketeers" segment, provides Rabbit with something he can use "professionally": an explanation of the "proverb" "Know thyself," which, as Jimmie explains, God understands to mean, "Be yourself." He winks and Rabbit winks back, knowing that he and Jimmie understand a higher truth: "Fraud makes the world go round." Television has amused its watchers sufficiently so that they do not realize that an ancient truth has been debased. In one's own home Greek spiritual teaching has become a social bromide. The viewer is intended to improve by following the proverb because it is reinforced by the analogy that "God doesn't want a tree to be a waterfall." But there is little effort made to show how difference alone will enable you to "be yourself" happily. Rabbit's problem is that he is keenly aware of his difference, but the world seems to demand conformity. Jimmie is thus an irresponsible secular priest giving a secular sermon.*

Another example from *RR* illustrates how much more real television is than life, and how it can intrude between a couple that needs desperately to work on their relationship. In the hospital after delivering her child, Janice watches a quiz show that offers money to people with the greatest tragedies. Janice enjoys the emotional program, but uses it to insulate herself from the problems in her own family. She shows more attention to quiz shows than to her husband or newborn, perhaps because she is anxious about Rabbit's commitment to her. *The Mickey Mouse Club* encouraged her to remain a child; the quiz show urges her to become a victim.

Ten years later Rabbit is addicted to television, but without Janice's involvement or his own ironic distance. He watches because he has become a watcher and has given up being a man of action. As *RRed* opens, Rabbit and his father, drinking at a bar, stare as though drugged at repeated showings of the *Apollo 11** moon launch. But, the narrator tells us, the lift-off leaves Rabbit and his father earthbound with their problems. While watching the moon landing with his mother and son, Rabbit can hardly see or hear the epochal event because of poor transmission: television is ineffective in bringing history* home. Since the moon is to Rabbit only "a big nothing," television has only aggravated his emptiness. Television does, however, bring Rabbit to consider problems beyond himself, but mainly through entertainment programs, not news reports. Although television brings the Vietnam* War into his living room, it fails to affect Rabbit emotionally. The treatment of the news on television is controlled, the narrator implies, by newscasters who oppose those protesting the war. The comedy program *Laugh-In*, in which black and white men kiss, does more to make Rabbit respond to racial problems than images of civil rights and city unrest on the screen. With his son, Nelson Angstrom,* Rabbit watches *The Carol Burnett Show*, which demythologizes Tonto and the Lone Ranger.* Though the point to the skit is the cuckolding of the Lone Ranger by Tonto, Rabbit does consider the plight of the Indians during America's expansion. He quickly ignores whatever illumination the skit provided when he argues about Vietnam later with Charlie Stavros,* the man who cuckolds Rabbit. The incursion of Charlie-as-Indian into territory of the white-man-as-Rabbit carries Burnett's skit into further comedy and shows that whatever Rabbit learns from television, he cannot use it in his own life. Rabbit realizes vaguely the kind of impact television has in forming Nelson's mind when he rejects his son's generation's interest in demonism by thinking that they "think life's one big TV." In *RIR* Nelson is thrilled by car wrecks on *Charlie's Angels*, and then wrecks three of his father's cars when they quarrel. But in *RaR* Rabbit encounters on television a film,* *The Return of Martin Guerre*, that stimulates him to think that it would be nice if men could change families now and then. He ignores the point to the film: the penalty for being caught in another man's identity is death.*

Like other critics of television, Updike has remarked that the processing of television images skips the creative interaction possible in film watching or reading. In addition, the everyday is given a kind of "shine." Even when it is off, the television is ominous with its "grave, gray-green Cyclops stare" (*Coup*). When it is on, it supplies a routine preceding Rabbit's sex* with Margaret Fosnacht and oversees the strenuous intercourse of Rabbit and Janice (*RRed*). In "A Soft Spring Night in Shillington" (*SC*) Updike expressed his admiration of Peter Sellers's portrayal of Jerzy Kosinski's Chauncy Gardner in the film *Being There*. Gardner learned all he knows from television, and his uncritical assimilation and regurgitation of that material makes him, ironically, pass for a seer among Washington politicians. In describing his own experience with television interviews,* Updike admits that "we love being on TV" (*CJ*). Television also loves making myths of those who appear on it, like Clark DeMott,* whose heroic killing of mad Jesse Smith* is shown repeatedly until Clark becomes tediously mythic (*IB*).

Bibliography: Updike, "Being on TV—I, II" (*OJ*); Ristoff, *UA*; Ristoff, *JU*.

Tertullian (Quintus Septimius Florens Tertullianus) (160?–230). A father of the church, Tertullian of Carthage, home of St. Augustine,* headed a group of Montanists in withdrawing from orthodox church beliefs. He wrote a defense of Christianity, *Apologeticus*, inspired by the persecutions of Emperor Septimius Severus. He also wrote about martyrs and baptism. In *RV* Roger Lambert* reads, in the Latin, Tertullian's *De resurrectione carnis* (written in 208) and finds "sickening" Tertullian's belief that the flesh lives everlastingly, which Updike had insisted upon in his poem, "Seven Stanzas at Easter" (*TP*). Ironically, immediately after his meditations, Lambert has a vision of his wife, Esther Lambert,* involved with the flesh of her lover, Dale Kohler.* Cleverly, he explains to her that in Tertullian's *Ad uxorem* Tertullian told his wife that if he predeceased her, she must remarry a Christian. Then in *De exhortatione castitatis* Tertullian told his wife not to remarry anyone. Lambert seems to be taunting Esther for his perception that she has been unfaithful. *See* **Classical Literature**.

Thomas Aquinas, St. (1225–1274). The major Scholastic philosopher of the Middle Ages, Thomas Aquinas studied at Monte Cassino and under Albertus Magnus became advisor to Pope Alexander IV. He debated the merit of the Islamic philosopher Averroës, whose commentaries on Aristotle held that truth could be discovered through reason, without divine revelation. Thomas's synthesis connected Augustine's* revealed faith with Aristotle's idea of truth arrived at through the senses. He explained in *On the Truth of the Catholic Faith* (1261–64) that though truths like Christ's Incarnation could be understood only by faith, other truths having to do with the material world could be apprehended only through sensory data, but God's existence could be known by both. Updike turned to Thomas during his religious crises (1954–60), and although his character Roger Lambert* is opposed to notions of God as a mere fact among facts, Updike, like Lambert, could not warm to Thomas's conception of a "locked-in" God (*RV*). Thomas is mentioned with Plato* and others as a "theorist of beauty," and since Thomas's aesthetic theories influenced James Joyce's* writings and Updike admired Joyce, Thomas's theories may have influenced Updike in "Commercial" (*P*). Thomas is cited as stating that God made the world "in play" ("Packed Dirt, Churchgoing, a Dying Cat, a Traded Car" [*PigF*]), a comment that is repeated by Jill Pendleton* in *RRed*. See **Barth, Karl; Dante; Kierkegaard, Søren; Ministers**.

Thoreau, Henry David (1817–1862). Radical, humanist and naturalist, Henry David Thoreau of Concord, Massachusetts, was a friend of Ralph Waldo Emerson* and Nathaniel Hawthorne.* He kept voluminous journals of his observations of nature* that were made into books about the Maine woods and Cape Cod, among other places. His *Walden* (1854) is an influence upon Updike, but like other literary influences on him (Vladimir Nabokov,* Marcel Proust* and Henry Green,* e.g.), the influence is diffuse and absorbed into Updike's idiosyncratic interests. Thoreau's heroic and pastoral* genres appear in Updike's work, especially in *C*, and with irony in *TE*, in which Ben Turnbull* is wise enough to laugh at his own return to nature and at his sophistication by recognizing the incongruity of his position in making love to the young "nymph" in the woods while fighting prostate cancer.* Critic Larry Taylor finds in Updike's story "The Hermit" (*MuS*) "absurd echoes of the Thoreauvian experience": Thoreau reads Homer, but Stanley the hermit in his hut reads poor nineteenth-century fiction; Thoreau bathes in the "depthless" pond, but Stanley in a rivulet that barely covers him; Thoreau's experience is affirmative, but Stanley's "leads to madness." For Taylor, the mad self-exiled hermit illustrates what happens to a modern Thoreauvian. One might also detect aspects of Thoreau's "Civil Disobedience" in the jeremiads of Skeeter* (*RRed*).

Bibliography: Taylor, *PA*; Margaret Atwood, "Memento Mori—But First, Carpe Diem," *New York Times Book Review* 12 Oct. 1997: 9–10.

Thorne, Freddy. A Tarbox dentist who oversees the many couples in *Couples* at social gatherings and games,* Freddy Thorne offers a philosophy to explain the situation of suburbia in the 1960s. Freddy sees religion* as having failed to alleviate modern man's fear of the unknown. He argues that the only way to truly stave off death* is through sex.* The couples are therefore seeking each other in order to "humanize" one another. Impotent himself, Thorne nevertheless is stung when his wife Georgene has an affair with the local contractor Piet Hanema.* He exacts revenge when Piet's affair with Foxy Whitman* requires an abortion.* Thorne arranges it, but demands Piet's wife Angela* in return. Although he is an avid reader of Sigmund Freud* and pornography and Angela is the most desirable of the wives, he fails sexually with her. When President John Kennedy* is assassinated, Thorne is tested: will his planned party alleviate the anxiety of his friends, or will it be inappropriate? He goes through with the party, and the couples comply, thus accepting him as the high priest of a new religion. As a dangerous and even malevolent character, Thorne looks back to the social engineer Stephen Conner* (*PF*) and forward to the devilish Darryl Van Horne* (*W*), whose name chimes with his.

Bibliography: Greiner, *JU*.

Thresher. On April 10, 1963, the atomic submarine *Thresher* sank two hundred miles off Boston, killing 129 men. This disaster is mentioned in *Couples* in a conversation centering on death* by crushing and thus contributes to the images of claustrophobia that appear repeatedly in the early novels from *RR* to *Couples*. See **Poe, Edgar Allan.**

Thurber, James (1894–1961). One of America's finest humorists and cartoonists, James Thurber was a staff writer for the *New Yorker** and then managing editor (1927–33). He shared an office with E. B. White, with whom he wrote *Is Sex Necessary?* (1929). (White had a hand in hiring Updike when they met in Oxford* in the fall of 1954.) Updike has said that the first books he read were Thurber's, and at age eleven he was impressed by the combination of drawings and prose, "a beautiful demonstration of artistic making," in *Fables for Our Time, My Life and Hard Times* and *The White Deer*. He found *Men, Women and Dogs* filled with New York* sophistication, amusing adult misery and carefree creativity. It seemed "a super way to live, to be behind such a book." Updike wrote to Thurber expressing his delight, and Thurber sent him a cartoon of a dog as a gift, which Updike has kept on his wall as a talisman for many years. Tragically, blindness made Thurber give up drawing after 1952. Thurber's drawings and stories often depicted the battle of the sexes, and often, as in "The Unicorn in the Garden," took the character of fable, complete with moral. This fable tells of the inability of a man's wife to believe that he has really seen a unicorn. The fantasizing Walter Mitty of "The Secret Life of Walter Mitty" has become a modern image of the repressed man who finds more heroic poses in fantasy than reality offers him.

Thurber's influence on Updike was wide-ranging. He may have led Updike to consider working for the *New Yorker*, to design his own dust jackets and to embellish stories and essays with drawings ("During the Jurassic" [*MW*]); *Jester's Dozen*; "At War with My Skin" and "A Soft Spring Night in Shillington" [*SC*]). Thurber's *Fables for Our Time* (1940) may have also provided a model for Updike's sophisticated "beast fables," such as "Brother Grasshopper" (*A*) and "During the Jurassic" (*MW*), which recalls Thurber's "The Unicorn in the Garden." The beast fables may have sparked Updike's use of Beatrix Potter's* *Tale of Peter Rabbit** in *RA*. Thurber's story "The Secret Life of Walter Mitty" (1942) resembles *RR*, since Harry "Rabbit" Angstrom* dwells on his past sports* heroics while living a second-rate life dominated by women. Thurber's interest in the personal reminiscence essay may have encouraged Updike to write of himself in "The Dogwood Tree"* and to continue this form throughout his life. Thurber's books for children,* such as *The Thirteen Clocks* (1950) and *The Wonderful O* (1957), may suggest some influence upon Updike's retellings of *A Midsummer Night's Dream*, "The Fisherman and His Wife,"* *The Ring* and *The Magic Flute*. Personal details suggest connections between Thurber and Updike. (But honesty compelled Updike to observe in a review of a posthumous book of Thurber's, "Logomachic tricks are asked to pass for wit and implausible pun-swapping for human conversation.") Each was afflicted as a child with a disability prolonged further into life: Thurber lost an eye; Updike had psoriasis. Each had an "eccentric" family. The affliction and the odd family encouraged solitariness, reading and writing. Despite this, in an interview* Updike remarked, "I never became James Thurber, but nobody could." *See* **Art; Cartooning; Drawing and Painting**.

Bibliography: Updike, "Credos and Curios" (*AP*); "An Answer to the Question . . . What Books Have Left the Greatest Impression on Me, and Why?" (*MM*).

Tiberius Claudius Nero (42 B.C.–37 A.D.). Updike quotes Christ's famous injunction "Render therefore unto Caesar those things which are Caesar's and unto God the things that are God's" (Matthew 22:21) to explain why he could not side with those wanting to withdraw from the Vietnam* War (*SC*). Christ explained that in matters of civic responsibility, citizens should respect the law and "render" what Tiberius Caesar commanded. Updike thus could support President* Lyndon Johnson* during the war while remaining a practicing Lutheran. The Roman emperor Tiberius is also mentioned in *Coup* by Enzian, who characterizes Col. Félix Ellelloû* as hiding on Capri while Kush became more pro-Russian, just as Tiberius had while Christ preached subversion. Ironically, modern historians consider Tiberius a supporter of republicanism. *See* **Bible; Classical Literature**.

Tilden, Samuel (1814–1886). American lawyer Samuel Tilden fought Tammany Hall and the Tweed Ring as governor of New York. Tilden became the 1876 Democratic presidential candidate but lost a contested election to Rutherford B. Hayes by one electoral vote. According to John Hook,* Tilden had the goodness of America in mind, and but for his forbearance another Civil War might have been fought. Hook, however, tended to demonize Republicans (*PF*), as did George Caldwell* (*C*). According to Caldwell, the town of Olinger was once called "Tilden" after "the man cheated out of the election." Since Tilden Creek still flows through Olinger, the memory of betrayal remains. *See* **Presidents**.

Tillich, Paul (1886–1965). A Lutheran philosopher, minister* and theologian, Paul Tillich emigrated from Germany to escape Hitler, whom he had openly opposed, and eventually became professor of theology at Harvard* University in 1954. In *Systematic Theology* (1951–63) Tillich explained that scientific thinking, as well as depth psychology and existentialist ideas, could be incorporated into Protestant religion. His "Protestant Principle" stated that every Yes has a corresponding No, that no human truth is ultimate. For him, the ultimate concern was "the God above God," and the quest for being rather than salvation is the goal. He has been called a "dialectical humanist." Tillich's ideas can be traced in many Updike works. Thus Harry "Rabbit" Angstrom's* sense of the "right way and good way," his personal needs and society's demands, brings him to an impasse at the end of *RR*, and this "yes, but"* theme echoes throughout Updike's work. The conflict between Rev. Jack Eccles* and Rev. Fritz Kruppenbach* (*RR*) resembles the opposition of Karl Barth* and Tillich, since Updike remarks that he thought that Tillich was a "traitor" to Christianity for "trying to humanize something that is essentially nonhuman" (*Time* 26 April, 1968: 54). Kruppenbach's Barthian insistence is a rebuke to Eccles and Tillich: "there is nothing but Christ" for ministers, and all else "is Devil's work." One might add to this criticism of Eccles-as-Tillich that Eccles feels especially drawn to Rabbit, who senses that no human truth is ultimate and feels that a "thing" exists beyond the church-approved God. Tillich, like Rabbit, could not accept, as Updike says, "the split between a faith unacceptable to culture and a culture unacceptable to faith."

Updike uses an epigraph* for *MS* taken from Tillich: "The principle of soul, universally and individually, is the principle of ambiguity." Updike selected it because his father-in-law was a "Tillich fan," but it helps to explain the contradictoriness of Rev. Tom Marshfield.* He loses his faith through sexual misconduct, then regains it through meditative journal writing, only to commit sexual misconduct with the manager of his motel. Marshfield's soul is ambiguous, as are many Updike characters* who are, as he says in a story, "perceptive men caged in their own weak character" ("Sunday Teasing" [*SD*]). Updike describes such ambiguity of motive in the stories about separation and divorce* of *TF*. Also, Dale Kohler's* belief that scientific discoveries can be blended with modern faith is criticized in *RV* by the Barthian Roger Lambert* as the ultimate in the humanization of God, and Kohler's failure to provide proof of God's existence denounces the usefulness of scientific knowledge in seeking God. Updike scores Tillich in one review for "trying to revivify the Christian corpse with transfusions of Greek humanism, German metaphysics and psychoanalytical theory." In another review he calls Tillich "puzzling" and "theologically dubious," yet Updike detects that Tillich's tolerance for uncertainty was "specifically Lutheran." *See* **Religion**.

Bibliography: Updike, "Tillich" (*AP*); "Religious Notes" (*PP*); "To the Tram Halt Together" (*HS*); View from the Catacombs," *Time* 91 (26 April 1968): 66–68, 73–75; Darryl Jodock, "Once a Lutheran Always a Lutheran? The Influence of Updike's Lutheran Roots," in Yerkes, *JU*.

"Tinkletum, Tankletum." "Tinkletum, Tankletum" is a bawdy Scots Jacobean song sung by Jane Smart* (*W*) and associated with witches, according to Margaret Murray's book *The Witch-Cult in Western Europe*.

Tippu Tib (c. 1830–1905). The Afro-Arab trader who was called Muhammad bin Hamid or Tippu Tib ruled an African empire (1860s–1890). Since he is constructing a Marxist state, Col. Félix Ellelloû* would have contempt for this man he called the last of the slave-traders (*Coup*). Tippu Tib initially resisted European influence, but later governed part of Belgian king Leopold II's Congo colony (1887–90). Though Ellelloû resists such a conflicted position, his underlings cannot.

Titans. In Greek myth the Titans were twelve children of Uranus and Gaea, Heaven and Earth. Though they were for a time the universe's supreme rulers, only Prometheus and Oceanus sided with Zeus against his father, the Titan Cronus. Titans are mentioned in "Playing with Dynamite" (*A*), and Prometheus and Zeus have human analogues in *C*. Peter Caldwell,* in his aspiration as an artist, represents Prometheus to his father's Chiron.* During a fever Peter suffers like Prometheus chained to a rock, his chest psoriasis a parallel to the eagle that pecked at Prometheus's liver. *See* **Classical Literature**.

Titles of Updike's Works. Concerned about every aspect of his books, Updike has (perhaps in conjunction with his editors) produced a great many arresting titles, attesting to his training at the *New Yorker** and his early career as a light-verse* poet. (To make my comments on Updike's titles clearer, I have dispensed with the customary abbreviations.) Sometimes he uses alliteration: *Rabbit, Run, Rabbit Redux, Rabbit Is Rich, Rabbit at Rest, Bech:*

A Book, Bech at Bay, Bech is Back, Toward the End of Time, Picked-up Pieces, Marry Me, "Paranoid Packaging" (*MM*), "Sirin's Sixty-Five Shimmering Short Stories" (*MM*), "Tummy Trouble in Tinseltown" (*MM*), "Pinter's Unproduced Proust Printed." Occasionally Updike employs rhyme: "Typical Optical" (*FM*), "Bech in Czech" (*BaB*), "Gender Benders" (*MM*). He sometimes uses allusion: *The Same Door* alludes to *The Rubaiyat* of Omar Khayyám. Updike often employs quotation: "More Stately Mansions" (*TM*) is a line from "The Chambered Nautilus" of Oliver Wendell Holmes*; *In the Beauty of the Lilies* is taken from "The Battle Hymn of the Republic," by Julia Ward Howe; "I Will Not Let Thee Go, Except Thou Bless Me" (*MW*) comes from Shakespeare's *Othello*; and *More Matter*, from the Bard's *Hamlet*. Updike also employs innuendo ("Cheever on the Rocks" [*MM*]) and pun (*Bech at Bay, Bech: A Book, Tossing and Turning, Trust Me, Self-Consciousness, Odd Jobs,* "Ace in the Hole" [*SD*], "What MOMA Done Tole Me" [*JL*], "Beattleniks" [*OJ*], "M.M. in Brief" [*MM*], and David Cox suggests in his *"An Examination of Thematic And Structural Connections between John Updike's Rabbit Novels"* that *Redux* may pun on *rédacteur,* "the one who makes." The titles may use domestic objects (*The Carpentered Hen*) or popular expression (*A Month of Sundays, Hugging the Shore, Odd Jobs*). Some titles are deliberately misleading (*Memories of the Ford Administration*), and others seem to refer to other books (*Rabbit Redux* to John Dryden's *Astraea Redux* and Anthony Trollope's *Phineas Redux, Roger's Version* to Roger Chillingworth of Nathaniel Hawthorne's* *Scarlet Letter* and *S.* to Thomas Pynchon's *V*). Titles of stories or poems may be in French, Italian, German or Latin. At times the titles yoke dissimilars ("Tao in the Yankee Stadium Bleachers" [*CH*], "At War with my Skin" [*SC*], "The Dance of the Solids" [*M*], "Duet with Muffled Brake Drums" [*CH*]) or produce shock ("Cunts" [*TT*] "Fellatio" [*M*], "The Man Who Became a Soprano [*A*]). Many of the titles of the reviews are clever ("How *How It Is* Was" [*AP*], "Witty Dotty" [*OJ*]). Rarely is the syntax problematic, but with *Of the Farm* Updike clarifies that the title really meant not "about the farm" but myths *of* the farm.

The titles of *Rabbit Angstrom* contain levels of meaning. *Rabbit, Run* concerns Harry "Rabbit" Angstrom's* habit of running when he played basketball,* or when he feels trapped, but Updike has asserted that the title is also a command to run. *Rabbit Redux* not only reintroduces the character of Rabbit to the reader, but also draws the reader back to Rabbit after a decade's hiatus and signals his return to health, as Updike's jacket note explains. *Rabbit Is Rich* points to Rabbit's success in business as well as his discovery that his real treasure is his wife and granddaughter. *Rabbit at Rest* suggests not only that Rabbit has retired to Florida* but also that his "rest" there has been interrupted, and he has been called from retirement to face the greatest dangers of his life. Rabbit never "rests in peace" until he dies. The titles of the saga are thus, as critic George Hunt notes, "controlling metaphors"

(Hunt, *JU*) and other titles contain the same metaphorical guidance (*The Centaur, Roger's Version, Facing Nature, The Coup* and *The Poorhouse Fair*).

Story and poem collections comment on their contents. *The Carpentered Hen* suggests that the poems are like the darning egg, crafted and useful for specific purposes. *Pigeon Feathers* points to the central story of David Kern's* crisis in "Pigeon Feathers," but it suggests that the stories themselves may each be like pigeon feathers. *Telephone Poles* implies that the poems are constructed imitations of nature* in the way that telephone poles imitate trees, and poems and poles assist communication while standing among us, ignored giants. *Tossing and Turning* suggests fitfulness in the author and his times and mimics the reader's turning pages, tossing the book aside. *Facing Nature* illustrates ways to face "nature," both directly and figuratively. Only the titles of *Olinger Stories* and *Too Far to Go* do not refer to a story in the collection. *Olinger Stories* was a compilation of previously published stories, except for "In Football Season." *Too Far to Go* contains seven stories not previously published. The British edition, *Your Lover Just Called*, is, however, titled after the story of the same name in the collection.

Too Far to Go: The Maples Stories (Greenwich, CT: Fawcett, 1979). *Too Far to Go: The Maples Stories* is a gathering of stories concerning Joan Maple* and her husband Richard Maple* that were written during 1956–76, all but seven having been collected in *SD, PigF, MuS, MW* and *P*; "Divorcing: A Fragment" had not been previously published. *TF*, which Updike has called a "quasi-novel," was intended to be a book tie-in when Robert Geller's drama *Too Far to Go*, based on some of these stories, was televised in 1979. The stories represent the most candid demonstration of how Updike turned autobiographical material into art. The galleys, as critic James Schiff notes, show that he even consulted his wife about Joan Maple's language (*TF*), and *Olinger Stories* are the only short-fiction* collections not named after a story in the collection.

TF covers twenty years in the Maples' marriage, from early difficulties to divorce.* The first four stories reveal the tensions between the Maples that lead to their estrangement, while the last four record their path to divorce. Various motifs (illness, the seasons, games,* Hansel and Gretel) link the stories, and the narrative voice* speaking through the images projects a tone sometimes sympathetic to Richard, sometimes to Joan. The first story, "Snowing in Greenwich Village," shows that early in their marriage the Maples had problems. When Richard escorts Joan's old friend Rebecca Cune to her apartment, at Joan's insistence, he feels attracted to Rebecca, though he stifles his impulse. Is Richard restless enough to leave Joan? Did Joan test Richard's fidelity by placing Rebecca in his path? If so, was Joan looking for renewal of his commitment or an escape from the marriage? Such questions control our response to the other stories as the reader explores the ambiguous motives and actions of Joan and Richard. The image of the snow suggests an exciting change in the weather, but the snow forms an ironic purity coating the cityscape. In "Twin Beds in Rome" the controlling image is the Coliseum, which resembles a rotting wedding cake; thus decaying grandeur and martyrdom symbolize their marriage. Most adventurously, Updike uses images from physics. In "Here Come the Maples" Richard reads a physics pamphlet about the four forces governing nature. Each force figuratively resembles Richard, Joan, his family and his lover. Gravity, the most mysterious force, is exerted by Richard's lover; against this force his own "weak force" must contend. Images in other stories such as blood ("Giving Blood") and a civil rights march ("Marching through Boston," which made the *New Yorker** editors anxious) suggest the depth of the Maples' pain. Such imagery* of natural forces, ancient ruins, biology and social protest places the dissolution of the marriage in larger cultural contexts. "Separating" uses, as a controlling image, Richard's refurbishing of the home he is about to leave in emotional disrepair. This is also the powerful controlling image governing the collection.

Updike probes the Maples' affection, understanding and empathy (they even kiss on being divorced), which makes the end of their marriage all the more painful and mysterious to them and the reader. It seems fitting that the Maples receive one of Massachusetts's first "no-fault" divorces. Interestingly, as a series of connected stories *TF* resembles Updike's *Scarlet Letter* trilogy (*MS*, *RV*, and *S.*), three novels illustrating the perspectives of modern characters* resembling those of Hawthorne. But in *TF* Updike draws attention to the reactive character of both narratives. In *The Scarlet Letter* all information about the affair of Hester Prynne and Arthur Dimmesdale has been withheld; in *TF* we know nothing of Richard's involvement with his lover. In each case the writers are concerned with the way in which the characters respond to their condition, rather than to the events that put it in motion. *TF* also resembles what Updike called a "quasi-novel," a term used by Vladimir Nabokov* for his *Pnin*.

TF gathers together many award*-winning stories: "Wife-Wooing" (*O. Henry Prize Stories of 1961*); "Nakedness" (*O. Henry Prize Stories 1976*); "Marching through Boston" (O. Henry Prize, 1967); "Your Lover Just Called" (O. Henry Prize, 1968); "Nakedness" (O. Henry Prize, 1975); "Separating" (O. Henry Prize, 1976); and "Gesturing" (Best Short Stories, 1980), which Updike also included in *The Best American Short Stories of the Century*.

Bibliography: Updike, "Note on 'Separating' " (*MM*); Paul Theroux, "A Marriage of Mixed Blessings," *New York Times Book Review* 8 Apr. 1979: 7, 34; Erica Jong, "*Too Far to Go*," *New Republic* 181 (15 Sept. 1979): 36–37; Greiner, *OJ*; Detweiler, *JU*; Luscher, *JU*.

Tossing and Turning (New York: Knopf, 1977). *TT*, Updike's fourth collection of poetry,* contains a picture of a head by Constantin Brancusi on the jacket that meant, Updike has said, to recall the same shape as the carpentered hen, the title of his first volume of poems. But since the sculpture is called *Sleeping Muse*, Updike may have thought it apt for poems about the difficulty of sleeping, about the effort to awaken the muse to relieve anxiety. The jacket blurb, perhaps written by Updike, says this is the poetry of a man past midpoint alert to "the double entendres of imagination." According to the book's title, such "doubleness" produces unease, and two serious sections (tossing?) bookend a section of humorous poems (turning?), continuing Updike's plan ever since *M* to showcase more serious poems. The epigraph* from James Joyce's* *Ulysses* contains an allusion to his second wife, Martha Ruggles Bernhard Updike,* whom he had recently married, but the poems predate that marriage and depict Updike in transition and often, for the first time in his life, alone.

In section I various poems inquire about forces tossing him through life. Chief among these is nature,* weaving in and out of this volume and the dominant concern of his next volume of poems, *FN*. The first poem, "You Who Swim" (1960), describes the precariousness of love, for at night her "dim" lips hold the "bubble" love. "Dream and Reality" finds the speaker in his dream* wondering, "There must be more than this," only to discover on waking that "reality" is what owls cough up. "The Solitary Pond" recollects a time when the speaker was thirteen and found ice skating on a country pond more treacherous than skating in the city. Again, reality befuddles the dream. Certainly the confusion in his home in "Leaving Church Early" (which seems to describe Updike's personal experience in Plowville*) provides only a vision of restless adulthood to the bookish speaker. In a note to this poem in *CP*, Updike explains that the poem has an "adolescent harshness" when the boy wonders "how to get out of here," both away from his family and away from the farm he detests. The retrospective *Envoi* to this poem tells his mother that there is never enough time for all the forgiving needed.

The restless question asked in "Query" is, why does nature persist? This poem, like "Late January" and "Touch of Spring," describes more alienation from nature: trees and cats are more comfortable with changing seasons than the speaker. "Melting," recalling Wallace Stevens,* alarms with an allusion in the last line to Proserpine freed from Hades as spring begins. "Bath after Sailing" records a brush with "death's* face" on the sea; in his bath he celebrates his penis, "emissary to darkness," in creating a future generation. Updike's note in *CP* relates a more graphic description of how he and his captain, Professor Manfred Karnovsky, "fought for our lives" in the tossing seas. "Wind" is an analogy of God's voice, which says, "Let go." The implied condition is one of stasis. Even in the tropics the situation is dire, as "Poisoned in Nassau" shows with its sea that seems evil. "Raining in Magens Bay" reminds man that he is a mixture of sun, salt, sea and shadow. "Sleepless in Scarsdale" recounts insomnia at a friend's home on the way to speak at a college. He fears that his "prosperity" and "success" have stolen his sleep. "Sunday in Boston" shows that cities offer no cure for the restless: Boston, with its winos and tarnished statues and jogging girls pale in July, is a "city of students and drunks." It is, perhaps, Updike's reply to Stevens's "Sunday Morning."

"Apologies to Harvard" was written "under the clear influence of L.E. Sissman," as Updike says in a note in *CP*, reflecting Sissman's "festive" air in his 1971 Phi Beta Kappa poem. Updike celebrates the "home of the hermit scholar" that took him in raw, then "spit him out a gentleman." He mentions his isolation from African Americans* as he adopted the Harvard* tone, "absurdly cheerful." He digresses to describe his meeting with his future wife, Mary Pennington Updike.* Though he reflects on courses and his homesickness his first year at Harvard, the poem mainly describes his meetings with his wife-to-be at Radcliffe. He asks Harvard's forgiveness for not being able to meet the standards carved by William James. The poem thus takes several turns and shows that even Harvard was unable to assuage his restlessness. But "Commencement, Pingree School" allows the speaker some relief as he watches his daughter graduate. "South of the Alps" parallels the speed of a hurtling car through Italy to the speaker's sense of the mutability of the driver's beauty and his own claims as a "word-hoarder" wishing to "smudge more proofs." Though the driver is "clean copy," she asks him, "Why doesn't anything last?" He is not alone in his anxiety, but no answer is offered to her question, unless "Calder's Hands" offers a reply. The sculptor Alexander Calder* tosses wire and metal in his "unresting" hands to make art.* The poem suggests an antidote to "tossing and turning," but the speaker leaves it tantalizingly untaken.

Section II, "Light Verse," seems to try to ignore the problems of alienation and depression of the first section by comic deflection. "The Cars in Caracas" offers a tour de force in onomatopoeia in which sounds of traffic are replicated through the sounds of words; then Updike turns this poem into Spanish onomatopoeia. He provides a sudden sharp epiphany in "Upon Shaving Off One's Beard," the only real transformation poem in the collection, but an alternative to the problems of section I. The poem contains the "soul of wit," brevity, four deft lines. The old restlessness returns in "Insomnia the Gem of the Ocean," as he ebbs and flows with his waterbed. Here, as in many of his light-verse* poems, notes from newspapers cue Updike's poems, and in a parody of "You Are Old, Father William" of Lewis Carroll, he creates a parody of a parody, but the poem has its cutting edge with the emphasis on aging. Updike plays with the residences of authors, such as Wallace Stevens's; imagines the response of Venus on being hit by radar (the goddess, not the planet) in "Milady Reflects"; and supplies "Seven New Ways of Looking at the Moon," recalling Wallace Stevens's "Thirteen Ways of Looking at a Blackbird" as well as Updike's golf* essay, "Thirteen Ways of Looking at the Masters" (*HS*). The poem suggests that a near anagram of "Second Coming" is "Moon Seducing," a provocative idea as we enter the age of space flight. Tossing and turning again arise in "Skyey Developments," as recent discoveries in astronomy "discomfort our philosophy."

Section III returns to serious poetry, developing the theme of "tossing" in section I, but seeking a way to turn from "discomfort." In "A Bicycle Chain" the speaker takes heart from "linked lines" observable in protein atoms and bicycle chains: nothing is without connection. But "The Melancholy of Storm Windows" develops a metaphysical conceit in which each window asks, "Am I clean?" Though they "resemble" us, we cannot say, "At last," once put in our place. In "Rats" the speaker finds that rats run parallel to "chambers" he inhabits in his home. Ironically, at least the rats show that he is not alone. A "Sand Dollar" cast on the sand suggests to the speaker a metaphorical clue to nature, but nature is enigmatic, casting clues from the sea, as dreams tease with leads. "Tossing and Turning," which gives this volume its name, advises the insomniac, "Unclench your philosophy" mainly by sleeping, where "another world" awaits. Like T. S. Eliot's* "Ash-Wednesday," "turning" becomes a positive thing.

"Living with a Wife: At the Piano, in the Tub, under the Sunlamp, during Menstruation, All the While" in its several sections finds in the speaker's wife images that aid that "turning." The images recall Stevens's "Peter Quince at the Clavier." In the tub she is a "pond" mirroring pink clouds; "During Menstruation" boldly describes the subject from a woman's point of view in which "eggs are hurled unripe from the furnace." In "All the While" the wife "walks through" his veins and remains a mystery. A wife diminishes the anxiety, but the speaker's "Who sent you?" remains unanswered. "Marching through a Novel" returns to the discipline of art to reduce angst.* The "speaker" is writing *RRed*. He returns to the first-person woman's voice to describe her "jewel" and "riddle" in "Cunts," Updike's boldest venture since "Midpoint" into the female anatomy. She commands, "Adore!" because it is the "tunnel of the world." Interspersed with such fervent metaphors are pornographic snippets from mail the author had received. Thus the poem provides a variety of tones in showing the ambiguity of the central mystery of life. It is also Updike's approximation to Walt Whitman* and to Allen Ginsberg. The poem comes closest in Updike's poetry to celebratory eroticism.* Less successful in this vein is "Pussy," since the tone is ironic, particularly when Updike uses the term Karl Barth* applies to the unknowable God, *totaliter aliter*.

"Phenomena" continues the theme of anxiety, perhaps made acute by the distance from sex* relief: "lying down, I cannot breathe." "Boil," closer to light verse, supplies a connection between reason and boils that makes a grotesque conceit: each "holds the terror in." "Mime" offers another look at arts as palliative: "Praise be mimesis." "Dutch Cleanser," like "Note to the Previous Tenants," celebrates the pleasure of being ready to take care of the dirt ahead, as the Dutch Cleanser girl "upholding the stick" is ready to do. "Heading for Nandi" ends without relief as the speaker, surrounded by honeymoon couples on a South Seas island, pleads, "I wish I had a woman."

Updike told interviewer Helen Vendler that poetry is a set of slides, whereas prose makes tableaux move "cinematically." He admitted that it was "always at the back of my mind to be a poet." Vendler called this slide collection "one of the year's major entries" ("John Updike on Poetry") and identified Updike as "a gifted poet" who with greater concentration could become "one of the foremost living practitioners of the art." Donald Greiner concurs, finding this volume of loneliness and loss a dramatic advance over Updike's previous poetry, and one that should relieve Updike of being known solely as a poet of light verse.

Bibliography: Helen Vendler, "John Updike on Poetry" (*HS*); Matthew Hodgart, "Family Snapshots," *Times Literary Supplement* 13 Oct. 1978: 1158; Greiner, *OJ*.

Tothero, Marty. Harry "Rabbit" Angstrom's* coach for the Mt. Judge* High School basketball* team, Marty Tothero befriends Rabbit when Rabbit returns after fleeing from his wife Janice Angstrom* and introduces him to Ruth Leonard Byer* when they double-date (*RR*). At dinner he and Rabbit relive old basketball games, Tothero reminding everyone that whoever succeeds in sports* cannot fail "in the greater game of life" because he has known the "sacredness of achievement." Tothero is the best evidence that this idea is questionable, since he is unfaithful and masochistic. Although Tothero had promised to discuss Rabbit's problem more fully, he only offers his judgment two months later when Rabbit accidentally meets him in the hospital where Tothero is being treated for a stroke. Tothero then tells Rabbit that goodness comes from concrete acts, not from the sky. The coach suggests a "do as I say, not as I do" rule that has little effect on Rabbit. Rabbit himself will ask the same of his son Nelson Angstrom* in *RIR* when he encourages him not to marry the woman he made pregnant. Tothero may be perceptive, but his weak character stymies him. Perhaps this is why his name, when written as a circle (like a basketball net), can spell either "Tot-hero" or "to-the-rot." The name Tothero appears on many cemetery plots in Plowville* Cemetery, where Updike's parents and maternal grandparents are buried. *See* **Names**.

Bibliography: Markle, *FL*; Detweiler, *JU*; Greiner, *JU*.

Tothero, Mrs. Marty. The suffering wife of basketball coach Marty Tothero* who endures his philandering and ministers to him when he has a stroke, Mrs. Marty Tothero may represent a person who knows the "sacredness of achievement" "even in defeat"—the ultimate goal for an athlete, as Tothero lectured his players (*RR*). She leads Rabbit to her husband, knowing that he would want to see his ex-star.

Toward the End of Time (New York: Knopf, 1997). Updike's novel *TE* blends, like *PF*, science fiction* and realism. As *IB* looked back upon America, 1909–90, *TE* jumps forward to the year A.D. 2020 and finds that America is not flourishing. In 2010 an atomic war destroyed China and the Midwest, the governmental infrastructure is reeling, and in this strange world new forms of life have emerged, "metallobioforms," which live on electricity and oil spots. A space station hovers in the sky containing dead and dying astronauts who cannot be returned to earth. A "torus" spaceship covers virtually the entire sky when it visits earth every thousand or million years (no one is certain). Since the narrator Ben Turnbull* is married to a shrew and has contracted prostate cancer,* his tone is understandably elegiac and sardonic. Yet his meditations on quantum theory, time and existence are unflinching, and his actions are calculated to stave off death* through games of golf,* eroticism* and advice on how to commit crime.

Surprisingly, much of eastern seaboard business goes on as usual (financial markets are intact, and Vivaldi is played on the radio), and so does nature,* as Turnbull provides minute and tender Thoreauvian* descriptions of nature throughout the cycle of the year, from January to late December. In addition, either through fantasy, free association from his *National Geographic* reading or quantum "branching," Turnbull slips into roles that, among others, feature him as a Neanderthal and a man awaiting the end of the world. Updike has thus used what he has referred to as the very "pliable" form of the novel* to tell the story of a reflective retired financial executive facing the end of his time on earth.

The narrative encompasses a full year, marked by pastoral* descriptions of great precision that firmly situate Turnbull in his natural environment but form a poignant contrast between his dying and the irrepressible vitality of nature. (Updike's mother, Linda Hoyer Updike,* had a passion for nature [*SC*], something reflected in her fictional guise Mrs. Mary Robinson's* love of her farm [*OF*]. Turnbull names the plants, flowers and ferns as they appear with the precision of Linda Updike.) At the same time, such pastoralism suggests the resilience of nature in the face of war: man may die; nature will not. But in the antipastoral theme, innocent "shepherds" squatting on Turnbull's property are extortionists; the young "swains" squatting on his land are cold-blooded murderers; and the beguiling milkmaid is a jaded thirteen-year-old groupie.

Apart from these squatters, Turnbull's life is uneventful. As the narrative begins, Turnbull, dominated by his wife Gloria Turnbull,* helps drive away a deer that is threatening the garden of their hillside home, then keeps a prostitute in the house while Gloria is at a conference (or perhaps she has been murdered by him, depending on which "branch" the reader chooses), visits his children and grandchildren, conspires with intruders, undergoes treatment for cancer and writes this book. His descriptions of the war are oblique and uninvolved—Turnbull alludes to the problem of "underpopulation." Since law enforcement has failed, "insurance" is provided by criminals, Phil and Slim, selling "protection," and later by the teenagers who eliminate their competition. FedEx has become the custodian of national protection, since its infrastructure has remained unimpaired. Meanwhile, Turnbull offers the teens advice on how to get his neighbors to pay protection by burning their barn, and as a result he gains sexual favors from thirteen-year-old Doreen. Adrift from Gloria, nostalgic about his first wife Perdita, irritated by his mistress-prostitute and suffering the indignities of prostate cancer, Turnbull finds in Doreen a momentary rejuvenation while he awaits death.

The novel takes up one of Updike's chief themes from *RA*, entropy, the winding down of everything. Turnbull witnesses the collapse of aspects of federal and local order, his home and his body. His prostate cancer reduces his lust to suckling. Cancer is sometimes described as an "irrational" action of cells, and Turnbull's metaphor for the disorder within him and around him is nature's incomprehensibility, which he describes through quantum physics,* a science that explores the counterintuitive behavior of subatomic particles. Turnbull theorizes that he might "branch" like a particle into another time and another life, as particles move enigmatically from position to position. Gloria appears to branch from a doe to the prostitute Deirdre. He does not know if Gloria is on a trip or if he has murdered her. As he himself branches, without warning each "new Turnbull" becomes an alter ego.* In other branches, at first presented carefully with transitions from his "real" life, he re-creates the world of Neanderthals, noting both their discovery of a hope for an afterlife and their probable cannibalism; then he becomes a grave robber trapped in a pyramid, then St. Paul's friend St. Mark, than a monk about to be murdered by a Viking, then a Nazi guard. The roles are arbitrary, but they replicate the history* of human life and embody both the spiritual and the brutal.

Such branching demonstrates "quantum leaps" in human history, as well as elements of magic realism.* In Turnbull's world of postatomic war, subatomic particles form the ruling trope, not gods, as in *C*, yet they supply the same sense of mystery at the heart of things. Such mystery cannot be apprehended for long in a materialist society without being reduced to scientific explanation, and Turnbull apparently sees his roles as paranoid episodes, explainable by his sense of failure and his fear of irrational attachments to creeds, religious or political. Since he rationally reflects upon these alter egos casually in his daily narrative as easily as he compares his own aching prostate to the bloody tail of a snake he has accidentally maimed, he is conscious of trying out other personas. (Turnbull's involuntary "branching" may be an updating and a warning of Harry "Rabbit" Angstrom's* wish, on seeing the film *The Return of Martin Guerre*, to change identities every decade or so [*RaR*]).

Sophisticated and aloof, Turnbull sardonically witnesses the triumph of materialism in America, the emasculation of men, the pandering to youth and the unheeded dangers of technology. He notes that his children had raised themselves with the help of television* and corporations trying to sell them something. He calmly admires the feral teens with whom he strikes a deal; he even calls them "entrepreneurs." They are tolerated as the dangerous new metallobioforms are endured even after they dispatch some of the young hoodlums. But Turnbull tries to maintain some connection to the lost cultural authorities in his self-conscious identifications of composer Dietrich Buxtehude and painter Mark Rothko. Also, Turnbull returns to his office to reconnect with the financial world where money is authority, and he plays golf to reestablish camaraderie within the authority of the game's rules. Yet Turnbull also knows that money, whether dollars or the new "wellers," has mere arbitrary value. In such a world it is little wonder that Turnbull finds quantum physics fascinating, since the weird behavior of subatomic nature fits the psychosocial world he inhabits.

As he had in *PF*, Updike challenges the reader to confront the near future of America: traditional values have a wispy strength, religion* has failed, and technological achievements like prostate laser surgery extend life, but the reasons for living and procreating are obscure. As usual with Updike, no one can move into the future without looking backward. Turnbull thinks, like Rabbit, how his identity was created by popular culture.* He loves to recall the popular music* that accompanied his courtship of Gloria and his sense of purpose. Despite his ten grandchildren, though, he finds himself growing increasingly outside the realm of his children, who tolerate homosexuality* (despite "underpopulation") more easily than Turnbull does a gay colleague. As new standards develop that Turnbull cannot accept, though he can playfully manipulate them, he finds solace only in the seasons, a young woman's body or the eccentricities of quantum mechanics. He is as nonjudgmental about the atomic war as he is about postwar morality; he allows us to see what morality has become through the clear glass of his meditations, which crystalize in aphorisms or expand into his alter egos.

TE reflects upon Updike's previous books. It recalls *PF* by its treatment of aging and the traditional community in a world hostile to both. Modern communities appear, usually negatively, in *Couples*, *RRed*, *MS*, *S.*, *RV*, *RaR*, *IB* and *W*. Like *RV*, *TE* takes us into the inner thoughts of a man at odds with his age, determined to hold to his own values, speculating with mordant wit or brilliant metaphor about the world around him, trenchant in his observations and troubled by women, like so many Updike heroes. Deirdre deserts Turnbull, as Janice Angstrom* left Rabbit in *RRed*. Deirdre's previous relation to one of the gangsters recalls Ruth Leonard Byer's fling with Ronnie Harrison,* and Deirdre's leaving him a note in which she says that his second wife Gloria controls him brings to mind Janice's note on leaving Rabbit in *RRed* and later telling him that he is controlled by his mother. Echoing Joey Robinson* (*OF*), Turnbull wonders if he had left his first wife because she gave him the freedom to ruin their marriage, or if he hates his second wife because she provides the sheltering he previously resented. Like Rev. Tom Marshfield* (MS), Turnbull is driven to record his thoughts for self-purgation as well as from love of the written word. Writing provides linear logic that counters the chaotic world of war and quarks. Like Rabbit, Turnbull feels erotically drawn toward a member of his family, and like Rabbit, he knows that he needs to confront his personal urges toward the divine and the infernal. His space is as restricted as Marshfield's (MS), and his temporal life is stretched over twelve months, like Clarence Wilmot's,* whose religious crisis caused him to seek alter egos in the movies (IB). Turnbull is, like George Caldwell* (C), a dying centaur, with his head in the sky seeking comets, his feet in the swamp of fecund nature. He imagines himself a million years hence alone with the only other life form, fungus. Turnbull contemplates the Hubble telescope's revelations with the same hope for answers that Clyde Gabriel had sought through his telescope (W) or Piet Hanema* had sought when he searched for the constellation Orion (Couples). Gabriel and Caldwell felt that science* was winning; Turnbull, like Caldwell, fears that science has won, and what it knows of the expanding-contracting universe brings small consolation for a world in which God is absent, faith contracting. Updike's observation of Herman Melville's* Ishmael could be applied to Ben Turnbull: " 'the intense concentration of self in the middle of such a heartless immensity' . . . [encourages'] speculations of a perilous profundity." Updike had speculated upon the "last man" in "Fanning Island" ("The Blessed Man of Boston, My Grandmother's Thimble, and Fanning Island" [PigF]), as well as in the science-fiction* story in OF about the last man on earth who struggles to reach the sea so that his cells may continue to live and thus give rise to life on the earth of the future, that is, the present. See **Magic Realism; Novel; Symbolism**.

Bibliography: Updike, "Introduction" to The Complete Shorter Fiction of Herman Melville; Taylor, PA; Robert Nadeau, "John Updike," in Readings from the New Book on Nature: Physics and Metaphysics in the Modern Novel (Amherst: University of Massachusetts Press, 1981), 95–120; Jim Yerkes, "Updike Offers Rich Reflections in 'End of Time,' " Allentown (Pennsylvania) Morning Call 13 Sept. 1997: A45, A52; James Schiff, "Updike's Meditation on Aging, Time and the Universe," Raleigh (North Carolina) News and Observer 7 Oct. 1997: D4; David Malone, "Updike 2020: Fantasy, Mythology and Faith in Toward The End of Time," in Yerkes, JU.

Transcendentalism. The transcendentalist movement generally accepted, in philosophy and literature, a belief in a reality beyond the senses and reason. The greatest transcendental philosopher is Immanuel Kant, who used the term to refer to pure mind and its a priori forms. Kant's descendants Johann Fichte, Friedrich Schelling, and Edmund Husserl made transcendentalism synonymous with metaphysical idealism. In America transcendentalism developed as a reaction against Puritan predestination and dogmatism, and the movement is said to begin with Ralph Waldo Emerson's* essay "Nature" (1836), which discloses the spiritual quality of physical reality. Henry David Thoreau* contributed to this idea in *Walden* (1854), and Walt Whitman's* *Leaves of Grass* (1855) provided a link between America as a "poem" with a plan for future spiritual evolution and America as a democratic country. American transcendentalism thus focused on individualism, self-examination, nature* and "organic" unity, connecting God, nature and creativity. Such ideas were publicized when the Transcendental Club, formed by Emerson and Thoreau in 1836, published the *Dial*, edited by feminist Margaret Fuller. The club also experimented in communal living at Brook Farm,* Massachusetts, which Nathaniel Hawthorne* satirized in *The Blithedale Romance* and Updike in *S*. Updike examines the movement in "Emersonianism"* and "Whitman's Egotheism."* *See* **Unitarianism**.

Bibliography: Updike, "Whitman's Egotheism" (*HS*); "Emersonianism" (*OJ*); "Elusive Evil" (*MM*).

Translations. Updike has translated foreign works, has been translated into a great many languages and has responded to works in translation that he has reviewed. Updike is particularly well grounded in French and has translated poems from Latin, Spanish and Russian, working from English adaptations in the latter two cases. His Latin translation has been declared quite competent. His Spanish translation of a poem was intended to approximate the jaunty sound effects of his own poem "The Cars in Caracas." He has also translated works by Jorge Luis Borges,* working from an adaptation in English. He translated the poems of Yevgeny Yevtushenko included in the Russian poet's *Stolen Apples*, also working from adaptations.

Since 1961, when *RR* was translated into Italian, Updike has been translated into at least twenty-one languages, including Spanish, Hebrew, Chinese and Hungarian. Thus Updike has a vast readership around the world. In some cases Updike's presence in translation has led to interviews* (in French and German) and original foreign publications (in Japanese). He has noted puns in the titles* (*RaR* became *Rabbit Rust* in Dutch) and has commented on occasional errors, such as showing president Richard Nixon on the cover of *RIR*, the dust-jacket artist's misunderstanding of Joan Maple (*TF*), and another artist's misrepresentation of the topography of Massachusetts (*TE*). Updike also notes the occasional jacket's beauty (novels in Danish and Japanese) or ugliness.

Updike has commented on the French translation of *FN*, saying that he would "gladly embrace" the possibility that the poems will be "better in French," a different response from the puzzled Henry Bech,* who was told that his work read better in French. He often makes lively remarks about translations of non-English books he has reviewed. In *MM* he notes that he finds that a translation of Camus's *Stranger* supersedes Stuart Gilbert's distinctly English one by a "closer simpler rendering" that makes Meursault "seem even stranger." Elsewhere he is "distracted by English awkwardnesses." A list of translated texts by and about Updike can be found in Jack De Bellis, *John Updike: A Bibliography, 1967–1993*. See **Languages**.

Bibliography: Updike, "Kiss Sixteen," translation from the Latin of "Basium XVI," by Ioannes Secundus, in *Poemata Humanistica Decem: Renaissance Latin Poems with English Translations* (Cambridge, MA: Friends of the Houghton Library, 1986), 12–13; "A Foreword to the French Edition of *Facing Nature*" (*MM*), Jack De Bellis, *John Updike: A Bibliography, 1967–1993* (Westport, CT: Greenwood Press, 1994), 253–70.

Trilling, Lionel (1905–1975). Lionel Trilling is an American psychological and sociological literary critic whose work is best exemplified by *The Liberal Imagination* (1950) and *Freud and the Crisis of Our Culture* (1955). His influential study of Jane Austen* is quoted in a critical book on Austen, which is the first connection between Betty and Rafe, who become adulterers ("A Constellation of Events" [*TM*]). See **Adultery; Freud, Sigmund**.

Tristan and Isolde (also Tristan and Isolt, Tristram and Iseult). Updike uses the story of the legendary doomed lovers Tristan and Isolde in three novels, several stories and a poem. Characters from Celtic legend, they appear in medieval love romances, the most well known being that of the thirteenth-century German poet Gottfried von Strassburg, and in *Le Morte Darthur* by the fifteenth-century English poet Thomas Malory. In the nineteenth century interest was renewed in the story, and the lovers became the subject of several poems and Richard Wagner's 1865 opera *Tristan und Isolde*. Updike was stimulated to explore the myth by two books by Denis de Rougemont. In the legend, Tristan and Isolde fall in love when Tristan brings her from Ireland to marry his uncle, King Mark of Cornwall. Mark discovers the truth and forces Tristan to flee to France, where he is wounded by a poisoned weapon. Tristan sends for Isolde, but is told that she is not coming, he dies in despair, whereupon Isolde kills herself. T. S. Eliot* used the myth* in *The Waste Land* to describe the failure of love in the modern world, and Denis de Rougemont used the legend to inquire into the narcissistic character of romantic love in *Love in the Western World* and *Love Declared*, which Updike examined critically. Ideas generated by his review fused with his treatment of Tristan and Isolde, employed in his work in the 1960s and remarkable for the versatility with which he approached the ancient story.

In reviewing de Rougemont's "psychoanalysis of the legend" in 1963, Updike paraphrases the argument of *Love in the Western World*: Tristan and Isolde are not in love with each other but with "*being* in love," which creates a false reciprocity disguising a "twin narcissism." They venerate spirit over flesh and in their "love-myth" hate creation. Love becomes a way of escaping the world; thus Iseult is the unreachable Lady, the woman "of his most intimate nostalgia." Updike finds this argument unconvincing because de Rougemont reaches beyond the facts of the legend to metaphysical conclusions, and Updike rejects the charge of narcissism against the lovers by countering with Freud's* argument that in making love the lover shares in the "glorification" of the beloved and himself becomes "lovely." Thus selfishness and altruism are wedded. In *Love Declared* de Rougemont planned a "mythanalysis of culture" in which he sought repressed religious material, starting with novels like Vladimir Nabokov's* *Lolita* as a variant on the Tristan myth: "Tristan and his underage Iseult" (*OJ*), Updike calls them. Then Updike discusses *Hamlet*, Søren Kierkegaard,* Don Juan and others. The result of this exploration for Updike is unconvincing. He wonders if de Rougemont's discovery of the power of love beyond its procreative aim might be explained without myth as a "Promethean protest" (*AP*) against death.* In love the lover corroborates "the supremely high valuation each ego secretly assigns itself" (*AP*). Marriage works against this by restricting freedom. The implications of the last thoughts reverberate throughout *RR*, *C*, *Couples*, "The Music School" (*MuS*) and many other novels and stories.

In the same year that Updike's review appeared, 1963, he wrote in the second of his "Erotic Epigrams" that Iseult to a condemned Tristan is like a letter of reprieve never delivered that he knows has been sent. Thus the knowledge of her love cannot save him, but it is enough to know that her love exists even if he dies, an idea carried into the short story "Four Sides of One Story," written in 1965 and collected in *MuS*, which produces a whimsical irony by retelling the legend from a medieval and modern vision at the same time through four letters from Tristan, two Isoldes (one is his wife, "Isolde White Hands") and Mark. As Robert Luscher observes, the letters reveal the lovers' separation, and since their letters are the second and third of the four letters, the women's lives are enveloped by the men. Tristan cannot choose between wife ("Isolde White Hands") and mistress ("Isolde the Fair") from fear of hurting either and himself. Tristan's letter complains that there is nothing to read on board his boat as he deserts his mistress and wife but the works of D'Annunzio,* and he notes that Mark thinks that he has a death wish. He tells mistress Isolde that he is the "perfect lover" because he permitted any agony on his behalf she wished. He offers a syllogism proving that they mirror each other; he reveals that Iseult is seeing a psychiatrist. Tristan's wife, "Iseult of the White Hands," writes to her brother, while the kids sleep and the dishwasher chugs, that Tristan has left her. "Iseult the Fair's" letter is unsent because Mark has withheld it for a lawsuit, adding that she is losing weight over Tristan's inability to commit to their marriage. Mark writes to his lawyer to agree that the magic potion will not hold up in court; anyway, he is having his alchemists find an antidote. Both women are more practical and more suffering than Tristan, but neither his mythic sense of the ideal woman nor Mark's practicality resolves the issues of love. The modernizing of the legend contains the enduring truth that love paradoxically causes pain; despite the demands of ego and the restrictions of marriage, whether ancient or modern, lovers threaten the social order. To critic Robert Luscher, Tristan appears cowardly.

Marry, the novel, was also conceived, according to Updike, in 1965, though it was published in 1976. It uses images from the myth to provide a sense of the union of the soul and body of Sally Mathias and Jerry Conant.* Such images include rose windows, chess* and French phrases like *amour de coeur*. Their airplane* flight whisks the lovers from earthly impediments, suspending them in the sky, as though they were heaven-borne souls. Yet Updike's conclusion is ambiguous; he provides alternative endings in which they separate and return to their mates, or leave their spouses and marry each other.

The legend also served Updike in *Couples*, in which he explores the adulterous affair of Foxy Whitman* and Piet Hanema.* As in the legend of Tristan and Isolde, their affair takes place by the sea, and Piet is "wounded" by the abortion* of their child. King Mark is transformed into Piet's nemesis Freddy Thorne,* but, countering the myth, Foxy's erotic love "cures" Piet of his fear of death, neither dies, and they do divorce their spouses and marry each other, unlike the ambiguous adulterers of *Marry*.

Critic George Hunt maintains that the Tristan theme "always betrays a masculine viewpoint." Perhaps to counter this implied attitude, Updike parodied the legend in "Tristan and Iseult" (*A*), in which the hero fantasizes while being attended to by a dental hygienist. But the masculine viewpoint may be seen in *B*, a tragic treatment of the legend in which time destroys the passionate affair of Tristão Raposo* and Isabel Leme.* Not even magic can save them. Updike acknowledged in his "Afterword" to *B* that he used Joseph Bédier's *Romance of Tristan and Iseult*, and in updating the myth, Updike substituted for adultery* the barrier of color—Tristão is black—and their love is richly tested by their fear of detection. After Isabel's use of magic makes him white, Tristão drifts from her and dies because he thinks that he can be self-sufficient as a white man.

Touches of the myth might remain in Updike's use of near incest in the sex* of Harry "Rabbit" Angstrom* and Teresa "Pru" Angstrom* in *RaR*, and in the intimacy of sixty-six-year-old Ben Turnbull* and thirteen-year-old Doreen in *TE*. Nearness in kin and distance in age make both pairs of lovers star-crossed. The tragic lovers Gertrude* and Claudius* also reflect something of Tristan and Isolde (*GC*).

Bibliography: Updike, "More Love in the Western World" (*AP*); "Tristan and Iseult" (A); Michael Harry Blechner, "Tristan in Letters: Malory, C. S. Lewis, Updike," *Tristania* 6 (Autumn 1980): 30–37; Hunt, *JU*; Luscher, *JU*.

Trust Me (New York: Knopf, 1987). The twenty-two stories of Updike's collection *TM* concern marriage, adultery* and, something new, homosexuality.* The characters* are mostly men in their fifties who experience moments of truth by confronting desire, aging and death.* Except for the symbolic "Leaf Season," the stories are strictly realistic and contain little experiment or variety of tone or point of view. Since few other collections are so focused in theme, the following description of each story will show how trust and distrust unify the volume.

"Trust Me," the first story, initiates the major themes of trust and misplaced trust in loved ones. It provides a montage of several examples of trust and failed trust. As a child, Harold is thrown by his father into a pool to learn to swim. He nearly drowns. Later Harold asks a girlfriend to ski with him on the advanced slope, and she is injured. Then his child makes brownies laced with hashish, and when Harold feels the effect, he calls his mistress, who refuses to help. He then examines a dollar bill, not for "In God We Trust" but for a "mystical eye" and the word "one," realizing that you can trust only "number one." As a minor theme, Updike suggests how abuse of trust begins with a misplaced effort to teach and ends with a malicious prank: abuse leads to intensifying abuse.

"Trust Me" echoes through "Killing," in which Anne assists her father in dying, only to discover that her trust in this experience is ironically related to her ex-husband's trust that she can provoke his virility. In "Deaths of Distant Friends" friends can be trusted to keep secrets only if they precede you in death. Physical well-being is again at risk in "The City," in which Carson must trust strangers and his ex-wife to treat his appendicitis. Carson's Kierkegaardian* "rotation" enables him to resituate himself toward the "city" of life, which he compares to an anonymous whore who services him and then disappears.

"Still of Some Use" is an especially good example of the casual way in which ordinary things take multiple meanings. From his divorced wife's house, Foster tosses out old children's games* (with their punning names, rules and counters) and feels the pang of knowing that the tokens and dice were "hieroglyphs whose code was lost." There is no "goodwill" to which to consign the games. Yet at the dump he tries to "protect" his son from the heaped-up "old happiness." Foster fails to recognize that his son showed that he trusted his father's protection, though Foster was deserted because he refused to play games with his marriage. Perhaps he and his wife were too full of games to sustain their marriage. "The Lovely Troubled Daughters of Our Old Crowd" provides another montage of failed trust in marriage, with the disconcerted narrator deciding that such failures reveal a visible absence of faith in life. Like Foster in "Still of Some Use," he wonders innocently, "What are they afraid of?" hardly realizing how much he needs reassurance that his divorce* and remarriage were the right decisions. "Unstuck" again finds a metaphor to control a depiction of a fading marriage, as bickering old marrieds wrestle their car from a snowdrift in language wryly recalling the unsuccessful intercourse they experienced the night before.

"A Constellation of Events" records the four-day winter diary of adultery abetted by a critical work on Jane Austen.* Despite the future pain of her affair, Betty sees her confidence in it not as a rainbow, but as scattered stars in a constellation. "Pygmalion" describes how the hero, named Pygmalion, creates his second wife unwittingly in the image of the first. The moral: do not trust a change of partners to change your life. "More Stately Mansions," set in 1968, treats, retrospectively, an adulterous affair between high-school colleagues against the background of the nation's loss of confidence in the Vietnam* War. As President Lyndon Johnson* agonizes, Francis emerges from the discovered affair successfully, but the husband of his lover Karen becomes an alcoholic and dies. The liaison is recalled when a student brings a chambered nautilus to "show and tell" class. Francis tells the class the shell's lesson: "We all must grow." But his own antigrowth has been shown by the story of national and personal betrayal he unwittingly reveals. "Learn a Trade" charts the Oedipal struggle of an artist, Fegley, and his children. His efforts to keep them from becoming artists fail as one becomes a potter, another writes a book, and the third goes into filmmaking. Hope for the fourth dies when he gives up carpentry for mobile making. Fegley's efforts to stop him fail, as his own father's efforts had failed to deter him from a career as a sculptor. The confidence of fathers is eroded by their inevitable love of their children.

"The Other" records Hank's infatuation for Priscilla's twin Susan; family myth labels the twins the artistic and scientific, respectively, but Hank decides that they are reversed. In seeking the "scientific" Priscilla, he has her "parade" nude to prompt and assuage his desire. Since he was raised poor and she rich, Susan and Hank are "other," though Priscilla and Susan do not think of this when they are together. Hank even imagines that Susan is present when he deflowers Priscilla, and his guilt over this shifts to a "twin of his own." As the years roll by, Hank has affairs, Susan's marriage dissolves, and they at last find one another. The story seems a reworking of "More Stately Mansions" to a happier conclusion for the lovers, though in the end Susan fears that she may not be "seen" except as the "Other" of Priscilla, and Hank realizes that the "ideal" she represented is illusory: she is a woman. He has grown to understand and accept reality over the course of thirty years. Like other Updike heroes, Hank has made his peace with the dualism of real and ideal. "The Other Woman" concerns Ed Marston's discovery that his wife is sleeping with a "trust officer." Ed keeps the secret so that he can end the marriage without guilt, but in the process his wife's lover's wife, Pat, is vulnerable to his knowledge and eventually to the community's when the affair becomes known. Ed becomes Pat's lover, and he wonders if she had known all along of her husband's affair and used Ed to gain a divorce. Pat had been entrusted to his care and, it seems, he to hers.

Other stories include "The Ideal Village," which examines the difficulty of accepting "paradise," once found, while "One More Interview" exposes a more anxious return to an Edenic hometown resembling Shillington.* Sardonic humor accompanies the social climbing into suburban heights in "Getting into the Set" (reminiscent of *Couples*), in which a status seeker has her possessions pilfered by the crowd she has idealized as her set. Also recalling *Couples*, as well as the story "When Everyone Was Pregnant" (*MW*), is "Leaf Season," in which a Columbus Day weekend in Vermont's autumnal beauty is the occasion for ritualized rediscoveries through fun and games by several friends, some of whom were former lovers. The discovery of cancer* leads a working-class man in "Poker Night" to rely upon the structure of the poker game to postpone his informing his wife of his impending death. He trusts in the turn of the cards and the balm of ritualized friendship instead of the confusion that might occur when he demands real trust from his wife. A gradual recognition of a man's attraction to men marks "Beautiful Husbands," in which a woman's lover discusses her husband as pillow talk. An exploration of middle-age loss tied to film* imagery* marks "The Wallet." "Made in Heaven" treats a man who overlooks his wife's physicality by entrusting himself to her spirit. "Slippage" recounts the growing awareness of Morrison, a history professor, that sex* and love are falling away from him as he prepares to die and become part of history. Morrison is the first of many Updike heroes to meditate upon his approaching death.

As is Updike's practice, these stories have been edited in small ways from their original magazine publications, but the ending of "Trust Me" reveals a major difference. *New Yorker** editor William Shawn published an ending in which Harold and Priscilla are apparently reunited, but for this collection Updike restored the original ending in which Harold, alone, examines a dollar bill.

Bibliography: Greiner, *OJ*; Christopher Lehmann-Haupt, "Books of the Times," *New York Times* 20 Apr. 1987: C-17; Michael Wood, "Hiding the Harm Away," *Times Literary Supplement* 9–15 Oct. 1987: 1106; Luscher, *JU*.

Turnbull, Ben. A retired Boston investment consultant in *TE*, Ben Turnbull, sixty-six, spends much of his time examining the change of seasons, visiting his grandchildren and his office and trying to maintain the integrity of his home. To do so, he must first pay "protection" to hoodlums and then consort with murderous teenage squatters. Law and order have broken down since the atomic war ten years before, and Turnbull suffers from cancer* that may have been a result of radiation. He reads and meditates and at times changes into other people, from Neanderthals to Nazis, as a result of "branching" (*TE*) (a theory derived from quantum physics*). Updike's description of John Cheever* could apply to Turnbull: "He thought fast, saw everything in bright, true colors, and was the arena of a constant tussle between the bubbling *joie de vivre* of the healthy sensitive man and the deep melancholy peculiar to American Protestant males (*OJ*)." *See* **Characters**.

Bibliography: David Malone, "Updike 2020: Fantasy, Mythology and Faith in *Toward the End of Time*," in Yerkes, *JU*.

Turnbull, Gloria. Ben Turnbull's* second wife in *TE*, Gloria dominates him, and when she is absent, he does not know if he killed her or if she is attending a conference. Gloria insists that Turnbull kill a deer that troubles her garden, but she herself may have "branched" (through quantum physics*) into the deer and then into Turnbull's lover, the prostitute Deirdre. The conflict between Gloria and Ben recalls that of Harry "Rabbit" Angstrom* and his wife Janice Angstrom,* particularly in *RaR* when Rabbit is in decline and Janice gains in vigor and control. Gloria is one of Updike's femmes fatales,* like Lucy Eccles* (*RR*), yet she cares for Turnbull when he contracts cancer* and tries to persuade him to avoid the trap of personalizing everything. *See* **Feminism**.

Bibliography: David Malone, "Updike 2020: Fantasy, Mythology and Faith," in *Toward the End of Time*, in Yerkes, *JU*.

2001: A Space Odyssey. The 1968 film* *2001: A Space Odyssey* by American film director Stanley Kubrick enters *RRed* twice, underlining structure, character and theme. *2001* provides an innovative depiction of the future in which a baffling message from an advanced civilization drives men to explore Jupiter, the outer reaches of the universe and inner reaches of themselves, beyond time and space. The hopeful future is tempered by shipboard betrayal by the master computer. In fact, Kubrick suggests that violence is basic to man, showing how the monolith somehow transfers to ancient apes toolmaking ability, which is immediately used to kill other apes. The film and the novel are connected by structure (passage, quest, flight); character (the similarity of the main characters* of each work); imagery* (the monolith and the presentation of space travel); and music (the novel's action echoes the film's recurrent ascending chord of three notes of Richard Strauss's *Also Sprach Zarathustra*, a tone poem that refers to philosopher Friedrich Nietzsche's work of the same name concerning the prophecies of the desert prophet Zarathustra).

Structurally, Janice Angstrom* is on her own quest, what her lover calls a "space odyssey," through her first extramarital affair; the film provides key images that establish her newly developed strength. Harry "Rabbit" Angstrom* is on a kind of passive quest, a "terrestrial astronaut" whose "mother ship" of a home is invaded by aliens Skeeter* and Jill Pendleton,* who teach him about America's history* through "teach-ins" and change his future, as the astronauts learn their strange destiny after destroying a murderous computer. Rabbit, who slept through most of the picture, is eager to see the film again, perhaps because he is more aware of how his personal quest can proceed. When the film returns to Brewer,* Janice and Rabbit reconcile and renew their marriage odyssey.

Characters in the film bear suggestive connections to those in *RRed*. Skeeter resembles the mysterious monolith because he is also black, enigmatic and a source of power attached to the future. Rabbit is linked to the computer HAL (their names have a common derivation) in his attachment to machines and his need to subvert his marital mission from fear of what might be discovered. Like Dave Borman, the sole survivor in *2001*, who voyages into the unknown, Janice's flight from Rabbit changes her forever. In addition, the imagery of the "star child" at the film's end suggests that Janice has forgiven herself for her baby's death ten years before and points the way to her psychological accommodation.

When the monolith appears at the beginning of the movie to a group of apes, three ascending notes sound, the famous leitmotif by which Strauss sought to remind his audience, intertextually, of Nietzsche's existential parable, because the notes were intended to recall Zarathustra's three-word epitaph, "God Is Dead." This is also the world of *RRed*: the Vietnam* War, racial riots, drug* addiction, technological obsolescence and sexual infidelity all demonstrate how men, left to their own existential anxieties, have disobeyed the Golden Rule. Strauss's music is used for subsequent entrances of the monolith in the film, but its last appearance leaves ambiguous whether or not the future of man without God will be liberating. (The ascending notes later became a cliché for suspenseful excitement, as in their use in the Kush National Anthem in *Coup*, and they signify in that novel that Col. Félix Ellelloû,* a virtual god, is dead, and that the atheistic state has erected the dollar as its new god.)

Strauss, like Kubrick, is not sure what the new freedom will bring, and this is a fitting question mark for a novel that leaves Rabbit at the end wondering "O.K.?" at his own passage through personal pain that mirrors the larger agony of Vietnam: his mother is dying, his young mistress has died through his carelessness, and his son hates him. Perhaps Updike wishes us to recall that when *2001* left town in *RRed*, it was followed by *True Grit*, as if courage is needed once God is dead. In *RaR* Rabbit recalls *2001* and the journey toward the stars (so like the golf* ball he struck in *RR*) and wonders if he will make it to the year 2000. He does not reach the millennium, partly because his courage fails him. *See* **Classical Music**.

Bibliography: Jack De Bellis, " 'The Awful Power': John Updike's Use of Kubrick's '2001: A Space Odyssey' in *Rabbit Redux*," *Literature/Film Quarterly* 21.3 (1993): 209–17; Jack De Bellis, " 'It Captivates . . . It Hypnotizes': Updike Goes to the Movies," *Literature/Film Quarterly* 23.3 (1995): 169–87.

U

Uncle Sam. The nickname for the personification of the United States and named by Congress a national symbol in 1961, Uncle Sam was adopted during the War of 1812. He was first shown in 1832 as a slender man in a long white beard, with high hat and tails, dressed in stars and stripes. James Flagg adopted this image for use in World War I recruiting posters. Updike's father, Wesley Updike,* led a July Fourth parade dressed as Uncle Sam in 1946. In the poem "How to Be Uncle Sam" (*TP*) Updike recounts how a man, incensed at being taxed, tried to punch his father, while a patriot shouted from the crowd that it was all right to hit Updike, but not Uncle Sam. The event is alluded to when Harry "Rabbit" Angstrom* leads the parade as Uncle Sam in *RaR*, unsteadily and with his beard and hat threatening to ruin his image. "Coming apart," he is unable to give anyone directions who asks; he symbolizes the United States in 1990. Based on Updike's experience of marching as Uncle Sam in Georgetown, Massachusetts, Updike's story "The Parade" concerns "Bobby," a writer for technical journals, who marches in a parade celebrating the seventy-fifth anniversary of "Hayesville," probably Shillington.* Bobby feels like a fool, wants to scream and realizes, "By ever leaving Hayesville, I had as good as died anyway." Though he is not dressed as Uncle Sam, his experience resembles that of Rabbit's (*OJ*). *See* **Presidents**.

Unitarianism. Unitarians generally reject the divinity of Christ, original sin and eternal punishment. For them, the Eucharist is not a sacrament, but a spiritual communion with Jesus. Though Unitarianism traces its origins to the Monarchians (250–300 A.D.) who rejected the Trinity for the belief in One God, Unitarians in England could practice their faith without persecution only after the Toleration Act of 1689. This "Arianism" flourished in New England in the eighteenth century as a counter to Puritanism and was adopted in 1796 by Boston's King's Chapel in breaking with Episcopalianism.

Updike's essay "Emersonianism" (*OJ*) celebrates the leading American advocate of Unitarianism, Ralph Waldo Emerson.* When he graduated from Harvard* Divinity School in 1829, Emerson became minister* of the Second Church (Unitarian) of Boston. However, he left in 1832 because he encouraged every person to become Christ, not merely imitate Him, a liberalism that would not be tolerated. Updike's first father-in-law, Rev. Leslie T. Pennington, was the Unitarian minister of the First Unitarian Church of Chicago, and Updike's first wife, Mary Pennington Updike,* was also a Unitarian, but Updike never joined the church.

Updike generally sees Unitarianism as having compromised itself into becoming too socially oriented and thus lacking in authority. Rev. Jack Eccles* describes his father as an Episcopalian who kept his church viable by nearly becoming a Unitarian himself (*RR*). Thus Updike's father-in-law is treated fictionally in *MS* as Wesley Chillingworth preparing a lecture for his ethics course, "Is the pleasant the good or not quite?" While Tom Marshfield* has sex* with Chillingworth's daughter, and Marshfield supplies a graphic sexual description of the history of their affair with a witty counterpoint of the ethical writers covered in Chillingworth's course. Marshfield relishes the irony because the Unitarians "epitomized" everything he hated about academic religion*: "its safe and complacent faithlessness, its empty difficulty, its transformation of the tombstones of the passionate dead into a set of hurdles for the living to leap on their way to an underpaid antique profession." Jerry Conant* says that the "Supreme Unitarian command" is "Face Things" (*Marry*). But Felicia Gabriel in *W* futilely faces the evil of demonism when she sermonizes in the Unitarian church to a sparse, indifferent congregation. Unitarianism is so liberal and lacking in the ability to identify evil that even the devil speaks in its church when Darryl Van Horne* delivers a sermon* against God's creation (*W*). *See* **American literature; Transcendentalism**.

United States Information Service (USIS). The United States Information Service (USIS) or United States Information Agency was founded in 1953 to provide people of other countries with an understanding of American foreign policy. Its principal vehicle is the Voice of America, which broadcasts to over 120 million people in forty-two languages as well as English. Cutbacks in funding for USIS mean that Jerry Conant* has no commercials to make (*Marry*). Updike and Henry Bech* had been good-will travelling writers for USIS.

Updike, David (1957–   ). John Updike's first son was born on January 19, 1957, in New York* City. He received his master of arts degree from Teachers College, Columbia University, has taught at City College of New York and now teaches in Roxbury Community College, Boston. David married a woman from Kenya, Njoki Githiora; a son, Wesley Doudi Githiora, was born in 1989, and they live in Cambridge, Massachusetts. His father, John Updike, dedicated *CP* to Wesley Doudi Githiora as the latest member of the family.

David Updike is the author of *Out on the Marsh* (Boston: David R. Godine, 1988), a collection of stories mostly published in the *New Yorker*,* and several children's books, including *A Winter Journey* (Englewood Cliffs, NJ: Prentice-Hall, 1985), with illustrations by Robert Andrew Parker. David Updike provided photographs to accompany his father's poems, *A Helpful Alphabet of Friendly Objects* (New York: Knopf, 1995), a book not only fitting for David's children, but that also balanced his father's "A Cheerful Alphabet of Pleasant Objects" (*CH*), which Updike had dedicated to David. David's photograph of his father appeared on the dust jacket of *TT*.

Like John Updike's other children, David may have been the model for fictional characters, such as the son in the stories "Wife-wooing" (*PigF*), "Avec la Bébé-sitter" (*MuS*) and "Son," in which he plays the guitar (*P*). He also may have been a source for the son in the stories delineating the dissolution of Updike's first marriage, particularly "Separating," in which the eldest son supplies a crucial epiphany for Richard Maple* when he asks of his decision to leave his family the unanswerable question, "Why?" (*TF*). Also, David might have modeled for two-year-old Nelson Angstrom* in *RR*. As Updike remarked, David and his siblings "said little, tactfully, of the odd versions of themselves and their home that appeared now and then in print" (*OJ*).

Bibliography: David Updike, "Writers as Progenitors and Offspring" (*OJ*); David Updike, "The Colorings of Childhood," *Harper's* Jan. 1992: 63–67.

Updike (Cobblah), Elizabeth Pennington (1955–   ). John Updike's first child, Elizabeth was born on April 1, 1955, in England, and in anticipation of the event Updike composed "March: A Birthday Poem," which asserts that father and daughter share the same month for their birthdays. Strictly speaking, since Updike was in New York and Elizabeth was born in London, he was five hours "behind" and consequently still in March when she was born on April 1. Elizabeth married August Tete Cobblah of Ghana, and they have two sons, John Anoff and Michael Kwame Nitiri, to whom Updike dedicated *SC* and to whom he addressed his genealogical essay-letter, "A Letter to My Grandsons" (*SC*). She received a degree from the Rhode Island School of Design.

Elizabeth appears in several stories as an infant, child and woman. Updike alludes to her birth in "Grandparenting" (*A*). Conceivably, she was a resource for Rebecca Angstrom* (*RR*). Updike identifies her in notes to *CP* as the child who failed to be amused by a bird mobile her father had brought home ("Toward Evening" [*SD*]). In "Incest" she is a year and seven months old (*SD*). In "Should Wizard Hit Mommy?" she resists her mother (*PigF*). She is included in "Avec la Bébé-sitter" (*MuS*) and as Alfred Schweigen's eight-year-old piano-playing daughter in "The Music School" (*MuS*). Possibly she was also a source for the eighteen-year-old leaving home in "Daughter, Last Glimpses of" (*P*), as well as Judith, the elder daughter who returns from a year in England in "Separating" (*P*). *See* **Babies; Updike, Mary Pennington.**

Bibliography: Carl Gray, "Perennial Promises Kept." *Time* 120 (1982): 72–74, 79–81; David Updike, "The Colorings of Childhood," *Harper's* Jan. 1992: 63–67.

Updike, Hartley Titus (1860–1923). Born in Pennington, New Jersey, John Updike's paternal grandfather, Hartley Titus Updike, was used as the model for Clarence Wilmot* (*IB*). He graduated from Pennington Seminary in 1879, orating on "Moral Courage," then attended Princeton University, 1879–83, and afterward Princeton Seminary for two years and Union Seminary in New York. Ordained in 1887, Hartley Updike preached in Presbyterian churches in Missouri, Illinois, Indiana, Nebraska and Arkansas. He married Virginia Emily Blackwood on July 21, 1891. He sustained a throat "affection" in 1896 in Livonia, Illinois, that curtailed and finally ended his preaching. He joined his father's real-estate and insurance firm, but it did not thrive, and after suffering pneumonia and strokes, he died in Florida.* Like Wilmot's, Hartley's life smelled "of financial failure and of the guilt and shame that attaches to such failure," which, Updike says, "ate away at my grandfather's life as if in some tale by Hawthorne" and left Updike's father, Wesley Updike,* feeling a "miserable helpless pity." Updike "envisioned" Hartley Updike as "like me, bookish and keen to stay out of harm's way; we aspired to the clerisy" (*SC*).

Bibliography: Updike, "A Letter to My Grandsons" (*SC*).

Updike, John. *See* the Chronology in the Preface to this volume.

Updike, John, in His Work. Updike is of course the subject of his memoirs, "The Dogwood Tree: A Boyhood"* (*AP*) and *SC*. He said that he wrote "Midpoint" (*M*) to explain his philosophy; he included family photographs within the poem, some of his parents, wife and children as well as of himself. Many other poems contain references to his family ("Leaving Church Early," "March: A Birthday Poem" [*TT*]; "Shillington," "How to Be Uncle Sam" [*TP*]; tributes to Harvard* ("Apologies to Harvard" [*TT*]); and descriptions of places Updike visited ("L. A." [*FN*], "Pompeii" [*M*], "Brazil" [*CP*], "Antigua" [*M*], "Spanish Sonnets" [*FN*], "Postcards from Soviet Cities" [*M*]); and family pets* ("Dog's Death" [*M*] and "Another Dog's Death" [*FN*]). His fiction uses his hometown of Shillington* and the nearby town of Mt. Penn*

Courtesy of Martha Updike

and the city of Reading* in various guises in novels (*RA*, *C* and *IB*) and stories (in *OS*, *PigF* and *A*). Updike's Massachusetts background appears in *Couples*, *RV* and *TE*. His home state and adopted state are subjects of many articles (*AP*, *PP*, *HS*, *OJ* and *MM*).

Updike's New York* writer Henry Bech* speaks directly to Updike in *BB*, advising him in the "Foreword" not to write about a writer, and he worries in "Bech Noir" that his creator might destroy him. Bech also interviewed Updike four times, on the appearances of *RRed* and *RIR*, *MF* and *BaB*. Updike also interviewed himself concerning his involvement in "Murder Makes the Magazine."* He has based upon himself, as models, not as self-portraits, the characters Joey Robinson* ("The Sandstone Farmhouse" [*A*]), Allen Dow ("Flight" [*PigF*], "His Mother inside Him" [*A*]), Rentschler ("The Other Side of the Street" [*A*]) and Lee ("The Black Room" [*A*]). Updike has been used as a model for the character Christopher in stories by his mother Linda Updike* in *The Predator* and *Enchantment*.

Updike explores the problem of having an identity ("I") and yet being known as "Updike," with whom he is frequently confused. He fears the day he will go to his study and find that "Updike" has not shown up: "I would attempt to do his work, but no one would be fooled" ("Updike and I").

Bibliography: Updike, "Bech Meets Me," "One Big Interview" (*PP*); "On One's Own Oeuvre," "Interviews with Insufficiently Famous Americans" (*HS*); "Literarily Personal" (*OJ*); "Updike and I" (*MM*); "Questions of Character: There's No Ego as Wounded as a Wounded Alter Ego," *New York Times* 1 Mar. 1999: E1, E7.

Updike, John, Reading. A historical review of Updike's reading shows his development as a writer, since, as he has said, every great writer is also a great reader. His reading can be divided into five overlapping phases: (1) pre-1946, recreational reading; (2) 1946–54, school reading; (3) 1955–present, professional reading for reviews, articles and the like; (4) 1968–present, research for novels, poems and other writings; and (5) 1969–present, re-reading for public talks on canonical writers. Here is a highly compressed description of the writers he encountered and how a few affected his writing during his career.

1. *Pre-1946: Recreational reading.* Like most professional writers, Updike began reading as a child. He fondly recalled the "Big Little Books" his mother gave him, particularly one about Mickey Mouse. This book provided him what he called a moment of "utter reading bliss." During his early school years, especially after leaving Shillington* in 1945, he read widely in *New Yorker** authors, including such poets as Ogden Nash, Phyllis McGinley and Morris Bishop; in fiction writers Mark Twain, Ring Lardner, James Thurber,* Robert Benchley, P. G. Wodehouse, Peter De Vries, Thorne Smith, John O'Hara, H. G. Wells, O. Henry and James Joyce*; and in essayists E. B. White and S. J. Perelman. He also read dozens of mystery writers, including John Dickson Carr, Agatha Christie,* Earl Stanley Gardner and Ellery Queen, all of whom influenced an aborted murder mystery Updike began in 1943 and another started in 1960. If "Pigeon Feathers" is evidence, he read historical works like Wells's *Outline of History*, perhaps led to it by way of Wells's *Time Machine* and *The Invisible Man*. At this time Updike wrote voluminously for the Shillington* High School *Chatterbox,** so he had practice presenting his views (primarily about films*) and imitating the poetry (and cartoons) of his favorites.

2. *1946–54; School reading.* Updike read Shakespeare and other major writers at Shillington High School, but the major turning point in his reading came at Harvard.* There he read the ancient classics and English* and American literature,* especially Henry Green,* Joyce Cary, Franz Kafka,* T. S. Eliot* and other modernists who would greatly affect his work, and he steeped himself in modern poets such as Robert Frost, Marianne Moore, E. E. Cummings* and, above all, Wallace Stevens,* in whom he discovered

a Reading writer. A crucial discovery was J. D. Salinger,* who showed him
that ambiguity in fiction was a primary goal. At Harvard Updike also delighted in the mellifluous poetry of Edmund Spenser and became interested
in Robert Herrick, finally writing his thesis on Herrick's indebtedness to
Horace. Updike had read widely in the Bible* and at Harvard read commentaries by Søren Kierkegaard,* Karl Barth* and Paul Tillich.* By the time
he graduated from Harvard in 1954, he had read authors important to his
spiritual development—Hilaire Belloc,* Thomas Aquinas,* Bertrand Russell
and C. S. Lewis. John Milton and Shakespeare's tragedies may have helped
to underline his fundamental sense, as he said, that the human condition is
tragic because there can be no final answers to any question. After graduation, Updike continued his omnivorous and varied reading program. He
wrote a poem using Anglo-Saxon devices in 1955 and, in the summer of that
year, read Cervantes's *Don Quixote* and wept at the end. It made him want
to write books as "vast and opaque" as life itself.

3. *1955–present: Professional reading for reviews, articles, and the like.* Updike
has estimated that between 1955 and 1991 he reviewed 369 books for the
New Yorker alone; *MM* includes reviews of another 63 books for that magazine. Since he also reviewed steadily for other magazines, at least another
100 books have been read for reviews since 1955. In addition to reading the
books he reviewed, he read other books in order to review art* and music
and to write prefaces, introductions, forewords and afterwords; also, he did
research for talks that were later published. Conservatively, then, Updike
read another 350 books in addition to those perused for *New Yorker* assignments. Naturally, Updike was reading books that did not immediately work
into reviews, including the works of philosophers, philosophical novelists,
and historians such as Sigmund Freud,* Jean-Paul Sartre, Albert Camus and
Will Durant, as well as novelists such as Henry Miller* and Vladimir Nabokov.* In the late 1950s he reread Marcel Proust,* James Joyce and Henry
Green in order to use their discoveries in technique and style in his first
novels, especially *PF* and *RR*. He selected Proust's *Remembrance of Things
Past* as another great moment of bliss. Jack Kerouac's* *On the Road* (1957)
was an important negative influence about 1958, since it made escape from
responsibility so willful that Updike wanted to show its ravages in *RR*. The
success of Vladimir Nabokov's *Lolita* (1955) encouraged Updike's desire to
explore eroticism in *RR*, to which Søren Kierkegaard supplied the context
of angst* and Barth religious ideas. About 1960 Updike discovered his first
wife's mythology book, which he relied upon in framing the myth of Chiron*
for *C*, and he used Barth as well.

Until about 1962, to help him through personal crises, Updike continued
his intensive reading in theology and philosophy with the works of Plato,*
Richard Hooker, Tillich, Arthur Schopenhauer and Miguel de Unamuno.
In 1968 he delved into psychologists, reading further in Freud (an important
influence on *Couples*) and Freudians such as Richard von Krafft-Ebing,

Theodore Reik, Wilhelm Reich and the Menningers. His acquaintance with Denis de Rougemont's *Love in the Western World* and *Love Declared* led him to use the Tristan and Isolde* story as underpinning to the love stories in *Marry* and *Couples*; he would use this legend throughout his career. By the 1970s, fellow *New Yorker* contributors became Updike's professed favorite writers—John Cheever,* J. D. Salinger, Saul Bellow* and Bernard Malamud; later he would endorse Alice Munro, Ann Beattie, Muriel Spark and Anne Tyler. Many of these writers are concerned, like Updike, with domestic difficulties and suburbia. Though he revered Ernest Hemingway,* in 1986 Updike admitted that he could not read William Faulkner,* and the absence of Southern writers in his reading is glaring. His reviews reflected this, as well as his interest in European authors such as Raymond Queneau, Robert Pinget and Julio Cortázar. He had read a Soviet literature anthology in 1968 and was clearly responsive to the French *nouvelle vague* writers Alain Robbe-Grillet and Marguerite Duras, as *BB* and *BIB* show. But he was very concerned to see how novelists of vastly different backgrounds approached their craft, so he began to read widely in African novelists, broadening this gradually to include writers from all prominent countries and many minor ones.

Updike continued to steep himself in American writers and praised Edward Hoagland and Sylvia Plath in particular. Hoagland was cited as "the best essayist of my generation" (*OJ*), and Updike notes that his nature* essays were "remarkable for their frankness, range and pungency (*OJ*). Updike seldom comments on poets, but he called Sylvia Plath "the best—the most exciting and influential, the most ruthlessly original—poet of her generation" (blurb for *Bitter Fame: A Life of Sylvia Plath*, by Anne Stevenson [Boston, Houston Mifflin, 1990]). Updike's sonnet "Upon Looking into Sylvia Plath's *Letters Home*" examines her as if her book were analogous to Chapman's Homer in John Keats's sonnet "On First Looking into Chapman's Homer." The poem concludes: "You, dead at thirty, leaving blood-soaked poems / for all the anthologies, and I still wheezing, / my works overweight; and yet we feel twins." These are only a few examples of Updike's reading as a reviewer.

To this one might add Updike's vast reading in order to write "special messages" for book-club editions; introductions to foreign editions like the Czech edition of *OF* and the French edition of *FN*; prepared talks such as "Why Write?" (*PP*), acceptances for awards such as Pulitzer Prizes, National Book Awards, and many others; travel commentary about Anguilla,* Brazil, London, Finland and China; introductions to books of cartoons by cartoonists such as David Levine and William Steig; introductions to collected stories of Kafka, Isak Dinesen and Herman Melville*; a foreword to a lengthy bibliography; and afterwords to a novel by Edmund Wilson* and a story by John Cheever. Updike's reading is all the more impressive when one realizes how kinetic it is, for in a review he will typically draw comparisons between a book in question and many others; his articles often create dialogues between books as he develops his theses. Additionally, one cannot calculate the breadth of Updike's personal reading that never contributed to a formal review or article—Barth's commentary on St. Paul; reading about golf,* computers or the history of Ipswich—or rereading the Bible, his own books, Proust, Joyce, Nabokov and others. Few writers of fiction and poetry in this century or any other can claim such extraordinary acquaintance with books.

4. *1968–present: Research for novels, poems and other writings.* Updike's first research project was *C*, which obliged him to use a great number of mythological figures. Next, he used science* from encyclopedias and magazines for "Midpoint" (*M*, 1969), but that was dwarfed by the nearly 200-page "Afterword," really an annotated bibliography (begun about 1968), on President James Buchanan* for *BD* (some items of which, including *BD* [!], were appended to the "Brief Bibliography" on the president for *MF*). As if to parody his Buchanan bibliography, Updike created a mock bibliography for Henry Bech* (*BB*, 1970), containing the names of real critics but fictitious works by them (real toads in imaginary gardens?). To write *RRed* the following year, Updike read deeply in African-American* writers, such as Frederick Douglass, and other writers such as William Styron, who wrote his novel about the slave Nat Turner in Turner's own voice. Reading in Nathaniel Hawthorne* prompted the trilogy based on *The Scarlet Letter* (*MS, RV, S.*). For *Coup*, Updike acknowledged numerous persons who supplied information as well as novels about Africa by T. C. Boyle and Evelyn Waugh and books on West African drought. For *RIR* he studied Toyota manuals; for *RaR* he learned about the treatment of heart disease and, from Barbara Tuchman's *First Salute*, the American Revolution.

W took Updike into researching witchcraft, including many novels treating the subject and Jules Michelet's *Satanism and Witchcraft*, which he first read at Harvard, Norman Cohn's *Europe's Inner Demons* and Margaret Murray's *The Witch-Cult in Western Europe* and *The God of the Witches*, as well as books by Erica Jong, Colin Wilson and many others. *RV* took him to tutorials in computing from MIT friends and the study of science books by Paul Davies, John Eccles and Fred Hoyle, among others. *S.* caused him to explore accounts of Rajneeshpuram and the work of Ajit Mookerjee, Mircea Eliade and Joseph Campbell, as well as Hindu sacred books. For *B* Updike researched Claude Lévi-Strauss, Theodore Roosevelt and many Brazilian novelists. *IB* brought him to explore books on the United States Postal Service, as well as books on the Paterson, New Jersey, silk strike, a great many on film* including Bob Thomas's *King Cohn*, and books on religious cults and crisis theology. Though *TE* acknowledges only a book by Paul Davies, a great deal of background reading on physics went into this novel.

5. *1969-present: Rereading for public talks on canonical writers.* Updike's rereading for public talks began with his exploration of Walt Whitman,* mainly "Song of Myself," for "Midpoint" (*M*, 1969). He returned to Whitman for his essay "Whitman's Egotheism" (1977), which after several revi-

sions was published as *Ego and Art in Walt Whitman* in 1980. Hawthorne's novels *The Scarlet Letter* and *The Blithedale Romance*, along with many of his stories, were explored in a talk in 1979 that was then revised and published as *Hawthorne's Creed* (1981). Hawthorne was instrumental in the writing of *MS*, and Updike returned to Hawthorne in writing *RV*, *S*. and *W*. Ralph Waldo Emerson* engaged Updike in preparation for a talk in 1983 that became "Emersonianism"* in 1984. The influence of Emerson is diffuse but can be detected in Updike's interest in transcendentalism* in *TE*, particularly by way of Emerson's disciple, Henry David Thoreau.* Despite a lifelong interest in the stories and novels of Herman Melville, begun with "Melville's Withdrawal" and continued in the 1997 "Introduction" to Melville's short fiction, Melville has had only a slight impact on Updike's creative work in *TE*. Nor have two writers associated with the genteel tradition, William Dean Howells and Edith Wharton, whom Updike reread in order to supply fresh appraisals. All along, Updike has stated, a continual instrument of bliss for him has been the *Encyclopaedia Britannica*.

When Updike prepares his reviews and articles for republication, he generally adds notes in order to update his readers on his further reading in the previously reviewed author. Updike has sometimes said that he looks forward to retirement so he can read more, and that, difficult to imagine, had he read more, he would have been a better writer. In his unsigned review of Nicholson Baker's *U and I: A True Story*, Updike explains the importance of reading: "Out of the books of others we sift a book of our own, wherein we read the lessons we want to hear" (*MM*). Updike has selected the ten greatest literary works providing such lessons from the past thousand years: *Summa Theologica*, by Thomas Aquinas*; *The Divine Comedy*, by Dante*; *Don Quixote*, by Cervantes (which left him in tears); the works of Shakespeare; *Candide*, by Voltaire*; *The History of the Decline and Fall of the Roman Empire*, by Edward Gibbon; *War and Peace*, by Leo Tolstoy; *The Possessed*, by Feodor Dostoevsky; *Remembrance of Things Past*, by Marcel Proust; and *Ulysses*, by James Joyce. *See* **Verisimilitude and Research.**

Bibliography: Updike, "Journeyers," "Hawthorne's Creed," "Melville's Withdrawal," "Whitman's Egotheism" (*HS*); "Leaving Home," "Emersonianism," "Howells as Anti-Novelist," "Re-reading Indian Summer" (*OJ*); "An Answer to a Question from *The Paris Review* on Humor," "Stevens as Dutchman," "Introduction to the Complete Shorter Fiction of Herman Melville," "Reworking Wharton," "Self Interview," "Five Remembered Moments of Utter Reading Bliss," "The Ten Greatest Works of Literature, 1001–2000: A Eurocentric List" (*MM*).

Updike, John, Residences. Born in West Reading, Pennsylvania, Updike lived the first thirteen years of his life in Shillington,* a Reading* suburb, moved to Plowville* in 1945, then left in 1950 to attend Harvard.* After graduation he lived a year in England, then nearly two years in New York*

City. Since 1957 he has resided in Massachusetts, within one hundred miles of Harvard, first in Ipswich,* briefly in Georgetown, then in Beverly Farms.

One could say that Updike's first home was the West Reading, Pennsylvania, Hospital, where he was born; he was quickly established at 117 Philadelphia Avenue, Shillington, from March 1932 to October 31, 1945. On Halloween 1945, his family moved to a sandstone farmhouse in Plowville,* Pennsylvania, a move Updike called "the crucial detachment of my life." Updike went to Harvard for four years (1950–54), living as a freshman in Hollis Hall, where Henry David Thoreau* had lived, and later in Lowell House*—the fifth floor during his junior year. When he moved to Oxford* on a Knox Fellowship, he lived in a basement flat on Iffley Road, and in London at 59 Cumberland Terrace (August 1954–55). Returning to New York in 1955 to work at the *New Yorker*,* Updike and his family lived at West Eighty-fifth Street and Riverside Drive, fifth floor, and at 153 West Thirteenth Street from August 1955 to April 1957. The Updike family moved to Massachusetts in 1957; all his residences since then have been in that state. Updike and his family lived at "Little Violet" on Essex Road and Heartbreak Roads, Ipswich, from April 1957 to April 1958. Then they moved to a seventeenth-century house, 26 East Street, Ipswich, from April 1958 to 1970, and Updike worked in an office above a restaurant in the Caldwell Building in downtown Ipswich after 1961. He moved to 50 Labor-in-Vain Road, Ipswich (1970–74), and he found a striking resemblance between this home and the locale of the film* *Dark Victory*. Then, while awaiting his divorce,* he lived alone for the first time at 151 Beacon Street, Boston (September 1974–June 1976). Before and after remarrying, Updike moved to 58 West Main Street, Georgetown (1976–82), then to his present home in Beverly Farms, twenty-five miles north of Boston (May 1982–present).

Updike's work is filled with references to the precise places people live, including their apartment numbers. For example, at the end of *RIR* Harry "Rabbit" Angstrom* reflects on the address of his new home: "their dead-end spur cuts off of: 14 1/2 Franklin Drive," Penn Park. Since the spur has no name, Rabbit thinks of calling it "Angstrom Way." He then thinks about his parents' home at 303 Jackson Road, and the apartment he shared with Janice Angstrom,* his wife, and their son Nelson Angstrom* at 447 Wilbur Street, Apartment #5, third floor. He remembers their ranch house in Penn Villas that was burned by arsonists: 26 Vista Crescent. His retirement place in Deleon, Florida,* is in Valhalla Village, Building B, no. 413. Updike's characters live in precise places, and this makes their temporality poignant in its specificity.

Bibliography: Updike, "Author's Residences" (*TT*); "Note to the Previous Tenants" (*TT*); "A Soft Spring Night in Shillington" (*SC*); "Remembering Reading, Pa.,"

"Two Answers to the Question of Why I Live in New England," "Home in New England" (*MM*).

Updike, Linda Grace Hoyer (1904–1989). Linda Grace Hoyer Updike, the mother of John Updike and a major force throughout his life, was born on June 20, 1904, in Plowville,* Pennsylvania, the daughter of John Franklin Hoyer,* a teacher, charcoal burner and farmer. She graduated in 1918 from Keystone Normal School and in 1923 earned a bachelor of arts degree at Ursinus College in Collegeville, Pennsylvania, where her son would receive an honorary D.Litt. in 1964. Updike noted that "she found her intellectual focus there, as well as her husband," Wesley Updike,* a cable tester for the American Telephone and Telegraph Company. They were married on August 31, 1925. Linda Updike entered Cornell University in 1924 and received a master's degree the same year. On March 18, 1932, she bore her only child, John Hoyer Updike, in the West Reading Hospital. When he was eighteen months old, Linda Updike went to work in Pomeroy's Department Store in Reading* as a drapery saleswoman for fourteen dollars a week, leaving her son in the care of her mother, Katherine Kramer Hoyer.* She decided to leave Pomeroy's, saying, "I'm going to stay home—and become a writer," though she did work during World War II in a parachute factory, like the proverbial "Rosie the Riveter," as Updike recalled. As Wesley Updike changed jobs frequently, he and Linda Updike travelled from 1925 to 1931, when they settled in Shillington,* but in 1945 they were able to buy her birthplace, her parents' former eighty-three-acre Plowville farm, with its 1812 farmhouse, satisfying her lifelong dream.

The acquisition proved crucial in accelerating John Updike's creative development. Though John Updike disliked the move from Shillington, he used the isolated farm to turn his avocation into his vocation, remarking: "It was probably a very good thing, looking back on it. Whatever creative or literary aspects I had were developed out of sheer boredom those two years before I got my driver's license." As she had in Shillington, Linda Updike encouraged her son's artistic interests in drawing* by arranging, when Updike was in grade school, for lessons from a local artist descended from the founder of Shillington. She took a correspondence writing course from Thomas H. Uzzell of Texas and was a serious writer, often moving her son, when he was a baby, from her lap to the floor so she could type more easily. As John Updike developed as a cartoonist and poet, he and his mother sent their work to various magazines, most notably the *New Yorker*.* Linda Updike supported his keen desire to be published, and also his desire to enter Harvard* in 1950. Her breakthrough came in 1965 with the publication of "Translation" in the *New Yorker*, and more acceptance from that magazine followed. Her 1971 *Enchantment: A Novel*, centered on an alter ego,* Belle Minuit, just as John Updike developed alter egos in Allen Dow, Joey Robinson,* Harry "Rabbit" Angstrom,* Richard Maple* and Henry Bech.* Her second collection, *The Predator*, portraying the old age of Ada, was published posthumously in 1990. When asked if she was happy for her son's international fame, Linda Updike said firmly, "I'd rather it had been me." Updike observed that she was never published "as much as her gifts deserved." When she died on October 10, 1989, Linda Hoyer Updike left manuscripts of nearly two hundred short stories and six novels. "Fall" (*CP*), a poem John Updike wrote ten days after his mother's death, describes how she was found after the house was broken into; it ends, " 'I didn't take very good care of you.' "

Apart from making writing as he said, "a plausible or possible activity" (Plath, *CU*), Linda Updike also provided her son with a character who appeared in poems ("Plow Cemetery," [*FN*] "Leaving Church Early" [*TT*] and "Midpoint" [*M*]) and short stories ("Flight" and "Pigeon Feathers" [*PF*], "Son" [*P*] and several in *A*, most notably the award*-winning "A Sandstone Farmhouse"). She has some kinship with the fictitious mothers of Rabbit (*RA*), Peter Caldwell* (*C*) and Joey Robinson (*OF*).

Collectively, her stories and her son's describe a woman who loves her farm, her son and her independence. Filled with energy, she leaves profound imprints on the farm she cherished and the rooms she inhabited. The narrators of Updike stories and the speaker of each poem are filled with a sense of wonder at her force and an ambivalence about her possessiveness and her irascible empathy, which create the family tensions apparent in the poem "Leaving Church Early." Updike provides vivid portraits of her throughout *SC*, and he has noted that he composed the death of Rabbit for *RaR* during his mother's final illness, but he called this a "shameless" use of her declining health. In a kind of private homage Updike set *RaR* in Florida,* where she had wished to locate a novel, and named the Angstrom retirement town Deleon,* after Juan Ponce de León,* whom Linda Updike had sought for years to make the hero of a novel.

Updike has asserted that his mother was "an ideal reader and an ideally permissive writer's mother." Linda Updike had an "un-middleclass appetite for the jubilant horrible truth" (Plath, *CU*). Updike explained that his mother was "never other than encouraging, even when old wounds were my topic" (Plath, *CU*), as in "Leaving Church Early." Confronted with this when interviewed for the video "What Makes Rabbit Run?" she said, "Someone has to tell the truth. I'd just as soon it were John." She understood that her son would be a success and helped him to understand Reading, fictional Brewer,* as the "substance and the poignancy of something slipping away."

Bibliography: Updike, "The Most Unforgettable Character I've Met," *Vogue* 174 (Nov. 1984): 441; "Fall" (*CP*); *SC*; *OJ*; "A Response to a Request, from *Life*, to Remember Pearl Harbor" (*MM*); Ancona, *WA*; Bruce Weber, " 'As Good a Writer's Mother as One Could Ask For,' " *New York Times Book Review* 14 Jan. 1990: 11; "Materials Added to the Linda Grace Hoyer Updike Literary Papers Collections," *Myrin Library News* (Ursinus College) 8 (1 Dec. 1994): 1; Jack De Bellis, "Linda

Grace Hoyer," in *American National Biography* (New York: Oxford UP, 1999), Volume 11, 372–73.

Updike, Martha Ruggles Bernhard (1937–   ). Updike's second wife received her B.A. at Cornell in 1959, her M.Ed. at Harvard* in 1964, and her M.S.W. at Simmons School of Social Work in 1988. While awaiting his divorce in 1976, Updike lived with her and her three children in his house, 58 West Main Street, Georgetown, Massachusetts. They were married on September 30, 1977, in a Lutheran service in Marblehead, Massachusetts. In writing of Vladimir Nabokov's* literature class at Cornell (where Updike's mother Linda Updike* had matriculated), Updike draws upon Martha Updike's memories of taking that course even with a fever because, as she said, Nabokov "could teach me how to read . . . give me something that would last all my life—and it has." What lasted was Nabokov's "central dogma": "style and structure are the essence of a book; great ideas are hogwash" (*HS*). Nabokov called her a genius (*HS*). In receiving the National Book Award for *RIR*, Updike thanked Martha for "standing foremost in that band of intimates who surround with forbearance the homely and sometimes hopeless-seeming labor of concocting fiction" (*HS*). Updike uses for an epigraph* in *TT* a passage from James Joyce's* *Ulysses* containing Martha's name, and he dedicated to her *IB*, *OJ* and *GC*. Martha Updike's photograph of Updike was used on the dust jackets of *S.*, *IB* and *TE*.

Updike, Mary (1898–1985). Updike's paternal aunt (his father's sister), Mary Updike married her first cousin Don and thus remained an Updike. For a time she was Edmund Wilson's* secretary at the *New Republic*, and she gave her younger brother's family a subscription to the *New Yorker* for Christmas 1944, which helped determine Updike's direction as a writer. To be a contributor to the *New Yorker* was his highest aspiration, for to the very young Updike, the magazine was the highest expression of art and literature. She may have been a source for Esther Wilmot in *IB* and appears in the vignette "My Uncle's Death" (*AP*). Mary Updike's husband mined copper in Chile and may thus be a source for Tristâo Raposo,* who mines gold in Brazil (*B*).

Bibliography: Updike, "A Letter to My Grandsons" (*SC*).

Updike, Mary Pennington (Mrs. Mary Weatherall) (1930–   ). Mary Pennington was Updike's first wife and the daughter of Elizabeth Daniels Pennington and Rev. Leslie T. Pennington, minister* of the First Unitarian Church of Chicago. After the University of Chicago High School and the Buckingham School in Cambridge, she attended Radcliffe College, majoring first in social science and then in fine arts. In her junior year she met Updike, who was at Harvard,* in a medieval art class. He courted her, he recalled, "essentially by falling down the stairs of Fogg Museum." She graduated in 1952, and they were married on June 26, 1953, at the end of his junior year. The Ipswich home of one of her father's parishioners served as their honeymoon retreat. Mary Updike taught ceramics and painting at the Browne and Nichols School during Updike's senior year. When he received a Knox Fellowship to the Ruskin School of Fine Art and Drawing,* Oxford,* England for 1954–55, Mary studied painting there. On their return to New York, Updike used his wife as the subject of his drawings* and paintings, one of his last serious efforts at the graphic art, apart from cartooning.*

Relocating to Ipswich in 1957, Mary actively participated in the Congregational Church, the Democratic town committee and the Fair Housing Committee and, with her husband, played in a recorder group; this group may have been recalled in "The Man Who Became a Soprano" (A). In 1964 she went with John Updike, who travelled for the State Department, to Moscow, Leningrad, Tbilisi, Yerevan and Kiev. Mary participated in the Selma to Montgomery Civil Rights March in 1967, used as the basis for "Marching through Boston" (MW), and six years later she travelled with her husband to Ghana, Nigeria, Tanzania, Kenya and Ethiopia as part of his Lincoln Lectureship, visiting nearby game preserves. Mary was a first reader of Updike's work, and though Updike remarked in an interview that she had reservations about the uneventful characters* and plots of PF and OF, the confusing use of myth in C and the indulgence in eroticism in Couples, he has also said that he found her a "pricelessly" sensitive reader who was almost always right. In an "Introduction" to Self-Selected Stories of John Updike (MM) he said that she thought that "A & P" (PigF) "reminded her rather too much of J. D. Salinger*" (MM).

Separated in 1974, they were issued one of Massachusetts's first no-fault divorces in March 1976. After the divorce Mary worked at the Atlantic Monthly as a first reader of fiction and poetry, was a hospice volunteer and studied landscape design and painting at the Montserrat College of Art, Beverly, Massachusetts. She is now a landscape painter. Mary married Robert Weatherall, director of the Careers and Placement Office at Massachusetts Institute of Technology, in 1982. They live in Ipswich. Mary and John Updike had four children: Elizabeth,* born in Oxford on April 1, 1955; David,* in New York City, January 19, 1957; Michael,* in Ipswich, May 14, 1959; and Miranda,* in Ipswich, December 15, 1960. In addition, Mary and John Updike have many grandchildren. An old book of Mary's containing the story of the centaur Chiron,* discovered in the early 1960s by Updike, stimulated his writing of C. In 1968 he dedicated Couples to Mary and for the only time placed his dedication with his two epigraphs* on the same page, perhaps because an epigraph quoting Paul Tillich* was selected with Mary's father in mind, since he was a "great Tillichite." The other epigraph, from a poem by the Russian poet Alexander Blok, was intended as a "personal touch," since the Updikes had just returned from Russia.

If one reads Updike's work biographically, the marital tensions spanning 1956–76 that led to the Updikes' dissolving their marriage can be detected in many short stories about Richard* and Joan Maple* collected in *TF* and three novels, *OF*, *Marry* and *Couples*. Thus "Snowing in Greenwich Village" (1959) presents Richard's realization that infidelity could be desirable. Additionally, *OF* and *Marry* (begun in 1965) show that divorce* and remarriage had become fictional material for Updike, and in *Couples* Piet Hanema* leaves cool, beautiful Angela Hanema* for warm, adventuresome Foxy Whitman.* Other postdivorce writing such as *MS*, *RV* and *MF* and story collections such as *MuS*, *P*, *TM* and *A* also draw upon Updike's first marriage. In the three novels the marriages are saved, despite adultery.* Rev. Tom Marshfield does return to his wife after realizing that infidelity does not disqualify him for spiritual renewal. Roger Lambert's* brief affair with Verna Ekelof* and his wife Esther's* with Dale Kohler* do not ruin their marriage in *RV*. Nor in *MF* does Alf Clayton's* affair destroy his marriage. Set at nearly the same time as the *TF* stories, the recreation of events in 1974 in *MF* shows the continual fictional use Updike made of his first marriage. Allusions to it can be discovered also in *TE*. Thus Updike's experience in his first marriage provided him with a rich vein of material that he would exploit creatively.

Bibliography: Updike, "Apologies to Harvard" (*TT*); *SC*; "View from the Catacombs," *Time* 26 April 1968: 66–68, 73–75.

Updike, Michael (1959–   ). Updike's second son and third child was born on May 14, 1959. He graduated from Massachusetts College of Arts in 1982 and now works in Newburyport, Massachusetts, as a sculptor and designer of serving ware. He married Janice Eaton of Ipswich in 1991; they have two sons, Trevor Leonard and Sawyer.

Updike, Miranda (1960–   ). Updike's fourth child and second daughter, born on December 15, 1960, Miranda may appear as a baby in diapers who bursts into tears when a cookie is called a gâteau ("Avec la Bébé-sitter" [MuS]) and as the four-year-old metaphorically described as a "lioness" in the poem "Daughter" (*CP*), as well as the child who cried at the party in "When Everyone Was Pregnant" (*MuS*) and Nancy Hanema,* the daughter of Piet* and Angela Hanema,* who fears death,* yet accidentally enables the family cat to kill the pet hamster (*Couples*). Miranda Updike married Donald Freyleue but kept her own name. They have two sons, Kai Daniels Freyleue, to whom *A* is dedicated in part, and Seneca Dunn Freyleue. *See* **Babies, Children**.

Updike, Wesley Russell (1900–1972). John Updike's father, Wesley Russell Updike, was born in Trenton, New Jersey. He met Linda Hoyer (Updike)* at Ursinus College and married her on August 31, 1925. He worked as a telephone lineman for American Telephone and Telegraph from 1927 to 1932. After accumulating education courses at Albright College, he taught mathematics at Shillington* High School, where he was noted for his pranks and personality. He taught his son for three years, acting as his homeroom teacher one year, and since Updike was a good mathematics student there was no conflict between them in class. Updike was proud "seeing him perform" (Plath, *CU*), and reveled in his humor that "would make the whole auditorium roar with laughter" (Plath, *CU*). Once, to emphasize that equations end with decimal points, he smashed a snowball against the blackboard. Updike credits his father and mother with "considerable" acting skills that led him to "dramatize" his youth. John Updike thought that his father displayed "the Protestant kind of goodness going down with all the guns firing—antic, frantic, comic, but goodness nonetheless."

Later Updike saw "the real struggle that teaching is" and "a sense of . . . the agony of the working teacher." Though Updike has warned, "My parents should not be held to the letter of any of the fictional fathers and mothers," he admits that "George Caldwell was assembled from certain vivid gestures" and qualities in his father; each of them "dies daily" by teaching in a small school to support his family (*C*). When John Updike was criticized for the "outrageous portrait" by a friend, Wesley defended his son by saying, "No, it's the truth. The kid got me right." He had deliberately set out to portray his father in *C* as a foil for Harry "Rabbit" Angstrom* (*RR*): the man who stayed and worked versus the man who ran and let the social fabric unravel. Yet his father, like Rabbit, "bridles at good advice," taking direction only "from his personal, also incorrigible God." In Updike's next novel, *OF*, a novel written, as Updike said, "after the centaur has died," Joey Robinson* (Updike's alter ego*) puts on his father's clothes to tend to the farm. Much later Updike returned to embellish episodes described in *SC* in the story "My Father on the Verge of Disgrace" (*LL*), of which he said in a "Note" on that story that the detail of robbing the ticket money to pay for food still "frightens me to divulge" (*MM*). Updike's early stories "The Lucid Eye in Silver Town" (*AP*) and "Pigeon Feathers" (*PigF*) also portray a figure like Wesley Updike.

Bibliography: Updike, "The Lucid Eye in Silver Town" (*AP*); "Midpoint" (*M*); "My Father on the Verge of Disgrace" (*LL*); "View from the Catacombs," *Time* 26 April 1968: 66–68, 73–75, Ancona, *WA*; Jack De Bellis, "Oedipal Angstrom," *Wascana Review* 24 (1989): 45–59.

V

Valéry, Paul (1871–1945). Paul Valéry is a French poet mentioned in *Coup*, in which a "Negritudinist" writes in Valéry's style of classical form with sensuous, natural description and a musical technique. *See* **French Literature**.

Van Horne, Darryl. Darryl Van Horne (a false name that Updike may have intended to chime with "Devil with horns") is a devilishly clever New York* entrepreneur in *W* who descends upon Eastwick* and changes the lives of five people: three witches, Sukie Rougemont,* Alexandra "Lexa" Spofford* and Jane Smart,* who become his mistresses and develop their talents under his tutelage as journalist, sculptor and cellist; Van Horne's wife, Jenny Gabriel; and her brother Chris. A parody of the modern Renaissance man, Van Horne is passionately involved in both art* and science.* As an artist, he is a virtuoso pianist and worships pop art* because it reveals the vulgarity and waste of a world empty of meaning. As a scientist, he seeks a "loophole" in the second law of thermodynamics by extracting electromagnetism from rocks or from organisms in the Great Salt Lake. He entertains the witches with mad improvisations on the piano, hot-tub dinners, drugs,* sex* and tennis, in which he makes tennis balls defy gravity. He tries to get the witches to stretch to new levels of "empowerment," prompting Lexa to make bigger sculptures, Sukie to write novels and Jane to become a cello virtuoso. Stung by the death of Jenny, Van Horne gives a sermon in the Unitarian church in which he lobbies to supplant God in the next "election" because His is a "terrible Creation." He then elopes with Chris Gabriel, leaving the witches to realize that they as well as Jenny had been manipulated.

Bibliography: Updike, "Special Message for the Franklin Library Edition of *The Witches of Eastwick*" (*OJ*); Diane Johnson, "Warlock," *New York Review of Books* 31

(14 June 1984): 3–4; Katha Pollitt, "Bitches and Witches," *Nation* 239 (23 June 1984): 773–75; Kathleen Verduin, "Sex, Nature and Dualism in *The Witches of Eastwick*," *Modern Language Quarterly* 46 (Sept. 1985): 293–315; Charles Berryman, "Updike and Contemporary Witchcraft," *South Atlantic Quarterly* 85 (1986): 1–9.

Verisimilitude and Research. Factual accuracy or verisimilitude, the cornerstone of Updike's realism, is based upon respect for actuality and diligent research. Updike's Proustian* recollection is called upon in the fiction rooted in his early work, but he refers to it throughout his fiction in memories of Berks County, sometimes transposed to other settings, such as Basingstoke, Delaware, in *IB*. Updike acknowledges that "my adolescence seemed interesting to me" (*PP*), and pronounced "the world of stones and trolley cars fit subjects for fiction" (Plath, *CU*) since everything is the product of God. Thus, "there is a great deal to be said about almost anything" (*PP*). His adolescence and that "world of stones" became for him charged with nearly inexhaustible meaning embedded in every detail. Recollection for verisimilitude thus had a dual purpose for Updike: to precisely depict the world he inhabited as a way of praising God, as he once put it; and to reach beyond his realistic boundary to God's boundary. As he said, "Details are the giant's fingers" (*PigF*), and they lead to discovery of God's patterns ("The Blessed Man of Boston, My Grandmother's Thimble, and Fanning Island" [*PigF*]). Updike has remarked that he found his own early life exceptionally rich, but that once a writer reaches adulthood, he needs to research his work in order to supply a felt sense of actuality. A writer's first subject, his early life, then, is his given subject, but once it is exhausted, he must rely upon more than memory and call all the more on his senses, of which a very early critic said that Updike had six or seven. His sensitivity for the period in which each of his books is lodged is so acute that, as Dilvo Ristoff has shown, future historians could reassemble a facsimile of America from his books.

In a sense, Updike's use of research to establish actuality is an effort to rediscover the "giant's fingers." The first fruit of Updike's use of research for verisimilitude in his fiction occurred with the publication in 1965 of his first Henry Bech* story, "The Bulgarian Poetess," which used his "number of impressions" about his travels in Eastern Europe and Russia (*PP*). When the story proved a success, he put together others about Bech fortified with similar impressions. Updike's methodical use of research actually began, though, when, in the British Museum, he began compiling information on President James Buchanan* for a projected fourth novel about Pennsylvania. Finding that he was very uncomfortable with the re-creation of a world removed from his senses, he set his research aside and returned to his "old friend" Harry "Rabbit" Angstrom* and the familiar world of Shillington* and Reading.* Yet Updike's voluminous reading in history* was not wasted, and in 1974 he published a "closet drama" about Buchanan, *BD*, appending a long descriptive bibliography to the book. His Buchanan research found fictional use in 1992 in the novel *MF*, whose narrator was not only interested in Buchanan but also faced a writer's block similar to the one Updike had experienced in the early 1970s. Immediately after publishing *BD*, Updike began researching Nathaniel Hawthorne's* work for three novels based on *The Scarlet Letter* (*MS*, 1975; *RV*, 1986; and *S.*, 1988), and he included Hawthorne material in *MF* and *W*. A tour of Africa resulted in *Coup*, a novel set in what is probably Ethiopia, as his trip to Brazil provided research for *B* and a short time in Florida* provided background for *RaR*. Typically, Updike mines all his experience.

The Rabbit books, especially *RRed*, *RIR* and *RaR* exhibit perhaps the best marriage of the "youthful" remembered actuality and research. In *RRed* he blends a steady account of the decline of Brewer* since *RR* with the raw data of civil unrest and the moon landing. In *RIR*, though, Updike depicted the farm country around Brewer with affection and steeped himself in textbooks of the automobile* trade so much that Philip Roth complained that Updike knew more about Toyotas than he, the owner of one. Updike reports in his introduction to *RA* that even while he described the beautiful Bradford pear trees of Reading, he collected eyewitness information from his mother's heart disease that would be useful to his depiction of Rabbit's condition.

But research without such youthful recollection has dominated Updike's verisimilitude in *RV*, *S.*, *W*, *B*, *IB* and *TE*, as well as in many stories, particularly those starring Henry Bech (*BB*, *BIB* and *BaB*). Updike's "heartfelt thanks" in *RV* show how he sought to provide a precise knowledge of the computer sufficient to give his hacker Dale Kohler* authority, as well as an exact understanding of recent discoveries in microbiology, cosmology and astrophysics. Updike clearly brushed up on the controversies swirling around the church fathers to give Roger Lambert* professorial credibility. In *W* he researched witchcraft and the cello, delving into novels about witchcraft. His "Author's Note" to *S.* assures us that his Sanskrit is accurate when he supplies an extensive "Glossary" of that language, as he had appended to *C* a "Mythological Index" for his characters.* His "Afterwords" to *B* and *IB* attest to thorough reading in Brazilian history, though some critics indicated that his research was not entirely accurate for the time in which the novel was set. For *IB* Updike steeped himself in crisis theology, the city of Paterson, the silk strike, gardening, the Branch Davidian cult and all phases of the film* industry.

Such minute attention to detail, remembered or researched, shows that Updike's realism can be relied upon to present the sense of here and now. Yet Updike is grateful if his verisimilitude is simply "convincing," since "one of the minimal obligations a book has to a reader is to be factually right . . . that you do at least *attempt* to imagine technical details as well as emotions and dialogue" (Plath, *CU*). But unlike other writers who use research in their fiction, such as Theodore Dreiser,* Updike does not merely heap his work with documentation. As V. S. Pritchett said in reviewing *RIR*, Updike could make the Sears, Roebuck catalogue "sound like a chant from the Book of Psalms." *See* **The Novel; Updike, John, Reading**.

Bibliography: Updike, "One Big Interview" (*PP*); "Introduction," in *Pigeon Feathers* (New York: Knopf, 1977); "Special Messages" to *W, RV, S*. and *RaR* (*OJ*); "Introduction," in *Rabbit Angstrom: A Tetralogy* (New York: Knopf, 1995); "Special Messages" to *MF, B, IB* and *TE* (*MM*); V. S. Pritchett, *New Yorker* 9 Nov. 1981: 201–6; Ristoff, *UA*.

Vermeer, Jan (1632–1675). A Dutch painter of portraits and "Dutch interiors," Jan Vermeer is famed for his exquisite use of light and extraordinary balancing of elements. The importance of Vermeer in Updike's work resides both in his characters'* aesthetic appreciation of these qualities and in Vermeer as a representative artist of the actual. In a 1964 story, "The Lucid Eye in Silver Town" (*AP*), Jay goes to New York* with his father to shop for a Vermeer book, but when grit gets into his eye, the money set aside for the book is spent on doctoring Jay. He turns his disappointment on his father, perhaps revealing his fear that the world of grit and accident will always interfere with his apprehension of Vermeer's luminescent world. But in *C* Peter Caldwell,* about twenty-five years old, looks back on his adolescent self with an artist's knowledge of Vermeer. He responds deeply to the painter's craftsmanship and use of the frozen moment, so that when he sees the blue outline on a loaf of bread, he finds such eternal beauty that he wants "so badly to be Vermeer." Also, Peter's love of Vermeer enables him to reevaluate his father, since Vermeer represents for Peter an orderliness that his father had apparently disrupted.

No doubt Peter's own artistic pleasure responded to Vermeer's poised portraits of readers and writers, as well as Vermeer's paintings of religious subjects, like *The Holy Ghost of My Adolescence*, which demonstrate that the transcendent is present in the ordinary. But critic Judie Newman contends that Peter's admiration for Vermeer may have kept him from recognizing the suffering an artist must pass through, as depicted in a print that scares him, *The Flaying of Marsyas*. No doubt Peter, like Updike, responded primarily to Vermeer's uncanny ability to capture a moment in time that reveals depths of character in his people. Critic Larry Taylor suggests that the subtlety of Vermeer also may be seen in "The Bulgarian Poetess" (*MuS*), for objects and surfaces are "captured with a painterly boldness and imagistic clarity." Updike also suggests that first wives grow as transcendent as Vermeer's "girl with the pearl earring" (*OJ*). Critic James Schiff refers to Updike simply as "the Vermeer of American authors." *See* **Art**.

Bibliography: Updike, "An Outdoor Vermeer" (*JL*); "The Frick" (*MM*); Taylor, *PA*; Newman, *JU*; Schiff, *JU*; James Plath, "Verbal Vermeer: Updike's Middle-Class Portraiture," in Broer, *RT*.

Vietnam. A country in Southeast Asia, Vietnam has experienced war since the 1930s, with its Communist forces led by Ho Chi Minh.* After World War II Ho Chi Minh fought the French who had colonized French-Indochina. U.S. president Harry Truman supported the French, but by 1954 Ho Chi Minh forced a peace treaty that divided the country into North and South Vietnam, though the United States did not abide by the treaty, fearing that a "domino effect" would topple pro-Western countries such as Laos and Cambodia. Eventually the U.S. entered the war at the arranged request of South Vietnamese leaders. Ho Chi Minh's Vietminh were resourceful and determined, so the U.S., under Presidents John Kennedy* and Lyndon Johnson,* and forty other countries stepped up the war, Johnson acting under congressional authorization in the Gulf of Tonkin Resolution of 1964. Air Force generals promised "to bomb them back to the Stone Age," but the Tet Offensive of 1968 nearly destroyed the gains made by bombing North Vietnam. The war cost $25 billion a year and eventually 58,000 American lives. Increasing resistance at home and a sense that the war could not be won forced the U.S. government to engage in protracted negotiations. U.S. forces finally left in 1973, with a settlement established in 1975.

Though Updike had already alluded to the war in *Couples*, virtually in answer to repeated criticism that he should become more socially conscious, he explored the war quite closely in *RRed*, surprising his critics by using a black Vietnam veteran, Skeeter,* to tell of the waste and horror of the war. Updike uses the war in several different ways. First, Harry "Rabbit" Angstrom* (pro) quarrels about it with Charlie Stavros* (con), revealing not only an opposition of conservative and liberal values (hawk and dove, in the pro- and antiwar parlance of the time) but the suppressed rage Rabbit feels about the loss of American traditions and his willingness to accept authority and nationalism as sufficient excuse to support the war. The quarrel also exposes Rabbit's racism toward blacks, Native Americans and Asiatics, revealed when the quarrelers allude to characters from *The Lone Ranger** radio and television* series. Images from the series recur throughout *RRed* to form a pattern that virtually makes the war part of popular culture.* Rabbit is convinced that the war was, as he tells his sister Miriam Angstrom,* "a head fake" to keep the Communists off balance. Thus the war simply extends the Cold War with Russia, and Rabbit admits that the Cold War put structure into his life. But Charlie Stavros thinks that Rabbit's hawkish sentiments are anachronistic: "We-them. America first. It's dead." Rabbit's "we-them" value really rests on a fear of "the Other" and takes the form of sexism and racism. Ironically, Rabbit admits into his home the black veteran Skeeter, thus ushering the war into his parlor. Skeeter's attempts to explain the meaning of the war as he understands it, however, are ineffectual. Rabbit cannot accept his theory that the war is the start of a "black hole" of chaos that will cause a general race war, led by Skeeter as "the Black Messiah." Rabbit finally remains outwardly unaffected, even after his home is fire-bombed by a white Vietnam veteran.

Updike frequently underlines, though, subtle ways in which such arguments change Rabbit: his sexual combats with Jill Pendleton* use the war images of napalm bombing, and his negotiations with Stavros about the return of his wife, Janice Angstrom,* mimic the Paris Peace Talks. Rabbit's unwillingness to interfere in Skeeter's hooking Jill Pendleton on heroin duplicates how Vietnam soldiers passively accepted drug* addiction or actively became drug dealers. As Rabbit and Skeeter watch the television news of body counts and civil disturbances, Rabbit's fear of Black Power parallels the fear of the Vietcong felt by American soldiers. The war really comes home when the disfigured Vietnam veteran, Eddie Brumbach, warns Rabbit about his public friendship with Skeeter and about their too-visible sex* with Jill. Since Brumbach sees Rabbit as similar to "wiseass" lieutenants he had "fragged," Brumbach no doubt set fire to Rabbit's house, as "hooches" in Vietnam were routinely burned for allegedly harboring Vietcong; the homes were burned in order to "save" them. The war that had pitted soldier against soldier now supplies a rationale for the returning soldier to attack defenseless civilians—even Rabbit, whose flag decal on his Ford Falcon proclaims that he is a hawk on Vietnam. Despite being irritated by Stavros, shaken by Skeeter, and burned out by Brumbach, Rabbit returns to a comfortable conservatism in which America is still, as he thinks, "the smartest kid on the block," bringing sanity with its bombers. Though Janice, through Stavros's influence, is a "dove," the Angstroms are united at the end, as Vietnam would be.

Updike professed ideas similar to those of Rabbit in "On Not Being a Dove" (*SC*) and in a statement in a collection of remarks by writers about the war. The major difference between Updike and Rabbit resides in Updike's defense of Lyndon Johnson rather than the war, and in his disgust with the antiwar protestors' vilification of the president.

The war also stands significantly in the background of *W*. The narrative is set, as Updike's dust jacket says, "during the national *Walpurgisnacht* of the Vietnam era." Though no quarrels take place and no veteran returns to tell his tale, Unitarian* minister* Ed Parsley* speaks against the war and later joins the Weathermen, a violent underground protest band. Parsley's bravery results in his death. The war is subtly offered as a general cause for Eastwick's* witchery since the country "is laboring under a malignant spell" because "the corporate power structure" profits from it, as newspaper editor Clyde Gabriel trumpets. Only Jenny Gabriel, the dying wife of devilish Darryl Van Horne,* connects the moral confusion of war and the Eastwick witches: their power was "something they had loosed on the air," like "Eisenhower refusing to sign the truce with Ho Chi Minh that would have ended all the trouble." Jenny is dying of cancer*; the Vietnam War might be America's cancer. To fuse Jenny's insights with her own, Brenda Parsley* speaks in the Unitarian church of her dead husband to condemn "evil wrought in Southeast Asia by fascist politicians and an oppressive capitalism, seeking to secure and enlarge its markets."

A variation on the Rabbit/Skeeter violence is shown in *IB*, where Updike offers another sinister legacy of the war in Jesse Smith,* a Vietnam veteran who becomes obsessed with America as a land possessed by the devil. On his compound he seeks to isolate believers in his church and, after a violent confrontation with authorities, begins killing his followers to save their souls. Clark DeMott,* a passive follower, like Rabbit, eventually rebels and kills Smith. Updike has noted that the story "The Indian" (*MuS*) is in fact about a Vietnam veteran. Perhaps the sight of that veteran eventually stimulated Updike to create Smith, as his sight of ex–basketball* players in Shillington* prompted the invention of Rabbit.

In *S.* Updike wryly offers an oblique perspective on Vietnam. Arthur Steinmetz (the Arhat*) avoids the draft by fleeing to India and after fifteen years there founds an ashram that attracts many Westerners. Though Sarah Worth* is disgusted by his disguise as a religious leader, the study of Buddhism rather than the study of war could have saved much suffering. *See* **American History; Chomsky, Noam; Presidents**.

Bibliography: Updike, untitled statement, in *Authors Take Sides on Vietnam: Two Questions on the War in Vietnam Answered by the Authors of Several Nations*, ed. Cecil Woolf and John Bagguley (London: Peter Owen, 1967): 150–51; "On Not Being a Dove" (*SC*); "A 'Special Message' for the Franklin Library's First Edition Society Printing of *The Witches of Eastwick*" (*OJ*); Detweiler, *JU*; Greiner, *JU*; Newman, *JU*.

Voltaire (François-Marie Arouet) (1694–1778). The French writer-philosopher Voltaire is mentioned in *Coup* as one who made Christianity untenable by his rational Deist assaults. His *Philosophical Letters* (1734) attacked French ecclesiastical institutions, and in his *Essay on the Character of Nations* (1756) Voltaire refuted supernaturalism, religion* and the clergy, although he made evident his own belief in the existence of God. His masterpiece *Candide* resembles *RR* in tracing the adventures of a man who is hopeful in the face of the hypocrisy of institutions, and who, for a while, tends his own garden.

W

Waring, Fred (1900–1984). The American director of the Pennsylvanians, a choral group famous for intricate harmonic arrangements, Fred Waring had programs on radio and television* during the 1950s. He is mentioned by Brad Schaeffer in "Made in Heaven" (*TM*).

Weber, Max (1864–1920). Referred to by history professor Morrison in "Slippage" (*TM*), Max Weber was a German economist who showed that the development of Western civilization was influenced by things other than Marxist economics. His work *The Protestant Ethic and the Spirit of Capitalism* reveals the impact of religious ideas on capitalism.

Where the Wild Things Are. In *Couples* Piet Hanema's* little daughter Nancy Hanema* reads *Where the Wild Things Are*, an illustrated children's tale (1963) by Maurice Sendak. Since Nancy needs to control her anger at thoughts of death,* Sendak's book about how the creation of a fantasy world allows the management of anger is quite apt. Georgene Thorne does not manage her anger well. Once she discovers that Piet has returned to his lover Foxy Whitman,* she tells Foxy's husband, precipitating the dissolution of the Hanema and Whitman marriages. Sendak and Updike shared an interest in Mozart's *Magic Flute*, Sendak doing set and costume design for a 1980 production and Updike writing a child's version of the opera in 1962. *See* **Art**.

Whitman, Elizabeth Fox "Foxy." Foxy Whitman, Ken Whitman's* pregnant wife, arrives in Tarbox, an upper-middle-class suburb (*Couples*). Generous, intelligent and neglected, she falls in love with Piet Hanema* while she is pregnant. Foxy is at first alarmed that others have detected their affair, but she continues it through the birth of her child. Foxy and Piet discontinue their affair but Foxy becomes pregnant by Piet when they meet one last time, has an abortion* and is exposed to Ken by Piet's disgruntled ex-lover, Georgene Thorne. When Ken begins divorce proceedings, she writes Piet voluminous love letters from her island retreat. They eventually marry and leave Tarbox to become, elsewhere, another couple. *See* **Games**.

Whitman, Ken. The husband of Foxy Whitman,* Ken Whitman is a microbiologist who, like George Caldwell* (*C*), believes that "all we are is chemicals" (*Couples*). Ironically, Ken explores the source of life while his wife and child drift from him. Like Harry "Rabbit" Angstrom* in *RR*, Ken is partly to blame for Foxy's abortion,* since his neglect of her led to her taking a lover, Piet Hanema.* Foxy says that Ken loves life only at the molecular level, and his rigid refusal to accept her back may support her claim. In this he resembles Rabbit, who refused to take his wife Janice Angstrom* back after her affair in *RRed*, though he eventually relented. In his adamant refusal, Ken contrasts to other Updike men such as Roger Lambert* (*RV*) and Richard Mathias (according to one of the endings of *Marry*) who take their wives back after their indiscretions. Nor do the spouse-swapping men in *RIR* divorce their wives. Rev. Tom Marshfield* virtually arranges his wife's seduction and does not hold it against her (*MS*), nor does Rabbit's son Nelson Angstrom* intend to divorce his wife Teresa "Pru" Angstrom,* even though she slept with his father (*RaR*).

"Whitman's Egotheism." Originally given as a talk at the Morgan library in New York City on October 4, 1977, Updike published it as "Walt Whitman: Ego and Art" (*The New York Review of Books* 25 [9 Feb. 1978]:33–36), and with this title it was published as *Ego and Art in Walt Whitman* (New York: Targ, 1980), a signed, limited edition. Finally, it was reprinted in *HS* as "Whitman's Egotheism." *See* **Whitman, Walt**.

Whitman, Walt (1819–1892). Walt Whitman has been called America's greatest poet for his frequently revised magnum opus *Leaves of Grass* (1855). It was a fresh breeze for poetry, which had been dominated by "Fireside Poets," such as Henry Wadsworth Longfellow. *Leaves of Grass* contains a new American poetry with freedom of verse forms, colloquial diction, daring symbolism and fresh subjects. Whitman's use of rhythm based on incantatory repetition, sometimes through long catalogues of images, brought something decisively new to American versification. His break with rhyme and standard structures like sonnets and odes signaled a new direction that would have a profound impact on modern poetry. In subjects, Whitman celebrated individualism and all things American, including the carnage of the Mexican-American War and the Civil War. In so doing, he devised a persona that sometimes spoke autobiographically, sometimes as a representative of America, sometimes as a "seer" or bard speaking prophetically.

Whitman continued the transcendentalist* philosophical viewpoint of Ralph Waldo Emerson* and Henry David Thoreau* by focusing upon the individual's senses and attitudes, which often included the frankest depiction of sex* to that time, and by seeking a path to the organic unity of the universe.

Whitman's poetry influenced Updike's "Midpoint" (M), particularly in Updike's direct treatment of personal experiences, Updike's "eye/I" pun and explicit descriptions of sex. In this poem Updike quotes many lines from Whitman's "Song of Myself," ending with the democratic "What is commonest, cheapest / nearest, easiest is Me." Updike's essay on Whitman was much revised, eventually appearing as "Whitman's Egotheism" (HS). In it Updike argues that Whitman was American poetry's first prophet, who created in "Song of Myself," "a god whose palms cover continents, but also a God who enters into 'the egos of the suffering.' " Such egotheism created, for Updike, the "metaphysics" of a distinctive American realism. In addition, Whitman's effort to act as a representative man takes him beyond simple egotism.

In IB Updike seeks to celebrate America in Whitman's special terms, to "absorb" and "hymn" this "great rectangular country" as Whitman had, using film* for its epical presentation of America and metaphorically embodying the "rectangular country" in the rectangular movie screen. Like Whitman, Updike peoples his novel with a kaleidoscope of Americans, from postmen to religious fanatics. In S. Sarah Worth* makes a "passage to India," to use the title of a Whitman poem, in seeking spiritual replenishment in the American West. Critic George Hunt finds Henry Bech's* Travel Light "Whitmanesque," and critic James Schiff calls Updike "our contemporary Whitman for his absorption of American attitudes and history." The story "Leaves" (MuS) ends with the narrator reading Whitman's Leaves of Grass. See Poetry.

Bibliography: Updike, "Midpoint" (M); "Whitman's Egotheism" (HS); Hunt, JU; Schiff, JU.

Williams, Robert F. (1925?–1996). A black activist who organized a chapter of the National Rifle Association composed of blacks in Monroe, North Carolina, Williams aided black demonstrators being beaten by police. The furor surrounding his return from China to Detroit excites Skeeter,* Jill Pendleton* and Nelson Angstrom,* despite the indifference of Nelson's father, Harry "Rabbit" Angstrom* (RRed). See African Americans.

Wilmot, Reverend Clarence. The problem set for ministers* in RV and MS, their inability to reconcile sex* with church law, changes in IB to a dramatic failure of faith. Clarence Wilmot's spontaneous leap of nonfaith arises from his inability to reply to the arguments of the proponents of crisis theology, to the assaults upon biblical truth or to the protestations of the

Apostles' Creed (*IB*). The minister of the Fourth Presbyterian Church in Paterson, New Jersey, in the 1910s, Clarence Wilmot suddenly loses his faith by reading Robert Ingersoll as well as German religious realists who challenged the divinity of Jesus. He rejects his ministry, choking on his final sermon, which his wife finishes. After a year's enforced sabbatical (compare Rev. Tom Marshfield's in *MS*), he can neither retrieve his lost faith nor accept the realistic compromises offered by a church elder. Wilmot gives up the ministry and becomes an encyclopedia salesman during a recession in Paterson, providing "the word" in a noble, massive book that purports to include all knowledge. The ritualistic entrance into homes and offices enables him to meet individually the congregation he could no longer address collectively. Since few can afford to buy the books, Wilmot spends his free time in nickelodeons and becomes captivated by the screen's magnified images of life and the ease with which nickelodeons transport him to real and imaginary places. As he slowly dies of tuberculosis, his son, Ted Wilmot,* curses God for not having provided Wilmot the faith he craved. (Like Harry "Rabbit" Angstrom,* Clarence Wilmot deserted his family to await some sign; neither receives that message.) Ted's daughter Essie Wilmot* keeps her grandfather's memory alive, since he kindled her interest in movies. Figuratively, she carries on his ministry, using the movie screen as a pulpit. Essie's son, Wilmot's great-grandson, Clark DeMott,* also feels Wilmot's spiritual energy by becoming involved with the fanatic Jesse Smith.* But Clark kills Smith when he realizes that the cult leader intends to massacre his congregation for the sake of their souls. As Wilmot had gathered a congregation, so does Smith with a charisma rooted in his convictions and tempered in the heat of the Vietnam* War. Smith's dedication to the Bible's* fundamental words provides the reply to the crisis theologians Wilmot could not devise.

Wilmot, Essie/Alma DeMott. The daughter of Ted Wilmot* and Esther Wilmot (*IB*), Essie Wilmot follows her dream of becoming a film* star and goes from ribbons to riches. She appears in high-school plays, models for a photographer and then goes to Hollywood, where she is interviewed by legendary mogul Harry Cohn, who rechristens her Alma DeMott. She quickly becomes a star and, since she has learned that sex* is Hollywood's currency, the bed partner of stars, as she glides from marriage to marriage and from film to television.* Alma senses that she has continued the work of her grandfather by ministering to millions as the "star" in the Hollywood "heaven"—"Alma DeMott," whose name could be translated the "soul of the demotic," the essence of the ordinary person.

The "Essie/Alma" chapter of secular transcendence is neatly sandwiched between chapters in which Clarence Wilmot* reduces God to rational scrutiny and the last chapter, in which biblical fanaticism sacrifices Alma's son to apocalypse. Alma offers a modern sort of transcendence through the identification of the mass audience with her screen roles. This carries forward the subjective conviction of her grandfather, Clarence Wilmot, in a positive way that is linked to public service. Clarence had been unable to reply to arguments of crisis theologians concerning the truth of the Word. She answers them by using screen images that are understood as self-transcending, without words. Alma's great discovery was that the material and the immaterial could be linked through film's art of illusion. Her dedication to this discovery leads to her neglect of her son, Clark DeMott,* who becomes mesmerized by the magnetic Jesse Smith's* understandings of the Bible.* Alma's conflicted feelings about helping him overturn Smith while she loses precious time away from advancing her career resemble Janice Angstrom's* decision to put her real-estate quiz before her husband Harry "Rabbit" Angstrom's* return from his frightening angioplasty (*RaR*).

Bibliography: Schiff, *JU*.

Wilmot, Ted. The son of Clarence Wilmot* in *IB*, Ted Wilmot rejects the chance to go to New York* with his brother Jared and live an exciting but shady existence, preferring to return to Baskingstoke, Delaware, a small town Updike lovingly re-creates, perhaps modeled on Shillington.* While working as a soda jerk, Ted meets Esther and later marries her. Eventually he becomes a postman in the 1920s, and as a mediator in communication, he supports his daughter Essie Wilmot's* interest in movies and the choices that lead her to fame. He rises steadily but without real ambition. In his enthusiasm for his daughter and in his ordinary life Ted resembles Harry "Rabbit" Angstrom.* As Rabbit could not understand why God did not save his drowning daughter and became increasingly unreligious, so Ted becomes an atheist because God did not help his father Clarence's unbelief.

Wilson, Edmund (1895–1972). An American literary critic, Edmund Wilson published a great number of books, including a study of symbolist poetry (*Axel's Castle* 1931), a ground-breaking Freudian* study of Henry James* in *The Triple Thinkers*, 1938, a survey of the literature of the American Civil War (*Patriotic Gore*, 1962) and a study of Canada (*O Canada*, 1965). Immensely interested in diverse subjects, Wilson also wrote about American Indians, the Dead Sea Scrolls and the Russian writer Alexander Pushkin. While producing these volumes, he gathered his reviews and articles by decades into chronicles of American writing and published them as *The Twenties*, *The Thirties*, and so on. Wilson edited the posthumous papers of F. Scott Fitzgerald, including *The Last Tycoon*. He also published several volumes of poems, plays and journals. In his review of a late journal volume, Updike notes Wilson's immense activity late in life, though Wilson was depressingly aware of "the relative feebleness and futility of human lives" ("Wilson as Cape Codder" [*MM*]).

Wilson dominated American criticism throughout the twentieth century because of "the force of his character, as much as his erudition and taste," in Updike's words. He helped establish Vladimir Nabokov* in America and championed writers who were attempting to break the hold of American Puritanism. His novel *I Thought of Daisy*, like the stories collected as *Memoirs of Hecate County* (which may have influenced *Couples*), was sufficiently sexually explicit to have been censored for a time. *Current Biographical Yearbook 1984* has called Updike "a legatee of the tradition of Edmund Wilson." *See* **American Literature**.

Bibliography: Updike, "Edmund Wilson's Fiction: A Personal Account," "An Earlier Day," The Cuckoo and the Rooster" (*HS*); "Edmund Wilson" (*OJ*); "Wilson as Cape Codder" (*MM*).

The Witches of Eastwick (New York: Knopf, 1984). Updike's novel *W* enters the occult for the first time in Updike's career by examining witchcraft in a contemporary setting, and the subject provides an opportunity to explore other religious matters regarding evil he had examined in the "*Scarlet Letter* trilogy" (*MS, RV* and *S.*). At the same time, Updike explores related issues of feminism,* satirically and seriously.

Three divorcées, journalist Sukie Rougemont,* cellist Jane Smart* and sculptor Alexandra "Lexa" Spofford,* exercise magical powers to disengage from their husbands, pursue their careers and take as their lover New York* entrepreneur Darryl Van Horne,* who encourages them to expand their talents. Meanwhile, they prankishly cast a spell over Felicia Gabriel, the wife of Sukie's editor and lover Clyde Gabriel, forcing house dirt to spew from her mouth. In despair over his affair and his wife's shrewishness, Gabriel murders his wife and hangs himself. Van Horne seduces the willing witches by lavishly entertaining them by playing the piano, giving them drugs* and exotic drinks and teaching them to fly. They are charmed and amazed by his collection of pop art,* his frank animality and his passionate scheme to find a loophole in the second law of thermodynamics, entropy. He urges Lexa to construct massive statues, not mere dolls, encourages Sukie to write novels, not hack journalism, and pushes Jane to greater challenges as a cellist. The witches consummate their Halloween Sabbath in Darryl's hot tub. After Gabriel's death, his daughter Jenny Gabriel and son Christopher Gabriel arrive, and after Jenny marries Van Horne and becomes pregnant, the scorned witches try to give her cancer* through an effigy doll. Jenny dies, perhaps from the spell. Meanwhile, Unitarian* minister Ed Parsley* runs away with teenager Dawn Polanski and is blown up making a bomb with which to protest the Vietnam* War; his wife Brenda* takes his place and sermonizes against the war and the witches. Van Horne, grieving for Jenny, provides a parodic sermon, "This Is a Terrible Creation," then leaves Eastwick* with his new lover, Christopher. The witches conjure new husbands and leave as Eastwick braces for the formation of a new witches' coven.

Two arresting themes of *W* are the emergence of evil in middle-class society and the relation of evil to feminism. Updike transferred Harry "Rabbit" Angstrom's* quest for "the thing that wants me to find it" to Van Horne's power that agitates and makes more unhappy modern women seeking some "thing" to empower them. Updike had always been concerned with such a demonic force, and Van Horne's origin can be traced to hard-hearted Stephen Connor* (*PF*) and impotent Freddy Thorne,* who saw the couples of Tarbox as "a magic circle of heads to keep the night out" (*Couples*). Since Thorne is from "Hell's Kitchen" and is thus a New Yorker, like Van Horne (their names even chime), he provides Updike with a sardonic reflection on New York, where he worked from 1955 to 1957. Thorne gains power during John Kennedy's* assassination, and Van Horne and the witches during the Vietnam War. The war represents intrinsic disorder that permits the emergence of witches and the devil. While they jealously plan the death of a rival, Van Horne seeks a way to circumvent natural laws while simultaneously unleashing evil in women through their craving for empowerment.

Updike has said that he wrote the novel as "a male attempt to look at . . . aspects of feminism," and to find out "what it's like to be a free woman . . . and the consolation that they find in each other." Such consolation was a threat to sexist characters like Rabbit, whose fears are realized in *W*: women with power take control, prove to be amoral and destructive and fail as mothers and productive citizens. Above all, they permit the arrival of Van Horne by dealing in the black arts. They cannot resist Van Horne's temptations, which flatter their craving for power, and such basic dependency on male support weakens their independence. The empowerment of women also causes suffering among men: the witches appear to have dispatched their husbands, lust for Sukie drives Clyde Gabriel to murder and suicide, and Van Horne publicly denounces all creation when his wife is afflicted with cancer. While playing a Bach suite, Jane Smart even discovers man's chief secret, the knowledge of death.* The very emergence of the witches seems to have prompted the presence of Van Horne in Eastwick. He provides them, Updike has said, with a "quality that women seem to like, of stirring them up and permitting them to *be*" (Plath, *CU*). The symbol of corrupt masculinity, Van Horne is not only a cynical womanizer (Jane is quick to see that his apparent sympathy with women's and witches' historical suffering was only a seduction ploy) but a betrayer of his wife, since he seems to have married Jenny only to seduce her brother. As a homosexual, he is incapable of progeny, what Updike may have meant by referring to Van Horne's homosexuality* as "nature's joke." He also adores pop art images that mock heterosexuality. Van Horne's effort to defy waste in nature only reveals his own disgust at creation. In mythology the Horned God is the giver of life and death, and the witches called him to Eastwick. Ironically,

Updike has called Van Horne an "educator . . . liberator . . . facilitator." Structurally, then, the relation of the witches to Van Horne is similar to that of Rabbit to Skeeter* (*RRed*).

The novel does not mock women's liberation so much as it unveils where its excesses might lead. Also, it roots the arrival of witchcraft in the Vietnam War, a particularly male event. But to keep the novel from becoming a tract, Updike employs comedy* rooted in magic realism* and black humor.* Tennis balls defy gravity, moths are emitted from a club woman's mouth, and storms are willed into existence. Laughs end in groans and vice versa, as in the character of Van Horne himself, with his head like a beer glass's handle, his patchwork clothes, his New York cab driver's accent and his vulgar renditions of popular musical* classics. Updike also uses images of hell and witches to keep the surface texture deceptively amusing: the witches cavort with Van Horne in his tub in a parody of the witches' cauldron and their burnings at the stake, while Van Horne explains the persecution of witches in terms of medieval doctors' fear of their loss of virility. A "red flag" to feminists, but only partly so, because neither sex can claim to be wholly good or evil, the narrative has exposed how casually the modern world takes evil. Updike thus continues what he called his "moral debates with the reader," in which he asks, what is goodness, what is a good man? (Plath, *CU*). The question has broadened to "What is a good society?" since in Eastwick Van Horne is permitted to castigate God's creation in the Unitarian church. As Clyde Gabriel observed, "I'm not sure the Unitarians care that much about God." Gabriel does, and he turns his telescope to the stars for his answers, but receives nothing definitive.

Bibliography: Updike, "Special Message for the Franklin Library Edition of *The Witches of Eastwick*" (*OJ*); Margaret Atwood, "Wondering What It's Like to Be a Woman," *New York Times Book Review* 13 May 1984: 1, 40; Diane Johnson, "Warlock," *New York Review of Books* 31 (14 June 1984): 3–4; Katha Pollitt, "Bitches and Witches," *Nation* 239 (23 June 1984): 773–75; Kathleen Verduin, "Sex, Nature and Dualism in *The Witches of Eastwick*," *Modern Language Quarterly* 46 (Sept. 1985): 293–315; Charles Berryman, "Updike and Contemporary Witchcraft," *South Atlantic Quarterly* 85 (1986): 1–9; Newman, *JU*.

Woolf, Virginia (1882–1941). The English novelist Virginia Woolf is mentioned by Harold little-Smith to display his knowledge of Woolf's difficult stream-of-consciousness novel *The Waves*, in which images and symbols are used as if they were musical themes to reveal the inner lives of characters (*Couples*). Woolf was influenced by James Joyce* and Marcel Proust,* writers Updike greatly admires. *See* **English Literature**.

Worth, Sarah. The letter-writing narrator of *S.*, Sarah Price Worth is, with Janice Angstrom,* Updike's most achieved female character. She abandons her rich "doctor husband" (as she calls him) to join an ashram in Arizona and study with the Arhat* in order to find inner peace. Her letters and audio tapes, which comprise this novel, tell how she rejected her much-loved upper-class life and pursued transcendence. Her elegant style is highly concrete, including advice on how to avoid beauty aids that harm hair sheen, how to operate a forklift truck and how to conceal money in Bermuda banks. Her epistles to her philistine friends are angry, sentimental, controlling, ironic and condescending. After she becomes the Arhat's secretary, she writes letters for him that are quasi-mystical, protective and cavalierly dismissive. Two letters to her husband form "bookends" to her narrative: in the first she tearfully, bitterly renounces him, his infidelity and his materialistic life. In the last she cleverly tries to manipulate him with erotic images. Her quest for enlightenment marks her related detailed descriptions of the inner workings of the ashram, her heterosexual and lesbian affairs there and her misunderstanding with the Arhat over the term "inner peace." Acquainted with the language of the *Kama Sutra** and of the Indian religions, she peppers her letters with dozens of Hindi words, using them casually even when writing to her mother. After the Arhat is unmasked as a fraud, Sarah still continues her spiritual quest, abetted by ashram funds she has embezzled. Updike uses Sarah as a satirical device in order to expose the hypocrisy of the Arhat, the absurdities of the Massachusetts North Shore elite and the inconsistencies in Sarah, who is caught between religion* and riches.

In addition to the satire, *S.* is the third novel of the "*Scarlet Letter* trilogy" (with *MS* and *RV*) and thus is Updike's version of Hester Prynne's story as told by Sarah. Consequently, Updike salts her digressive letters with allusions to Hawthorne's* novel: Sarah's "S" is crimson on the book's dust jacket, an explicit scarlet letter; she has monogram embroidery recalling Hester's intricately woven badge of shame; she insists on the wonders of vitamin A, thus becoming associated with the letter *A* as Hester was; she makes herself, like Hester, integral to the community; she tries to instruct her daughter to fend off her father, as Hester did with Pearl and Chillingworth; she pursues the holiest man in the community; and like Hester, Sarah retreats to a little house by the ocean. Updike merges the Hawthorne allusions to the Hindu imagery* when he blends Hester's scarlet "S" to the image of the Hindu serpent "Kundalini," the source of Sarah's sexual and spiritual power.

Like Hester, Sarah is used as a moral touchstone, exposing the hypocrisy of her community, but Updike also reveals comically her self-interest and hypocrisy, as when she interferes in the marital plans of both her daughter and her mother and then her ex-friend Midge and Charles Worth. She is a goad to feminist critics like Mary Allen and Mary Godwin who find Updike's portraits of women reprehensible, and particularly to Alison Lurie, who sees Sarah as "a wholly hateful woman," offended that Updike deigns to use as a model Hester Prynne, the strongest woman in American literary history and therefore a feminist saint. Even so, Sarah represents Updike's persistent effort to explore the mystery of womanhood.

Bibliography: Alison Lurie, "The Woman Who Rode Away," *New York Review of Books* 35 (12 May 1988): 3–4.

Writing Routine of Updike. Updike has explained that he writes every day but Sunday for three hours in the morning. As he notes, "Like snowflakes falling a certain accumulation will result." Different kinds of writing take place in several different rooms: books in one, correspondence in another (mostly on postcards with blue return-address hand-stamp, and dated but without the year), and in another room Updike uses the computer for novels. Until the arrival of the computer he wrote in pencil, and he still writes poems and essays in pencil or pen. He writes poetry* mainly on airplanes* and in hotels and composed "Seagulls" (*TP*) on the beach. When Updike wrote *Couples*, he said, he plotted it "almost entirely in church—little shivers and urgencies I would note down on the program" (Plath, *CU*). He usually only begins a book when he knows where it is going. Part of his writing routine, therefore, is to discover if a work "has legs," and if it does not, he sets it aside. The short story "Couples," he discovered, had hidden legs, and he later expanded it into the novel. He has remarked that "there isn't a lot of revision in my work," since things either "grind to a halt or keep on moving." Yet many of his manuscripts reveal a good deal of reworking, though to create such a volume of work, Updike must be capable of writing at speed with little second-guessing.

Bibliography: Updike, "One Big Interview" (*PP*); Jane Howard, "Can a Nice Novelist Finish First?" *Life* 61 (4 Nov. 1966): 74–74A, 74C, 74D, 76, 79–82; Charles Thomas Samuels, "The Art of Fiction XLII John Updike," *The Paris Review* 12 (Winter 1968): 84–117.

"Wynken, Blynken and Nod." "Wynken, Blynken and Nod" is a poem written in 1892 by an American writer of children's verse, Eugene Field (1850–1895), notable for "Little Boy Blue." It is quoted in "Conjunction" (*A*).

Y

Yalta Conference. The Crimean city of Yalta on the Black Sea was the site where, three months before the end of World War II, Joseph Stalin, Franklin Roosevelt* and Winston Churchill* discussed postwar Europe. The Yalta Declaration stated that Germany would never again be a military power, war criminals would be tried in court, and reparations would be demanded of Germany, which would be divided into zones controlled by England, France, the United States and the Soviet Union. Free elections would be held throughout Europe, and a conference of nations would meet in April. Poland was ceded to the Soviet Union, which agreed to declare war on Japan. In *C Minor* contends that the Yalta Declaration betrayed Europe and that communism would capture France and Italy. Though Peter Caldwell* thinks that Minor's "black republican stupidity" is irrational, he reminds him that the Yalta Declaration was intended to map a plan that would beat Adolph Hitler, and that communism is inevitable and a good idea. The argument reveals the paranoia some felt toward communism while displaying Peter, as Prometheus, providing knowledge in the face of madness. *See* **History; Presidents**.

Bibliography: Updike, "Descent of an Image," "A Response to a Request, from *Life*, to Remember Pearl Harbor" (*MM*).

"Yes, but." In an interview* Updike stated that his early novels intended to treat seriously both the need for freedom and the requirements of society. As he said: "Yes, in *Rabbit, Run*, to our inner urgent whispers, but—the social fabric collapses murderously. Yes, in *The Centaur*, to self-sacrifice and duty, but—what of a man's private agony and dwindling? No, in *The Poorhouse Fair*, to social homogenization and loss of faith, but—listen to the voices, the joy of persistent existence. No, in *Couples*, to a religious community founded on physical and psychical interpenetration, but—what else shall we do, as God destroys our churches?" (Plath, *CU*). The comments suggest a dualism* that pulls man in opposite directions, toward personal aggrandizement and toward concern for others.

Updike's *RR* and *C* were written to address both sides, the "private agony" that causes Harry "Rabbit" Angstrom* to desert his family for "the thing" that represented his lost sense of specialness, and his very real desire to be a husband and father. He makes love to Ruth Leonard Byer* "as he would to his wife," then deserts her when she threatens his family. It is tragic that he must, in the end, choose between his family with his wife, Janice Angstrom,* and a family with Ruth, whom he has impregnated. In *C* George Caldwell* is capable of rejecting a goddesslike gym teacher in order to preserve his family, even though his wife is hardened to him and his son Peter* wishes that he would die. He sacrifices himself daily for his son, something Peter does not understand until he is an adult. Caldwell is unusual among Updike heroes in being able to restrain his fear of "inner dwindling."

RA continues to explore "yes, but" as Rabbit repeatedly jeopardizes his family for his freedom, most sensationally in *RRed*, but at the end of his life in *RaR*, although he comes out of retirement to help repair the damage his son has done to the family business, he nearly ruins his son's family by giving in to his daughter-in-law Teresa "Pru" Angstrom's* overtures, exactly the temptation Caldwell avoided. The pattern persists in many other novels. For example, in *IB* Clarence Wilmot* must affirm the truth of his loss of faith, but that means losing his ministry and reducing his family to poverty. When his granddaughter, Essie Wilmot,* follows her star to become a great film* actress, her neglect of her son contributes to his death. In *TE* Ben Turnbull's* wish for freedom causes a "branching" in which he thinks that he may have murdered his wife; unworried, he has a tryst with a prostitute, as though he were Rabbit sleeping with Ruth Leonard. But later Ben's pursuit of a teenager carries no consequences. This may be Updike's only novel in which the "inner urgent whispers" are pursued, but the social fabric does not unravel.

Perhaps Ben is like Karl Barth,* whom Updike characterized as "a bit of a 'yes, but' and a master at having it both ways" (Plath, *CU*). With "but" gone, Updike suggests, what remains but "yes"? The opposition of "yes, but" is related to many other dualisms in Updike's work, like the pastoral* and antipastoral, science* and religion,* heaven and earth, and heart and brain. Often they are mixed together, as when Rabbit, observing the naked Pru, thinks, "Paradise," or when Dale Kohler* follows his affirmation that God is discoverable with an ambiguous image of Him on his computer monitor (*RV*). Updike suggested that the "yes, but" dualism resembles Søren Kierkegaard's "either/or," so that "no sooner do you look at one side than you see the other again" (Plath, *CU*). The "yes, but" formula is persistent in

Updike's work because it offers the best chance to display the ambiguity and truth at the heart of human action.

Bibliography: Charles Thomas Samuels, "The Art of Fiction XLII: John Updike" *The Paris Review* 12 (Wint. 1968): 84–117.

Yin and Yang. In Chinese philosophical naturalism the universe was viewed through the duality of yin and yang, opposed natural forces, most often imaged as male and female. When a nurse takes vials of his blood in treating his psoriasis, the narrator of "From the Journal of a Leper" wants to "counteract" the flow of blood by sucking her breasts, thinking, "Yin and Yang, mutually feeding" (*P*). Since change is of considerable importance to him (as he changes his leprosy for clear skin, his pottery declines artistically and he loses his mistress), the reference to yin and yang may involve the Chinese *I Ching*, a book that gives directions for divinations. *See* **Dualisms**.

Z

Zimmerman, Louis. The Olinger High School principal, Louis Zimmerman tries to discredit and destroy science* teacher George Caldwell* in *C*. When Zimmerman visits Caldwell's science class, he tries to seduce one of the students and then writes a negative report on Caldwell's teaching. Zimmerman later writes Caldwell's premature obituary and hounds him over lost basketball* tickets. Meek Caldwell accepts this and, though he had seen Zimmerman in a compromising situation, does not try to use this against him. Instead, his son Peter Caldwell* confronts Zimmerman and defends his father's loyalty and honesty. Zimmerman's mythic analogue is Zeus, head of Olympus, seducer of Io (Iris Osgood) and squelcher of rebellious Prometheus. Caldwell as Chiron* thinks that Zeus fears being "transmuted into pure irrelevance" by beings such as centaurs, a dangerous middle ground between gods and animals. In human terms, this is the customary fear of administrators that the faculty might usurp their power and prerogatives. *See* **Myth**.

Bibliography: Hamilton and Hamilton, *EJ*.

Appendix I: Chronological List of the Works of John Updike

The Carpentered Hen and Other Tame Creatures (1958)

The Poorhouse Fair (1959)

The Same Door (1959)

Rabbit, Run (1960)

The Magic Flute (1962)

Pigeon Feathers (1962)

The Centaur (1963)

Telephone Poles (1963)

The Ring (1964)

Assorted Prose (1965)

A Child's Calendar (1965)

Of the Farm (1965)

The Music School (1966)

Couples (1968)

Bottom's Dream (1969)

Midpoint and Other Poems (1969)

Bech: A Book (1970)

Rabbit Redux (1971)

Museums and Women and Other Stories (1972)

Seventy Poems (1972)

Buchanan Dying (1974)

A Month of Sundays (1975)

Picked-up Pieces (1975)

Marry Me: A Romance (1976)

Tossing and Turning (1977)

The Coup (1978)

Problems and Other Stories (1979)

Talk from the Fifties (1979)

Too Far to Go (1979)

Rabbit Is Rich (1981)

Bech Is Back (1982)

Hugging the Shore (1983)

Jester's Dozen (1984)

The Witches of Eastwick (1984)

Facing Nature (1985)

Roger's Version (1986)

Trust Me (1987)

S. (1988)

Just Looking (1989)

Self-Consciousness (1989)

Rabbit at Rest (1990)

Odd Jobs (1991)

Memories of the Ford Administration (1992)

Collected Poems, 1953–1993 (1993)

Love Factories (1993)

The Afterlife and Other Stories (1994)

Brazil (1994)

A Helpful Alphabet of Friendly Objects (1995)

Rabbit Angstrom: A Tetralogy (1995)

Scenes from the Fifties (1995)

Golf Dreams (1996)

In the Beauty of the Lilies (1996)

Toward the End of Time (1997)

Bech at Bay (1998)

Of Prizes and Print: Remarks Delivered on the Occasion of His Receiving the 1998 National Book Foundation Medal for Distinguished Contribution to American Letters (1998)

More Matter (1999)

Gertrude and Claudius (2000)

Licks of Love (2000)

Appendix II: Films and Film Personalities in the Works of John Updike

Like other subjects such as science, religion, history and sports, film constantly appears in Updike's work, but unlike the other interests, film proliferates in all his work except the nineteenth-century drama *BD* and the sixteenth-century *GC*. His novels constantly use film allusions to underline character, and film plots often counterpoint Updike's plots and underscore theme. In *IB* Updike explores the rise of a film actress. In his poetry he eulogizes movie theaters, and in his essays and reviews in his last nonfiction collection, *MM*, he shows the enthusiasm of a true devotee. Additionally, Updike wanted to work as a Disney animator when he was young and undertook the integration of film and fiction techniques in his early fiction. An investigation of individual films, like *2001: A Space Odyssey*, or film personalities, like Doris Day, reveals much about Updike's craft of fiction, his conception of the artist and the interrelation of popular culture and art. A study of other films and film personalities in the following lists may also prove worthwhile.

The work abbreviation after each entry indicates Updike's earliest use. Conjectured titles are indicated by titles in brackets [ ]. Possibly fictitious titles are marked "F?"

FILMS

Adam's Rib (IB)

The Adventures of Marco Polo (MM)

Affair in Trinidad (IB)

Agatha (RIR)

The Age of Innocence (MM)

Air Force One (BaB)

Aladdin (MM)

Alexander Nevsky (IB)

Alice in Wonderland (MM)

Alien (RIR)

All That Heaven Allows (OJ)

All the Way (RIR)

All You Need Is Love (OJ)

American Beauty (LL)

An American in Paris (MM)

The Amityville Horror (RIR)

Anatomy of a Murder (IB)

Anchor's Aweigh (MM)

And God Created Woman (*JL*)

L'Année des méduses (*OJ*)

Annie Laurie (*HS*)

The Apartment (*Concerts at Castle Hill*)

Apocalypse Now (*IB*)

The Assault (*OJ*)

Baby Breaks the Bank (*IB*; F?)

Baby Doll (*IB*)

The Bad and the Beautiful (*MM*)

Bambi (*MM*)

Barbarella (*SC*)

Beau Geste (*IB*)

Beauty and the Beast (*MM*)

[Bedtime for Bonzo] (*IB*)

Being There (*SC*)

Bell, Book and Candle (*RR*)

Ben Hur (*OJ*)

The Bicycle Thief (*IB*)

The Big Sleep (*Chatterbox*, 25 Oct. 1946)

Bitter Rice (*IB*)

Black Orpheus (*MM*)

The Black Watch (*IB*)

Blade Runner (*IB*)

Blow-up (*IB*)

The Blue Angel (*OJ*)

Bob and Carol and Ted and Alice (*IB*)

La Bohème (*HS*)

Bonnie and Clyde (*IB*)

Das Boot (*SC*)

Breaking Away (*RIR*)

The Bridge on the River Kwai (*IB*)

Broadcast News (*OJ*)

Bugs Bunny cartoon (*C*)

Bus Stop (*IB*)

Butch Cassidy and the Sundance Kid
    (*RRed*)

But Now Is Forever (*IB*; F?)

Calder's Hands (*CP*)

Call to Arms (*IB*)

Camille (*SD*)

Campus Confidential (*MM*)

The Canary Murder Case (*HS*)

Caprice (*HS*)

Carry On Cleo (*OJ*)

Casablanca (*S.*)

Casey and His Strawberry Blond (*IB*; F?)

Cass Timberlane (*MM*)

La Chartreuse de Parme (*IB*)

Chicago Confidential (*MM*)

Christmas Holiday (*MM*)

Circus (*RRed*)

Citizen Kane (*HS*)

City Lights (*OJ*)

[Civil War] (*MF*)

Cleopatra (*OJ*)

Close Encounters of the Third Kind (*RIR*)

Cocoon (*IB*)

Colored Entrance (*IB*; F?)

Con Air (*BaB*)

Cousin, Cousine (*MF*)

Cover Girl (*MM*)

Cream Cheese and Caviar (*IB*; F?)

Creepshow II (*OJ*)

Cross My Heart (*Chatterbox*,
    14 Mar. 1946)

Cyrano de Bergerac (*MM*)

Dangerous Liaisons (*MM*)

Dark Victory (*MM*)

Deer Hunter (*SC*)

The Delinquents (*IB*; F?)

Depraved (*RRed*; F?)

The Devil and Daniel Webster (*PP*)

The Devil in Miss Jones (*PP*)

Dr. Bull (*PP*)

Dr. Jekyll and Mr. Hyde (*HS*)

La Dolce Vita (*HS*)

Duel in the Sun (*IB*)

Due notte con Cleopatra (*OJ*)

Dumbo (*RaR*)

Easter Parade (*MM*)

Easy Rider (*IB*)

Ecstasy (*JL*)

Elephant Walk (*IB*)

Elvira Madigan (*PP*)

The Enemy (*HS*)

Les Enfants terribles (*IB*)

Escape from Alcatraz (*RIR*)

E.T. (*RaR*)

Ethan Frome (*MM*)

Ethiopia: The Unknown Famine (*OJ*)

Face/Off (*BaB*)

False Dawn (*IB*; *F?*)

Fantasia (*A*)

Fantastic Voyage (*SC*)

Film noir (*MF*)

Flesh and the Devil (*IB*)

Flying Down to Rio (Interview, *Good Morning America* 2 Feb, 1994)

Forever Amber (*IB*)

For Me and My Gal (*MM*)

For Whom the Bell Tolls (*OJ*)

Frankenstein (*AP*)

The French Connection (*MM*)

From Here to Eternity (*IB*)

Funny Face (*IB*)

Funny Girl (*RRed*)

The Gang's All Here (*MM*)

The Gadsden Purchase (*IB*; *F?*)

Gaslight (*OJ*)

Ghostbusters (*IB*)

Gigi (*RR*)

Gilda (*IB*)

The Godfather (*MM*)

The Godfather: II (*MF*)

Gone with the Wind (*MM*)

The Graduate (*IB*)

The Great Barrier Reef (*IB*)

The Great Gatsby (*OJ*)

The Great Train Robbery (*IB*)

The Group (*OJ*)

Hall, Jon, movie, possibly *South of Pago Pago* (1939), *The Tuttles of Tahiti* (1941) or *Hurricane Island* (1950) (*RIR*)

Hamlet (Olivier, director) (*Chatterbox*, 25 Feb. 1949)

Hamlet (Branagh, director) (*GC*)

Harem Girls (*RIR*)

The Harvey Girls (*IB*)

The Heiress (*IB*)

High Noon (*IB*)

His Girl Friday (*MM*)

Hobby Heaven (*RRed*)

Holmes, Sherlock, film (*P*)

Honeymoon in Swapland (*RRed*; *F?*)

Howl from the Streets (*IB*; *F?*)

How to Sleep (*MM*)

I Am Curious Yellow (*RRed*)

The Imitation of Life (*MM*)

I'm on My Way to Dublin Bay (*IB*; *F?*)

The Incredible and Sad Tale of Innocent Erendira and Her Heartless Grandmother (*MM*)

[*Indiana Jones and the Last Crusade*] (*IB*)

The Inn of the Sixth Happiness (*RR*)

[*International Squadron*] (*RIR*)

In the Heat of the Night (*IB*)

Invitation to the Dance (*MM*)

It (*IB*)

It Happened in Brooklyn (*Chatterbox*, 1 Apr. 1946)

It's Always Fair Weather (*MM*)

Ivanhoe (*IB*)

Japanese films (*SD*)

Jaws II (*RIR*)

The Ox-Bow Incident (IB)

[*The Pajama Game*] *(PF)*

Pal Joey (MM)

Pandora's Box (HS)

[*Penny Serenade*] *(IB)*

Peyton Place (MM)

Pinocchio (SC)

The Pirate (MM)

A Place in the Sun (RIR)

Plane Crazy (MM)

Platoon (SC)

Popeye cartoon *(C)*

Pornographic video *(IB)*

Postcards from the Edge (Esquire, Aug. 1992)

The Postman Always Rings Twice (IB)

The Prince and the Pauper (IB)

The Prisoner of Zenda (IB)

Pulp Fiction (Salon interview, 1 Dec. 1996)

Rabbit, Run (HS)

Ragtime (OJ)

Rebecca (IB)

Red River (IB)

*Red Rock Afternoon (IB)*F?

Reds (HS)

The Red Shoes (IB)

Reluctant Dragon (MM)

Remembrance of Things Past (SD)

The Return of Martin Guerre (RaR)

Road to Rio (MM)

Romance on the High Seas (HS)

The Roommates (OJ)

Rope (IB)

Running (RIR)

The Russia House (MM)

*Safe at Your Peril (IB)*F?

Saludos Amigos (MM)

Samson and Delilah (MM)

The Scarlet Letter (HS)

Scenes from the Class Struggle in Beverly Hills (MM)

The Searchers (SD)

See Here, Private Hargrove (MM)

*Sepia Follies (RRed)*F?

Sergeant York (OJ)

The Seventh Seal (OJ)

Sex, Lies and Videotape (IB)

The Sex Life of the Polyp (MM)

The Shaggy Dog (RR)

*The Sharpened Knife (IB)*F?

Showboat (IB)

The Sign of the Cross (HS)

Le Silence de la mer (IB)

Silk Stockings (TM)

Sinbad the Sailor (MM)

Singin' in the Rain (MM)

Snow White and the Seven Dwarfs (Couples)

Some Like It Hot (RR)

Something's Got to Give (MM)

[*The Song of Bernadette*] *(IB)*

Song of the South (MM)

The Sound of Music (MM)

Spanish film *(PF)*

Starting Over (RIR)

Star Wars (OJ)

Steamboat Willie (S.)

A Stitch in Time (IB)

The Strawberry Blond (IB)

Stromboli (MM)

Summer Stock (MM)

*Sweet and Low (IB)*F?

[*The Sweet Smell of Success*] *(IB)*

A Tale of Two Cities (IB)

The Temptress (IB)

10 (RIR)

That's Entertainment, Part II (MM)

They Won't Forget (MM)

The Three Caballeros (MM)

The Three Musketeers (MM)

Till the Clouds Roll By (IB)

Time-Marches-On (HS)

The Time of Your Life (MM)

Titanic (MM)

To Catch a Thief (MF)

To Have and Have Not (OJ)

Tom and Jerry cartoon *(C)*

Tom Jones (Couples)

Tommy (MF)

Too Far to Go (OJ)

The Torrent (HS)

Transfusion advertised as the Russian film *The Radiant Future (OJ)*

Travelogue of Thailand *(IB)*

The Treasure of Sierra Madre (HS)

The Treasurer's Report (MM)

*Trouble in Memphis (IB)*F?

True Grit (RRed)

Two-faced Woman (IB)

2001: A Space Odyssey (RRed)

*Uh-Oh, My Show Is Slipping (IB)*F?

Ulysses (BB)

Uncle Tom's Cabin (IB)

The Unsinkable Molly Brown (MM)

Viva Zapata! (MM)

Volunteers (OJ)

War movie *(Wake Island? Never So Few?) (Couples)*

West Side Story (MM)

White, Pearl, movie *(Concerts at Castle Hill)*

White Dwarf (MM)

Who Framed Roger Rabbit? (MM)

Who's on First? (Concerts at Castle Hill)

The Wild One (RIR)

The Wind (HS)

Wings (IB)

Witches' Brew (MM)

The Witches of Eastwick (OJ)

The Wizard of Oz (SD)

Working Girl (RaR)

The Wrecked Lady (Chatterbox, 1 Oct. 1947)

Xala (HS)

Year of the Torturer (OJ)

Yes (RRed)

Young Hunger (HS)

Young Man with a Horn (C)

You Only Live Twice (IB)

Ziegfeld Girl (MM)

FILM PERSONALITIES IN UPDIKE'S WORKS

Abbott, Bud *(Hub Fans Bid Kid Adieu,* "Preface," xii)

Adams, Alice *(IB)*

Adrian, Gilbert *(MM)*

Allen, Woody *(RIR)*

Allyson, June *(C)*

Andrews, Julie *(Couples)*

Antonioni, Michelangelo *(TM)*

Arbuckle, Fatty *(IB)*

Arnold, Edward *(MM)*

Arthur, Jean *(TM)*

Astaire, Fred *(HS)*

Auer, Mischa *(IB)*

Bacall, Lauren *(SD)*

Ball, Lucille *(IB)*

Bankhead, Tallulah *(OJ)*

Bardot, Brigitte (*M*)

Barrymore, John (*MM*)

Benchley, Robert (*MM*)

Bennett, Constance (*IB*)

Benny, Jack (*OJ*)

Bergen, Candace (*OJ*)

Bergman, Ingmar (*PP*)

Bergman, Ingrid (*RR*)

Berkeley, Busby (*OJ*)

Bernhardt, Sarah (*IB*)

The Big Bad Wolf (*IB*)

Biograph (*IB*)

Black, Karen (*IB*)

Bloom, Claire ("One Cheer for Literary Biography," *The New York Review of Books* 2 Feb 1999:5)

Bogart, Humphrey (*HS*)

Bolger, Ray (*SD*)

Bond, James (*HS*)

Bonzo (*IB*)

Borgnine, Ernest (*IB*)

Bow, Clara (*IB*)

Boyer, Charles (*MM*)

Bracken, Eddie (*MM*)

Brando, Marlon (*RIR*)

Brewer, George (writer) (*MM*)

Brooks, Louise (*HS*)

Bugs Bunny (*MM*)

Buñuel, Luis (*TM*)

Burns, George (*OJ*)

Burton, Richard (*OJ*)

Caan, James (*OJ*)

Cagney, James (*HS*)

Capra, Frank (*IB*)

Carioca, Joe (*MM*)

Caron, Leslie (*MM*)

Carson, Jack (*IB*)

Chaney, Lon (*IB*)

Chaplin, Charlie (*AP*)

Charisse, Cyd (*TM*)

Clift, Montgomery (*TM*)

Close, Glenn (*OJ*)

Coburn, Charles (*TM*)

Cohn, Harry (*HS*)

Colbert, Claudette (*HS*)

Colman, Ronald (*OJ*)

Columbia Pictures (*IB*)

Connery, Sean (*HS*)

Cooper, Gary (*HS*)

Costello, Lou (*Hub Fans Bid Kid Adieu*, "Preface," xii)

Crawford, Joan (*HS*)

Crosby, Bing (*OF*)

Cukor, George (*MM*)

Curtis, Tony (*IB*)

Curtiz, Michael (*HS*)

Daffy Duck (*MM*)

Dailey, Dan (*MM*)

Darnell, Linda (*IB*)

Davis, Bette (*HS*)

Day, Doris (*PF*)

Day, Laraine (*IB*)

Dean, James (*MM*)

De Carlo, Yvonne (*C*)

Dee, Sandra (*MM*)

DeHaven, Gloria (*MM*)

de Havilland, Olivia (*MM*)

Del Rio, Dolores (*IB*)

De Mille, Cecil B. (*BIB*; spelled "DeMille" (no space) in *HS*, "deMille" in *MM*)

Depardieu, Gerard (*RaR*)

Derek, Bo (?) (*RIR*)

De Wolfe, Billy (*HS*)

Dietrich, Marlene (*Marry*)

Dimbleby, Jonathan (*OJ*)

Disney, Walt (*M*)

Donald Duck (*IB*)

Donat, Robert (*RR*)

Donlevy, Brian (*Wake Island*? *Never So Few*?) (*Couples*)

Douglas, Kirk (*C*)

Dreyer, Carl (*MM*)

Dreyfuss, Richard (*RIR*)

Dunne, Irene (*RaR*)

Durbin, Deanna (*MM*)

Edison, Thomas (*IB*)

Eisenstein, Sergei (*HS*)

Fairbanks, Douglas (*MM*)

Farrow, Mia (*OJ*)

Faye, Alice (*IB*)

Fellini, Federico (Gado, Frank, "A Conversation with John Updike," *The Idol* LXVII [Spring 1971]: 3–32)

Fernandel (*PP*)

Ferrer, José (*IB*)

Fields, W. C. (*HS*)

Fisher, Carrie (*OJ*)

Fisher, Eddie (*CH*)

Flynn, Errol (*RR*)

Foch, Nina (*MM*)

Fonda, Jane (*SC*)

Fontaine, Joan (*IB*)

Ford, John (*IB*)

Forman, Milos (*HS*)

Foster, Jodi (*IB*)

Fox Studio (*IB*)

Freed, Arthur (*MM*)

Gabin, Jean (*PP*)

Gable, Clark (*Coup*)

Garbo, Greta (*SD*)

Gardner, Ava (*MM*)

Garfield, John (*MM*)

Garland, Judy ("Notes and Comments," The *New Yorker* July 5, 1969: 19)

Garner, James (*HS*)

Garr, Teri (*MM*)

Garrett, Betty (*MM*)

Garson, Greer (*W*)

Gaynor, Janet (*HS*)

Gazzara, Ben (*IB*)

Gilbert, John (*IB*)

Gish, Lillian (*HS*)

Godard, Jean-Luc (*PP*)

Goldwyn, Samuel (*MM*)

Goofy (*MM*)

Grable, Betty (*MM*)

Graham, Sheila (*MM*)

Granger, Farley (*SD*)

Granger, Stewart (*CH*)

Grant, Cary (*S.*)

Grant, Hugh (*MM*)

Grant, Kathryn (*IB*)

Grayson, Kathryn (*SD*)

Greenstreet, Sydney (*S.*)

Greenwood, Charlotte (*HS*)

Greer, Jane (*IB*)

Griffith, D. W. (*HS*)

Griffith, Melanie (*RaR*)

Guétary, Georges (*MM*)

Guinness, Alec (*Couples*)

Gwynne, Fred (*HS*)

Hagen, Jean (*MM*)

Haley, Jack (*IB*)

Hall, Jon (*RIR*)

Halliwell's Film Guide (*MF*)

Hardy, Oliver (*TM*)

Harlow, Jean (*MM*)

Harris, Julie (*MF*)

Hawn, Goldie (*OJ*)

Hayes, Helen (*MM*)

Hayes Code (*MF*)

Hayworth, Rita (*RRed*)

Heflin, Van (*MM*)

Henderson, Dell (*IB*)

Hepburn, Audrey (*RR*)

Hepburn, Katharine (*HS*)

Hermann, Edward (*OJ*)

Hitchcock, Alfred (*PP*)

Holden, William (*IB*)

Hollywood stunt man (*OJ*)

Hope, Bob (*Coup*)

Horne, Lena (*IB*)

Horsecollar, Horace (*SC*)

Horton, Edward Everett (*TM*)

Houseman, John (*OJ*)

Hudson, Rock (*Marry*)

Hughes, Howard (*IB*)

Hunter, Holly (*MM*)

Hunter, Tab (*Concerts at Castle Hill*)

Huston, Walter (*PP*)

Irving, Amy (*MM*)

Jaffee, Rona (*OJ*)

James, Harry (*C*)

Jannings, Emile (*IB*)

Jones, Jennifer (*IB*)

Jourdan, Louis (*MM*)

Kaprisky, Valerie (*OJ*)

Keaton, Diane (*RIR*)

Keel, Howard (*MM*)

Kelly, Gene (*MM*)

Kelly, Grace (*MM*)

Kenyon, Doris (*HS*)

Kidd, Michael (*MM*)

Kibbee, Guy (*TM*)

Konwicki, Tadeusz (*OJ*)

Krazy Kat (*HS*)

Ladd, Alan (*SD*)

Lake, Veronica (*IB*)

Lamarr, Hedy (*JL*)

Lamour, Dorothy (*IB*)

Lancaster, Burt (*RIR*)

Lang, Walter (*IB*)

Lassie (*TM*)

Laughton, Charles (*IB*)

Laurel, Stan (*TM*)

Leigh, Janet (*IB*)

Leigh, Vivien (*IB*)

Lemmon, Jack (*HS*)

LeRoy, Mervyn (*MM*)

Levant, Oscar (*MM*)

Lewis, Daniel Day (*MM*)

Lewis, Jerry (*TM*)

Lillie, Beatrice (*HS*)

Linder, Max (*IB*)

Littin, Miguel (*OJ*)

Lloyd, Harold (*IB*)

Lombard, Carole (*HS*)

Loren, Sophia (*OJ*)

Lorre, Peter (*S.*)

Losey, Joseph (*HS*)

Loy, Myrna (*MM*)

Lumière Brothers (*IB*)

Lupino, Ida (*RIR*)

MacDonald, Jeanette (*IB*)

MacGraw, Ali (*MF*)

MacLaine, Shirley (*MM*)

MacMurray, Fred (*RR*)

Madden, John (*MM*)

Madonna (*MM*)

Mailer, Norman (*OJ*)

Mankiewicz, Joseph (*MM*)

Massey, Raymond (*MF*)

Mature, Victor (*MM*)

Marx, Groucho (*RaR*)

Massen, Osa (*IB*)

Mastroianni, Marcello (*HS*)

Mayer, Louis B. (*MM*)

McCrea, Joel (*IB*)

McDowell, Andie (*IB*)

McQueen, Steve (*IB*)

Melcher, Marty (*PP*)

Méliès, Georges (*IB*)

Menjou, Adolphe (*AP*)

Metro Studio (*IB*)

Mickey Mouse (*S.*)

Miller, Ann (*MM*)

Minnelli, Vincente (*MM*)

Minnie Mouse (*RaR*)

Minter, Mary Miles (*IB*)

Miranda, Carmen (*IB*)

Mitchum, Robert (*HS*)

Monroe, Marilyn (as "Marilyn Moronrow") (*Couples*; also *MM*)

More, Kenneth (*MM*)

Moreno, Antonio (*IB*)

Morgan, Frank (*OJ*)

Murphy, Eddie (*OJ*)

Murphy, George (*MM*)

Neal, Patricia (*C*)

Neeson, Liam (*MM*)

Negri, Pola (*IB*)

Newman, Paul (*Concerts at Castle Hill*)

Nicholas Brothers (*MM*)

Nichols, Mike (*PP*)

Nielsen, Asta (*IB*)

Nolan, Lloyd (*CP*)

Novak, Kim (*CP*)

Oakie, Jack (*IB*)

O'Brien, Pat (*IB*)

O'Connor, Donald (*IB*)

Olive Oyl (*PP*)

Olivier, Laurence (*IB*)

O'Neal, Ryan (*RIR*)

Pabst, Georg (*HS*)

Paget, Debra (*CP*)

Papas, Irene (*OJ*)

Paramount Studios (*IB*)

Parton, Dolly (*MM*)

Pearce, Alice (*MM*)

Pfeiffer, Michelle (*OJ*)

Plimpton, George (*OJ*)

Popeye (*PP*)

Porky Pig (*MM*)

Presley, Elvis (*MM*)

Price, Vincent (*IB*)

Pudovkin, Vsevolod (*HS*)

Raft, George (*HS*)

Rains, Claude (*S.*)

Raitt, John (*RaR*)

Ray, Martha (*CP*)

Reagan, Ronald (*RIR*)

Redford, Robert (*OJ*)

Reynolds, Burt (*MM*)

Reynolds, Debbie (*CP*)

RKO Studios (*IB*)

Robards, Jason (*MF*)

Roberts, Julia (*MM*)

Robinson, Bill (Bojangles) (*BIB*)

Rogers, Ginger (*BIB*)

Rogers, Roy ("Untitled Mystery," in *First Words: Earliest Writing from Favorite Contemporary Authors*, ed. Paul Mandelbaum [Chapel Hill: Algonquin Books, 1993])

Rogers, Will (*PP*)

Rooney, Mickey (*JL*)

Ross, Katharine (*IB*)

Rossellini, Isabella (*IB*)

Rossellini, Roberto (*MM*)

Russell, Jane (*MM*)

Russell, Kurt (*OJ*)

Russell, Rosalind (*TM*)

Ryder, Winona (*MM*)

Sanders, George (*BIB*)

Schneider, Maria (*IB*)

Schwarzenegger, Arnold (*IB*)

Scorcese, Martin (*MM*)

Sellers, Peter (*SC*)

Sennett, Mack (*IB*)

Sharif, Omar (*RIR*)

Shore, Dinah (*OJ*)

Sinatra, Frank (*MM*)

Smith, Maggie (*IB*)

Snodgress, Carrie (*OJ*)

Snow White (*IB*)

Spacek, Sissy (*IB*)

Spielberg, Steven (*IB*)

Stanwyck, Barbara (*SD*)

Stewart, Jimmy (*OJ*)

Streep, Meryl (*OJ*)

Streisand, Barbra (*RRed*)

Swanson, Gloria (*IB*)

Tarantino, Quentin (*Salon* Interview 1 Dec. 1996)

Taylor, Elizabeth (*Couples*)

Taylor, Robert (*OJ*)

Taylor, William Desmond (*IB*)

Temple, Shirley (*P*)

Thalberg, Irving (*MM*)

Tracy, Spencer (*HS*)

Trevor, Claire (*MF*)

Turner, Lana (*TM*)

Universal Studios (*IB*)

Valentino, Rudolph (*IB*)

Van Dyke, Dick (*IB*)

Vera-Ellen (*MM*)

Von Stroheim, Erich (*IB*)

Wagner, Bruce (*MM*)

Warner Brothers Studios (*RaR*)

Wayne, John (*SD*)

Weaver, Sigourney (*RaR*)

Webb, Clifton (*MM*)

Weismuller, Johnny (*C*)

Welch, Raquel (*SC*)

Welles, Orson (*HS*)

Wellman, Billy (*HS*)

West, Mae (*IB*)

Whimpy (*PP*)

White, Pearl (*Concerts at Castle Hill*)

Whitty, Dame May (*Couples*)

Widmark, Richard (*HS*)

Wilder, Billy (*IB*)

Williams, Esther (*CH*)

Williams, Robin (*SC*)

Withers, Jane (*MuS*)

Wood, Natalie (*IB*)

Woody Woodpecker (*MM*)

Wyman, Jane (*OJ*)

Yevtushenko, Yevgeny (*OJ*)

Young, Loretta (*IB*)

Zinneman, Fred (*IB*)

Zuckmayer, Carl (*OJ*)

General Bibliography

BOOKS

Ancona, Francesco Aristide. *Writing the Absence of the Father: Undoing Oedipal Structures in the Contemporary American Novel.* Lanham, MD: University Press of America, 1986. 81–91.

Baker, Nicholson. *U and I.* New York: Random House, 1991.

Bloom, Harold, ed. *John Updike: Modern Critical Views.* New York: Chelsea House, 1987. (Includes Harold Bloom, "Introduction"; John W. Aldridge, "The Private Vice of John Updike"; Richard H. Rupp, "John Updike: Style in Search of a Center"; David Lodge, "Post-Pill Paradise Lost: John Updike's *Couples*"; Tony Tanner, "A Compromised Environment"; Joyce Carol Oates, "Updike's American Comedies"; Mary Allen, "John Updike's Love of Dull Bovine Beauty' "; James M. Mellard, "The Novel as Lyric Elegy: The Mode of Updike's *The Centaur*"; Jane Barnes, "John Updike: A Literary Spider"; Cynthia Ozick, "Bech, Passing"; Donald J. Greiner, "*The Coup*"; Chronology; and Bibliography.)

Broer, Lawrence R., ed. *Rabbit Tales: Poetry and Politics in John Updike's Rabbit Novels.* Tuscaloosa: University of Alabama Press, 1998. (Includes Lawrence R. Broer, "Introduction"; Donald J. Greiner, "No Place to Run: Rabbit Angstrom as Adamic Hero"; Charles Berryman, "Updike Redux: A Series Retrospective"; Jeff H. Campbell, " 'Middling, Hidden, Troubled America': John Updike's Rabbit Tetralogy"; Dilvo I. Ristoff, "Appropriating the Scene: The World of *Rabbit at Rest*"; Edward Vargo, "Corn Chips, Catheters, Toyotas: The Making of History in *Rabbit at Rest*"; Matthew Wilson, "The Rabbit Tetralogy: From Solitude to Society to Solitude Again"; Joseph J. Waldmeir, "*Rabbit Redux* Reduced: Rededicated? Redeemed?"; Ralph C. Wood, "Rabbit Angstrom: John Updike's Ambiguous Pilgrim"; Paula R. Buck, "The Mother Load: A Look at Rabbit's Oedipus Complex"; Jack B. Moore, "Sports, Basketball and

Fortunate Failure in the Rabbit Tetralogy"; Judie Newman, *"Rabbit at Rest*: The Return of the Work Ethic"; James Plath, "Verbal Vermeer: Updike's Middle-Class Portraiture.")

Burchard, Rachael C. *John Updike: Yea Sayings.* Carbondale: Southern Illinois University Press, 1971.

Campbell, Jeff H. *Updike's Novels: Thorns Spell a Word.* Wichita Falls, TX: Midwestern State University Press, 1987.

Cox, David Michael. "An Examination of Thematic and Structural Connections between John Updike's Rabbit Novels." Ohio University Press, 1978.

De Bellis, Jack. *John Updike: A Bibliography, 1967–1993.* Westport, CT: Greenwood Press, 1994. ("Foreword" by Updike.)

Detweiler, Robert. *Breaking the Fall: Religious Readings of Contemporary Fiction.* Louisville, KY: Westminster John Knox, 1996.

———. *John Updike.* Rev. ed. Boston: Twayne, 1984.

Falsey, Elizabeth. *The Art of Adding and the Art of Taking Away: Selections from John Updike's Manuscripts.* Cambridge, MA: Harvard College Library, 1987.

Greiner, Donald J. *John Updike's Novels.* Athens: Ohio University Press, 1984.

———. *The Other John Updike: Poems/Short Stories/Prose/Play.* Athens: Ohio University Press, 1981.

Hamilton, Alice, and Kenneth. *The Elements of John Updike.* Grand Rapids, MI: Eerdmans, 1970.

Hartman, Susan Beth. "The Role of the Berks County Setting in the Novels of John Updike." 1987. University of Pittsburgh.

Hunt, George. *John Updike and the Three Great Secret Things: Sex, Religion and Art.* Grand Rapids, MI: Eerdmans, 1980.

Luscher, Robert M. *John Updike: A Study of the Short Fiction.* New York: Twayne: 1993.

Macnaughton, William R., ed. *Critical Essays on John Updike.* Boston: Hall, 1982. (Includes William R. Macnaughton, "Introduction: A Survey of John Updike Scholarship in English"; Whitney Balliet, "Writer's Writer"; Granville Hicks, "A Little Good in Evil"; Arthur Mizener, "Behind the Dazzle Is a Knowing Eye"; Renata Adler, "Arcadia, Pa."; Jonathan Miller, "Off-Centaur"; Anthony Burgess, "Language, Myth and Mr. Updike"; Michael Novak, "Son of the Group"; Jonathan Raban, "Talking Head"; Charles Samuels, "Updike on the Present"; William T. Stafford, from "The 'Curious Greased Grace' of John Updike"; Tony Tanner, "The Sorrow of Some Central Hollowness"; D. Keith Mano, "Doughy Middleness"; Gilbert Sorrentino, "Never on Sunday"; Alfred Kazin, from "Alfred Kazin on Fiction"; Joyce Carol Oates, *"The Coup* by John Updike"; Paul Theroux, "A Marriage of Mixed Blessings"; Gerry Brenner, *"Rabbit, Run*: John Updike's Criticism of the 'Return to Nature' "; H. Peter, "John Updike's Metaphoric Novels"; Alice Hamilton and Kenneth Hamilton, "Metamorphosis through Art: John Updike's 'Bech: A Book' "; Robert Detweiler, "Updike's *Couples*: Eros Demythologized"; Larry Taylor, "The Wide-hipped Wife and the Painted Landscape: Pastoral Ideals in *Of the Farm*"; Clinton S. Burhans, Jr., "Things Falling Apart: Structure and Theme in *Rabbit, Run*"; Suzanne Henning Uphaus, *"The Centaur*: Updike's Mock-Epic"; Victor Strandberg, "John Updike and the Changing of the Gods"; Bernard A. Schopen, "Faith, Morality and the Novels of John Updike"; George W.

Hunt, "Reality, Imagination and Art: The Significance of Updike's 'Best' Story"; James M. Mellard, "The Novel as Lyric Elegy: The Mode of Updike's *The Centaur*"; George J. Searles, "*The Poorhouse Fair*: Updike's Thesis Statement"; Gordon E. Slethaug, "*Rabbit Redux*: 'Freedom Is Made of Brambles' "; Kathleen Verduin, "Fatherly Presences: John Updike's Place in a Protestant Tradition"; Gary Waller, "Stylus Dei or the Open-Endedness of Debate? Success and Failure in *A Month of Sundays*"; and Joyce Markle, "*The Coup*: Illusions and Insubstantial Impressions." The article by Brenner is reprinted from *John Updike: A Collection of Critical Essays*, ed. David Thorburn and Howard Eiland. Englewood Cliffs, NJ: Prentice, 1979. The essay by Mellard is reprinted in *John Updike: Modern Critical Views*, ed. Harold Bloom. New York: Chelsea House, 1987.)

Markle, Joyce B. *Fighters and Lovers: Theme in the Novels of John Updike*. New York: New York University Press, 1973.

Modern Fiction Studies 37 (Spring 1991). "John Updike Special Issue." (Includes Matthew Wilson, "The Rabbit Tetralogy: From Solitude to Society to Solitude Again"; Basem Ra'ad, "Updike's New Versions of Myth in America"; Derek Wright, "Mapless Motion: Form and Space in Updike's *Rabbit, Run*"; Stacey Olster, "Rabbit Rerun: Updike's Replay of Popular Culture in *Rabbit at Rest*"; Barbara Leckie, " 'The Adulterous Society': John Updike's *Marry Me*"; John N. Duvall, "The Pleasure of Textual/Sexual Wrestling: Pornography and Heresy in *Roger's Version*"; Sanford Pinsker, "John Updike and the Distractions of Henry Bech, Professional Writer and Amateur American Jew"; Malani Schueller, "Containing the Third World: John Updike's *The Coup*"; Jack De Bellis, "Updike: A Selected Checklist, 1974–1990.")

Neary, John M. *Something and Nothingness: The Fiction of John Updike and John Fowles*, Carbondale: Southern Illinois University Press, 1992.

Newman, Judie. *John Updike*. New York: St. Martin's, 1988.

O'Connell, Mary. *Updike and the Patriarchal Dilemma*. Carbondale: Southern Illinois University Press, 1996.

Plath, James. *Conversations with Updike*. Jackson: University of Mississippi Press, 1994.

Ristoff, Dilvo I. *John Updike's "Rabbit at Rest": Appropriating History*. New York: Lang, 1998.

———. *Updike's America: The Presence of Contemporary American History in John Updike's Rabbit Trilogy*. New York: Lang, 1988.

Samuels, Charles Thomas. *John Updike*. Minneapolis: University of Minnesota Press, 1969.

Schiff, James A. *John Updike Revisited*. Boston: Twayne, 1998.

———. *Updike's Version: Rewriting "The Scarlet Letter."* Columbia: University of Missouri Press, 1992.

Searles, George J. *The Fiction of Philip Roth and John Updike*. Carbondale: Southern Illinois University Press, 1985.

Stafford, William T., ed. *Modern Fiction Studies* 20 (Spring 1974). "John Updike Number." (Includes Robert McCoy, "John Updike's Literary Apprenticeship on *The Harvard Lampoon*"; Joseph Waldmeir, "It's the Going That's Important, Not the Getting There: Rabbit's Questing Non-Quest"; John B. Vickery, "*The Centaur*: Myth, History, and Narrative"; Paula Backscheider and Nick Backscheider, "Updike's Couples: Squeak in the Night"; Alan T.

McKenzie, " 'A Craftsman's Intimate Satisfactions': The Parlor Games in *Couples*"; Wayne Falke, "*Rabbit Redux*: Time/Order/God"; Robert Alton Regan, "Updike's Symbol of the Center"; Robert S. Gingher, "Has John Updike Anything to Say?"; Alfred F. Rosa, "The Psycholinguistics of Updike's 'Museums and Women' "; Albert J. Griffith, "Updike's Artist's Dilemma: 'Should Wizard Hit Mommy?' "; William T. Stafford, "Updike FourFiveSix, 'Just Like That': An Essay Review"; and Arlin G. Meyer and Michael A. Olivas, "Criticism of John Updike: A Selected Checklist." The last item was reprinted in Michael A. Olivas, *An Annotated Bibliography of John Updike Criticism, 1967–1973, and a Checklist of His Works*. New York: Garland, 1975.)

Tallent, Elizabeth. *Married Men and Magic Tricks: John Updike's Erotic Heroes*. Berkeley, CA: Creative Arts, 1982.

Taylor, Larry E. *Pastoral and Anti-pastoral Patterns in John Updike's Fiction*. Carbondale: Southern Illinois University Press, 1971.

Thorburn, David, and Howard Eiland, eds. *John Updike: A Collection of Critical Essays*. Englewood Cliffs, NJ: Prentice-Hall, 1979. (Includes David Thorburn, "Introduction: 'Alive in a Place and Time' "; Richard Gilman, "An Image of Precarious Life"; Dean Doner, "Rabbit Angstrom's Unseen World"; Richard Locke, "Rabbit's Progress"; Robert Alter, "Updike, Malamud and the Fire This Time"; Joyce Carol Oates, "Updike's American Comedies"; Howard Eiland, "Play in *Couples*"; David Lodge, "Post-Pill Paradise Lost: *Couples*"; George Steiner, "*A Month of Sundays*: Scarlet Letters"; Josephine Hendin, "Updike as Matchmaker: *Marry Me*"; Joyce Markle, "*The Poorhouse Fair*: A Fragile Vision of Specialness"; Larry E. Taylor, "*The Centaur*: Epic Paean and Pastoral Lament"; Martin Price, "A Note on Character in *The Centaur*"; Edward P. Vargo, "Shrine and Sanctuary: *Of the Farm*"; Charles Thomas Samuels, "Family Quarrels in *Of the Farm*"; Robert Towers, "Updike in Africa"; Deborah McGill, "Boy's Life"; Robert Detweiler, "*The Same Door*: Unexpected Gifts"; Arthur Mizener, "Memory in *Pigeon Feathers*"; Michael Novak, "Updike's Search for Liturgy"; Charles Thomas Samuels, "*The Music School*: A Place of Resonance"; Jack Richardson, "Keeping Up with Updike: *Bech: A Book*"; Rosemary Dinnage, "At the Flashpoint: *Museums and Women*"; Richard Todd, "Disengagement in *Museums and Women*"; "Chronology"; and "Selected Bibliography." The articles by Lodge and Oates were reprinted in *John Updike Modern Critical Views*, ed. Harold Bloom. New York: Chelsea House, 1987.)

Trachtenberg, Stanley. *New Essays on Rabbit, Run*. New York: Cambridge University Press, 1993. (Includes: Emory Elliott, "Preface"; Trachtenberg, "Introduction"; Philip Stevick, "The Full Range of Updike's Prose"; Sanford Pinsker, "Restlessness in the 1950s: What Made Rabbit Run?"; Erik Kielland-Lund, "The Americanness of *Rabbit, Run*: A Transatlantic View"; Stacey Olster, " 'Unadorned Woman, Beauty's Home Image': Updike's Rabbit, Run"; and selected bibliography.)

Uphaus, Suzanne Henning. *John Updike*. New York: Ungar, 1980.

Vargo, Edward P. *Rainstorms and Fire*. Port Washington, NY: Kennikat Press, 1973.

Vaughan, Philip H. *John Updike's Images of America*. Reseda, CA: Mojave, 1981.

Yerkes, Jim, ed. *John Updike and Religion: The Sense of the Sacred and the Motions of Grace*. Grand Rapids, MI: 1999. [Includes: "Preface," by James Yerkes; "Earthworm," by John Updike "Remarks upon Receiving the Campion Medal" by John Updike; "As Good as It Gets: The Religious Consciousness in John Updike's Literary Vision" by James Yerkes; "The Obligation to Live: Duty and Desire in John Updike's *Self-Consciousness*, by Avis Hewitt; "The Pocket Nothing Else Will Fill: Updike's Domestic God," by James A. Schiff; "When Earth Speaks of Heaven: The Future of Race and Faith in Updike's *Brazil*," by Dilvo I. Ristoff; "Updike 2020: Fantasy, Mythology and Faith in *Toward the End of Time*," by David Malone; "An Umbrella Blowing Inside Out: Paradoxical Theology and American Culture in the Novels of John Updike," by Kyle A. Pasewark; "What Is Goodness? The Influence of Updike's Lutheran Roots," by Darrell Jodock; "Writing as a Reader of Karl Barth: What Kind of Religious Writer Is John Updike Not?" by Stephen H. Webb; "The World and the Void: *Creatio ex Nihilo* and Homoeroticism in Updike's *Rabbit Is Rich*," by Marshall Boswell; "Learning to Die: Work as Religious Discipline in Updike's Fiction," by Wesley A. Kort; "Faith or Fiction: Updike and the American Renaissance," by Charles Berryman; "Giving the Devil His Due: Leeching and Edification of Spirit in *The Scarlet Letter* and *Witches of Eastwick*," by James Plath; "Guru Industries, Ltd.: Red-Letter Religion in Updike's S.," by Judie Newman; "Chaos and Society: Religion and the Idea of Civil Order in Updike's *Memories of the Ford Administration*," by George S. Diamond; "The Word as Host: John Updike and the Cultural Affirmation of Faith," by Donald J. Greiner. Bibliography.)

ARTICLES AND CHAPTERS IN BOOKS

Amis, Martin. "Updike: Life under a Microscope." Reading (Pa.). *Eagle* 4 Oct. 1987: E–18.

Atlas, James. "John Updike Breaks Out of Suburbia." *New York Times Sunday Magazine* 10 Dec. 1978: 60–61, 63–64, 68–70, 72, 74, 76.

Atwood, Margaret. "Wondering What It's Like to Be a Woman." *New York Times Book Review* 13 May 1984: 1, 40.

———. "Updike's Metamorphosis." *New York Times Book Review* 12 Oct. 1997: Sec. 7, 9–10.

Binkerts, Sven. "Roth, Mailer, Bellow Running out of Gas." *New York Observer* 13 Oct. 1997: 1.

Caldwell, Gail. "Bech to His Old Tricks; John Updike Sends His Alter Ego into Dubious Battle with Mortality." *Boston Globe* 25 Oct. 1998; Sunday City Ed., Books: N1.

Crews, Frederick. "Mr. Updike's Planet." *New York Review of Books* 33 (4 Dec. 1986): 7–10, 12, 14.

Detweiler, Robert. "John Updike and the Indictment of Culture-Protestantism." In *Four Spiritual Crises in Mid-Century American Fiction*. Gainesville: University of Florida Press, 1963. 14–24.

———. "Updike's *A Month of Sundays* and the Language of the Unconscious." *Journal of the American Academy of Religion* 47 (Dec. 1979): 611–25. (Rpt. in *Essays in Honour of Erwin Stürzl on his 60th Birthday*, ed. James Hogg. Salzburg:

Institut für Englische Sprache und Literatur, 1982. 76–100. Rpt. as a "short version" in Detweiler's *Story, Sign, and Self*. Philadelphia: Fortress, 1978. 154–64.)

Galloway, David. "The Absurd Man as Saint" in *The Absurd Hero in American Fiction: Updike, Styron, Bellow, Salinger*. 2nd rev. ed. Austin, TX: University of Texas Press, 1981. 32–40.

Gass, William H. "Cock-a-Doodle-Doo." *New York Review of Books* 11 Apr. 1968: 3. (Rpt. in his *Fiction and the Figures of Life*. New York: Knopf, 1970. 206–11.)

Gray, Paul. "Perennial Promises Kept." *Time* 120 (18 Oct. 1982): 72–74, 79–81.

———. "We Lost It at the Movies." *Time* (29 Jan. 1996): 78.

Greiner, Donald J. *Adultery in the American Novel: Updike, James, and Hawthorne*. Columbia: University of South Carolina Press, 1985. 3–71, 97–131.

———. "John Updike." *American Poets Since World War 2*. Detroit: Gale, 1980. 327–34.

———. "John Updike." In *Contemporary Authors Bibliographical Series*, vol. 1, ed. James J. Martine. Detroit: Gale, 1986. 347–82.

———. "John Updike." In *Dictionary of Literary Biography: Documentary Series: An Illustrated Chronicle*, vol. 3, ed. Mary Bruccoli. Detroit: Gale, 1983. 251–320.

———. "John Updike." In *Dictionary of Literary Biography Yearbook: 1980*. Detroit: Gale, 1981. 107–16.

Hardwick, Elizabeth. "Citizen Updike." *New York Review of Books* 36 (18 May 1989): 3, 4, 6, 8.

Harper, Howard M. "John Updike: The Intrinsic Problem of Human Existence." In *Desperate Faith: A Study of Bellow, Salinger, Mailer, Baldwin and Updike*. Chapel Hill: University of North Carolina Press, 1976. 162–90.

Kakutani, Michiko. "Tristan and Iseult as Latin Lovers." *New York Times* 25 Jan. 1994: C 19.

Lathrop, Kathleen. "*The Coup*: John Updike's Modernist Masterpiece." *Modern Fiction Studies* 31 (Summer 1985): 249–62.

Lehmann-Haupt, Christopher. "How One Small Ball Holds the Whole Universe." *New York Times* 19 Sept. 1996. Final, Sec. C. 17.

Lodge, David. "Bye-Bye Bech." *New York Review of Books* 19 Nov. 1998: 8–10.

Pritchard, William H. "His Own School of Criticism." *New York Times Book Review* 26 Sept 1999: Sunday Final, Sec. 7: 7.

Roth, Robert N. "A Closet Episcopalian." *New York Times Book Review* 3 Mar. 1996: 4.

Schiff, James A. "Updike Ignored: The Contemporary Independent Critic." *American Literature* 67 (Sept. 1995): 531–52.

Scott, A. O. "God Goes to the Movies." *The Nation* 12 Feb. 1996: 25–28.

Skube, Michael. "Updike Has Moved Beyond the Nobel, Work by Work." *Atlanta Constitution* 27 Sept. 1998.

Steiner, George. "Supreme Fiction." *New Yorker* 11 March 1996. 105–6.

Stubbs, John C. "The Search for Perfection in *Rabbit, Run*." *Critique* 10 (1968): 94–101.

Suderman, Elmer F. "The Right Way and the Good Way in *Rabbit, Run*." *University Review* 36 (Oct. 1969): 13–21.

"View from the Catacombs." *Time* 91 (26 Apr. 1968): 66–68, 73–75.

Walton, David. "Faces of the Nation." *The New York Times* 12 Sept. 1999, Sunday, Late Edition-Final, Sec. 7:26.

Wilson, Raymond, III. "*Roger's Version*: Updike's Negative-Solid Model of *The Scarlet Letter*." *Modern Fiction Studies* 35 (Summer 1989):241–50.

Wood, Michael. "God's Country." *New York Review of Books* 29 Feb. 1996: 5–6.

Wood, Ralph C. "John Updike as an Ironist of the Spiritual Life," and "The Strange Moral Progress of Harry ('Rabbit') Angstrom." *The Comedy of Redemption: Christian Faith and Comic Vision in Four American Novelists*. South Bend, IN: University of Notre Dame Press, 1988. 178–206, 207–29.

Index

Note: Main entry page numbers are set in **boldface** type.

Cleveland, Grover, 348
Clinton, Bill, 349
Cockaigne, **113**
Cohen, Orlando, 59, 60
Coleman, Ann, 79, **113**; and death,
134, 135; and drugs, 146
Coleridge, Samuel Taylor, **113**
Collected Poems, 1953–1993, **113–14**
Collecting Updike, **114–15**
College: *See* Academia
Comedy, **115–17**; and *The Centaur*, 95;
and Joyce, 229; and *Rabbit Is Rich*,
362, 364; and *Witches of Eastwick*, 491
"Commencement, Pingree School," 444
Commercialism, 229
Con, **117**
Conant, Jerry, **117**; and abortion, 1;
and airplanes, 11; and automobiles,
41; and Barth, 49; and Bible, 67; and
chess, 104; and Dante, 132; and di-
vorce, 139; and Gabriel Marcel, 262;
and Machiavelli, 258; and *Marry Me:
A Romance*, 263, 264; and *Ripley's Be-
lieve It or Not*, 378; and science, 396
Conant, Ruth, **117**; and abortion, 1;
and art, 33; and automobiles, 41; and
Bach, 46; and child psychologist, 104;
and death, 134; and eating, 152; and
Marry Me: A Romance, 263
Concerts at Castle Hill, **117–18**
"Conjunction," 493
Conner, Stephen, **118–19**; and cancer,
89–90; and Claudius, 112; and death,
133; and dualism, 148–49; and
Emerson, 158; and Jesse Smith, 414;
and John Hook, 206, 207; and *The
Poorhouse Fair*, 340, 341, 342; and
presidents, 347; and symbolism, 426,
427; and *Witches of Eastwick*, 490
"Constellation of Events, A," 11, 37,
456
Contras, the, **119**
Coup, The, **119–20**; and America, 15;
and Beckett, 64; and black humor, 70;
and characters, 98; and death, 135;
and Eliot, 156; and epigram, 160;
and Koran, 239; and magic realism,
259; and Nabokov, 253, 297; and
popular music, 345; and research, 479;

and sex, 407; and Tiberius Claudius
Nero, 437
Couples, **121–23**; and America, 15–16;
and Brook Farm, 78; and calendar,
88; and Camelot, 89; and characters,
97, 98; and children, 106; and classical music, 111; and creative process,
125; and death, 136, 287; and Eliot,
156; and epigram, 160; and femmes
fatales, 172; and film, 175; and homosexuality, 206; and Ipswich, Massachusetts, 222; and *Kama Sutra*, 232;
and Kennedy, 233; and Khrushchev,
236; and *Marry Me: A Romance*, 264,
263; and ministers, 276; and music,
118; and Poe, 337; and popular
music, 345; and Rougemont, 34; and
satire, 392; and science, 394, 396;
and symbolism, 426; and therapy,
183; and Tristan and Isolde, 454; and
Trust Me, 457; and Updike's life, 475;
and women, 171; and "Yes, but," 494–
95
"Couples," 263
"Crab Crack," 167
Craven, Frederick, 3
Creative process, 91, **123–27**, 140
Criticism by Updike, **127–29**
Critics/criticism, 207–10; and Bech, 52,
56, 57, 59, 60; and death, 135; hostile, 207–10, 329, 424; and James,
223; and Mailer, 259; and poetry,
338; and *The Poorhouse Fair*, 342; and
style, 424; Updike as, 69
Crosby, Harry Lillis "Bing," **129–30**
Cuban missile crisis, **130**
Culture: and Brewer, Pennsylvania, 77;
popular, 314, **343–44**, 449; and *The
Same Door*, 391; and sex, 404, 405–7;
and Updike's reading, 467
Cummings, E(dward) E(stlin), **130**
Cune, Rebecca, 246
Cunningham, Candace "Candy," **130**
"Cunts," 445

Dakar, **131**
Dalai Lama, **131**
"Dance of the Solids, The," 395
D'Annunzio, Gabriele, **131**

About the Author

JACK DE BELLIS is Professor of English at Lehigh University.